FOOTPRINTS IN PARCHMENT

ROME VERSUS CHRISTIANITY
30-313 AD

Sandra Sweeny Silver

authorHOUSE®

AuthorHouse™
1663 Liberty Drive
Bloomington, IN 47403
www.authorhouse.com
Phone: 1-800-839-8640

Published by AuthorHouse 5/14/2013

ISBN: 978-1-4817-3373-1 (sc)
ISBN: 978-1-4817-3374-8 (e)

Library of Congress Control Number: 2013905912

Front Cover Image: Eadwine the Scribe from The Eadwine Psalter c. 1160 AD

Also by Sandra S. Silver

NONFICTION
A Cosmos In My Kitchen: The Diary Of a Beekeeper
Pocket Full Of Posies
Abortion: A Biblical Consideration
The--Trust Me On This--Really Good Food Cookbook

FICTION
Snowtime

To my mother, Carmen Kniffin Sweeny,
who inspired me and believed in me

TABLE OF CONTENTS

PREFACE

"History" comes from the Greek word *historia* meaning "inquire." The author inquired how a 1st century group of Christians with no power, no leader, no money, no army and no country could, over a period of 300 years, contend with and overcome Rome, the most powerful pagan empire in the history of the world. Over three long centuries, there were no armed battles, no decisive victories or defeats, not even one military skirmish-to-a-standstill between these two enemies. How could that be? This book is the "account of my inquiries," a history of that inevitable conflict and the final outcome of one of the most important battles in the history of the world.

The book covers the years from the birth of Jesus of Nazareth (c. 6-4 BC) in the time of Caesar Augustus to the Resurrection of Jesus and Pentecost in c. 30 AD. It continues through the 300-year contest between the new faith of Christianity and the might of ancient Rome until the defeat of Rome by the Christians in 313 with the Edict of Milan.

Because of the thousands of certified, reliable ancient texts that have been carefully preserved and passed down to us over the millennia and because of the diligent work of archaeologists, epigraphists, philologists, linguists and cryptanalysts over the last 300 years, modern writers have an embarrassment of riches to use in their histories of ancient times.

In order to illustrate and to validate certain points without distortion, the author has tried "to pluck, as it were, flowers from the literary fields of the ancients themselves." Eusebius, *Church History 1.1* It is an assumption that the ancients speak more authoritatively about their times than scholars hundreds or thousands of years later. The author hopes that fiction and bias will submit to the purifying process of truth and reason in this book. Where these are found wanting, the author begs the indulgence of the reader.

Contemporary accounts by contemporary people are snapshots of history. Full-canvas paintings of history are later attempts to assemble and to paint a picture of history. Both the snap-shots and the full-canvas paintings are useful, but the contemporary accounts, the footprints in the parchments, are the primary materials used by historians to assemble their works. This book grounds its probable reasonings and its narrative upon these ancient texts.

With the integration of so many and varied ancient documents into the book, the reader will have the pleasure of reading extensive, first-hand accounts of events by people who were there or were within a suitable time frame from the events. Because of the predilections of the author, the book takes the reader down many ancient byways to examine the catacombs, explore the origins of words, experience the deaths of the early Christian martyrs in hopes of acquainting readers with seldom-seen sites. The main highway, however, will be the straight one that leads from Bethlehem to Milan. Comparing the focus of this book to the vast amount of ancient literature available, the writer had to exercise judgment and is aware that many relevant and pertinent texts have been omitted.

Ancient Rome, Judaism and early Christianity are the foundations upon which Western civilization has been built. If one wants to understand the modern world, it is necessary to examine the principles and the fundamentals of these three ancient behemoths.

Hopefully the book will attract not only readers who are engaged in the study of the Early Church and of the Greco-Roman period but will entice interested lay people and all readers who are warmly curious about the beginnings of Christianity. This work does not pretend to be an exhaustive study of either Rome under the Empire Period or of the Early Church in its first 300 years. The author urges the reader to consider this effort a modest contribution to the long list of admirable books on the conflict between paganism and Christianity.

Note: The author dislikes footnotes at the bottom of the page, at the end of the chapter or at the end of the book. It imposes an undue burden on the reader. Authors and works cited are integrated into the text where any interested reader can immediately and easily check the accuracy, context and/or relevance of the quote.

All Old and New Testament quotes are, unless otherwise designated, from The Holy Bible, New International Version, Zondervan Corporation, 2005.

TIMELINE OF THE PERIOD

"I warn and advise everyone from the start, that no one should ever pretend that he can be completely certain about matters of chronology.... no one...should believe that he is calculating dates with full accuracy and be deceived in that way." Eusebius, *Chronicle 1* (c. 325 AD) The author endorses Eusebius' advice and cautions the reader to assume a "c." (an abbreviation of the Latin word *circa* meaning "approximately") in front of every date.

BC

753   Rome (Roma) founded by Romulus as a Republic

612   Nineveh destroyed

605   Daniel and other Jews deported to Babylon

586   Babylonian Nebuchadnezzar destroys Jerusalem and Solomon's Temple

551   Confucius, founder of Chinese Confucianism, is born

539   Babylon conquered by Cyrus the Great

509   Founding of Roman Republic

500   Horatio saves Rome from the Etruscans

483   Death of Gautama Buddha in India

415   Socrates is instructing Plato

335   Aristotle is writing his *Poetics*

335   Alexander the Great begins his conquests

326   Circus Maximus is built

323   Alexander the Great dies in Babylon

96	Apostle John exiled to Isle of Patmos under Domitian; writes Book of Revelation
96	Domitian murdered; Nerva becomes emperor
98	Nerva dies; Trajan becomes emperor
99	John, Jesus' Apostle, dies a natural death at c. 100 years old
100	The Jewish canon is set
100	Building of Christian catacombs begins
117	Ignatius, disciple of John, thrown to lions in Rome
117	Trajan dies; Hadrian becomes emperor
122	Hadrian's wall is built in northern England
125	Fragment of John's Gospel (p52) dates to this time
126	Aristides presents his *Apology* to Hadrian
132	Jewish revolt against Romans under Bar Kokhba begins
135	Hadrian crushes the Bar Kokhba Rebellion
135	Hadrian begins to rebuild Jerusalem and names it Aelia Capitolina
135	Hadrian renames Judea "Palestinia"
138	Hadrian dies; Antonius Pius becomes Emperor
150	Justin Martyr is writing his Apologies for the Christian faith
155	Polycarp, disciple of John, martyred in Smyrna (Turkey)
161	Antonius Pius dies; Marcus Aurelius becomes Emperor
165	Justin Martyr is martyred
167	Roman Empire attacked by Barbarians
177	Marcus Aurelius kills Christians in Lyons and Vienne, France
180	Marcus Aurelius dies; teenage son Commodus becomes Emperor
183	Irenaeus is writing against the heresy of Gnosticism
192	Commodus is murdered
193	Septimus Severus seizes power, becomes Emperor
193	Severus massacres Christians for 18 years
211	Severus dies; sons Caracalla and Geta become co-emperors
212	Caracalla murders his brother Geta
212	Caracalla grants Roman citizenship Empire-wide
212	Caracalla begins to build his Bath in Rome
217	Caracalla murdered; succeeded by Macrinus, head of Praetorian Guard
218	Macrinus murdered; succeeded by 15-year-old Elagabalas

I.

On August 6, 258 AD Sixtus the new Bishop of Rome and six of his deacons wended their way down the stone steps to the subterranean chambers of the dead in the Catacomb of Praetextatus on the outskirts of Rome. Carrying small oil lamps to fend off the darkness, they assumed they would be safe to praise their God and to celebrate the Eucharist.

Safety was important in those days of persecution. A year before in 257 the Roman Emperor Valerian had issued a strong Edict targeting Christian leadership:

"…Valerian (has) sent a rescript to the (Roman) Senate to the effect that bishops and presbyters and deacons should immediately be punished…. that senators and men of importance and Roman knights should lose their title and moreover be deprived of their property; and if, when their means were taken away, they should persist in being Christians, then they should also lose their head….that matrons should be deprived of their property and sent into exile. Moreover, people of Caesar's household, whoever of them had either confessed (Christ) before, or should now confess, should have their property confiscated and should be sent in chains by assignment to Caesar's estate (to work as slaves). The Emperor Valerian also added to this address a copy of the letters which he sent to the governors of the provinces concerning us (the Christian leadership), and we daily await the arrival of these letters, bracing ourselves, each according to the strength of his faith, for the suffering that is to be endured and looking forward to the help and mercy of the Lord and the crown of eternal life. But know that Sixtus was martyred in the cemetery on the eighth day of the Ides of August, and with his deacons. Moreover the prefects in the City are daily urging on this persecution; so that, if any are presented to them, they are martyred and their property claimed by the treasury." Bishop Cyprian of Carthage in North Africa, *Epistle 81* (beheaded in 258 shortly after he wrote this letter)

The Romans were once again trying to eradicate this new religion that threatened social order and denied that Valerian was a god.

Valerian's Edict of August, 257 not only hoped to wipe out the ecclesiastical leaders by killing them all and scattering the sheep, but the order was, also, aimed at high-born Romans who had become Christians: senators, Roman knights, men from patrician families, wealthy women and even members of Caesar's own household. It was a broad, bold strike at the hierarchy of Roman society and of the Church.

Valerian had banned all Christian public assembly and forbade them to enter their catacombs: "Under no circumstances will you or any others be permitted to hold assemblies or enter the so-called cemeteries." Bishop Dionysius, *Letter to Hermammon*

Sixtus and his deacons were followed to their "so-called cemeteries" by the Roman authorities. Sixtus, underground, small oil lamps flickering, sitting on his portable, armless, curved back chair (Latin *cathedra*), was perhaps reading to them from the Psalms or from one of the Gospels. Maybe the group was in the act of taking Communion. The soldiers burst into the little underground room and with their heavy 23" swords beheaded all seven of them. One imagines so much chaos, noise and blood in such a small, dank space.

Later that night when the believers descended the steps to the scene of slaughter, they washed and wrapped the Bishop with his head and his deacons with their heads in linen burial cloths. Bishop Sixtus II, who had been Bishop for only a year, and four of his deacons Januarius, Magnus, Stephanus and Vincentius, were taken to the nearby Catacomb of Callixtus and buried. The Bishop's chair, covered with his blood, was buried behind his grave found in the Crypt of the Popes in 1854 by archaeologist Giovanni Battista de Rossi. The other two deacons, Felicissimus and Agapitus, were buried where they died in the Catacomb of Praetextatus.

It was Emperor Valerian who had said, "I'd rather hear of a threat to the throne than of another bishop in Rome." But the emperor had not always hated the new sect of Christians. In the early years of his reign (253-260) Valerian had opened his palace to many Christians as Dionysius (c. 190-265), the Bishop of Alexandria, relates:

"Both aspects of Valerian are astonishing. His earlier conduct was mild and friendly to God's people: no emperor before him was so kindly disposed toward them...as he clearly was in receiving them in close friendship at the start. Indeed he filled his whole palace with godly people, making it a church of God. But the teacher and leader of the assembly of Egyptian magicians, Macrian, persuaded Valerian to persecute and kill pure and holy men as rivals who impeded his own disgusting incantations....(Macrian) also encouraged Valerian to perform unholy rites...and ill-omened sacrifices such as cutting the throats of boys and tearing out the vital organs of newborn babies."
Letter to Harmammon

After that, Valerian's Edict to kill the Christian leadership of Rome was not hard.

One of the most revered martyrs of the Early Church is a Spaniard named Lawrence (San Lorenzo). Sixtus had been Lawrence's teacher and he brought the young man to Rome with him when he became Bishop and put him in charge of church treasures and administering to the poor. When Sixtus and his deacons were killed that day in August of 258, Deacon Lawrence knew he would be next.

When Lawrence was arrested, Valerian demanded all the assets of the church be delivered to him immediately. Lawrence said it would take three days to gather the treasure together. At the end of three days Lawrence presented to Valerian the poor, the blind, the maimed and the suffering.

"These," he said, "are the treasures of the church."

This bold affront enraged Valerian. He demanded the insolent deacon be immediately roasted to death on a grill.

His naked body was strapped to a gridiron and the wood was ignited. After many hours roasting on the grill, the still defiant Lawrence cried out, "I am already roasted on one side. Turn me over!" Butler, *Lives of the Saints*, Vol.8, August 10 When his charred and shredded body was claimed by church members, they buried it in the Catacomb of Cyriaca on the Via Tiburtina. Lawrence was martyred August 10, 258, just four days after bishop Sixtus and his fellow deacons were beheaded while worshiping in the Catacomb of Praetextatus.

The catacombs and the Rome of the early Christians are still there in modern Rome. The ruins of the Colosseum, built with the plunder taken from Jerusalem by Titus when he destroyed the Jewish capital in 70 AD, dominate. Since 63 BC when the Roman general Pompey had conquered the Jews, they had actively resisted the rule of Rome. There were constant uprisings, constant claims of Roman offenses against their one God. The Jews, like the early Christians, were a cantankerous bunch. They had to be destroyed.

The 50' high marble Arch of Titus, commemorating the Fall of Jerusalem, still stands on the Via Sacra close to the Colosseum. The Inscription on the Arch reads: "The Roman Senate And The People (dedicated this arch) To Deified Titus Vespasian Augustus, Son Of Deified Vespasian." High up in the relief is toga-clad Titus in his chariot in triumphal procession followed by men carrying treasures from the sacked Temple in Jerusalem: the golden Menorah, silver trumpets, the Table of the Shewbread. All the gold and silver plundered from Jerusalem was used to finance the building of the Colosseum and Jewish captives were the slave labor for the construction. The Colosseum, covering six acres and seating 87,000 people according to Philocalus' *Chronographia of 354*, was finished in 80. Most of the huge amphitheater survives as a symbol of Rome.

The weed-wrapped rubble of ancient Rome's political and religious center, the Forum, with its broken Ionic columns and weatherworn steps leading nowhere sit stoically on Palatine Hill. Toppled columns, the cobbled Via Appia and the relics of caved-in, carved-out ancient buildings intimately intermingle with the 17th century Baroque architecture of papal Rome and with the buildings of modern Rome. The Romans and their buildings will not go away. The early Christians, their religion, their God, their catacombs would not and did not go away either.

The catacombs are subterranean burial sites with labyrinthine, dark passages containing little rooms and small burial niches. There are 600 miles of these underground burial sites that ring Rome. Laid end to end they would stretch almost the entire length of Italy. About 6,000,000 Christians, Jews and Romans are buried in the catacombs.

All the underground chambers have not been found. As late as 1955 the Via Latina Catacomb was discovered when workmen were driving piles into the ground for a new apartment building on the Via Latina. They broke into an underground spacious chamber of wonder and beauty. Inside were perfectly preserved frescoes of early 4th century Christian art. Most of the paintings are vividly colored and of exceptional quality. Often called the "Sistine Chapel of the Early Christian World," appointments to see the Via Latina Catacomb can be petitioned through the Vatican Commission of the Catacombs.

The catacombs that are partially open to the public are: St. Callixtus (by far the largest and most visited); Domitilla (near Callixtus with a good bookstore); St. Sebastian (the oldest and most venerable); St. Agnes (named for the martyred girl) and Priscilla (way out on the Via Salaria).

The Via Salaria is the old Salt Road that pre-dates Rome itself. Salt was to the ancient world what crude oil is to the early 21st century--- the couch upon which the civilization reclined. Salt is a preservative, an additive with the power to protect against decay. Covering meat and fish in salt removes the moisture that causes spoiling. Salted food is sun-dried and can be eaten for months and sometimes for years. Ancient armies fought on brined and dried fish and meat. Fleets of trading ships plied the waters of the Mediterranean and the Atlantic on brined fish and meat. Salted and dried food was the staple of the ancient world. Roman housewives flavored their food with salt and pickled and preserved vegetables in salt water. Salt was used in sacrifices to God

(Leviticus 2:13) and Hebrews had a "covenant of salt" symbolizing faith, loyalty and longevity with their God (II Chronicles 13:5). Salt was a "good influence" (Matthew 5:13) and "eating salt together" meant sharing a meal. Roman soldiers were often paid in salt (*sale*). Salt was their *salarium*, their salary. The Roman author Petronius in his novel *Satyricon 57* coined the expression "not worth his salt" about a Roman soldier who was so bad he was not worth his pay, his salt. Not only to Rome but to all the ancient world, salt was white gold.

In 800 BC the Via Salaria ("Salt Road") ran all the way from a tiny settlement on the Tiber River to the Adriatic Sea where they evaporated the water from the salt ponds and caravanned the precious crystals back to the village that would become Rome. All roads, salt or not, would eventually lead to her.

In 28 AD, an ocean away from Imperial Rome, a popular young rabbi in the Galilee region of Judea stood on a mountainside and told His followers they were "the salt of the earth." (Matthew 5:13) Did He mean they were the preservers of the world? Salt was money, so were they to be a new currency? Were they to be a vital flavor to the world? Covenants were sealed with the exchange of salt, so were they to be a new covenant? Were they to be the stinging, healing disinfectant on the festering and the rotting? What did the Jewish rabbi mean? Rome would soon find out.

II.

"Gerusale, Civitas Et Ornamentum Martyrum Dei"

"Jerusalem, City And Honor Of God's Martyrs." A pilgrim carved this Latin graffiti into the walls of the Roman Catacomb of St. Callixtus in c. 300. To that visitor, this underground city of the dead, hallowed with the blood and the honor (*ornamentum*) of those who had given their lives for Christ, reminded him of the heavenly Jerusalem in Revelation 21:2.

The early Christians called these underground burial sites *koimeteria*, in Greek meaning "sleeping or resting places," the origin of our word "cemetery." The believers knew they were only sleeping, resting until the resurrection of the dead would come. This world was not the final answer. The very first catacomb, the Catacomb of St. Sebastian on the Appian Way, was at the site of a pre-existent pozzolana (volcanic ash) quarry that had been dug or hollowed out (Greek *kumbas*) by the side of the Via Appia road. Beginning in the late 200's AD all the underground cemeteries began to be called *kata kumbas*, catacombs, from the two Greek words meaning "at the hollows" or "hollowed out places."

By that time there had been many martyrs for the new faith and hosts of pilgrims came to Rome from all over the empire to see the graves of the martyrs. The Catacomb of St. Sebastian was the most important underground burial site of the heroic witnesses. The remains of Peter and of Paul, the great Apostles of the Early Church, were buried there.

When the early pilgrims from Africa, the Middle East and Europe arrived in Rome, all they wanted to know was: Where are Peter and Paul? The directions were simple: Go out of Rome beyond the city walls (*extra muros*) on the Via Appia. Walk until you see the hollows and the wide sandstone cavities. Peter and Paul are there.

It is ironic that Peter's bones remained for a while in that catacomb on the Appian Way because Peter had fled Rome along that same road in order to escape his martyrdom. The story of Peter's death, the *Quo Vadis* story, is a very famous one. It dates back to about 100 years after Peter was martyred and there are parts of the narrative that sound very much like the Biblical Peter. The Early Church fathers and J. B. Lightfoot, the incomparable 19th century Biblical scholar, believed the account to be true.

Peter was killed in the first big persecution of Christians under the Roman emperor Nero. When Claudius died, Nero became emperor on October 13, 54 AD when he was just 17 years old. The most vile of the Roman emperors, Nero committed every *cide* ("kill") you can name--matricide, homicide and finally suicide in 66. He sexually corrupted little boys and murdered his mother, his wives, his lovers and other men so he could molest their wives. He was a fornicator, a homosexual, a cross-dresser and a pederast. The Roman historian Tacitus (c.56-117AD) who lived during Nero's reign says: "Nero polluted himself by every lawful or lawless indulgence (and did not) omit a single abomination which could heighten his depravity." *Annals 14*

His dying words, *Qualis artifex pereo* ("What a great artist dies in me"), illustrate how deluded this malevolent man was. Theatric and effete, he loved to dress up and recite poetry as he played the lyre. From his youth, Nero had fancied himself a great singer. As emperor, he constantly gave concerts in public places to captured audiences:

"While he was singing, no one was allowed to leave the theater even for the most urgent reasons. And so it is said that some women gave birth to children there, while many who were worn out with listening and applauding, secretly leaped from the wall, since the gates at the entrance were barred, or (they) feigned death and were carried out as if for burial." Suetonius, *Lives of the Caesars: Nero*

Pertinent to the *Quo Vadis* story, Nero as Emperor had every thing, but he hated Rome and thought it looked like a pigsty. He envisioned Rome as Nero's Golden City if he could only get rid of squalid, crooked, cramped Rome. He wanted a Rome of shining buildings, straight thoroughfares and clean streets.

In 64 he instructed his lackeys to burn Rome to the ground so he could start over. The fire started on July 19th in the wooden shops inhabited by cooks, astrologers and prostitutes in the southeast angle of the Circus Maximus. Tacitus, who was a young boy when Rome burned, gives an account:

"...the conflagration both broke out and instantly became so fierce and so rapid from the wind that it seized in its grasp the entire length of the circus....The blaze in its fury ran first through the level portions of the city, then rising to the hills, while it again devastated every place below them, it outstripped all preventive measure; so rapid was the mischief and so completely at its mercy the city, with those narrow winding passages and irregular streets which characterized old Rome. Added to this were the wailings of terror-stricken women, the feebleness of age, the helpless inexperience of childhood, the crowds who sought to save themselves or others, dragging out the infirm or waiting for them, and by their hurry in the one case, by their delay in the other, aggravating the confusion...they found that, even places which they had imagined to be remote, were involved in the same calamity....And no one dared to stop the mischief because of incessant menaces from a number of persons who forbade the extinguishing of the flames...others openly hurled brands and kept shouting that there was one who gave them authority....a rumor had gone forth everywhere that at the very time when the city was in flames, the emperor appeared on a private stage and sang of the destruction of Troy, comparing present misfortunes with the calamities of antiquity. At last, after five days, an end was put to the conflagration at the foot of the Esquiline hill, by the destruction of all buildings on a vast space, so that the violence of the fire was met by clear ground and an open sky. But before people had laid aside their fears, the flames returned, with no less fury this second time....the temples of the gods and the porticoes which were devoted to enjoyment fell in a yet more widespread ruin. And to this conflagration there attached the greater infamy because it broke out on the Aemilian property of Tigellinus (a co-conspirator with Nero in the burning of Rome), and it seemed that Nero was aiming at the glory of founding a new city and calling it by his name." *Annals 14. 38-40*

Cassius Dio, writing one hundred years after the Great Fire that destroyed ten of Rome's fourteen districts, says:

"...while the whole people was in this state of excitement and many driven mad by the calamity were leaping into the blaze, Nero mounted upon the roof of the palace where almost the whole conflagration was commanded by a sweeping glance. (He) put on the professional harpist's garb and sang 'The Taking Of Troy'...although to common minds it seemed to be 'The Taking Of Rome.'" *Roman History 62.16-18*

In the aftermath of the Great Fire, the Roman people suspected arson and they suspected their insane ruler Nero. The palace servants spread the word that "the emperor had fiddled while Rome burned." The people, already willing to believe that he had started the fire, became riotous. They chanted, *Nero Incendiarius* ("Nero the Arsonist"). In order to stave off a public lynching, Nero immediately accused a new sect called "Christians." He rounded up Christians, dipped them in tar and burned them as torches for his dinner parties. He sewed them in animal skins and threw them to the dogs at the circus near Vatican Hill. His cruelty was so extreme that the people began to have sympathy for the Christians.

Even Tacitus who had little regard for Christians was repulsed:

"Consequently, to get rid of the report (that he had started the fire), Nero fastened the guilt and inflicted the most exquisite tortures on a class hated for their abominations, called Christians by the populace. Christus, from whom the name had its origin, suffered the extreme penalty during the reign of Tiberius at the hands of one of our procurators, Pontius Pilatus, and a most mischievous superstition (Christianity), thus checked for the moment, again broke out not only in Judea, the first source of the evil, but even in Rome, where all things hideous and shameful from every part of the world find their center and become popular. Accordingly, an arrest was first made of all (Christians) who pleaded guilty; then, upon their information, an immense multitude was convicted, not so much of the crime of firing the city, as of hatred against mankind. Mockery of every sort was added to their deaths. Covered with the skins of beasts, they were torn by dogs and perished, or were nailed to crosses, or were doomed to the flames and burnt to serve as a nightly illumination when daylight had expired. Nero offered his gardens for the spectacle and was exhibiting a show in the circus while he mingled with the people in the dress of a charioteer or stood aloft on a car. Hence, even for criminals who deserved extreme and exemplary punishment, there arose a feeling of compassion (for the Christians). For it was not, as it seemed, for the public good, but to glut one man's cruelty that they were being destroyed." *Annals 15.44*

The persecution of Christians under Nero began as a means to deflect blame but was the beginning of Imperial Rome's concerted effort over hundreds of years to stamp out another "source of evil" that had wandered into Rome to vex and to corrupt people like Nero. Over 150 years later, the North African Early Church apologist, Tertullian (c. 160-220), called the persecution of Christians the *institutum Neronianum* ("Nero's institution"):

"Consult your (Roman) records: you will there find that Nero was the first emperor who wreaked his fury on the the blood of Christians when our religion was just springing up in Rome. But we even glory in being first dedicated to destruction by such a monster. For whoever knows him can understand that it could only have been something of supreme excellence that called forth the condemnation of Nero." *Apology 5*

This State persecution of Christians was the first time the Roman government officially distinguished Christians from Jews. From Nero's reign until the Edict of Milan in 313 AD it was a capital crime to be a Christian. It was *Non licet esse Christianos*: "It is illegal to be a Christian."

In his wide net of blame, Nero targeted Peter and Paul, the co-founders of the church in Rome, who had labored to spread the news of a risen Christ all over the Roman Empire.

In this frenzied maelstrom of arrests and deaths, Roman Christians implored Peter to leave Rome. He who knew Jesus face to face must survive, they said, to spread the word of the resurrection. They begged him to flee from certain death. Peter did flee. He fled down the burned-out streets of Rome and reached the Via Appia which lead from Rome to Brindisi where he could find a ship to Judea. Near the 1M mark on the Appian Way, Peter saw Jesus coming toward him. He fell at His feet and said, "*Domine, quo vadis?*" ("Lord, where are you going?")

Jesus said to Peter, "I go to Rome to be crucified again." ("*Eo Romam iterum crucifigi.*")

This cut Peter to the quick. Once before he had denied Jesus and had fled from His crucifixion. He was doing it again. Jesus' last words to Peter had been "Follow me." (John 21:19) He realized he must go back and suffer the cross.

About thirty years before this encounter on the Appian Way, Jesus had asked His disciples, "Who do you say that I am?" Peter had immediately responded, "You are the Christ, the Son of the living God."

Jesus had looked at Peter and said, "And you are Peter and on this rock (Greek *petros*) I will build my church and the gates of hell will not prevail against it." Matthew 16:15-17

In the gospels and in this Quo Vadis encounter from the *Acts of Peter and Paul,* Peter is more a stone than a huge rock. But even a tiny pebble is hard, firm and can vex. A stone is more substantial---hard, firm, not easy to crush. A whole bunch of stones placed artfully together can build a structure, like the Appian Way, like the Christian church that can last for thousands of years.

Peter and his wife were eventually captured in Rome and taken outside the city walls to the Circus of Nero near Vatican Hill, one of the Seven Hills of Rome. Clement of Alexandria (c.150-211) writes: "When the blessed Peter saw his wife led away to death, he rejoiced that her call had come and that she was returning home. He called out to her by name in encouragement and comfort, 'Remember the Lord!' Such was the marriage of the blessed and their perfect affection." *Stromata Book 7*

The Acts Of Peter and Paul written in the 2nd century AD is an apocryphal, often bizarre account of Peter's life. But there are parts of the book scholars consider true. Peter's request to be crucified upside down has been embraced by many reputable early writers as well as by academics: "I (Peter) beseech you executioners, crucify me thus, with the head downward and not otherwise....And when they had hanged him up after the manner he desired, he began again to say unto them..." *37. 38*

The Early Church father and scholar Origen says in c. 240's: "Peter was crucified at Rome with his head downwards as he himself had desired to suffer." Eusebius, *Church History 3.1* The church scholar Jerome (c. 340-420) in *The Book Of Illustrious Men* says that when Peter's time came to be crucified, he asked to be crucified upside down: "(Peter) was crucified his head being down and his feet upward, himself so requiring, because he was, he said, unworthy to be crucified after the same form and manner as the Lord was." Because Peter was considered a common criminal, his body was interred in a hastily dug grave on the northeast slope of Vatican Hill in a section reserved for the poor. A few tiles were thrown over his body.

Both Peter and Paul were condemned when Nero was Caesar, but Paul was a Roman citizen and that citizenship gave him the "privilege" of a quick death. He was beheaded at the same time as Peter in c. 64-67 on the Via Ostiensis. There are no Early Church records or legends of Paul's martyrdom. In addition to being one of the greatest intellects of the western world, Paul had suffered often and much to spread the Evangel (Greek *euangelion*):

"(I) have been in prison...been flogged...been exposed to death again and again. Five times I received...the forty lashes minus one. Three times I was beaten with rods; once I was stoned; three times I was shipwrecked....I have been in danger from rivers; in danger from bandits; in danger from my own countrymen; in danger from Gentiles; in danger in the city; in danger in the country; in danger at sea....I have known hunger and thirst and have often gone without food; I have been cold and naked." II Corinthians 11:23-27

Paul had been hardened and toned by suffering. It is sure he died a fearless and faithful death. He was originally buried where he was beheaded on the Ostian Way in Rome.

One hundred years after the death of the two Apostles, Bishop Dionysius of Corinth in a letter to the Roman Bishop Soter said of the two most important leaders of the Early Church: "You have also by your very admonition brought together the planting that was made by Peter and Paul at Rome and at Corinth; for both of them (Peter and Paul) sowed in our Corinth and instructed us together; in Italy too they taught jointly in the same place (Rome) and were martyred at the same time." Eusebius, Church History 2.25

Thirty years later in c. 200 Tertullian writes of the deaths of the two Apostles in Rome:

"But if you are near Italy, you have Rome....What a happy church that is, on which the apostles poured out their whole doctrine with their blood; where Peter had passion like that of the Lord (crucifixion), where Paul was crowned with the death of John the Baptist by being beheaded." *Demurrer Against The Heretics 36*

"Let us see what milk the Corinthians drained from Paul; against what standard the Galatians were measured for correction....what even the nearby Romans sound forth to whom both Peter and Paul bequeathed the gospel and even sealed it with their blood." *Against Marcion 4.5*

Caius, a Christian author at the beginning of the 3rd century, remarked he could lead a visitor to the graves of Peter and Paul: "But I can show the trophies of the Apostles. For if you will go to the Vatican or to the Ostian Way you will find the trophies of those who laid the foundations of this church." Eusebius, *Church History 2.25*

Sometime between their deaths in c. 64-67 and the 200's, the bones of Peter and Paul were transferred to the Catacomb of St. Sebastian on the Via Appia. The persecutions were raging during those centuries and perhaps the Christians hid the bones for safekeeping. The catacomb became a mecca for believers who called it *Memoria Apostolorum*, "In Memory of the Apostles." Attesting to the presence of their remains, more than 600 graffiti invoking Peter and Paul are etched into the walls of St. Sebastian by pilgrims:

"*Domus Petri*" ("House of Peter")

"You that are looking for the names of Peter and Paul, you must know that the saints have lived here."

"Peter and Paul. Remember us."

"Paul and Peter. Intercede for Victor."

"Peter. Paul. Pray for us."

It personalizes these great Apostles to see a small painting of them in the Catacomb of Domitilla. Peter looks robust and has a full head of short hair. Paul looks a little haggard and is balding with a ring of hair reaching from ear to ear. A gilt etching on glass in the Vatican Library from the 300's shows the busts of two toga-clad men in profile looking at each other. "Petrus" is etched into the glass on the left next to the man with a short beard and a full head of short hair. "Paulus" is etched next to the man on the right. He is balding and has a long beard.

In the Apocryphal book, *The Acts Of Paul and Thecla* from the 2nd century, there is a verbal picture of Paul: "A man rather small in size, bald on the head, crooked thighs, handsome legs, hollow-eyed;

had a crooked nose; full of grace; for sometimes he appeared as a man, sometimes he had the countenance of an angel." *1.7*

The vast majority of Old and New Testament men portrayed in catacomb art are clean-shaven and have short hair. The archetype is Jesus, the disciples and all ancient men had long hair and beards. It is true that some Jewish men had long beards and long hair, but by the time of Jesus, the Greek influence had spread all over the Western world and most Jews had short hair and were clean-shaven like the Greeks. In Roman, Greek and even Etruscan art the men have short hair. It can be deduced from I Corinthians 11:13-16 that Paul and most of the men in his world had short hair:

"Judge for yourselves. Is it proper for a woman to pray to God with her head uncovered? Does not the very nature of things teach you that if a man has long hair, it is a disgrace to him, but that if a woman has long hair, it is her glory? For long hair is given to her as a covering. If anyone wants to be contentious about this, we have no other practice, nor do the churches of God."

Paul could not have been more emphatic. It is unnatural and a disgrace for men to have long hair. The early churches were filled with short-haired men like Peter and Paul. There was "no other practice."

When the short-haired Roman emperor Constantine converted to Christianity, he and his co-emperor Licinius issued the Edict of Milan in 313. The proclamation gave religious freedom to all peoples, especially Christians, within the Roman Empire: "We might grant to the Christians and others full authority to observe that religion which each preferred....we thought to arrange that no one whatsoever should be denied the opportunity to give his heart to the observance of the Christian religion." The persecution of Christians was over. Shortly after the Edict of Milan, the remains of Peter and Paul were taken from the catacomb of St. Sebastian and buried at the places of their martyrdoms on Vatican Hill and on the Via Ostiensis.

In 324 Constantine, called The Great, built the Basilica of Constantine at the foot of Vatican Hill to contain the bones of the martyred Peter. Legend says that Constantine took off his royal robes and with his own hands began digging the foundation of the Basilica. The apse of his Basilica was centered directly over Peter's tomb. Over the centuries that Basilica crumbled and eventually was torn down in 1505 by Pope Julius II. The new church was designed by the Renaissance architect Donato Bramante (1444-1514) who envisioned St. Peter's as "the Pantheon on top of the Basilica of Maxentius." He died long before it was finished, but the modern observer can see his concept came to fruition. It took over 100 years to build St. Peter's Basilica. Consecrated November 18, 1626 by Pope Urban VIII, it is the largest Catholic Church in the world holding over 60,000 people.

St. Peter's is sited on the huge tract of land called the Circus of Nero where Peter was killed. "Nero had a space in the Vatican valley enclosed where he might practice his chariot-racing. At first he raced in private, but soon he was inviting the public in to cheer him on." Tacitus, *Annals 14.14* Nero used his private Circus, not as large as the Circus Maximus, for personal as well as public entertainments such as the killing of Christians. Today St. Peter's Square occupies most of the oval area of that ancient playground.

There is a crude brick tomb below the Papal Altar of Confession in St. Peter's Church. It can be accessed by two semi-circular ramps that descend to the 4th century Constantinian Basilica. The ancient brick tomb, covered with red plaster, is scribbled with the names of people who had visited the tomb in ancient times and there are many invocations to Christ on it. One graffiti bears the ancient inscription: *Petr...en...,* "Peter is here."

Almost two thousand years after Peter's death in Pope Pius XII's Christmas message on December 23, 1950, he startled the world with the announcement that the tomb of Peter had been found: "The relics of St. Peter have been identified in a way we believe convincing." Another Pope, John Paul VI, confirmed the discovery 18 years later on June 26, 1968: "We believe it our duty...to give you this happy announcement.... we are right in believing that the few but sacred mortal remains have been traced of the Prince of Apostles, of Simon son of Jonah, of the fisherman named Peter by Christ." Apparently, the analyses of the bones of a c. 67-year-old man from the 1st century found in that 2,000-year-old brick tomb under the Papal Altar of Confession in St. Peter's Church was convincing enough for the judicious Vatican to justify the announcements. Perhaps *Petr...en*, "Peter is here."

In 2005 Vatican archaeologists announced they had identified the tomb of Paul under the Basilica in Rome that bears his name, St. Paul's Outside The Walls. An 8-foot-long marble sarcophagus inscribed with the words *PAULO APOSTOLO MART* ("PAUL APOSTLE MARTYR") was discovered in 2002 during excavations around the church on the Via Ostiense. In June of 2009 Pope Benedict XVI announced that carbon testing on the bone fragments found in the marble sarcophagus dates to the 1st century AD. The journey of the two most famous Christian martyrs and their bones continues.

The soil under the city of Rome is of volcanic origin. The second layer of the earth contains a rock called tufa, a soft, malleable and porous rock made of compacted volcanic ash. Because of tufa's softness, it was the perfect medium for fashioning an underground cemetery. When it is exposed to air, tufa hardens enough that these underground catacombs have survived for over two thousand years.

Roman tombs, Christian or not, were protected. Roman law considered burial places sacred. Tomb violation risked deportation to the mines, exile or even death. In the Basilica of the Catacomb of Domitilla there is inscribed an ancient Roman warning: *Sacer locus. Sacrilege. Cave malu.* ("Sacred place. Sacrilege. Beware evil.") If you violate this sacred grave, evil will befall you.

There are over 40,000 inscriptions in the catacombs:

"May You Live With The Saints In Heaven In God In Christ In The Holy Spirit Forever"
"I Septimius Fronto Servant Of God Repose Here
I Shall Have No Regret For Having Lived An Honest Life
I will Serve You Lord Also In Heaven
And I Will Praise Your Name Forever
I Gave Back My Soul To God At The Age Of 33 Years And 6 Months"

"Sweet Simplicius Live In Eternity"
"Deacon Deusdedit Who Melted The Hearts Of The Obstinate With
Goodness
He Was Devoted To Justice And Led An Upright Life
He was Rich To The Poor And Poor To Himself"
"The Gentle And Innocent Severianus Rests Here In The Sign Of
Christ
He Lived More Or Less 50 Years
His Soul Was Received Into The Light Of The Lord"
"To The Sweet Repose To The Singular Piety To The Innocence Of Life
And The Marvelous Wisdom Of A Most Dear Youth Who Chose His
Mother's Religion
Augustine Lived 15 Tender Years And 3 Months
A Most Devoted Mother To Her Sweetest Son In Eternal Peace"
"Dionisia In Pace"
"Provopius In Pace"
"Eliodora In Pace"
"Laid To Rest In Pace"
"Arcireus Aged 75 In Pace"

In Pace, "In Peace" is the most common inscription in the catacombs indicating the deceased was a Christian. "Reborn" (*Renatus*) and "Born Again In Jesus" are common inscriptions. The "Day of Birth" (*Dies Natalis*) into eternal life gives a fresh meaning to death on several Christian graves. "DM" meaning "Highest God" (*Deo Maximo*) is a prominent inscription.

Many graves have *Deposito* inscribed on them. Our word "deposit" comes directly from that Latin word. A deposit is something laid aside or given in trust. The dead body is the frail deposit given for the solid hope of life eternal as the New Testament indicated:

"Now we know that if the earthly tent we live in is destroyed, we have a building from God, an eternal house in heaven, not built by human hands. Meanwhile we groan, longing to be clothed with our heavenly dwelling....so that what is mortal may be swallowed up by life. Now it is

God who has made us for this very purpose and has given us the Spirit as a deposit, guaranteeing what is to come. Therefore we are always confident and know that as long as we are at home in the body, we are away from the Lord. We live by faith, not by sight." II Corinthians 5:1-7

"...having believed, you were marked in him with a seal, the promised Holy Spirit who is a deposit guaranteeing our inheritance until the redemption of those who are God's possession." Ephesians 1: 13, 14

"He anointed us, set his seal of ownership on us, and put his Spirit in our hearts as a deposit, guaranteeing what is to come." II Corinthians 1:22

The catacomb Christians believed their dead bodies were the necessary seed deposit for the resurrection of the spiritual body in the life to come. In mortal life they had been officially sealed by the Holy Spirit as a sure guarantee of their resurrection in the life to come.

Today a Notary places his official seal on important documents like deeds and wills. Seals were even more important in the ancient world than they are now. As far back as Daniel 6:17 (c.600 BC) we learn that official documents and official acts were notarized with official seals: "A stone was brought and placed over the mouth of the (lions') den, and the king (Darius) sealed it with his own signet ring and with the rings of his nobles so that Daniel's situation might not be changed." The Median King Darius and his officials impressed their royal seals into the soft clay on the stone that had entombed Daniel with the lions. Official acts required official seals.

Signet rings, worn on the finger or on a cord around the neck, were inlaid with hard stones such as agate, onyx or jasper on which were carved emblems (a lion, a bird, letters) that were engraved in reverse on the ring. When the ring was pressed into soft wax or clay, the official signature was revealed. Signet rings were more functional jewelry than decorative and were often made of gold. When King Tutankhamun's tomb (c. 1340 BC) was found in 1921, his official gold signet ring was among the many treasures.

Six hundred years before King Tut, another Egyptian pharaoh gave his own signet ring to a Jew named Joseph who had been sold into slavery by his jealous brothers. Because he could interpret dreams, Joseph was brought from his dungeon to divine Pharaoh's troubling dream:

"Then Pharaoh said to Joseph, 'In my dream I was standing on the banks of the Nile, when out of the river there came up seven cows, fat and sleek, and they grazed among the reeds. After them, seven other cows came up, scrawny and ugly and lean....The lean, ugly cows ate up the seven fat cows....Then I woke up.'" Genesis 41:17-21

Joseph tells Pharaoh that the seven good cows are seven years of plenty and the seven scrawny cows are seven years of area-wide famine. Joseph suggests Pharaoh collect and store grain during the next fat years so the nation will survive the ensuing seven lean years:

"Then Pharaoh said to Joseph, 'Since God has made all this known to you, there is no one so discerning and wise as you. You shall be in charge of my palace and all my people are to submit to your orders. Only with respect to the throne will I be greater than you.' So Pharaoh said to Joseph, 'I hereby put you in charge of the whole land of Egypt.' Then Pharaoh took his signet ring from his finger and put it on Joseph's finger. He dressed him in robes of fine linen and put a gold chain around his neck....Thus he put him in charge of the whole land of Egypt." Genesis 41:39-43

Signet rings were only given to and used by people in authority. The ends of official documents were sealed with wax. The ring was pressed into the warm wax and the distinctive image came out positive. This ensured the contents were official and tamper-proof. To the dead Christians, God was their authority, notary and ruler. The promise of eternal life was sealed by His Spirit and guaranteed their eternal existence and inheritance. At the resurrection the seal would be broken and they would rise from the dead into eternal life.

To early Christians' *Deposito* on a tomb also meant---deposited in corruption, raised incorruptible. They believed the dead body had to be sown (deposited) in order to reap the spiritual body. Your dead body was your deposit on eternal life with God Who is spirit. John 4:24 *Deposito* shortens Paul's words in I Corinthians 15:35-45:

"But someone may ask, How are the dead raised? With what kind of a body will they come?....What you sow does not come to life unless it dies. When you sow, you do not plant (deposit) the body that will be but just a seed perhaps of wheat....So will it be with the resurrection of the dead. The body that is sown is perishable...it is sown a natural body; it is raised a spiritual body."

The physical body is like an acorn, perhaps, or a seed of corn. When it is planted in the earth, it must first rot and die. Only then can it become the huge oak tree or the graceful stalk of corn.

The "deposited" in the catacombs lie 25' to 65' below the surface of Rome. Descending the deep stairways, one enters a maze of underground passageways. Prudentius (348-392), an early Christian poet, describes his 4th century descent into this stygian darkness:

"Not far from the city walls among the well-trimmed orchards there lays a crypt buried in darksome pits. Into its secret recesses a steep path with winding stairs direct one, even though the turnings shut out the light. The light of day, indeed, comes in through the doorway and illuminates the threshold of the portico; and when, as you advance further, the darkness as of night seems to get more and more obscure. Through the mazes of the cavern, there occur at intervals apertures cut in the roof (*luminaria*) which convey the bright radiance of the sun down into the cave. Although the recesses, winding at random this way and that, form narrow chambers with darksome galleries, yet a considerable quantity of light finds its way through the pierced vaulting down into the hollow bowels of the mountain. And thus throughout the subterranean crypt it is possible to perceive the brightness and enjoy the light of the absent sun." *Liber Peristephanon*

In spite of the presence of these *luminaria* or light shafts, the overwhelming experience of a modern visitor to the catacombs is one of darkness. In the catacombs open to the public, dull light bulbs punctuate the blackness.

The passages are about 3' wide---just wide enough for the gravediggers to have maneuvered. The walls are lined three to five-stories high with small *loculi* (burial places) stacked on top of each other like berths on a large ship. Most of the graves are 16"-24" high and 47"-59" long, a tight squeeze. The body was wrapped in linen and laid in the hollow. The burial niches were covered with pottery tiles fixed by mortar or a thin marble slab. Sometimes graves had brief inscriptions or recognition signs. In order to commemorate the dead and probably to identify the exact grave among the packed walls of the galleries, loved ones would press a little lamp, a coin, a small toy, a figure in glass paste, a shell, a piece of ivory, buttons, necklaces, small metal bells, a doll or statuette made of bone or some other remembrance into the new mortar. The tiles that once covered their bodies have long ago been pillaged. The empty graves gape open.

In the 200-300's *arcosolia* became popular. These graves were much larger niches with arches above them that held private graves in a discrete area. Wealthy families often had an arcosolium.

There are numerous small rooms called *cubicula* carved into the catacombs. Most of the cubicula are square or polygonal and contain many graves. In 1853 de Rossi, an explorer of the catacombs, found one family cubicle closed by an engraved marble slab: "Marcus Antonius Tatutus Made This Sepulcher For Himself And His Own Who Are Confident In The Lord." The cubicles were usually family mausoleums with separate niches for the burial of bodies, but guilds of bakers or coopers also had cubicles. The famous Crypt Of The Popes in the Catacomb of St. Callixtus is a cubiculum. Almost all of the Christian paintings and iconography in the catacombs of Rome are found in these small rooms and in the arched arcosoliums.

From the inscriptions and paintings in the catacombs, it can be deduced that most of the Christians came from the working class in Rome. One of the critics of early Christianity, Celsus, sarcastically said that only "weavers, cobblers and fullers, the most illiterate persons" held to the "irrational faith" and taught it to "women and children." Origen, *Against Celsus IV* In Domitilla there is a badly damaged picture of an anonymous woman standing by a table where her vegetables are displayed. On the walls of the catacombs a man bakes bread; a fishmonger sits in his shop; a farmer has a sickle in one hand and vegetables in the other; a man sits upon a wagon drawn by oxen; eight men stand by two large barrels; a man is beside a boat filled with casks of oil; men carry bags of grain on their backs and, attesting to the Italian's abiding love of pancetta and prosciutto, there is in the Catacomb of St. Agnes a very good drawing of a ham with the Latin word *perna* meaning "ham" engraved under it. Tools of their trade are incised into the walls: wine barrels, spindles, compasses, instruments for measuring grain, hammers, scissors, chisels, scales, musical instruments and a pair of pliers holding an extracted molar. The epigraphy, the inscriptions in the catacombs testify to diverse occupations: butchers, bakers, milkmen, pastry makers, glass blowers, barbers, engravers of gems and stone, acrobats, gymnasts, gladiator instructors, shafts of wheat indicate farmers and female merchants sell oil. These were people with everyday occupations that kept the everyday life of the Romans clipping along at an everyday pace. Sculptors, gladiators, soldiers, charioteers, teachers, physicians, surgeons and even an exorcist declare their occupations. These "last words" and "last paintings" illustrate the pride and honor people have always felt in a life devoted to a profession.

There are few names on the graves but some survive. "Cucumio" worked in the Baths of Caracalla and another man was a "cloak room attendant" there. "Deuterius. Interpreter Of Ancient Seers And Teacher Of Latin And Greek, Rests In Tranquil Peace" as does "Primenius The Food Seller," "Jovinus The Carriage Builder," "Aurelius Aurelianus The Centurion Of The V Cohort" and "Faustus The Waiter."

Most of the names in the catacombs are Latin or Greek ones. The most common Christian names are: Aurelius (411 mentions); Flavius

(149); Julius (94); Aelius (84); Valerius (64); Claudius (52); Ulpius (24) and Antonius (20). Obviously names of emperors and famous men were popular. Some were named after pagan deities: Eros, Hercules, Hermes. Perhaps these men came from pagan families and converted to Christianity. Others were clearly born in Christian families and were given names with a theological meaning: Irene (Peace), Spes (Hope), Agape (Love) and Anastasius (Resurrection).

The exact number of catacombs under Rome varies from scholar to scholar. Some say there are 45. Others say 50 or 69.

It is unclear exactly when Christians began to use the catacombs to bury their dead. Probably in the beginning or middle of the 2nd century wealthy Christians began to allow fellow-believers to be buried underground on their country estates along the consular roads. The catacombs of Praetextatus, Domitilla and Priscilla are named after these benefactors.

When the Goths sacked Rome under Alaric the Visigoth in 410, burial in the catacombs ceased, but they continued to be the destination of holy pilgrimages to Rome. In the 700's the Roman Church could no longer maintain them and feared the relics of the martyrs would be pillaged in the continuing attacks on Rome. They transferred the relics to various churches and sites inside the walls of Rome. The pilgrims, no longer able to experience the catacombs and to see where the holy martyrs were interred, stopped coming to Rome. The catacombs were abandoned. Their entrances became clogged with vegetation and refuse. The underground cities were lost, forgotten for almost a thousand years.

Antonio Bosio (1575-1629), called the "Columbus of the Catacombs," was inspired to look for catacombs when in 1578 there was an accidental discovery of a part of a catacomb on the Via Salaria. Bosio spent the rest of his life trying to find and finding entrances to catacombs. He cleared away rubble, climbed into cramped tunnels, dug into ancient volumes to discover the names and locations of these old tombs. He recorded and drew everything he had discovered, and after his death, *Roma Sotterannea* (*Underground Rome*), the work of his lifetime, was published.

Bosio had called attention to the catacombs, but unfortunately that attention led to the pillaging of all the individual burial sites within the catacombs. Looters, some lawless, some official, opened all the graves searching for the bodies and relics of martyrs, gouged out rings and necklaces from the soft tufa, shattered the cement of each grave in search of pieces of bone or gold. The gaping graves, the broken marble, the frescoes with graffiti on them---the catacombs as they are seen today---all date from this post-Bosio period.

After the initial frenzy and looting following Bosio's finds, the catacombs were again forgotten and deserted. Two hundred years later an Italian boy named Giovanni Battista de Rossi ((1822-1894) was given Bosio's *Roma Sotterannea* for his 11th birthday. At the age of 27, de Rossi rediscovered the entrance to the Catacomb of Callixtus on the Via Appia. He devoted the rest of his life to the scholarship of the catacombs, to its epigraphy, its frescoes, its graffiti, its topography. In 1867 de Rossi published his own book named *La Roma Sotterranea Cristiana, Christian Underground Rome*, in imitation of and homage to Antonio Bosio whose book had first kindled his interest.

The catacombs are the property of Italy, but since the Lateran Agreement in 1929, they are under the care of the Vatican. Today, they are just one of the many things one can see in Rome. They are not the reason one comes to Rome as they were in the earliest years, but because of Bosio and de Rossi they are not now forgotten and unknown.

The unsung heroes of these underground cities are the men who dug the catacombs: the *fossores*, the gravediggers. Over a period of three hundred years (c. 100-400) these men accomplished one of the most amazing feats of underground construction ever endeavored. With just metal picks and shovels they dug out millions and millions of tons of tufa rock and disposed of it basketful by basketful. The ash from this volcanic rock, pozzolana, was the secret ingredient in Roman cement that was so strong the domed Parthenon has been standing in tact for 2,000 years. Soon the whole ancient world wanted Rome's amazing cement and the fossors and others went into business selling the excavated tufa. It was shipped abroad from the bridge on the Tiber River that is to this day called the Porto di Pozzolana.

The fossors worked in total darkness with only small oil lamps to guide their work. If their lamps went out, they could easily lose their way and be stranded in the maze of tunnels for days. Giovanni Battista de Rossi took a gun with him when he entered the tunnels. If he got lost, he would fire the gun up through a luminaria and rescuers could find him.

In the early centuries of construction, the gravediggers carried the volcanic dirt out of the long passageways and then up the steep steps into the daylight. Later on, they built the luminaria. The skylights took care of several problems: the stench of rotting bodies and the need for light and air. Because the fossors could hoist the tons of dirt up basketful by basketful through the skylights, construction became much more efficient.

There are several pictures of fossors in the catacombs. Diogenes the Gravedigger is buried in the Catacomb of Callixtus. A fresco of him shows a mature man in a tunic with a lamp in his left hand and a pick over his right shoulder. At his feet are scattered levers, picks and other tools of his trade. "Diogenes Fossor. In Pace. Depositus Octabu Kalends Octobris." The inscription "In Pace" ("In Peace") over his tomb identifies Diogenes as a Christian. Another very young fossor is depicted in the Catacomb of Peter and Marcellinus on the Via Labicana. Barefoot, with a closely shaved beard and wearing a short tunic, he is excavating the rock with a pick. A lamp hangs by his side. In the Catacomb of Commodilla a roughly incised image depicts a fossor, wearing an apron to hold his tools, with a lamp in his left hand and in his right hand a pick cavalierly thrown over his shoulder. Before him is a body wrapped for burial. In addition to digging the underground tombs, the fossors usually buried the dead.

Eventually the gravediggers formed a guild and were loosely attached to the infant church. Over the centuries they became very powerful. Many of them bought underground land and sold burial sites. One inscription in illiterate Latin reads: "The Place Of Filumenus Which He Bought For His Family From The Fossor Florentius." Some gravediggers became very wealthy.

When the persecution of the Church ended in 313, Christians

continued to be buried in the catacombs for another hundred years. At this time the fossors referred to themselves as "clergy" and even tried to get military exemption. But they had overreached and were soundly denied both title and exemption: "(Exemption is) refused to them who protect themselves by the title of clerics when they are really occupied in the gloomy obsequies of the dead."

History was moving on. Christians began burying their dead in the churches or in cemeteries above ground. The fossors became obsolete. By c. 440 this cadre of daring and brilliant engineers who shovelful by shovelful had forged underground cities that would endure and amaze for millennia had ceased to exist.

The fossors were not the only Romans who did amazing engineering feats. Sextus Julius Frontinus (c. 40-130). We know his name and we know what he did. In 96 AD he was appointed *Curator Aquarum*, Curator of Water, of the city of Rome. After an outstanding career as a soldier, governor and politician, Frontinus at age 56 became superintendent of the water works of Rome:

"Inasmuch as every task assigned the Emperor demands special attention; and inasmuch as I am incited, not merely to diligence, but also to devotion, when any matter is entrusted to me...and inasmuch as Nerva Augustus (Emperor from 96-98)...has laid upon me the duties of water commissioner, an office which concerns not merely the convenience but also the health and even the safety of the City, and which has always been administered by the most eminent men of our State; now therefore I deem it of the first and greatest importance to familiarize myself with the business I have undertaken, a policy which I have always made a principle in other affairs."

So begins Frontinus' valuable, detailed and highly interesting book *The Aqueducts Of Rome.*

As the fossors were constructing their underground architectural wonders, the builders of the aqueducts of Rome were erecting and perfecting the system of arched aqueducts and underground pipes that brought billions of gallons of fresh water every day into the capital city of the world.

How many people did this ingenious system of waterworks serve? Modern scholars are scattered on the number of people living in Rome at that time. Most think there were about a million people. But Augustus Caesar who was living at that time and was in charge of taking censuses of his people says:

"...in my sixth consulate (28 BC) I made a census of the people with Marcus Agrippas as my colleague...in which...4,063,000 heads of Roman citizens (were counted)....Then again (in 8BC)...I conducted a lustrum (purification rite after the taking of a new census) in which ...were counted 4,233,000 heads of Roman citizens. And the third time (in 14 AD) with my son Tiberias as a colleague...counted 4,937,000 of the heads of Roman citizens."

This first-hand account of what Caesar Augustus did is taken from *Res Gestae Divi Augusti* (*The Deeds Of The Divine Augustus*) written in 14 by Augustus himself when he was 76 years old. In the 16th century *The Deeds* were found inscribed on marble in a building in Ankara, Turkey that had been dedicated to Augustus. Called *Monumentum Ancyranum*, it is considered to be the most famous inscription of antiquity.

There is some speculation that the censuses taken by Augustus were Empire-wide. But during a 1941 excavation at Ostia, Italy at the mouth of the Tiber River, an inscription was found indicating that at the time of Augustus' successor Tiberias (14-37), the population of Rome was 4,100,000.

When Frontinus was head of water works in 96, there were probably about four million people living in greater Rome. Frontinus had charge of 11 aqueducts. Rome's main aqueduct alone, the Aqua Marcia, brought 51,511,000 gallons of water each day into Rome. Combining all 11 aqueducts, billions of gallons, some estimate 264,019,630,000 gallons, of sweet water flowed into greater Rome every 24 hours. In comparison, today in the Capital of the United States, Washington, D.C., DC WASA delivers about 108,000,000 gallons of sweet water per day to c. 5,000,000 people living in the greater metropolitan area. Per day/per person ancient Rome's aqueducts provided many more times the amount of water to its customers than WASA does to its customers in our modern-day capital. Strabo, the Greek historian (c. 64 BC-24 AD), in his *Geography 5.3.8* marveled at the Roman aqueducts and their scope and efficiency:

"...so plentiful is the supply of water from the aqueducts that rivers may be said to flow through the city (Rome) and the sewers, and almost every house is furnished with water pipes and copious fountains."

After Frontinus had done his due diligence and had inventoried the water system, detailed the monitoring system and corrected existing problems, he had the Senate enact standards for water maintenance and construction. He who came from politics and the military was, like Strabo, awed by the workings of Rome's aqueducts. "I ask you!" he shouted. "Just compare this vast array of indispensable structures carrying so much water with the idle pyramids or the world-famous but useless monuments of the Greeks!" The Roman water system was living, evolving and imminently useful. For a pragmatic man like Frontinus they far outweighed the inert, useless architectural wonders from the past.

When the eleven aqueducts that supplied water to Rome were completed, their combined lengths were over 300 miles. Only 29 miles of this water system was above ground. The rest carried the water underground through lead pipes into Rome. (Gibbons in *The Decline And Fall Of The Roman Empire* cites these lead pipes as a contributing factor to the eventual fall of the Romans because of the debilitating effects of lead poisoning over the years on Roman bodies and minds.)

The underground pipes and above ground arched aqueducts were constructed over, under and through all types of terrain. The continual flow of the water relied entirely on gravity. The sources of most of the water were underground springs. Once these were identified, the surveyors (*librators*) moved in. They had to calculate not only the beginning and the end of an aqueduct but the gradient that had to be maintained to keep the water running but not rushing along many miles. The *chorobates* was a rod 20' long with legs on either end used to level and to determine these gradients. A *groma* was a surveying instrument used to measure straight lines and right angles. Pictures of groma show sticks and stones attached to the instrument. One of these groma was found in the ruins of Pompeii. These two instruments, crucial to building the aqueducts, seem very primitive. With considerably less than modern equipment, the Romans built a water delivery system that was unrivaled for the next 2,000 years.

When the aqueducts were completed, the regulation of the water became an official matter. Private villas as well as commercial consumers paid for their water. It was delivered into their homes and businesses just like we dispense water today. The common people collected their water from hundreds of fountains scattered throughout Rome while massive cisterns held water for emergencies. The cistern outside of Naples, Italy that held the fresh water supply for the entire Roman fleet can still be seen at Misenum.

Above ground and below ground Roman technical skill and pragmatic ingenuity would be the plumb line for 2,000 years after her fall. But as the catacombs were being hollowed out of the soft earth under her city and the aqueducts were spanning her countryside with ribbons of clean water, serious hairline cracks were beginning to weaken the entire foundation of Roman civilization.

III.

"...they rounded up some bad characters from the marketplace, formed a mob and started a riot in the city (Thessalonica). They rushed to Jason's house in search of Paul and Silas in order to bring them out to the crowd. But when they did not find them, they dragged Jason and some other brothers before the city officials shouting: 'These men who have caused trouble all over the world have now come here....They are all defying Caesar's decrees, saying that there is another king, one called Jesus.'" Acts 17:5-7 (c. 63 AD)

Arma virumque cano. "I sing of arms and the man." So begins the first book of Virgil's poem *The Aeneid* (written c. 29-19 BC). It is the epic story of Aeneas, Virgil's founder of Rome, who fled from burning Troy in c. 1200 BC carrying his father Anchises on his back. He and his band of homeless Trojans sailed the Mediterranean and landed on the shores of Carthage. The aristocratic and beautiful queen Dido welcomed them. Dido fell in love with her guest Aeneas. They had a love affair. But Aeneas remembered his destiny was to found a great city. He sailed away from Dido and Carthage. Besotted Dido killed herself with Aeneas' sword. Aeneas founded Rome. There were endless wars (Punic Wars 264-146 BC) between Dido's Carthaginians and Aeneas' Romans. They did not live happily ever after.

The ruins of Dido's ancient city of Carthage are in Tunisia on the northern coast of Africa. In the time of the building of the aqueducts and the catacombs, Carthage, with a population of about 300,00 people, was one of the principal cities of the Roman Empire. It was a wealthy city because its location commanded the trade routes from the eastern to the western Mediterranean. Romans had lived there for centuries. Caesar Augustus (63 BC-14 AD) who ruled Rome when Jesus of Nazareth was born gave many land grants in Carthage to soldiers who had distinguished themselves in battle or in service to the emperor.

Wherever Romans went, they took their *circus* ("ring") with them. Roman circuses were huge circular or oval arenas used for contests and spectacles (*spectaculum*). The Roman satirist Juvenal (65-140 AD) in *Satires 10* said, "All the people of Rome care about is the grain supply and circuses (*panem et circenses*)." This famous analysis of a declining culture has been appropriated to: "All the people care about is bread and circus."

In the eleventh-hour of their culture a great percentage of the Roman people lived on handouts from the State. As long as they had free food and free entertainment, they could be kept in check and the imperial throne was secure. That had not been so in the years of the Republic (c. 509-45 BC) when the Roman people were responsible for electing their leaders, conferring honors on worthy citizens and running the Roman legions. But over the years the Roman people abdicated significant rights for material needs and pleasures. During the years of its persecution of Christians (c. 60-313), Rome was in a slow decline. The Barbarians were at the steppes if not at the gates.

Carthage as a prominent Roman colony had a huge amphitheater. Recently archaeologists have found in the ruins of ancient Carthage remnants of a structure they believe to be the walls of a church dedicated to Carthage's most famous Christian martyr, Perpetua. The church is outside the south gate near the amphitheater.

Emperor Septimius Severus who ruled from 193-211 took the eradication of Christians seriously. He passed an edict in 202 that all people under the rule of Rome were forbidden under penalty of death to become Christians. New converts or "catechumens" were to be sought out and killed publicly in the circus.

Carthage had a vibrant and growing Christian community in 200

A.D. One of the great Early Church intellects was the Carthaginian Tertullian (c. 160-220). His conversion to Christianity in his 30's was occasioned in part by his observations of how heroically Christians died in the arenas. Some have hypothesized Perpetua was a member of Tertullian's home church. He who said in his *Apologeticus* that "the blood of the martyrs is the seed of the church" may have been there that day in March of 203 when the five young, new Christians Perpetua, Felicitas, Saturus, Revocatus and Saturninus were killed in the arena.

Perpetua wrote *The Passion of St. Perpetua* in Latin as she awaited martyrdom. It is the most ancient document extant by a Christian woman. It has been reproduced and read since the day she died. No serious scholar has ever doubted its authenticity.

Perpetura came from a noble family in Carthage. She was twenty-two, married and had an infant son who was still nursing. We do not know how long she had been a Christian or how she became a Christian. Written during her imprisonment, her diary begins by recounting the conversations the new convert had with her father. He knew the deadly implications of her faith and constantly tried to get his beloved daughter to recant. From her diary:

"When we (Christians) were still under legal surveillance (before the arrest), my father was liked to vex me with his words and continually strove to hurt my faith because of his love: Father, said I, Do you see this vessel lying, a pitcher or whatsoever it may be? And he said, I see it. And I said to him, Can it be called by any other name than that which it is? And he answered, No. So can I call myself nought other than that which I am, a Christian."

Because of the Emperor's edict, Perpetua, her servant Felicitas and the three young men were arrested and thrown into prison:

"(I was) much afraid because I had never known such darkness....I was tormented there by care for my child. Then Tertius and Pomponius, the blessed deacons who ministered to us, (bribed the guards) with money that for a few hours we should be taken forth to a better part of the prison and be refreshed. Then...I suckled my child who was now faint with hunger. And being careful for the child, I spoke to my mother and strengthened my brother and commended my son unto them. I pined because I saw they pined for my sake. Such cares I suffered for many days (until) the child (came to be) with me in prison; and straightaway I became well and was lightened of my labor and...suddenly the prison was made a palace for me."

Perpetua, her baby and the others waited in prison for a trial date. When the trial date was announced, her father rushed to the prison:

"...the report went abroad that we were to be tried. My father returned from the city spent with weariness; and he came up to me to cast down my faith saying: Have pity, daughter, on my grey hairs; have pity on your father, if I am worthy to be called father by you; if with these hands I have brought you into this flower of youth and I have preferred you before all your brothers; give me not over to the reproach of men. Look upon your brothers; look upon your mother and mother's sister; look upon your son who will not endure to live after you. Give up your resolution; do not destroy us all together; for none of us will speak openly with men again if you (die in the arena)."

Perpetua knew how painful this was for her father and had compassion for him:

"This he said fatherly in his love, kissing my hands and groveling at my feet and with tears he named me, not daughter, but lady. And I was grieved for my father's case because he would not rejoice at my passion... and I comforted him saying: Whatsoever God shall please that shall be done at this trial; for know that we are not established in our own power, but in God's. And he went from me very sorrowful."

The day of their trial arrived. The whole city had talked of nothing else but of this noble girl who by her conversion to Christianity had betrayed her family, her baby, the emperor and the gods. Perpetua writes:

"(When) we were at meal we were suddenly snatched away to be tried; and we came to the forum....A report spread abroad through the parts near the forum and a very great multitude gathered together. We went up to the tribunal. The others being asked (Are you a Christian?), confessed. So they came to me. And my father appeared there also, with my son, and would draw me from the step saying: Perform the sacrifice! Have mercy on the child! And Hilarian the procurator...said: Spare your father's grey hairs; spare the infancy of the boy. Make sacrifice to the Emperor's prosperity. (But) I answered: I am a Christian. And when my father stood by me yet to cast down my faith, he was bidden by Hilarian to be cast down and was smitten with a rod. And I sorrowed for my father's harm as though I had been smitten myself; so sorrowed I for his unhappy old age. Then Hilarian passed sentence upon us all and condemned us to the beasts; and cheerfully we went down to the dungeon. Then because my child had been used to being breastfed, and to staying with me in prison, straightaway I sent Pomponius the deacon to my father, asking for the child. But my father would not give him. And as God willed, no longer did he need to be suckled, nor did I take fever that I might not be tormented by care for the child and by the pain of my breasts."

Felicitas, eight month's pregnant, was Perpetua's slave and was apprehended with her. Perhaps Felicitas was in the faith before Perpetua. So many slaves had led their masters to Christ. When the Apostle Paul wrote the letter to the Philippians from his prison cell in Rome in the early 60's, he ends the epistle with "All the saints send you greetings, especially those who belong to Caesar's household." (Phil. 4:22) Only thirty years after Jesus' resurrection in Jerusalem, faith in the new Savior had infiltrated the palace of Nero in Rome, probably through his slaves.

Felicitas was distraught. Roman law forbade the execution of pregnant women. She wanted to die with her friends and not "shed her blood after (her delivery), among strangers and malefactors. Also her fellow martyrs were much afflicted lest they should leave behind them...

their fellow traveler on the road of the same hope. (So) with joint and united groaning they poured out their prayer to the Lord three days before the games....After their prayer her pains came upon her."

In her cell Felicitas screamed out in pain. One of the jailers yelled to her, "You...make complaint now, what will you do when you are thrown to the beasts!" She had a baby girl on March 4, 203 "whom a sister reared up to be her own daughter."

In prison Perpetua had many beatific dreams of battle and victory that encouraged her and her friends as they approached the hour of their death. After the final vision of victory, "I awoke and understood that I should fight, not with beasts, but against the devil; but I knew that mine was the victory."

Perpetua ends her diary on March 6, 203 the day before her contest in the arena: "Thus far I have written this, till the day before the games; but the deed of the games themselves, let him write who will."

Someone, perhaps the deacon Pomponius who had ministered to the new believers in prison, recorded the deaths of the young people at the end of her diary: "...we are unworthy to finish the recounting of so great glory," he wrote, "yet we accomplish the will of the most holy Perpetua...adding one testimony more of her own steadfastness and height of spirit."

The original diary was written in Latin. But within a hundred years, there were many copies in both Greek and Latin. For us almost two thousand years later, the narrative is not only touching and painful, but it is a valuable primary source of information about the deaths of Christians and others in the Roman arenas.

The amphitheater in Carthage held 70,000 people. On March 7, 203 the games would honor the emperor. The young catechumens were to be the entertainment. "Now dawned the day of their victory and they went forth...cheerful and bright of countenance." When they entered the arena, Perpetua's "piercing look" at the crowd, caused them to "cast down their eyes."

All Roman games were dedicated to gods and goddesses. The young Christian men, Saturas, Revocatus and Saturninus, were compelled to put on the robes of the priests of Saturn (a god of harvest). Perpetua and Felicitas were ordered to don the dress of the priestesses of Ceres (goddess of grain).

Perpetua would not. She cried out, "For this cause we came willingly that our liberty might not be obscured. For this cause we give our lives that we might do no such thing as this!" The tribune gave up and "led them forth as they were." Perpetua began to sing hymns as she walked around the great arena. Revocatus, Saturninus and Saturas "threatened the people" with God's judgment.

When they came to the box where the Roman procurator Hilarian presided, "they (said) to Hilarian, stretching forth their hands and nodding their heads: You judge us...and God will judge you. At this (outburst) the crowd became enraged and demanded they should be beaten with scourges." They each were beaten thirty nine times with cat 'o nine tails. "They gave thanks because they had received somewhat of the sufferings of the Lord."

Their sufferings had only begun. Bold Saturninus had said when he was imprisoned that he "wished to be thrown to every kind of beast so that indeed he might wear a more glorious (heavenly) crown. At the beginning of the spectacle therefore Saturninus and Revocatus first (were mauled by) a leopard and afterwards torn by a bear (as they were tied down) on a raised bridge." They died and were dragged out of the arena.

Next was Saturus. He had told the soldier Pudens that he would die by "one bite of a leopard....Therefore when he was being given to a wild boar, the gladiator who had bound him to the boar was torn to pieces by the same beast and died after the days of the games. Saturus was no more than dragged around. Moreover when he had been tied on the bridge to be assaulted by a bear, the bear would not come forth from his den. So Saturus was called back unharmed a second time....at another gate Saturus exhorted Pudens the soldier saying: So then indeed, as I trusted and foretold, I have felt no assault of beasts until now. And now believe with all your heart. Behold, I go out and shall perish by one bite of a leopard. And immediately at the end of the spectacle, the leopard was released and with one bite Saturus was covered with so much blood that the people in witness to his second baptism cried out to him: Well washed! Well washed!"

A man, covered with blood, caused the people in the stadium to cry out, "Well washed! Well washed!" We can deduce from this first hand account that "Well washed!" was a typical chant of the crowd after a gladiator or criminal or Christian was particularly bloodied in the arena. We see, also, from the account of Saturninus' and Revocatus' deaths that more than one animal could be released on the prisoners and that a prisoner was often tied down so the animal did not have to chase him.

Sometimes a victim was tied to a wild animal. In the case of Saturus, a gladiator who was strapping Saturus to the wild boar was himself gored to death. There were hazards even for those not condemned to die.

They abandoned the boar scenario, Instead they tied Saturus to a bridge, but the bear would not leave his den. The master of the beasts had overfed the bear. One would imagine that the people would give a "thumb's up" to a man who had cheated death twice. But Saturus was forced to enter the arena a third time to face a leopard.

As he lay dying, he said to Pudens:

"Farewell. Remember the faith and me. Let not these things trouble you, but strengthen you....Saturus took from Pudens' finger a little ring...(dipped) it in his wound...leaving Pudens a pledge and memorial of his blood. Then as the breath left him, he was cast down with the rest in the accustomed place for his throat to be cut."

We learn from this passage that there was a pit for the dead in the arena and that the Romans did a final dispatch on all bodies before they were burned or buried. Just in case.

For the next spectacle, Perpetua and Felicitas were brought forth. A savage she cow was chosen for their deaths. The manuscript says the cow was "prepared for this purpose against all custom." What laws or breeding practices they violated in order to produce such a cow is not known. The two young women had been stripped naked and "made to put on nets; and so they were brought forth. The people shuddered seeing one a tender girl (Perpetua) and the other her breasts yet dropping from her recent childbearing (Felicitas)." Even the bloodthirsty crowd was made uneasy by the sight of the naked young mothers:

"So (the two girls) were called back and clothed in loose robes. Perpetua was attacked first and thrown. She fell on her loins. When she sat upright, her robe being torn at the side, she drew it over to cover her thigh mindful rather of modesty than of pain. Next (she looked for a hairpin) and pinned up her disheveled hair; for it was not meet that a martyr should suffer with hair disheveled lest she seem to grieve....So she stood up. She saw Felicitas smitten down. She went up and gave her hand and raised her up. Both of them stood up together and the hardness of the people now subdued they were called back to the Gate of Life."

As can be gleaned, death in the circus sometimes took a long time. After the cow mauled the young women, Perpetua covers her nakedness and pins up her hair. She helps Felicitas get up. The crowd's mood changes. It is not fun anymore. They are led out of the arena to the Gate of Life.

Another believer, Rusticus, comforts the women. Perpetua is dazed and asks him, "When are we going to be thrown to the cow? When she heard that this had been done already, she would not believe it until she saw some marks of mauling on her body and her dress...she called her brother and Rusticus to her and spoke to them. Stand fast in the faith and love you all one another. Don't be offended because of our passion, our suffering."

One would imagine that being sent to the "Gate of Life" in a Roman circus would be a blessed reprieve. It was, in fact, where the condemned waited to be beheaded. Felicitas was dispatched with one blow.

But "the swordsman was a novice...Perpetua was pierced between the bones and shrieked out." He had missed. Her neck was mangled and blood was everywhere. "When the swordsman's hand wandered still, (Perpetua) set the sword upon her own neck." She guided her nervous executioner to the place. That chop was final.

IV.

"Other writers of history record the victories of war and the trophies won from enemies, the skill of generals and the manly bravery of soldiers defiled with blood and with the innumerable slaughters for the sake of children and country and other possessions. But our narrative of the government of God will record in ineffaceable letters the most peaceful wars waged in behalf of the peace of the soul and I will tell of men doing brave deeds for truth rather than country, and for piety rather than dearest friends. I will hand down to imperishable remembrance the discipline and the much-tried fortitude of the Athletes Of Religion, the trophies won from demons, the victories over invisible enemies and the crowns placed upon their heads." Eusebius, *Church History 5*

As Perpetua's Diary has left us a unique and personal account of the heroic deaths of Christian martyrs during the Roman persecutions, Eusebius of Caesarea (c. 260-339) in his *Church History* wrote the definitive history of the first three hundred years of the Christian faith.

Eusebius was the Bishop of Caesarea Maritima a city of 50,000 on the Mediterranean half way between modern Tel Aviv and Haifa. Herod the Great, the Herod under whom Jesus was born, was known for his massive building projects. The building of the harbor in the port city of Caesarea in just 12 years (c. 22-10 BC) was one of the most amazing engineering projects in the ancient world. In order to make the harbor navigable for ships, Herod built two breakwaters of Roman concrete, one 1,800' long and the other 900' long. 44 shiploads carrying 400 tons each brought the pozzolana and the lime for the concrete from Rome to Caesarea. Divers worked underwater to lay the wooden forms for the concrete. Huge barges were floated out to sea and the cement was poured into the forms until they sank. Herod named the new harbor Sebastos, the Greek word for "Augustus," his patron. For thousands of years, until the excavations at the harbor in the 1980's-1990's proved the truth of the ancient accounts, technicians and scholars did not believe that underwater engineers 2,000 years ago had the ability to do what Herod's engineers had done.

Caesarea Maritima became the most important harbor in the Mediterranean, second only to the harbor in Alexandria. The Roman centurion Cornelius lived in Caesarea (Acts 10:1). Philip the Evangelist and his four daughters who were prophetesses lived there for a while (Acts 21:8,9) and Paul the Apostle was imprisoned in Caesarea for two years (Acts 23:23-26:32). It was the seat of the Roman Prefect in Judea and after the destruction of Jerusalem in 70 AD, the Romans ruled Judea from Caesarea.

In the first 350 years of the Christian faith, Caesarea was considered one of the hubs of the faith and had its own influential bishops, one of whom was the learned Eusebius who wrote the invaluable *Church History*. He was the only man who wrote a comprehensive history of the Early Church in its first 300 years. He sifted through mountains of material and culled information from scholars and writers who had lived through the years from c. 60 to 324. Many of the manuscripts he references and the writers he quotes have been lost. Were it not for the Bishop of Caesarea, our knowledge and understanding of Christianity in its infancy would be fractional. His *Church History* is the work upon which later church historians must and did build. Eusebius' purpose was not only to chronicle the people, events and doctrines crucial to the development of the Early Church, but also to commit to history the "Athletes Of Religion" who contended for the faith in the sandy arenas of Rome and the distant reaches of her empire.

Athletes (Latin *athlos* meaning "contest") and sports have been with us since man began. The word "sport" is an Anglo-Saxon word that grew to mean "pastime, recreation, pleasure." Probably the first sports derived from hunting needs and wars:

Who could throw the spear better than anyone else?

Who was the most accurate at shooting an arrow?

Who best wrestled a man to the ground and pinned him?

From the archers 30,000 years ago seen in the caves of Altimira in Spain and Lescaux in France to the 1500 BC ball courts in Mesoamerica and the first Olympic games of Greece in 776 BC, the need for competition and sports has been universal and central to man's existence.

The first Olympics were held in the town of Olympia in the district of Elis, Greece. There was only one contest---the 200-yard dash. It was won by a naked runner named Coroebus, a cook from Elis. He was crowned with a wreath of olive leaves taken from the grove near the Temple of Zeus there in Olympia and that humble crown was worn for almost a thousand years by winners of Roman games and by rulers of Rome.

The Greeks held the Olympic Games every four years. The 400-yard dash was added in 772 BC. Gradually boxing and the pentathlon consisting of discus throwing, javelin toss, long jump, running and wrestling became events. Every four years for over a thousand years the Olympics were held in Greece until the emperor Theodosius I, a Christian convert, abolished the games in 393 because of their paganism. Long before that date the Romans had devised other contests and many Christians were killed in those games.

Some scholars think the popular gladiator contests originated with the Etruscans and were adopted by the Romans. Others believe they grew out of funeral rites that had involved human sacrifice. Rufius Festus (c. 369 AD) says the combat was a substitute for the sacrifice of prisoners and slaves at the grave of an important person.

The first gladiator contest occurred in 264 BC in the cattle market in Rome. Marcus and Decimus Brutus staged the event to honor their dead father. The honoring of the dead was a Roman duty, a *munus*. That day three pairs of slaves fought. The people loved the novel sword-to-sword combat. Other men began holding similar munera for the dead. The Roman contests had begun.

Even older than the gladiator contests were the chariot races in Rome dating back to c. 600 BC. The races were held in a natural declivity in the Murcian Valley between the Palatine and Aventine hills. The Circus Maximus, built in 326 BC and appropriately named Biggest Circle, was a gigantic amphitheater. The oval racetrack was 2,037' long and 387' wide. The Circus suffered a devastating fire in 31 BC. When the 33-year-old Caesar Augustus became emperor in 27 BC, he restored the buildings and enlarged the seating capacity to 250,000 people. (Two thousand years later, the largest stadium in the modern world, the Indianapolis Speedway, holds the same amount of people.)

The Circus Maximus was designed for chariot racing, but other events were held there. There were processions for and celebrations of their gods and goddesses, especially the goddess of the moon Luna and Ceres, goddess of grain, as well as gladiatorial contests and wild animal hunts. Because the wealthy in Rome organized and paid for these entertainments, they were free to the public. The Roman public was insatiable. By the time of Augustus, almost a fourth of every year was devoted to a Circus. In order to curry favor with the plebeians, Emperor Domitian once sponsored one hundred chariot races in one day.

Chariot racing was the most popular sport in Rome. There were four racing companies (Latin *factiones*): the Red Faction, The Blue Faction, the White Faction and the Green Faction named for their racing colors. The Romans were as fanatically devoted to one of the four Factions as people today are devoted to the Yankees (the Blues and Whites) or the Steelers (the Blacks and Golds).

Pliny the Younger (63-113) in his *Letters 9.6* could not understand this enthusiasm:

"I am the more astonished that so many thousands of grown men should be possessed...with a childish passion to look at galloping horses and men standing upright in their chariots. If...they were attracted by the swiftness of the horses or the skill of the men, one could account for this enthusiasm. But...it is the color of the tunic they favor....And if during the running the racers were to exchange colors, their partisans would change sides and instantly forsake the very drivers and horses whom they were just before...clamorously cheering by name."

Pliny, also, did not understand team loyalty. Pliny's uncle, Pliny the Elder, was of the same opinion. He is incredulous when he records that during the Republic in the 70's BC, a charioteer for the Reds had been killed and a distraught fanatic fan (both words come from the Latin *fanaticus* meaning "crazy") threw himself on his funeral pyre and died with his hero. Both Plinys were far removed from teams and team loyalties. Nowadays if a Red Sox player (Reds) joins the Yankees (Blues), a Red Sox fan does not abandon the Red Faction. It's not the players. It's the team.

The crazy-connection with the word "fan" may be a mild one when one reads the thousands of lead "curse tablets" that have been found with imprecations to the gods to cause evil and vile things to happen to these ancient teams and drivers:

"I adjure you, demon whoever you are, and I demand of you from this hour, from this day, from this moment that you torture and kill the horses of the Greens and Whites and that you kill in a crash their drivers...and leave not a breath in their bodies."

"Help me in the circus on 8 November. Bind every limb, every sinew, the shoulders, the ankles and the elbows of Olympus, Olympianus, Scortius and Juvencus, the charioteers of the Red. Torment their minds, their intelligence and their senses so that they may not know what they are doing, and knock out their eyes so that they may not see where they are going---neither they nor the horses they are going to drive."

"Bind the horses whose names and images are on this implement. I entrust to you of the Red...of the Blues. Bind their running, their power, their soul, their onrush, their speed. Take away their victory, entangle their feet, hinder them, hobble them so that tomorrow morning in the hippodrome they are not able to run or walk about or win or go out of the starting gates or advance on the racecourse or track, but may they fall down with their drivers."

"Bind every limb, every sinew, the shoulders, the ankles and the elbows of…the charioteers of the Reds. Torment their minds, their intelligence and their senses so that they may not know what they are doing and knock out their eyes so that they may not see where they are going--- neither they nor the horses they are going to drive."

"I conjure you up, holy beings and holy names, join in aiding this spell and bind, enchant, thwart, strike, overturn, conspire against, destroy, kill, break Eucherius, the charioteer, and all his horses tomorrow in the circus at Rome. May he not leave the barriers well; may he not be quick in contest; may he not outstrip anyone; may he not make the turns well; may he not win any prize."

After reading these curses, one can believe that following the end of the chariot races in ancient times, there were often rioting and deaths. 30,000 people were killed in c. 550 AD in Constantinople over "loyalty to colors." Soccer games in Europe and South America are still times of heavy police presence because of the deaths inspired by team loyalty.

The circus was, also, a place for flirting and sex. Ovid (43-17 BC), best known for his erotic poetry, takes us to a typical race at the Circus Maximus where his mind and his eyes are on the woman he wants to seduce:

"Though I am sitting here, it's not in the least because I am interested in the racing….I've come here to talk to you, to sit near you and to tell you how tremendously I love you….Why do you keep trying to edge away from me? We've got to sit close because of the seats. That's an advantage I owe to the Circus arrangements….you behind her; don't thrust out your legs…don't let your hard knee dig into her back….Mind, darling, you're letting your dress drag on the ground….Ah, jealous dress, how you like to cover her beautiful legs….I can just imagine from what I've seen what those other charms are like that you conceal so well under your dainty dress….a horrid black smut has come and settled on your white dress. Begone, base smudge, from those snowy shoulders. But here they come….Now's the time to clap; the procession is coming in all its splendor. First of all comes Victory with wings outspread….Next three

cheers for Neptune, you rash people that put your trust in the sea….You, my soldier friend, shout aloud for Mars, he is your god. I loathe fighting. Let Phoebus be propitious to the augurs and Phoebe to the huntsmen, and you, Minerva, receive the salutations of the craftsmen. And you, you tillers of the soil, give hail to Ceres and to kindly Bacchus. May Pollux hearken to the gladiators' prayers and Castor to the horseman's. For 'tis thee, sweet Venus, thee and the Loves, thy bowmen, that we greet with cheers. Oh, help me, tender goddess; change thou my fair one's heart that she may let herself be loved. See, Venus nods, and seems to tell me I shall win….and all the gods that shine in that procession I call to witness, you shall ever be my darling mistress….They've cleared the course now and the big races are going to begin. The praetor's given the signal. The four-horsed chariots are off….Ye gods, how wide he takes them round the turning-post. Wretched creature, what are you about? Now you've let your rival get ahead of you. He went round ever so much more closely….For heaven's sake pull your left rein hard. Oh, he's an idiot, our man. Come on, Romans, have his back, wave your togas there. See, they're calling him back. But mind they don't ruffle your hair, dearest, waving their togas about like that: come and hide your head in the folds of mine. Look, now they're starting again, the bars are down. Here they come with their differing colors, driving like mad….you've got a clear field in front of you. See that my mistress has her way, and see that I have mine. Well, (he won), she's got her way, but I must wait….She smiled, the darling, and there was a promise in her look. That's enough for here. Elsewhere you'll let me have the rest."
The Loves 3.2

Ovid's love poetry is valuable because he gives so much information about typical Roman life and, in the quote used, about a day at the Circus Maximus. The seating was cramped. 250,000 people and up to 30 horse races a day kicked up lots of black dirt and his mistress got a dark smudge on her white dress. The procession of the gods begins the race day. The goddess of Victory, leads the procession into the stadium. Neptune, god of the sea, followed her and was cheered by all mariners. The shouts were loud for Mars, the god of war. Diviners cheered Phoebus;

hunters cheered their patron goddess Phoebe; craftsmen cheered for Minerva; farmers cheered Ceres, goddess of grain, and many cheered Bacchus, god of the wine from their vineyards; Pollux was special to the gladiators and Castor to the horsemen. Trailing the others, Venus, goddess of love, was Ovid's favorite deity and from the huge cheer, one surmises the crowd loved her, too. The stone idols of the gods were placed in niches near the emperor so they could enjoy the races given in their honor.

The race that day was a four-horse race. Ovid picked his mistress' favorite and follows the progress. The driver took the turning-post too wide and a rival team gets ahead of him. Ovid calls him, "wretched creature," "foolish one," "an idiot" and tells him to pull his left rein harder. There's a foul. Romans wave the edges of their togas in the air. The officials give in to the crowd and call for the race to stop and start over. Every charioteer has to turn around and head back to the starting gate. This waving of togas in the air to declare real or supposed fouls at the Circus could happen as many as 10 times in one race and it became such a problem over the years that the number of times a race could start over was finally limited. When the bars at the starting gate jump down, the race began again. This time her favorite wins. Ovid hopes he will win, too. The excitement of the races and romantic seduction often went hand in hand.

There were superstar charioteers like we have superstar sports figures today. One of them was Scorpus of the Green Faction who raced under the reign of Domitian (81-96 AD). By the time he was 27, he had won 2,048 races. One day in one hour he collected fifteen bags of gold thrown to him by grateful spectators. The satirist Juvenal complained that Scorpus earned one hundred times more than lawyers. We do not know exactly how he died, but it was on the racetrack when he was 27 years old.

Martial in his *Epigrams 10.50* wrote: "Ah villainy! Scorpus, cheated of your first youth, you die. So soon you yoke black horses." Many charioteers died near the turning posts. A relief in the Pergamon Museum in Berlin shows a fallen charioteer being pummeled to death by another team's horses. Perhaps that is how young Scorpus died.

One of the most famous charioteers was the Spaniard Gaius Diocles of the Red Faction. Many of the drivers were from Spain, home to most of the stud farms that bred the best race horses. Diocles drove his first race at age 18 (122 AD) for the White Faction. His admirers erected a stone monument to him when he retired in 146. It survives (*Inscription CIL VI, no. 10048*) and recounts intimate details of his career. The *Inscription* begins:

"Gaius Appuleius Diocles, charioteer of the Red stable, a Lusitanian Spaniard by birth, age 42 years, 7 months, 23 days. "

The monument says "he raced four horse chariots for 24 years." The number of horses hitched to a chariot seems to vary. The usual number was a four-horse chariot, but in Diocles' monument it mentions he rode two-horse, three-horse, four-horse, six-horse and seven-horse chariots. There were twelve starting gates. When a white flag was dropped, the gates sprung open and the race began. Each race consisted of seven lapses around the track, a distance of 2.7 miles from start to finish. It was run in eight to nine minutes as was the famous chariot race in the movie *Ben Hur*.

The *Inscription* continues:

"...he started in 4,257 races and won 1,463 times....he won 92 major prizes. Of these 32 were of 30,000 sesterces, three of them with six horse teams....two of them in races with six horse chariots...one of these in a seven-horse chariot....he tied a Blue 10 times, a Green 91.... Grand totals: He drove chariots for 24 years, ran 4,257 starts and won 1,463 victories, 110 in opening races. In single entry races he won 1,064, winning 92 major purses, 32 of them, including 3 with six-horse teams at 30,000 sesterces, 28, including 2 with six-horse teams at 40,000 sesterces, 29, including 1 with a seven-horse team, at 50,000 sesterces and 3 at 60,000 sesterces....he won a grand total of 35,863,120 sesterces."

It is difficult to calculate what Diocles' lifetime winnings would be in dollars or in any modern currency. We can, however, put his financial assets in perspective. The common soldier was paid 900 sesterces a year before deductions. A person was considered wealthy if his property totaled 400,000 sesterces. In order to be a senator, a man had to own property worth 1,000,000 sesterces. Diocles' 35,863,120 sesterces definitely put him in a class all by himself.

The description of his career is quite long:

"…(Diocles was) the most eminent of all the charioteers….Diocles is outstanding with respect to new sorts of prizes never before recorded… on one day…he won the prize both times with a six-horse chariot… and with a seven-horse team without a yoke…he won 50,000 sesterces in the contest with Abigaeus (his inside trace horse who set the pace) as his lead horse and in other contests without using a whip he won 30,000 sesterces….he seems to be crowned with double glory from these novelties."

That we still have this inscription and cite it is triple glory for the most successful charioteer of them all.

Modern readers can understand teams, men and horses pitted against each other, betting, winning and losing. We can understand the Circus Maximus. What is impossible for us to understand is blood sport. Not the drawing of blood during sport, but the spectacle of humans led into a sports arena to be torn to shreds by wild animals or forced to fight to the death while tens of thousands of people are watching, cheering, taunting, eating, talking and laughing.

Ignatius, the Christian Bishop of Syrian Antioch, was torn to pieces by lions in the Colosseum as 87,000 Romans approved and applauded. The following is a rendition of his trial in c. 107 before the Roman Emperor Trajan (reigned 98-117). It is taken almost verbatim from the ancient manuscript *Martirium Colbertinum* aka *The Martyrdom of Ignatius*:

Emperor Trajan looked down at the man in his seventies who was clasping iron chains around his stomach. "Who are you, wicked wretch, who transgress our commands and persuade others to do the same so that they should miserably perish like you will?" he growled.

Ignatius replied, "No one ought to call Theophorus a wicked wretch! All the evil spirits and demons you worship have departed from us who are the servants of the one God." Ignatius, dragging his chains, moved closer to the Roman emperor. "But if because I am an enemy to these spirits, you call me wicked in respect to them, I quite agree with you. For because I have Christ the King of heaven within me, I destroy all the devices of these evil spirits."

Trajan asked the scribe to hand him the list. He began to read the names of the people who were coming before him that day. This old wretch in front of him was supposed to be the leader of an unruly group in Antioch called Christians. Trajan was fresh from his victories over the Dacians (Romania/Bulgaria). While he was in Antioch taking care of this type of local business, he had instructed 80 million cubic yards of earth and rock be removed from Quirinal Hill in Rome in order to construct the Forum of Forums to celebrate this victory. At his death, his ashes were set into the base of the 125-foot column topped with a statue of him. Trajan's Column is still standing.

Powerful and omnipotent, the conqueror Trajan was confident he could deal with these commoners who were defaming the gods all over his empire. His Procurator in Antioch had been lobbying him to come to his city for some time.

"Theophorus. Theophorus," Trajan said. "I see no 'Theophorus' on this list. Why are you talking about Theophorus? Who is Theophorus?" The emperor threw down the list.

"I am Theophorus, the one who has Christ within his breast."

"I was told you were Ignatius. Well then," said Trajan, " be whoever you want to be. But, a question. Do I, your emperor, not seem to you to have the gods in my mind, too? The very gods whose assistance we enjoy in fighting against our enemies like the Dacians?"

Ignatius was emboldened. "You are in error, emperor, when you call the demons of your nation gods. For there is but one God who made heaven, earth, the sea and all that are in them. And one Jesus Christ, the only-begotten Son of God."

"Jesus. Oh, yes, that Jesus." The emperor knew the sect of Christians. He knew they believed that some Jew named Jesus was the Christ and had risen from the dead. It was there in Antioch that the people first called them "Christians" meaning "little christs" after *christos* the Greek word for "messiah." Both the Hebrew word *moshiach* (messiah) and the Greek word *christos* mean "anointed one."

"You mean the Jesus who was crucified under our Procurator Pontius Pilatus?"

Ignatius jumped in. "I mean the one who crucified sin along with its inventor, Emperor. And all the deceit and malice of the devil he has put under the feet of those who carry Him in their heart. That's the Jesus I mean."

"Carry Him in their heart!" Trajan smiled and leaned forward. "So you are saying you carry within you that Jesus who was crucified. That's not believable. How can you carry a god within you?" The emperor stood up and pointed to the marble statue of Justitia (Justice). "I can't take this statue of Justitia and shove it inside me! I've heard enough."

Trajan turned to the scribe. "I command that Ignatius who says that he carries about within him this Jesus who according to our *Acta* was crucified, dead and buried, I command that he be bound by soldiers, carried to the great Rome, and be there devoured by the beasts for the gratification of the people of Rome. Get him out of here!"

As Ignatius was hurried away by the soldiers, he cried out, "I thank you, Lord, that You have honored me with a perfect love toward You and that I will be bound with these chains like your apostle Paul!"

Trajan walked over to the scribe. "These Christians are insane! He's going to be torn to pieces by a lion and he's happy. Who's next on the list?"

The account of Ignatius' trial before the emperor in c. 107 in Antioch (modern Antakya in southern Turkey) is reputed to have been written by two eyewitnesses---Philo, a deacon from Tarsus and Rheus Agathopus, a Syrian. Scholars consider the account to be accurate. (For the original wording of the trial and the account of Ignatius' long journey to Rome, see the *Martirium Colbertinum* or *The Martyrdom of Ignatius*.)

News of the Bishop of Antioch's inspired eloquence and boldness before the emperor and of his death sentence spread swiftly throughout the nascent Christian communities in Asia Minor. All along the journey to Rome, Ignatius was greeted by Christians who comforted, encouraged and revered him.

Ignatius was already famous among early Christians because Jesus Himself had embraced him. Ignatius was the little child Jesus took into His arms in Matthew 18:1-5, Luke 9:46-48 and in Mark's gospel 9:33-37:

"They came to Capernaum. When he (Jesus) was in the house, he asked them (the disciples): 'What were you arguing about on the road?' But they kept quiet because on the way they had argued about who was the greatest. Sitting down, Jesus called the Twelve and said, 'If anyone wants to be first, he must be the very last, and the servant of all.' Jesus took a little child and had him stand among them. Taking him in his arms, he said to them. 'Whoever welcomes one of these little children in my name welcomes me, and whoever welcomes me does not welcome me but the one who sent me.'"

Ignatius called himself *Theophorus* meaning in Greek "God-Bearer" because Jesus had taken him as a young child into His arms. By this appellation, Ignatius witnessed to that event and to the God within his heart.

Ignatius had known many of Jesus' Apostles. Before Peter was martyred in Rome, he had appointed Ignatius Bishop of Antioch. All the believers knew that Ignatius and his young friend Polycarp had been disciples of the venerated Apostle John. Until his death in c. 99, John taught and ministered with Ignatius and Polycarp. Now, less than 20 years later one of the Apostle John's most intimate friends was on his way to the greatest city in the world to seal his belief with his blood.

It was about a 1,500 mile journey from Antioch to Rome. At least half of Ignatius' trip would be on foot. Up until the 20th century, most people in the history of the world have walked from one place to another. There have always been trails and routes. The American Indians had thousands of miles of well-worn trails all over America. Early trappers and traders used Indian trails to bring their goods to market. The pioneers followed the Oregon Trail and other Indian trails as they went west. On the other side of the world the ancient Chinese had their routes: the fabled Silk Road from China to the Mediterranean Sea and The Tea Horse Road from Tibet to India. The Incas of Peru had 14,000 miles of trails the most famous of which was the 3,200 mile Camino Real from Quito, Ecuador to Tucaman, Argentina. People everywhere have always traveled. All cultures had trails and routes. But the Romans had---roads.

Their roads were built to last. Roman roads and structures have survived for millennia for one reason---cement. The Romans "invented" cement (Latin *caementum*). Roman cement made possible the durability of Roman roads and revolutionized architecture by enabling previously impossible construction like the enormous domed and vaulted spaces of the Pantheon and all the Imperial Baths. After the demise of the Roman Empire, the formula for cement was lost until John Smeaton, a British engineer, rediscovered it in 1756 by mixing clay with limestone.

To build the Roman roads, a foundation pit was dug and filled with carefully placed rocks. Then broken stones, cement and sand were laid down. Another layer of cement mixed with broken tiles was added. The roads were surfaced with stone paving blocks crowned to shed water. Curb stones at the sides held the paving blocks in place. On either side of the road were drainage ditches. The roads were built to move conquering armies and to facilitate communications and supplies from one end of Rome's vast empire to its most remote frontiers. Every long stretch of road had *mutationes* for changing horses and *mansiones* for lodging at night. Julius Caesar and his army traveled so fast on those roads that it took them only eight days to go from Rome to the Rhone. By using the relay and refreshment stations all along the highways, couriers could cover 500 miles on horseback in just 24 hours.

Rome's roads carried official documents, personal letters and news from Rome to all parts of the Empire. The Via Appia, called the "queen of roads" (Latin *regina viarum*), was built in c. 312 BC by Appius Claudius when he was Censor (in charge of taking the census and of public morality) of Rome. Normal, unofficial communications traveled usually on foot the c. 350 miles from Rome to Brindisi on that road in about six days and visitors to Rome today still travel to some of the catacombs on the Via Appia. Official orders and military communications from Rome took only 33 days to go all the way to the Roman colony in Britain called Londinium by the Romans, a distance of c. 900 miles. *London* seems to have been derived not from a Latin word but from a pre-Celtic word *Lonidonjon* meaning "boat river" or "swimming river." The Romans established Londinium on the Thames River and seemed to have Latinized the word the native Britons were using. The origin of the word "London" is hotly debated in circles where these things are important.

Many Roman roads have survived. The ancient Roman Via Emilia is today the SS9 superhighway that leads to the Adriatic coast. The Roman road from Dover to London now called Watling Street was used all through the Dark Ages, the Middle Ages, during the Renaissance and part of it is still used today. In Jordan the milestones of the Roman Via Traiana are still standing and the road is semi-passable. All over the world today ruins of Roman roads are still in existence: in Turkey, Syria, Israel, Ireland, France, Germany, England. The Romans built over 50,000 miles of roads.

Even though Ignatius, his deacon Philo, his friend Rheus and the ten soldiers had a long journey ahead of them, part of that trip would be on those Roman roads. It is doubtful the thirteen of them had a closed carriage drawn by horses. That was reserved for the wealthy. Some who passed them on the roads must have been military regiments being deployed to another post or messengers on horseback from the *cursus publicus*, the State-run postal service, or rich men and their wives in chariots or in litters carried by slaves. But most of their fellow travelers would have been walking either alone or in groups as did Jesus and His disciples.

The trip was grueling for the older man. In one of Ignatius' letters he says: "From Syria even to Rome I fight with wild beasts, by land and sea, by night and by day, being bound amidst ten leopards...a company of soldiers who only grow worse when they are kindly treated." The long journey with rough Roman soldiers prodding him on was a training camp for his contest in the Colosseum and he knew it.

The closer Ignatius got to Rome the more he anticipated his death:

"How I look forward to the lions that have been prepared for me! All I pray is that I will find them swift. I am going to make overtures to them so that...they will devour me with all speed. And if they are reluctant, I shall have to use force on them...Fire, cross, beast-fighting, hacking and quartering, splintering of bone and mangling of limb, even the pulverizing of my whole body. Let every horrid and diabolical torment come upon me provided only that I can win my way to Jesus Christ!"

Not surprisingly, Ignatius, like so many Christians who were martyred in the arenas, used the language of the ubiquitous Roman games to describe their contests and their deaths. They would win, receive a crown and be glorified.

Many athletic allusions to the Christian life and to the battles for holiness are found in the letters of the New Testament. Paul often compared the challenging and persecution-filled life he led to the endurance a long distance runner must have:

"Do you not know that in a race all the runners run, but only one gets the prize? Everyone who competes in the games goes into strict training. They do it to get a crown that will not last; but we do it to get a crown that will last forever." I Corinthians 9:24,25
"I press on to take hold of that for which Christ Jesus took hold of me....I press on toward the goal to win the prize for which God has called me heavenward in Christ Jesus." Philippians 3:12-14
"However, I consider my life worth nothing to me, if only I finish the race and complete the task the Lord Jesus has given me." Acts 20:24

Shortly before he was beheaded, Paul wrote these famous last words:

"For I am already being poured out like a drink offering, and the time has come for my departure. I have fought the good fight. I have finished the race. I have kept the faith. Now there is in store for me the crown of righteousness which the Lord, the righteous Judge, will award to me on that day." II Tim. 4:6,7

As a Roman citizen, Paul had seen many contests and races. He had, also, seen victorious generals parading their spoils of war and doomed captives behind them through the streets of the Empire. In I Corinthians 4:9 Paul envisions himself and his fate in these terms: "For it seems to me that God has put us apostles on display at the end of the procession, like ones condemned to die in the arena."

Ignatius, a contemporary of Paul, must have read those words in I Corinthians many times. Now it was he who was on display and was condemned to die in the arena. But, like his hero Paul, Ignatius knew the crown that awaited him.

On his journey to the Colosseum in Rome, Ignatius wrote seven letters. In all of these he has great resolve about his impending death for Christ. In his *Letter to Polycarp* he is "encouraged, resting without anxiety in God...if by means of suffering I may attain to God...and be found a disciple of Christ."

In the *Letter to the Ephesians* he asks them for their prayers that he "be permitted to fight with beasts at Rome that by martyrdom I may indeed become the disciple of Him who gave Himself for us."

Ignatius says, "of (my) own free choice (I have) accepted to die unto His passion" in his *Letter to the Magnesians.*

The people in Thralles in Asia Minor admired Ignatius and all those who had given their lives for the faith. In his letter to them, he gently chastises this admiration: "I have many deep thoughts in God, but I take the measure of myself lest I perish in my boasting. For now I ought to be the more afraid and not to give heed to those who would puff me up, for they that say these things to me are a scourge to me. For though I desire to suffer, yet I know not whether I am worthy."

In the *Letter to the Smyrnaeans* he gives counsel on a heresy that was bothering the church. People were saying that Jesus rose from the dead symbolically and spiritually but not physically. "For if these things were done by the Lord (symbolically), then am I also a prisoner (symbolically). And why then have I delivered myself over to death, to fire, to sword, to wild beasts? But near to the sword, near to God. In company with wild beasts, in company with God. Only let it be in the name of Jesus Christ."

In the *Letter to the Philadelphians* he courts their prayers "because I am not yet perfected. But your prayer will make me perfect unto God that I may attain unto the inheritance wherein I have found mercy."

The church in Rome had many influential believers who wanted to intercede with the authorities on behalf of Ignatius. In his letter to them, he begs them to allow his death: "Permit me to be an imitator of the passion of my God. If any man has Him within himself, let him understand what I desire....If you (will) remain silent and leave me alone, I am a word of God. But if you save my flesh, then shall I be a mere cry."

Apparently on the last leg of the journey to Rome, "(the lead soldier) Christophorus was pressed by the other soldiers to hasten to the public spectacles in the mighty Rome." Emperor Trajan who had condemned Ignatius to death had proclaimed 123 days of contests in the Colosseum to celebrate his victory over the Dacians. They had to hurry to get Ignatius to Rome before the period of celebration was over.

They were sailing for Puteoli, a major commercial shipping center in the Bay of Naples. Ignatius was excited they would be landing in Puteoli because his hero, the Apostle Paul, had landed there (Acts 28:13, 14), stayed seven days and then walked c. 150 miles to Rome where he was martyred:

"But a violent wind...did not (suffer the ship to land in Puteoli)...and (they) sailed by....continuing to enjoy fair winds. We (here Philo injects himself for the first time into the narrative) were reluctantly hurried on in one day and a night, mourning over the coming departure (death) of this righteous man (Ignatius). But to him this happened just as he wished, since he was in haste as soon as possible to leave this world that he might attain to the Lord whom he loved. Sailing then into the Roman harbor (Ostia) and the unhallowed sports being just about to close, the soldiers began to be annoyed at our slowness, but the bishop joyfully yielded to their urgency."

Ostia situated on the Mediterranean at the mouth of the Tiber River was the port of Rome. The group walked the Via Ostiensis into Rome where the soldiers would deliver their prisoner to the master of the games at the Colosseum. The soldiers were vexed "at (their) slowness" because Ignatius was to be killed on that particular day.

The many Christians who had come to Ostia to greet Ignatius further delayed them: "…the fame relating to the holy martyr being already spread abroad we met the brethren full of fear and joy." The soldiers were not happy.

Some of the Christians "were saying that they would appease the people so that they should not demand the destruction of this just one. (Ignatius) begged them" not to deprive him of the privilege of dying for his Lord. When the soldiers and the band of Christians were near the Colosseum, Ignatius knelt in prayer: "(He) entreated the Son of God on behalf of the churches that a stop might be put to the persecution and that mutual love might continue among the brethren."

After the prayer, the soldiers quickly hustled Ignatius into the amphitheater:

"Then, being immediately thrown in according to the command of Trajan given some time ago, the spectacles (were) just about to close… it was a solemn day (dedicated to a god)…the people were assembled in more than ordinary numbers. They came together zealously (and Ignatius) was thus cast to the wild beasts close beside the temple."

The narrative indicates that Ignatius' death was just one of many gory events squeezed into a day at the Circus. When they arrived at the Colosseum, he was "immediately thrown" into the arena. After months of preparation for this battle, it seems Ignatius had a hasty, gruesome death at the end of a long day. It is certain that Ignatius died well. He had trained a lifetime for his ultimate contest.

The soldiers had been with Ignatius for months. Their long trip with the old man was over. They had done their duty as Roman soldiers. Maybe they stayed around to watch him being torn to pieces by lions. Or maybe they were so excited to be in Rome that they handed him over and left for the nearest taverna.

The old martyr had been disappointed that he could not land in Puteoli like Paul had done before his martyrdom. Because Ignatius was not familiar with Rome, he did not know that his hero Paul had been beheaded on the same road, the Via Ostiensis, which Ignatius had taken from the port of Ostia into Rome. Ignatius would have been happy to know that he and Paul traveled the same road to their deaths.

When Philo and Rheus claimed Ignatius' body, "only the harder portions of his holy remains were left." The lions had eaten all of him except his bones. His friends wrapped the gnawed bones in linen and took them back to Antioch. His relics were removed to Rome in the 7th century where they reside under the high altar in the Basilica di San Clemente.

A bus to "Colosseo" takes the modern tourist to the Basilica. The ruins of that blood-soaked amphitheater are very near the crypt that contains Ignatius' revered relics. Almost 2,000 years after the old Bishop's death in 107, there are over 900 Christian churches in Rome. Ignatius of Antioch, the great Christian athlete, would not be amazed.

V.

"Hear, O Israel: the Lord our God, the Lord is one."
Deuteronomy 6:4

These eleven Old Testament words, the historic Shema, set the Jews apart for thousands of years from all the polytheistic cultures around them. The Jews (shortened form of the Hebrew word "Y'hudah" "Judah") have always been monotheists. They have always believed there is only one God.

When Abraham, a monotheist, began his long journey from Ur of the Chaldeans about 2,000 BC (Genesis 12), he left the pantheon of gods and goddesses that had surrounded him since his birth. Tammuz, a fertility god, and his consort Inanna and her sacred prostitutes were principal deities along with Sin, the moon god, and his wife Nina. (Nineveh was named after Nina.) Oannes, a fish god, enlightened the Mesopotamians about science and history. Namma, Ki and Ishtar were mother goddesses. Marduk was the god of light. Each god and goddess had children and sisters and brothers who were, also, gods and goddesses who demanded veneration, human sacrifices and oblations.

When Abraham arrived in Canaan, new gods and goddesses were worshipped. Asherah, mother of seventy gods, was the goddess of fertility. Baal, the storm god, was the chief of the gods. His worship required periodic sacrifice of babies to calm his wrath or to thank him for favors. Mot was the god of death and Yam was god of the sea. The

61

chief god of the Ammonites was the chthonic Moloch. Large stone idols of him were made emphasizing his huge open mouth. A fire was kindled in his mouth and babies and little children were thrown into the fire to appease Moloch in times of flood or drought, attack or victory. Abraham and his small family of believers in only one god were surrounded by Chemosh, the god of the Moabites; Tammuz had migrated from Sumeria and became a nature god, worshipped by the Syrians; Dagon was worshipped by the Philistines. All of these gods were accompanied by an extensive and intricate panoply of gods and goddesses.

When Abraham and his family left Canaan and its idols, they entered Egypt. In Pharaoh's land they encountered more gods and goddesses with different names and rigid rituals associated with their worship. Here Amon-Re was the king of Egyptian gods. Hathor, depicted as a cow, was the goddess of love. Horus, god of the sun, was worshipped as a falcon. Osiris and his popular sister/wife Isis, Serapis, Nut, Mut, Anubis, Apis, Ptah, Seth and Thoth and all their sisters and brothers and mothers and fathers and sons and daughters were venerated as gods. For thousands of years the monotheistic Jews lived around and among peoples who worshipped each facet of emotional as well as physical creation as a god or goddess.

The Jews and early Christians swam against the religious current of the entire world. Today we call that stream pagan. "Pagan" comes from the Latin word *paganus* meaning "rural, from the countryside." Orosius (c. 375-418), a Christian historian and disciple of St. Augustine, said many of the major cities in his day had been Christianized, but in the countryside, the rustics still practiced the old heathen ways. These rural people were called "pagans." *Seven Books Of History Against The Pagans*

The dictionary defines "pagan" as "one of a people or community observing a polytheistic religion, as the ancient Romans or Greeks." It was this clash between monotheism and polytheism that defined the struggle between the pagan Romans and the Jews and early Christians.

The Jewish Apostle Paul traveled all over the pagan world from

c. 46-64 proclaiming one god. When he reached Athens, Greece "he was greatly distressed to see that the city was full of idols." He started talking to a group of Stoic and Epicurean philosophers. They wanted to hear more and took him to the Areopagus, a rocky outcrop near the Acropolis where Athenians did public business and philosophized. "You are bringing some strange ideas to our ears, and we want to know what they mean," said the assemblage. Paul boldly proclaimed only one god and the resurrection:

"Men of Athens! I see that in every way you are very religious. For as I walked around and looked carefully at your objects of worship, I even found an altar with this inscription: TO AN UNKNOWN GOD. Now what you worship as something unknown, I am going to proclaim to you. The God who made the world and everything in it is the Lord of heaven and earth and does not live in temples built by hands. And he is not served by human hands, as if he needed anything, because he himself gives all men life and breath and everything else….we should not think that the divine being is like gold or silver or stone, an image made by man's design and skill….For he has set a day when he will judge the world with justice by the man (Jesus) he has appointed. He has given proof of this to all men by raising him from the dead." Acts 17:16-32

The Romans had conquered the Greeks in 146 BC, but from the end of Alexander's conquest of the world in 323 BC into the first centuries AD, it was Greek language and ideas that dominated the world. When Roman writers complained about the "Asiatic influence" in Rome, they were deriding the new gods (e.g. Isis, Mithra) that were constantly wandering into Rome through Greece and corrupting the worship of their own gods. Paul's One God, though well received in Hellenized ("Greek-influenced") cities like Ephesus and Corinth was not welcome in Rome, the city of the world, the city that mattered.

It is impossible after 2,000 years of Judeo-Christian teaching and influence for anyone in the West to understand how unique, foreign and threatening the early Christians were in their proclamation of one God to a world of many gods and goddesses.

We cannot understand how the Roman Bishop Sixtus and his six deacons who were simply singing and praying in an underground catacomb could be such an affront to Rome that they were hacked to death. After all, Rome had for centuries tolerated the competing gods of the nations it conquered. Were Peter's and Paul's one God and message of salvation such unpardonable sins that they had to die? What fatal blow could be dealt to mighty Rome by a young mother named Perpetua, her pregnant slave girl and an old man named Ignatius that they were condemned to be torn apart by wild beasts in the arena? Why did Christians have to die?

In order to understand the Roman hatred for and persecution of Christians and, indeed, the death-world of the gladiators, the cruelty of the Colosseum and the open perversity of ancient Rome, the paganism of Rome must be acknowledged and understood. It was the belief in the Roman pantheon of deities that formed, allowed and required the culture and the acts that most of us today consider unspeakable and despicable.

One of the most popular and enduring of the Roman gods was the Greek god Dionysius known in Rome as Bacchus, the god of wine. When Jupiter, king of the Roman gods, had intercourse with a human woman, Bacchus was conceived. The woman, Semele, was destroyed in a fit of jealousy by Jupiter's wife Juno. Jupiter rescued the fetus, sewed him into his thigh and carried him to birth. When Bacchus was a man, he took as a lover a young boy called Ampelos who was killed by a bull. Bacchus turned the dead boy's body into a vine and wrung from his blood the elixir called wine. Bacchus became the god of wine and intoxication.

Bacchus is represented on vases and in sculptures as a pretty, long-haired youth. The Greek playwright Euripides (480-406 BC) in his *Bacchantes* describes him as "this effeminate stranger." In the play the young King Pentheus attempts to stamp out the worship of Dionysius. The homosexuals and the women devoted to him, who included his own mother Agave, exact their revenge on him by literally tearing him to pieces in their wine-fueled frenzy. When confronted by her father Cadmus with the chest filled with the mangled and bloody pieces of her son Pentheus, Agave laments:

"Father, you see how all has changed for me....
the mother of a king, I'm now transformed---
an abomination, something to fill
all people's hearts with horror, with disgust---
the mother who slaughtered her only son,
who tore him apart, ripping out the heart
from the child who filled her own heart with joy---
all to honor the god Dionysius....
Alas, for my poor son, my only child,
Destroyed by his mother's Bacchic madness.
How could these hands of mine which loved him so,
Have torn these limbs apart, ripped out his flesh.
Here's an arm that has held me all these years....
His feet....His face was handsome, on the verge of manhood.
See the soft down, still resting on these lips,
Which have kissed me thousands of times or more....
It makes no sense---it's unendurable.
How could the god have wished such things on me?"

Androgynous and besotted, Bacchus' most ardent devotees were women and homosexuals. Beginning in c. 200 BC, Bacchanalian festivals were celebrated all over Italy.

Livy (59 BC-17 AD) in his *History of Rome 39* gives a detailed description of the religious rites of Bacchus:

"To their religious performances were added the pleasures of wine and feasting to allure a greater number of proselytes. When wine, lascivious discourse, night and the intercourse of the sexes had extinguished every sentiment of modesty, then debaucheries of every kind began to be practiced....From the same place, too, proceeded poison and secret murders so that in some cases not even the bodies could be found for burial....the violence (was concealed) on account of the loud shouting and the noise of drums and cymbals so that none of the cries uttered by persons suffering (sexual) violation or murder could be heard abroad.... When any person was introduced, he was delivered as a victim to the priests....where he must first suffer (rape) and afterwards commit every thing that was abominable....there was nothing wicked, nothing flagitious that had not been practiced among them. There was more frequent pollution of men with each other than with women. If any were less patient in submitting to dishonor or more averse to the commission of vice, they were killed and sacrificed as victims....nothing unlawful (is) the grand maxim of their religion....the evil increases and spreads daily."

All these abominations were committed in the name of and for the delectation of the popular god Bacchus. There were decent men and women in Rome who recognized the evil for what it was. They had tried to stamp out the rites. As early as 186 BC the Roman Senate passed the *Senatus Consultum de Bacchanalibus* that decreed:

"Regarding the Bacchanalia, it was resolved to give the following directions to those who are in alliance with us: No one of them is to possess a place where the festivals of Bacchus are celebrated....No man is to be a Bacchantian....no man is to be a priest....no one shall observe the sacred rites either in public or private or outside the city....if there are any who have acted contrary to what is written above...a proceeding for a capital offense should be instituted against them. The senate has decreed that you should inscribe this on a brazen tablet and that you should order it to be placed where it can be easiest read....the revelries of Bacchus...(are) disbanded within ten days after this letter shall be delivered."

In Calabria, Italy in 1640 an ancient Roman bronze tablet was found engraved with the entire text of the Senate's ban on the Bacchanalia to which Livy referred. Once again archaeology vindicates, confirms and supplements not only Biblical texts but also ancient historians.

Roman deities required temples built for them and sacrifices given to them because Rome did not want any god or goddess to be displeased with the city. Each Roman household had a host of gods to placate. Each and every corner of a home had a protector god. The god Roculus protected the door. A separate spirit, Cardea, protected the hinges of the door. And Limentinus guarded the threshold of the door. The broom even had a guardian spirit named Deverra. Vesta, the most important household goddess, protected the hearth of the home. The Penates protected the food and drink in the home. When a Roman moved from one house to another, he had to take the Penates with him. Every thing and place in the home was "owned" by some god or goddess.

Juno and Mena assured a good menstrual flow. Sexual intercourse was presided over by the gods down to the minutest detail. Cinxia was in charge of taking off the woman's clothes. Prema made sure there was a good penetration. Liber allowed the ejaculation. If a child was conceived, Alemons nourished the baby in the womb; Nona and Decima were there when the child was ready to be delivered; Partula managed and directed the birth and Lucina was in charge of bringing the child into the light of day. Rumina was implored to give good milk to the nursing child; Statina was worshipped when the child first walked; Locutinus (from whom we get our word "locution") taught the child to talk. Every aspect of life and living no matter how big or small had a god or goddess presiding over it. These deities all had limited jurisdiction and competing agendas. They were never bound by any code of conduct or consistency and all their actions were ad hoc.

Pagan religion was mostly occupied in bribing or bargaining with the gods: if I do 'x', give me 'y'; if I do 'x,' Juno, please persuade Jupiter to give me 'y.' The ritual and sacrifice for each and every deity were rigorously spelled out. If a Roman did not do it right or had omitted a single step, he had to start all over again. Plus, each god and goddess had many names by which they were known. It was so confusing that even the elegant poet Horace in his *Odes* implores "Diana" to protect mothers but hedges "whether you prefer to be addressed as Lucina or as Genitalis." In Apuleius' *The Golden Ass* the Queen of Heaven is addressed as Ceres, Venus, Proserpina or "by whatever name with whatever rite in whatever appearance it is right to invoke thee." There was even confusion about the sex of some divinities. In that case, the Roman would pray, *"Sive deus, sive dea"* ("Whether you be god or goddess, male or female").

Prayers were formulaic and chanted. In Virgil's *Eclogues 8* a lover's prayer had to be repeated nine times. The Roman worshipper had to face north, south, east or west when reciting a prayer. Sometimes the supplicant had to chant and hop in step to the chant. Prayers had to be accompanied by a sacrifice to the god or goddess. The sacrifice was a symbol of life in some form. Cheese, milk, fruit, vegetables and wine were commonly used by individuals, but for State gods and collective worship animal or human sacrifice was required. A bull or calf had its throat cut. It was disemboweled and priests would examine the entrails. If the entrails showed a bad omen, another animal would often be sacrificed until a good omen was seen.

All of this is strange and puzzling to sensibilities that have been formed by 2,000 years of monotheism in the West. It is refreshing to know that some people of that time found the pantheon of gods and goddesses to be silly, too. Lucian of Samosata was a Greek satirist who lived from c. 125-180 AD. In his *Dialogues Of The Gods* he has the Greek gods conversing with each other:

"Hermes (messenger of the gods)
'Mother, I am the most miserable god in heaven.'
Maia (his mother and a great mother symbol)
'Don't say such things, child.'
Hermes
'Am I to do all the work of heaven with my own hands, to be hurried from one piece of drudgery to another and never say a word? I have to get up early, sweep the dining room, lay the cushions....then I have to wait on Zeus (king of the gods) and take his messages up and down all day long; and no sooner am I back again and there was the nectar to pour out, too, till his new cup-bearer was bought....and I have to go to Pluto (god of the underworld)...and play the usher in Rhadamanthus' Assembly....why should Alemena and Semele, paltry women, why should

they feast at their table and I, the son of Maia, the grandson of Atlas, wait upon them?....I am half dead with it all. Mortal slaves are better off than I am. They have the chance of being sold to a new master.'
Maia
'Come, come, child. You must do as your father bids you like a good boy. Run along now to Argos and Boeotia. Don't loiter or you will get a whipping.'"

There are many comical exchanges in Lucian's book. Another is between Eros, the cupid of love, and Zeus, king of the gods. Eros was constantly smiting Zeus with love for a human woman and turning him into various forms so he could have intercourse with her:

"Eros
'You might let me off, Zeus! I suppose it was rather too bad of me. But there. I am but a child, a wayward child.'
Zeus
'A child....You bad old man. Just because you have no beard, and no white hairs, are you going to pass yourself off for a child?'
Eros
'Well, and what such mighty harm has this old man ever done you that you should talk (of putting me) in chains?'
Zeus
'Ask your own guilty conscience what harm. The pranks you have played on me. (You have turned me into) a satyr, bull, swan, eagle, shower of gold. I have been everything in my time and I have you to thank for it. You never by any chance make the women in love with me. No one is ever smitten by my charms....(the women) like the bull or swan well enough, but once let them set eyes on me, and they are frightened out of their lives.'
Eros
'Well, of course. They are mortals. The sight of Zeus is too much for them....Now shall I tell you the way to win hearts? Keep that aegis of yours quiet and leave the thunderbolts at home.'"

Lucian's book is a delightful and satirical send-up of the gods. He understood, as we do today, that Greek and Roman gods and goddesses were only personified humans with magical powers, were figments of the collective imagination.

Human sacrifice to the gods and goddesses was prevalent in the ancient pagan world. Julius Caesar (July 13, 100 BC-March 15, 44 BC) in his *Gallic Wars 6.16* (51-58 BC) describes a unique way of sacrificing people to the gods:

"The nation of all the Gauls (Germany, France, Netherlands, Belgium) is extremely devoted to superstitious rites; and on that account they who are troubled with unusually severe diseases and they who are engaged in battles and dangers either sacrifice men as victims or vow that they will sacrifice them and employ the Druids as the performers of those sacrifices; because they think that unless the life of a man be offered for the life of a man, the mind of the immortal gods cannot be rendered propitious, and they have sacrifices of that kind ordained for national purposes. Others make (human) figures of vast size, the limbs of which are formed by branches and twigs (and) they fill (this wicker figure) with living men, which when they set on fire, the men perish enveloped in flames."

The "wicker man" has caught the imagination of the modern world. With the revival of paganism in the West in the late 20th century, Wiccans in Europe burn huge effigies of wicker men at their festivals and keep smaller ones as talismans. In Scotland there is a rock 'n roll Wickerman Festival every year and the British have made a horror film entitled *The Wicker Man*. One wonders if any but the Wiccan know the origin of their activities.

Archaeologists have found bones of babies and children in the cornerstones of buildings all over Mesopotamia and the near East. These sacrifices were thought to perform the magic needed to protect the home or building. During the reign of the Biblical king Ahab (c. 850 BC), a Canaanite king rebuilt Jericho that had been destroyed by the Israelites c. 1450 BC. He made "foundation sacrifices" of his oldest and youngest sons: "In Ahab's time, Hiel of Bethel rebuilt Jericho. He laid its foundations at the cost of his firstborn son Abiram, and he set up its gates at the cost of his youngest son Segub." (I Kings 16:34) Most of these "foundation sacrifices" were of babies or young children. However, in Megiddo the sacrifice of a 15-year old girl was found attached by a layer of mortar to the foundation of a fortress.

In 1971 archaeologists excavating at Pozo Moro in Spain found the remains of a stone tower dating to c. 500 BC. On the relief of the tower is a ghastly depiction of child sacrifice. A two-headed monster god with his tongue hanging out is ready to eat a small child scrunched in a bowl. A priestly figure in an animal mask is ready with a curved sword to sacrifice another small child for the god's "feast."

In most of the ancient pagan world, sacrifice of children and babies to appease, pacify and court the favor of the gods was common. In the martyr Perpetua's city of Carthage in northern Africa, there is a cemetery called the Tophet (the "roasting place," "fire place") or Precinct of Tanit. There archaeologists have found more than 20,000 urns, some with two children in them, containing the ashes and bones of infants and children up to the age of four burned in the fire of sacrifice. Similar precincts have been found in Sardinia, Tunisia and Sicily.

Inscriptions on the Carthage urns indicate these infants and toddlers were sacrificed to their mother goddess Tanit and her consort Ba'al. One inscription to the goddess explains the reason the man sacrificed his child: "To our lady, to Tanit, the face of Ba'al and to our lord, to Ba'al Hammon that which was vowed by PN, son of PN, son of PN. Because he (Ba'al) heard his (PN's) voice and blessed him." PN had vowed to sacrifice his child if he was "blessed." He got his blessing; he threw his child into the fire. A Carthaginian man named Tuscus inscribes that he gave Ba'al "his mute son Bod'astart, a defective child, in exchange for a healthy one." Human sacrifice always implied placating, bribing or bartering with the gods.

The 1st century BC author Diodorus Siculus in his *The Library Of History 20.14* was an eye-witness of these sacrifices to the god Kronos who in mythology was famous for eating his own children: "There was in (Carthage) a bronze image of Kronos extending its hands, palms up and sloping toward the ground, so that each of the children (to be sacrificed) when placed thereon rolled down and fell into a sort of gaping pit filled with fire." Notice the difference between Siculus' matter of fact description of child sacrifice and the post-Christian Plutarch (c. 45-120) when describing the same area of child sacrifice: "The whole area before the statue (of Kronos) was filled with a loud noise of flutes and drums so that the cries of wailing (children) should not reach the ears of the people....the Carthaginians offered up their own children, and those who had no children would buy little children from poor people and cut their throats as if they were so many lambs or birds. Meanwhile, the mothers stood by without a tear or moan." *Moralia 171D* In the pagan Plutarch's narrative, the influence of the Christian's abhorrence of human sacrifice can be gleaned from his description of the dehumanizing of little children as "so many lambs or birds" and his offense at the fact that their own mothers "stood by without a tear or a moan." Plutarch, like so many educated Romans, was viewing time-immemorial rites in a totally different way than Siculus did just 100 years previously. Christian ideas were working their way into the fabric of Roman society, very slowly but surely.

Polybius (c. 200-118 BC) blamed the population decline in Greece on zealous infanticide by parents. *Histories 6* As late as 225 AD Tertullian, a native of Carthage, decried the still extant Carthaginian custom of sacrificing their children to gods. The teenage Roman Emperor Elagabalus sacrificed young girls and boys to his god in 218, but by then it was considered wrong.

In the Americas before the Europeans came, the Aztec, Maya and Inca cultures all sacrificed children, virgins and prisoners to propitiate their many angry gods. The victim's heart was torn out by a flint knife and given to the priests. The victim was thrown down from the top of a pyramid temple. His arms and legs were eaten by humans and the rest of his body was given to animals. Cortez and his men were horrified by the number of people sacrificed daily and by the dried and fresh blood all over the Mesoamerican temples. Some estimate 250,000 were sacrificed each year, but others say the number was 40,000. Fernando de Alva Cortes Ixtlilxochitl, a 16th century Aztec royal, says in his

Codex Ixtlilxochitl, now in the Bibliotheque Nationale in Paris, that in addition to sacrificing 80,000 to 125,000 people yearly, the Aztecs sacrificed one out of every five of their own children annually. There are many pictorial depictions of these sacrifices in the Aztec's own codices: e.g. *Codex Tudelea, Codex Ixtlilxochitl.*

By the time of the Empire, Rome had outlawed human sacrifice in 97 BC. It was occasionally practiced in the ecstatic rituals of Ceres, Bacchus or Diana, but it was rare in Rome. What was not rare was the Roman custom of exposing their newborn babies to die. When a child was born, the father, the "paterfamilias" of the family determined whether the child was acceptable and could be kept or was not acceptable and would be abandoned at the cesspools or outside the city on the garbage dumps. A legal document, *Dionysarion's Letter*, was written by Dionysarion in the 1st century BC to her in-laws in order to get back the dowry her family had given them for her marriage to their son. Their son, her husband, had died and she was pregnant. The legal document says Dionysarion is "…not to sue for childbirth….(but) she is permitted to expose her baby or to join herself in marriage to another husband." Juvenal mentions children "abandoned by cesspools" and a 1st century letter from a man to his pregnant wife says: "If it is a boy, keep it. If it is a girl, discard it."

Roman law, religion and the entire ethos of their world saw nothing morally wrong with infanticide or with abandoning newborns. Romulus, the founder of Rome, had ruled back in the 8th century BC that no child could be killed "before" his third year "unless" he was deformed. Even the so-called refined and educated Cicero (106-43 BC) in his *On the Laws 3.8* states: "Deformed infants shall be killed." The "deformity" could be an unwanted child (Latin *exposti*), a sickly child, a deformed child or simply a wrong sex child. The Stoic philosopher Seneca (4 BC-65 AD) comments casually in *On Anger 1.15*: "…mad dogs we knock on the head…unnatural progeny we destroy; we drown even children at birth who are weakly and abnormal."

Plutarch in *Lives: Lycurgus 16* writes that in State-controlled Sparta:

"Nor was it in the power of the father to dispose of the child as he saw fit (as was his right in most heathen societies). He was obliged to carry (the newborn) child before certain men at a place called Lesche; these men were some of the elders of the tribe to which the child belonged; their business was to carefully view the infant, and, if they found it stout and well made, they gave order for its rearing and allotted to it one of the nine thousand shares of land above mentioned for its maintenance, but, if they found it puny and ill-shaped, ordered it to be taken to what was called the Apothetae ("depository"), a (large cave) under Mt. Taygetus (in the Peloponnese); as thinking it neither for the good of the child itself, nor for the public interest, that it should be brought up, if it did not, from the very outset, appear to be healthy and vigorous."

Some exposed Roman newborns were no doubt taken home by infertile couples. Some were picked up and raised as house or field slaves. Some of these children were rescued to play with the couple's natural children, or as court-jesters, or for pedophilic gratification and some were genuinely loved and educated by their masters. In the Catacomb of Praetextatus there is a grave with the name "Stercorius" on it. Some are kind and translate the Latin name "abandoned in the garbage." But the true translation of the name of this abandoned child, undoubtedly raised as a slave, is "little shit." The catacomb names of Projectus and Projecticus convey that these people were abandoned on the dung hills and garbage heaps of Rome.

The catacombs are filled with very tiny graves with the epitaph "adopted daughter of…" or "adopted son of…" inscribed on them. These inscriptions refer to the many babies and young children Christians rescued from the trash over the centuries. Tertullian says Christians sought out the tiny bodies of newborn babies from the refuse and dung heaps and gave them a decent burial or tended to them before they died or raised them as their own. The Christian idea that each individual person had worth because they were created by God was foreign to pagan society where the State, the tribe, the collective was the only value they knew. There are numerous tombs of small dimensions in the catacombs. Out of a total of 111 burials in one gallery of the Catacomb of Panfilo, 83 are of children and only 5 have inscriptions.

Abortion was practiced on a regular basis among the poor, slave, merchant and royal classes. To ancient people and the Romans an abortion was amoral. There was nothing in Roman law or in the Roman heart that said, "It is wrong to kill your baby in the womb." Tertullian, the early Christian apologist, describes how doctors of the time performed abortions:

"Among surgeons' tools there is a certain instrument which is formed with a nicely-adjusted flexible frame for opening the uterus first of all and keeping it open. It is further furnished with an annular blade by means of which the limbs of the child within the womb are dissected with anxious but unfaltering care; its last appendage being a blunted or covered hook, wherewith the entire fetus is extracted by violent delivery....There is also (another instrument in the shape of) a copper needle or spike, by which the actual death is managed in this furtive robbery of life. They give it, from its infanticide function, the name of *embruosphaktes* meaning 'the slayer of the infant' which of course was alive." *A Treatise on the Soul 25*

Romans agreed with the Greek view of abortion. Some of the most eminent and respected Greek philosophers encouraged and condoned abortion. Aristotle recommends that parents should be compelled by law to expose deformed or handicapped babies. In *Politics 7.1335b* Aristotle says:

"As to exposing or rearing the children born, let there be a law that no deformed child shall be reared; but on the ground of number of children, if the regular customs hinder any of those born being exposed, there must be a limit fixed to the procreation of offspring, and if any people have a child as a result of intercourse in contravention of these regulations, abortion must be practiced on it."

Aristotle (384-322 BC) feared population explosion. In the days of Caesar Augustus (27 BC-14 AD), he knew by censuses that the population of Romans in the world was declining. He had tried to curb lax morals and encourage marriages by implementing in 18 BC a law making adultery a crime and 27 years later in 9 AD he enacted *Lex Papia Poppaea* to promote and reward marriage because the number of Roman men who were unmarried was greater than the number of married men. He blamed the low marriage rate on homosexuals and on men who preferred the licentiousness of the single life to the responsibilities of married life and children. As Caesar, Augustus saw lax morals and low birthrate as threats to the Roman State. He addressed publicly in the Forum this problem. He praised the married men for:

"helping to replenish the fatherland....For is there anything better than a wife who is chaste, domestic, a good house-keeper, a rearer of children; one to gladden you in health, to tend you in sickness, to be your partner in good fortune....And is it not a delight to acknowledge a child who shows the endowments of both parents, to nurture and educate it at once the physical and spiritual image of yourself so that in its growth another self lives again?....I love you and praise you...and I not only bestow the prizes I have already offered but will distinguish you still further by other honors and offices....After this speech he made presents to some of them at once and promised to make others; he then went over to the other crowd (of unmarried men).... O, what shall I call you? Men? But you are not performing any of the offices of men. Citizens? But for all that you are doing, the city is perishing. Romans? But you are undertaking to blot out this name altogether....you are bent on annihilating our entire race and...upon destroying and bringing to an end the entire Roman nation. For what seed of human beings would be left, if all the rest of mankind should do what you are doing?.... introducing customs and practices which, if imitated, would lead to the extermination of all mankind, and, if abhorred, would end in your own punishment....you are committing murder in not begetting in the first place those who ought to be your descendants....Moreover, you are destroying the State by disobeying its laws and you are betraying your country by rendering her barren and childless....For it is human beings that constitute a city...not houses or porticos or market-places empty of men." Cassius Dio, *Roman History 56.1-5*

In the 1st century AD Augustus, thinking strategically, saw Rome's corrupt morals and low birth rate as threatening to the defense and sustainability of the Roman State. But c. 300 years earlier Aristotle had been worried about the danger to the Greek State of too many children. Both cultures blamed their ills upon the dearth of children or the proliferation of children. In *The Republic 461a-461c* Plato argues that in the ideal state governed by Philosopher Kings, women should be forced to have an abortion when the city-state becomes too populous. Zero Population Growth (ZPG) and China's One Child Policy promote the same doctrine in our modern world. The pagan practice of abortion bolstered by the idea of the primacy of the State over individual liberties was deeply engrained in all heathen cultures.

But as with all generalities, there are always exceptions. It is enigmatic to find Ovid, the ultimate 1st century roué, despoiler of women and libertine of love, not only against abortion but wishing that his mistress who had just attempted an abortion had died in the process:

"She who first essayed to expel from her womb the tender fruit she bore therein, deserved to perish in the struggle she had invited....If in the childhood of the world mothers had followed this wicked custom, the human race would have vanished from the face of the earth....Who would have overthrown the kingdom of Priam (Troy) if Thetis, goddess of the seas, had not been willing to bear her fruit until the term allotted by nature? If Ilia had smothered the twins she bore within her (Romulus and Remus), the founder of the ruling city of the world (Rome) would never have been born. If Venus had slain Aeneas in the womb, the earth would have been bereft of Caesars. And thou (Ovid's mistress), who was born so fair, would have perished had thy mother done that act thou has just tried....Why with cruel hand tear away the fruit ere it be ripe?....let it increase at will; to bring new life into the world is meet reward for a few months of patience....O women, why will you desecrate your entrails with the instruments of death? Why offer dread poisons to infants yet unborn?....The Armenian tigresses behave not thus, nor dares the lioness destroy an offspring of her own....Many a time she slays herself who slays her offspring in the womb. She dies herself and with disheveled hair is born away upon her bed of anguish, and all who see her cry, 'Well was her doom deserved.'" *The Loves 2.14*

In our modern Judeo-Christian culture even the most fervent Anti-Abortionists would never wish any woman dead from an abortion. What to make of pagan Ovid whose name is forever linked to licentiousness.

The early Christian apologist Minucius Felix (c. 150-270), indicting the Roman gods writes: "I see that you expose your children to wild beasts and to the birds... and that you crush (them) when strangled with a miserable kind of death....those things assuredly come down from your gods....Saturn (aka Kronos) did not expose his children but devoured them." *Octavius 30*

Against the grain of the pagan world, the Jewish-Christian God and teachings stood strongly against both abortion and infanticide:

"You must not worship the Lord your God in their (pagan) way, because in worshiping their gods, they do all kinds of detestable things the Lord hates. They even burn their sons and daughters in the fire as sacrifices to their gods." Deuteronomy 12:31 (c. 1450 BC)

"Thou shalt not murder a child by abortion nor kill him when born." *Didache 2.2* (c.50-100 AD)

"The (Mosaic) law, moreover, enjoins us to bring up all our offspring and forbids women to cause abortion of what is begotten or to destroy it afterward; and if any woman appears to have so done, she will be a murderer of her child by destroying a living creature and diminishing human kind." Josephus, *Against Apion 2.25* (c. 80 AD)

"The embryo therefore becomes a human being in the womb from the moment that its form is completed. The law of Moses, indeed, punishes with due penalties the man who shall cause abortion, inasmuch as there exists already the rudiment of a human being which has imputed to it even now the condition of life and death, since it is already liable to the issues of both, although, by living still in the mother, it for the most part shares its own state with the mother." Tertullian, *A Treatise on the Soul 37* (c. 200 AD)

"If men fight and hurt a woman with child so that she gives birth prematurely, yet no harm follow, he shall surely be punished accordingly as the woman's husband imposes on him; and he shall pay as the judges determine. But if any harm follows (the death of mother or child), then you shall give life for life." Exodus 21:22, 23

"You shall not abort a child, nor again, commit infanticide." *Letter of Barnabas 19.5* (c.130 AD)

Abortion and infanticide were outlawed after the age of Constantine. Customs and practices associated with their pagan gods and goddesses that had been common for thousands of years were declared immoral and legally wrong.

Were there people in Rome and its provinces who were appalled at the behavior of the Roman gods and who were morally repulsed by the everyday culture of Rome? There is always a remnant of sane and decent people. Many Roman writers decried what was happening to Rome. Juvenal (c. 60-140 AD) in his *Satires* lampoons in detail the whole host of evils that had infected the Roman State: homosexuality, abortion, drunkenness, pederasty, prostitution, adultery, over-eating, over-indulgence in luxury. In the *Satires 6*, he blames his bloated society on no Empire-wide wars, too much money, too much idle time and corrupt women:

"You ask where these monsters (evils) come from....Poverty made Latin women chaste in the old days, hard work and a short time to sleep and hands calloused and hardened with wool-working and Hannibal close to the city, and their husbands standing guard at the Colline

Gate that kept their humble homes from being corrupted by vice. But now we are suffering from the evils of a long peace. Luxury, more ruthless than war, broods over Rome and takes revenge for the world she has conquered. No cause for guilt nor deed of lust is missing now that Roman poverty has vanished. Money, nurse of promiscuity, first brought in foreigners' ways and effete riches weakened the sinews of succeeding generations."

In *Satires 3* Juvenal chronicles Rome as the melting pot of the late 1st and early 2nd centuries AD. The passage is quoted at length to give the reader a feel for the city of Rome c. 100 when the infant Church was developing:

"What can I do at Rome? I cannot lie; if a book is bad, I cannot praise it and beg for a copy; I am ignorant of the movements of the stars....I have never examined the entrails of a frog....The Syrian Orontes (river) has long since poured into the Tiber (river of Rome) bringing with it its lingo and its manners....Out upon you, all you that delight in foreign whores with painted headdresses!....Your country clown now trips to dinner in Greek-fangled slippers....One comes from lofty Sicyon (Greece), another from Asmyudon or Andros (Greek island), others from Samos (Greek island), Tralles (Turkey) or Alabanda (Turkey); all making for the Esquiline (a fashionable living area of Rome)....all ready to worm their way into the houses of the great and become their masters....these people (immigrants) are experts in flattery and will commend the talk of an illiterate, or the beauty of a deformed and compare the scraggy neck of some weakling to the brawny throat of Hercules...or go into ecstasies over a squeaky voice not more melodious than that of a cock when he pecks his spouse the hen....they (the Greeks) are a nation of play-actors. If you smile, your Greek will split his sides with laughter; if he sees his friend drop a tear, he weeps....Besides all this, there is nothing sacred to his lusts: not the matron of the family, nor the maiden daughter, not the as yet unbearded son-in-law-to-be not even the unpolluted son. If none of these be there, he will debauch his friend's grandmother....the first question they ask is about the wealth, the last about the character....

in Rome you pay a big rent for a wretched lodging, a big sum to fill the bellies of slaves and buy a frugal dinner for yourself....In Rome....we all live in a state of pretentious poverty....here we inhabit a city supported for the most part by slender props, for that is how the bailiff holds up the tottering house, patches up gaping cracks in the old walls....(there are) nightly fires and nightly alarms....Who but the wealthy get sleep in Rome?....The crossing of wagons in the narrow winding street, the slanging of drovers when brought to a stand (make) sleep impossible.... we are blocked by a surging crowd in front (of us) and by a dense mass of people pressing in on us from behind: one man digs an elbow into me, another a hard sedan pole; one bangs a beam, another a wine-cask against my head. My legs are beplastered with mud; huge feet trample on me from every side and a soldier plants his hobnails firmly on my toe....You will be robbed by a burglar or perhaps a cut-throat will do you quickly with cold steel....Happy, you would say, were the forebears of our great-grandfathers, happy the days of old which under Kings and Tribunes beheld Rome satisfied."

For a long look at Roman low life in the 1st century, read the *Satyricon* by Petronius (c. 27-66). The author gives a biting and detailed description of Rome's moral depravity. The book is not for the faint of heart or those with delicate sensibilities. Suetonius (c. 69-130) in his *Lives of the Caesars* chronicles in less graphic but highly effective prose the perversions, crimes and downward spiral of Rome's emperors and upper classes in the centuries during its fall.

Petronius, Juvenal and other Roman writers place some of the blame for the decline and depravity of Rome on the many immigrants, especially the "Asians" (Greeks and people from Asia Minor), who had traveled into Rome on its superb highways bringing with them their decadent morals, prurient gods and insatiable needs. The decline of the infrastructure of Rome, the decline in educational and cultural standards, the decline in moral values, the overcrowding of the city and the demand on housing and services Juvenal blames on immigrants. The result of Roman conquest was a huge influx of Roman subjects from all over the Empire longing to see Rome and to be a part of it.

Martial (c. 38-104) took this anti-immigrant sentiment and used it to ingratiate himself to the Emperor Domitian (81-96). The foremost writer of epigrams turned a problem into a praise:

"What race is so distant from us, what race is so barbarous, O Caesar, that from it no spectator is present in your city! The cultivator of Rhodope (Bulgaria) is here….The Scythian (Ukraine) who drinks the blood of his horses is here; he, too, who quaffs the water of the Nile (Egypt)….The Arabian (Saudi Arabia, Iran, Iraq) has hastened here; the Sabaeans (Yemen) have hastened; and here the Cilicians (Turkey) have anointed themselves with their native perfume. Here come the Sicambrians (Netherlands) with their hair all twisted in a knot and here the frizzled Ethiopians (Africa). Yet though their speech is all so different, they all speak together hailing you, O Emperor, as the true father of your country." *Epigrams 9.3*

But Rome was corrupt long before the immigrants crowded all the roads that led to Rome. The pagan gods and goddesses that the Romans had worshipped from the very beginning of the Republic (c. 509 BC) were anthropomorphic personifications of the worst instead of the best in the heart of man.

Jupiter, the king of the gods, was an adulterer and womanizer. His wife Juno was, also, his sister. She regularly killed Zeus' many lovers. Minerva, Jupiter's daughter, caused wars, protected from wars and killed anyone who was better than she was. Mars was Jupiter and Juno's son who became the god of war and raped a vestal virgin who conceived the founders of Rome, Romulus and Remus. Vesta was the goddess of the hearth and her Vestal Virgins had been holy whores in her incarnation in Ephesus. Ceres, goddess of grain, was the daughter of Saturn and Ops (another wife/sister of Jupiter) and was the mother of Proserpina who was raped by the god of the underworld Pluto. Diana was the goddess of the moon and another of Jupiter's many children by many women. Even though she was supposed to be chaste, she chased and was often a raving lunatic (Latin *luna* means "moon").

Venus, the famous goddess of love, was born in this way: When the Titan god Kronus severed his father's genitals and flung them into the ocean, the blood and semen caused foam. She was born out of that foam. Mercury was another of promiscuous Jupiter's many children. He was a kleptomaniac from the beginning so Jupiter always put a message for him to deliver into his sticky hands. Neptune, god of the sea, was one of Kronus' children. Kronus ate most of his children, but Neptune was spared by his mother who gave Kronus a baby owl to eat instead of his son. Vulcan was the god of fire. He was born deformed and was cast out of heaven to earth by his parents. He caused lots of earthquakes and volcanic eruptions trying to work out his early traumas. Apollo was the brother of Diana. His father Jupiter pretending to be a swan had raped the human Leto. She became pregnant. Again Jupiter's queen Juno stepped in and banned Leto from giving birth on dry land. The island of Delos had just been created. Leto gave birth to Apollo and his sister Diana there and then Jupiter anchored the island to the earth. Apollo was a womanizer like his father, but he was bisexual like many of the lesser gods. He accidentally killed his young male lover Hyacinthos. But he turned him into a flower.

The above jumbled litany is a minute fraction of the confusing stories of the Olympian Twelve. (See LaRousse's *Mythology* for a comprehensive look at ancient Greco-Roman deities.) Josephus, the Jewish historian of the 1st century AD, critiques the Greek/Roman pantheon of gods as ludicrous in comparison to the God of the Old Testament:

"…(their gods) may be allowed to be as numerous as they have a mind to be; they are begotten one by another….They are distinguished in their places and ways of living as (one) would distinguish several sorts of animals; as some to be under the earth; as some to be in the sea; and the ancientest of them all to be bound in hell; and for those gods to whom they have allotted heaven, they have set over them one, who in title is their father, but in actions a tyrant and a lord; whence it came to pass that his wife and brother and daughter, which daughter (Athena) he brought forth from his own head, made a conspiracy against him to seize upon him and confine him just as he had himself seized upon and confined his own father before….some of the gods are beardless and young and others of them are old with beards....some are set to trades... one god is a smith and another goddess is a weaver....one god is a warrior and fights with men...some of them are harpers or delight in archery... mutual seditions arise among them and they quarrel about men and they not only lay hands upon one another, but they are wounded by men and lament....But what is the grossest of all in point of lasciviousness are those unbounded lusts ascribed to almost all of them....which how can it be other than a most absurd supposal....Moreover, the chief of all their gods, and their first father himself, overlooks those goddesses whom he had deluded and begotten with child and suffers them to be kept in prison or drowned in the sea. He is also so bound up by fate that he cannot save his own offspring, nor can he bear their deaths without shedding tears. These are fine things indeed! Adulteries truly are so impudently looked on in heaven by the gods that some of them have confessed they envied those that were found in the very act. And why should they not do so, when the eldest of them who is their king also, has not been able to restrain himself from the violence of his lust.... some of the gods are servants to men and will sometimes be builders for a reward and sometimes will be shepherds; while other of them, like malefactors, are bound in a prison of brass. What sober person is there who would not be provoked at such stories and rebuke those that forged them and condemn the great silliness of those that admit them to be true?" *Against Apion 2.34.35*

It is crucial to the survival of a civilization that the ideals it holds high and the deity or deities it worships be worthy of veneration. Otherwise, the culture at its inception is fated to become corrupt and fall. Rome's gods were self-absorbed, predatory and destructive idols using their magical powers for whimsy and human exploitation. Roman culture reflected them.

The poet William Blake (1757-1827) said, "We become what we behold." If the gods a people worship kill their children, so will they. If the gods a people worship pimp, prostitute and fornicate, so will they. If the gods a people worship have sex with boys and men, so will they.

If the gods a people worship kill indiscriminately and with impunity, so will they.

Ancient Rome, the open perversity of its rulers and subjects and the tens of thousands of people they killed for sport and recreation in their circuses and arenas cannot be fathomed without understanding their paganism. The God or gods a civilization worships determine their concept of right and wrong, of good and bad, of acceptable and unacceptable. With the gods of Rome, everything under the sun was acceptable.

The Christians and Jews said there was only one God and not many gods. The Christians publicly insisted fornication, adultery, prostitution, homosexuality, pederasty, abortion, infanticide and killing humans for sport were immoral. They said their God Who is Spirit was real and the Roman gods, according to their Scriptures, were not real, were false lifeless idols fashioned of wood and stone:

"Of what value is an idol, since a man has carved it?
Or an image that teaches lies?
For he who makes it trusts in his own creation;
He makes idols that cannot speak.
Woe to him who says to wood, 'Come to life!'
Or to lifeless stone, 'Wake up!'
Can it give guidance?
It is covered with gold and silver.
There is no breath in it.
But the Lord is in his holy temple;
Let all the earth be silent before him." Habakkuk 2:18-20

From Isaiah 44:9-21 we learn that in addition to craftsmen making idols, ordinary blacksmiths and carpenters, using cypress, oak and cedar, often fashioned the idols people worshipped:

"All who make idols are nothing,
and the things they treasure are worthless....
The blacksmith takes a tool

and works with it in coals;
he shapes an idol with hammers,
he forges it with the might of his arm....
The carpenter measures with a line
and makes an outline with a marker;
He roughs it out with chisels
and marks it with compasses.
He shapes it in the form of man,
of man in all his glory,
that it may dwell in a shrine.
He cut down cedars,
or perhaps took a cypress or oak....
It is man's fuel for burning;
some of it he takes and warms himself,
he kindles a fire and bakes bread.
But he also fashions a god and worships it;
he makes an idol and bows down to it.
Half of the wood he burns in the fire;
over it he prepares his meal,
he roasts his meat and eats his fill.
He also warms himself....
From the rest he makes a god, his idol;
he bows down to it and worships.
He prays to it and says,
'Save me; you are my god.'
They know nothing, they understand nothing....
No one stops to think
no one has the knowledge or understanding to say,
'Half of it I used for fuel,
I even baked bread over its coals,
I roasted meat and ate it.
Shall I make a detestable thing from what is left?
Shall I bow down to a block of wood?'
...He cannot save himself or say,
'Is not this thing in my right hand a lie?'

...Remember these things, O Jacob,
for you are my servant, O Israel,
I have made you."

Isaiah reminds that God created people. People did not create God. The Biblical one God supernaturally revealed Himself to man. The pagan gods and goddesses, their attributes, their histories and antics, all the myths and stories about them were incrementally conjured up from the imaginations and fantasies of the people who projected on to them their adulterated needs, aspirations and fears. Fashioning and then worshipping metal, stone and wooden gods and trying desperately, unthinkingly to imbue feelings and sensory organs into the metal, stone and wood, pagans had become like the statues they created. Christians pointed out the futility, folly and falsity of paganism with its mute, blind, deaf pieces of wood, metal and stone.

The Romans correctly intuited from the very beginning that the Christian message was dangerous and could topple the military might, the wealth, the grandeur, the social structure and the very bases of their entire civilization. If the Christians were right, Rome and everything it meant, had meant and had become were founded on a lie. That is why Christians had to die.

VI.

"It has been said that the lives of early Christians consisted of 'persecutions above ground and prayers below ground.' Their lives are expressed by the Colosseum and the catacombs." John Foxe, *Book Of Martyrs 2* (1563)

Not only did the Romans have a complex pantheon of gods and goddesses who resided on Mt. Olympus, they, also, had a flesh and blood god in Rome---Caesar, the Emperor, their Pontifex Maximus, the highest priest in the Roman pagan religion.

Imperial Rome had begun as a Republic in c. 509 BC. Supreme power had resided in the citizens who voted for men to represent them and their interests in the Roman Senate. The Greek idea of democracy, meaning "rule by the people," was then and still is always held in tension with the people's need for and love of charismatic leaders. Julius Caesar was the first of ancient Rome's dynamic leaders to consolidate his military power into a dictatorship. When he crossed the Rubicon River with his troops in 49 BC, that unlawful act plunged Rome into civil war. Julius killed off all strong opposition and in 45 BC he forced the Senate to declare him "dictator for life." Even though he was beloved by the people, the Senate correctly saw these power grabs as the end of the Roman Republic. Sixteen members of the Senate, calling themselves "Liberators," assassinated him on the 15th (Ides) of March in 44 BC. Brutus, Caesar's former friend and one of the assassins, was so pleased to have Caesar dead that he issued a denarius coin, called the EID MAR for Ides of March. On the reverse is EID MAR with two daggers and a liberty cap. On the obverse is Brutus' proud image.

Rather than restoring the representative Republic, Caesar's assassination threw Rome into civil war. Ironically, Caesar's grandnephew and adopted son Octavian eventually emerged from the wars not as a Republican Liberator but as the Caesar/Emperor of the new Roman Empire. Octavian took the name Augustus ("respected one") and immediately declared his dead stepfather *"Divus Julius"* ("Divine Julius"). The cult of the Emperor as a god had begun.

Octavian Augustus, who was Caesar when Jesus was born and came of age (Luke 2:1), ruled from 27 BC to 14 AD and was declared "divine." All the successive Emperors either declared themselves divine or were called by the Senate and people "divinity."

For the next three hundred years temples were built and sacrifices were made to the Emperors. Julius Caesar had allowed a statue of himself to be made with the inscription *"Deo Invicto"* on it. "The unconquered god" became the description of the Emperors of Rome. The many gods and goddesses of the Roman pantheon now had a flesh and blood brother whom the people could see, hear and worship. A human as god/king was the inevitable consequence of the pagan view of the world, but it was one that would have dire consequences for the early Christians.

Perpetua and her friends were killed because they would not participate in the Imperial cult and perform a sacrifice to the Divine Emperor Septimus Severus. "Perform the sacrifice!" "Make sacrifice to the Emperor," her father and even the Roman procurator of Carthage implored the young woman. It would have been such an easy thing to throw some incense on the altar of the Emperor in order to avoid her death. But the young Christian knew that Caesar was not God or even a god. She chose to die for that belief.

One of the very early, mid 2nd century apologists, "defenders" of the faith, was Theophilus, the 7th Bishop of Antioch. Extant are his books explaining Christianity to his pagan friend Autolycus. He describes to Autolycus how Christians view Roman emperors:

"I shall pay homage to the emperor, but will not adore him; I shall instead pray for him. I adore the true and only God, by whom I know the sovereign was made. Well now, you might ask me: 'Why don't you adore the emperor?' The emperor, given authority by God, must be honored with proper respect, but he must not be adored. You see he is not God; he is only a man whom God has placed in that office not to be adored, but in order that he exercise justice on earth. In a way this authority was entrusted to him by God. As the emperor may not tolerate that his title be taken over by those subject to him, so no one may be adored save God. The sovereign must therefore be honored with sentiments of reverence; we must obey him and pray for him. In this way, God's will is done....Grace guards (us); peace protects us; the Sacred Word guides us; wisdom teaches us; eternal life directs us. God is our King." *Apology To Autolycus 1.2; 3.15*

Christians were not to adore Caesar as a god. They were to respect him as a God-appointed man placed by God in a position of authority to execute justice. That attitude was not enough for Rome's emperor god.

One of the ways the Roman authorities could ferret out those defiant Christians was to command all people to make sacrifice to the Emperor or to the pagan gods:

"Emperor Maximinus I (235-238) issued edicts that all the people should offer sacrifice and the rulers of the city should see to this diligently and zealously. Heralds went through the whole city of Caesarea by the orders of the governor summoning men, women and children to the temples of the idols...the imperial edicts...commanded that the altars of the idols should be rebuilt with all zeal and that all men together with the women and children, even infants at the breast, should offer sacrifice and pour out libations." Eusebius, *Martyrs of Palestine 4*

If a man, woman or child refused to sacrifice, it meant he or she was a Christian, a monotheist and they were killed. The church historian Eusebius was an eyewitness to many of these executions:

"I myself saw some of these mass executions (in Thebes, Egypt) by decapitation or fire, a slaughter that dulled the murderous axe until it wore out and broke in pieces while the executioners grew so tired they had to work in shifts. But I also observed a marvelous eagerness and a divine power and enthusiasm in those who placed their faith in Christ. As soon as the first person was sentenced, others would jump up on the tribunal in front of the judge and confess themselves Christians." Eusebius, *Church History 8.9*

Many Christians in Thebes (Egypt) refused to sacrifice to the Emperor god. The authorities devised diabolical means of killing these men, women and children:

"Their whole bodies were torn to shreds with claw-like potsherds until they expired. Women were tied by one foot and swung high in the air, head downward, by machines, their bodies totally naked without a stitch of clothing....Others died fastened to trees: they bent down their strongest branches by machines, fastened one of the martyr's legs to each, and then let the branches fly back to their natural position, instantly tearing apart the limbs of their victims. This went on not for a few days but for...whole years. Sometimes ten or more, at times more than twenty were put to death, or thirty, or almost sixty; at other times a hundred men, women and little children were condemned to a variety of punishments and killed in a single day." Eusebius, *Church History 8.9*

The Empire had found the litmus test to flush out Christians---perform the sacrifice or die. A rough calculation starting with Nero's persecution of Christians in 64 and ending with the Edict of Milan in 313 yields about 120 years of persecution and 129 years of toleration and uneasy peace.

In the 400's the Church made a list of 10 Imperial persecutions, not counting the numerous local persecutions:

Persecution under Nero (64-68)
Persecution under Domitian (81-96)

Persecution under Trajan (98-117)
Persecution under Marcus Aurelius (161-180)
Persecution under Septimus Severus (193-211)
Persecution under Maximinus the Thracian (235-238)
Persecution under Decius (249-251)
Persecution under Valerian (253-260)
Persecution under Aurelian (270-275)
Persecution under Diocletian (284-305) and Galerius (305-311)

Many Christians over the centuries cracked under the pressures of torture or fear of torture and death. These people performed the sacrifice to the Emperor or gods and were let go. After the persecution was over, most of them wanted to be back in fellowship with the Christian body. This produced a dilemma in the Early Church: should we allow them back after they had denied Christ and sacrificed to pagan gods or should we exclude them permanently from the Church?

Those who avoided martyrdom and other forms of torture by publicly renouncing their faith in Christ were called *lapsii* meaning "to fall away." They had lapsed from the faith. The believers broke into two camps. There were those who believed that once you publicly renounced faith in Christ and performed the sacrifice, you had removed yourself permanently from Christian fellowship. The other faction believed that because Jesus had forgiven Peter and forgives all repentant sinners, the lapsii should be readmitted to the Church after a period of penance.

Because there had been repeated persecutions over the centuries, this issue was hotly debated at the end of every persecution. One side argued that if a particular lapsi had watched her mother, father, husband and sister die, she who had "chickened out" was a *traditor,* a "traitor" and should definitely not be allowed back into the Church. The other side argued that her spirit was willing, but her flesh was weak just like Jesus had said in Matthew 26:41. Jesus would forgive her just like He forgave Peter who had publicly denied Him three times on the night before His death.

One can imagine the heat this problem generated. So many had family and friends tortured and killed. Most had chosen to die rather than to betray their Lord. Just because the persecution was over for a while, why should these lapsii be admitted back into the Church? What kind of faith did they have that could so easily be broken? Could we ever trust them under torture not to betray us to the authorities?

The other side conceded the questions but pleaded for forgiveness. Jesus had forgiven Peter who betrayed Him just several hours after that Apostle had declared to Jesus, "Even if all fall away (lapsi), I will not.... Even if I have to die with you, I will never disown you!" (Mark 14:29, 31) Jesus not only forgave Peter, but later commissioned him to do great things. Jesus died to forgive sinners. That was the reason He came to earth. Who are we, they argued, to deny the repentance of the lapsii if our Lord would not? The problem of the lapsii had been argued for a long time. The two sides became so contentious in the early 4th century they caused public rioting in Rome. The leaders of the two factions were sent into exile by Emperor Maxentius (306-312).

Bishop Damasus (c. 304-384) is called the Poet of the Catacombs because his sometimes banal verses memorialize many people in the catacombs. One of the leaders of the "forgivers" side of the lapsii controversy was Bishop Eusebius (not the same man who wrote *Church History*). The Emperor exiled him to Sicily where he died of starvation. Damasus' description of this deadly internal division is inscribed over Eusebius' tomb in the Catacomb of St. Callixtus:

"Heraclius (leader of the hardliners) did not admit that the lapsii
Could do penance for their sins.
But Eusebius taught that these unhappy ones
Should weep for their faults.
From the passionate rage of the people,
Divided into two factions,
Came seditions, slaughters, war, discord, strife
Till suddenly the tyrant (Maxentius) banished both.
The pontiff (Eusebius) who stood for the integral pledges of peace
Bore exile serenely, awaiting divine judgment
And left the world and earthly life on the Sicilian shores."

Even though Damasus' poetry is wanting, his renowned calligrapher Philocalus engraved this tribute and other beautiful writings in the catacombs. Philocalus wrote and illuminated the legendary *Chronographia of 354*, an extensive and historically valuable calendar of Roman history and public figures.

After a period of persecution, many of the churches in the Roman Empire had weighed in on the problem of the lapsii. Emperor Marcus Aurelius, in spite of his subsequent reputation as a benevolent Stoic Philosopher King, unleashed one of the most violent periods of persecution against Christians. During his reign (161-180), thousands of Christians in Lyons and Vienne, France were martyred. A letter from the churches in Lyons and Vienne to the churches in Asia and Phrygia survives. It describes the horrors their fellow Christians had endured. When the persecution was over, the Bishop of Lyons, Pothinus, and 19,000 Christian men, women and children had been butchered. Previous to the killings, the Christians in Gaul had been excluded from the public baths, the markets and all public places. Mobs beat them, dragged them through the town, stoned them, took their clothes and finally imprisoned them until the Roman governor arrived. When he sat in judgment on them, the governor asked, "Are you a Christian?" If the person said, *"Christianus sum"* ("I am a Christian"), he or she was set aside for capital punishment. Day after day hosts of people were presented to the governor and condemned.

When the killing began:

"...the sufferings of the blessed martyrs are beyond description or writing....Sanctus (a deacon from Vienne)...resisted with such tenacity that he did not even tell them his own name, race, city of origin or whether he was slave or free but replied to every question in Latin, 'Christianus sum' ('I am a Christian'). The governor and the torturers were eager to master him and when all else failed, they finally pressed red-hot plates of brass against the most tender parts of his body. These were burning, but he remained steadfast in his confession....his body was all one wound, mangled and shorn of human shape....The blessed Pothinus, Bishop of Lyons, was more than ninety years old and physically weak. He could scarcely breathe….He was dragged before the tribunal by soldiers…and with the populace howling at him….he gave a noble witness. When the governor asked him, 'Who is the god of the Christians?' he replied, "If you are worthy, you will know.' Then he was dragged about mercilessly, pummeled by hands and feet that showed no respect for his age, while those at a distance hurled whatever was at hand at him, all imagining that they were avenging their gods. He was thrown into prison, barely breathing, and died two days later….(Christians) ran the gauntlet of whips, the mauling by beasts, and whatever the crazed mob demanded, and finally the iron chair, which roasted their bodies and clothed them with the stench….Attalus, when roasting in the iron chair with the stench rising from his body, told the crowd in Latin: 'Look! Eating men is what you are doing'…. Blandina was filled with such (heavenly) power that those who tortured her from morning to night grew exhausted and admitted that they were beaten, for they had nothing left to do to her… since her whole body was smashed and lacerated….Maurus, Sanctus, Blandina and Attalus (after much torture) were taken to the beasts in a special public exhibition…(where) Blandina was hung on a stake and offered as food to wild beasts…(but) none of the beasts would touch her (so she was) returned to jail to be reserved for another ordeal….On the last day of the games (in the amphitheater) Blandina was again brought in….(she) rejoiced at her departure as if invited to a wedding feast. After the whips, the beasts and the gridiron, she was finally put into a net and thrown to a bull…she was tossed by the animal for some time before being sacrificed. The heathen admitted that never before had a woman suffered so much for so long….they threw to the dogs those who had been strangled (in jail)….Then they threw out the remains (of those) left by the beasts and the fire, torn and charred…denying them burial." Eusebius, *Church History 5.1*

Because of Blandina's sex, her suffering and her witness to the pagans, she became a heroine of the Early Church. There are many early paintings and icons of her and, even today, two communes in France are named Sainte-Blandine. In Lyons, France in the ruins of the Roman amphitheater called Amphitheatre des Trois Gaules, there is a pole in the arena as a mute memorial to all the Christians who were killed there c. 1,800 years ago.

After pages and pages of gory and glory-filled deaths, the churches of Lyons and Vienne addressed the subject of those among them who had not been strong enough to resist such physical torture, the lapsii:

"...the first martyrs clearly and eagerly made their confession of martyrdom ('I am a Christian'). Others, however did not seem ready. Having failed in training, they were not equal to the struggle, and ten of them proved stillborn, causing us much grief and restraining the enthusiasm of those not yet arrested....At that point we were all tormented by uncertainty about their confession, not fearing (our own) impending punishment but afraid lest anyone fall away." Eusebius, *Church History 5.1*

Clearly those who faltered in their faith and courage at such crucial times were not only dispiriting to other Christians but also caused concern among the clergy for the salvation of those who had "fallen away," who had lapsed from the faith.

The churches eventually came down on the side of the forgivers. The church in Rome wrote to the church in Carthage that if the lapsii were left to their own resources, their fall would be irreparable and they would be lost. The bishop encouraged them to extend their hands to the fallen that they may rise again. Dionysius, a contemporary of Origen, argued that before their martyrdom by Decius in 249-251, even some martyrs had accepted lapsii back into their fellowship. Who were they after the persecution was over to "grieve mercy and overturn order?" The chalice of mercy was ever full during the centuries of Christian persecution.

The hard-liners had made some good points philosophically and practically, but the wise men of the Early Church followed the Gospel of Forgiveness and Jesus' injunction in Matthew 18:21,22: "Then Peter came to Jesus and asked, 'Lord, how many times shall I forgive my brother when he sins against me? Up to seven times?' Jesus answered, 'I tell you, not seven times, but seventy times seven.'" It is interesting to note in this passage that Peter the Denier was the one who asked the question about forgiveness that Jesus answered with the doctrine of Infinite Forgiveness.

In order to weed out Christians in his Empire, Emperor Decius (249-251) issued an edict requiring all citizens of the Empire to sacrifice to him in the presence of a Roman official and to obtain a Certificate Of Sacrifice called a *libellus*. This posed another moral problem for Christians. They could sacrifice and live. They could refuse to sacrifice and be killed. They could pay or bribe an official for one of these libelli and be in the clear. Forty-four of these libelli have been discovered. One reads:

"To those appointed to see the sacrifices: From Aurelia Charis of the Egyptian village of Theadelphia. I have always continued to sacrifice and show reverence to the gods and now, in your presence, I have poured a libation and sacrificed and eaten some of the sacrificial meat. I request you to certify this for me below."

Another from the Rylands Library in Manchester, England reads:

"It has always been my practice to sacrifice to the gods. Now, in your presence and in accord with the command (of Decius), I have sacrificed, poured a libation, and tasted the offering. I beg you to certify this statement....I, Aurelia Demos, have presented this declaration. I, Aurelius Ireneus (her husband), have written for her since she is illiterate. I, Aurelius Sabinus, the commissioner, saw you sacrificing."

The bishops of Rome, Antioch and Jerusalem refused to buy a certificate or sacrifice and they were killed. The bishop of Smyrna and others performed the sacrifice. It is likely that some Christians bribed an official to forge the certificate or bought a libellus at an exorbitant price.

In the libellus cited above, Aurelia Demos had to get a certificate "proving" she was not a Christian. She was illiterate and her husband had to write for her. It is a truism that the majority of early Christians were from the lower socio-economic classes. Jesus had attracted the masses and repelled the wealthy class of priests.

Most people in the working class were illiterate. A contract by a flute-player named Aurelius of Egypt survives:

"In the consulship of our lords, Licinius Augustus and Licinius Caesar (c. 320 AD).

To Aurelius Eugenius, gymnasiarch and senator of Hermopolis, greetings from Aurelius Psenymis, son of Kollouthos and Melitene, a flute-player from Hermopolis.

I agree that I have contracted and pledged myself to you, the squire, to present myself at the village at the vintage-time in the vineyards with the appointed grape-treaders. There I will serve, without fail, the grape-treaders and others with my flute-playing. I promise not to leave the grape-treaders till the end of the vintage in the coming prosperous 10th special fiscal year. For the flute-playing and the pleasure I give, I shall receive the agreed sum from the contracting party.

Signed the 24th of Choiak, in the above-named consulship,

Aurelius Psenymis

I will fulfill the conditions as stated.

I, Aurelius Pinoution, his assistant, have written for Aurelius since he is illiterate."

But not all Christians were illiterate or from humble walks of life. Flavia Domitilla after whom the Catacomb of Domitilla is named was a devout Christian. She and her husband Titus Flavius Clemens were both from the royal family of the Flavians. The Flavian family of emperors comprised the last three Caesars. Emperor Titus Flavius Vespasian who ruled from 69-79 was the first of the Flavian Caesars. His two sons succeeded him: Titus from 79-81 and Domitian from 81-96. (There were many emperors of Rome, but only the first twelve are considered Caesars. See Suetonius, *Lives of the Caesars*.)

All three Flavian Emperors were opponents of the Jews and the Christians. Following his father Vespasian's orders, Titus destroyed the city of Jerusalem in 70 and began the eventual Diaspora of the Jews that lasted for the next two thousand years. Titus assumed the throne in 79 at the death of his father. His brother Domitian was the most ruthless of the three. He allowed his brother Titus to die of a fever that ceded Domitian the throne in 81. Domitian led one of Rome's most concerted efforts to stamp out Christianity. He killed thousands of Christians and sent John, the last living Apostle of Jesus, into exile on the Isle of Patmos in c. 96.

Flavia Domitilla was very well-connected to this royal family. She was the granddaughter of Emperor Vespasian. Her mother was the daughter of Vespasian and the sister of both Emperors Titus and his brother Domitian. Domitilla was married to her cousin, Titus Flavius Clemens. Their two sons had even been adopted by her uncle Domitian to succeed him as emperors. When Domitilla and her husband Clemens became Christians, Domitian showed no mercy to his relatives. Their lives and that of their sons were destroyed. Domitian had his cousin Clemens executed and he exiled his niece Domitilla. History is silent about the fate of their two sons.

Cassius Dio (c. 150-235) in his *Roman History 67.14* confirms Domitian's ruthlessness:

"...Domitian slew, along with many others, Flavius Clemens the consul, although he was a cousin and had to wife Flavia Domitilla who was also a relative (niece) of the emperor's. The charge brought against both of them was that of atheism (did not believe in the Roman gods), a charge that many others who drifted into Jewish ways were condemned. (Christianity was then still associated with the Jews.) Some of these were put to death and the rest were deprived of their property. Domitilla was...banished."

But not before she had given a large plot of land to the Christians. The Catacomb of Domitilla was dug under that donated land. Wealthy Christians occasionally gave land for underground burial because so many of their fellow believers were poor and could not afford burial sites. In the catacombs named after Domitilla, there is a marble slab with her name on it and the designation that she was the *neptis*, the "granddaughter" of Emperor Vespasian. When Paul had written the Letter to the Philippians in c. 60 and had sent greetings from the believers in "Caesar's household," it was only a matter of time before the mother, sister, daughter or granddaughter of an Emperor would be converted and have to suffer death and/or exile because of that choice.

Many wealthy and patrician men and women became Christians and were often martyred for their faith. One of the first known patrician converts was Pomponia Graecina, the wife of Plautius who helped subdue Britain. Tacitus in *Annals 13.32* tells us that she was accused in 57-58 of some "foreign superstition and handed over to her husband's judicial decision." "Foreign superstition" was a very early Roman term for Christianity. He held a trial and exonerated her, but she was thereafter a pariah in royal circles. DeRossi who rediscovered the catacombs in the 1850's identified the Crypt of St. Lucina in the catacombs of Callixtus as that of Pomponia Graecina and her family. Pomponia was her Roman name and when she was baptized, she received the name of Lucina, meaning "illumination."

Felicitatis whose name means "happiness" was a daughter of wealth who was widowed and had seven sons. She was a pious and educated woman who had raised her boys as Christians. She and her seven sons were arrested in c. 165 in Rome under the persecutions of Marcus Aurelius. Before she was beheaded, the Romans forced her to watch as her seven sons were killed---one by one. Januarius, the oldest, was scourged and pressed to death with weights. Felix and Philip had their brains bashed out with clubs. Her fourth son, Silvanus, was thrown to his death from a high precipice. Her three youngest sons, Alexander, Vitalis and Martialis, were beheaded. This most unhappiest of mothers must have gladly surrendered her head to the chopping block. De Rossi found the tomb of her first son Januarius in the Catacomb of Praetextatus on the Via Salaria. His mother Felicitatis' grave was next to his.

Wealthy Christians not only gave their lives for Christ, they, also, donated land for the catacombs as Domitilla had done. They allowed believers to use their homes for religious services, gave missionaries money for travel expenses, provided food, money and clothing to their needy brothers and sisters and gave money for the poor in other parts of the Empire. When Bishop Ignatius was on his way to be martyred in the Colosseum, rich Roman Christians wanted to use their influence to save his life. Christianity was status-blind and was embracing male and female, slave and free, rich and poor, plebeians and nobility.

Wealthy pagan Romans gave a lot of money to feed and to entertain the population of the Empire. Most of Rome's wealth was inherited or acquired through business. There was a minute layer of aristocracy at the top of the Roman Empire and a gigantic mass of poverty and need under that thin upper crust. In order to keep the populous from rioting and overthrowing the Emperor and the ruling class, the Emperors, the Senators and the wealthy had to keep the people distracted and contented. This they did with periodic outbursts of generosity.

Augustus Caesar in his previously mentioned summary of the good deeds of his life, chronicles in detail his generosity:

"I paid to the Roman plebs ("common people") HS 300 ("HS" equals sesterces) per man from my father's (Julius Caesar) will and in my own name gave 400 sesterses from the spoils of war (in 29 BC)....(in 24 BC) I again paid out a public gift of 400 sesterces per man...from my own patrimony....(in 23 BC) twelve doles of grain personally bought were measured out; and in my twelfth year of tribunician power (12-11 BC) I gave 400 sesterses per man for the third time. And these public gifts of mine never reached fewer than 250,000 men." *The Deeds 15*

All of the Roman people, of course, were not eligible for Caesar's State welfare. He mentions 250,000 plebs above, but he later gave 200,000 people 240 sesterces per person. Another time he gave 240 sesterces to 350,000 plebs in addition to the doles of grain they regularly received. In order to receive the grain, a Roman had to present to the authorities every month his *tessera frumentaria*, his pottery token to prove he was entitled to receive the grain. A significant number of Roman citizens were on the dole (State welfare) in Augustus' time. In order to pacify the masses, the Roman State had to keep adding public benefits. Marcus Aurelius added pork and wine to those on the dole and later Septimus Severus added olive oil. Their national poet Virgil in *The Georgics* had glorified the Roman State as supreme. For that privilege, the State must provide for the people: "All is the State's; the State provides for all."

Augustus and all the Caesars paid heavily for the crowns they wore. When the public treasury or the military got in trouble, Augustus had to bail them out:

"Four times I helped the senatorial treasury with my money, so that I offered 150,000,000 sesterces to those who were in charge of the treasury. And when Marcus Lepidus and Lucius Arruntius were consuls (in 6 AD), I offered 170,000,000 sesterces from my patrimony to the military treasury."

After Augustus' death, several entries were added to his *Deeds*. One of them calculated his personal public donations as Caesar: "All the expenditures which he gave either into the treasury or to the Roman plebs or to discharged soldiers: 2,400,000,000 sesterces." With olive oil costing 3 sesterces a quart, Augustus was wildly wealthy but it was very expensive to be Caesar.

Money and handouts were one way to keep the rabble quiet. An even more potent way was to provide them with increasingly sophisticated and violent entertainment.

In the early days of the Empire, the chariot races at the Circus Maximus and the periodic distribution of doles of grain kept the people at bay. "Bread and circus." With full bellies they madly cheered for their teams and applauded the Emperor. New attractions were constantly added: animal hunts with wild animals from Africa, theatrical productions, gladiator fights.

But the people always demanded newer, bigger, better, more.

VII.

"Rome's order, Rome's justice, Rome's peace (the *Pax Romana*) were all built on a savage exploitation and suppression....The empire which had pushed back the barbarian tribes that threatened its borders had erected a greater barbarism at the very heart of its dominium, in Rome itself. Here the prospect of wholesale destruction and extermination from which the city had largely escaped, thanks to Roman arms, came back in the acting out of even more pathological fantasies." Lewis Mumford, *The City in History, p. 297*

The people's rapacious demands were met with the inauguration of the Colosseum in 81 AD. This most famous of buildings was originally called the Flavian Amphitheater after the Emperor who built it, Flavius Vespasian. In 67 Nero had sent his general, Vespasian, to Jerusalem to put down a Jewish rebellion. The next year Nero committed suicide under pressure from the Senate. General Vespasian came back to Rome and seized the throne. Vespasian left his son Titus in Jerusalem to settle the Jewish problem once and for all. In 70 Titus dismantled Jerusalem stone by stone as Jesus had foreseen forty years earlier. Matthew 24:1,2; Mark 13:1,2; Luke 21:5,6

Vespasian was so pleased with Jerusalem's fall that he had a bronze sestertius struck in 71 with *"Judaea Capta"* ("Judea Captured") written on the reverse and his own double-chinned, craggy features on the obverse. Caesars and Emperors had sole power over the mint and used coins to spread their name, face and message throughout the Empire. The coin Jesus was given by a Pharisee that prompted His famous "Render unto Caesar the things that are Caesar's and unto God the things that are God's" (Matthew 22:15-21) was a silver denarius used to pay the Roman poll tax. It had "Tiberius Caesar, Son Of Divine Augustus" and his laureled head on the obverse and his mother Livia seated as *Pax* (Peace) with a scepter in her right hand and an olive branch in her left on the reverse. Jesus had avoided a Pharisaic trap by pointing out Caesar's image on the coin and saying, Give back to Caesar what is his and give to God what is His. When Vespasian's son Titus became Emperor in August of 79, he had a silver denarius minted. On the obverse he had etched a realistic depiction of himself as a full-faced, bull-necked, middle-aged man looking very much like his father Vespasian.

Suetonius (c. 69-130) in *Lives of the Caesars: Titus* says of Titus in the campaign against Jerusalem:

"Titus displayed great valor and military talents in the prosecution of the enterprise (the war in Judea). After an obstinate defense by the Jews, that city, so much celebrated in the sacred writings, was finally demolished, and the glorious temple itself, the admiration of the world, reduced to ashes."

Jerusalem, the Temple and the treasury contained untold millions of dollars worth of money and religious objects. The relief on the Arch of Titus near the old Roman Forum shows the Romans parading the looted Temple treasures through the streets of Rome. As the buildings of Jerusalem burned, the flames melted much of the gold and silver. The Romans extracted the molten metals from the stones and debris and used the plundered treasure to finance the building of the Colosseum. 97,000 Jews captured as slaves were forced to build it.

The site of the Colosseum was near another legendary building, the Golden Palace, the *Domus Aurea* that Nero had built after he started the great fire in 64. Suetonius gives a description of Nero's Golden House:

"Its size (300 acres) and splendor will be sufficiently indicated by the following details. Its vestibule was large enough to contain a colossal statue of the emperor 120' high….(the house) was so extensive that it had a triple colonnade a mile long. There was a pond, too, like a sea, surrounded with buildings to represent cities, besides tracts of countryside, varied by tilled fields, vineyards, pastures and woods, with a great number of wild and domestic animals. In the rest of the house all parts were overlaid with gold and adorned with gems and mother-of-pearl. There were dining rooms with fretted ceilings of ivory whose panels could turn and shower down flowers and were fitted with pipes for sprinkling the guests with perfumes. The main banquet hall was circular and constantly revolved day and night like the heavens. He had baths supplied with seawater and sulphur water. When the edifice was finished in this style and he dedicated it, he deigned to say nothing more in the way of approval than that he was at last beginning to be housed like a human being." *Lives Of The Caesars: Nero*

A 120' nude, bronze statue of Nero graced the vestibule of his Golden House. It was so huge the people called it the *Colossus* meaning "gigantic." That nickname gradually became the site-name of Vespasian's Amphitheater.

The Colosseum, built of travertine marble, is elliptically shaped and c. 1,729' in circumference on a foundation of six acres. It has four stories and is c. 157' high. On the top story was an enormous awning, the *velarium* that protected the spectators from the sun and inclement weather. It required 1,000 men to open and to close this ingenious device. The four arches at the four axes of the building were the main entrances, but 76 other entrances provided easy access to the seats. Moderns calculate the seating capacity at 50,000. But the *Chronographia of 354*, written in 354, says the stadium held 87,000 spectators.

Admission to the Colosseum was generally free, but the plebs had to have a ticket, a *tessare*. They lined up the night before to get these coveted prizes. The pottery ticket was presented to the usher who indicated the seat. If a shard read "CVN II GRAD VI LOC IV," it meant the ticket holder was in Section 2, Row 6, Seat 4. For the plebs the seats were wooden planks placed over the marble tiers. The senators and patricians had the choice cushioned seats at the bottom of the arena. Women and children were relegated to the highest tier far from the action.

And what action there was. Never before or since has the world seen the likes of the spectacles in the Colosseum. When the giant amphitheater was inaugurated in 81, there were one hundred days of celebration. On opening day, 5,000 wild animals and 4,000 tame animals were "hunted" and killed by *venatores*, slaves trained to put on a good show before they slew the animals. These wild animal hunts in a contained area (Latin *venationes*) had been going on for years before the Colosseum. They were originally held in the Circus Maximus, but often the cornered animals jumped into the stands and killed or mauled spectators. Even after a moat was dug around the Circus, the animals were not predictable. The arena of the Colosseum was designed so that no man or beast could vault, jump, crawl or claw his way to the spectators. Men and beasts were trapped. That was the point.

For wild animal hunts, the entire arena was landscaped to resemble a lush jungle. Lions, leopards, bears, wild boars, jaguars, panthers, ostriches, tigers, ibex, rhinos, wild sheep, elephants and any animal that was not tame and was foreign and unusual was captured, presented to the Roman people for their pleasure and then killed. Roman ships sailed to Africa and Asia to hunt exotic animals for the venationes.

The orator and statesman Cicero (106-43 BC) saw nothing strange about capturing wild animals to be killed in the Circus Maximus. In fact, his friend Rufus constantly asked him to provide *"pantherae"* for all the games. *Pantherae* was generic for leopards, lions, jaguars or panthers. Cicero was at this time governor of Cilicia in Asia Minor and had access to people who hunted wild animals. Cicero wrote to Rufus:

"About the panthers, the usual hunters are doing their best on my instructions. But the creatures are in remarkably short supply....the matter is receiving close attention, especially from Patiscus....Whatever comes to hand will be yours, but what that amounts to I simply do not know." *Letters 2.11.2*

In addition to his governorship in that outpost region of Cilicia in modern Turkey, Cicero seems to have had a vigorous side business in procuring animals for the Circus. He wrote to one hunter:

"In almost all my letters I wrote to you about panthers. It will embarrass you that Patiscus has sent ten panthers to Curio and that you have not sent me many more than that. Curio gave me those ten panthers plus another ten African ones...if you will only remember and procure panthers from Cibyra (in Turkey) and likewise send a letter to Pamphylia (in Turkey) because they say more panthers are captured there, you will accomplish your purpose...for as soon as they are captured, you have people available whom I sent to feed and ship them." *Letters 8.9.3*

Panthers were the animals Romans most wanted to see in the arenas. In the 1st century AD Pliny the Younger wrote a tactfully ambiguous letter to his friend Maximus about the gladiatorial show Maximus had given in Verona. First, he congratulated him on it, but made clear how bad Maximus' reputation would have been had he refused to do something grand for the people of Verona since his dead wife came from that town. Pliny was, however, disappointed in the absence of pantherae. Pliny hints at his friend's reticence to spend money on a show (the Veronese had to beg him) and the longer the letter, the more cutting Pliny becomes:

"You did perfectly right in promising a gladiatorial combat to our good friends the citizens of Verona, who have long loved, looked up to and honored you; while it was from that city too you received that amiable object of your most tender affection, your late excellent wife. And since you owed some monument of public representation to her memory, what other spectacle could you have exhibited more appropriate to the occasion? Besides, you were so unanimously pressed to do so that to have refused would have looked more like hardness than resolution. The readiness too with which you granted their petition and the magnificent manner in which you performed it, is very much to your honor; for a greatness of soul is seen in these smaller instances, as well as in matter of higher moment. I wish the African panthers, which you had largely provided for this purpose, had arrived on the day appointed, but though they were delayed by the stormy weather, the obligation to you is equally the same since it was not your fault that they were not exhibited. *Letters 72*

One wonders if pantherae had even been procured for the celebration or had just been promised. There was such a need for wild animals from Africa in the arenas all over the Roman Empire that some breeds were becoming extinct or were "lost at sea."

Many Roman intellectuals like Cicero who scorned, commented on or satirized the Circus, the Colosseum and its contests had no real objection to the violence or the bloodshed. They just did not understand, or pretended not to understand, how the masses could get so excited over the chariot races in the Circus Maximus or the events in the Colosseum. They looked down on the plebs. Tacitus says: "The peculiar vices of this city are love of theater and a manic zeal for gladiators and horses." *A Dialogue On Oratory 29* They, as the educated class, were above those vices. There is no moral outrage among these intelligentsia, just a smug superiority.

On the 1,000th anniversary of the founding of Rome, the State presented these uneducated people with an orgy of blood. 1,000 pairs of gladiators fought and died. 32 elephants, 10 tigers, 60 lions, 30 leopards, 10 hyenas, 10 giraffes, 20 wild asses, 40 wild boars, 10 zebra, 1 rhinoceros and 6 hippopotami were killed.

The soldier-Emperor Probus (reigned 276-282) in order to give gifts to the Romans and to celebrate his many military victories released into the Colosseum 1,000 ostriches, 1,000 stags, 1,000 boars as well as deer, ibexes, wild sheep and other semi-tame animals. The plebs themselves hunted the animals in an elaborately landscaped forest setting complete with the chirping of exotic birds. Whatever the people could kill, they could keep.

Martial, the Spanish poet and father of epigrams gives us a very detailed account of all that went on in a typical day at the Colosseum.

Humans and animals were indiscriminately slaughtered for the amusement of the Roman people:

"Amidst the terrible contests by which Caesar imitates the sports of Diana (goddess of the hunt), a light spear having pierced a pregnant she-boar, one of her litter leaped forth from the wound of its wretched mother. Oh! cruel Licina (goddess in charge of delivery of babies)! Was this a delivery? She should willingly have died wounded by more weapons, that this sad way to life might not have been opened to all her young ones. Who will now deny that Bacchus owed his birth to the death of his mother? You may believe that a deity was so produced; for thus has a beast been born." *On The Spectacles 12*

"As first bound down upon the Scythian rock, Prometheus with ever-renewed vitals feasted the untiring vulture, so has Laureolus (a notorious robber), suspended on a cross, offered his defenseless entrails to a Caledonian bear. His mangled limbs quivered, every part dripping with gore, and in his whole body no shape was to be found." *On The Spectacles 7*

Even though Cicero was making money by capturing and shipping animals to be killed in the hunts, he seemed to have had a few qualms when he actually saw a hunt:

"The rest of the hunt took place twice a day for five days. They were magnificent, nobody denies that. But what pleasure can there be for a civilized man when either some powerless man is ripped to shreds by a powerful beast or some magnificent animal is transfixed by a spear?" *Letters 7.1.1-3*

Any of the living, man or beast, was fodder for the pagan Romans' arena of entertainment. It must be stressed that each of these "spectacles" was carefully planned, choreographed and appointed by "normal" Roman people whose jobs were to set up everything and make sure it all worked well as if one were planning and executing a performance in a modern stadium.

One of the definitions of a "civilized man" is a "humane man." What people like Cicero and other intellectuals of the ancient world failed to comprehend is that they were born, bred and lived in a barbarous, inhumane culture, in a culture that was not kind, not compassionate not humane.

For killing was what the Colosseum was all about. There were feeble pretensions of art called *silvae*. These were choreographed and splendidly staged reenactments of famous myths. The story of the master artificer Daedalus who fashioned wings for himself and his son Icarus to escape prison on Crete ended with Daedalus, dangling high above the arena, falling to his death and being eaten by a bear. Martial in his *On The Spectacles 8* comments sarcastically: "Daedalus, while you were being thus torn by a Lucanian bear, how must you have desired to have those wings of yours."

No myth was so appalling that Romans did not want to see it reenacted for their titillation. The story of the Cretan minotaur, the half-man, half-bull, who was born as a result of intercourse between King Minos' wife Pasiphae and a bull, was presented as a *silva:* "Believe that Pasiphae was enamored of a Cretan bull; we have seen it. The old story has been confirmed. Let not venerable antiquity boast itself, Caesar; whatever fame celebrates, your arena reproduces for you." Martial, *On The Spectacles 5* Called zoophilia or bestiality, this act was not uncommon in the pagan world and at this public display there seemed to be no public outcry.

Nor was there hue and cry at the frequent reenactment of the castration of Attis, the Phrygian god and lover of the mother goddess Cybele. Tertullian watched many spectacles before his conversion to Christianity. He describes what he personally saw:

"We have often witnessed in a castrated criminal your god...Attis; (we have seen) a wretch burnt alive as Hercules. We have laughed at the sport of your midday game of the gods when Father Pluto, Jove's own brother, drags away, hammer in hand, the remains of the gladiators; when Mercury with his winged cap and heated wand...tests whether the bodies were really lifeless or only feigning death." *To The Nations 1.10*

Slaves or criminals were forced to play the fatal parts in these early "snuff films." Martial (c.38-104) wrote *De Spectabilis* (*On The Spectacles*) in 81 in honor of the opening of the Colosseum and dedicated his work to Emperor Titus. Here he praises the Emperor for the realistic scenery behind the death of the mythic musician Orpheus. Orpheus' death is incidental:

"Whatever the Thracian mountain Rhodope (mountain range in Balkan Peninsula) is said to have witnessed during Orpheus' performance, the arena exhibited to you, Caesar. Rocks crawled and the forest amazingly moved quickly just as it is believed the grove of the Hesperides did. Rapt, every type of wild animal intermingled with the tame herd was listening as was many a bird suspended in air above the poet (Orpheus). But ultimately our Orpheus lay on the ground mangled by a displeased bear." *On The Spectacles 2*

The most amazing spectacles of them all were the *naumachia*, mock sea battles. These were reenactments on water of historical naval battles with condemned criminals as sailors. The first naumachia was given by Julius Caesar in 46 BC to celebrate his victories in Egypt. Caesar created a basin near the Tiber River on the Campus Martius and flooded it. Sixteen life-size ships manned by 4,000 rowers and 2,000 slaves reenacted a battle between the Egyptians and the Tyrians. It was a fight to the death for men and rowers. Caesar had a special coin minted portraying this first-of-a-kind spectacle.

Emperor Augustus, the adopted son of Julius Caesar, celebrated the inauguration of a temple to Mars, the god of war, in 2 BC with the second naumachia. He describes it in his *The Deeds 23*:

"I gave the people a naval battle in the place across the Tiber where the grove of the Caesars is now, with the ground excavated in length 1,800', in width 1,200', in which 30 beaked ships, biremes and triremes, but many smaller, fought among themselves. In the ships about 3,000 men fought in addition to the rowers."

In that small pretend ocean, the pretend sailors with real weapons were packed in like sardines. They reenacted the Battle of Salamis (480 BC) in which a powerful Persian army attacked a weak Greek contingent off the island of Salamis. The Greeks won. In this sham naval battle, the criminals were dressed like Persians and Greeks.

It boggles the mind to imagine the sophisticated engineering and the minute preparations for this and other naumachia: the construction and filling of the basin by a specially built aqueduct (remains of which are still visible in Rome below the monastery of St. Cosimato), the making and fitting of the costumes, the brief education the combatants had to receive in order to know what they were doing, the building of the bleachers for the spectators, the advertising for the event, secure transportation of the criminals to the scene and getting them on the boats and deciding when the battle would begin, and.... Think of how many thousands of men/slaves had to spend thousands of hours for an afternoon of entertainment for the masses. And the bloody cleanup.

Of course, for Augustus' naumachia he had his eye on Julius' naumachia forty-four years earlier and wanted to make sure his spectacle exceeded that of his adoptive father. The cost? Who knows? The criminal actors were free. Free slave labor dug the basin, built the aqueduct, built the ships, made the costumes. And there had to have been highly educated Romans who engineered and profited from this whole extravaganza. In this mock battle, if you multiply the number of fighting men (3,000) by two, there were 6,000 rowers. A total of 9,000 men, more than a standard Roman fleet, fought. It is unlikely that many of them survived the battle. Again, that was the point.

Nero in 57 was the first to give a naumachia in an amphitheater. The amphitheater was a wooden one on the Campus Martius. We do not know much about this building, but Suetonius in *Lives Of The Caesars* relates an interesting incident that occurred one day at that amphitheater. It was during one of the reenactments of the popular Icarus' and Daedalus' "attempt at flying" story:

"Icarus (played by a condemned criminal) at his very first attempt (at flight from the top of the building) fell close by (Nero's) couch and bespattered the emperor with his blood, for Nero very seldom presided at the games, but used to view them while reclining on a couch."

Suetonius' whole point in telling this bloody story was not to call attention to doomed Icarus but to emphasize the fact that Nero rarely presided at the games. He "peeked" at them from an opening in the curtain and was besmirched.

When the marble Colosseum was opened and officially inaugurated in 81, Emperor Titus declared one hundred days of celebration. On the first day of the celebration, Titus treated the people to a twenty-four hour extravaganza. Everything he had organized was like the finale of a fire-works display:

"...remarkable spectacles....a battle between cranes and also between four elephants; animals both tame and wild were slain to the number of 9,000....women, but not those of any prominence, took part in dispatching them....and naval battles. For Titus suddenly filled this same theater (Colosseum) with water and brought in horses and bulls and some other domesticated animals that had been taught to behave in the liquid element just as on land. He also brought in people on ships who engaged in a sea fight there, impersonating the Corcyreans (from Corfu) and the Corinthians....There, too, on this first day there was a gladiatorial exhibition and wild beast hunt." Cassius Dio, *Roman History 66.25.1-5*

Scholars have speculated for centuries on how the Colosseum was filled with water sufficient for a mock battle to take place. Martial who was at the Colosseum that day in 81 says:

"There was land until a moment ago. Can you doubt it? Wait until the water, draining away puts an end to the combats. It will happen right away and you will say: the sea was there a moment ago." *On The Spectacles 24*

The arena was obviously flooded and drained seamlessly. After the opening animal hunt was dismantled, landscaping carted away, dead animals dragged out and the area cleaned up, the people talked, laughed and waited for the next show. What's that? Water! Gushing and rushing in. Some in the audience start the rumor that a naumachia will take place. The last spectacle like that was twenty-five years ago. Some in the crowd were too young to have seen one. The water continues to fill up the arena until it is of sufficient depth. Then what? Do they bring in the big, life-size triremes and all the thousands of combatants dressed like Corcyreans and Corinthians? How did they get those standard-sized ships with all the combatants aboard into the flooded arena without letting out the water? Maybe they first placed the ships and men into the arena and then turned the floodgates loose? We know there were pipes for carrying the water into the arena, but exactly how did they get the water for the naumachia into and then out of the arena in such a short time? Was the arena watertight? It had to have been. Many, many questions over the last 2,000 years. The fact remains: we do not know exactly how the Romans placed all the "soldiers" and paraphernalia into the arena and then flooded and drained the Colosseum just as we do not know how the Egyptians built the Pyramid of Cheops.

We do know that on that first day of celebration, the animal hunt was first, the naval battle was second and then the amphitheater was drained and dry (not muddy) because next "there was a gladiatorial exhibition and (another) wild-beast hunt." The second day there was a chariot race. The third day there was another flooding of the Colosseum with "a naval battle between 3,000 men....The Athenians conquered the Syracusans...(who) made a landing on the islet (that had been created in the middle of the Colosseum) and assaulted and captured a wall that had been constructed around the monument. These were the spectacles that (Titus) offered, and they continued for a hundred days." Cassius Dio, *Roman History 66.25*

At the end of the 100th day of celebration, Titus took his bows before the people. They were wildly appreciative. Titus had exceeded their expectations. As he stood before the cheering crowds on that last day, he wept bitterly and all the people saw him crying.

Cassius records:

"The next day, in the consulship of Flavius and Pollio, after the dedication of the building mentioned (Colosseum), he passed away at the same watering-place (Aquae Cutiliae in province of Rieti) that had been the scene of his father's death....Titus, as he expired, said: 'I have made but one mistake.' What this was he did not make clear." *Roman History 66.26*

Titus had destroyed Jerusalem eleven years earlier. The money looted from the holy Temple in Jerusalem had financed the building of the Colosseum that he had so lavishly inaugurated. Was his destruction of the holy Temple and Jerusalem and the looted treasure the mistake Titus had made? We will never know.

But the Romans and all ancients believed in the retribution of the Furies if a man had done something terrible. They, also, believed in signs and portents of coming events. On the night before Julius Caesar's assassination, his wife dreamed that the foundation of their house fell down and her husband was stabbed in her arms. Caesar was not feeling very well the next day and decided not to go to the Senate, but Brutus, one of the conspirators, urged him to go. He left for the Senate about 11:00 in the morning. Julius had been warned by the soothsayer Spurinna to "Beware the Ides of March." When he was on his way to the Senate that morning, he passed the soothsayer and said, "This is the Ides of March." The seer said, "Yes, but it has not passed."

Droughts, famines, unusual weather, a comet or the appearance of a special star like the star that sent the Arabian Magis on their long journey to Bethlehem---all of these extra-ordinary phenomena were imbued with ultimate meanings. The Jewish historian Josephus only five years after Jerusalem's destruction wrote of and seemed to believe in the omens that happened in Jerusalem prior to Titus' destruction of that city:

"...a few days after that feast on the one and twentieth day of the month Artemisius (June 8), a certain prodigious and incredible phenomenon appeared. I suppose the account of it would seem to be a fable were it not related by those that saw it and were not the events that followed it of so considerable a nature (destruction of Jerusalem) as to deserve such signals. For before sun setting, chariots and troops of soldiers in their armor were seen running about among the clouds and surrounding the cities (of Judea). Moreover, at that feast which we call Pentecost, as the priests were going by night into the inner court of the Temple, as their custom was, to perform their sacred ministrations, they said that, in the first place, they felt a quaking and heard a great noise, and after that they heard a sound as of a great multitude saying, 'Let us remove hence.'" *Wars Of The Jews 6.5.3*

Some fifty years later, the reliable Roman historian Tacitus corroborates the portents that occurred in the city before Jerusalem's fall:

"Prodigies had occurred, but their expiation by the offering of victims or solemn vows is held to be unlawful by a nation (Jews) which is the slave of superstition (belief in one god) and the enemy of true beliefs (the Roman gods). In the sky appeared a vision of armies in conflict, of glittering armor. A sudden lightning flash from the clouds lit up the Temple. The door of the holy place abruptly opened, a superhuman voice was heard to declare that the gods were leaving it, and in the same instant came the rushing tumult of their departure. A few (Jews) placed a sinister interpretation upon this. The majority were convinced that the ancient scriptures of their priests (the Old Testament) alluded to the present as the very time when the Orient would triumph and from Judaea would go forth men destined to rule the world." *Histories 5*

Another important historical event is associated with Titus. He became Emperor on June 24, 79 just two months before the eruption of Mt. Vesuvius in August of 79. The ashes and lava from the eruption buried and preserved in tact the Roman towns of Pompeii and Herculaneum. In spite of Roman attempts to resuscitate the towns, over the centuries earth, grass, trees, vines and vegetation gradually reclaimed them. Even people living near the site of Pompeii forgot its name. They called it simply "*la civita*," the city. It was not until 1763 that it regained its name when archaeologists recovered its identity.

There are two ancient accounts of the eruption. One is by Pliny the Younger whose uncle Pliny the Elder died in the eruption. The other is by Cassius Dio in *Roman History 66. 21-23*:

"In Campania remarkable and frightful occurrences took place. For a great fire suddenly flared up at the very end of the summer. It happened on this wise....This was what befell....There were frequent rumblings, some of them subterranean that resembled thunder, and some on the surface, that sounded like bellowings. The sea also joined in the roar and the sky re-echoed it. Then suddenly a portentous crash was heard, as if the mountains were tumbling in ruins, and first huge stones were hurled aloft, rising as high as the very summits. Then came a great quantity of fire and endless smoke so that the whole atmosphere was obscured and the sun was entirely hidden as if eclipsed. Thus day was turned into night and light into darkness. Others believed that the whole universe was being resolved into chaos or fire. Therefore they fled, some from the houses into the streets, others from outside into the houses, now from the sea to the land and now from the land to the sea....While this was going on, an inconceivable quantity of ashes was blown out which covered both sea and land and filled all the air. It wrought much injury of various kinds, as chance befell, to men and farms and cattle, and in particular it destroyed all fish and birds. Furthermore, it buried two entire cities, Herculaneum and Pompeii, the latter place while its populace was seated in the theater. Indeed, the amount of dust, taken all together, was so great that some of it reached Africa and Syria and Egypt, and it also reached Rome, filling the air overhead and darkening the sun....the people (in Rome) did not know and could not imagine what had happened, but like those close at hand, believed that the whole world was being turned upside down, that the sun was disappearing into the earth and that the earth was being lifted to the sky....Titus accordingly sent two ex-consuls to the Companians to supervise the restoration of the region."

Titus ruled for only two years before his abrupt, and some would say Furies-plagued, death on September 13, 81 AD at age 41, but he is forever associated with the destruction of Jerusalem and the eruption of Mt. Vesuvius, two significant historical events. That he was the first to flood the Colosseum for a naumachia is notable but historically insignificant.

But all the naumachia put together could not match the one that Emperor Claudius had staged in 52 on Lake Fucine (now called Lago di Fucino) 60 miles east of Rome.

Every year when the spring rains came, the prime farmland around Lake Fucine was flooded for miles around because the lake had no natural outlet. The Romans were crack engineers. It took 30,000 men over eleven years to dig a tunnel 3½ miles long through a mountain of solid rock to reach the Liris River. When the rains came, the excess water in the lake ran off through the brick-lined tunnel and emptied into the river. The farmer's land remained dry for spring planting.

To dedicate the opening of this amazing tunnel, Claudius decided to give a naval battle on Lake Fucine, Italy's largest inland lake:

"The tunnel through the mountain to drain the Fucine lake into the river Liris had now been completed. In order that as many people as possible might admire the impressiveness of the achievement, a naval battle was arranged on the lake itself….Claudius put 19,000 armed combatants into two fleets of ships with both three and four banks of oars. He positioned rafts around the edge of the lake to block off any escape routes, leaving enough space in the middle for the display of the power of the oarsmen, the skill of the coxswains, the speed of the ships and all the other arts of such a contest. Platoons and companies of the praetorian cohorts were stationed on the rafts, protected by ramparts, from behind which they fired catapults and missile-throwers. Covered ships manned by marines occupied the rest of the lake….The battle, though contested by criminals, was fought as bravely and spiritedly as if the combatants were men of free will, and after considerable bloodshed, the survivors were excused death." Tacitus, *The Annals 12.56*

What is interesting here is not just the battle but the contingent of 19,000 armed-to-the-teeth criminals. It is estimated that in addition to Claudius, his fourth wife Agrippina and a sizable contingent of people from Rome, there were tens of thousands of people from the surrounding area in attendance at this event. 19,000 men already condemned to death and armed with deadly weapons posed a security problem. To counter this threat, covered ships with armed mariners patrolled the lake itself. Rafts with ramparts filled with platoons of soldiers and companies of guards were positioned all around the perimeter of the lake to block any escape route. From these rafts they could fire catapults and missile-throwers to sink or to burn the ships if there was a problem.

A problem did develop at the beginning of the battle when the criminal "soldiers," dressed and armed as Rhodians and Sicilians, sailed close to the emperor to pay homage to him. Claudius, covered in royal purple and his queen in a mantle of gold, sat on a raised dais. 19,000 voices shouted out, "Hail, Caesar. We who are about to die salute thee!" The shout of that many men blasted and rippled across the countryside. Claudius who was a little daft, yelled back, "Or not."

"….(at that reply) all of them refused to fight, maintaining that they had been pardoned. Upon this (Claudius) hesitated for some time (and thought) about destroying them all with fire and sword, but at last (he) leaped from his throne and running along the edge of the lake with his ridiculous tottering gait (polio as a child?), he induced the men to fight, partly by threats and partly by promises." Suetonius, *Lives of the Caesars: Claudius*

It is more likely that the criminals decided to fight the battle not because they feared bumbling Claudius but because they feared his power to unleash thousands of trained Roman soldiers on them.

"Ave, Emperor, morituri te salutamus." The "we who are about to die" salute given to Claudius in Suetonius' text is the only place where this phrase is mentioned in ancient literature. Most have heard this salute and assume it was said by all gladiators before they fought. There

is no evidence for this textually. However, because everything in the Colosseum's arena was staged and dramatic, there was probably some type of salute, maybe this one, given by gladiators to the emperor at the games.

The signal for the beginning of the naval battle on Lake Fucine was given by a mythological figure called Triton, son of the god of the sea Neptune, who miraculously rose from the middle of the lake and blew on a golden conch shell. This was, in and of itself, quite a mechanical tour de force. A facsimile of Triton, made of pure silver, was submerged in the middle of the lake until at a certain time, a certain mechanism was triggered and the figure rose out of the lake and actually blew a loud trumpet blast. At this signal, the two fleets of ships began the battle. The music was playing, the people were shouting, the ships were moving toward confrontation.

Tacitus says the criminals fought "bravely and spiritedly." They gave a good show. Some ships were rammed by the iron beaks in the prows of other ships. A rammed trireme sunk very quickly and all aboard usually drowned. That was the easy way to dispatch an enemy ship. Most of the ships plowed through the engine (the oars) of the galleys. All the oarsmen were mangled and crushed as the oars were forced into them. Dead in the water, deprived of its rowers, the ship was boarded by a gangplank. Wielding swords and knives, the men fought to the death.

When the battle was over, Lake Fucine had turned red with blood. We are not told how many of the original 19,000 combatants survived. The survivors were not executed as was sometimes the custom. They were given the privilege of living to fight and to die another day on a bloody lake or in the sandy arena of the Colosseum.

In addition to these sham naval battles and the wild beast slaughters, there were small dramas, music and poetry readings performed in the Colosseum. But make no mistake about it. The Colosseum was built for blood. Tens of thousands of people were killed in over three hundred years of active use. If one extends that number to the 250 amphitheaters built all over the Roman Empire, the number of the dead multiplies by thousands.

It is vital to remember that the pagan gods and the emperor/god presided over and approved all of these activities. Martial praises the emperor god: "Whereas piously and in suppliant guise the elephant kneels to thee, Caesar, that elephant which erewhile was so formidable to the bull his antagonist, this he does without command, and with no keeper to teach him: believe me, he too feels your present deity." *On The Spectacles 17*

Every person murdered, every animal killed, every artifice and spectacle was sponsored by, dedicated to, and for the honor and pleasure of the pagan gods and their human god. At the beginning of each spectacle, the gods (e.g. Diana, Ceres, Apollo, Flora, Hercules, the Emperor) were acknowledged with great pomp and ceremony involving priests, priestesses, standards, banners, music and great festooned processions. Everything in a day at the Colosseum was cloaked in religious trappings. All eyes were, however, always on the arena. *"Arena"* in Latin means "sand." The Romans covered the area of the arena with sand in order to soak up the blood. We still use the Latin word for "sand" to designate the "central stage, ring or area used for sports or other forms of entertainment surrounded by seats for spectators." Blood-soaked sand was scooped up by slaves after every gore-imbrued spectacle and replaced with clean tan sand as if nothing had transpired.

A typical day at the Colosseum began in the early morning. Often a *lotteria* or lottery was given. The emperor or man who sponsored the lottery (Greek *euergetes*) had numbered pieces of parchment or pottery thrown into the stands. Those who grabbed them presented their number to the redemption booth and received their prize. Often the prizes were roasts of chicken or a pretty vase, but sometimes people hit the jackpot with gold and silver pieces, a piece of furniture, a horse or even an estate. The lottery excitement of never knowing but always hoping was the same as it is today and we have the ancient Romans to thank for that type of chancy game.

The *venationes*, the animal hunts were first after the musical procession to the gods. At noon, some spectators left for lunch, but most brought or bought lunch from the vendors who hawked their wares of sausages, pastries and wine all over the stadium as they do today. Prostitutes waited under the many arches of the amphitheater for customers. Our word "fornication" comes from the Latin word for "arches" (*fornix*). The origin and survival of the word "fornication" indicate the brisk trade carried on under the fornices for hundreds of years. Circus days were profitable for both vendor and fornicator.

Midday was, also, the time when criminals were executed. Public execution was done in order to warn the spectators against committing any of these acts. Murderers, arsonists and Christians were thrown to wild beasts (*damnatio ad bestias*) or made to fight each other as impromptu gladiators. Often they were beheaded, crucified or burned alive by dipping a tunic, called a *tunica molesta,* in a naphtha-soaked substance and setting it on fire.

The Christians were grouped with other criminals because they were guilty of atheism. An atheist is usually defined as a person who does not believe there is a god. But atheists to the Romans were those who did not believe in or would not acknowledge their gods or their emperor as a god. Christians had no images or idols to worship and performed no outward sacrifices. Their internal rather than external worship of God was totally incomprehensible to pagans. Rome was a syncretic society that had accepted all the gods and goddesses their conquered people held sacred. Yet the Christian god was not only an affront to them but was a threat to society and to their gods because Christian atheism was a belief in only one god who repudiated all other gods and idols as false and demonic. That was a capital crime.

The Stoic philosopher Seneca (4 BC-65 AD) went to the Colosseum one noonday to see what was going on. In a letter to his friend Lucilius he wrote:

"The other day I chanced to drop in at the midday games, expecting sport and wit and some relaxation to rest men's eyes from the sight of human blood. Just the opposite was the case. Any fighting before that was as nothing. All trifles were now put aside. It was plain butchery. The men had nothing to protect them. Their whole bodies were open to the thrust, and every thrust told. The common people prefer this to matches on level terms or request performances. Of course they do. The blade is not parried by helmet or shield, and what use is skill or defense? All these merely postpone death. In the morning men are thrown to bears or lions, at midday to those who were previously watching them. The crowd cries for the killers to be paired with those who will kill them and reserves the victor for yet another death. This is the only release the faux gladiators have. The whole business needs fire and steel to urge men on to fight. There was no escape for them. The slayer was kept fighting until he could be slain. 'Kill him! Flog him! Burn him alive!' The spectators roared. 'Why is he such a coward? Why won't he rush on the steel? Why does he fall so meekly? Why won't he die willingly?' Unhappy as I am, how have I deserved that I must look on such a scene as this? Do not, my Lucilius, attend the games, I pray you. Either you will be corrupted by the multitude, or, if you show disgust, be hated by them. So stay away!" *Epistles 7*

The prudish and shocked attitude of Seneca at the high noon killing of Christians and criminals is disingenuous: "How have I deserved that I must look on such a scene as this?" Seneca was a licentious man who was exiled for committing adultery with Emperor Caligula's young niece. He served with wile and guile the crazy Caligula, the quixotic Claudius and the evil Nero. He had even been Nero's tutor. He had seen many people killed or forced to commit suicide by those emperors. He had lived in Rome for years and was conversant with the lifestyles of the rich and famous. It was not, to be sure, the first time Seneca had wended his way to that amphitheater. To pretend offense at what he saw at the Colosseum was pretentious and self-serving.

Later, Nero forced his tutor Seneca to kill himself by opening his veins. The blood wouldn't flow out and Seneca was in pain. He drank poison but it did not work. Finally, he threw himself into a hot bath and died of suffocation from the steam. (Tacitus in *Annals 15* describes his death scene.)

The 2nd century Christian apologist Tertullian was of a judicial and more refined state of mind than Seneca. After his mid-life conversion to Christianity, he was disgusted by the games, gods and events represented in Roman arts and arenas. One of his classic arguments against Rome's persecution of Christians and their God is the Roman's obvious contempt for their own gods:

"Other of your (Roman) writers, in their wantonness, even minister to your pleasures by vilifying (your) gods. Examine those charming farces of your Lentuli and Hostilii where in the jokes and the tricks it is your... deities which afford you Romans merriment....Your dramatic literature, too, depicts all the vileness of your gods. The Sun (Apollo) mourns his offspring (Phaeton) cast down from heaven and you (Romans) are full of glee; Cybele (a mother goddess) sighs after the scornful swain (her son/paramour Attis who castrated himself), and you do not blush.... When the likeness of a god is put on the head of an infamous wretch, when one impure and trained up for the art in all effeminacy represents a Minerva or a Hercules, is not the majesty of your gods insulted and their deity dishonored? Yet you not merely look on, but applaud. You are, I suppose, more devout in the (Colosseum), where after the same fashion your deities dance on human blood, on the pollutions caused by inflicted punishments, as they act their themes and stories, doing their turn for the wretched criminals, except that these too often put on divinity and actually play the very gods....we must explain all these things by the contempt in which (your) gods are held by those who actually do these things and by those for whose enjoyment they are done." *Apology 15*

After the midday slaughter, the afternoon was the highlight of a day at the Colosseum for the Romans. That was when the gladiators fought. Gladiators were usually slaves from conquered nations who were trained in a gladiator school to fight each other in the arena. When they fought, they were dressed in costumes to resemble the Barbarian tribes Rome had conquered.

The fights had originated as munera, as ritual sacrifices in honor of the dead. By the time of the Colosseum, the duel as a funerary ritual had morphed into forced mortal combat. The crowd just wanted to see highly trained men fight to the death for their delectation. The people were so avid for new thrills that Julius Caesar once had his gladiators clad in armor made of silver. The people were dazzled. Other wealthy patrons imitated him in their games, but the people were bored and booed.

With the gladiators, the Roman populace had found their ultimate thrill. The fights were between skilled, trained men and the deadly outcome was unpredictable. The people favored those men who fought valiantly with contempt for their own lives. They ridiculed gladiators who played it safe or fought hard to preserve their lives. Often a fighter made a mistake and went down. Gladiators were taught how to die. Vanquished, they would kneel on one knee and grasp the thigh of the victor. The victor waited for the sponsor (*editor*) of the game to give a thumb's up or down. Occasionally the gladiator had fought so vigorously that the crowd would rise, wave their handkerchiefs or togas in the air, put their thumbs up and yell, *"Missus! Missus!"* ("Let him go!"). Most of the time the people wanted blood and would thrust their thumbs down and yell, *"Jugula! Jugula!"* ("Throat! Jugular Vein!"). The winner would grasp the head of the kneeling warrior with one hand. With the other he rammed his sword into his neck.

Scholars in the 19th and 20th centuries have debated and divided over the position of the determinative thumb in gladiator contests. For some "thumbs down" means "kill him." Others say "thumbs down" means "let him go." The Latin phrase *pollice verso* meaning "turned thumb" only indicates the crowd turned their thumbs without saying whether the thumbs were turned up or down. The Christian Prudentius (348-c.405) hated the inhumanity of the games and gives another ambiguous description of the turning of the thumb:

"(The Vestal Virgin) sits conspicuous with the awe-inspiring trappings of her head-bands and enjoys what the trainers (of the gladiators) have produced. What a soft, gentle heart! She rises at the blows and every time a victor stabs his victim's throat she calls him her pet; the modest virgin with a turn of her thumb (*converso pollice*) bids him pierce the breast of the fallen foe." *Against Symmachus 2*

Most of the peoples and nations of the world use and have used "thumbs down" to indicate disapproval and "thumbs up" to indicate approval. It seems logical that "pollice verso" meant "turned down."

After the "thumbs down" was executed, a man dressed like the god of the dead ran out and smashed a mallet into the head of the dead gladiator signifying, "He's mine." Another god-impersonator (often Mercury) ran out, poked the dead man with a red-hot poker to make sure he was dead. The dead gladiator was dragged out of the arena by a hook. Often his throat was slit as a final coup. Rammed with a sword. Smashed with a mallet. Poked with a red-hot poker. Hooked and dragged. Throat slit. Blood and violence was what the people wanted and they got it in spades.

Few spectators in the early centuries of Christian persecution seemed to have what we would call pity on the gladiators or on the Christians. If a gladiator went down, the crowd yelled callously, "He's had it!" (*"Habet, hoc habet!"*) When the Christian woman Blandina suffered severe torture for so many days in Lyons, the crowd admitted they had never seen a woman suffer so nobly. The Carthaginian spectators at Perpetua's and her servant's ordeal recoiled slightly when the women were brought out half-naked and they realized they were young mothers. Those moments of conscience did not, however, stop the killings.

When Christian men, women and children were in the arena to be killed, the people often cried out, *"Usque quo genus tertium!"* ("How long must we endure this third race!") The Romans considered themselves the First Race. Jews, as monotheists, were the Second Race but were allowed exemption from participating in the cult of the emperor or of the other gods. Upstart Christians, monotheists like the Jews, were the Third Race but were not exempt from emperor worship. The ancients usually divided themselves into just two races: themselves and all the others. The Jews said there were Jews and Gentiles (people from other nations). The Greeks said there were Greeks and all those who spoke a strange language that sounded to Greeks like "bar, bar, bar" hence Barbarians. The Romans had conquered the known world and incrementally made the Barbarians part of the First Race of Romans.

Romans, the First Race, wanted all their victims in the Colosseum to fight bravely and to die nobly like their warrior soldiers who had conquered the whole world had done. The amphitheater became the medium for the common man to relish in Rome's power and to see first-hand the violence of the many wars their soldiers had waged to make Rome and the Romans masters of the world.

"Kill him!

"Flog him!"

"Burn him alive!"

"Why is he such a coward?"

"Why won't he rush the steel?"

"Why does he fall so feebly?"

"Why won't he die willingly?" the people yelled at Christians and criminals who obviously had no physical defensive or offensive weapons or skills.

In the gladiators the Romans found the ideal representation of their brave soldiers. Here were the strongest, the most elite of the conquered tribes. Here were trained, trim and toned men fighting for their lives.

There were four schools to train gladiators in Rome, the largest of which, Ludus Magnus, was connected to the Colosseum by an underground tunnel. On the day of the fight, the pairs of gladiators walked the long dark tunnel to the arena and watched as their friends fought and died. They waited their turn.

The gladiators were paired according to their defensive and offensive weapons. A Thracian with his curved short sword and armor on his left arm was paired with a Mirmillo who had a small shield, a lance and a crested helmet with a vizor. A Retarius had a net, a trident, a dagger and scaled armor covering his left arm. He would be paired with a Secutor who had a shield, a sword and a full helmet.

Attesting to the wild popularity of these fighters, archaeologists have unearthed stunning mosaics of gladiators all over the Roman Empire. At the Borghese estate in Torrenova in 1834, they found the floor of a dining room from c. 320 rimmed with sixteen fields of mosaics relating to gladiators. In one square a gladiator is being prodded by a hot iron to continue fighting. Many of the squares show them fighting, dying, bleeding. An interesting square shows musicians playing. This confirms what some ancient authors have written. An orchestra played extemporaneously along with the fights, with a slow tempo as they circled each other and a fast tempo as one moved in for the kill.

Another mosaic found in 2007 in the ruins of Emperor Commodus' palace in Rome depicts a Retarius gladiator named Montanus being proclaimed victor by a referee named Antonius. Commodus was the handsome, muscular Emperor (reigned 180-192) who fashioned himself a gladiator. He often performed mock feats of Hercules to prove his virility and even fought naked in the arena to the disgust of the spectators. Of course, he always won because the whole charade was an exercise in vanity.

In the Museo Nazionale in Rome there is a limestone relief of a Roman gladiator with helmet and shield fighting off a leopard attacking him on the left but looking to an approaching lion on his right that is being goaded to attack him by a man holding an iron prod. It is unclear whether this gladiator is a trained fighter or a criminal or Christian dressed like a gladiator, but there are rare instances where gladiators were made to fight wild animals.

Another exquisite mosaic of a gladiator was unearthed on the coast of Libya in 2000. An exhausted, victorious gladiator is seated on the arena sand and is staring at his dead opponent. Those who have seen the mosaic and gazed into the gladiator's eyes say the sad, exhausted and jaded look is worthy of a Botticelli.

Lactantius (c. 240-320), who was an advisor to the first Christian Emperor Constantine, critiques the Colosseum contests and adjures Christians not to go to them:

"He who finds it pleasurable to watch a man being killed even though the man has been legally condemned, pollutes his conscience just as much as though he were an accomplice or willing spectator of a murder committed in secret. Yet they call these 'sports' where human blood is shed! When you see men placed under the stroke of death, begging for mercy, can they be righteous when they not only permit the men to be killed but demand it? They cast their cruel and inhuman votes for death, not being satisfied by the mere flowing of blood or the presence of gashing wounds. In fact, they order the (gladiators), although wounded and lying on the ground, to be attacked again and their corpses to be pummeled with blows to make certain they are not merely feigning death. The crowds are even angry with the gladiators if one of the two isn't slain quickly. As though they thirsted for human blood, they hate delays....By steeping themselves in this practice, they have lost their humanity. Therefore, it is not fitting that we who strive to stay on the path of righteousness should share in this public homicide." *Divine Institutes 7.20*

Constantine outlawed the contests in 325 AD. One of the triumphs of Christianity was the last gladiator fight in Rome on January 1, 404.

Certainly these brave gladiators were worthy of praise. The best among them became public idols---valiant men fighting and vanquishing opponent after opponent, year after year. The crowd loved the superstar gladiators. So did the women.

"Gladiator," coming from the Latin word for the 23" steel sword they used (the *gladius*), was, also, a slang term for "penis." Gladiators who won consistently became national heroes and had groupies. Young women, middle-aged women and old women hung around the gladiator barracks just to get a look at a famous fighter. Because Pompeii was destroyed in one day and entombed in volcanic ash, many wall inscriptions and artifacts have survived in tact. Written on the wall of a gladiator school is: "The Thracian Celadus is the heartthrob of all the girls." In that same school was found the skeleton of a richly adorned woman. Was she having a liaison with a gladiator? Or did she just take shelter from the rain of volcanic ash? We will never know.

But we do know the story of Eppia and her gladiator lover Sergius. It is the most famous ancient account of a romance between a gladiator and a noble woman. Juvenal (c. 57-127) tells the story in his *Satires 6*:

"Eppia, though the wife of a senator, went off with a gladiator to Pharos and the Nile on the notorious walls of Alexandria, though even Egypt condemns Rome's disgusting morals. Forgetting her home, her husband and her sister, she showed no concern whatever for her homeland...and her children in tears…When she was a baby she was pillowed in great luxury in the down of her father's mansion in a cradle of the finest workmanship…She didn't worry about the dangers of sea travel---She had long since stopped worrying about her reputation….With heart undaunted she braved the waves of the Adriatic and the Ionian Sea to get to Egypt….Yet what was the glamour that set her on fire, what was the prime manhood that captured Eppia's heart? What was it she saw in him that would compensate for her being called 'gladiatrix?' Note that her lover, dear Sergius, had now started shaving his neck and was hoping to be released from duty (as a gladiator) because of a bad wound on his arm. Moreover, his face was deformed in a number of ways. He had a mark where his helmet rubbed him and a big wart between his nostrils and a smelly discharge dripping from his eye. But he was a gladiator! That made him…beautiful. This is what she preferred to her children and her homeland, her sister and her husband. It's the sword they're in love with!"

Not all gladiator fights resulted in the death of one of the gladiators. If both had fought valiantly to a draw, the crowd insisted they both be spared. On the opening day of the Colosseum in 81, two famous gladiators, Priscus and Verus, were to fight each other to the death:

"As Priscus and Verus each lengthened the contest and for a long time the battle was equal on each side, repeatedly loud shouts petitioned for the men to be released. But Caesar (Titus) followed his own law. It was the law to fight without shield until a finger was raised….But an end was found to the equal division: Equals to fight, equals to yield. Caesar sent wooden swords to both and (victor's) palms to both. Thus skillful courage received its prize. This took place under no prince except you, Caesar, when two fought, both were victor." Martial, *On The Spectacles 29*

Sometimes the loser had fought so well that the emperor and the crowd wanted him to live. Occasionally a superstar gladiator was given his freedom if he had fought victoriously for many years. Some gladiators had fought and won so many times over so many years that they were retired with acclamation. Suetonius writes of one such gladiator:

"....when (Claudius) had granted the wooden sword to a gladiator whose four sons had begged for his discharge, the (public) act (in the arena) was received with loud and general applause." *Lives of the Caesars: Claudius*

Wounded and scarred as he was, Eppia's lover Sergius, the victorious veteran of many fights, was probably retired. When a gladiator was given retirement, he was presented with a wooden sword, a symbol of "no more blood." Often the man chose to remain at the school as an instructor. Not Sergius. He left for Egypt and took his Eppia with him.

Emperor Claudius (41-54) had four wives. His third wife Messalina loved men. Period. And gladiators were supermen. At a game sponsored by her husband, one of her gladiator lovers lost the fight. Claudius and the crowd wanted him killed, but Empress Messalina intervened and saved his life. Juvenal has much to say about this royal nymphomaniac:

"Hear what the Emperor Claudius had to put up with. As soon as his wife (Messalina) thought that he was asleep, this imperial whore put on the hood she wore at night, determined to prefer a cheap pad to the royal bed, and left the house with one female slave only....hiding her black hair in a yellow wig, she entered the brothel, warm with its old patchwork quilts and her empty cell, her very own....She took her stand, naked, her nipples gilded, assuming the name of Lycisca....She obligingly received customers and asked for her money and lay there through the night taking in...all comers....When the pimp sent the girls home, she went away sadly....her face dirty and bruised, grimy with lamp smoke, she brought back to her pillow the smell of the brothel." *Satires 6*

Messalina's profligacy finally sealed her fate. Hundreds of lovers. Thousands of lies. Claudius' courtiers had had enough. Afraid that cuckolded Claudius would pardon Messalina for bigamy (she married another man while still married to the Emperor), they killed the 30-year-old woman in the gardens of Lucullus:

"Claudius was still at the banquet when they told him that Messalina was dead, without mentioning whether it was by her own or another's hand. Nor did (Claudius) ask the question, but called for a cup of wine and finished his dinner as usual." Tacitus, *Annals 38*

The wife of an Emperor with a gladiator. The wife of a senator with a gladiator. The mother of Nero's Praetorian prefect, Nymphidius, was so in love with the gladiator Martinus that she divorced her husband of many years and married the man with the sword. This graffiti from Pompeii praising a retarius, "Crescens the nocturnal netter of young girls," testifies to the groupies that have always followed super stars.

The criminals, the Christians, the wild animals, the plays, the music, the elaborate sets, the presence of the Emperor. Everything paled in comparison to the gladiator fights. Every large city and small town in the Roman Empire had an amphitheater for the contests.

In Pompeii many advertisements for gladiator fights at the local amphitheater have been found appended to walls: "The gladiatorial troop of the *aedile* (magistrate responsible for games) Aulius Suettius Certus will fight at Pompeii May 31. There will be a hunt and awnings will be provided." Hoping to lure Pompeians to the fights, country organizers tried to get the best fighters with the best records: "Freedman Oceanus won 13 times. Araciatus won 9 times and 1 loss. Albanus won 13 times and 1 loss." After the contests were over, the results were posted: "3 killed. 6 spared. 9 victorious." The odds of survival in the arena were 1 in 7 in the 1st century AD. As the bloodletting went into the 2nd, 3rd and 4th centuries, the odds declined.

It can be surmised that all gladiators did not go willingly into the ring. Diodorus Siculus (90-21 BC) in the *Library Of History 36.10.2-3* tells of hundreds of captive slaves from Sicily who were bound for the gladiator school in Rome. Rather than fighting with wild beasts and against each other, they committed mass suicides at public altars all over

Rome. Another gladiator went to the bathroom in the Colosseum and never returned. They found he had taken the stick with a sponge on it used for wiping and shoved it down his throat. In 73 BC the gladiator Spartacus led his famous slave revolt from the renowned school for gladiators in Capua.

Even if they had adulation, women, money and fame, a gladiator was still on the bottom rung of the social ladder. He was a slave, bound by a fearful oath: "I will endure to be burned, to be bound, to be beaten and to be killed by the sword." He had a master at the barracks and a mistress in the arena. Over hundreds of years, the few gladiators who rose to prominence have become archetypes of bravery, endurance and masculine skill. The thousands of gladiators who died in anonymous agony in the arena have become nothing. They just died. But the fact remains they were always meant to be fodder, expendable.

The number of gladiators killed in the Colosseum is dwarfed by the number of Christians killed. The gladiator had a fifty-fifty chance of survival. The Christian men, women and children had a zero chance of living to contend for the faith another day. They were untrained in the art of physical combat, but they proved to be professionals in the discipline of spiritual warfare. As a lion tore off one arm, the other arm was raised in praise. Unarmed, they endured, rather than parried, the thrusts of spears, lances, fire, beasts, crucifixion, mauling. "And yet, notwithstanding all these continual persecutions and horrible punishments, the Church daily increased, deeply rooted...and watered plenteously with the blood of saints." Foxe, *Book Of Martyrs*

Like "imperishable seeds" (I Peter 1:23), thousands were planted and blood-watered in the sands of the Colosseum. Ironically, that arena, built with the monies plundered from the foundational structure of the Jewish religion in Jerusalem, became the unlikely nursery for a new religion and ethic that sprouted and flourished in Rome, in Gaul, in Britain and then in the whole world.

VIII.

"As for the triumph of Christianity, no student of civilization will ever underestimate its importance. Here, again, conjecture loses itself asking what would have become of arts, laws and letters if the Germanic invaders had conquered a world knowing no better deities than Jupiter or Isis. The victory of Christianity over paganism was, as the great German scholar Ulhorn has well said, 'the purest ever won. For it was won by witnessing and enduring, by loving and suffering, by pouring out innocent blood.' It was won by weak men and women, slaves often, opposed to the mightiest of governments and all the social and intellectual pride and prejudice of the civilized world." William Stearns Davis, *Readings In Ancient History: Rome And The West, p. 285*

During the infant years of the Christian faith, society was divided into two classes: slave and free. That division had been in place as far back in history as organized communities can be traced. All ancient civilizations had slaves. The concept of slavery as immoral or abusive was nonexistent. There were slaves just like there were the four elements---fire, earth, air and water. To question whether there should be people who are owned by other people never occurred to the ancient mind.

In *Hammurabi's Code* (c. 1792-1750 BC), engraved on a 7.5' tall black basalt stone discovered in 1900 at the acropolis in ancient Susa, there were intricate laws regarding slaves: on the subleasing of slaves, on bearing children by slaves, on punishment of sassy slaves. Slavery could be imposed upon negligent landowners and even upon spendthrift wives. Runaway slaves were a constant problem in ancient Babylon:

"If any one take a male or female slave of the court, or a male or female slave of a freed man, outside the city gates, he shall be put to death."

"If any one receive into his house a runaway male or female slave…and does not bring it out at the public proclamation of the major domus, the master of the house shall be put to death."

"If any one find a runaway male or female slave in the open country and bring them to their masters, the master of the slaves shall pay him two shekels of silver."

Obviously, the only people in the ancient world who questioned slavery were the slaves.

The Old Testament assumed slavery:

"If a man beats his male or female slave with a rod and the slave dies as a direct result, he must be punished; but he is not punished if the slave gets up after a day or two since the slave is his property." Exodus 21:20.

"Your male and female slaves are to come from the nations around you; from them you may buy slaves." Leviticus 25:44

Aristotle, Plato and Socrates took it for granted that each household had slaves. In *Nicomachian Ethics 8.11* Aristotle states:

"There is nothing common to ruler and ruled, there is not friendship either, since there is not justice between a craftsman and a tool, between soul and body, master and slave; the latter in each case is benefited by that which uses it, but there is no friendship nor justice towards lifeless things. But neither is there friendship towards a horse or an ox nor to a slave qua slave. For there is nothing common to the two parties; the slave is a living tool and the tool is a lifeless slave. Qua slave then, man cannot be friends with him. But qua man one can."

Those revered philosophers, considered the best the pagan world had to offer, encouraged humane treatment of slaves by reasoning that slaves who were treated well performed their work better than abused slaves. But as Aristotle stated, a slave and a master had nothing in common. There was no such thing as friendship or justice in the slave/master relationship because "a slave is a living tool and the tool is a lifeless slave." Slaves were not human. To the man who co-founded Western philosophy slaves were just tools like hammers devoid of life.

The Augustan poet Horace (65-8 BC) who coined the still-popular Latin phrase *"carpe diem"* ("seize the day") asserted a gentleman required ten slaves. Wealthy Romans owned many slaves: Senator L.P. Secundus in the 1st century AD had 400 slaves; the wealthy freedman Caecilus Isidorus (8 BC) who had once been a slave owned 4,116 slaves; Pudentilla, wife of Apuleius in the 2nd century AD divided 400 slaves among her sons. The normal free Roman who lived a moderate to low-income life owned between one and ten slaves. The idea that the institution of slavery was wrong went unquestioned in the pagan world.

The slave as tool and the right to have slaves were embedded in the laws of every people in the ancient world. The 2nd century AD Gaius writes: "Slaves are the *patestas* (those under authority) of their masters, and this is acknowledged by the laws of all nations." *Institutes 1.52*

Slaveholding was accepted as the natural order of things for thousands of years. In all cultures there were never enough people to do all the work that needed to be done. Slaves were the work force. No citizen wanted to volunteer to dig in the copper mines or to build the temples or to hollow out the tunnels---for free. Who was going to pay 100,000 Egyptians to work eighteen-hour days to build Cheops his pyramid?

The origins of slavery are lost in the mists of time. But there had to have been a tribe who conquered another tribe and took their land, their possessions, their animals, their women, their children and their men as chattel, slaves, property. The victor's tribe became stronger with this free labor. They could make more products to barter or to sell, dig more wells, breed more cattle and mount a stronger defense. They could become richer, more prosperous. The pragmatic and economic applications of slavery have always been its driving forces.

In ancient slavery's hoary history there was never a people or a race of people who were singled out as slave workers. The Babylonians conquered the Jews and had Jewish slaves. The Jews conquered the Canaanites and had Canaanite slaves. The Africans conquered Africans and had African slaves. The Chinese conquered Chinese and had Chinese slaves. The Aztecs conquered other Mesoamerican tribes who became their slaves. Rome conquered most of the known world and took their most talented people and their soldiers to Rome as slaves. Slaves were always victims of war and opportunity.

A census taken by the despot Demetrius Phalereus who ruled Athens from 317-301 BC found there were 21,000 Greek citizens, 10,000 foreigners and 400,000 slaves living in the city. Slaves outnumbered free people by more than 13 to 1. In Athens' neighboring city of Sparta the "helots" or state-owned slaves outnumbered the Spartans 10 to 1.

It is impossible to number the Egyptian slaves because we do not have textual or inscriptive evidence. But Thutmose II (1493-1479 BC) returned from a campaign against Canaan with 90,000 captured soldiers who became slaves. Egypt had temple slaves, farm slaves, household slaves, slaves in professions (e.g. scribe), royal slaves and slaves who built cities and pyramids. By deduction slaves were a sizable percentage of ancient Egypt's population.

It is estimated that 40% to 50% of Roman Italy were slaves. Plautus, the Roman writer of comedies (254-184BC), refers to scores of slaves in his works: grooms, stewards, fowlers, singers, cooks, doorkeepers, hairdressers, masseurs. Cato the Elder (234-149 BC) in *De Agricultura* says that all agricultural work was done by slaves: swineherds, shepherds, ploughmen, managers. Rome and all ancient civilizations were undergirded, built and sustained by slave labor. The Greek historian Plutarch (c. 45-120 AD) in writing about the Roman general and politician Crassus advertently describes slaves as "the living tools of housekeeping:"

"(Crassus) had many silver mines and much valuable land, and laborers to work in it, yet all this was nothing in comparison to his slaves, such a number and variety did he possess of excellent readers, amanuenses, silversmiths, stewards and table waiters whose instruction he always attended to himself, superintending in person while they learned, and teaching them himself, as counting it the main duty of a master to look over the slaves, that are, indeed the living tools of housekeeping." *Lives, Life of Crassus 2.3*

Even though some slaves were educated and had interesting jobs, slaves in Rome were at the bottom of the human heap. They were "speaking tools," *res mancipi*, "a hand-bought thing". Slaves were part of the property of a master along with his home, his cattle, his jewelry, his money and his personal possessions. They were considered corporeal moveable property that could be bought, sold, transferred or inherited.

In the 1st century Christianity introduced an entirely new view of slaves and slavery into the pagan world. In the New Testament letter to Philemon Paul urges Philemon to take back and to forgive his runaway slave Onesimus. *Onesimus* meaning "useful" was a common name for slaves. Onesimus had run away from his master Philemon in Colosse (modern day Turkey) and had stolen from him. The runaway had ended up in Rome where Paul was imprisoned. Paul led Onesimus to Christ and was sending him back to Philemon with this letter:

"I am sending him, who is my very heart, back to you. I would have liked to keep him with me so that he could take your place in helping me (being "useful") while I am in chains for the gospel....you might have him back for good, no longer as a slave, but better than a slave, as a dear brother....welcome him as you would welcome me. If he has done you any wrong or owes you anything, charge it to me." Philemon 12,16,17

Onesimus was now Philemon's brother, not his slave. That social distinction had been obliterated by Onesimus' conversion. The Christian belonged to a family of spiritually related people. Each Christian was brother or sister to every other Christian. Lucian of Samosata, a Greek satirist in c. 170, wrote in a letter to his friend Cronius a derogatory description of Christians. He makes light of their counter-cultural beliefs and their belief that they were all brothers once they were Christians:

"The Christians, you know, worship a man to this day---the distinguished personage (Jesus Christ) who introduced their novel rites, and was crucified on that account....You see, these misguided creatures start with the general conviction that they are immortal for all time, which explains the contempt of death and voluntary self-devotion which are so common among them; and then it was impressed on them by their original lawgiver that they are all brothers from the moment that they are converted and (they) deny the gods of Greece and worship the crucified sage and live after his laws. All this they take quite on faith, with the result that they despise all worldly goods alike, regarding them merely as common property." "The Death Of Peregrinus"

Clearly the Christian concept of a slave was not "a bought thing." Philemon was to treat Onesimus as he would treat his own brother. The social distinction between master and slave had been vitiated by the new faith. (There is a tradition that Onesimus became Bishop of Berea and was martyred.)

The word "slave" is translated from the Latin word *servus* from which we get our English word "servant." A Roman slave greeted his master by saying, *servus humillimus* meaning "your most humble slave." But the etymological origin of the English word "slave" comes from the Middle English words *sclave, slav* used to designate those people who lived in eastern, southeastern and central Europe. Around 800 they were conquered and for centuries were serfs (free men who were bonded to the land) for other Europeans.

Christian teachings and texts introduced into the ancient world new ideas, revolutionary ideas, ideas whose time had come. The new faith redefined the historic definition of a slave:

"Were you a slave when you were called (converted to Christ)? Don't let it trouble you---although if you can gain your freedom, do so. For he who was a slave when he was called by the Lord is the Lord's freedman; similarly, he who was not a slave when he was called is Christ's slave. You were bought with a price (by the blood of Christ), do not become slaves of men." I Corinthians 7:21-23

The New Testament writings turned the definition and terms of slavery on its ear. If you are a physical slave, you are free. If you are a free person, you are a slave. All believers in Christ are free people. All Christians are slaves. That was a new idea to the ancients, a revolutionary oxymoron.

Paul in Colossians puts slaves and masters under the same subjection to a heavenly Master:

"Slaves, obey your earthly masters in everything...with sincerity of heart and reverence for the Lord....Masters, provide your slaves with what is right and fair, because you know that you also have a Master in heaven." 3:22; 4:1

Letter by letter, word by word Christian beliefs and sensibilities began influencing and overturning core assumptions of the pre-Christian pagan world.

The Greek writer Plutarch (45-120 AD) was contemporary with the rise of the Early Church. As a Platonist philosopher and as one of the priests at the Temple of Apollo at Delphi, he was current with all the newest ideas including those of Christianity. When writing in his *Lives* about Cato the Elder (234-149 BC), Plutarch displays some of the Christian attitudes that had begun to penetrate his world:

"(Cato never bought) a slave for above 1,500 drachmas; as he did not seek for effeminate and handsome ones, but able, sturdy workmen, horse keepers and cowherds: and these he thought ought to be sold again when they grew old, and no useless servants fed in a house....Yet certainly, in my judgment, it marks an over rigid temper, for a man to take the work out of his slaves as out of brute beasts, turning them off and selling them in their old age, and thinking there ought to be no further commerce between man and man than whilst there arises some profit by it. We see that kindness and humanity has a larger field than bare justice to exercise itself in....It is doubtless the part of a kind-natured man to keep even worn-out horses and dogs, and not only take care of them when they are foals and whelps, but also when they are grown old." *Lives: Life of Marcus Cato The Elder 4.5*

This "kind-natured" sensitivity to slaves, even calling them "man" as Plutarch does, is certainly not the same attitudes Plutarch's 4th century BC teachers, Aristotle and Plato, had when they called slaves "lifeless things" and "living tools."

The New Testament was written in Koine Greek, the common dialect of Greece. At the time of the writing of the New Testament, Koine (pronounced "coin-ay") was the lingua franca of the Hellenized Roman world. *Doulos* meaning "slave" was the Greek word used to designate all those in the ancient world who were born slaves or had become slaves. The social condition opposite to *doulos* was *eleutheros* meaning "free." Paul the Apostle was a free-born (*eleutheros*) Roman citizen. Yet in his writings he calls himself a *doulos*, a slave:

"Am I now trying to win the approval of men or of God? Or am I trying to please men? If I were still trying to please men, I would not be a slave (doulos) of Christ." Galatians 1:10
"Paul, a slave (doulos) of God and an apostle of Jesus Christ." Titus 1:1

Slaves were just things (Latin *res*), a bought thing, totally owned by their master and never free to leave. It was scandalous that Paul and other Christian writers identified themselves with the most reviled and worthless members of society. Even Jesus' brothers, James and Jude, said they were slaves:

"James, a slave of God and of the Lord Jesus Christ." James 1:1
"Jude, a slave of Jesus Christ and a brother of James." Jude 1

Simon Peter called himself a "doulos," a slave: "Simon Peter, a slave and apostle of Jesus Christ." (II Peter 1:1) *Mirabile dictu*, the entire New Testament says that all people, slave or free, who become Christians become slaves:

"The Lord's slave (believer) must not quarrel; instead, he must be kind to everyone; able to teach, not resentful." II Timothy 2:24
"Epaphras who is one of you and a slave of Christ Jesus, sends greetings." Colossians 4:12
"The revelation of Jesus Christ which God gave him to show his slaves what must soon take place." Revelation 1:1

The very early Christian church was largely composed of slaves and of those on the socio-economic fringes of society. The revolutionary concept was that a believer in Christ is a slave to Him regardless of the believer's social situation. The Christian is a free person even if he is a slave. In *The Acts Of Martyrdom Of St. Justin And Companions* written in 165 by an anonymous witness to the trial, the prefect Rusticus asks one of Justin Martyr's companions: "'And what are you?' Euelpistus, a slave of Caesar, answered, 'I too am a Christian, having been freed by Christ; and by the grace of Christ I partake of the same hope.'" Right before his beheading, the slave Euelpistus testifies to the freedom and the hope that he, on the lowest rung of society, had found in Christ. This new definition of slavery as spiritual bondage rather than physical bondage and of freedom as a spiritual state rather than a physical state was a radical one that appealed to hordes of people. But the redefinition of slavery by the new faith was even deeper than that. Their Christ, Jesus of Nazareth, was a slave:

"Your attitude should be the same as that of Christ Jesus: Who, being in the very nature of God…made himself nothing, taking the very nature of a slave (doulos), being made in human likeness." Philippians 2:5,7

The Christian Savior identified Himself as a slave. The idea that a god would serve man was explosive. Gods are served. They are not servants. Instead of "slave" being a pejorative word, the Christian God and Christian writers were sanctifying and even glorifying the word "slave."

Jesus enjoined his followers to be slaves. The ancient world, much like the modern world, worshipped royalty and admired those who had power and money. They aspired to be rulers, to be somebody important. Even Jesus' closest friends and their families wanted to be elevated to positions of authority. They wanted to have human adulation:

"Then the mother of Zebedee's sons (James and John) came to Jesus with her sons and kneeling down, asked a favor of him. 'What is it you want?' (Jesus) asked. She said, 'Grant that one of these two sons of mine may sit at your right and the other at your left in your kingdom.' 'You don't know what you are asking,' Jesus said to them. 'Can you drink the cup I am going to drink?' 'We can,' they answered. Jesus said to them, 'You will indeed drink from my cup, but to sit at my right or left is not for me to grant. These places belong to those for whom they have been prepared by my Father.' When the ten (Apostles) heard about this, they were indignant with the two brothers. Jesus called them together and said, 'You know that the rulers of the Gentiles lord it over them and their high officials exercise authority over them. Not so with you. Instead, whoever wants to become great among you must be your servant, and whoever wants to be first must be your slave---just as the Son of Man did not come to be served, but to serve, and to give his life as a ransom for many." Matthew 20:20-28

Jesus wanted His followers to seek to serve, not to seek to be served. In a social world composed of nothing but slaves or masters this was a hard teaching.

The New Testament further expanded its unsettling doctrines. Not only were all believers slaves, but they were adopted people. Adoption was prevalent in the Roman world. It was considered a great honor to be adopted. The royal and wealthy classes of Rome often adopted sons. If a man had no male heir, he adopted a boy or young man as his son.

Sometimes the adopted son was from the plebeian class, but more often the adoptee was from the upper class. Roman emperors sometimes adopted sons to succeed them as emperor. Caesar Augustus had been adopted by his great-uncle Julius Caesar to succeed him. Augustus adopted his stepson Tiberias to succeed him. The adoptee no longer belonged to his natural family. He took the adopter's name and rank as his own and became the adopter's legal heir. An adopted child had the full and absolute rights of primogeniture and inheritance.

Believers knew the high honor of adoption. That they in their meager circumstances were worthy of adoption by God, the Ruler of the Universe, with the full inheritance implied in that adoption was another radical idea:

"In love (God) predestined us to be adopted as his sons through Jesus Christ..." Ephesians 1:4, 5
"...that we might receive the full rights of sons. Because you are sons, God sent the Spirit of his Son into our hearts, the Spirit who calls out, 'Abba, Father.' So you are no longer a slave, but a son; and since you are a son, God has made you also an heir." Galatians 4:5-7

The Christian God adopted all believers and wanted them to call him Father, even wanted them to call Him the more affectionate *Abba* meaning "Daddy." The idea that God chose to become we so that we could inherit what only God owns and that we had an eternal inheritance and familiar access to the Father God of All was astounding. Such intimacy between God and the believer and between believers of all classes began to affect the names they called each other. Christian slave masters began to call their Christian slaves *alumna/alumnus*, "foster daughters/sons" indicating the changing view toward the enslaved and toward relationships to brothers and sisters in Christ. Many Christians freed all their slaves. In the Catacomb of Callixtus there is a short, tantalizing inscription from c. 200:

"The Freedmen Of Petronia Auxentia, The Highly Born Lady Who Died At The Age Of 30, Made The Grave Where She Rests In Peace."

The patrician Petronia, a Christian resting "In Pace," had obviously freed her slaves sometime before she died at the young age of 30. One wonders where her high-born parents, siblings, relatives and friends were because it was left to her freed slaves to dig her grave and to bury her. Maybe Petronia had been ostracized by her family and friends when she became a Christian. (The Greek word *ostrakon* from which comes our word "ostracize" were broken pieces of black pottery used by voters in the democratic city of Athens to write down the names of citizens they did not want in office or that they wanted to be sent into exile. We still use the term "blackball" to mean excluding someone from membership.) It was not an unusual occurrence for those who became Christians to be exiled or ostracized by their families. Petronia's family, the Auxentia, perhaps had one of the hundreds of above-ground marble sepulchers that lined the Via Appia. If so, she was obviously denied burial in the family grave and was buried by her loyal freedmen in a small, obscure underground niche beside her low-born Christian brothers and sisters.

The slaves and the poor who were eagerly receiving the Christian message were awed. They were free people who were the slaves, not of earthly people, but of Christ. Even their converted masters were slaves of Christ. If the Emperor himself would become a Christian, he would be a slave. All Christians were slaves and had been adopted by God. They had been adopted into the ultimate universal royal household. This was a freedom and an inheritance unthinkable to most Romans.

The slave, the poor who had been at the nadir of Roman and of all of ancient society were suddenly elevated into the supreme household of the God of the universe. Everyone, slave or free, who became a Christian was the adopted child of God.

The new faith proclaimed yet another unthinkable concept---all people who are Christians are of one body:

"Here there is not Greek or Jew, circumcised or uncircumcised, barbarian, Scythian, slave or free, but Christ is all and is in all." Colossians 3:11
"For we were all baptized by one Spirit into one body---whether Jews

or Greeks, slave or free---and we were all given the one Spirit to drink."
I Corinthians 12:13

"There is neither Jew nor Greek, slave nor free, male nor female, for you
are all one in Christ Jesus." Galatians 3:28

There was no difference, the new religion said, between a Jew
and a Greek or between a Roman and a Barbarian. The tribal and
national distinctions that had been in place since man began were being
challenged by the new faith. It was preposterous to think of the world
as one people. The world had always been divided into "us" and "them."
Yet Christianity said it was not a tribe or a nation that united people. It
was an invisible, spiritual bond that bound all people as one.

The genealogies and the lines of ancestors that were so important
to the order and the influence of the ancient world were not important.
All the endless lists of descent (x was the father of y) and ascent (y was
the son of x) that were so crucial to land inheritance and to the rights
of hereditary privilege were abolished.

If you were a believer in Christ, you were of the family of God
and your father, your mother, your sister and your brother were fellow
believers. Their own Lord had said:

"Then Jesus' mother and brothers arrived. Standing outside, they sent
someone in to call him. A crowd was sitting around him and they told
him, 'Your mother and brothers are outside looking for you.' 'Who are
my mother and my brothers?' he asked. Then he looked at those seated
in a circle around him and said, 'Here are my mother and my brothers!
Whoever does God's will is my brother and sister and mother." Mark
3:31-35

Christians were members of a new family, a spiritual family under
one God stretching back to the father of the faith---Abraham. Bloodlines
were obliterated. Christianity was smashing all historic barriers and
distinctions.

The new Gospel went further. It said whether you were a man
or a woman, you were equal in Christ. Jesus and the new faith even

challenged the distinction between a man and a woman. Jesus had freely conversed with women. There were women, some of them even married, who traveled with Him and His disciples. They provided for the needs of His ministry out of their own pockets:

"...Jesus traveled about from one town and village to another, proclaiming the good news of the kingdom of God. The Twelve were with him, and also some women who had been cured of evil spirits and diseases. Mary, called Magdalene, from whom seven demons had come out; Joanna the wife of Cuza, the manager of Herod's household; Susanna and many others. These women were helping to support them out of their own means." Luke 8:3

"Many women were there (at the crucifixion), watching from a distance. They had followed Jesus from Galilee to care for his needs." Matthew 27:55

Here was a young Jewish rabbi who not only talked freely with women and took their questions and concerns seriously, but He openly traveled all around the Galilee and Judea with them in His entourage. This was totally contrary to what Jewish custom was at that time. In the synagogues, men and women were separated. Women could not study the Torah or teach it. Women could not testify at trials. They were either under their fathers' or their husbands' care. It was a major transgression for a Jewish man to talk with a woman other than his wife, daughters and the women of his household.

Jesus defied the customs of His time and consistently interacted with and treated women as the equals of men. Mary sat at His feet when He visited their home and discoursed on subjects regarding the kingdom of Heaven. (Luke 10:38-42) He initiated a discussion with a Samaritan woman at a well. (John 4:7-27) He violated a particularly strong Jewish ritual prohibition against menstrual blood by healing a woman who had been suffering with that issue for twelve years. ((Mark 5: 25-34) Even the seminal event in the Gospels, Jesus' resurrection from the dead, was first revealed to women. Matthew 28:1-10; Mark 16:1-8; Luke 24:1-11; John 20:1-18

His followers would have the same attitude toward women as He did. Rather than being prohibited from full worship in the synagogues like women had been they, individually or with their husbands, held church services in their homes where all worshipped together as equals: Priscilla with her husband Aquila (Romans 16:3). There was a church in the home of Philemon and his wife Apphia (Philemon 2). Many single Christian women even held religious services in their own homes: Mary, John Mark's mother (Acts 12:12); Chloe (I Corinthians 1:11); Lydia, the first European convert to Christ (Acts 16:14.15); Nympha (Colossians 4:15) and other women all hosted home churches.

The status of women in the ancient world had always been precarious. Sometimes they, like slaves, were property to be bought and sold. Sometimes women had considerable liberties, but they never had the complete freedom of men. The idea that there was no innate difference between a man and a woman, that there was no male or female in Christ was unimaginable to the ancients.

These New Testament ideas about relationships and social distinctions began to fracture the ideological foundations of the pagan world. Christianity had embraced and nuanced the status of a slave. It had granted adoption by God to all believers. It said a Roman was the same as any other person, that Romans were no better or worse than Greeks or Huns or Africans or Britons. A woman or a daughter was as equal as a man or a son. It did not matter to the new faith if you were slave or free, rich or poor, male or female, ruler or subject, Roman or Carthaginian, sick or whole, black, white or brown. Christians of all nations and colors and classes and circumstances were to accept each other as family, as brother and sister, and they were to worship together as one body because the Christian God saw no differences between people:

"God does not show favoritism." Romans 2:11

"Masters.....do not threaten (your slaves), since you know that he who is both their master and your master is in heaven, and there is no partiality with him." Ephesians 6:9

In c. 60 AD Paul, a Roman citizen, enunciated another new doctrine to the Roman citizens of Phillipi (in ancient Greece): "Our citizenship is in heaven." (Philippians 3:20) Believers in Christ were not Roman citizens or citizens of Jerusalem, Antioch or Alexandria. Their growing numbers were all citizens of heaven. Their allegiance was not to an earthly kingdom like Rome but to a spiritual, heavenly kingdom. The vast number of Gentile believers in the Jewish Jesus as the Messiah had been predicted by Jesus in c. 29 AD when one day in Capernaum a Roman centurion asked Jesus to heal his paralyzed servant and told Jesus He did not even have to come to his house. All He had to do was say the word and his servant would be healed:

"When Jesus heard this, he was astonished and said to those following him, 'I tell you the truth, I have not found anyone in Israel with such great faith. I say to you that many will come from the east and the west and will take their places at the feast with Abraham, Isaac and Jacob in the kingdom of heaven.'" Matthew 8:10,11

The Christian kingdom and their king, their Caesar, was not an earthly, flesh and blood king, but a heavenly king. Peter went so far as to say that believers were an alien race of strangers here on earth: "...a chosen people, a royal priesthood, a holy nation, a people belonging to God....Dear friends, I urge you, as aliens and strangers in the world.... Live such good lives among the pagans that, though they accuse you of doing wrong, they may see your good deeds and glorify God." I Peter 2:9-12

Eschewing any earthly connection and especially Roman citizenship was a direct challenge to Rome. In a world dominated by Rome the highest honor a non-Roman could acquire was Roman citizenship. Only those born of two citizens were automatically Roman citizens. Citizenship had many benefits: a citizen was entitled to the protection of the Roman State; was granted the right to vote in Roman elections; the right to do business and to buy and sell real estate; the right to run for political office; the right to sign legal documents; the right to sue; the right to hold property; the right to a legal trial in a Roman court and the right to appeal verdicts. A Roman citizen could not be subjected to degrading forms of punishment such as scourging with whips, searing with iron rods or crucifixion. A convicted citizen had the right to a quick death by beheading.

As Roman dominion grew, citizenship could be inherited from ancestors on whom it had been conferred. This seems to have been the case with the Apostle Paul from Tarsus who used the fact of his Roman citizenship to escape being flogged in Acts 21:30; 22:22-29:

"The crowd listened to Paul until he said this. Then they raised their voices and shouted, 'Rid the earth of him! He's not fit to live!' As they were shouting and throwing off their cloaks and flinging dust into the air, the commander ordered Paul to be taken into the barracks. He directed that he be flogged and questioned in order to find out why the people were shouting at him like this. As they stretched him out to flog him, Paul said to the centurion standing there, 'Is it legal for you to flog a Roman citizen who hasn't even been found guilty?' When the centurion heard this, he went to the commander and reported it. 'What are you going to do?' he asked. 'This man is a Roman citizen.' The commander went to Paul and asked, 'Tell me, are you a Roman citizen?' 'Yes, I am,' he answered. Then the commander said, 'I had to pay a big price for my citizenship.' 'But I was born a citizen,' (in c. 2-5 AD) Paul replied....The commander himself was alarmed when he realized he had put Paul, a Roman citizen, in chains."

Claudius Lysias was the commander, the chilliarch, of the Roman regiment of 1,000 soldiers there in Jerusalem. (Acts 23:26) He had paid a lot of money to obtain his citizenship and was terrified he had unlawfully laid hands on a man who was a Roman citizen by birth. At the time of this incident in c. 57 Roman citizenship was coveted, but by the middle of the 3rd century Roman citizenship was not the prize it had been in Paul's day and a weakened Rome liberally extended citizenship to freed slaves, whole cities and even the Barbarian auxiliary forces that fought in their army.

The Christian faith was saying that Christians were not citizens of this world and their king was not Caesar. Earthly citizenship, even the coveted citizenship of Rome, was irrelevant. Tribal and geo-political ties were subordinated to the believer's King Jesus and His kingdom was not of this world:

"Jesus said (to Pontius Pilate). 'My kingdom is not of this world.'" John 18:36.
"Once, having been asked by the Pharisees when the kingdom of God would come, Jesus replied, 'The kingdom of God does not come with your careful observation, nor will people say, Here it is, or There it is, because the kingdom of heaven is within you.'" Luke 17:20,21
"For here we do not have an enduring city, but we are looking for the city that is yet to come." Hebrews 13:14
"They (Christians) are all defying Caesar's decrees, saying that there is another king, called Jesus." Acts 17:7

Not only were all slaves free and all masters slaves, not only was there no difference between a Roman and a Barbarian or between a Jew and a Gentile or between a man and a woman, but all Christians on earth were strangers in a strange land, were under the suzerainty of a spiritual kingdom whose ruler was God almighty.

The new faith that had wandered into Rome was abolishing accepted distinctions with an egalitarianism that had never before been broached. Not only was Christianity's monotheism aggressively striking at the heart of paganism, its subsequent teachings were slowly corroding the social structures of the entire ancient world. It is little wonder that Christians were considered troublemakers, people who were turning the world upside down and inside out:

"…they (in Thessalonica) dragged Jason (a believer) and some other brothers before the city officials, shouting: 'These men who have turned the world upside down have come here, too!'" Acts 17:6 in c. 60 AD.

Perhaps the most revolutionary idea that Christianity introduced into the pagan world was the concept of redemption from sin. All cultures everywhere have known there was something wrong with man. There was a bad thing in him. The bad thing, the evil thing was defined in different ways by tribal taboos or complex legal systems. But all men have always known there was an innate propensity for evil lodged irrevocably in the heart of the human soul.

This bad seed grew into deeds that wreaked havoc on the social order. Societies and tribes have always constructed elaborate systems and complicated religious rituals to deal with the pollutions caused by these sinful acts.

Imbedded, also, in the heart of man is the concept of a supreme being or beings. Man knew he would have to mollify, pacify whatever gods he had offended by these evil deeds. The long history of the gruesome pacification of the gods and the expiation of human sin is filled with child sacrifice, human sacrifice, ritual bloodletting and other horrendous attempts at purification.

All cultures believed there was something "holy," something pure about blood. On the other side of the world, pre-Columbian cultures in the Americas practiced auto-sacrifice, the self-letting of blood. Archaeologists have found bloodletting instruments made of obsidian, shark's teeth, the spines of stingrays and thorns in private and public buildings dating back to 1200 BC. The magnificent, well-preserved wall paintings at Bonampak (c. 580-800) depict Mayan royals piercing their genitals and sprinkling the blood on pieces of bark paper that were then burned as blood-offerings to their gods. The Mayans, Aztecs, Toltecs and Incas attempted to atone for their sins by sacrificing young children and virgins. In formal public religious rituals, they would insert an obsidian knife into a victim's chest and tear out the still-beating heart as an offering to their gods. Children were pure. Virgins were pure. Blood was pure. Blood was the only thing that could mollify the gods and purify from sin.

When in c. 1450 BC the Israelites entered Canaan, all the tribes there sacrificed babies and children to their gods. The Hebrew Scriptures decried and condemned that practice:

"Do not give any of your children to Moloch (to be burned alive) for you must not profane the name of your God. I am Lord." Leviticus 18:21 "When the king of Moab saw that the battle had gone against him, he took with him seven hundred swordsmen to break through to the king of Edom, but they failed. Then he took his firstborn son who was to succeed him as king and offered him as a sacrifice on the city wall." II Kings 3:26,27

The pressure to perform human sacrifice was so ubiquitous that hundreds of years later in c. 600 BC the Israelites had abandoned the one God and succumbed to the pagan practices around them:

"The word of the Lord came to Jeremiah....'the people of Israel and Judah have provoked me by all the evil they have done....They set up abominable idols....They built high places for Baal in the Valley of Ben Hinnom to sacrifice their sons and daughters to Moloch.'" Jeremiah 32:26-35

The Canaanites, the Sumerians, the Assyrians, the Mycenaeans, the Carthaginians, the Minoans, the northern European tribes, the Chinese, most of the ancient world sacrificed the undefiled blood of their children and victims to their many gods. There was a universal belief in the atoning and the expiatory power of blood.

The Hebrew Scriptures, alone in the ancient world, railed against human sacrifice, but they sacrificed animals as expiation for their sins and taught: "it is the blood that makes atonement for one's life." (Leviticus 17:11) In the beginning, in Genesis the very first acceptable sacrifice was the shepherd Abel's offering of a lamb from the first-born of his flock. (Genesis 4:1-5) Some person, some animal had to shed his or its blood in order for sin to be expiated. Blood atonement for sin was stamped into man's DNA.

The new faith declared that the bad seed, sin, had been dealt with finally and for all by the bloody death of Jesus of Nazareth on a cross in Jerusalem. This long-prophesied Messiah, they declared, was the fulfillment of thousands of years of Old Testament prophecy, was the willing One, the Sin-Bearer, the pure Lamb/Man, the culmination of and the final act of human sacrifice:

"...the law requires that nearly everything be cleansed with blood, and without the shedding of blood there is no forgiveness....But now (Jesus) has appeared once for all at the end of the ages to do away with sin by the sacrifice of himself....so Christ was sacrificed once to take away the sins of many people." Hebrews 9:22,26,28

"Then he took the cup, gave thanks and offered it to them saying, 'Drink from it all of you. This is my blood of the new covenant which is poured out for many for the forgiveness of sins.'" Matthew 26:27,28

"For you know that it was not with perishable things such as silver or gold that you were redeemed (bought back) from the empty life handed down to you from your forefathers, but with the precious blood of Christ, a lamb without blemish or defect," I Peter 1:18,19

"...because you (Jesus) were slain and with your blood purchased men for God from every tribe and language and people and nation." Revelation 5:9

"...(Jesus) did not enter by means of the blood of goats and calves; but he entered the most holy place once for all by his own blood, having obtained eternal redemption." Hebrews 9:12

The new faith was saying believers were blood-bought people, that Jesus of Nazareth willingly gave his life's blood for everyone, that Jesus' blood atonement for sin was a once-and-for-all act obliterating the need for any other human or animal blood.

Paul often couched the essence of the Christian message in the vernacular everyday Romans would readily understand:

"...for all have sinned and fall short of the glory of God, and are justified freely by his grace through the redemption that came by Christ Jesus. God presented him as a sacrifice of atonement through faith in his blood." Romans 3:25

"Justification" was the language of the Roman court. A judge declared a defendant "justified," "not guilty." A "sacrifice of atonement" was the language of Roman religion where a sacrifice offering was given to take the place of the guilty. "Redemption" was the common language of commerce and slavery. Goods or slaves could be bought back, "redeemed," for a price. A redeemed slave was called a *liberti*, "freed one." Romans understood the idea of redemption, understood all these New Testament words and concepts that were given different meanings by the new religion.

Sometimes a master would free a slave who had been particularly faithful or who had done an extraordinary thing for the family. Occasionally a slave who was a household or business slave could save up enough money to buy his freedom. That money was called the ransom money, the *redimo*, "the buy back, the purchase price."

The new faith said the cost to free mankind from its enslavement to sin, from its congenital bad seed was paid by Jesus of Nazareth on a cross in Judea:

"For there is one god and one mediator between god and men, the man Jesus Christ, who gave himself as a ransom for all men." I Timothy 2:5,6

The Christian message to the ancient world was they were all, slave or free, born "slaves to sin" (Romans 6:17,20), that their gory sacrifices were in vain and that Jesus Christ had paid once and for all the time-immemorial blood ransom required to absolve sin.

Instead of paying money to ransom the slaves of sin, this Jesus became a voluntary slave and paid for the freedom of all the sin-enslaved with His own blood. He "bought back, ransomed, obtained the release of, purchased, redeemed" men with his life-blood. Christianity had combined the time-immemorial blood sacrifice of people/animals to atone for sins with the fact of sin and had finessed the two as Jesus of Nazareth, the Sin-Bearer, the Ransom-Payer, the Redeemer.

Christianity ushered in a flood of troubling yet liberating ideas where slaves were free, the free were slaves, all people were equal, women were equal to men, the slave was equal to the master, they were all

155

citizens of an eternal kingdom, the new believer was an adopted child of God and the Christian God had sent his own Son to pay the blood ransom required for human redemption from sin.

As these radical ideas were spreading throughout her empire, Rome's world was falling apart. When the Barbarians were finally at the gates of Rome (Visigoths under Alaric in 410), the mightiest empire on earth was already on its knees. But the new Christian ideas that had honeycombed its realm were just beginning to stand up and to flex their muscles.

During the long Dark Ages in Europe after Rome fell, the work force was composed not of slaves but of serfs who worked the land of a feudal master. Serfs were, however, free to leave the land and to work for another master. After the fall of Jerusalem in late August 70 AD, the Jews ceased to sacrifice animals to atone for their sins. After the conversion of Constantine at the Battle of Milvian Bridge in 312, the pagan world became nominally Christian and the sacrifice of children and innocents to atone for sin was abolished in the West. After the Christian Spaniards conquered the Aztecs and Incas in the New World, human sacrifice ceased. And three of the early Popes, Clement of Rome (92-99), Pius I (158-167) and Callixtus (217-222) were former slaves. Christian values were slowly erasing thousands of years of core pagan practices and beliefs.

Rome had believed her armies and her grandeur were invincible and they were for a time. But civilizations survive not just by might but by the power of their ideas. Ideas trump might. Unlike Greece, Rome was never a culture of thought and transcendent concepts. The philosophical and religious underpinnings of her society were retreads from Greece. Rome was not something to believe in. She was something to submit to.

The new ideas and the Christian spirit that had swept into Rome in the middle of the first century had been embraced by "weak men and women, slaves often…opposed to the mightiest of governments and all the social and intellectual pride and prejudice" of the ancient world.

As Paul, the Apostle to the Gentiles and the co-founder of the Roman Church, said to the early believers:

"Brothers, think of what you were when you were called. Not many of you were wise by human standards; not many were influential; not many were of noble birth. But God chose the foolish things of the world to shame the wise; God chose the weak things of the world to shame the strong. He chose the lowly things of this world and the despised things---and the things that are not---to nullify the things that are." I Corinthians 1:26-28

The Christian religion, its tenets and the stubborn insistence on its veracity by the early believers were seen as a threat to the Roman State. Unarmed and despised, the new believers were killed. They died willingly and heroically for their God and their beliefs. It became obvious to Rome and to the Romans that this new "superstition" would be hard to kill.

IX.

"When I was a boy at Rome, and was being educated in liberal studies, I was accustomed, with others of like age and mind, to visit on Sundays the sepulchers of the apostles and martyrs...often did I enter the crypts, deep dug in the earth, with their walls on either side lined with the bodies of the dead, where everything is so dark." St. Jerome, *Commentary in Ezekiel 40.5* (c. 354)

Mostly poor and having no earthly status, the early believers were driven underground---to the catacombs. There, deep in the earth, they could worship, honor their martyred and their dead and celebrate Communion (from Latin *com* meaning "with, together" and *unus* meaning "union, oneness"). Most importantly, they could in the tartarean darkness openly display the symbols and the iconography of their faith.

The hundreds of miles of underground tunnels that cincture Rome are filled with Christian inscriptions, sculptures, symbols and wall paintings. The iconography ranges in execution from very primitive to Grandma-Moses charming to respectable attempts at classical Greco-Roman renderings. None of the artistic presentations in the catacombs would be considered high art, but they are invaluable indications of what the very earliest Christians believed and what they considered important to their faith.

They were, first of all, People Of The Book. They had all of what is now called the Old Testament. Because of the subject matter in the catacomb paintings, we know that by the early 100's AD they had all of what is now called the New Testament. They had the Bible. The word "Bible" comes from the name of an ancient coastal town in Lebanon called Byblos, just north of Beirut. Because of its natural harbor and its location at the foot of a Lebanese mountain range with an endless supply of cedar groves, Byblos had exported lumber from its prized cedars of Lebanon all over the Mediterranean world since c. 3000 BC. King Solomon in c. 950 BC contracted with the Sidonian King Hiram for all the cedar that would be used in the building of his Temple:

"'...give orders that cedars of Lebanon be cut for me. My men will work with yours, and I will pay you for your men whatever wages you set. You know that we have no one so skilled in felling timber as the Sidonians'.... Hiram sent word back to Solomon: 'I have received the message you sent me and will do all you want in providing the cedar and pine logs. My men will haul them to the sea, and I will float them in rafts by sea to the place you specify. There I will separate them and you can take them away...grant my wish by providing food for my royal household.'" I Kings 5:6-9

The Bible says that Solomon provided Hiram's royal household with 115,000 gallons of olive oil and 125,000 bushels of wheat every year in exchange for the lumber from those stately, tall trees.

Arid Egypt especially needed that Lebanese lumber for its buildings and the oils and resins from the cedars for mummification, medicinal and cosmetic purposes. Cedar oil is a preservative, insecticide, has anti-bacterial properties and has always been prized for its aroma. In return for the cedar logs, Byblos imported from Egypt metals, cedar oil infused perfumes and especially papyrus. Over the centuries Byblos became famous for the manufacturing and exporting of papyrus to the Mediterranean, Aegean and Roman world. When the Greeks first received papyrus, they called it *biblia* meaning "Byblos things." Intimately associated with Egyptian papyrus, "Byblos" is the root of the later Greek word *biblion* meaning "book, scroll, parchment." The word "Bible" means "the book."

In c. 3000 BC the Egyptians had begun making sheets of papyrus from the reed that grows in the marshes along the Nile. That was the beginning of what would become books. Pens for writing on the papyrus were made from whittled reeds, metal, bone or sharpened quills. Quills made from goose feathers were the most common although calligraphers preferred swan feather quills. Quill pens needed to be frequently sharpened by a knife called a "pen-knife." "Pen" comes from the Latin word "penna" meaning "feather, quill." From antiquity until 1808 in England and 1810 in America when a metal pen point or nib was affixed to a wooden shaft, quills were man's main writing instruments in the West.

For ink the ancients combined carbon (soot or lampblack), water and natural gums. The gum most often used was gum arabic, a natural gum from the acacia tree used to control the ink's viscosity when applied to the papyrus. Thousands of small clay containers used as inkwells have been found.

Pliny the Elder (23-79 AD) gives a description of the making of sheets of papyrus:

"Paper is made from the papyrus plant by separating it with a needle point into very thin strips....paper of whatever grade is fabricated on a board moistened with water from the Nile. The muddy liquid serves as a bonding force. First there is spread flat on the board a layer consisting of strips of papyrus running vertically...with their ends squared off. After that a cross layer completes the construction. Then it is pressed in presses, and the sheets thus formed are dried in the sun and joined one to another....there are never more than twenty sheets in a roll." *Natural History 13.74-82*

The sheets of papyrus were glued together to form long sheaves rolled into scrolls. Some Egyptian scrolls were over 100' long, but the Hebrew scrolls rarely exceeded 30' in length. Jeremiah the 6th century BC prophet dictated a prognostication of the fall of Jerusalem in 586

BC on a scroll and had his scribe Baruch read it to all the people in Jerusalem. King Jehoiakim had the scroll read to him by a scribe: "Whenever Jehudi had read three or four columns of the scroll, the king cut them off with a scribe's knife and threw them into the firepot until the entire scroll was burned in the fire." (Jeremiah 36:23) King Jehoiakim and his people had contempt for God's warnings to repent or they would go into captivity. Clearly, Jeremiah's papyrus scroll was long enough to be cut into pieces and burned but not powerful enough to cause repentance.

Occasionally, a scroll had writing on both sides (Ezekiel 2:10; Revelation 5:1). These are called opisthographs. A normal scroll was read by unrolling it with one hand while rolling it up again with the other hand. Official scrolls were sealed with clay imprinted with the sender's personal seal or signet ring.

The choice quality of papyrus, "hieratic," came from the center of the rush and was used for priestly writings. "Amphitheatic," another high quality paper, was developed in Rome at the workshop of a man named Fannius. Inferior scraps of papyrus called "saitic" and "taeneotic" were sold not by the sheet but by weight and were used for everyday letters and communications. The lowest grade of papyrus called "emporitic" was used for envelopes and as wrapping paper in shops.

The demand for papyrus lasted from c. 3000 BC to c. 1000 AD when China's use of rags and other plant fibers began to filter into Europe. Papyrus was in constant use longer than any other product in the history of the world and has stamped its imprimatur on our English word "paper." Modern paper made from wood pulp is a very recent invention when in the 1840's the German F.G. Keller developed the process of mechanical pulping. No one in the Bronze Age, however, could have imagined that the wood exchanged for Egyptian papyrus would end up being the paper of the Information Age. It is one of the many ironies in this branch of knowledge called "history," etymologically from the Greek word *historia* meaning a story or learning by "inquiry."

For thousands of years people, also, wrote on parchment, a material made from the hides or skins of sheep, goats and calves. Parchment is different from leather because it is not tanned. The hide is cleaned, rinsed, scraped, stretched and dried to produce a stiff, white, translucent surface for writing. For important documents vellum, made only from calf skin, and parchment were preferred over papyrus because they were able to be more easily inscribed on both sides, were not as subject to humidity or tearing, were able to weather a tool that scrapes away mistakes and were much more durable. The important Isaiah Scroll (aka 1QIsa) discovered in 1947 in the caves near Qumran is written on 24' of parchment with black ink made from carbon mixed with natural gums. Testifying to the superiority of parchment, it has been preserved in tact for over 2,000 years.

Parchment, also, could be reused for another book. To get rid of the current writing on the parchment, the page was scraped (erased) and the scribe wrote over whatever was previously there. This type of parchment is called a palimpsest from the Greek words *palin* ("again") and *psan* ("to rub"). The most famous palimpsest in modern times is the *Archimedes Palimpsest*. On October 29, 1998 in New York City, Christies auctioned off a small, 13th century, 174 page Byzantine prayer book written in Greek. It had been charred by fire, was moldy and was almost illegible. It sold for 2.2 million dollars because the erased texts under the prayers included treatises by the greatest mathematician and inventor of the classical world, Archimedes of Syracuse (c. 278-212 BC). Two of his works, *The Method* and *Stomachion*, are found nowhere else. The prayers in the prayer book, or euchologion, are of interest, but the group of scientists that have been studying the palimpsest are recovering, using modern imaging tools, seven treatises of Archimedes leading them to conclude that the majority of the pages in the prayer book came from an 11th century parchment book containing the works of Archimedes. They have, also, found under the prayers some unknown works by the 4th century BC orator Hyperides, an unknown commentary on Aristotle's *Categories* and 20 pages from four unidentified authors. The American owner of the *Archimedes Palimpsest* has not been identified and is known as Mr. B, but on that afternoon at Christies he finessed the Greek Orthodox Patriarch of Jerusalem who had said it should be returned to them because it was stolen from their library centuries ago, and Mr. B outbid the Minister of Culture in Greece for one of the most important erased and reused parchments ever discovered.

For the Hebrews and Christians their parchments and scrolls, their books, their holy writings were and still are the priceless, common links that connect them to their faith and to each other.

Paul, imprisoned in Rome, alone, deserted by all but Luke, knowing that he will be executed, writes his final letter to his protege and young friend Timothy:

"For I am already being poured out like a drink offering, and the time has come for my departure. ....Do your best (Timothy) to come to me quickly, for Demas, because he loved the world, has deserted me.... Crescens has gone to Galatia, and Titus to Dalmatia. Only Luke is with me....When you come, bring the cloak that I left with Carpus at Troas, and my scrolls, especially the parchments." II Timothy 4:6-13

Days or months before his beheading and knowing that he had not faltered in the fight, not failed in the faith Paul wanted to be surrounded by his son in the Lord and his cherished scrolls and parchments, the Words of Life.

Pergamum, one of the seven churches in the Book Of Revelation (2:12-17), became famous for its excellent quality parchments. The English word "parchment" is an evolution from the name of that Turkish city famous for its library of 200,000 parchments. Around the time of Jesus, parchment began to be cut into pages that were bound or sewn together and then covered with painted or illuminated wooden blocks. They looked like modern books and are called "codices" (singular "codex").

Pergamum had the second most famous library in the ancient world. The first was the Library at Alexandria in Egypt that contained 700,000 to a million books. Julius Caesar is accused of inadvertently destroying that library during a war in 48 BC when, as a defensive ploy, he set fire to his ships in the harbor of Alexandria. The fire spread to the docks and burned the adjacent library. (See Plutarch's *Lives 7*) Mark Antony, Caesar's romantic rival for Egypt's queen Cleopatra, later plundered the library at Pergamum and gave the books to her as a wedding gift in compensation for Caesar's reckless crime.

During the first four centuries of the Christian faith, codices, scrolls, parchment and papyrus were common all over the Roman world. The Jews had always been devoted to their Torah and to all the books of the Old Testament. The Gentile Christians were equally dedicated to the books of the Old Testament and of the New Testament. They believed these books contained the inerrant words of God. The *Biblion*, the Bible, was for them the Book of Books. Scrolls of parchment, sheets of papyrus and codices, all containing writings from the Bible, are recurring motifs in catacomb art.

A particularly good painting in the Catacomb of Peter and Marcellinus depicts a short-haired man in a toga holding in his hands an open book of parchment and earnestly imploring us to read it. In the Catacomb of Domitilla, a young martyr in a tunic and *palla* (draped shawl) with "Petronilla Martyr" inscribed near her head introduces a woman named Veneranda to heaven. The deceased Veneranda, wearing a loose *dalmatica* (gown) and a veil, has her hands raised in praise. Petronilla points to a round casket filled with scrolls. Veneranda has followed the Bible's teachings. The books have been opened and she is welcomed into paradise by Petronilla.

Petronilla was an early 1st century Christian martyr who is often identified as the daughter of the Apostle Peter. We know Peter was married because Jesus healed his mother-in-law of a fever in Mark 1:29-31. The 2nd century writer Clement of Alexandria wrote in *Stromata 3.52-53* that "Peter and (the Apostle) Philip fathered children and Philip gave his daughters in marriage," and Ignatius, the disciple of the Apostle John, said: "For I pray that, being found worthy of God, I may be found at their feet in the kingdom; as at the feet of Abraham and Isaac and Jacob; as of Joseph and Isaiah and the rest of the prophets; as of Peter and Paul and the rest of the apostles that were married men. For they entered into these marriages not for the sake of appetite, but out of regard for the propagation of mankind." *On The Philadelphians 4.1:81* In *The Roman Martyrology* the Church acknowledges Petronilla as Peter's daughter: "St. Petronilla, Virgin (and Martyr), daughter of the blessed apostle Peter, who refused to marry the nobleman Flaccus. Given three days for consideration, she spent them in fasting and prayer. On the third day, having received Christ sacramentally, she gave up her spirit."

Some have speculated that Petronilla was Peter's "spiritual daughter," but there is no historic reason to believe this. It does not disparage Peter or his importance or his election to believe that children were a natural outcome of his marriage. One of the early 2nd century heresies of the Church was the doctrine pronounced by both Tatian and the Encratites that marriage was evil. Irenaeus (c.120-c.202) who was a disciple of Polycarp who was a disciple of the Apostle John wrote *Against Heresies* to refute this and other radical departures from Biblical and Apostolic thought:

"....those who are called Encratites preached against marriage, thus setting aside the original creation of God, and indirectly blaming God, Who made the male and female for the propagation of the human race....(Tatian) was excited and puffed up by the thought of being a teacher, as if he were superior to others, composed his own peculiar type of doctrine....he declared that marriage was nothing else than corruption and fornication." *1.28*

Constant vigilance was and is required to combine theology with sound, consistent Biblical teaching. Peter and his wife, probably parents of Petronilla, were martyred together under Nero as Clement of Alexandria reveals in his *Stromata Book 7*. In the 700's the Church transferred Petronilla's remains from the Catacomb of Domitilla to the Vatican. In the 16th century her relics were taken to St. Peter's where an altar was dedicated to her.

There is a well-preserved and well-executed painting in the Catacomb of Peter and Marcellinus of Christ, seated on a cushioned, backless seat with an opened scroll in His hand. The Greek letter "A" for *Alpha*, (the beginning) is to the right of His head and a Greek "W" for *Omega* (the end) is to the left of His head. A wiry, tall bald Paul is to His right and Peter, bearded and short-haired, is to the left of Jesus and is pointing to

Him with his right hand. These three, Jesus, Peter and Paul, were for the early Christians of the catacombs the celestial triad. Jesus is clearly the Book, the Logos, the Alpha and Omega, and Paul and Peter are His two most important witnesses, martyrs. Below and separated from the triad are the martyrs Peter and Marcellinus for whom that catacomb is named and two other martyrs. All four praise and point toward a lamb standing on another throne. In this painting Jesus, as the Word, holding the Word in His hands, is surrounded by those who had given their lives for Him, who believed He was the Passover Lamb seen by John in Revelation 5:6-9: "Then I saw a Lamb, looking as if it had been slain.... (the Lamb) came and took the scroll from the right hand of him who sat on the throne....You are worthy to take the scroll, and to open its seal, because you were slain, and with your blood you purchased men for God from every tribe and language and people and nation."

Jesus was the Logos, the Word:

"In the beginning was the Word and the Word was with God and the Word was God. He was with God in the beginning. Through him all things were made; without him nothing was made that has been made. In him was life, and that life was the light of men." John 1:1-4

The sacred words in the Old Testament had predicted His coming and the sacred words and deeds in the New Testament had shown Him as fulfillment of the prophecies. The Bible was for them the embodiment of God's relationship to man. It was the very words of God and Jesus was the incarnation of those words, God's Word in flesh. Christians took the words in their parchments very seriously.

In the Catacomb of the Giordani on the Via Salaria there is a fresco in the crescent-shaped lunette of an arcosolium that depicts a man in a toga holding an open book. "The resting place of Silvestri" is inscribed in the book. The catacomb Christians believed their names were written in the Book of Life (Revelation 20:15), the ultimate Book that would be opened on the Day of Judgment. They followed the Book. They had faith in the Word.

In the Coemeterium Maius there is a 4th century painting of Christ seated on a small throne with boxes of books around Him. In Domitilla, a well-executed painting of Christ, flanked by six Apostles on either side of Him, is seated on a throne with the scrolls of the Scripture at His feet. As these paintings are in a necropolis, it is clear they depict the Judgment that John recorded in the book of Revelation 20:12: "I saw the dead, great and small, standing before the throne, and the books were opened....And the dead were judged by what was written in the books, by what they had done."

The catacomb dead are the saved people of the resurrection. They are figured on the catacomb walls as *orants*, worshipers with their hands and arms raised in prayerful praise. Tertullian (c.160-220) testifies that in worship "we (Christians) not only lift up our hands, but we spread them out, modeling them after the Lord's passion." *Treatise On Prayer*

On the catacomb walls Noah's hands are raised in praise. Daniel, surrounded by two lions, has raised hands. Even petulant Jonah who is only half-out of the large fish's mouth has his hands raised in praise. Hippolytus of Rome (c. 236) surely had his hands raised in praise as he prayed:

"O crucified One, Thou leader of the mystical dances! O this spiritual wedding feast! O divine Pasch that passes from heaven to earth and rises up again to heaven! O Joy of the universe, honor, ecstasy, exquisite delight by which dark death is destroyed. Life returns to all and the gates of heaven are opened! God appeared as a man and man rose up as God when He shattered the gates of hell and burst the iron bolts thereof. And the people that were in the depth arise from the dead and announce to all the hosts of heaven: 'The thronging choir from earth is coming home!'"

Because of their Bible, their holy book, and the salvation they accepted, these dead fear no condemnation or judgment. As the hymnist Frederick Faber has said, "There is no place where earth's failings have such kindly judgment given" as in the Roman catacombs.

Because the books of the Old and the New Testaments were venerated as the inspired words of God, the Christian iconography in the catacombs all proceeds from the Scriptures and reflects stories and events in these books.

The most frequent story depicted in catacomb paintings is the scene of Christ raising Lazarus from the dead in the town of Bethany. The catacomb Christians in the early 100's had by then the complete Gospel of John because only in John is this miracle recorded. Lazarus and his two sisters were friends of Jesus. Lazarus died. Jesus arrived four days later when Lazarus was in his tomb:

"It was a cave with a stone laid across the entrance. 'Take away the stone,' (Jesus) said. 'But, Lord,' said Martha, the sister of the dead man, 'By this time there is a bad odor, for he has been dead there four days.' Then Jesus said, 'Did I not tell you that if you believed, you would see the glory of God?' So they took away the stone. Then Jesus looked up and said, 'Father, I thank you that you have heard me. I knew that you always hear me, but I said this for the benefit of the people standing here, that they may believe that you sent me.' When he had said this, Jesus called in a loud voice, 'Lazarus, come out!' The dead man came out, his hands and feet wrapped with strips of linen, and a cloth around his face. Jesus said to them, 'Take off the grave clothes, and let him go.'" John 11:38-44

Msgr. Joseph Wilpert, a pioneer in catacomb archaeology in the early 20th century, found 53 paintings of the Lazarus miracle and several more have been found since then. One of the most noteworthy portrayals is in the Via Latina Catacomb. The Via Latina Catacomb is not open to the public, but inside it is completely painted from the vaults to the cubicles, from the walls to the columns. This catacomb is considered the greatest gallery of ancient Christian art. Painted on the right of a panel is a tomb containing the dead Lazarus. Jesus is in the middle of the fresco about to address Lazarus. Behind Jesus and surrounding him on an adjacent wall is one of the few crowd scenes in the catacombs. The artist has jammed hundreds of people side by side as far as the eye can see. It is a unique and artistic presentation.

In an arcosolium near a staircase in the Catacomb of Domitilla is a detailed mosaic decoration of Christ with hands outstretched toward the tomb at the moment He is saying, "Lazarus, come forth." Lazarus is still dead, wrapped in mummy-like grave cloths. Companion to the resurrection of Lazarus in this site are two other scenes: the Three Holy Children in the furnace and the sacrifice of Isaac. The artist seems to be saying in this artful juxtaposition: the Christian dead will be resurrected like Lazarus even amidst the fires of persecution because God the Father sacrificed His Own Son. The Christians knew Daniel's account of Shadrach, Mesach and Abednego emerging whole from Nebuchadnezzar's fiery furnace. They knew that at the last moment God substituted a ram for the sacrifice of Isaac. They believed this substitution was a foretelling of God saying to Abraham: "Not your son. Mine." An inscription on the wall reads: "Whom The Son Spoke the Father Made." Christ, speaking to Lazarus is the Word, the Logos in John 1:1-3 who speaks, calls forth into existence the impossible.

Excavations carried out by the Franciscans at Bethany (today called el-Azariyeh meaning "The Place of Lazarus") have uncovered the remains of Christian churches dating back to the 300's. Eusebius says that in his time (263-339) people made pilgrimages to the site of Lazarus' tomb in Bethany. The Lazarus story was for the catacomb Christians an historic act prefiguring their own resurrection from the dead.

Christians believed in the immortality of the soul. Most pagan religions believed that at death, the candle went out. After death, there was nonentity or a vague eternity of mournful, shadowy shades wandering listlessly in Hades, hell. None of the catacomb Christians believed that death was final. Their tomb art and inscriptions depict their vibrant hopes, their peace and their fervent beliefs in an afterlife:

"May you live with the saints in heaven, in God, in Christ, in the Holy Spirit forever."
"Agrippina, the day of death was the day she entered into light."
"I lived here as in a tent for forty years. Now I live eternally."
"Sweet Simplicius. Live in Eternity."

In contrast pagan tomb inscriptions are cynical and carping:

"I lift my hands against the gods who took me away at the age of twenty though I had done no harm."

"Traveler, curse me not as you pass. For I am in darkness and cannot answer."

"Live for the present hour since we are sure of nothing else."

Many pagan tombs have a famous abbreviation on them: *nf,f,ns,nc.* It represents the Latin saying: *Non fui. Fui. Non sum. Non curo* meaning "I was not. I was. I am not. I care not." The prevalence of the inscription attests to the nihilism and existential despair that permeated pagan societies.

The inscriptions over the tombs of very young children especially illustrate the difference between the pagan view of death and the Christian perspective. An inscription in the Lapidarian gallery mirrors the painful despair and rebellion those without the hope of an afterlife can feel:

"Caius Julius Maximus (aged) 2 years and 5 months. O relentless fortune who delights in cruel death, why is Maximus so suddenly snatched from me? He who lately used to lie joyful in my bosom this stone now marks his tomb. Behold his mother."

There are many Christian inscriptions memorializing little children:

"Eutychius the father (has erected) the gravestone to his sweetest little son Eutychianius the child who lived 1 year, 2 months, 4 days. The servant of God."

"To Julius Acutianus who lived about 10 years. Well deserving in peace. In this tomb which you see rests a boy witty of mind despite his tender age. A lamb snatched to heaven and given to Christ."

"The body of sweet Severa is buried here until she shall rise again. And the Lord, who has taken from me (father Deacon Severus) her chaste, pure and forever inviolable soul with her saintly spirit, will give it back

adorned with spiritual glory. She lived nine years, eleven months and fifteen days. Thus she passed from this earthly life."
"Aproniane, five years and five months old. Aproniane, you believed in God. You will live in Christ."

For the pagan, this world was it. It was all there was or would be. For the Christian, this world was important, but it was not all there was or would be. The pain, sorrow and loss Maximus' pagan mother felt at the death of her child Caius was the same that Julius', Severa's, Eytychianius' and Aproniane's parents felt when their child died. The difference was the Christian parent believed there was an afterlife. The pagan parent did not. The pagan saw death as an impersonal blow of Fortune or Fate. The Christian saw death as the personal call of a loving God to an eternal home. That belief was the difference between despair and hope.

The second most repeated story from the Bible in catacomb art is the Old Testament story of Jonah, the reluctant prophet to Nineveh.

The message of the Lazarus story is very straightforward. The believer would come forth from his tomb as Lazarus had done. The Jonah story on the other hand is layered with many meanings only one of which is the obvious resurrection motif. Jesus had used Jonah's experience of being swallowed by a large fish and being vomited up on the shore three days later to prefigure his own resurrection from the dead:

"(Jesus) answered, 'A wicked and adulterous generation asks for a miraculous sign! But none will be given it except the sign of the prophet Jonah. For as Jonah was three days and three nights in the belly of a huge fish, so the Son of Man will be three days and three nights in the heart of the earth. The men of Nineveh....repented at the preaching of Jonah, and now one greater than Jonah is here.'" Matthew 12:39-41

In the Catacomb of Peter and Marcellinus and in the Cubicles of the Sacraments in St. Callixtus there are well-preserved paintings of Jonah being thrown into the sea by men on a boat. A sea monster, a *pistrix* waits to devour him. In representing Jonah, the believer was saying that he, like Jonah imprisoned in the body of a large sea creature and like Christ dead in the garden tomb, would rise from the dead.

Jonah is, also, a symbol of baptism. Sinful and disobedient to God, Jonah was cast into water and emerged chastened and obedient. His immersion for three days in the waters of the sea followed by his deliverance to dry land mirrored the Christian belief in the washing away of sin by baptism, the transformation from disobedient and lost to saved.

In the Catacomb of St. Sebastian in the Cubicle of Jonah there are four paintings on the walls. The first painting shows Jonah being thrown into the sea. In the second scene Jonah is vomited up on shore. On the south wall of the cubicle the third painting shows the monster fish half-in, half-out of the water. Jonah, both hands raised in praise to God, is left naked and compunctious on a rocky shore. In the fourth scene Jonah, legs crossed and head bent, is sitting under a bower of withered vines.

This fourth scene represents a third layer of meaning in the many depictions of Jonah in the catacombs. God had sent the recalcitrant Jonah in c. 775 BC to proclaim repentance and salvation to the Gentile people of evil Nineveh, the ancient capital of Assyria on the banks of the Tigris River. The catacomb Gentiles appreciated God's love for those ancient Ninevites. It was proof that God had always reached out to the Gentiles and not just to the Jews:

"But Jonah was greatly displeased (when the people of Nineveh repented and were saved) and became angry. He prayed to God, 'O Lord, is this not what I said when I was still at home! That is why I was so quick to flee to Tarshish. I knew that you are a gracious and compassionate God, slow to anger and abounding in love, a God who relents from sending calamity. Now, O Lord, take away my life for it is better for me to die than to live.'" Jonah 4:1-3

The painting of an angry Jonah pouting under the dead vine after the Ninevites had been saved was a poignant symbol for the Gentiles. The Jew Jonah did not want those wicked Gentiles to be saved, but God did. God's continued concern and compassion for all Gentiles were implied in this scene and echoed His words to sulking Jonah:

"You have been concerned about this vine, though you did not tend it or make it grow....But Nineveh has more than a hundred and twenty thousand people who cannot tell their right hand from their left, and many cattle as well. Should I not be concerned about that great city?" Jonah 4:10,11

The joy the early Gentile Christians felt in being included in God's plan of salvation jumps from the walls of subterranean Rome. They portrayed many Old and New Testament stories that reflected God's use of and inclusion of Gentiles.

Balaam, the greedy prophet whose ass tried to deter him from cursing Israel (Numbers 22-24), is often portrayed in catacomb paintings. "Balaam, son of Beor from Pethor in Aram" (Deuteronomy 23:4) was a powerful and famous diviner in the ancient world. He was an Arab from a town near the Euphrates. Not only is he mentioned in the Old Testament, but a fragmentary plaster inscription about him was found in 1967 at Deir 'Alla, Jordan 25 miles north of the plains of Moab where the Israelites had camped. The inscription, written in black and red ink on a plaster wall, dates to between 800-700 BC. The long inscription begins: "The misfortunes of the Book of Balaam, son of Beor. A divine seer was he."

The Arab Balaam was, also, a descendant of Abraham through his son Ishmael. He had been summoned by Balak, king of the Moabites, to curse the Israelites who were conquering the land of Canaan. The Hebrews, lean and hungry for land, had emerged from their 40 years in the wilderness a disciplined and invincible force. Balaam, tempted by the money King Balak had offered him, tried to utter curses on the Jews but could only pronounce praises upon the Jews. (Numbers 23-24) In one of Balaam's prophecies he says:

"I see him, but not now;
I behold him, but not near.

173

A star will come out of Jacob;
A scepter will rise out of Israel."
Numbers 24:17

These four verses are memorialized in catacomb art not only as a
Messianic prophecy but as a prediction of the Star of Bethlehem. In
the Via Latina Balaam, wearing a Roman toga, is looking at us and
pointing with his right arm raised and his forefinger extended to an
eight-pointed star in the sky. Scientists and scholars have speculated for
millennia about the astronomical nature of the Star of Bethlehem. Was
it a nova, a sudden bright star; a triple conjunction called a *conjunctio
magna* of Jupiter and Saturn in Pisces that took place in May of 7
BC and occurs once every 900 years; a conjunction of the Moon and
Jupiter in Aries that occurred in April 6 BC; a slow-moving comet; a
special astronomical manifestation created by God; or was the Star of
Bethlehem something else? We will never know for sure.

Some scholars believe the words in Numbers 24:17 belonged to
an early collection of *Testimonia* or passages from the Old Testament
prefiguring the coming of the Messiah. In the Qumran scrolls discovered
in 1947, Balaam's prophecy is one of the most frequently quoted
Messianic texts. Balaam and his star appear several times in Peter and
Marcellinus, in the Catacomb of Priscilla and in the Catacomb of St.
Sebastian.

In the Museo Civilta Romana in Rome a plaster sarcophagus slab
from the 200's covered the tomb of one "Severa." It depicts Mary and
the toddler Jesus sitting on a chair with Balaam behind them pointing to
his star in the sky. In front of the Mother and Child are three men with
arms and hands outstretched toward the toddler, rushing with scarves
blowing in the wind, to present their gifts to young Jesus whose arms
are reaching out to them. This representation is crude but the sculptor
has caught the eagerness of the Magi to deliver the gifts to Jesus and the
excitement of the little boy Jesus. In the Catacomb of Priscilla Balaam
stands beside a seated Madonna with the nursing Child in her lap.
Balaam is looking at the Infant and pointing to the star in the sky. This
same scene with the star is repeated in a greatly deteriorated picture in

Domitilla. A particularly strange (humorous) Madonna and Child are on an arcosolium, an arched niche in the Coemeterium Maius. Mary, looking like a Roman matron, is lavishly dressed, perfectly coiffed, wearing earrings and a necklace. She is seated with her hands raised in praise like an orant worshipper. On her lap is Jesus. One writer kindly explains: "The Child sits on her lap, but has now passed well beyond babyhood." J. Stevenson, *The Catacombs* The truth is baby Jesus has morphed into a diminutive 25-year-old man. In catacomb art there are many primitive paintings that cause a sympathetic smile. This well-executed painting is the only one that could cause gasps and laughs. To Mary's right is the six-pointed star of Balaam, the "star of Jacob."

Of great importance to the catacomb Christians was that God used the sinful and Gentile Balaam to foretell not only Christ's birth but to specify the star the Magi would follow to worship Him. They were echoing in their paintings the famous Messianic quote in Isaiah 49:6: "I will also make you a light for the Gentiles, that you may bring my salvation to the ends of the earth." In their tomb art the people of the Book were rejoicing that God includes the Gentiles in His plan of salvation and they were anchoring their faith in New Testament events to Old Testament prophecies.

There are at least 85 paintings of the coming of the Magi in the catacombs. They not only show the believer's adoration of Christ, but they shout, "Gentiles were the first people to recognize who Jesus was and to worship Him as the Messiah!" The birth of Jesus was the most important event in history according to the Christians. The Gentile Roman Christians deliberately linked Gentile Balaam's star to the star the Gentile Magi followed.

Early Christians identified many Old Testament Scriptures with the coming of the Magi:

"Nations will come to your light and kings to the brightness of your dawn....Herds of camels will cover your land, young camels of Midian and Ephah, and all from Sheba will come bearing gold and incense and proclaiming the praise of the Lord." Isaiah 60:3,6
"The kings of Tarshish and distant shores will bring tribute to him. The

kings of Sheba and Seba will present him with gifts. All kings will bow down to him and all nations will serve him." Psalm 72:10,11

"This is what the Lord says---the Redeemer the Holy One of Israel---to him who was despised and abhorred by the nation, to the servant of rulers: Kings will see you and rise up, princes will see and bow down, because of the Lord who is faithful, the Holy One of Israel who has chosen you." Isaiah 49:7

The word "Magi" comes from the Greek word *magos* meaning "magician, sorcerer." In the ancient world these Magi were trusted advisors to kings, were learned men proficient in the knowledge of mathematical calculations, astronomy, medicine, astrology, alchemy, dream interpretation and history as well as practitioners of magic and paranormal arts. As far back as 604 BC King Nebuchadnezzar of Babylon had a troubling dream and "summoned the magicians, enchanters, sorcerers and astrologers to tell him what he had dreamed." (Daniel 2:2) His wise men could not interpret the dream. Daniel was able to ascertain the meaning and Nebuchadnezzar made him his Prime Minister. Ancient kings needed and relied upon Magi for advice and discernment as modern rulers rely on their advisors.

The Magi in the Bible came "from the east." (Matthew 2:1) The East at the time of Christ's birth meant Media, Persia, Assyria and Babylonia, countries now encompassed by Iran and Iraq. Justin Martyr in 160 said, "Magi from Arabia came to Herod." Clement of Alexandria (c.150-215) in the *Stromata* says they came from Persia.

In addition to their own sacred writings, the Gentile magi/scholars in the ancient Middle East had read and pondered the books of the Old Testament they had acquired when the Jews in northern Israel were defeated by Sargon II and taken into exile in 722 BC.

Those ten tribes that lived in northern Israel never returned from the Assyrian Captivity. Many exotic and interesting theories swirl around the Lost Ten Tribes of Israel: they went to China; they became the Druids in England; they went to India; they went to Ireland; they became the Indians of the Americas; they went to Africa, to Japan. The Pashtuns in Afghanistan and a tribe in Ethiopia as well as certain clans in India all claim descent from one or more of the lost ten tribes of Israel. Some Jews may have wandered from Babylonia to other parts of the world, but most of the lost tribes probably became assimilated over the centuries into the general population of Assyrian/Babylonian Arabs.

It should be noted, however, that on the day of Pentecost (perhaps Sunday, May 24, 30 AD according to the Julian calendar) many Jews from the Middle East were there in Jerusalem to celebrate Passover: Parthians from regions near the Tigris River, Medes from Persia, Elamites from the Persian Gulf, and Mesopotamians from the lands between the Euphrates and Tigris Rivers. (Acts 2:9-11) Over seven hundred years after the Assyrian Captivity, some Jews from Northern Israel had still maintained their discrete identity and made yearly pilgrimages to their Holy City of Jerusalem.

About a hundred years after the northern tribes went into captivity and oblivion, Judah and Benjamin, the two tribes of Judea in southern Israel, were conquered and taken to Babylon in 586 BC. They took the books of the Old Testament with them. The Arabian Magi, renowned for their hunger for wisdom and knowledge, had many centuries to pour over the Jewish writings and the prophecies and signs of a coming Messiah.

"After Jesus was born in Bethlehem in Judea, during the time of King Herod, Magi from the east came to Jerusalem and asked, 'Where is the one who has been born the king of the Jews? We saw his star in the east and have come to worship him.'" Matthew 2:1,2

There is an interesting, if not phantasmagoric, account of the reason for the coming of the Magi entitled *Narrative Of Events Happening In Persia On The Birth Of Christ*. It was written in the early 200's AD by Julius Africanus who is praised by ancient authors for his erudition and scholarship. Unfortunately, most of his legendary works are lost. Africanus traveled all over the world seeking first-hand knowledge of places and events relating to the Bible. He visited Mt. Ararat to see the place where Noah's ark rested and he went to Mesopotamia where he purportedly saw and transcribed from golden plates the events that transpired in the temple of their high goddess, Juno, on the night Jesus was born. Africanus begins his narrative:

"Christ first of all became known from Persia. For nothing escapes the learned jurists of that country who investigate all things with the utmost care. The facts therefore which are inscribed upon the golden plates and laid up in their royal temples, I shall record; for it is from the temples there, and the priests connected with them, that the name of Christ has been heard of."

On the night Jesus was born, angels were the first to proclaim the birth of Jesus to shepherds. The shepherds saw "Mary and Joseph and the baby, who was lying in the manger. When they had seen him, they spread the word (locally) concerning what had been told them (by the angels) about this child, and all who heard it were amazed at what the shepherds said to them." (Luke 2:16-18) But Africanus is correct. The first people who spread the news of the birth of the Christ throughout the Middle East and beyond were the Magi, the priests and others within the royal court in Persia.

At the time of Jesus' birth, Mesopotamia was ruled by a people of obscure origin called the Parthians. In 247 BC the leader of an army of nomads, Arsaces, led a revolt that toppled the frail hold the Seleucid remnant of Alexander the Great's conquest had on the region. Arsaces and his brother Tiridates founded the Parthian Empire. Over the next one hundred years, succeeding Parthian kings battled their way to hegemony over the Tigris/Euphrates River Valley and the rest of Mesopotamia (modern Iran and Iraq). By the time of Jesus' birth in c. 6-4 BC, the Parthians in the East and the Romans in the West controlled most of the Western and Middle Eastern world.

According to the writing on the golden plates, there were shocking events in the goddess Juno's temple on the night Jesus was born. The Parthian king at the time had come to the temple to have some of his dreams interpreted by the priest. Harps began to play without a player, muses to sing, gold and silver idols of animals and birds were given voices, huge statues of gods and goddesses fell over and were shattered. Other statues cried out that the mighty god Sol has embraced Juno, but Juno is now called Myria "for she bears in her womb, as in the deep, a vessel of a myriad talents' burden....This stream of water sends forth the perennial stream of spirit, a stream containing a single fish, taken with the hook of Divinity, and sustaining the whole world with its flesh as though it were in the sea."

The king is terrified and wants to run from the temple, but the priest urges him to stay and see the final revelation:

"...the roof of the temple was opened, and a bright star descended and stood above the pillar of Pege (mother goddess), and a voice was heard to this effect:...'the mighty Son has sent me to make the announcement to you....the child begotten by extraordinary generation is called the Beginning and the End, the beginning of salvation and the end of perdition'....the king gave orders to bring in all the interpreters of prodigies and the sages who were under his dominion...when they saw the star above Pege... the statues lying on the floor they said: 'O king, a root divine and princely has risen, bearing the image of the King of heaven....and the star is a celestial announcement of portents to fall on the earth. Out of Judah has arisen a kingdom which shall subvert all the memorials of the Jews....Now, O king, send to Jerusalem. For you will find the Christ (Messiah, Avatar) of the Omnipotent God borne in bodily form in the bodily arms of a woman'....The king...sent some of the Magi under his dominion with gifts, the star showing them the way. And when they returned, they narrated to the men of that time those same things which were written on the plates of gold."

At the time Jesus was born, the king of Persia was the Parthian Phraates IV (reigned 38-2BC). He was not the type of person one would consider devout in either the Christian or the pagan sense. When he became king in 37 BC, he methodically purged his family of pretenders to the throne. He killed his father, all thirty of his brothers and sent five of his sons as hostages to Caesar Augustus. According to

Josephus, Phraates was persuaded to exile his sons to Rome by an Italian concubine:

"When Phraates had had legitimate sons of his own, he had, also, an Italian maidservant whose name was Thermusa whom Phraates called the Goddess Musa….He first made her his concubine; but he being a great admirer of her beauty, in process of time having a son by her, whose name was Phraataces, he made Thermusa his legitimate wife and had a great respect for her. Now she was able to persuade him to do anything that she said and was earnest in procuring the government of Parthia for her son; but still she saw that her endeavors would not succeed, unless she could contrive how to remove Phraates' legitimate sons. So she persuaded Phraates to send his sons as pledges of his fidelity to Rome; and they were sent to Rome accordingly, because it was not easy for him to contradict her commands." *Jewish Antiquities 18.2.4*

It was not a kindly king that sent his Magi with the gifts to Bethlehem. Phraates was, perhaps, trying to buy alliance and good will with this new king of the Jews whose birth was announced by supernatural events as far away as Persia. With so many family enemies at home, Phraates was, like Herod in Jerusalem, paranoid with reason. Phraates must have been relieved when the Magi returned with the news that the new king came from humble origins. He need not have worried about the infant Jesus. Phraates was murdered in 2 BC by his son Phraataces, whose mother Thermusa crowned him Phraates V. Herod the Great, also, must have been relieved when he had all the males two years old and under slaughtered in Bethlehem. He need not have worried about the toddler Jesus. In 4 BC Herod died of an excruciating disease:

"Herod's illness progressively worsened as God exacted punishment for his crimes. A slow fire burned inside him, less obvious to the touch. He had an insatiable desire for food, ulcers in the intestines, terrible pain in the colon, and a clammy edema in his feet. His bladder was inflamed and his genitals gangrenous, breeding worms. His breathing was rapid and extremely offensive due to its stench, and every limb was convulsed intolerably. Wise onlookers declared that God was exacting retribution from the king for his many wicked deeds." Josephus, *Jewish Antiquities 17.6.5*

The late Professor of Archaeology at Hebrew University, Ehud Netzer, announced on May 7, 2007 that he had found the tomb of Herod the Great right where Josephus had said it was at a hill called Herodium outside of Jerusalem. Inside the tomb was Herod's broken sarcophagus but no body. It is ironic and sad that Netzer, who had searched for Herod's tomb for over 35 years, died several years later in October of 2010 as a result of a fall at the ruins of Herodium.

Two prominent ancient kings were associated with Jesus' birth. Instead of his kingdom rebelling, Herod's own body turned against him and his tomb was looted. And Phraates' favored son murdered him in his royal bed and the crown of Persia was placed upon his own young head.

Africanus transcribed from the golden plates in Phraates' Persia not only the supernatural events in the temple of Juno, but also the story of the Magi's journey, their reception by Herod and their encounter with Mary and Jesus:

"And we (Magi) came to that place then to which we were sent and saw the mother and the child, the star indicating to us the royal babe. And we said to the mother: 'What are you named, O renowned mother?' And she says: 'Mary, masters.' And we said to her: "Whence are you sprung?' And she replies: 'From this district of the Bethlehemites.' Then we said: 'Do you not have a husband?' And she answers: 'I was betrothed with a view to the marriage covenant, my thoughts being far removed from this. For I had no mind to come to this. And while I was giving very little concern to it, when a certain Sabbath dawned, and straightway at the rising of the sun, an angel appeared to me bringing me suddenly the glad tidings of a son. And in trouble I cried out, Be it not so to me, Lord, for I have not a husband. And he persuaded me to believe, that by the will of God I should have this son.' Then we said to her: 'Mother, mother, all the gods of the Persians have you blessed. Your glory is great; for you are exalted above all women of renown, and you are shown to be more queenly than all queens.' The child, moreover, was seated on the ground, being, as she said, in his second year, and having in part the likeness of his mother. And she had long hands, and a body somewhat delicate; and her color was like that of ripe wheat (golden brown); and she was of a round face, and had her hair bound up. And as we had along with us a servant skilled in painting from the life, we brought with us to our country a likeness of them both; and it was placed by our hand in the sacred temple, with this inscription on it: 'To Jove the Sun, the mighty God, the King of Jesus, the power of Persia dedicated this.' And taking the child up, each of us in turn, and bearing him in our arms, we saluted him and worshipped him and presented to him gold, and myrrh, and frankincense, addressing him thus: 'We gift you with your own, O Jesus, ruler of heaven'....And the child leaped and laughed at our caresses and words. And when we had bidden the mother farewell, and when she had shown us honor, we came again to the place in which we lodged. And at eventide there appeared to us one of a terrible and fearful countenance saying, 'get out quickly, lest you be taken in a snare'…. And we made speed to depart thence in all earnestness; and we reported in Jerusalem all that we had seen."

Africanus' transcribed record must be interpreted against the pagan cultures in which not only the Persians but, also, the Christian Africanus lived. His veracity is normally reliable and has undergone intense scrutiny over the centuries. But few scholars have in recent times given much credence to this fanciful account. The reader is encouraged to read all of Africanus' *Narrative of Events Happening in Persia On The Birth Of Christ*.

There were not three wise men. The Magi were not kings. They did not come to the manger scene and their names were not Gaspar, Melchior and Balshasar. Origen in c. 250 was the first to give them these names. By the 7th century, and even now, the most educated accepted as fact that there were three wise men. The Bible does not tell us how many Magi came to Palestine. It only says: "Magi from the east came to Jerusalem." Matthew 2:1

In one catacomb painting in St. Peter Cemetery there are 2 Magi. In the Lateran Museum and in Peter and Marcellinus there are 3. In Domitilla there are 4. A vase painting in the Kircherian Museum in Rome has 8 wise men crowding the house where Jesus and Mary reside. The number of Magi in very early Christian art ranges from two to a gaggle. Legend and Christmas carols have blindly assumed there were three wise men because there were three gifts and because Origen had given them three names. All we know for sure is that some Magi made the long journey to adore "the one who (had) been born king of the Jews." Matthew 2:2

There are four paintings of Mary and Jesus in the catacombs. The most ancient fresco dates from the 100's and is in Priscilla. Mary is seated and appears to be nursing the infant Jesus. The prophet Balaam points to his star. The Madonna and Child in the Coemeterium Maggiore was done in the 300's as was the Madonna and Child in the Catacomb of Domitilla. The enthroned Virgin and Child in Commodilla dates from the late 400's. The four paintings are not autonomous. Each appears as one of a group of paintings and decorative wall art. Mary, unless paired with Jesus in the above examples, is not a subject of catacomb tomb art. After the Council of Ephesus in 430, Mariology and art depicting her alone or with Jesus blossomed for the next 1,200 years. But there are numerous paintings in the catacombs of the Coming of the Magi with their bloused pants and their crooked Phrygian caps that look like the ones worn by the seven dwarfs in Disney's 1937 animation.

In the Greek, Matthew 2:11 specifies: "And having come into the house, (the Magi) found the little child with Mary, his mother, and having fallen down did homage to him." The Greek uses the word *oikos* meaning "house, building" to denote the location of Jesus and Mary and uses the word for "young child" (*paidion*) to denote the approximate age of Jesus. Two of the four paintings of Jesus and Mary in the catacombs show Jesus as a toddler (16-24 months) or as a young child. The Gentile Magi were the first to worship, to acknowledge and to give homage to Jesus, but they did not arrive until Jesus, Mary and Joseph had found lodging in a house in Bethlehem.

The only beings at the birth of Jesus were Mary, Joseph and the animals, if any, that shared the stable/cave with the family. On the night Jesus was born, however, an angel announced the birth of the Messiah to a group of shepherds:

"And there were shepherds living out in the fields nearby, keeping watch over their flocks at night. An angel of the Lord appeared to them, and the glory of the Lord shone around them, and they were terrified. But the angel said to them, 'Do not be afraid. I bring you good news of great joy that will be for all people. Today in the town of David a Savior has been born to you; he is Christ the Lord. This will be a sign to you: You will find a baby wrapped in cloths and lying in a manger'....So they hurried off and found Mary and Joseph and the baby who was lying in a manger." Luke 2:8-12,16

Sheep were only tended at that time of year and near a town if the sheep were destined for sacrifice at the Temple services. The Temple-appointed shepherds who left their doomed flock and hurried through the dark to the cave/barn to see the heaven-announced baby found Him lying in a manger, a feed trough for animals made of clay and straw. The only people who came to see the Good Shepherd on the night He was born were shepherds who tended sheep intended for sacrifice. The symbolism reverberates.

The Greek uses the word *brephos* meaning an "unborn or newborn" baby to denote the infancy of Jesus in the manger passage. In contrast, when the wise men arrived, Jesus was a *paidion*, a "young child" and the family was living in a house not in a stable.

After the star had appeared to the Magi, they had a long journey to Jesus. Depending upon where they came from (and we will never know for sure), it was an 880-1,300 mile trip. Even before they left the Middle East, the wise men had to ponder the new star, look for its meaning in all their sacred books including the Old Testament, decide to follow the star and make preparations for such a long trip. These considerations could take months or even over a year.

Ezra, the priest who returned from Babylon to Jerusalem with a group of Babylonian exiles in 457 BC:

"...arrived in Jerusalem in the fifth month of the seventh year of the king (Artaxerxes of Persia). He had begun his journey from Babylon on the first day of the first month and he arrived in Jerusalem on the first day of the fifth month, for the gracious hand of his God was on him." Ezra 7:8,9

It took Ezra, with God's speed, only four months to travel from Babylon to Jerusalem, a distance of c. 880 miles following ancient routes. We can deduce then from Ezra's account that caravanning, the choice of the routes traveled and with stops along the way, it took an average traveler considerably more time than four months to journey from Babylon to Jerusalem. When the Magi arrived, it is certain Mary, Joseph and Jesus were not still living in a stable.

Over the millennia, there have been many conjectures regarding the dates of Jesus' birth, the coming of the Magi and of His death. We know in Scripture that Jesus was born "during the time of King Herod." (Matthew 2:1) According to Josephus in *Wars Of The Jews 1.33.5-8*, Herod died at Jericho in 4 BC. Jesus' birth then had to have occurred toward the end of Herod's life in c. 6-4 BC. Most Biblical scholars posit 6-4 BC as the date of Jesus' birth.

In the interest of truth and inquiry, the date for Jesus' birth given by Eusebius of Caesarea in his *Church History 1.5* must be put forth:

"It was in the 42nd year of the reign of Augustus and the 28th after the conquest of Egypt and the deaths of Antony and Cleopatra, the last of the Ptolemaic dynasty, that our Savior and Lord, Jesus Christ, was born in Bethlehem of Judea in accordance with the prophecies concerning him. This was at the time of the first census, which took place while Quirinius was governor of Syria, a registration mentioned also by Flavius Josephus."

Eusebius calculated the reign of Augustus from the death of Julius Caesar in 44 BC. That would place Jesus' birth at 2 BC. Antony and Cleopatra died in 30 BC. So twenty-eight years later, 2 BC, neatly coincides with the 42nd year of the reign of Augustus. Eusebius in the early 300's was much closer to documents and oral tradition than we are 2,000 years later. However, his 2 BC date obviates the interaction between Herod and Jesus by conflicting with the date Josephus gives for the death of Herod in 4 BC. That discrepancy has always been the problem with Eusebius' later date of 2 BC. Discrepancies in ancient dates may, however, be accounted for by the use of different calendrical calculations. There are Hebrew calendar dates, AUC Roman calendar dates, Julian calendar dates and Gregorian calendar dates. As Eusebius says in the Preface to his *Chronicle* detailing chronological tables from the very earliest times down to his own time in the 320's AD: "...no one...should believe that he is calculating dates with full accuracy and be deceived in that way." For the dates of Jesus' birth, life, death and His resurrection we do have markers.

The successor of Augustus was Tiberias who ruled from 14-37 AD. He was Caesar during Jesus' late adolescence and adulthood. Tiberias appointed Pontius Pilate as procurator of Judea (from 26-36 AD). Tiberias is usually given short shrift by historians. But tucked away in Eusebius' *Church History 2.2* is an interesting story about him and his efforts to get the Roman Senate to appoint Jesus a god:

"Our Savior's extraordinary resurrection and ascension into heaven were by now famous everywhere (c. 35AD). It was customary for provincial governors to report to the emperor (by a document called an *Acta*) any new local movement so that he might be kept informed. Accordingly, Pilate communicated to the emperor Tiberius the story of Jesus' resurrection from the dead as already well known throughout Palestine, as well as information he had gained on Jesus' other marvelous deeds and how many believed him to be a god in rising from the dead. They say that Tiberius referred the report to the Senate which rejected it, allegedly because it had not dealt with the matter before. According to an old law, still in effect, no one could be deemed a god by the Romans unless by vote and decree of the Senate, but the real reason was that the divine message did not require human ratification. In this way, the Roman council rejected the report submitted to it regarding our Savior, but Tiberius maintained his opinion and made no evil plans against the teaching of Christ."

Over one hundred years before Eusebius wrote of Tiberias' sentiments regarding the deity of Jesus, the Carthaginian lawyer and apologist for Christianity Tertullian had written about the same matter in c. 197:

"...there was an old decree that no god should be consecrated by a general without the approval of the Senate....among you (Romans) divinity is weighed out by human caprice. Unless a god shall have been acceptable to men, he shall not be a god. Man must now have mercy on a god! Accordingly Tiberius, in whose time the Christian name first made its appearance in the world, laid before the senate tidings from Palaestina which had revealed to him the truth of the divinity (of Jesus) there manifested and (Tiberias) had supported the motion by his own vote to begin with. The Senate rejected it because it had not itself given its approval. Caesar Tiberias held to his own opinion and threatened danger to the accusers of Christians." *Apologeticus 5*

Whether or not the debauched Emperor Tiberias accepted the resurrection and divinity of Christ, we do know that Jesus was crucified under his appointed procurator Pontius Pilate on a Friday before the Saturday Passover in the month of Nisan (March-April). Astronomically, the only relevant 1st century years that Nisan 14 (Passover was on the 14th day of the first month) fell on a Friday were 30, 33 and 36 AD. Some scholars opt for Nisan 14, 33 as the date of Jesus' death. But Nisan 14, 30 is the traditional date for Jesus' crucifixion. That would make Him about 34-36 when He died. With Biblical and historical markers, we have an approximate, if not totally accurate, chronology of the dates of Jesus' birth, the coming of the Magi, His death and the resurrection.

The Roman Catholic and some Protestant churches celebrate the coming of the Magi or Epiphany twelve days after Christmas on January 6. Epiphany, a Greek word meaning "manifestation," is an old church festival dating back to the 3rd century in the Eastern Church. At that time, however, Epiphany commemorated the Baptism of Jesus by John. (Matthew 3:13-17) That meaning was gradually lost in the Western churches and the feast morphed into the celebration of the coming of the Magi. The Eastern Orthodox churches still celebrate Epiphany as the baptism of Jesus. Knowing this conflicting history, it is not prudent to place the arrival of the Magi 12 days after Christ's birth.

Herod, known as Herod the Great because of his many building projects, was king of the Jews when Jesus was born, but he was not a Jew. His father was an Idumean (Edomite Arab) convert to Judaism and his mother was a Nabatean (Arab). Herod was not the rightful heir to the throne of Israel. He had aligned himself with the Romans and had been appointed king of the Jews by the Roman senate in 40 BC. He spent the next three years violently suppressing and killing all opposition to his rule. Herod murdered his wife, his relatives and his friends. He had such a tenuous and paranoid hold on power during his 36-year reign that he even suspected his own sons of treason and had them executed. That caused the Roman Caesar Augustus to pun: "I'd rather be Herod's pig (Greek *hus*) than his son (Greek *huios*)." As a converted Jew, Herod could not kill an abhorred pig.

When the Magi arrived and inquired where the King of the Jews should be born, the illegitimate King Herod began plotting the new king's destruction. If important ambassadors from the East were interested in this newborn, maybe armies from Arabia would join forces with his Jewish opposition and depose him. Herod was always on alert.

"Herod called the Magi secretly and found out from them the exact time the star had appeared." (Matthew 2:7) From their answers, Herod determined the child was two years old or under. After the Magi left his territory, Herod "gave orders to kill all the boys in Bethlehem and its vicinity who were 2 years old and under, in accordance with the time he had learned from the Magi." (Matthew 2:16) The Slaughter Of The Innocents took place as Joseph, Mary and Jesus were escaping in the dead of night with the valuable, portable gifts of gold, frankincense and myrrh given to them by the Gentile Magi, gifts that would pay for their stay in Gentile Egypt.

During His ministry, Jesus initiated important and inclusive contacts with Gentiles:

"Now on his way to Jerusalem, Jesus traveled along the border between Samaria and Galilee.....ten men who had leprosy met him. They stood at a distance and called out in a loud voice, 'Jesus, Master, have pity on us!' When he saw them, he said, 'Go, show yourselves to the priests.' And as they went, they were cleansed. One of them, when he saw he was healed, came back, praising God in a loud voice. He threw himself at Jesus' feet and thanked him---and he was a Samaritan. Jesus asked, 'Were not all ten cleansed? Where are the other nine? Was no one found to return and give praise to God except this foreigner?'" Luke 17:11-18

Because of the location on the border between Galilee and Samaria, the ten lepers were probably a combination of ostracized and quarantined Jews and Samaritans. Jesus healed them all. Jesus ironically noted that the Samaritan, or "foreigner, stranger" as He called him, was the only one who returned to thank Him.

The phrase, "a good Samaritan," comes from one of Jesus' most famous parables:

"On one occasion an expert in the law (a scribe) stood up to test Jesus. 'Teacher,' he asked, 'what must I do to inherit eternal life?' 'What is written in the law?' (Jesus) asked. 'How do you read it?' The man answered: 'Love the Lord your God with all your heart and with all your soul and with all your strength and with all your mind and love your neighbor as yourself.' 'You have answered correctly,' Jesus replied. 'Do this and you will live.' But he wanted to justify himself, so he asked Jesus, 'And who is my neighbor?' In reply Jesus said: 'A man was going down from Jerusalem to Jericho when he fell into the hands of robbers. They stripped him of his clothes, beat him and went away, leaving him half dead. A priest happened to be going down the same road, and when he saw the man, he passed by on the other side. So, too, a Levite, when he came to the place and saw him, passed by on the other side. But a Samaritan as he traveled, came where the man was; and when he saw him, he took pity on him. He went to him and bandaged his wounds, pouring on oil and wine. Then he put the man on his own donkey, took him to an inn and took care of him. The next day he took out two silver coins and gave them to the innkeeper. 'Look after him,' he said, 'and when I return, I will reimburse you for any extra expense you may have.' Which of these three men do you think was a neighbor to the man who fell into the hands of the robbers?' The expert in the law replied, 'The one who had mercy on him.' Jesus told him, 'Go and do likewise.'" Luke 10:25-37

In this parable Jesus was challenging the thinking of the Jewish holy men. They believed that God chose the Jews, which He did, and that the Jews were the only righteous people in the world, which they were not. In the parable Jesus chooses the most holy of Jews, a priest and a Levite from the priestly class, to be the ones who ignore the stranger in trouble. We are not told in the parable whether the injured man was a Jew or a Gentile, but Jesus chooses a Gentile from Samaria to be the kind, obedient and Godly person.

The New Testament Samaritans were a mixed race of Jews and Gentiles. In Jesus' time to be called a "Samaritan" was as odious as being called a "heathen" or a "tax collector." One day when Jesus was teaching in the Temple, the Pharisees began to revile Him. They did not hold back. They called Him a bastard by birth and accused Him of being not only demon-possessed but a Samaritan. Three damning charges:

"'We are not illegitimate children,' they protested. 'The only Father we have is God himself'....The Jews answered him, 'Aren't we right in saying that you are a Samaritan and demon-possessed?'" John 8:41,48

The Samaritans were descended from the population exchange affected by the Assyrians after the captivity of Northern Israel 700 years before Jesus was born. The Assyrians had deported the Jewish elite and educated back to Assyria and had left the farmers and the illiterate to tenant the land. They replaced the Jewish elite with a mixture of lower caste people from the Mesopotamian areas of Sepharvaim, Avva, Hamath and Cuth. Over the centuries of assimilation, the Samaritans had come to believe in Yahweh, in the Pentateuch of Moses and in the coming of the Messiah/Prophet predicted by Moses in Deuteronomy18:15-19:

"The Lord your God will raise up for you a prophet like me (Moses) from among your own brothers. You must listen to him….The Lord said to me: 'What they say is good. I will raise up for them a prophet like you from among their brothers; I will put my words in his mouth, and he will tell them everything I command him. If anyone does not listen to my words that the prophet speaks in my name, I myself will call him to account.'"

But the Samaritans were not pure Jews.They were half-breeds physically and theologically. They were shunned and hated by the Jews. "He who eats the bread of a Samaritan, is as one who eats swine's flesh," says the rabbi in Mishnah Shebiith 8.10.

Tensions were particularly high during Jesus' lifetime between the Jews and the Samaritans. John Hyrcanus, a relative of the Maccabees, had destroyed the Samaritan temple on Mt. Gerizim in 128 BC. There were minor skirmishes between the two groups for years. In c. 6-7 AD, the Samaritans had scattered bones all over the temple in Jerusalem during Passover. A good Jew did not associate with Samaritans.

The story of Jesus and the woman at the well figures several times in catacomb art. When Jesus met this Samaritan woman, he was on his way back to the Galilee region:

"…he had to go through Samaria. So he came to a town in Samaria called Sychar (modern Askar) near the plot of ground Jacob had given to his son Joseph. Jacob's well was there (and still is at modern Bir Ya'Qub), and Jesus, tired as he was from the journey, sat down by (Jacob's) well. It was about the sixth hour (noon). When a Samaritan woman came to draw water, Jesus said to her. 'Will you give me a drink?' His disciples had gone into the town to buy food. The Samaritan woman said to him, 'You are a Jew and I am a Samaritan woman. How can you ask me for a drink? For the Jews do not associate with Samaritans.' Jesus answered her, 'If you knew the gift of God and who it is that asks you for a drink, you would have asked him and he would have given you living water.' 'Sir,' the woman said, 'you have nothing to draw with and the well is deep. Where can you get this living water? Are you greater than our father Jacob, who gave us the well and drank from it himself, as did also his sons and his flocks and herds?' Jesus answered, 'Everyone who drinks this water will be thirsty again, but whoever drinks the water I give him will never thirst. Indeed, the water I give him will become in him a spring of water welling up to eternal life.' The woman said to him, 'Sir, give me this water so that I won't get thirsty and have to keep coming back to draw water.' He told her, 'Go, call your husband and come back.' 'I have no husband,' she replied. Jesus said to her, 'You are right in saying you have no husband. The fact is, you have had five husbands, and the man you now have is not your husband. What you have said is quite true.' 'Sir,' the woman said. 'I can see that you are a prophet. Our fathers worshipped on this mountain (Mt. Gerizim), but you Jews claim that the place where we must worship is in Jerusalem.' Jesus declared, 'Believe me, woman, a time is coming when you will worship the Father neither in the mountain nor in Jerusalem. You Samaritans worship what you do not know; we worship what we do know for salvation is from the Jews. Yet a time is coming and has now come when the true worshipers will worship the Father in spirit and truth, for they are the kind of worshipers the Father seeks. God is spirit, and his worshipers must worship in spirit and in truth.' The woman said, 'I know that Messiah…is coming. When he comes, he will explain everything to us.' Then Jesus declared, 'I who speak to you am he'…. leaving her water jar, the woman went back to the town and said to the people, 'Come, see a man who told me everything I ever did. Could this be the Christ?'….Many of the Samaritans from that town believed in him because of the woman's testimony.…they urged him to stay with them, and he stayed two days. And because of his words many more became believers." John 4:4-41

Jacob's well is in a Greek Orthodox Compound in Bir Ya'Qub near the Palestinian city of Nablus in the West Bank. It is revered by Jews, Christians, Muslims and modern-day Samaritans. In November of 1979 a Zionist group appeared at the monastery and demanded all Christian icons and crosses be removed because it was a Jewish site. Later that month a monk, Philoumenous, was found tortured and hatcheted to death inside the crypt that led to the well. No arrests have ever been made. Today the c. 135' deep well with a circumference of 7.6' has a new church over it and visitors are led down the steps to the crypt that houses the 4,000 BC well where 2,000 years later Jesus had his friendly encounter with the Samaritan woman and where 2,000 years after Jesus, there occurred a heinous, deadly encounter between Jews and a Christian priest.

In a primitive painting in the Via Latina of Jesus' encounter with the woman, the artist has done a remarkable job with the face of the Samaritan woman. She is on the left side of Jacob's well and has a bucket tied to a rope in her left hand. Jesus, to the right of the well, is painted as a short-haired young man wearing a Roman toga. The painting is stilted and flat, but the solemn, quizzical look in the woman's eyes and the rapt set of her face exactly reflect the dialogue from the Gospel of John. Jesus called the woman at the well away from sin when He pointed out her adulterous relationships. He offered her His water. The early Gentile Christians were excited and awed that Jesus Himself when He was on earth had offered salvation to Gentiles, had offered the sinful Samaritan woman the living water of baptism, the water that washes away sins and births the new life.

This story further underlines Jesus' independent outreach to Gentiles. The woman at the well, adulterous, promiscuous, outcast, drew her water at noontime when the respectable women had gone. Jesus had even violated a Jewish taboo by talking to a woman. Most importantly, it was to this Gentile woman that Jesus first publicly revealed that He was the long-awaited Messiah:

"The woman said (to Jesus), 'I know that Messiah is coming. When he comes, he will explain everything to us.'
Then Jesus declared, "I who speak to you am he.'" John 4:25,26

She believed and began to evangelize her whole Samaritan town of Sychar. It was this group of half-breeds who first openly received Jesus and declared him "the savior of the world" and in the Greek "the Christ, the Messiah." (4:42) The Gentile Christians painted the walls of the catacombs with Biblical events that showed God's abiding love for them as well as for the Jews.

After the stoning of Stephen in c. 34, "a great persecution broke out against the church at Jerusalem, and all except the apostles were scattered throughout Judea and Samaria." (Acts 8:1) Christians fled Jerusalem and were "scattered; they preached the word wherever they went." (8:4) Philip went north to Samaria and is reputed to have preached in Sychar. He was so successful among the Samaritans that the Jerusalem church sent Peter and John to help Philip with his outreach. (8:14) His Apostles were continuing the work that Jesus had begun several years earlier in that reviled yet receptive small Samaritan region. Today in areas around Nablus there are still hundreds of people who call themselves Samaritans.

After Philip left Samaria, he was commanded by the Lord to go to the 50-mile stretch of road that led south from Jerusalem to Gaza where a Godly, seeking and eager black eunuch from Ethiopia became the first black Gentile whose conversion story is detailed in the New Testament:

"Now an angel of the Lord said to Philip, 'Go south to the road, the desert road, that goes down from Jerusalem to Gaza. So (Philip) started out, and on his way he met an Ethiopian eunuch, an important official in charge of all the treasury of Candace, queen of the Ethiopians. This man had gone to Jerusalem to worship, and on his way home was sitting in his chariot reading the book of Isaiah the prophet. The Spirit told Philip, 'Go to that chariot and stay near it.' Then Philip ran up to the chariot and heard the man reading Isaiah the prophet. 'Do you understand what you are reading?' Philip asked. 'How can I,' he said, 'unless someone explains it to me?' So he invited Philip to come up and sit with him. The eunuch was reading this passage of Scripture: 'He was led like a sheep to the slaughter and as a lamb before the shearer is silent, so he did not open his mouth. In his humiliation he was deprived of justice. Who can speak of his descendants? For his life was taken from the earth.' (Isaiah 53:7,8) The eunuch asked Philip, 'Tell me, please, who is the prophet talking about, himself or someone else?' Then Philip began with that very passage of Scripture and told him the good news about Jesus. As they traveled along the road, they came to some water and the eunuch said, 'Look, here is water. Why shouldn't I be baptized?' And he gave orders to stop the chariot. Then both Philip and the eunuch went down into the water and Philip baptized him. When they came up out of the water, the Spirit of the Lord suddenly took Philip away, and the eunuch did not see him again, but went on his way rejoicing." Acts 8:26-39

That unnamed, everlastingly renowned Ethiopian eunuch was chosen to be the first to bring the Gospel to Africa. Though he was castrated and unable to have children, the promises in Isaiah 56:3-5 aptly apply to him:

"…let not any eunuch complain, 'I am only a dry tree.' To the eunuchs who keep my Sabbaths, who choose what pleases me and hold fast to my covenant---to them I will give within my temple and its walls a memorial and a name better than sons and daughters; I will give them an everlasting name that will not be cut off."

At about the same time as Philip's encounter with the memorialized eunuch (c. 35), a truculent, angry Christ-hating Jew named Saul who was destined to become Paul the Apostle to the Gentiles was knocked down and blinded on the road that led north from Jerusalem to Damascus:

"Meanwhile, Saul was still breathing out murderous threats against the Lord's disciples. He went to the high priest (Caiaphas) and asked him for letters to the synagogues in Damascus, so that if he found any there who belonged to the Way (an early name for Christianity), whether men or women, he might take them as prisoners to Jerusalem. As he neared Damascus on his journey, suddenly a light from heaven flashed around him. He fell to the ground and heard a voice say to him, 'Saul, Saul, why do you persecute me?' 'Who are you, Lord?' Saul asked. 'I am Jesus whom you are persecuting,' he replied. 'Now get up and go into the city and you will be told what you must do.' The men traveling with Saul stood there speechless; they heard the voice but did not see anyone. Saul got up from the ground, but when he opened his eyes, he could see nothing. So they led him by the hand into Damascus. For three days he was blind and did not eat or drink anything. In Damascus there was a disciple named Ananias. The Lord called to him in a vision, 'Ananias!' 'Yes, Lord,' he answered. The Lord told him, 'Go to the house of Judas on Straight Street and ask for a man from Tarsus named Saul, for he is praying. In a vision he has seen a man named Ananias come and place his hands on him to restore his sight.' 'Lord,' Ananias answered, 'I have heard many reports about this man and all the harm he has done to your saints in Jerusalem. And he has come here with authority from the chief priest to arrest all who call on your name.' But the Lord said to Ananias, 'Go! This man is my chosen instrument to carry my name before the Gentiles and their kings and before the people of Israel. I will show him how much he must suffer for my name.' Then Ananias went to the house and entered it. Placing his hands on Saul, he said, 'Brother Saul, the Lord---Jesus who appeared to you on the road as you were coming here---has sent me so that you may see again and be filled with the Holy Spirit.' Immediately, something like scales fell from Saul's eyes and he could see again. He got up and was baptized and after taking some food, he gained his strength. Saul spent several days with the disciples in Damascus. At once he began to preach in the synagogues that Jesus is the Son of God. All those who heard him were astonished and asked, 'Isn't he the man who raised havoc in Jerusalem among those who call on this name? And hasn't he come here to take them as prisoners to the chief priests?' Yet Saul grew more and more powerful and baffled the Jews living in Damascus by proving that Jesus is the Messiah." Acts 9:1-22

That first Jewish persecution of Christians in c. 34-35, intended to quash the new religion, became instead the vehicle for its expansion into Africa and into Asia Minor.

But God's chosen vessels were still unformed, unfired clay. Paul would spend three years in Arabia before he was ready for his ministry and Peter had a lot to learn about God's love and care for each of His creations. The story of Peter and the Roman centurion Cornelius in Acts 10 is represented in the catacombs. Up until the conversion of Cornelius, Peter's world of evangelism had been confined to spreading the Good News to the Jews throughout Israel and visiting new Jewish believers. Peter was 32 miles away from Jerusalem in the port city of Joppa where 800 years before the Jewish Jonah had fled to escape God's command to go to Gentile Nineveh and preach repentance. Around noon one day in c. 40 AD Peter had a vision of a large sheet containing all kinds of clean and unclean animals, reptiles and birds. A voice commanded, "Get up, Peter. Kill and eat." Peter replied he would never eat anything unclean. The voice said, "Do not call anything impure that God has made clean."

Meanwhile Cornelius had been told by God to send men to Joppa and bring back "a man named Simon who is called Peter. He is staying with Simon the tanner whose house is by the sea." Cornelius was the first recorded Roman Gentile in the New Testament after Pentecost to initiate contact with Jewish Christians. Peter was told by the Spirit to accept the invitation of an unknown, unclean Roman soldier and go to his home in Caesarea. When he arrived at Cornelius' home, a hesitant Peter began his speech to those assembled Romans by telling them it was against Jewish law for him to be in Cornelius' home or even to speak to them:

"You are well aware that it is against our law for a Jew to associate with a Gentile or visit him. But (in visions) God has shown me that I should not call any man impure or unclean." Acts 10:28

As Peter was telling the Gentile gathering about Jesus, the resurrection and the forgiveness of sins, the Holy Spirit fell on Cornelius, his family and friends. They started speaking in tongues like the Apostles at Pentecost. An astonished Peter "ordered that they be baptized in the name of Jesus Christ."

In the Catacomb of Commodilla there is a fresco of Gentile soldiers dressed in Roman military garb. A man on the left has a wand and he has struck a rock from which water is flowing. The soldiers are drinking the water. In Exodus 17:1-6, God commanded Moses to strike a rock with his rod. Water gushed out to quench the thirst of the parched and complaining Israelites. The catacomb artist has made the connection between the Cornelius story, Peter whose name means "rock," the Moses incident and the hidden water in the rock that quenches spiritual thirst and symbolizes baptism. Reluctant Peter, who by baptizing the soldier Cornelius opened the floodgates of Gentile conversions to the freedom of salvation, becomes a type of Moses who led the Israelites out of slavery in Gentile Egypt.

Word of the conversion of the Roman Cornelius' family spread quickly among the Jewish Christians:

"...the apostles and the brothers throughout Judea heard that the Gentiles also had received the word of God. So when Peter went up to Jerusalem, the circumcised believers (Jews) criticized him and said, 'You went into the house of uncircumcised men and ate with them!'" Acts 11:1-3

Rather than rejoicing in the conversion of Cornelius, the Apostles and brothers in Jerusalem were furious with Peter for entering the house of an unclean Gentile. When Peter explained what had occurred, these very early friends of Jesus became resigned to the fact that Jesus was for Gentiles, too:

"When they heard this (Peter's explanation), they had no further objections and praised God saying, 'So then, God has granted even the Gentiles repentance unto life.'" Acts 11:18

After Pentecost and after the persecution following the stoning of Stephen, Christian Jews had fanned out and were preaching the Good News, the *Euangelion* (in Greek means "proclaim good news") solely in Jewish synagogues all over the Hellenized world. As far as the Jews were concerned, Jesus was their Jewish Messiah and He rose from the dead for the redemption of Jews only. But the Cornelius episode began to crack that certainty. For one feisty disciple of Christ, Paul of Tarsus, that exclusive focus on the Jews changed dramatically one Sabbath day in c. 46 AD in the Turkish city of Pisidian Antioch.

3,600' above sea level, Pisidian Antioch was in Roman times a substantial city with good roads, active trade routes and a large Jewish population. Paul was born in c. 5 AD during the reign of Caesar Augustus (27 BC-14 AD) when Pisidian Antioch was an outlaw city besieged and surrounded by pirate kingdoms. In order to bring the Roman Peace to that part of his empire, Augustus bequeathed many land grants to Roman legionnaires who settled there. He sent engineers to construct the Via Sebaste Road that went straight through the city. Under the Roman tactics of military might and mighty roads, Pisidian Antioch had become in Paul's day a stable Roman colony and the capital city of that region.

One of only three surviving copies/fragments of Augustus' *The Deeds* was found in Pisidian Antioch. The first and only complete copy was found by a Dutch scholar named Ogier de Busbecq in 1555 engraved in Latin and Greek on the walls of a ruined Temple to Augustus in Ankara, Turkey. There were, no doubt, numerous copies of *The Deeds* in bronze and stone placed throughout the empire after Augustus' death. Suetonius mentions *The Deeds*:

"(Augustus) made a will a year and four months before his death (14 AD)....consisting of two skins of parchment, written partly in his own hand, and partly by his freedmen Polybius and Hilarian; and they had been committed to the custody of the Vestal Virgins, by whom (at Augustus' death, they were) produced, with three codicils under seal, as well as the will. All these were opened and read in the senate….With regard to the three codicils…in one of them he gave orders about his funeral; another contained a summary of his acts which he intended should be inscribed on brazen plates and placed in front of his mausoleum; in the third he had drawn up a concise account of the state of the empire." *Lives of the Caesars: Augustus*

The copy inscribed on bronze pillars and placed in front of Augustus' mausoleum is lost. Another fragment has been found in Apollonia in eastern Turkey. The Pisidian copy of Augustus' *The Deeds* was found in the early 20th century engraved on the front of the Temple of Augustus. This copy was on display that Jewish Sabbath day in c. 46 in the deified Augustus' temple in Pisidian Antioch near the synagogue where Paul and Barnabas went to worship and to proclaim a new kind of king:

"…(they) sat down. After the reading from the Law and the Prophets, the synagogue rulers sent word to them saying, 'Brothers, if you have a message of encouragement for the people, please speak.' Standing up, Paul motioned with his hand and said: 'Men of Israel and you Gentiles who worship God, listen to me!'" Acts 13:15,16

Paul gave a brief synopsis of God's election of and care for Israel starting with the centuries in Egypt and ending with King David. He genealogically tied Jesus to David, noted the Jerusalem Jews' rejection of Jesus, recounted Jesus' crucifixion and resurrection and ended with the risen Messiah's power to remit sins.

There had always been Gentiles who believed in the one God of the Jews and in the laws of the Mosaic Pentateuch. They were called "God-fearers" and worshipped with the Jews in synagogues all over the Roman Empire. That Saturday Sabbath in c. 46 the Jews and Gentiles received Paul's message and asked him and Barnabas to talk again the next Sabbath:

"On the next Sabbath almost the whole city gathered to hear the word of the Lord. When the Jews saw the crowds, they were filled with jealousy and talked abusively against what Paul was saying. Then Paul and Barnabas answered them boldly. 'We had to speak the word of God to you first. Since you reject it and do not consider yourselves worthy of eternal life, we now turn to the Gentiles'....When the Gentiles heard this, they were glad and honored the word of the Lord." Acts 13:44-48

In the ruins of Pisidian Antioch archaeologists have been digging under the 4th century Basilica of Saint Paul since the early part of the 20th century. They have found what they believe to be the remnants of that 1st century synagogue where Paul preached his first recorded sermon and deliberately decided to become the Apostle to the Gentiles.

X.

"With all the examples from sacred Scriptures before them, the blessed martyrs (in Alexandria Egypt) did not hesitate, but, with the eye of the soul toward God, and a resolve to die for their faith, they held fast to their calling, knowing that our Lord Jesus Christ became man for our sakes to destroy sin and enable us to enter into eternal life. Equal with God, he emptied himself to assume the form of a slave who humbled himself unto death, even death on a cross. So, eagerly desiring the greater gifts, the Christ-bearing martyrs endured suffering and torture devices of every kind….odious torments, some with hands tied behind them were hung from gallows and all their limbs were pulled apart by machines….others were suspended by one hand from a colonnade and hauled up with excruciating pain in their joints and limbs. Others were lashed to pillars with their feet off the ground their body weight pulling the ropes tighter and tighter. This they endured not only while the governor was speaking to them at his leisure but for most of the day….Only at the last gasp were they to be taken down and dragged off….Some died under torture….Others were locked into prison half dead….The rest in time recovered and gained confidence from their imprisonment. But when they were again ordered to choose between touching the abominable sacrifice and gaining an accursed freedom, or not sacrificing and incurring death, without hesitation they went to their death gladly. They knew what the sacred Scriptures have ordained for us: 'Whoever sacrifices to other gods shall be destroyed,' (Exodus 22:20)

and 'You shall have no other gods but me' (Exodus 20:3)." Eusebius, *Church History 8.10*

The first martyrs for Christ were Jewish Christians. Stephen, the first Christian martyr, was stoned to death in Jerusalem in c. 34. James, an Apostle and the elder brother of the Apostle John, was killed by a sword under Herod Agrippa in c. 43. (Acts 12:1,2) Philip the Apostle was scourged, thrown into prison and crucified in c. 54 in Hieropolis (Turkey). The Apostle Matthew, author of the Gospel of Matthew, was killed by a sword while he was preaching in Ethiopia in c. 60. James the Just, Jesus' brother, was thrown from a parapet in Jerusalem and then clubbed to death in c. 62. In c. 62 the Apostle Andrew, Peter's brother, was crucified in Edessa (Turkey) on a cross with two ends affixed to the ground (the St. Andrew's Cross). During the persecution in Rome under Nero in c. 64-67, the Apostle Peter was crucified upside down and Paul, the Apostle to the Gentiles, was beheaded. Mark, Peter's amanuensis and author of the Gospel of Mark, was dragged to pieces in Alexandria (c. 68). Luke, the Greek physician and author of the Gospel and the Book Of Acts, was hanged in Greece. Matthias, chosen to replace Judas as the twelfth Apostle, was stoned and then beheaded in Jerusalem. The Apostles Jude aka Thaddeus and Simon the Zealot were both crucified in c. 72, Jude in Edessa, Simon in Britain. Doubting Thomas went all the way to India to preach the Gospel. He was martyred there in c. 72. His fellow Apostle known as Nathaniel in the East and Bartholomew in Judea was skinned alive in India at about the same time.

Behind the altar of the Sistine Chapel in Rome is a massive fresco called *The Last Judgment* depicting the Biblical Day of Judgment of all souls. St. Bartholomew is painted displaying the empty envelope of his flayed skin in his left hand. The distorted, tortured face on the limp skin is supposedly the face of the painter Michelangelo. Of all the paintings in the Sistine Chapel where Michelangelo could have chosen to hide his own face, he chose the limp skin of the Biblical character he most admired whom Jesus described as "a true Israelite in whom there is nothing false." (John 1:47) Michelangelo was a complicated genius who believed his talent came from God. When he first accepted the commission to do the Sistine Chapel ceiling, he refused pay. Later, he wrote to his brother Lionardo: "Many believe, and I believe, that I have been designated for this work by God....I do not want to give it up; I work out of love for God and I put all my hope in Him."

Many of the very earliest martyrs who put all their hope in Him were not only the Jewish men who had known Jesus and had accepted Him as the Messiah, but they are the Jewish Apostles of the faith. As the first three centuries of Christianity progressed, however, there were more Gentiles killed because they accepted the Jewish Messiah than there were Jews.

In the 20th century AD there were more Christians killed because of their faith in the Jewish Messiah than in all the centuries of Christian persecution combined. 65% of all Christians who have ever been persecuted or martyred lived in the years from 1900-2000. Antonio Socci, an Italian journalist, estimates that 45 million Christians were martyred in the 20th century. *The New Persecuted: Inquiries into Anti-Christian Intolerance in the New Century Of The Martyrs* This number is considered high by some. Most of the organizations that monitor human rights and Christian agencies that calculate Christian persecutions and deaths estimate the number of Christians killed in the last century as 15-20 million---still a shocking number.

The 20th century commenced with the Massacre of the Armenian Christians beginning on April 24, 1915 and continuing in the years after World War I. The Turkish Muslim government decided that the Christian "race" was a danger to their national unity. In order to settle what they called "the Armenian question," they systematically killed 1.5 million Christian Armenians.

When the atheist Communists took over Russia in 1917, they spent the next seven decades deliberately suppressing, exiling and killing an estimated 20 million Christians (17 million Russian Orthodox and 3 million Roman Catholic).

After the Communist revolution in Mexico and the new Constitution in 1917, the atheist government began a vigorous campaign against the Catholic Church. The State outlawed religious orders, took away the clergy's right to vote and restricted rights to worship. A people's army, the Cristeros (Fighters for Christ), rose up against the atheists and more than 30,000 of them were killed. 40 priests were assassinated between 1926-1934. By the end of 1934, there were only 334 priests licensed to minister to 15,000,000 Mexicans.

In Spain 13 bishops, 4,172 priests and seminarians, 2,364 monks and 283 nuns were killed by atheist Leftists during the Spanish Civil War (1936-1939). Synagogues, Protestant churches and Catholic churches were burned, pillaged or closed. In Franco's Fascist Spain (1939-1975), the country's 30,000 Protestants were persecuted and many were forced to leave the country. All non-Catholic Bibles were prohibited and were confiscated by the police.

When Hitler came to power in Germany in 1933, his avowed purpose was "to settle the Jewish question" forever. When Titus had destroyed Jerusalem in 70, the Romans felt they "had settled the Jewish problem" forever. Before World War II there were 9,000,000 Jews living in Europe. When World War II was over, there were 3,000,000 Jews in Europe. Hitler had killed 90% of the Jews in Poland; 70% of the Jews in Yugoslavia, Hungary, the Netherlands and Greece; 50% of all the Jews in Norway, Estonia, Romania and Belgium; over 30% of all the Jews in Russia and 25% of the Jews in France and Italy. The Nazis killed two out of every three people who were of the same race and ethnicity as was Jesus of Nazareth.

Hitler and his propagandists correctly linked the religion of Christianity with the Jews:

"The Fuhrer is deeply religious, though completely anti-Christian. He views Christianity as a symptom of decay. Rightly so. It is a branch of the Jewish race....Both (Judaism and Christianity)...in the end, they will be destroyed." Joseph Goebbels (Nazi Minister Of Propaganda), *The Goebbels Diaries: Entry on December 29, 1939*

Germany was a nominally Christian country. The Nazis first forced believing Christians underground. They became the Confessing Church. When the Confessing Church was taken to the death camps, there was no longer a Christian opposition to Hitler. The German people, like the Turkish people during the Armenian genocide, went along with the Nazis even when the killings included their Christian neighbors, Gypsies, Communists, the mentally handicapped (target of the Euthanasia Project), homosexuals and Jehovah's Witnesses.

Hitler and the Nazi ideology were antithetical to both God and the better angels of human nature. In trying to build a Darwinian/ Nietzschean race of fit, smart, blue-eyed, blond-haired people, the dark-haired Hitler massacred 60,000,000 people all over Europe. His experiments in conquest and eugenics should have been a final lesson to mankind. They were not.

During Mao Zedong's ten-year Cultural Revolution Of The Proletariat (1966-1976), it is estimated he killed from 30-70 million Chinese. People who wore glasses were killed because they knew how to read and cared about learning. Untold numbers of Christians were killed because they were theists and would not renounce their faith in Christ. The atheist Communist "Great March Forward" ended with Mao's death in 1976. In the decades following his death, however, the number of Christians in China has exploded to between 60-80 million believers. The Christians in China are today the largest single persecuted community.

In 1983 in the Sudan, the northern, fundamentalist Muslim government, the Khartoum, declared "holy war" (*jihad*) against the Christians in southern Sudan. As in all attempts at genocide, the object was to kill only certain people. In the last three decades the Janjaweed, the Arab-speaking Muslim militia, have killed 2 million Sudanese Christians and 4 million people have been displaced and are in refugee camps.

When the jihadists capture a Sudanese, they ask, "Are you Christian or Muslim?" If it is a man and he replies, "Christian," he is slaughtered. Christian women are gang-raped, have their breasts cut off and are left to die as an example to others. In the days of Rome's persecution of Christians, they were asked, "Are you a Christian?" If they answered, "I am a Christian," they were killed. 2,000 years later Christians in the Sudan are martyred by their answer to that same question.

On July 9, 2011 the Republic of South Sudan was born in a ceremony attended by the head of the United Nations, dozens of heads of state and a quarter of a million southern Sudanese who sang and danced to a Christian hymn, "I Have Decided To Follow Jesus." Dr. Daniel Madit Thon Duop who had left the Sudan at age 13 returned on that day to live and to serve as a Christian surgeon in this new land of freedom. "Our crime of being a Christian in the United Sudan is over," he cried. Not true, unfortunately. Northern Sudan continues to bomb, rape and kidnap Christians from South Sudan.

The radical group Boko Haram, meaning "Western education is sin," is an anti-Christian Islamist group in Nigeria dedicated to establishing Sharia (wide-ranging body of Muslim fundamentalist laws) in that country and cleansing it of Christians. Boko Haram killed over 600 Christians in 2011-2012. On August 7, 2012 three men from Boko Haram entered a Bible study in a Christian church in Otite, Nigeria and opened fire, killing at least 19 Christians at the Deeper Life Church. In the middle of the night of December 2, 2012 they slaughtered 10 Christians in Chibok, Nigeria and then burned down their houses.

When World Vision, a Christian relief organization dedicated to working with children and the world's most vulnerable people, was in Islamabad, Pakistan working with victims of the 2005 Kashmir earthquake that killed 80,000 people, its offices were broken into and six people were dragged one by one into a room and shot because the terrorists said that Christian aid organizations were "working against the tenets of Islam and hampering Islam's efforts to raise their standard of living." *CBN.COM March 12, 2010*

In most Muslim countries there are anti-conversion laws in effect. Such laws prohibit a citizen from converting from Islam to any other religion on penalty of fines, imprisonment and/or death. These laws against "religious freedom" are strictly enforced in Afghanistan, Pakistan, Iran, Saudi Arabia and other Muslim countries. Predominantly Hindu India, also, has anti-conversion laws.

The largest Christian population in any Muslim country are the Coptic Christians of Egypt whose faith was established by St. Mark in the 60's AD. Ever since the fall of Egypt to Muslim forces in the

7th century AD, Egypt's Coptic Christians have been a provocation to sporadic persecutions by the majority Muslims. In 1956 when Gamel Abdul Nassar came to power, he nationalized all private businesses, most of them owned by Christians, and tens of thousands of Copts were forced to flee to Europe and America. The uprising of Egyptians demanding freedom and jobs in Tahrir Square on Tuesday, January 25, 2011 seemed a hopeful sign for Egyptian Christians and Muslims who demonstrated side by side. Their sectarian dictator, Hosni Mubarak, resigned on February 11, 2011 and the military junta took over. Within a month Christian persecutions began. 13 Christians were killed and 140 injured in Cairo by Muslims on March 8, 2011 during a Christian demonstration against attacks upon their churches. On Sunday October 9, 2011 Coptic Christians in Cairo marched in protest against the burning of a Christian church in Aswan. Military tanks plowed into them and live ammunition was fired. 24 Christians were killed. During their burial service in St. Mark's Cathedral in the Abassiyeh section of Cairo, some of the congregants held up the blood-stained shirts and trousers of the dead and cried, "With our souls and blood we sacrifice ourselves for the cross." Those words could have been confessed by their brothers and sisters all over the world for the last 2,000 years. In China and in Arab countries, as in ancient Rome, it is *non licet esse Christianos.* It is forbidden to be a Christian.

Some of these anti-conversion laws have been challenged by the evangelical Christian community's missionary efforts in the 10/40 Window. Those countries in the eastern hemisphere located between 10 and 40 degrees north of the equator hold two-thirds of the world's population and have the most restricted access to the Christian message. Since the 1990's Christians have progressively targeted that Window for evangelization. As the Christian faith has spread to and throughout these countries, the governments have reacted with the same restrictions and persecutions as the early Romans did. The Age of the Martyrs is not confined to the Early Church.

In the Early Church there was what is called the Cult of the Martyrs. The Greek word *marty*r or *martus* means "witness" or "testifier." The word *martus* was originally a judicial word used for a witness or testator in legal proceedings. The word, also, was used to denote someone who testified about what he/she had seen or heard. Originally, a Christian martyr was one who witnessed or testified to his/her faith in Christ by the life he/she lived or one who bore testimony to the power of Christ and to God's faithfulness. In Revelation 2:13 a man named Antipas is described as "my faithful witness (*martus*) who was put to death in your city" (Pergamum). But it was not until the martyrdom of Polycarp in c. 155 that the word "martyr" evolved to denote exclusively one who witnessed to his/her faith by dying for Christ. In the early years of the catacombs a martyr's grave was designated by "MRT" or simply "M."

Today "martyr" has many connotations in addition to a "person who willingly dies rather than renounce his/her faith." A martyr can be a person who seeks sympathy by exaggerating his/her pain, circumstances, deprivation; a person who undergoes constant suffering. Muslims use the word "martyr" for those who willingly kill themselves and others for Allah. Islam likely appropriated the word "martyr" from Christian terminology and Muslims have used the word since the 700's. The difference between the Christian context of the word and the Islamic application is the difference between being killed for your faith and killing for your faith.

It is natural and appropriate to venerate those who are killed not because they have done illegal acts but simply because they believe certain things. It is, also, natural to want to see the places where religious martyrs are buried. Early believers, however, went to inordinate lengths to pay homage to martyrs.

When some Christians died, they wanted to be buried close to the spot in the catacombs where a martyr was laid to rest. Those who could afford it paid exorbitant prices to the fossors to get a choice spot near Agnes or Sebastian or other Christian martyrs. There are places in the catacombs where tombs have been dug perpendicular to a popular martyr or under the tomb of a martyr. These graves are called *retro sanctos* meaning "behind the holy one." Tombs dug into the floor of a crypt are called *formae*. *Formae* are very numerous near martyr's tombs. There seemed to be the belief that if your dead body lay physically close to a martyr's dead body, you would not be overlooked at the resurrection of the dead.

The Cult of the Martyrs began very early after Peter and Paul were killed in c. 64-67. In the second century, pilgrims began to scribble messages to Peter and Paul and other prominent martyrs on the walls of the catacombs:

"Paul and Peter. Intercede for Victor." Catacomb of St. Sebastian
"Peter and Paul. Pray for us." Catacomb of St. Sebastian

These scribbles or graffiti are the first evidence in Jewish or early Christian writing of a belief in the intermediating power of the dead no matter how holy they were when alive. The Old and the New Testaments are totally silent on the ability of a dead person to intercede with God on behalf of anyone. The New Testament states:

"For there is one God and one mediator between God and men, the man Christ Jesus, who gave himself a ransom for all men." I Timothy 2:5

The Old Testament states:

"I am the Lord your God....You shall have no other gods before me. You shall not make for yourself an idol....You shall not bow down to them to worship them." Exodus 20:2-5

As the centuries progressed, the natural veneration of the martyrs became the worship of the martyrs, the Cult of the Martyrs. "Cult" comes from the Latin word *cultus* meaning "cultivation, tending, care." Its common use was in connection with agriculture and farming. A man "cult-ivated" his land. The cultivation of the Cult of the Martyrs was a slow and organic process that had nothing to do with Biblical injunctions but everything to do with peoples' natural inclinations.

Because of the heroic nature of their deaths, the martyrs were thought by the masses to have great power in heaven. With that increased power went the ability to intercede to God on behalf of the living. The martyr was, the humble people reasoned, particularly favored by God. Thus God would listen to them rather than to plebeian "Victor" or "Hermes" or "Agatha."

It was common for people to extract from those about to be martyred the promise to win from God pardon for sins committed by those still alive. After the martyr's death, therefore, a lapsed petitioner believed that his forgiveness had been achieved by the martyr's promise and that he should be readmitted into the fellowship of the church without the onerous process of penance.

Cyprian, bishop of Carthage in North Africa from c. 248-258, resisted these strange, non-Biblical beliefs. He was opposed to the Cult of the Martyrs and to the easy grace some priests extended to those who had betrayed the faith or had committed outrageous sins. Rather than petition martyrs to win their way back into fellowship, Cyprian argued for true and prolonged repentance for sin as the only Biblical way to absolution and restoration. From exile he wrote to the church in Carthage:

"...control the minds of the lapsed by counsel and by your own moderation according to the Divine Precepts. Let no one pluck the unripe fruit at a time as yet premature. Let no one commit his ship, shattered and broken with the waves, anew to the deep before he has carefully repaired it. Let none be in haste to accept and to put on a rent tunic unless he has seen it mended by a skillful workman and has received it arranged by the fuller." *Epistle 11.3*

In spite of the good and poetic counsel of Godly men, the people and the local priests continued their adoration and worship of martyrs. Some of the martyrs became famous for their method of martyrdom or their age of martyrdom or their journey to martyrdom. These laudable men and women were idolized over the years by the growing body of Christians and were incrementally imbued with heavenly powers that would or could affect earthly actions. Prayers to these dead martyrs as if to gods became common and were scrawled on the walls of the catacombs from the very earliest times:

"Martyrs. Holy. Good. Blessed. Help Quiracus." Catacomb of Pamphilus

"Marcellinus and Peter. Intercede For Gallicanos The Christian." Catacomb of Peter and Marcellinus

"O, Sixtus. Remember In Your Prayers Aurelius Repentinus." Catacomb of St. Callixtus

"Holy Spirits. Pray That Verecundus May Be Safe At Sea With His Dear Ones." Catacomb of St. Callixtus

After eons of paganism and polytheism, some Christian converts had a difficult time invoking and worshiping only one God. The local priests and bishops tolerated and often encouraged the adoration of and prayers to local or popular martyrs. But there were always Christian churches and leaders who were able to negotiate the difference between venerating a martyr and idolizing a martyr. After Polycarp and eleven other Christians were martyred in c. 155, the church in Smyrna (in Turkey) wrote to the other churches:

"...we can never abandon Christ to worship anyone else. Him we worship as the Son of God, the martyrs we love as disciples and imitators of the Lord....We worthily venerate the martyrs as disciples and imitators of the Lord and for their supreme fidelity towards their King and Master, and may it be granted to us also to become their companions and fellow-disciples....Having collected the bones of Polycarp, more precious than rare gems and purer than the finest gold, we laid them to rest in the appointed place. And meeting in this place of exultation and joy whenever we can, the Lord will allow us to celebrate the anniversary of his martyrdom, remembering all who have faced the same struggle and asking for strength for those who will face it in the future." *Martyrium Polycarpi 18. 2-3*

The leaders of the church in Smyrna hewed to the Biblical position of veneration and honor to martyrs rather than quasi-deification. Several hundred years later Eusebius in *Church History, 8.6* dismisses the idea that any dead martyr would ever be adored as a god by Christians:

"Whole families and groups (in Nicomedia) were butchered with the sword by imperial command, while others were fulfilled by fire.... Executioners bound many others and threw them into the sea from boats. As for the imperial servants already buried with appropriate honors, their bodies were dug up and thrown into the sea also, under the absurd notion that otherwise in their very graves they would be worshipped (by us) as gods!"

After the first Christian martyr Stephen was stoned, "Godly men buried Stephen and mourned deeply for him." (Acts 8:2) The first believers did not make of Stephen an idol to petition and to worship. The Old and New Testament positions have always been that upon death, holy and Godly or martyred people should be mourned, revered and held up as examples to the Jewish and Christian communities. There is no Biblical example of praying to a dead person or petitioning God through a dead person.

The very earliest formal statement of Christian beliefs, The Apostles' Creed (c. 125 AD or earlier), makes no mention of martyrs. The Nicene Creed of 325 makes no mention of an elevated heavenly status for those killed for the sake of Christ. Scripture and the early statements of Christian belief are silent about the efficacy of prayers to and through martyrs and about a martyr's ability to act as an intermediator between God and man.

It was many centuries before the universal Church began to grapple doctrinally with the people's Cult of the Martyrs. Almost 1,000 years after the resurrection of Christ, the Church in Rome declared its first Saint, St. Ulrich of Augsburg, in 993. His name begins a list called the "canon" composed of people over the centuries who have been the subjects of popular devotion by the faithful. Some of these men and women had been martyred, but many were faithful people who had lived exemplary lives. In the 13th century Pope Gregory IX (1227-1241) further organized the list of people in the canon, but it was Sixtus V (1585-90) who first set up a formal procedure for canonization and beatification.

When a person is beatified by the Roman Catholic Church, he or she is fiatly declared "ascended to Heaven." There he/she has the capacity to intercede with God on behalf of individuals who pray in his/her name. The process of canonization that posthumously declares a person a "saint" is a rigorous trial of the proposed person's life and subsequent miracles. If the legal-like trial finds the person worthy, he/she is canonized and is publicly declared to be an effective intercessor on behalf of the living. The canonized person is henceforth called Saint Basil or Saint Theresa, et al. There are currently about 10,000 Saints in the Roman Catholic Church's canon. Over a 1,500-year period the Roman Church gradually meandered its way to a man-made doctrine that caters to the same innate needs of worship and adoration of the honorable we see scribbled on the walls of the Roman catacombs in the early years of the Christian faith.

The word "saint" comes from the Latin word *sanctus* meaning "holy, consecrated." In the New Testament, "saint" only denotes a believer in Christ. According to the Bible, any one who has accepted Jesus as Savior is a Christian saint:

"As Peter traveled the country, he went to see the saints in Lydda." Acts 9:32
"To all in Rome who are loved by God and called to be saints." Romans 1:7
"Greet one another with a holy kiss. All the saints send their greetings." II Corinthians 13:13
"To all the saints in Christ Jesus at Philippi…Grace and peace to you." Philippians 1:1

The Church in Rome incrementally appropriated the word "saint" (abbreviated to "St./Ste.") to denote only those who had lived lives of uncommon virtue and "whom the Church honors as saints….by a solemn definition called canonization. The Church's official recognition of sanctity implies that the persons are now in heavenly glory (have been beatified), that they may be publicly invoked everywhere, and that their virtues during life or martyr's death are a witness and example to the Christian faithful." *Modern Catholic Dictionary*

The Biblical use of the word "saint" and the Roman Catholic use of the word "saint" are not congruous. However, there were, are and will be men and women dedicated to the Lord who live saintly lives or who serve as examples of sanctity and holiness or who were/are/will be killed because they are Christians.

One of these examples for us of holiness and dedication to the Lord was a little 12 to 13-year-old girl named Agnes. She was a widely revered martyr in the Church. After her martyrdom, probably under the persecution of Diocletian (c. 304), Agnes became a heroine and an intercessor to God for some believers.

Pope Damasus (c. 304-384) who encouraged hagiolatry composed a panegyric to her. The visitor to the Catacomb of Agnes on the Via Nomentana can see his poem engraved on a marble slab at the foot of the stairs leading into the catacombs:

"It is told that one day the holy parents recounted that Agnes, when the trumpet sounded its sad tunes, suddenly left the lap of her nurse while still a little girl and willingly trod upon the rage and threats of the cruel tyrant (Emperor). Though he desired to burn the noble body in flames, with her little forces she overcame immense fear and gave her loosened hair to cover her naked limbs lest mortal eyes might see the temple of the Lord."

Agnes was tortured, set on fire and finally beheaded. St. Ambrose (c. 340-397) was the first to write of her in *De virginibus 1.2.5-9*. He says only that she was a young virgin who was beheaded. Prudentius in c. 405 further embellished Agnes' story in a hymn extolling her. *Peristephanon 14*. He states that she was taken to a brothel to be violated. A young man who lusted her was struck blind.

The Early Church rightly venerated young Agnes for her valor, her virginity and her boldness. *Agnus* is the Latin word meaning "lamb, sheep." Her sacrifice as a young "lamb" and the holiness of the Lamb of God for whom she died resonated. She is frequently pictured and sculpted with a little lamb in her arms or by her feet.

Agnes was the first person to be buried in the catacomb that bears her name on the Via Nomentana. There are only about 7,000 people buried in her humble, cramped and neglected Catacomb. Outside her catacomb is an imposing dome-shaped mausoleum built by the Emperor Constantine for his daughter Constantina. She was devoted to Agnes and was buried there in c. 360.

During the excavations at the Baroque Church of St. Agnes in the Piazza Navona in 1901, a silver sarcophagus was found. It contained the headless bones of a young girl. Today those bones rest in a 17"-18"silver sarcophagus under the altar of the church at her Catacomb. Over her tomb there had been a slab with the inscription Agne Sanctissima, "Agnes the Holiest." In about 1652 her head was found and given to the church that bears her name in the Piazza Navona, the modern site of the ancient Roman Circus of Hadrian where Agnes was martyred. An examination of the skull has determined it is that of a 12 to 13-year-old girl.

The Catacomb of St. Sebastian on the Via Appia is named after a famous Christian martyr of the 3rd century---Sebastian. Sebastian was born in Narbonne, France in c. 256 to Italian parents and raised in Milan. We do not know when he became a Christian. His biographies, written a hundred years after his martyrdom, open with Sebastian as a soldier in the Roman army:

"…his natural inclination gave him an aversion to military life, but to be better able, without suspicion, to assist the confessors and martyrs in their suffering, he went to Rome and entered the army under Emperor Carinus about the year 283." *Acts Of St. Sebastian* (c. 400)

The Roman military was a fruitful mission field for the Christian message. A Christian soldier did not, however, have divided loyalties. An inscription in the Catacomb of St. Callixtus memorializes a Christian soldier:

"His friends' memories keep the record of Theodulus who died with military honors. His loyalty was outstanding among non-commissioned officers. He was faithful to all fellow-soldiers and friends. His reputation declares him a servant of God rather than of money and an upright official of the city prefecture. If I were able, I would sing his praise forever so that he may be granted the promised gifts of light."

Sebastian like Theodolus was "a servant of God," was a soldier with a mission. He felt God had called him to the military to evangelize and to help soldiers like the twin brothers, Marcus and Marcellinus, who were sentenced to death because of their faith in Christ. The boys' heathen parents and friends had come to the prison to visit the twins and by their tears, supplications and pleadings, they had weakened the brothers' resolve:

"Sebastian…stepped in and made them a long exhortation to constancy, which he delivered with the holy fire that strongly affected all his hearers….the parents of Marcus and Marcellinus, the jailer Claudius, and sixteen other prisoners were converted." *Acts Of Sebastian*

The twin brothers were released but later rearrested and died after being nailed together on a cross and then stabbed. The Catacomb of Marcus and Marcellinus on the east side of the Via Ardeatina is named after them.

Sebastian not only had gifts of exhortation and evangelism, but he had the gift of healing. While he was preaching in that jail, the warden's wife was healed of a stroke that had left her mute. This miracle led to a chain reaction. Her husband, the warden Nicostratus, freed all the prisoners, took them to his home and called for a priest to baptize all of them. When Chromatius, the governor (mayor) of Rome heard that Tranquillinus, the twins' father, had been healed of gout the moment he was baptized, he wanted to be healed of his gout. He sent for Sebastian, was healed and he and his son Tiburtious were baptized. After his conversion, governor Chromatius resigned his prefecture with the Emperor's consent, freed all his slaves and "retired into the country of Campania taking many new converts along with him." *Acts Of Sebastian*

Sebastian was a powerful force for Christ in the military. Many soldiers were converted and subsequently martyred for their faith. Soon it was Sebastian's turn:

"St. Sebastian, having sent so many martyrs to heaven before him, was himself impeached before the Emperor Diocletian (284-305), who... delivered him over to certain archers of Mauritania (country in western Africa), to be shot to death. His body was covered with arrows and left for dead. Irene the widow of Castulus, going to bury him, found him still alive and took him to her lodgings, where...he recovered his wounds, but refused to flee and even placed himself one day by a staircase where the Emperor Diocletian was to pass, whom he...accosted, reproaching him for his unjust cruelties against the Christians. This freedom of speech, and from a person, too, whom he supposed to have been dead, greatly astonished the Emperor; but, recovering from his surprise, he gave orders for him to be seized and beat to death with cudgels, and his body thrown into the common sewer. A pious lady called Lucina... got (the body) privately removed and buried it in the catacombs at the entrance of the cemetery of Callixtus." *Acts Of Sebastian*

Before he was killed, Sebastian had requested that he be buried "*ad catacumbus*, at the entrance of the crypt, near the memorial of the Apostles." *Acts Of Sebastian* After his death in c. 288, Sebastian's body was placed in the catacombs, since named after him, where the remains of Peter and Paul had once been. In 826 Pope Eugenius II gave Sebastian's body to the Abbot of St. Denys in France. Pope Sergius later gave Sebastian's head to St. Willibrord in Luxemburg. Other relics of Sebastian and parts of his body are scattered all over Europe: in Paris, Mantua, Malacca, Seville, Toulouse, Munich, Tournay, Antwerp and in a chapel in Brussels. In the hierarchy of the Cult of the Martyrs Sebastian was very popular and any tiny relic of him was desired and cherished.

Almost two thousand years after St. Sebastian's death, the Roman Catholic Church still seeks and reveres relics from the holy dead. Marie-Bernade Soubirous, St. Bernadette, a young French girl from Lourdes, France had a series of visions of "a small young lady" in 1858. The Catholic Church declared the "lady" the Virgin Mary, Our Lady of Lourdes. Lourdes subsequently has become a mecca for the sick and needy who have been healed there. Bernadette went into a convent where she died of tuberculosis in 1879 at the age of 35. Her well-preserved body has been disinterred twice to obtain relics. In April of 1919, Drs. Talon and Comte wrote that they "removed the rear section of the 5th and 6th right ribs as relics…(as well as) a piece of the diaphragm…. two patella bones….muscle fragments right and left from the outsides of the thighs." Again on August 3, 1925, they disinterred her body and Dr. Comte took as relics "two right ribs." Supposedly, these bone and muscle parts have found their way around the world as have the relics of St. Sebastian. Thomas Merton (1915-1968), Trappist monk and religious syncretist, listed among his many relics "bone fragments from St. Bernadette Soubirous" accompanied by a certificate of authenticity. Any physical fragment of a holy one has always been venerated.

Attitudes toward martyrs and the Cult of the Martyrs were not the only sources of friction in the Early Church. In the Judeo-Christian religion there has always been fierce disagreement between those who believe it is acceptable to fashion and to enjoy images of deity or holiness and those who believe it is a violation of God's commandment in Exodus 20:4:

"You shall not make for yourself an idol in the form of anything in heaven above or on the earth beneath or in the waters below. You shall not bow down to them or worship them: for I, the Lord your God, am a jealous God."

No images of God or of Christ have been found during the first two hundred years of the catacombs. It was wise to display symbols that were cryptic and would be understood only by the believers such as the *Chi-Rho*, a symbol of an "X" with a "P" superimposed over it.

"Chi=X" and "Rho=P" are the first two letters of the name "Christ" in Greek. "Christ" in Greek means "anointed" and is a direct translation of the Hebrew word "Masiah" (Messiah) meaning "anointed one." The use of the Chi-Rho denoted believers who acknowledged Jesus as the Jewish Messiah, as the Christ. In a world where the Greek language was preeminent, the early Christians were called such because of their reverence for the Christ, the Messiah of the Jews. Christians are not named after Jesus but after His Messiah-ship.

The Pio Cristiano Museum at the Vatican contains many early Christian sculptures, gravestones and sarcophagi. Most of the sarcophagi in the days of the Early Church are of marble or stone, but original sarcophagi were often made of limestone. A limestone sarcophagus reportedly consumed the entire corpse within 40 days. Attesting to this phenomenon, the word "sarcophagus" comes from two Greek words meaning "flesh-eating."

One gravestone in the Pio Cristiano has a perfectly chiseled Chi-Rho surrounded by a victor's wreath. To the left of the monograph is a decent rendering of a wine or cooper's barrel signifying the profession of the dead Christian. To the right of the Chi-Rho is his name "SEBERUS." The engraver did not correctly calculate the amount of space left on the stone. After "S-E-B-E-R-U," there was no space left for "S." It is crudely added below under the first "E." In the catacombs, Chi-Rhos, *Chrismons* meaning monograms of Christ, and other Christograms are etched into the walls by visitors as well as carved on marble sarcophagi. The Chi-Rho symbol is still used on altar cloths, priestly vestments and on church banners in both Protestant and Catholic churches.

The British Museum has a fine collection of early Christian engraved objects. There are many Christian rings. Most of the rings display symbols meaningful to the faithful: an anchor, fish, dove, sheep, olive and palm branches, the word *ICHTHUS* (the acrostic for Christ/Fish) and the phrase *Vivas In Deo*, ("May You Live In God"). There are 5th century Christian engravings on ivory: large pieces sculpted with scenes from the Passion that originally formed the sides of a casket; panels representing Pilate washing his hands, Christ carrying His cross and Judas hanged. In the early centuries of Christianity when the

220

movement was still under the influence of the Jews, it would have been blasphemy to depict Jesus carrying a cross or to draw a cross, but the superimposed Greek letters Chi-Rho resemble a cross. The cross as a symbol of Christianity did not become popular until the 5th century.

The trial before Pontius Pilate, the Crucifixion and the Resurrection are never represented in catacomb art. The early Christians were tied to Jewish traditions and Old Testament commandments that forbade any depictions pictorially or materially that could possibly become iconic. In the Jewish Catacombs in Rome there are paintings of the shofar and the menorah, but none of deity. Jews had and some still have a taboo against pronouncing even the tetragrammaton, the four syllable name of God. The four Hebrew letters *YHWH* signifying "Yahweh" (meaning "I AM") were considered too holy to be spoken. If uttering God's name was forbidden, it was double anathema to attempt to portray His image.

As the Jewish influence began to wane in the 3rd century, however, paintings of a Romanized Christ began to appear in catacomb art: seated at a Communion table with His disciples; talking to the woman at the well; looking back at the woman who touched the hem of His garment and was healed of a bleeding issue. Eusebius claims to have seen in c. 300 an old bronze statue of Jesus related to this miracle :

"Since I have mentioned this city (Caesarea Philippi), I should not omit a story that should be recorded also for those who follow us. The woman with a bleeding hemorrhage who was cured by our Savior, as we learn from the holy Gospels (Mark 5:25-34), came from here, they claim. Her house was pointed out in the city and amazing memorials of the Savior's benefit to her were still there. On a high stone base at the gates of her home stood a bronze statue of a woman on bent knee stretching out her hands like a suppliant. Opposite to this was another statue of the same material---a standing figure of a man clothed in a handsome double cloak and reaching his hand out to the woman. Near his feet on the monument grew an exotic herb that climbed up to the hem of the bronze double cloak and served as an antidote for diseases of every kind. This statue, they said, resembled the features of Jesus and was still extant in my own time. I saw it with my own eyes when I stayed in the city. It is not surprising that those Gentiles who long ago were benefited by our Savior should have made these things, since I have examined likenesses of his apostles also---Peter and Paul---and in fact of Christ Himself preserved in color portrait paintings. And this is to be expected since ancient Gentiles customarily honored them as Saviors in this unreserved fashion." Eusebius, *Church History 7.18*

In this passage we learn for the first time that the Biblical woman "subject to bleeding for twelve years" was a Gentile who lived in Caesarea Philippi within the Golan Heights. To honor her healing, she had commissioned two statues, one of her and one of Jesus, to be placed at the gates of her home. Eusebius did not believe in fashioning religious images and gently chides the woman's "ancient Gentile" propensity to create images "in this unreserved fashion" that could become idols or, as he says, "Saviors."

This same Eusebius was upset with a letter he had received from Constantia, Constantine the Great's sister, asking to see portraits of Jesus and the Apostles still extant in their day (c. 325). In a fragment of his letter that still survives, he replies:

"Such practices (of painting portraits of Jesus or other holy people) are illegal for us....Are not such things (paintings and icons) excluded and banished from churches all over the world. (The icons should be destroyed) lest we appear, like the idol worshippers, to carry our God around in an image." *Letter to Constantia*

The orthodox Church in the 4th century clearly held to the views of the Jews and of the Old Testament's 2nd commandment.

The most represented image in catacomb art is of Christ as the Good Shepherd. In the ancient world sheep provided wool, milk, cheese and meat and the shepherd of the sheep was the person who led the sheep to good pastures, risked his life to protect them from wild animals, gave help to the sheep who were injured, kept an accurate account of them, looked for those who were lost and made sure they were safe at night.

Hammurabi of Babylon (c. 1750 BC) and other rulers throughout Mesopotamia were all called "shepherds." The kings of Israel were expected by God to be shepherds of His people (II Samuel 5:2) and the New Testament word for "pastor" from the Latin *pastorem* literally means "shepherd."

Most of the Good Shepherd images in catacomb paintings and in sculptures portray a young Roman shepherd with a sheep flung over his shoulders meant to evoke passages in Scripture about Christ as the shepherd who goes after the lost sheep, finds it and brings it home as well as the shepherd who protects, pastures and lays down his life for his flock:

"I am the good shepherd. The good shepherd lays down his life for his sheep....I am the good shepherd. I know my sheep and my sheep know me---just as the Father knows me and I know the Father---and I lay down my life for the sheep." John 10:11-15

"Suppose one of you has a hundred sheep and loses one of them. Does he not leave the ninety-nine in the open country and go after the lost sheep until he finds it? And when he finds it, he joyfully puts it on his shoulders and goes home. Then he calls his friends and neighbors together and says, 'Rejoice with me; I have found my lost sheep.' I tell you that in the same way there will be more rejoicing in heaven over one sinner who repents than over ninety-nine righteous persons who do not need to repent." Luke 15:4-7

"The Lord is my shepherd, I shall not be in want. He makes me to lie down in green pastures. He leads me beside quiet water. He restores my soul." Psalm 23:1,2

Sometimes Jesus as the Good Shepherd has a goat flung over his shoulders: "When the Son of Man comes in his glory...he will sit on his glorious throne. All the nations will be gathered before him and he will separate the people one from another as a shepherd separates the sheep from the goats. He will put the sheep on his right and the goats on his left." Matthew 25:31-33 How the catacomb Christians rejoiced. They, the goats, the ones who had been shut out of the heavenly kingdom and lost in paganism, had been found and rescued by Jesus, the Good Shepherd. The early Christians artistically used the Biblical metaphor of the shepherd to evince the redeeming work of Christ and of His care for believers---Jew and Gentile. There is no attempt to depict Jesus as the man He was in catacomb art. An idyllic young Roman shepherd could not become an icon, they reasoned.

Religious paintings and sculptures are by nature visual and tangible. The flock could become attached to them and turn them into objects of veneration if not actual worship as the pagans had done for thousands of years with their idols. "Idol" comes from the Greek word *eidolon* meaning "appearance, reflection in water or a mirror." That Greek word was appropriated by the New Testament writers (e.g. I Corinthians 8:4) as an accurate description of the narcissistic nature of the images worshipped by pagans. The man-made images were, as the word implies, simply a reflection of the man who made them. When man looked at his idols, he was looking at himself, not at God.

Those who believed that "God is Spirit" (John 4:24) and that it is not possible and even sacrilegious to worship the immaterial through the material were called "Iconoclasts," "image-breakers." They vehemently objected, as did the Early Church, to religious portrayals and icons and often physically smashed them to pieces to the horror and wrath of those who believed that illiterate people needed tangible objects of worship and veneration and that God Himself became tangible in Jesus. Those who defended icons were called "Iconophiles," "image lovers."

As in the dispute over the *lapsii* in the years of Roman persecution, the Church hardened into two factions. The Iconoclasts Tertullian, Clement of Alexandria, Eusebius of Caesarea and Origen had all rejected any representation of Jesus or martyrs in art. John of Damascus, Theodore the Studite and Patriarch Nikephoros I were Iconophiles who wrote Apologies favoring the use of icons.

During the time of Pope Gregory the Great (590-604) in Rome, the worship/veneration of icons had reached a boiling point. Gregory, an Iconophile, declared: "...painting can do for the illiterate what reading does for those who read." That seemed to settle the dispute for a while, but the real battle had not been decisively won.

The first serious outbreak of Iconoclasm (730-787) erupted in the Eastern Church at Constantinople. In 726 the Eastern Byzantine Emperor Leo III, under the influence of the Eastern Orthodox Church, had published a decree declaring all images were idols and ordering their destruction. Monks and local priests, who were the chief defenders of icons, were persecuted and their church images were destroyed. In 730 the Western Pope Gregory III formally condemned Iconoclasts, declared them heretics and excommunicated them. In defiance, the Eastern Emperor Constantine V convened the Synod of Hieria in 754 and condemned all icons of Christ or saints:

"Supported by the Holy Scriptures and the Church Fathers, we declare unanimously, in the name of the Holy Trinity, that there shall be rejected and removed and cursed...every likeness which is made out of any material and color whatever by the evil art of painters....If anyone venture to represent the divine image of the Word after the Incarnation with material colors, let him be anathema! (cursed)....If anyone shall endeavor to represent the forms of the saints in lifeless pictures with material colors which are of no value---for this notion is vain and introduced by the devil--and does not rather represent their virtues as living images in himself, let him be anathema!" *Epitome Of The Definition Of The Iconoclastic Conciliabulum*

Persecution and idol smashing followed Constantine's edict. The Eastern Church held that the veneration of icons had become consubstantial with the reality and had gone beyond the level of art or symbolism into the realm of paganism and heresy. These were fighting words. After many deaths and much destruction, after many theological wranglings and wars, in 780 the Iconophile Eastern Empress Irene, the widow of the Iconoclast Leo V and regent for their 10-year old son Constantine, met with the Roman Emperor and reversed her late husband's position against icons in 787 at Nicea: "...representational art...is quite in harmony with the history of the spread of the gospel as it provides confirmation that the becoming man of the Word of God was real and not just imaginary....the revered and holy images, whether painted or made of mosaic or of other suitable material, are to be exposed in the holy churches of God, on sacred instruments and vestments, on walls and panels, in houses and by public ways." Second Council Of Nicea September 24, 787

The war over icons between the Byzantine East and the Roman West had been settled---temporarily. A Second Iconoclasm War (814-842) erupted less than a century later between the Eastern and the Western churches. The war ended in 843 when an empress again intervened. Theodora, regent for the minor heir Michael III, proclaimed that all icons should be restored to all churches in the East. The Eastern Church who hated icons became so iconophilic that it still celebrates the first Sunday of Lent as the feast of "The Triumph of Orthodoxy" over Iconoclasts, the smashers of idols. The wars were over. The lovers of icons, the Iconophiles, had triumphed.

What began with the Cult of the Martyrs in the primitive church grew into such an intense desire for and veneration of material representations of holy people that the Church had split in two. The Western Roman Church and its icons won that long battle---temporarily.

Nine hundred years later an internecine war broke out again when on October 31, 1517 a Catholic monk named Martin Luther tacked 95 Theses to the door of the Castle Church in Wittenberg, Germany. The battles over doctrine and the veneration/worship of icons were renewed. Riots occurred between Iconoclasts (Protestants) and Iconophiles (Catholics) in European cities sporadically from 1523 to 1562. Five hundred years later the dispute, though muted, continues.

XI.

"But concerning baptism, thus shall ye baptize.
Having first recited all these things, baptize in the name of the Father
and of the Son and of the Holy Spirit in living water.
But if thou hast not living water, then baptize in other water;
And if thou art not able in cold, then in warm.
But if thou hast neither, then pour water on the head thrice in the name
of the Father and of the Son and of the Holy Spirit.
But before the baptism let him that baptizeth and him that is baptized
fast, and any other also who are able;
And thou shalt order him that is baptized to fast a day or two before."
Didache 7:1-4 (c. 60-100 AD)

Since the very beginning of the faith, Christians have disagreed over doctrines and rituals. To this day those who believe the only Biblical form of baptism is total immersion in water frown upon other forms of baptism. Some churches insist on infants being baptized. Others are sure baptism should only occur when the initiate is mature enough to accept Jesus as Savior. Serious intramural wars and the casualties and denominations that accompany such wars have been fought over the correct way to baptize---immerse, dunk, dip, sprinkle, pour. And over the correct age of baptism---infants, 12-year-olds, any age.

It is enlightening to read the *Didache* subtitled *The Teaching Of The Twelve Apostles*. In another document the subtitle is *The Teaching of the*

Lord to the Gentiles. The writer is anonymous, but the Teachings reflect a person who was living at a very early period when Jewish influence was still important to the Church. The *Didache* (pronounced "did-ah-kay" or "did-ah-key")) is a catechism of early Christian teachings taken from the Old and New Testaments. Perhaps it was meant as a pastoral doctrinal guide to core Christian beliefs. The current consensus dates the original manuscript between 60 AD (some 30 years after Jesus) and 100 AD. The early dates make the Teachings contemporary with most of the Apostles and, therefore, highly relevant to the practices of Christians under Apostolic influence.

Those, for instance, who want to marry themselves as accurately as possible to the beliefs and practices of the infant Church will find the *Didache's* teaching on Baptism liberating.

The preferable way is to baptize in "living water." "Living water" is "running water." It denotes a river, an ocean, a stream, a spring, a groundwater well or a lake with outlets. Living or running water has the baptismal advantage of being able, metaphorically, to purify and to wash away as it is flowing.

If a river, ocean, stream, spring, well or lake is not available, you can be baptized "in other water." "Other water" could be a pond, a lake without outlets, a swimming pool or any receptacle that has enough water in it to contain the baptizer and the baptized, or "other water" could just mean "water." The important ingredient here is "water."

"Cold" (running) water is preferred, but if you do not have cold water, then you can baptize in "warm" (standing) water.

If cold or warm water is not available, then "pour water on the head three times in the name of the Father and of the Son and of the Holy Spirit." It can be deduced that any kind of available water will suffice for sprinkling/pouring.

One important injunction in the *Didache* not followed by the modern church is: "Before the baptism, let him that baptizeth (pastor, priest, minister) and him that is baptized fast, and any other who are able; And thou shalt order him that is baptized to fast a day or two before." This dictate has been abandoned, yet "fasting and prayer" together appear 509 times in the Bible. (e.g. Psalm 35:13; Daniel 9:3; Matthew 17:21; Luke 2:37; I Corinthians 7:5)

Cleansing with water for physical as well as spiritual purity was commanded in the Old Testament. Moses bathed Aaron and his sons before their ordination as priests. (Leviticus 8:6) Clothing contaminated by mold or mildew had to be washed. (Leviticus 13:58) A diseased, unclean person had to be quarantined outside the camp until the infection ceased. (Leviticus 13:45,46) When the disease was gone, the person had to "wash his clothes, shave off all his hair and bathe with water." (Leviticus 14:8) Diarrhea and urethral discharges meant disease, uncleanness and the ill person as well as all those around him had to wash their clothes and "bathe in fresh (running) water." (Leviticus 15:13) Semen and menstrual blood were unclean and required water cleansing (Leviticus 15:16-33) The seemingly tedious lists in Leviticus of "clean" and "unclean" that required water cleansing were in reality prescient medical methods of preventing the spread of infectious diseases as well as practical practices that reinforced the need to be "clean" outside. To be clean outside was a metaphor for inward, spiritual purity.

The Jews were, of all ancient peoples, the most aware of how sinful they were before their God and how much they needed to be cleansed from their sins:

"…your iniquities have separated you from your God; your sins have hidden his face from you….your hands are stained with blood, your fingers with guilt. Your lips have spoken lies and your tongue mutters wicked things. No one calls for justice; no one pleads his case with integrity….They hatch the eggs of vipers and spin a spider's nest…. Their feet rush into sin…Their thoughts are evil thoughts; ruin and destruction mark their paths….our offenses are many in (God's) sight and we acknowledge our iniquities." Isaiah 59:2-5,7,12

The strongest example in the Old Testament of spiritual cleansing is the annual release of the Scapegoat on the Day of Atonement (Yom Kippur):

"When Aaron has finished making atonement for the Most Holy Place, the Tent of Meeting and the altar, he shall bring forward the live goat. He is to lay both hands on the head of the live goat and confess over it all the wickedness and rebellion of the Israelites---all their sins---and put them on the goat's head. He shall send the goat away into the desert in the care of a man appointed for the task. The goat will carry on itself all their sins to a solitary place; and the man shall release it in the desert. Then Aaron is to go into the Tent of Meeting and take off the linen garments he put on before he entered the Most Holy Place, and he is to leave them there. He shall bathe himself with water in a holy place and put on his regular garments." Leviticus 16:20-24

The Scapegoat, carrying in its body the collective sin of the Israelites, is, typologically, one who bears all the blame for something he did not do. The Yom Kippur Scapegoat, let loose to die in the barren desert, was released year after year after year. Sin could be put away for a time but it was not eliminated. After officiating at the sin/atonement ceremonies, the high priest would have to "bathe himself with water in a holy place" to cleanse himself physically from the spiritual filth of sin.

By the time of Christ, ceremonial cleanliness by water had become institutionalized into a purity ritual involving full immersion in a *mikveh* (or *miqveh*), a "collection of water." Mikveh purification was required of all Jews before they could enter the Temple or participate in major festivals. Hundreds of thousands of pilgrims converged on Jerusalem for Passover and other major feasts. One hundred mikvehs, attesting to the need for water purification before entering into Temple rites, have been found by Hebrew University's Benjamin Mazar around the wall adjacent to Herod's Temple. Mikvehs, resembling large bathtubs or small garden ponds, have been found in Jericho and elsewhere in Israel.

The Jews tried to make sure their family's mikveh was connected to a source of "living water" like a spring or well, but that was not always possible. Tap water could not be used as the primary source of water for the mikveh, but the rabbis decided you could "top off" the mikveh to a suitable level with a little tap water. The rule of thumb was that the mikveh should be big enough to hold 40 *seahs* of water. When asked how much volume a seah was, the rabbis said it was enough to fit 144 eggs. If there were less than 40 seahs of water (enough to hold 5,760 eggs) in a mikveh, you could not add even 3-4 more pints of water from an unnatural source because that would render the mikveh unfit for use. It would have to be drained and refilled. A simple ritual had been turned into a legalistic nightmare prefiguring the disputes of the Christians over methods of baptism. It has been a temptation in all religions to replace the ritual for the reality it was meant to reflect. One rabbi had suggested that the mikveh contain enough water to cover the body of an average-sized man. There have always been sensible people.

The teaching concerning baptism in the *Didache* is eminently sensible and should give comfort to all the various sects of Christendom. But those who baptize in "living water" have a slight edge. It is these "slight edges" and often "hard edges" that have divided Christians from the beginning.

In Acts 6:1-6 one of the first recorded divisions in the Church pitted the Grecian Jews against the Hebraic Jews. The Grecians (Hellenized Jews born and raised outside of Jerusalem who spoke only Greek and some Hebrew or Aramaic) said their widows "were being overlooked in the daily distribution of food." Apparently the Hebrews gave more food to Hebrew-speaking widows than to Greek-speaking widows. The Apostles settled that dispute by choosing seven men to evenly distribute the food, all of whom had Greek names and one of whom, Nicholas, was a Gentile convert to Judaism. That left the Apostles free to tend to major rather than to minor issues. Stephen, the first Christian martyr, was one of those seven deacons (Greek *diakonos*).

In Acts 11:2-18 Peter was chastised and castigated by the Apostles and brothers for meeting with the Gentile centurion Cornelius: "'You went into the house of uncircumcised men and ate with them!'" In order to appease the brothers, Peter had to recount the entire supernatural history of how God Himself led him to uncircumcised Cornelius and why he ate a meal with him. "To eat with Gentiles or not to eat with Gentiles?" That was the question. Peter won that round, but Paul was always in trouble.

Everywhere he went, Paul was plagued by legalists and dogmatists called Judaizers who insisted new Gentile Christians needed to observe all Jewish laws and customs. These Jewish Christians from Jerusalem had come to Antioch and were telling the Gentile converts they had to be circumcised or they could not be saved: "This brought Paul and Barnabas into sharp dispute and debate with them." Acts 15:2

The two men and "some other believers" left for Jerusalem to have this issue resolved. In c. 50 AD the first organized Council in the Church's history took place in Jerusalem to solve the problem of whether or not the male Gentile believers needed to be circumcised. (Acts 15:1-35) To circumcise Gentiles or not to circumcise Gentiles? Peter, who had been castigated regarding Cornelius about 10 years previously, offered an impassioned defense of Paul's position before the Council. (This instance is the last mention of Peter in the book of Acts.) James and the other fathers finally resolved: "...not to burden (Gentiles) with anything beyond the following requirements: You are to abstain from food sacrificed to idols, from blood, from the meat of strangled animals and from sexual immorality." Acts 15:29

The debate over Gentile circumcision had been settled. Gentiles need not be circumcised. However, the few prohibitions the early Jerusalem Fathers pronounced on Gentiles were later countermanded by Paul and, except for the prohibition against sexual immorality, were dismissed.

In the Early Church there was, also, a debate about certain types of asceticism. Many strong believers in Egypt had taken refuge for their souls in the Egyptian desert and lived solitary lives of physical deprivation including celibacy and abstention from certain foods. Most of them refused to eat meat and many of them subsisted on just bread and water. The monk-like life of the Desert Fathers (3rd century AD) appealed to many Christians in other parts of the ancient world. An interesting anecdote on very early asceticism is tucked away in the account of the martyrs of Lyons and Vienne in 177-178 referred to in Chapter VI of this book:

"A certain Alcibiades, who lived a very austere life among them (in Lyons) refused everything but bread and water. But after his first contest in the amphitheater, it was revealed to Attalus (who was later roasted alive) that Alcibiades was not doing well in failing to use what God had created (all foods) and (he was) offering offense to others. Alcibiades was persuaded and started to eat everything freely and gave thanks to God." Eusebius, *Church History 5.3*

The question of vegetarianism versus meat eating has preceded the 21st century by at least 2,000 years. By the early 2nd century AD, heresies abounded and Irenaeus, a disciple of Polycarp, attacked them in *Against Heresies 1.28.* He called vegetarianism "one of numerous heresies…. they insist upon teaching. Some…have introduced abstinence from animal food, thus proving themselves ungrateful to God Who formed all things." Paul, the pragmatist who always hewed to basic truths and eschewed irrelevancy, hit this contentious subject head-on. The Christian can eat meat, can eat anything his/her conscience allows:

"Accept him whose faith is weak without passing judgment on disputable matters. One man's faith allows him to eat everything, but another man, whose faith is weak, eats only vegetables. The man who eats everything must not look down on him who does not, and the man who does not eat everything must not condemn the man who does…. He who eats meat, eats it to the Lord, for he gives thanks to God; and he who abstains, does so to the Lord and gives thanks to God….As one who is in the Lord Jesus, I am fully convinced that no food is unclean in itself. But if anyone regards something as unclean, then for him it is unclean." Romans 14:1-14

"So then, about eating (meat) sacrificed to idols. We know that an idol is nothing at all in the world….Some people are still so accustomed to idols that when they eat such food, they think of it as having been sacrificed to an idol, and since their conscience is weak, it is defiled. But food does not bring us near to God. We are no worse if we do not eat, and no better if we do." I Corinthians 8:4-13

Paul was not positing a new theology. He was expanding upon what Jesus had taught about clean and unclean foods:

"…Jesus called the crowd to him and said, 'Listen to me, everyone, and understand this. Nothing outside a man can make him unclean by going into him. Rather it is what comes out of a man that makes him unclean.' After he had left the crowd and entered the house, his disciples asked him about this parable. 'Are you so dull?' he asked. 'Don't you see that nothing that enters a man from the outside can make him unclean? For it doesn't go into his heart but into his stomach and then out of his body.' In saying this, Jesus declared all foods clean." Mark 7:14-19

The question of vegetarianism versus meat eating seems to have been doctrinally settled by Paul rather quickly in the Early Church, but it was not to die. Nor was the question of circumcising Gentiles. About seven years after the 50 AD Council, Paul is in Jerusalem and is grilled again by "James and all the elders." He was at first greeted warmly, but then taken to task: "(Judaizers) have been informed that you teach all the Jews who live among the Gentiles to turn away from Moses, telling them not to circumcise their children or live according to our customs." James and the elders decided that Paul should purge himself of these charges and mollify the Judaizers by joining four men in Jewish purification rites:

"There are four men with us who have made a vow. Take these men, join in their purification rites, and pay their expenses, so that they can have their heads shaved. Then everybody will know there is no truth in these reports about you, but that you yourself are living in obedience to the law.…The next day Paul took the men and purified himself along with them. Then he went to the temple to give notice of the date when the days of purification would end and the offering would be made for each of them." Acts 21:17-26

Paul's gesture did not end the matter. A week later he was beaten and almost killed by a mob stirred up by Jews from Asia (Turkey, Greece). The Roman commander of the troops in Jerusalem, Claudius Lysias, had to rescue him. Acts 21:27-36

The Jewish Christians who felt the Law should be a primary tenet of the belief in and observance of early Christianity would not budge on their convictions. Years later, the question of Gentile circumcision was still rattling around. Paul in his letter to the Colossians radically redefined the meaning of circumcision:

"In him (Christ) you were also circumcised, in the putting off of the sinful nature, not with a circumcision done by the hands of men but with the circumcision done by Christ, having been buried with him in baptism and raised with him through your faith in the power of God, who raised him from the dead." Colossians 2:11-13

Here Paul nullifies the Abramic Old Testament covenant of physical circumcision. (Genesis 17:1-14) In the new covenant, the sinful nature of man is itself circumcised, is dealt with by the spiritual work of Christ upon the cross. The rite of baptism, the washing away of sin, becomes the new circumcision, the new outward manifestation of an inward reality.

The incessant insistence of the Judaizers on the primacy of outward works and circumcision eventually causes Paul to redefine all of the Jewish religion and its nascent offshoot Christianity by replacing works and circumcision with one word---faith:

"For we maintain that a man is justified by faith apart from observing the law. Is God the God of Jews only? Is he not the God of Gentiles, too? Yes, of Gentiles, too, since there is only one God, who will justify the circumcised by faith, and the uncircumcised through that same faith. Do we then nullify the law by this faith? Not at all! Rather, we uphold the law. What then shall we say that Abraham our forefather, discovered in this matter? If, in fact, Abraham was justified by works, he had something to boast about---but not before God. What does the Scripture say? 'Abraham believed God, and it was credited to him as righteousness.' Now when a man works, his wages are not credited to him as a gift, but as an obligation. However, to the man who does not work but trusts God who justifies the wicked, his faith is credited as righteousness....Is this blessedness only for the circumcised, or also for the uncircumcised? We have been saying that Abraham's faith was credited to him as righteousness. Under what circumstances was it credited? Was it after he was circumcised, or before? It was not after, but before! And he received the sign of circumcision, a seal of the righteousness that he had by faith while he was still uncircumcised. So then he is the father of all who believe but have not been circumcised, in order that righteousness might be credited them. And he is also the father of the circumcised who not only are circumcised but who also walk in the footsteps of the faith that our father Abraham had before he was circumcised. It was not through law that Abraham and his offspring received the promise that he would be heir of the world, but through the righteousness that comes by faith....Therefore, the promise comes by faith, so that it may be by grace and may be guaranteed to all Abraham's offspring---not only to those who are of the law but also to those who are of the faith of Abraham. He is the father of us all." Romans 3:28-31; 4:1-5, 9-13, 16

Divisive words. Fighting words. But Paul was not the first to contend that being a physical descendant of Abraham was not the sole prerogative of the Jews. John the fiery Baptist in c. 26 AD proclaimed that God could produce heirs of Abraham from stones if He so desires:

"John said to the crowds coming out to be baptized by him, 'You brood of vipers! Who warned you to flee from the coming wrath? Produce fruit in keeping with repentance. And do not begin to say to yourselves, We have Abraham as our father. For I tell you that out of these stones God can raise up children for Abraham.'" Luke 3:7, 8

The Baptist was saying that God requires righteousness not works. The Jews took great tribal pride in two facts: that they were, of all peoples on the earth, chosen by the one God to receive the Law and Commandments on Mt. Sinai and that only they could trace their ancestry back to Abraham and his lawful wife Sarah. The Law and Abraham. Those two defined their *raison d'etres*, were the two things that advantageously set Jews apart from all other tribes and nations. Paul insisted those advantages were nullified:

"Understand, then, that those who believe are children of Abraham.... (Christ) redeemed us in order that the blessing given to Abraham might come to the Gentiles....If you belong to Christ, then you are Abraham's seed and heirs according to the promise." Galatians 3:7, 14, 29

Paul was replacing concrete laws of ancestry and inheritance with an amorphous Faith and was daring to call anyone of any color, tribe or race a child of Abraham. To the Jews Abraham was their father, was the father of their circumcision and their religion. Circumcision was their rite, their sign of uniqueness.

No wonder Paul wrote: "Five times I received from the Jews forty lashes minus one...once I was stoned...I have been in danger...from my own countrymen; in danger from Gentiles; in danger in the city; in danger in the country." II Corinthians 11:24-26

The conclusion of Paul's stand on circumcision was:

"A man is not a Jew if he is only one outwardly, nor is circumcision merely outward and physical. No, a man is a Jew if he is one inwardly; and circumcision is circumcision of the heart, by the Spirit, not by written code." Roman 2:28, 29

Reversing thousands of years of history and belief, Paul declared a Jew is not a physical connection and is not defined by bloodlines. A Jew is a spiritual condition defined by faith and a circumcised heart, not defined by laws, codes, cultural ethos or ancestry. All who have faith in Christ are Jews, spiritual Jews.

The men, the Judaizers who opposed Paul and dogged his journeys, were not evil men. They were trying to adhere to every letter of the Mosaic Law and all the rabbinic emendations. They wanted to please God by their works and by doing exactly what He or His representatives commanded. They sincerely believed that Gentiles should observe the core practices of the Jews if they wanted to become Christians. Jesus was a Jew and was promised to the Jews. Surely, they reasoned, the new faith in Jesus as Messiah and Savior did not abrogate Jewish and rabbinic laws, rituals and methods of interpretation.

The fears of the Judaizers were real. Paul's teachings incrementally separated the Jerusalem believers from the Gentile believers. The Christian Church under Paul, the Apostle to the Gentiles, grew from a vibrant Jewish sect to an international movement. Paul repealed and redefined circumcision, abolished clean and unclean foods and taught that the believer was saved by grace through his faith and not by the works of the Mosaic Law:

"For it is by grace you have been saved through faith---and this not from yourselves, it is the gift of God---not by works, so that no one can boast." Ephesians 2:8,9

The proud emblem of the Early Church is marked with questions and arguments and struggles between earnest men who sought after and fought for righteousness and Biblical truth. Even an arcane question about an allegorical interpretation of Scripture was not too small to address seriously. Dionysius, the Bishop of Alexandria, journeyed all the way from Alexandria down the Nile to Arsinoe in c. 255 just to resolve a heresy based on the "Jewish fashion" of Scriptural interpretation that said:

"...there would be a sort of millennium of bodily indulgences on this earth....When I (Dionysius) arrived at Arsinoe where, as you know, this teaching had long been prevalent....I convened a meeting of the presbyters and teachers of the village congregations....I sat with them for three days in a row, from morning until night, criticizing what had been (taught)....I was greatly impressed by the soundness, sincerity, logic and intelligence of the brethren as we discussed methodically and with restraint the difficulties and points of agreement. We refused to cling blindly to prior opinions or avoid problems but tried our utmost to grapple with the issues and master them. Nor were we ashamed to alter our opinions, if convinced, but honestly and trusting in God, we accepted whatever was proved by Holy Scriptures." Eusebius, *Church History 7.24*

As can be gleaned, the Early Church through confrontations, councils, days and nights of discussions, prayer, wisdom and Godly inspiration gradually worked out early disputes. The Orthodox (Greek *"orthos"* meaning "right, true, straight" and *"doxa"* meaning "opinion") clung tenaciously to Apostolic teaching and to *Sola Scriptura*, Only The Scriptures. Any one who deviated from the Scriptures was confronted. If he refused to conform to Biblical Apostolic teaching, he was shunned as a heretic by the early leaders of the church.

Polycarp, one of the Apostle John's disciples, recounted John's reaction to a heretic named Cerinthus. In Mark 3:17 John and his brother James were called the Sons of Thunder (*Boanerges*) by Jesus because of their fiery, fervent temperaments. The following story is emblematic of John's volatile reactions:

"According to Polycarp, the apostle John one day went into a therma (bath-house) to take a bath, but when he found Cerinthus inside, he leaped out of the place and ran for the door, since he could not endure to be under the same roof (with that heretic). He urged his companions to do the same, crying, 'Let's get out of here lest the place fall in. Cerinthus, the enemy of the truth, is inside!'" Irenaeus, *Against Heresies 3*

It is to be noted that John, leaping up, running and yelling to his friends, was in his late 80's or early 90's at the time of the bathhouse incident. Obviously, his thunderous zest and zeal for "the Truth that will set you free" (John 8:32) had not abandoned him.

Many of the early doctrinal clashes were between the letter of the law and the spirit of the law. The letter of the law was important. There were the Ten Commandments delivered by God Himself to the Jews. There was the Biblically-mandated act of circumcision as a sign that a Jew was in a special covenant with God. But about four hundred years before Jesus was born, rabbis in Judaism had begun to formulate their own laws of behavior extrapolated from Torah laws. These extra-Biblical oral laws were variously called "the tradition of the elders" (Mark 7:3-5) or "the works of the law" (Romans 3:20-28). Over the years the rabbis counted 613 individual laws in the Pentateuch. They divided these into "heavy, great" laws and "light, little" commandments. The original purpose of these rabbinic laws was to make sure it was abundantly clear what was accepted orthodox behavior. By the time of Jesus, these rabbinic extrapolations, called Halakhah meaning "walk," had become a prison for the Jews.The rules from the Halakhah governed the daily lives and religious practices of the Jews. Every aspect of Jewish life was hemmed in by a tangled web of prohibitions. These man-made laws had more power over the everyday life of the people than Biblical laws.

You could not carry a "burden" on the Sabbath. The lowest standard of a "burden" was anything heavier than a dried fig such as pieces of papyrus or a piece of broken pottery. After Jesus healed the man lying at the pool of Bethesda (John 5:1-16), He told him, "Get up! Pick up your mat and walk....The day on which this took place was a Sabbath, and so the Jews said to the man who had been healed, 'It is the Sabbath. The law forbids you to carry your mat.'" It was heavier than a dried fig.

You could not touch grain on the Sabbath. You could not remove the husks (guilty of harvesting), rub the heads (guilty of threshing), clean or bruise ears (guilty of sifting) or throw them up by hand (guilty of winnowing). However, if you wanted to remove a sheaf of grain, you could lay a spoon on it and in the process of removing the spoon, you could or might remove the sheaf, also. That ruse was not a sin. In Matthew 12:1-8 "Jesus went through the grain fields on the Sabbath. His disciples were hungry and began to pick some heads of grain and eat them. When the Pharisees saw this, they said to him, 'Look! Your disciples are doing what is unlawful on the Sabbath.'" They were guilty of harvesting.

You could do no work whatsoever on the Sabbath. Fishing was considered harvesting. To pick fruit, or even to lift it up from the ground, was reaping. Walking more than 2,000 cubits (c. ½ a mile) from your home on the Sabbath violated rabbinic law. Some Jews wriggled around this law by continuing their journey by walking backwards after the prescribed 2,000 cubits forward. A person had to "work" to avoid working on the Sabbath.

Sabbath law applied even to inanimate objects. Wool could not be dyed because the color of a fabric could not be altered (sin of changing). Even animals had Sabbath laws of rest. Only those ornaments necessary for leading out, bringing in or the safety of animals could be put on them. All else was a "burden." Even something put on an animal to prevent the rubbing of a wound was forbidden on the Sabbath.

Women were not allowed to look at themselves in a mirror on the Sabbath because they might find a white hair and attempt to pull it out. That would be the sin of work. If a person had an earache and had wadding dipped in oil in his ear on the Sabbath and the wadding fell out, he could not bend down to pick it up because that would be the sin of work. And there was the added danger of the sin of healing.

Healing was work and was not permitted on the Sabbath. In Luke 13:10-17 a crippled woman was in one of the synagogues where Jesus was teaching on the Sabbath. He healed her and the ruler of the synagogue was "indignant because Jesus had healed on the Sabbath." The ruler reasoned, "There are six days to work. So come and be healed on those days, not on the Sabbath." Jesus was guilty of the sin of working on the Sabbath and the woman was guilty of being healed on the Sabbath.

The Jewish scholar Alfred Edersheim (1825-1889) converted to Christianity at a young age and wrote *The Life And Times of Jesus the Messiah* (1883). In the chapter examining the rabbinic laws of the Sabbath, "The Law Of The Sabbath From The Mishnah And The Jerusalem Talmud," he explains:

"...its object (Rabbinic law) is to make the Sabbath Laws more bearable. For this purpose, it is explained how places, beyond which it would otherwise have been unlawful to carry things, may be connected together, so as, by a legal fiction, to convert them into a sort of private dwelling. Thus, supposing a number of small private houses to open into a common court, it would have been unlawful on the Sabbath to carry anything from one of these houses into the other. This difficulty is removed if all the families deposit before the Sabbath some food in the common court, when a connection is established between the various houses, which makes them one dwelling….(or) when narrow streets or blind alleys were connected into a private dwelling by laying a beam over the entrance, or extending a wire or rope along such streets and alleys. This, by a legal fiction, make them a private dwelling so that everything was lawful there which a man might do on the Sabbath in his own house."

As is obvious, the rabbis even enacted complicated laws that could cleverly circumvent the laws they had established regarding the Sabbath. Sabbath laws were, as Edersheim says so succinctly, "legal fictions." The day of rest became a burden rather than a day of spiritual, mental and physical rest. What was originally intended by the rabbis and elders as an explanation of what the "Sabbath day of rest" meant became an intricate game of ingenious casuistry. It cannot be over-emphasized how Jesus' continual breaking of these fictitious Sabbath laws brought Him not only into conflict with the religious establishment but led eventually to His death on the cross.

Decades before the radical Paul, the revolutionary Jesus had challenged and threatened the foundations and the viability of the Jewish social order and His followers, the early Christians, would later challenge the bases of Roman culture. Jesus railed often and publicly against those restrictive, non-Biblical laws and pronounced His famous Seven Woes on the ruling priests:

"Woe to you, teachers of the law (scribes) and Pharisees, you hypocrites!…. Woe to you, teachers of the law and Pharisees, you hypocrites!….Woe to you blind guides!….Woe to you….You blind guides! You strain at a gnat but swallow a camel….Woe to you teachers of the law and Pharisees, you hypocrites! You clean the outside of the cup and dish, but inside you are full of greed and self-indulgence….Woe to you…you are like whitewashed tombs which look beautiful on the outside but on the inside are full of dead bones and everything unclean. Woe to you…. You snakes! You brood of vipers!" Matthew 23:13-3

Needless to say, the ruling Pharisees, Sadducees, Herodians and scribes kept a wary and suspicious eye on this firebrand Jesus and tenaciously followed Him wherever He went. They made the 90-mile journey up to the Galilee area and were there one day when His disciples did not wash their hands before they ate:

"The Pharisees and some of the teachers of the law who had come from Jerusalem gathered around Jesus and saw some of his disciples eating food with hands that were unclean, that is, unwashed. The Pharisees and all the Jews do not eat unless they give their hands a ceremonial washing, holding to the tradition of the elders. When they come from the marketplace they do not eat unless they wash, And they observe many other traditions, such as the washing of cups, pitchers and kettles. So the Pharisees and the teachers of the law asked Jesus, 'Why don't your disciples live according to the tradition of the elders instead of eating their food with unclean hands?' (Jesus) replied, 'Isaiah was right when he prophesied about you hypocrites; as it is written: These people honor me with their lips, but their hearts are far from me. They worship in vain; their teachings are but rules taught by men. You have let go of the commands of God and are holding on to the traditions of men.'" Mark 7:1-8

Jesus did not mince words when He lashed out against those religious men who had traveled so far to observe Him. He used Isaiah 29:13 to rebuke them for following rabbinic traditions and laws rather than the commands of God. He called them "hypocrites" and called their religion "vain." Jesus never tried to ingratiate Himself to the ruling class of Jews nor did He want their stamp of approval. He hated the rabbinic laws, "the traditions of the elders," that made a mockery of God's laws and imprisoned rather than freed people .

The ruling elders, however, kept inviting Jesus to have dinner with them:

"...a Pharisee invited (Jesus) to eat with him, so he went in and reclined at the table. But the Pharisee, noticing that Jesus did not first wash before the meal, was surprised. Then the Lord said to him, 'Now then you Pharisees clean the outside of the cup and dish, but inside you are full of greed and wickedness. You foolish people! Did not the one who made the outside make the inside also? But give what is inside the dish to the poor, and everything will be clean for you'....One of the experts of the law (scribes who were mostly Pharisees) answered him, 'Teacher, when you say these things you insult us also.' Jesus replied, "And you experts of the law, woe to you, because you load people down with burdens they can hardly carry, and you yourselves will not lift one finger to help them'....When Jesus left there, the Pharisees and teachers of the law began to oppose him fiercely and to besiege him with questions, waiting to catch him in something he might say." Luke 11:37-53

First Jesus attacked the Pharisee who had invited him to dinner. When a scribe who was reclining, Roman-style, at the table observed that Jesus had not only insulted the host but also the scribes who were there, Jesus turned His wrath on him. There was nothing in the Torah or Old Testament writings that commanded the washing of hands before eating. The Pharisaic emphasis on external purity versus internal purity infuriated Jesus. (The saying, "Cleanliness is next to Godliness," originated from the late 2nd century AD Rabbi Phineas ben-Yair and is only Biblically true in an inward, spiritual sense.)

By the time of this dinner table encounter, Jesus had already raised Jairus' daughter from the dead and had healed a man with leprosy, a paralytic, the centurion's slave, a woman subject to hemorrhaging, a boy with an evil spirit, and a man who was mute. He had given the Sermon on the Mount and had taught many of His most famous parables. Instead of questioning Him about His works and words, the Pharisees and scribes had focused on a minor infraction of a trifling rabbinic law. Jesus was irate.

Jesus was a volatile guest, but the invitations to dinner kept coming. At first these invitations were out of curiosity about his teachings and identity. As Jesus' ministry grew and His antipathy to the religious leaders became apparent, they invited Him to discredit and to entrap Him:

"One Sabbath when Jesus went to eat in the house of a prominent Pharisee, he was being carefully watched. There in front of him was a man suffering from dropsy (swelling as a result of the accumulation of fluids in the body). Jesus asked the Pharisees and experts in the law. 'Is it lawful to heal on the Sabbath or not?' But they remained silent. So taking hold of the man, he healed him and sent him away. Then he asked them, "If one of you has a son or an ox that falls into a well on the Sabbath day, will you not immediately pull him out?' And they had nothing to say." Luke 14:1-6

Jesus saw the snare. They had placed the man with dropsy right in front of Him to see if He would break the laws of the Sabbath and heal the afflicted man. Jesus asked the Pharisees: "What do you think I should do with this man? It is the Sabbath. Should I heal him or not?" Jesus had turned the tables on them. "They remained silent." Jesus healed the man and then asked the Pharisees whether they would rescue their own son on a Sabbath day if he fell into a well. The question answered itself: "Of course, you would. You would immediately pull him out so that he would not drown." The Bible says, "And they had nothing to say."

Just because they remained silent did not mean the Pharisees concurred with Jesus. The Nazarene was a worthy sparring partner. They may even have remembered that several Sabbaths before this one Jesus had healed a crippled woman in a synagogue and had demolished the objections of the ruler of that synagogue. (Luke 13:10-17) But they knew for sure if they said it was lawful to heal on the Sabbath, they would betray rabbinical teachings. And if they said it was not lawful to heal on the Sabbath, they would have no Biblical backing. The Pharisees were trapped into silence.

One hundred and thirty years after the destruction of Jerusalem in 70 AD, the Jews in Judea began to feel that the oral traditions of the Pharisaic rabbis would be lost or forgotten. So a rabbi from the kingly line of David, Rabbi Judah haNasi (135-c. 217), compiled all the oral laws into a work called the Mishnah. Over the next centuries the Mishnah was added to and redacted by the rabbis into Gemara (c. 350-400). These two worthy and fascinating compilations make up The Talmud. The Rabbi Jesus of Nazareth, however, would have had choice epithets for these thrice-removed-from-Scripture rabbinic works if they are ever cited with the force of Biblical authority rather than as fountains of human wisdom.

Dialogues between Jesus and the religious leaders were one of the hallmarks of His ministry. Over the millennia, they have been referenced to keep in check the human desire to be accepted by God through good works and punctilious doctrine. Working one's way to God, the letter of the Law, was the Way of the Pharisees.

For man innately knows he is not good enough for God. Even "all his righteous acts are as filthy rags." (Isaiah 64:6) But he has always tried to get to that holy place, to God, to gods, to Paradise, back to Eden. Always and forever man keeps trying through elaborate rituals or self-mutilation or self-deprivation or silent meditation or dogma or deeds to get clean.

XII.

"In the flood, too, there was a figure anticipating baptism….what is the flood, if not a means of preserving the just man so that he will propagate justice, while destroying sin? To that end, the Lord seeing men's faults multiplying, preserved only the just man and his descendants while he ordered water to overflow even the peak of mountains. Thus the flood destroyed all corrupted flesh, while the race, the model of the just man, alone subsisted. Is baptism not precisely such a flood, wherein all sins are erased while alone the spirit and the grace of the just man resurrect?" Ambrose of Milan (c. 340-397), *About The Sacraments 2. 1*

People have always wanted to be clean. "Clean" as "free from dirt; unsoiled; unstained; free from pollution; unadulterated; fresh; free from defects or flaws; wholesome; morally pure; innocent; upright; honorable; pure." There is physical dirt to be washed away and there is moral dirt to be expunged.

Water covers 70% of the earth's surface. To space travelers we seem an agate of azure, void of all but water life. Water is found on the surface of the earth, within the rocks of the earth, in the bowels of the earth and in the clouds that cover the earth. Water is a trinity of liquid, solid and gas. During its poetic cycle, it evaporates from the oceans into the atmosphere where it condenses and falls to land again to regenerate and to perpetuate. We cannot live without this liquid of life and, some argue, people cannot live without its symbolic refreshment. Ubiquitous and salvific, water is the medium and the metaphor for "life" and for "clean."

In Ambrose of Milan's quote, he extrapolates the Noahic flood as "a figure" or metaphor of the cleansing of sin from the earth and the preserving of the just and Godly. "Is baptism not precisely such a flood?" he asks. The account of the Flood in Genesis 6-9 is one of the seminal stories of the Bible. The veracity of the story has never been questioned by orthodox believers, but few modern believers automatically connect Noah's story to baptism.

The Christians of the catacombs did. There are many representations of Noah in the catacombs. In the Via Latina God is pouring water from the heavens to cleanse the earth. In the Catacomb of Peter and Marcellinus Noah stands, waist-deep, in a small container. His hands are raised in praise. A dove flies above his right hand. In a series of contiguous paintings from Old and New Testament stories in Peter and Marcellinus, Noah stands in a little four-legged chest with his hands raised in praise like an orant. This time a raven is above his left hand and a dove above his right.

The tiny size of the Ark in catacomb representations is particularly interesting given the dimensions of the Ark in Genesis 6:14-17:

"…(God said to Noah) make yourself an ark of gopher wood; make rooms in it and coat it with pitch inside and out. This is how you are to build it: The ark is to be 450 feet long, 75 feet wide and 45 feet high. Make a roof for it and finish the ark to within 18 inches of the top. Put a door in the side of the ark and make low, middle and upper decks."

Noah's Ark was massive, far bigger than any wooden ship ever built or even imagined until the 20th century. The six-masted gaff schooner *Wyoming* was built in 1909 in Bath, Maine. Its overall length was 450' just like the Ark's. It had a cargo capacity of 303,621 cubic feet and could carry 6,000 long tons of coal. The ship foundered and sank with all on board on March 24, 1924. The *Wyoming*, constructed of 6" planks of yellow pine, is the longest wooden ship ever built since Noah's Ark.

The Hebrew for "gopher wood" does not correspond to any wood now existing. Perhaps it was a pre-diluvian tree. In some Biblical translations "cypress wood" replaces "gopher wood."

Given the extraordinary size of the Ark, it is puzzling that the catacomb artists chose such confining containers to encase Noah. Perhaps the dimensions given in the Genesis account were so beyond imagination that representation was impossible. Or maybe the dimensions meant nothing because the doctrine was the point.

Peter in his First Epistle 3:20, 21 makes the connection between the water of the Deluge and baptism: "....God waited patiently in the days of Noah while the ark was being built. In it only a few people, eight in all, were saved through water, and this water symbolizes baptism that now saves you also---not the removal of dirt from the body but the pledge of a good conscience toward God." As the waters of the Flood washed away collective sin, the waters of baptism wash away individual sin. The Flood is emblematic of the baptismal rite.

Water and dove are potent Old and New Testament symbols and they are both in the Noah/Flood story. When Jesus was baptized by John in the waters of the Jordan River, the minute He came up out of the water "heaven was opened and he saw the Spirit of God descending like a dove and lighting on him. And a voice from heaven said, 'This is my son, whom I love; with him I am well-pleased.'" Matthew 3:16, 17

The Holy Spirit, descending as a dove on Jesus as He emerges from the water, announces the initiation of a new spiritual life for mankind. In the Flood story the dove, returning to the Ark with an olive branch in its beak, heralds the arrival of a new earth, an earth renewed by water.

There are few statues or marble carvings in the catacombs, but in the above ground area of the Catacomb of St. Callixtus there is an exquisitely executed marble sarcophagus called the Sarcophagus Of The Child (Sarcofago dei Bambino). Across the entire front of the sarcophagus important Biblical stories are depicted. Noah in the ark with a dove above him is first. The prophet Habakkuk, holding the scroll of the Torah is next. Daniel in the lion's den follows and the dead child, his hands raised in orant praise, is between two men. Jesus turns the water into wine at Cana. Lazarus comes forth from his grave and in the last sculpture, Mary, Lazarus' sister, is seated at the feet of Jesus.

We have in these carvings on the small child's sarcophagus a catechism of core Christian beliefs: Noah---the Christian is saved from judgment by baptism; Habakkuk---the new life in Christ is nourished by the Word of God (and Jesus is the Logos, the Word); Daniel---this world is filled with perils, but God will save; the little child---the one who "becomes a little child" (Luke 18:17) will be saved; Jesus turning water into wine is a Eucharist symbol, the wine of His blood shed for man; Lazarus---the Christian will, like Lazarus, be resurrected; Mary at Jesus' feet---Mary chose the best thing: to listen, to be taught by the Word, the Book.

It must be emphasized that the catacomb Christians and all peoples living at that time were much more attuned to symbols and arcane meanings than people of the 21st century. They were steeped in myths and mysteries and metaphors and omens and divinations and allegories. Everything that happened meant something and every thing had a riot of meanings around it. To enter the world of catacomb paintings and of early Christian symbols is to enter a very rich, deeply intellectual and poetic world of meanings.

One of the most interesting and ingenious early 1st century Christian symbols is what is called The Roman Square or The Rotas Square:

SATOR
AREPO
TENET
OPERA
ROTAS

When the five-letter Latin words are read in line order horizontally or vertically or backwards or forwards or bottom to top or top to bottom, they mean: "The sower, Arepo, holds or works the wheels with care." Another translation is: "He who works the plow sows the seed." The Roman Square is a combination of a palindrome where the words read the same backwards and forwards and, in this case, line by line either vertically or horizontally and a cryptogram where all the words are written in such a form or order that a key is required to understand the sense.

The 1st century Christians were a persecuted minority forced to identify themselves to each other by secret signs and actions, the most common of which were the primitive fish sign and the spilling of a little wine on the ground. The obvious meaning of the Rotas Square to a Christian would have been Jesus' Parable of the Sower in Matthew 13:3-9 when He likened the spreading of the word of the kingdom of God to a farmer who sows seeds. Christians were spiritual farmers spreading the seeds of the *Evangel*, the Good News. But hidden in the Roman Square is an anagram when positioned in the form of a cross. By rearranging the 25 letters, a new phrase, extremely beloved by Christians down through the ages, is formed:

```
        P
        A
       ATO
        E
        R
PATERNOSTER
        O
        S
       OTA
        E
        R
```

Pater Noster ("Our Father") is the beginning of The Lord's Prayer in Latin. The 25 letters arranged in this cross fashion say "Our Father" twice, vertically and horizontally, with two "A's" and two "O's" left over and placed as palindromes. "A" and "O" are the first and the last letters in the Greek alphabet and mean "Alpha, the Beginning" and "Omega, the End." Jesus called Himself the First and the Last in Revelation 1:8: "I am the Alpha and Omega...who is and who was and who is to come, the Almighty." The Greek letter Tau (pronounced Taw) in the middle of the two palindromes simulates the cross of Christ (T) as does the arrangement of the Pater Noster letters. The interpretation of "ATO" and "OTA" would be: Christ on the Cross, the Alpha and Omega.

Tao (pronounced Dow) means "the way, the path" in Chinese. Taoism had been known in learned circles in the Middle East since the 4th century BC. Jesus says in John 14:6 "I am the way, the truth and the life; no man comes to the Father but by me." Christianity in its earliest days was called "the Way," (Acts 9:2; 24:14) and the Christian way is "the narrow (way) that leads to life, and only a few find it." (Matthew 7:14) It is impossible, however, to ever know whether Lao Tzu's "Tao" has an intentional, unintentional or even a tangential relationship to the Christian "way" (Greek *odos*).

To the uninitiated the Roman Square may seem confusing, obscure and recondite, but it has been understood and reproduced since shortly after Jesus' resurrection. It was found at Herculaneum on a pillar of the west wall in a wrestling school and in Pompeii etched into the wall in the house of one Publius Paquius Proculus. The two cities were buried in August of 79 AD when Mt. Vesuvius erupted, so these very early Christian Squares were incised before then. The Roman Square is in an 822 Carolingian Bible; in the 1100's it was inscribed on the masonry of the Church of St. Laurent near Ardeche, France and in the Keep of the Castle of Loches, France. Starting in the 1200's, the Square began to lose its original meaning and turned up as a help to women in labor. By the 1400's it was used to quench fires and in the 1500's the Square is a cure for insanity. R. P. Kirchner (1602-1680) found in his travels in Africa that the Christian Ethiopians invoked the Savior by naming the five nails that pinned Him to the cross: SADOR, ALADOR, DANET, ADERA, RODAS, an obvious corruption of the five words in the Roman Square. In 1954 archaeologists digging an ancient Roman site near Budapest found a Roman Square on a roof tile from the residence of a Roman provincial governor. At a redevelopment site in Manchester, England in 1978, a worker unearthed a 2nd century Roman pottery shard that had parts of the Rotas Square on it. Other examples have been found in Portugal, France and in Dura-Europos in Syria. The very early appearance of the Roman Square, its geographical reach and the centuries of use attest to its popularity and to the power of its message, no matter how artfully encrypted it was.

As with the Roman Square, nothing represented in catacomb art means only what is represented. The Biblical stories not only portray historical events, but, also, admit to many allegorical as well as anagogical interpretations. Noah is the just man saved from destruction. Noah is saved upon the waters of baptism, is the prototype of the baptized, is the "new creature in Christ" of II Corinthians 5:17. The Flood is judgment, redemption, baptism, resurrection. The Ark is salvation, Divine protection, God's provision and man's obedience. The dove is the bearer of good news, the harbinger of life, the gentle spirit, peace between God and man, the Holy Spirit.

But of all the symbols commonly used by early Christians, the fish was the most mystic. One recalls Africanus' translation of the narrative of events that supposedly happened in Persia at the time of Christ's birth when the statues cried out: "(Mary) bears in her womb, as in the deep, a vessel of myriad talents' burden....This stream of water sends forth the perennial stream of spirit, a stream containing a single fish, taken with the hook of Divinity, and sustaining the whole world with its flesh as though it were in the sea." If these golden plates go back to the Magi and the birth of Jesus, this is the earliest allusion to Christ as Fish.

Tertullian (c. 160-220) in his treatise on baptism, *De Baptismo 1*, reasons that as water sustains fish, "we, little fishes, after the image of our *ichthus*, Jesus Christ, are born in the water (of baptism) nor are we safe but by remaining in it."

By calling Christians "little fishes," Tertullian evokes Mark 1:16-18 where Jesus, the Big Fisherman, called fishermen to become fishers of men: "As Jesus walked beside the Sea of Galilee, he saw Simon and his brother Andrew casting a net into the lake, for they were fishermen. 'Come, follow me,' Jesus said, 'and I will make you fishers of men.' At once they left their nets and followed him."

Tertullian calls Jesus Christ "our ichthus." *Ichthus* is a Greek word meaning "fish." Clement of Alexandria (c. 150-215) who was the teacher of Origen recommends his readers have their personal seals engraved with either a dove or a fish. *Pedagogus 3.11* Since Clement does not explain why he suggests a dove or a fish, it can be inferred that the symbols were common and needed no explanation.

Most of these very early literary references to Jesus as Fish probably postdate the Christian practice of referring to Christ as Ichthus:

```
I---------IESOUS-------JESUS
CH----- CHRISTOS---CHRIST
TH------THEOU-------OF GOD
U--------UIOS----------SON
S--------SOTER-------SAVIOR
```

"JESUS CHRIST, SON OF GOD, SAVIOR." This holy acrostic was the original credo, the fundamental article of faith for the earliest Christians. It was perhaps used as an abecedary, as a mnemonic tool for new believers. Abecedaries were, and still are, rhymes or lists used to teach the alphabet to young children as in the English Alphabet Song. Groups of individual letters of the Greek and Latin "alphabet," itself a word derived from the first two letters of the Greek alphabet (*alpha* and *beta*), have been found on ancient gravestones and in the catacombs. The letters obviously meant something then, but defy translation now. If the meaning of the grouping of the letters "I-CH-TH-U-S" had not been preserved through the ages, it would, also, be mystifying.

Augustine (354-430) elaborates: "Of these five Greek words (Iesous, Christos, Theou, Uios, Soter), should you group together the first letters, you would form the word ichthus, fish, the mystical name of Jesus the Christ who, in the abyss of our mortality, as though in the depths of the sea, was able to remain alive, that is, free from sin." *The City of God 23*

Symbols, allegories, acrostics, similes and metaphors are forms of poetic thought and must be caught rather than taught. One of the things Augustine was saying is that Jesus, the mystical big fish, was in the waters, in the sea of human mortality, yet He did not succumb to sin as we do but remained alive, remained free from sin, remained clean. (The fish has the added advantage of its association with baptismal water as well as its Greek acrostic resonance.) The early Christians caught it.

And they comprehended that if Christians were fishers of men and, by induction, fishes, then Jesus who called them to be little fishes and fishermen would Himself be the Big Fish, the Ichthus.

Nobody in extant literature took the symbol of Christ as the Big Fish further than Abercius, Bishop of Hieropolis. In c. 163 the 72-year-old Bishop journeyed to Rome and home again where he composed a sixteen-verse Epitaph for himself. In it he talks of eating the "fish of exceeding great size" along with "the choicest wine…mixed with bread." His description of the Eucharist is hermetical, fanciful, gnostic and has provoked animated controversies:

"The citizen of an eminent city, this monument I made while still living,….My name is Abercius, the disciple of the Holy Shepherd Who feeds His flocks of sheep on the mountains and plains, who has great eyes that see everywhere….everywhere Faith was my guide and everywhere provided as my food the Fish of exceeding great size and pure whom the spotless virgin caught from the spring. And Faith ever gives this food to his disciples to eat, having the choicest wine and administering the mixed drink with bread….Let him who understands these words and believes the same pray for Abercius."

Some think Abercius was the priest of a mother-goddess or of the mountain goddess Cybele. A. Harnack, an eminent Biblical scholar, in 1895 proffered Abercius as a religious syncretist. The likely truth is that Abercius is the man named Avircius Marcellus that Eusebius mentions in his *Church History 5.16* who wrote a treatise against the heretical Montanists. And the possible truth is that Abercius, like so many Christian intellectuals of his time who were bathed in allegories, symbols and mysticism, was writing an abstruse, orphic epitaph to be understood only by "him who understands these words."

Pectorius of Autun would have understood. June 24, 1839 a marble gravestone inscribed in Greek was discovered in the cemetery of St. Pierre l'Estrier at Autun in southern France:

"Divine race of the heavenly fish preserve a pure heart having received among mortals the immortal source of divine waters. Refresh, O friend, your soul with the ever-flowing waters of treasure-bestowing wisdom. Receive the sweet food of the Savior of the saints. Eat with delight holding the fish in your hands. Nourish with the fish, I pray, Master and Savior. Sweetly may mother slumber, I beseech You, Light of the dead. Ascandios father, beloved of my heart with sweet mother and my brothers in the peace of the fish, remember Pectorius."

Nothing is known of Pectorius. Because of its paleographic characteristics, the tablet is dated c. 290. The first five lines in this Greek inscription begin with the Greek letters "I, CH, TH, U, S," Ichthus, Fish, Christ. Pectorius closes his inscription "in the peace of the fish." Clearly, the symbol of Christ as Ichthus, as the Fish was known in France as well as in Rome from earliest times.

Pectorius' *Inscription* has, also, provoked controversy. He mentions "holding the fish in your hands" during the Lord's Supper (also called Holy Communion and the Eucharist). The modern Eucharist (from the Greek *eucharistia* meaning "thanksgiving") is composed of two elements, the bread and the wine, not of three elements. Mysticism, metaphor, reality? Or perhaps Pectorius meant that the bread and the wine together compose the Body of Christ, the Ichthus or that Christ/Ichthus is "present" at the Eucharist? What to make of Pectorius and Abercius? Certain it is that modern-day Christians who place stickers of a fish or of the word "Ichthus" on the bumpers of their cars or who wear a fish around their necks as a symbol of their faith are not thinking of Abercius and Pectorius. But the ancient acrostic and the symbol of Christ as Fish are powerful and have survived.

There are many frescoes in the catacombs connecting fish with the celebration of the Eucharist. In the Catacomb of Callixtus in the Cubicles of the Sacraments there is a unique representation of the *imposito manum*, the laying on of hands, the blessing of the Communion bread. A tripod/altar holds a loaf of bread and a fish. A man is laying his hands on the bread. A female on the right has her hands raised in praise. There is another tripod in the same Cubicle with bread on it and seven baskets full of bread on the floor. The most interesting fresco relating to Communion in Callixtus is in the Crypt of Lucina (c. 180). Two large fish face each other, each bearing on its back a wicker basket overflowing with loaves of bread. Each basket contains a cup of red wine hidden among the loaves. Bread, wine and fish, as metaphor or as a part of the sacrament? All three were depicted on the table at early Christian Communions in catacomb art.

Jesus' intimate association with fish/meals/the Eucharist is further illustrated in His third post-resurrection appearance to seven disciples by the Sea of Galilee. (John 21:1-14) The seven had been fishing all night but had caught nothing. As morning dawned, Jesus stood on the shore and called out to them, "Friends, haven't you any fish?" "No," they answered. He said, "Throw your net on the right side of the boat and you will find some." Some fishermen on the Lake used a dragnet hundreds of feet long, but Simon and the disciples were probably using a 55 square foot circular fishing net. They obeyed Jesus and caught 153 large fish. John immediately said to Peter, "It is the Lord!" Peter impetuously jumped into the water, swimming to Jesus as the other disciples towed the net full of fish to the shore. When they all arrived:

"...they saw a fire of burning coals there with fish on it and some bread....Jesus said to them, 'Come and have breakfast.' None of the disciples dared ask him, 'Who are you?' They knew it was the Lord. Jesus came, took the bread and gave it to them and did the same with the fish."

This post-resurrection breakfast was a type of Communion meal prepared and served by Jesus. He took the bread and gave it to them and He took the fish and gave it to them just like He had taken the bread and the wine and given it to them at the Seder meal the night before He was killed:

"While they were eating, Jesus took bread, gave thanks and broke it, and gave it to his disciples saying, 'Take it; this is my body.' Then he took the cup, gave thanks and offered it to them, and they all drank from it. 'This is my blood of the covenant which is poured out for many,' he said to them." Mark 14:22-24

Rather than emphasize Jesus' sacrifice on the cross as the Passover meal in the Upper Room did, this seaside breakfast obviously included the command to "go fish," to evangelize. It included a miracle of fish, the fishermen, the Great Fisherman Himself, fish and bread.

At Jesus' first post-resurrection appearance to His Apostles, He showed them His hands and feet and tried to allay their astonishment and to demonstrate He was a body and not an apparition by asking, "'Do you have anything here to eat?' They gave him a piece of broiled fish, and he took it and ate it in their presence."(Luke 24:40-42) The eating of the fish convinced the Apostles that Jesus was alive again. Eating fish, meals of fish, miracles of fish. It is not totally enigmatic that the early Christians may have had fish on the Communion table and portrayed Jesus as the Ichthus, the Fish, the *Christos*. Even in Greek, the lingua franca of their world, His acrostic name was Fish.

One of Jesus' miracles most represented in the catacombs is the Multiplication of the Loaves and Fishes. This miracle perhaps illuminates more profoundly the prominence of the fish in early Communion celebrations:

"...the crowds followed him on foot from the towns. When Jesus landed and saw a large crowd, he had compassion on them and healed their sick. As evening approached, the disciples came to him and said, 'This is a remote place, and it's already getting late. Send the crowds away, so they can go to the villages and buy themselves some food.' Jesus replied, 'They do not need to go away. You give them something to eat.' 'We have here only five loaves of bread and two small fish,' they answered. 'Bring them to me,' he said. And he directed the people to sit down on the grass. Taking the five loaves and the two fish and looking up to heaven, he gave thanks and broke the loaves (as He had done in the Upper Room). Then he gave them to the disciples, and the disciples gave them to the people. They all ate and were satisfied, and the disciples picked up twelve basketfuls of broken pieces that were left over. The number of those who ate was about five thousand men, besides women and children." Matthew 14:13-21

It was supernatural for Jesus to heal physical infirmities. But there were, are and will be miraculous healers in the world. It was, however, beyond human imagination or comprehension to cause two brined, dried fish and five loaves of small, flat, unleavened barley bread to increase exponentially into enough food to feed five thousand men, not including women and children. It was considered important enough to be the only miracle of Jesus mentioned in all four Gospels. (Matthew 14:31-44; Mark 6:31-44; Luke 9:10-17; John 6:1-15). Two of the Gospel writers record a second miracle of multiplication that fed four thousand people from just seven loaves of bread and "a few small fish." (Matthew 15:29-39; Mark 8:1-10) These two miracles involving bread and fish are often pictured in catacomb art.

The *Fractio Panis* ("Breaking of Bread") fresco in the Catacomb of Priscilla on the Via Salaria is liturgically and theologically one of the most famous of catacomb paintings. Seven people are reclined/seated at a table where there is a cup of red wine and two large plates. One plate contains five loaves of bread, the other two fish, replicating the numbers in the multiplication miracle from the Gospels. A man (presbyter/priest?) at the end of the table has a small loaf in his hands. His arms are stretched out in front of him to show he is breaking the bread as Jesus broke the bread at the Last Supper and before He fed the five thousand and the four thousand. Near the man is a two-handled cup. On one side of the painting are four wicker baskets overflowing with bread. On the other side there are three baskets filled with bread representing the "seven basketfuls of broken pieces that were left over" (Mt. 15:37) after Jesus had fed the four thousand.

The *Fractio Panis* fresco, early 100's, is the clearest example we have in catacomb art of the ritual of the Eucharist in the first one hundred years of the Gentile Church in Rome. In the New Testament book of Acts (c. 63-70) there are references to Christians gathering to "break bread:"

"They devoted themselves to the apostles' teaching and to the fellowship, to the breaking of bread and to prayer." 2:42

"They broke bread in their homes and ate together with glad and sincere hearts." 2:46

The *Fractio Panis* fresco illuminates more clearly how the early catacomb Christians celebrated the Lord's Supper. We see the Communion bread is broken and blessed by the laying on of hands. A cup of wine is present as are two fish. All three elements are on the table. Two millennia later Christian Communion is exclusively celebrated (Latin *celebrare* meaning "to assemble to honor") as reflecting the Last Supper when Jesus pronounced the Bread His Body and the Wine His Blood. According to their iconography, the catacomb Christians gave the Eucharist a much broader context by including fish in the ritual.

There is a very early description of the correct way to celebrate the Eucharist in the *Didache*, a work cited by the Christian writers Clement of Alexandria (c. 150-215), Eusebius of Caesarea (263-339) and Athanasius (c. 293-373). Though known through those authors, the *Didache* in manuscript form had been lost for over 1,400 years until it was re-discovered in 1873 by a Greek Orthodox Metropolitan, Philotheos Bryennios, in the Jerusalem Monastery of the Most Holy Sepulcher in Istanbul. Bryennios published the *Didache* in 1883. It was immediately recognized as one of the most important manuscripts (Latin *manu* meaning "by hand" and *scriptus* meaning "written") of the Early Church because it was obviously written before church hierarchy was firmly in place and was very close to the Jewish Apostolic Age.

The *Didache* begins: "The teaching of the Lord through the twelve Apostles to the Gentiles (meaning 'nations')." According to the Teaching, this is how the Eucharist should be celebrated:

"And with respect to the thanksgiving meal, you shall give thanks as follows.

First with respect to the cup: 'We give you thanks, our Father, for the holy vine of David, your child, which you made known to us through Jesus your child. To you be the glory forever.'

And with respect to the fragment of bread: 'We give you thanks, our Father, for the life and knowledge that you made known to us through Jesus your child. To you be the glory forever.

As this fragment of bread was scattered upon the mountains and was gathered to become one, so may your church be gathered together from the ends of the earth into your kingdom. For the glory and the power are yours through Jesus Christ forever.'

But let no one eat or drink from your thanksgiving meal unless they have been baptized in the name of the Lord. For also the Lord has said about this, 'Do not give what is holy to the dogs.'

And when you have had enough to eat, you shall give thanks as follows:

'We give you thanks, holy Father, for your holy name which you have made reside in our hearts, and for the knowledge, faith and immortality that you made known to us through Jesus your child. To you be the glory forever.

You, O Master Almighty, created all things for the sake of your name, and gave both food and drink to humans for their refreshment, that they might give you thanks. And you graciously provided us with spiritual food and drink and eternal life through your child.

Above all we thank you because you are powerful. To you be the glory forever.

Remember your church, O Lord; save it from all evil, and perfect it in your love. And gather it from the four winds into your kingdom, which you prepared for it. For yours is the power and the glory forever.

May grace come and this world pass away. Hosanna to the God of David. If anyone is holy, let him come; if any one is not, let him repent. Maranatha! ("Come, Lord!") Amen. ("So be it.")

But permit the prophets to give thanks (or: 'hold the eucharist') as often as they wish."' *Didache 9. 10*

Several centuries later the 4th century Gentile theologian Cyril of Jerusalem left a more detailed and ritualistic instruction for Communion. While the *Didache* concentrates on prayer and thanksgiving, Cyril's instructions emphasize technique:

261

"Approaching (Communion)…come not with your palms extended and stretched flat nor with your fingers open. But make your left hand as if a throne for the right, and hollowing your palm receive the body of Christ saying after it, Amen. Then after you have with care sanctified your eyes by the touch of the holy Body, partake…giving heed lest you lose any particle of it (the bread). For should you lose any of it, it is as though you have lost a member of your own body, for tell me, if any one gave you gold dust, would you not with all precaution keep it fast, being on the guard lest you lose any of it and thus suffer loss? How much more cautiously then will you observe that not a crumb falls from you, of what is more precious than gold and precious stones. Then having partaken of the Body of Christ, approach also the cup of His blood; not extending your hands, but bending low and saying in the way of worship and reverence, Amen, be you sanctified by partaking, also of the blood of Christ." *Catechetical Lecture 5*

The celebration of the Lord's Supper was for the early Christians an extremely solemn occasion. Cyril describes the Bread/Body as more precious than gold or costly gems and admonishes them not to let a crumb of it fall to the ground. At the time of Cyril of Jerusalem, a 12-year-old boy in Rome, Tarcisius, was charged with carrying the consecrated bread down the street to some shut-ins. The Spanish Pope Damasus (c. 304-384) has inscribed what happened:

"When a wicked group of young fanatics flung themselves
On Tarcisius who was carrying the Eucharist,
Not wanting to profane the sacrament,
Thereby preferred to give his life rather than yield up
The Body of Christ to the rabid dogs."

The holy boy, Tarcisius, is called "the Eucharist martyr." He was beaten to death rather than let the Communion bread fall on the ground. He is buried in the Catacomb of Callixtus where the poem of Damasus honors his sacrifice.

One thing is sure. The early Christians reverently and reflectively celebrated the Eucharist with bread and wine. But it is moot whether they ate the fish with the sacrament or included the fish as symbol of the totality of the bread and wine, Christ's Body, Ichthus. Perhaps the fish depicted on Communion tables in the catacombs has a meaning yet to be comprehended by modern Christians.

After Jesus had fed the loaves and fishes to the thousands of people who had followed him across the Sea of Galilee (John 6:1-24), his Twelve Apostles got into a boat and began to row back to Capernaum. It was dark. A storm developed. Violent storms come up quickly on the Lake from the Mediterranean Sea through a wind tunnel formed by the Arbel Pass. After "three or three and a half miles" of rowing in rough seas, they saw Jesus walking on the water and approaching their boat. They were terrified---not by the storm, but of Jesus. He tells them not to be afraid and it is indeed He. They take Him into the boat and immediately reach Capernaum.

When Jesus was expelled from his hometown of Nazareth (Luke 4: 16-31), Jesus' Apostle Matthew, a native of Capernaum, informs us in his Gospel: "Leaving Nazareth, (Jesus) went and lived in Capernaum." (4:13) As a resident, Jesus conducted much of His public ministry from this small town located about 25 miles northeast of Nazareth on the 14 miles long and 6 miles wide beautiful Sea of Galilee (aka Tiberias aka Gennesaret aka Kinnereth). Though an insignificant town, Capernaum was a stop on the very ancient Via Maris Highway between Damascus and Caesarea Maritima on the Mediterranean. As a customs or tax collector (Matthew 9:9), Matthew, son of Alphaeus, could have exacted the Roman tax on the Via Maris from travelers either entering or leaving Herod Antipas' Tetrarchy. Roman tax collectors like Matthew were notoriously dishonest and were considered traitors. They were expelled from synagogues and were prohibited from serving as witnesses or judges in courts. Matthew could have been in charge of collecting the Roman tax for licenses to fish and then for the additional tax on the fishermen's daily catch. Peter, Andrew, James and John were partners in a fishing business in Capernaum and would have exported fresh as well as dried fish to Damascus, Tyre, Jerusalem and the villages around the Galilee. Fishing was an important part of the Galilean economy and the tilapia, sardines and carp from this large fresh water lake were prized all over the region. Until he became an Apostle, the four businessmen would, no doubt, have had little regard for the tax collector Levi (Hebrew "joined"), whose name was later changed to the Greek Matthew ("gift of Jahweh").

"The Jesus Boat," so called by archaeologists who in 1986 found a 1st century fishing boat on the northwestern shore of the Sea of Galilee, shows the size of the typical fishing boat used by fishermen like Peter and John who lived along the Lake's shores. Made of scraps of many different types of wood including cedar and oak, the Jesus Boat measures 26.5' long, 7.5' wide and 4.5' deep. These dimensions could carry a crew and ten passengers if used as a ferry boat or if used as a fishing boat, could hold about five crew members and a catch of up to a ton of fish. Carbon-14 dating on a piece of the wood from the Galilee boat gives c. 40 AD as its date, plus or minus 80 years.

Archaeologists have found the ruins of a large house in ancient Capernaum they believe to be the home of Peter. It is in a cluster of some twelve houses dating from the 1st century AD, close to the ruins of a synagogue. The walls of the home are plastered and painted with stylized flowers, pomegranates, figs, geometric figures and hundreds of crosses. On the limestone floor were found many fragments of votive lamps, signifying this house had been singled out from earliest times for special veneration. On the walls of the home are graffiti in many languages: "Lord Jesus Christ, Help;" "Christ Have Mercy;" "Most High God." There are 124 inscriptions in Greek, 18 in Syriac (one mentioning the Eucharist), 15 in Hebrew and 2 in Latin. One in Latin says, "Peter, Helper Of Rome." So many inscriptions in so many languages suggest this was a place of pilgrimage for early believers.

When Emperor Constantine's mother, Helena, made a tour of Palestine in c. 325-327, this home in Capernaum was pointed out to her as the home of Peter. She made the home into a church that was visited 50 years later by the Spanish pilgrim Egeria who wrote in the diary of her pilgrimage: "In Capernaum the house of the prince of the apostles became a church. The walls, however, of the house have remained unchanged to the present day."

Jesus lived in Capernaum (probably with Peter) and performed some of his most memorable miracles there: the healing of Peter's mother-in-law (Mt. 8:14-17); the healing of the palsied man whose friends lowered him down from the roof of a home where Jesus was teaching (Mt. 9:1-8; Mark 2:1-12; Luke 4:40,41); the raising from the dead of Jairus' daughter (Mt. 9:18, 23-25; Mark:22; Luke 8:40-56); the woman healed from an issue of blood (Mt. 9:20-22); the healing of the man with a withered hand (Mt. 12:9-14; Luke 6:6-11) the healing of two blind men (Mt. 9:27-30); the healing of a mute man (Mt. 9:32,33); the miracle of the coin used to pay the Temple tax (Mt. 17:-27).

It is interesting to note that so many of the miracles done in Capernaum are recorded by the eyewitness testimony of Matthew who was a native of Capernaum. Of particular interest to the tax collector Matthew must have been Jesus' command to Peter in Matthew 17:24: "…go to the lake and throw out your line. Take the first fish you catch; open its mouth and you will find a four-drachma coin. Take it and give it to them (the Temple tax collectors) for my tax and yours." It is certain that Matthew had never seen any kind of tax, Temple or Roman, paid in that fashion.

In Capernaum Jesus healed the servant of the Gentile Roman centurion who was in charge of the small military garrison there and had built the local synagogue for the Jews:

"When Jesus had finished saying all this in the hearing of the people, he entered Capernaum. There a centurion's slave, whom his master valued highly, was sick and about to die. The centurion heard of Jesus and sent some elders of the Jews to him asking him to come and heal his servant. When they came to Jesus, they pleaded earnestly with him, 'This man deserves to have you do this, because he loves our nation and has built our synagogue.' So Jesus went with them. He was not far from the house when the centurion sent friends to say to him: 'Lord, don't trouble yourself, for I do not deserve to have you come under my roof. That is why I did not even consider myself worthy to come to you. But say the word, and my servant will be healed. For I myself am a man under authority, with soldiers under me. I tell this one, Go, and he goes; and that one, Come, and he comes. I say to my servant Do this, and he does it.' When Jesus heard this, he was amazed at him, and turning to the crowd following him, he said, 'I tell you, I have not found such great faith even in Israel.' Then the men who had been sent returned to the house and found the servant well." Luke 1:1-10

It was in this synagogue in Capernaum, built by a Roman centurion sympathetic to the Jews and to Jesus, that Jesus would make one of His most controversial claims.

After the suppertime miracle of the loaves and fishes, the next morning the thousands of well-fed people realized Jesus was not there. Some crossed the Sea of Galilee in boats from Tiberias and found Him in that synagogue in Capernaum. They began to question Him: How and when did you get to Capernaum? What works does God require of us? Will you do a miracle like Moses did when he made manna come out of heaven to feed our forefathers? What will you do to make us believe in you? Jesus rebuked them:

"...you are looking for me...because you ate the loaves and had your fill. Do not work for food that spoils, but for food that endures to eternal life....it is not Moses who has given you bread from heaven. For the bread of God is he who comes down from heaven and gives life to the world. 'Sir,' they said, 'from now on give us this bread.' Then Jesus declared, 'I am the bread of life. He who comes to me will never go hungry, and he who believes in me will never be thirsty'....At this the Jews began to grumble about him because he said, 'I am the bread that came down from heaven'....'Stop grumbling among yourselves!' Jesus answered....'I am the bread of life. Your forefathers ate the manna in the desert, yet they died. But here is the bread that comes down from heaven....I am the living bread that came down from heaven. If anyone eats of this bread, he will live forever. This bread is my flesh, which I will give for the life of the world....unless you eat the flesh of the son of Man and drink his blood, you have no life in you....For my flesh

is real food and my blood is real drink....Just as the living Father sent me and I live because of the Father, so the one who feeds on me will live....This is the bread that came down from heaven. Your forefathers ate manna and died, but he who feeds on this bread will live forever.'"
John 6:25-59

A lot had happened in a twenty-four hour period. Jesus had healed many people, had fed the five thousand, had walked on the waters of the Lake and then had a lengthy, contentious debate in the Capernaum synagogue. He had declared Himself to be the living fulfillment prefigured by the manna/bread from heaven in the wilderness. He had asserted that He is the bread of life and that in order to have eternal life, you had to eat His flesh and drink His blood. He was establishing the new covenant:

"While they were eating, Jesus took bread, gave thanks and broke it, and gave it to his disciples, saying, 'Take it; this is my body.' Then he took the cup, gave thanks and offered it to them, and they all drank from it. 'This is my blood of the covenant which is poured out for many.'"
Mark 14:22-24

He was saying to these astonished and offended Jews in Capernaum that He was the living bread that comes from heaven, the eternal daily nourishment given by God versus the temporal manna given to their starving ancestors in the Desert of Sin (Exodus 16:1-4). He hallowed the wine as the life-sustaining water from the rock given to the Jews when they were dying of thirst in the desert (Exodus 17:1-7). Bread and water; body and blood. He said He was the embodiment of the desert miracles that had kept their people alive.

It had been a crucial twenty-four hour period in which Jesus radically defined who He was by His miracles and His words. It was a pivotal time that forced His followers to ask the question, Who in the name of God is this man?! Many of His followers balked at His saying, "unless you eat the flesh of the son of Man and drink his blood, you have no life in you." Some of His disciples said, "This is a hard teaching. Who can accept it?" So "from this time many of his disciples turned back and no longer followed him." (John 6:60, 66) Jesus had about a year before He would be crucified. He was not mincing words. He was separating the wheat from the chaff.

The New Testament Christians graced the walls of the catacombs with frescoes portraying their celebration of the events of that 24-hour period in Galilee when Jesus took fish, broke bread and fed thousands; declared His Body, bread; His Blood, wine; Himself the Ichthus---the Christ, Son of God, Savior.

Through the rites of Baptism and Communion the Christian faith washes away sin and maintains spiritual purity. The pagan Romans among whom the early believers lived also wanted to be clean---physically clean.

In Ankara the capital of Turkey are the ruins of a Roman bath built by Emperor Caracalla and dedicated to Asclepios, the god of healing. Ankara, then known as Ancyra, was the capital city of Galatia, an ancient area in Asia Minor principally known today for its association with the Apostle Paul's letter to the Galatians (c. 48-52) in the New Testament. Galatia had been conquered by Caesar Augustus and annexed to Rome in 25 BC. Two bronze tablets inscribed with Augustus' *The Deeds* have been found in the ruins of his temple in Ankara, formerly known as Angora. In order to maintain the Roman Peace, the Pax Romana, Augustus settled soldiers and their families in all conquered cities and regions. Over the centuries thousands of Romans were living in the Galatian area and they wanted the hallmark of their culture---a Roman Bath.

In 212 Emperor Caracalla built them their bath. In that same year Caracalla (aka Antononius) had issued a decree, the *Constitutio Antoniana*, declaring that all free men in the entire Empire were Roman citizens and all free women had the same rights as Roman women. This declaration vastly increased the number of people who would pay taxes to Rome, took away ambivalent identity ("Am I a Gaul or a Roman?") and gave Caracalla much more money to build baths.

The Bath in Ancyra, a symbol of Rome and of the Galatians' new Roman citizenship, was large. The main hall was 262' wide and 427' long. Off the main hall were auxiliary buildings. In the buildings were hot pools, warm pools, a swimming pool, recreation facilities and rooms for cultural events. The ancient Turks loved this bath so much that the modern-day Turkish people with their famous Turkish baths are the only people in the world who have for thousands of years maintained a direct historical link to the fabled Roman Baths.

In 212 Caracalla, also, began to build in Rome the most famous of all the Baths, the Baths of Caracalla. Covering over 33 acres, it was the second largest Roman Imperial Bath, exceeded in size only by the Baths of Diocletian dedicated 100 years later in 306. Caracalla built his Baths, called in Latin *thermae* ("warm springs"), near Aventine Hill close to the Via Appia, the main road of entry into Rome, where every visitor could see and be impressed with his massive, multi-billion sesterces homage to the art of bathing.

The water to supply his Baths was diverted from the largest of Rome's eleven aqueducts, the Aqua Marcia that carried into Rome the cool and sweet waters of the Aniene River 57 miles away. The water for the Baths was stored on the premises in a double row of 64 cisterns behind the seats of a stadium near one of the two rectangular buildings (*palaestrae*) where athletes practiced and competed in sporting events. Special athletic events were staged in the Bath's stadium. It had only one bank of tiered seats. The rest of the stadium was left open so people who were exercising or strolling could see the contests.

13,000 recently captured Scottish slaves had leveled the land for the Bath. 21 million bricks faced the outside of the buildings. 600 marble workers from Greece were employed to carve the 6,400 square yards of marble and granite columns, facings, friezes, entablatures and statuary that adorned the inside rooms and courtyards.

Caracalla spared no expense for the stones and marbles inside his Bath. He imported grey granite from Egypt, yellow marble from Numidia, a green-veined marble from the island of Carystus in the Mediterranean, green porphyry from Sparta and the prized purple porphyry from a quarry in Egypt. Purple was the color of royalty and the royal Emperor Constantine's casket was made of this purple porphyry. The porphyry from that one quarry in Egypt was very expensive and rare. Its fame was so great that even to this day, the road from that quarry to an ancient city on the Nile is called The Porphyry Road (Via Porphyrites).

Bathing was usually done in the afternoon because the Roman citizen's workday was typically over at midday. The beating of a great copper gong announced the opening of all the Baths. The Roman orator and philosopher Cicero said the sound of that gong was for him "sweeter than the voices of all the philosophers in Athens."

The central building of the Baths of Caracalla was a gigantic 253,000 square feet. The Baths could hold 1,600 bathers not counting the hundreds of other people who came just for social or business reasons. Sometimes the baths were free, but usually there was a small fee paid at one of the four entrances. The main entrance was on the northeast where the cloak and changing rooms (*apodyterium*) were. To show they were socially prominent, patrician men and women often brought a large contingent of slaves with them. Slaves carried all the paraphernalia needed for an afternoon at the Baths: linen towels, exercise and bathing clothes, boxes for jewelry and other sundry items, dishes for scooping water, a toilet kit containing flasks of perfumed oils, olive oil as soap (the very poor used lentil flour as soap) and a curved tool made of metal or bone called a "strigil" used for scraping off dirt, water and oil.

Olive oil was one of the staples of the ancient world. It was burned as fuel for their lamps. Doctors prescribed it, externally and internally, for the sick. James 5:14 urges olive oil as a medicine: "Anoint the sick with oil." We now know olive oil contains not only the potent antioxidant oleocanthal but also salicylic acid, the active ingredient in aspirin. Athletes were massaged with olive oil to relieve aches and pains. As soap, it burrowed deep into the skin and unclogged pores. As a shampoo, it killed head lice and other critters. Olive oil was used for cooking, for embalming, as a food, as a perfume and in sacred rites. There is a 3,500-year-old recipe for a fragrant and sacred anointing oil in the Bible:

"...Take the following fine spices: 12½ lbs. of liquid myrrh, half as much of fragrant cinnamon, 6¼ lbs. of fragrant cane, 12½ lbs. of cassia…and 4 qts. of olive oil. Make these into a sacred anointing oil, a fragrant blend, the work of a perfumer. It will be the sacred anointing oil." Exodus 30:22-25

The Jews anointed their dead with fragrant spiced oils. In John 19:38-40, Joseph of Arimathea and Nicodemus anointed Jesus' dead body in preparation for His burial in the garden tomb:

"…Joseph of Arimathea asked Pilate for the body of Jesus….He was accompanied by Nicodemus….Nicodemus brought a mixture of myrrh and aloes, about 75 pounds. Taking Jesus' body, the two of them wrapped it, with the spices, in strips of linen. This is in accordance with Jewish burial customs."

The brisk Roman trade with Arabia and India was driven by the demand for the East's plants and spices used to flavor their food and to perfume their olive oil. Rome had its perfumeries, but only the wealthy could afford olive oil-based perfumes containing decoctions of frankincense, narcissus, saffron, aloes, myrrh, calamus, cinnamon and other expensive plants, roots or secretions. At Pompeii, shops that sold perfumes have been identified by inscriptions and wall paintings and the House of Perfumer has gardens indicating the types of plants and plant oils that were processed and used in ancient perfumes.

Several days before Jesus was crucified, He had dinner at the home of Simon the Leper with the resurrected Lazarus and his two sisters in Bethany two miles from Jerusalem on the eastern slope of the Mount of Olives. Mary, one of the sisters, "took about a pint of pure nard, an expensive perfume. She poured it on Jesus' feet and wiped his feet with her hair. And the house was filled with the fragrance of the perfume." John 12:3

A pint of pure nard had cost 300 silver denarii, as much as a worker at that time made in one year. (John 12:4) Nard or spikenard is a flowering plant from India. Its rhizomes were crushed and distilled into a thick oil. The aromatic oil had been imported from India as far back as King Solomon's reign in c. 950 BC. The poet Solomon uses the perennial herb to describe the sensual pleasures of his love: "You are a garden locked up, my sister, my bride; you are a spring enclosed, a sealed fountain. Your plants are an orchard of pomegranates with choice fruits, with henna and nard." (Song of Solomon 4:12,13) Because nard was undiluted, it was one of the most expensive perfumes in the world and was called *nardinium*. Lazarus and his sisters were obviously very wealthy. Today one of the most expensive perfumes in our world is Clive Christian's "Imperial Majesty." For women, it comes in essences of bergamot, white peach, Indian jasmine or sandalwood. A 16.9 oz. bottle costs $215,000. But---the bottle is Baccarat crystal and has an 18 carat gold cap adorned with a 5-carat diamond. Mary's 16 ounces of pure unadorned nard was more expensive in her world than the most expensive gold/diamond/ with a little perfume in a little bottle is in ours.

Horace's lyric *Odes* were popular in Mary's time. In *Odes 4.12* he invites his friend Virgil to feast with him as long as he brings a flask of precious nard with him as a gift: "If you would drink a cup of choice wine at my house, bring a flask of precious nard with you. It will draw forth the wine bottle which now lies in the Sulpician vaults." The guarded Sulpician Vaults was a communal wine cellar/cave at the foot of Aventine Hill used by the wealthy to store their wine collections. Horace assures that he will go and pick out a choice bottle of expensive aged wine if Virgil brings him a flask of "precious nard."

Olive oil itself was relatively inexpensive. The Roman poor-on-the-dole got it for free. Today no one uses olive oil as soap, unless Castile soap is in the tub. But when the Romans entered their public baths, they scrubbed and rubbed with their soap, olive oil.

Some slaves remained in the changing room to watch the clothing. A young boy's entry in a Roman schoolbook quotes him as saying to his slave, "Do not fall asleep on account of the thieves." If you did not have a slave to watch your belongings, you could rent one (a *capsarius*) or take your chances with the many thieves.

After you had changed, the entire complex was at your disposal. Before entering the pools, male and a few female bathers liked to work up a sweat in one of the two great open courtyards, each three times the length of a football field, surrounded by colonnades on three sides and filled with trees, gardens, sculptures and splashing fountains made of marble and polished silver. The Romans did not have our team sports but they played hand games and dice (3's and 6's were best; 3's and 1's terrible). In these pastoral open fields, men could run, roll hoops, wrestle, fence, box, lift weights, practice for events in the Olympic games or play handball with a leather ball. (Rubber from the Americas was 1,300 years in the future. Ancient Rome was in ruins when a new continent would be discovered.)

After exercising and resting, you could go into one of the many massage rooms called *unctoriums* and have a soothing rubdown with olive oil. The normal bather, however, entered the *tepidarium*, the room with the tepid pool. It was the largest, the most luxurious and the most visited bath in the complex. Rigidly symmetrical, the room soared over 100' toward the domed and glass-windowed ceiling. It was adorned with grand marble sculptures and entablatures and the floors were covered with exquisite patterned mosaics. Each room in the entire Bath was assembled to astonish. The tepidarium was where your pores opened up and your body was rubbed with oil. When you were ready to leave the warm waters for the next room, all the body dirt and the oils were scraped away with the strigil. You were clean. We are not told how often the waters in the tepidarium were changed, but the philosopher Emperor Marcus Aurelius (121-180) gives us a piece of his mind about the waters of a tepidarium: "What is bathing when you think about it---oil, sweat, filth, greasy water, everything loathsome." At the end of that quote Aurelius, the cynical Stoic, extends his negative view of the Baths to life in general: "... greasy water, everything loathsome, so is every part of life and everything else." *Meditations 8.24*

If you were an aristocratic, pessimistic germaphobe like Aurelius or just wanted privacy in bathing, you could rent rooms with basins for private baths. In all the rooms of the Baths, however, there were provisions in the floor for draining the pools. The dirty water and the water from the toilets drained into a sewer far under the Baths and were eventually carried by the main sewer of Rome, the Cloaca Maxima, into the Tiber River. (The Cloaca was so well-constructed that it continues to function today as an auxiliary sewer connected to the main sewer of modern Rome.) Other than the philosopher king, it is hard to find an ancient who felt anything but joy at the Baths.

A Roman could do anything he or she wanted to do in any order they wished to do it. But it appears from all ancient evidence that a person went from the tepidarium to the *caldarium*, a circular, capacious room 4/5th the size of the Pantheon. Our word "cauldron" comes from that word and the caldarium in the bath, though only three feet deep, was very hot. Caldariums appear to have been a combination of a pool heated to 100-110 degrees F. and a steam bath. It was the hottest room in the complex. Some Baths in Rome had a hot, dry, sauna-like area called a *laconicum* to induce sweating. All the hot rooms in Roman baths were covered with domes to enclose the heat and were sited toward the southwest to take advantage of the solar heat of the afternoon sun.

After the caldarium, you could get a massage or another anointing and scraping, but the normal progression from the caldarium was into the *frigidarium*, a majestic, partially open-air room containing a cold bath. The covered part of the frigidarium normally had skylights of unglazed glass at the top of the room. The experience was a cold dip and a lounge and tan in the sun. In the winter months of Rome, the plunge into the waters in the frigidarium shocked the system and closed the pores of the body. We are not told how they kept the waters in that pool cold during the hot summer months, but Romans were known to have brought snow from distant mountains into Rome in the summertime and flavored it with fruit juices like snow cones. Long before refrigeration when Philip II (1527-1598) ruled Spain, ice and snow were routinely brought to Madrid from the mountains 40 miles away, stored in snow pits and sold all summer long for cool drinks and sherbets. The Romans were ingenious and, it is sure, they devised a way to keep the cold pool cold.

There would have been no Roman baths if Roman engineers had not perfected hypocaust heating ("heating from below"). The heating system kept the rooms in the Bath heated and the hot pools hot. Today their system is called radiant heat, heated floors. Underneath the central building of the Baths on the lowest floor were massive furnaces fueled by wood. The caldarium, the hottest room, was built over the central furnace. The heat generated by the furnaces warmed the floors of the baths and was funneled by an intricate system of pipes and flues to the floors of any part of the building that required heat. The heat could, also, be channeled through the walls of the complex by leaving a gap between the external wall and the internal wall. Modern studies on the ancient hypocaust system have shown that in the Baths the tepidarium was heated to between 64-70 degrees Fahrenheit and the caldarium to between 100-110 degrees F. Slaves worked the furnaces and had to stoke up to 10 tons of wood per day to keep the Baths of Caracalla hot. It took 2-3 days to fire up the furnaces, so the fires were banked at night.

The service world was, also, on the lowest of the four levels of the Baths. There were corridors wide enough and tall enough for horse-drawn carts to bring in wood for the furnaces and supplies for the Baths. This was the world of the stokers, the lamplighters, and all the thousands of slaves who worked underground to keep the baths operational. Manholes and hidden staircases opened all along the central building so the slaves, without being seen by the bathers, could restock the linens, repair plumbing or roofing and do all the tasks needed to keep the Baths running seamlessly.

After your baths, the entire 33-acre recreational complex was available. Perhaps you wanted a swim in the open-air, Olympic-sized swimming pool (*natatio*) with colorful awnings for shade and bronze mirrors mounted overhead to reflect sunlight into the pool area. Maybe you wanted to get your hair done and have a manicure in the beauty salon. You could read in one of the two libraries with their niches for codices, scrolls and parchments. In case there was a chill, one of the libraries was heated by flues in the ceiling. The pagans were constantly inventing new gods. If you were a convert to the Persian god Mithras, there was a small Mithraeum attached to the Baths where you could perform the mysterious rites.

A daily papyrus newspaper, the *Acta Diurna* (*Daily Events*), was distributed in locations around the Baths. Probably the low-grade saitic or taenotic paper was used for daily publishing, no doubt one of the reasons that no scraps of the *Acta Diurna* have ever been found.

Whitewashed boards with news of the day were, also, posted in public places.

The ancient world kept in touch with each other and with current events. In c. 715 BC during the reign of the Jewish king Hezekiah, "couriers went throughout Israel and Judah with letters from the king and from his officials....the couriers went from town to town in Ephraim and Manasseh, as far as Zebulun." (II Chronicles 30: 6,10) Herodotus in his *Histories 8.98* describes the 6th century BC Persian/Mede postal system: "It is said that as many days as there are in the whole journey, so many are the men and horses that stand along the road, each horse and man at the interval of a day's journey; and these are stayed neither by snow nor rain nor heat nor darkness from accomplishing their appointed course with all speed." Even though the US Postal Service does not have an official creed, Herodotus' quote about a postal system 2,600 years ago has been embraced by them. The Chinese devised their first system of distant communication during the Han Dynasty (206 BC-220 AD). In the Middle Ages in Europe homing pigeons were used as postal carriers. In the 1400's AD the Incas in Peru had couriers carrying messages over its 2,000 miles of roads in just 7 days. Civilizations have always desired to communicate.

The Cursus Publicus, the Roman Regal Post System, was only for Imperial and military letters and dispatches. Couriers traveled about 100 miles a day, but when Nero was forced to commit suicide, the news of his death traveled 332 miles in only 36 hours. Ordinary Romans sent letters either through servants, friends or traders. A brother to brother letter, written c. 150 AD, illustrates the universality of ordinary letters no matter when or where they have been written:

"Tusticus Barbarus to his brother Pompeius, greetings!
How come you haven't answered my last letter if you received the loaves of bread I sent you? First I sent you 15 loaves with Popillius and Dutoporis, then I sent you another 15 as well as a vase with the carter Draco. Do you realize how much wheat that used up! Please have me some decorated knives made by the fort blacksmith for my personal use and make them as beautiful as possible. Write to me so that I can send

you some more bread in payment or even some money, whichever you wish. I want you to know that I am getting married. Once I am married, I will let you know so that you can come and visit us.

Goodbye,

Regards to Julius"

Pompeius was obviously a soldier at a fort because his brother Barbarus asks him to have the blacksmith at the fort make him a set of decorated knives. Barbarus had already sent Pompeius 30 loaves of bread and a vase and still had not heard a word from his ungrateful brother. Letters, communications, the daily newspaper and even 30 loaves of bread were disseminated all over the Empire by couriers and friendly carriers.

The *Acta Diurna* kept Romans current on events of interest: weddings, births, deaths, crimes, trials, monies in the treasury from the provinces, the cost of the supply of grain, movements and events in the Imperial family, gossip columns on the latest amatory adventures of the rich and famous, gladiator events, military and political news as well as some human interest stories (dog lost far away finds way home) and astrological readings.

From the *Chronographia of 354* we know what Roman astrologists considered propitious and inauspicious for each of the 7 days of the week. Saturn's day (Saturday) reads:

"The day of Saturn and its hours, whether day or night, all things become obscure and laborious; those born will be sickly; those who hide will not be found; those who fall ill will perish; the hidden deed will not be found out."

Wednesday was Mercury's day (*mercredi* in French):

"The day of Mercury and its hours, whether day or night, it is advantageous to negotiate with a farm-manager, actor or shopkeeper. Those born will be healthy; those who hide will be found; those who fall ill will quickly recover; the hidden deed will be found out."

People were as anxious then for such prognostic pablum as they are today.

When Julius Caesar was Consul in 59 BC, he began the *Acta Diurna* and ordered it posted in markets, on the doors of temples and in all public places. Because no pieces of the daily newspaper are extant, we know about the gazette and its popularity only through ancient writers. In the writing of his *Lives of the Caesars* Suetonius used the *Acta Diurna* for dates and places of births, deaths and events. Through Tacitus we learn the newspaper was carried by courier throughout Rome's vast empire and was eagerly read for current news from Rome. Describing a bit of intrigue between Nero and one of Nero's opponents in the Senate named Thrasea, Tacitus says: "The journal of the Roman people is scanned through the provinces and armies with double care for news of what Thrasea has done." *Annals 16.22* Tacitus does, however, want to separate his great works of history from common journalism: "It has been held fitting to consign great events to the pages of history and details such as these (the foundation and beams of Nero's amphitheater) to the urban gazette." *Annals 13.31* The daily gazette published in Rome continued until c. 330 when Constantine moved the seat of government to Constantinople.

After you had read the daily newspaper, you could go to the lecture hall and hear a poetry reading or listen to a philosopher expound or visit and gossip with friends or conduct business meetings. Jugglers, magicians, acrobats, musicians and prostitutes roamed the extensive grounds plying their trades and hoping to make money. There were private rooms where you could have an assignation with a prostitute or with a paramour. The bathing was often segregated, but in the Baths of Caracalla naked men and women swam together, flirted and had sex in the pools. Clement of Alexandria (c. 150-202), a convert to Christianity and the Christian leader of the Catechetical School in Alexandria, says of the baths:

"And of what sort are their baths….gold-plated chairs and silver ones, too, and ten thousand vessels of gold and silver….besides these, there are even braziers of coals; for they have arrived at such a pitch of self-indulgence that they sup and get drunk while bathing...the dirt of wealth, then has an abundant covering of censure....the baths are opened promiscuously to men and women; and there they strip for licentious indulgence...as if their modesty had been washed away in the bath." *Pedagogus, 3.5*

The Baths became such arenas of licentiousness that the Christians called them "cathedrals of the flesh."

There was a two-story arcade filled with small shops where you could buy wool, linen and cotton *stolae* (the female equivalent of a toga), tunics, togas, shawls (*pulla*), other loose-fitting garments (the Romans considered pants barbaric), jewelry, leather sandals, writing paper (papyrus, parchment) or *tabellae* (wood tablets covered with wax for writing), writing implements (*stylus*) and inks made from fish oil or the red dye of the octopus, perfumes, silk scarves from China and other choice merchandise. Mattresses and cushions made of feathers, wool or straw were sold to cover stone or wooden sleeping and dining couches. There were shops specializing in *candelabrum* that held many candles and in armless, backed chairs called *cathedra*. In the Early Church all the bishops used a *cathedra*, leading to the expression *ex cathedra*, from the official chair. It is, also, the origin of the English word "cathedral," a seat of worship. One could purchase *clepsydras* or water clocks. The Greek word *clepsydra* means "water thief." Apparently the expression "thief of time" is very ancient.

While you whiled away time, you could listen to a concert in the music pavilion or stroll the museum filled with Greek and Roman sculptures and paintings. In the sixteenth century some of the sculptures from the ruins of the Baths of Caracalla were retrieved by Cardinal Farnese to adorn the palace he was building near the Campo di Fiori in Rome. He rescued two large stone bathing tubs, turned them into fountains and put them in front of his home. They still give the Piazza Farnese its special interest and timeless beauty.

In 1534 Farnese became Pope Paul III and commissioned Michelangelo to finish his palace. The artist in Michelangelo must have gasped as the excavations at the Baths of Caracalla unearthed discoveries that far exceeded all expectations. In 1545 the *Group of the Bull* was found. It is the largest sculptural group to survive from antiquity and is the stunning work of two brothers from Rhodes. A year later the resplendent nine foot tall *Hercules* by the Greek sculptor Glykon (c. 200 AD) was unearthed. A weary, reflective Hercules rests temporarily from his Twelve Labors and leans on his club, draped with the skin of the Nemean lion he had killed in his first Labor. His right hand is hidden behind him but clutches the fruits of his 11th Labor, the golden apples of the Hesperides. Hercules, massive and muscular, meditates his 12th and final task, the descent into the Underworld to bring back the vicious, many-headed dog Cerberus who guards the gates of Hell. Such works of ancient Greek genius, now in the National Archaeological Museum in Naples, were commonplace in the Baths and continue to astound the world.

Food was a big part of the Roman spa experience. Vendors with their heated carts sold hot sausages, fish, pastries and, the forerunner of the modern pizza, bread sprinkled with olive oil and cheese. At Herculaneum, buried by the eruption of Mt. Vesuvius in August of 79, a list of foods for sale in their small Bath has been found: Nuts and drinks---14 *as* (*as* are chunks of bronze money); Hogsfat---2 as; Bread---3 as; Cuttlefish 3---12 as; Sausage 4---8 as. Martial says a friend of his ate eggs, lettuce and fish at the Bath. They ate their foods on terracotta pottery with knives and spoons. The fork was not widely used in the West until the 17th and 18th centuries.

The normal Roman's daily diet was restricted, but not exclusively, to choices of: fresh, honey-preserved or salted fish, shellfish, eels, oysters, snails and a fermented fish sauce called *garum* used as an all-purpose condiment like we use catsup or mustard; domestic fowl and game, rabbits, dormice, lamb, pork, wild boar but not beef as cattle were considered work animals only; breads (most of their grains were imported from Egypt) made from barley, rye, wheat, spelt, millet and rice; cheeses made from cow and goat milk, butter, eggs, asparagus, beans, lentils, peas, onions, garlic, cabbage, celery, turnips, parsnips, cucumbers, greens, carrots, apples, plums, raisins, cherries, peaches, quinces, pears, figs, apricots, lemons, melons, nuts, pastries, honey, fruit juices (especially grape juice called *mustum*), beer, water and the favorite drink of Romans of all ages---red and white wine diluted with water or sweetened with honey.

Romans, following the Greek tradition, considered it barbaric and provincial to drink undiluted wine. Even though they had a profitable trade with Gaul (France and environs) exchanging wine for slaves, the Romans looked down on the Gauls as a besotted people because they drank their wine undiluted. The Romans mixed one part wine to two parts water. The Greeks diluted their wine with three-four parts water. When the early Christians talk of using "mingled wine" in Communion, they are meaning wine diluted with water. *Mulsum* was wine sweetened by honey. *Conditum* was wine to which herbs, spices and pepper were added. Mixed wines had a number of applications. Wine mixed with barley made a good household vinegar. The wine blended with myrrh offered to and turned down by Jesus on the cross in Mark 15:23 was used as an anesthetic.

The original Greek name for Italy was *Oenotria* meaning "wine country." Its modern name "Italy" seems to come from a legendary king of the Oenotrians called Italos/Italus. Even though wine and winemaking has been around for thousands of years, by the end of the 2nd century BC, the Romans had perfected viticulture and winemaking. The basic winepress consisted of an upper vat where the grapes were trodden with bare feet and a deeper lower vat to receive the juices. In order to get all the juices out, the grape husks were pressed down by a wooden plank covered with heavy stones. More sophisticated winepresses have been found with three or four vats to refine and reduce the amount of sediment in the wine. The juice fermented in the lowest vat for about a week and then was poured into wineskins or jars called *amphorae* for two to four months when the normal fermentation process was complete.

Wines were graded and priced according to the grapes used and the location of the vineyards. The fabled Falernian wine, grown from imported Greek grape vines at Cumae in the Bay of Naples, was the most expensive wine and could withstand aging up to 150 years. It was a white wine, normally aged 10-20 years until it was amber-colored. The daily drink of Romans was a plebeian red wine not more than a year old. Most wines were bottled in 100-gallon amphorae that were sealed and labeled.

In Paphos, Cyprus a floor mosaic from the 200's AD has been found in an antique villa. Called *The First Wine Drinkers*, it recalls the mythological story of Ikarios from Athens who was kind to the god Dionysius. As a reward, Dionysius gave him the gift of wine which Ikarios gave to his shepherds. They thought from the effects of the wine they had been poisoned and killed Ikarios. The mosaic depicts two of Ikarios' shepherds, one lying drunk on the ground holding his head, the other gesturing aggressively. Over the mosaic are the Greek words, "The First Wine Drinkers." Obviously, the wealthy builders of the villa were making a statement on the floor of their dining room. Was it the dangers of drink since it harks back to the murder of Ikarios? Was it the celebration of drinking in a rich man's home? Or was it something else?

This villa in Cyprus seems to have been the permanent dwelling place of the owners, but many wealthy Romans had elaborately furnished and sited second homes outside of Rome in Baiae, Pompeii and Capri where they escaped the summer heat of Rome. Pliny the Younger (61-112AD) loved villas and had four of them in addition to his Roman residence. Two of his villas were north of Rome on beautiful Lake Como where he was born. He could find local people to build his summer villas, but it is staggering to imagine the architects for his villas, the painters and paints for the wall frescoes, the mosaic artists and the tiles for the floors, the sheets of marbles and all the extravagant furnishings and accoutrements for the villas being dragged 400 miles from Rome over uncertain terrain to this popular but relatively impassable place. The lovely Hotel Villa Serbelloni on a rocky promontory in Bellagio is thought to be on the site of Pliny's 1st century AD Villa Tragedia. In a letter to his friend Romanus, Pliny describes his villas on Lake Como:

"I am pleased to find by your letter that you are engaged in building; for I may now defend my own conduct by your example. I am myself employed in the same sort of work....your buildings are carried on upon the sea-coast, mine are rising upon the side of the Larian lake. I have several villas upon the border of this lake, but there are two particularly in which I take most delight. They are both situated like those at Baiae (on the Mediterranean coast): one of them stands upon a rock and overlooks the lake. One, by a gentle curve, embraces a little bay....The former (at Bellagio) built upon a greater height commands a wider...view of the lake....Here you have a straight walk extending itself along the banks of the lake....(the villa) does not feel the force of the waves....from this (villa) you fish yourself and throw your line out of your room and almost from your bed, as from a boat. It is the beauties these agreeable villas possess that tempt me." *Letters 9.7*

By such letters Pliny lured many people from Rome up to Bellagio where they had pleasant days of fishing and sumptuous banquets at night under the flickering torches and oil lamps.

Today pastas and tomatoes are intimately associated with Italy, but it was Marco Polo many hundreds of years after the fall of Rome who introduced Italy to the Chinese pasta (the noodle) in c. 1295. The tomato was a gift to the world from the Americas (post 1492) as were potatoes, corn, coffee and chocolate. The Roman's only sweetener was honey. Sugar from the cane was a closely guarded secret kept by the Arabs for centuries. But the "honeyed reed," as sugar was first called, was brought back to Europe in the 12th century by the Crusaders.

If the normal Roman's diet was somewhat restricted, the wealthy ate lavishly and imaginatively. Hundreds of thousands of sesterces were squandered on dinner parties where guests were regaled with foods from all over Rome's Empire. So that the pleasures of eating might be prolonged, some ate and then vomited so they could consume more delicacies. But homes did not have a vomitorium. The arenas did. Vomitoriums were passageways that "spewed forth" the people at the end of performances.

With the upper classes every thing was exaggerated as they sought more and more meaning in their empty lives. Poppaea Sabina, Nero's wife, took 500 asses, all shod in gold and silver shoes, on a journey with her so she could have their milk for her cosmetic baths. Her husband fished with nets of gold threads. Unnatural and unrequited longings impelled the upper classes and new thrills, unearned gifts and blood thirst at the games drove the lower classes. Normal became a boring word. Virtue was mocked. Unambiguous obscenity had ruled the Roman Empire for centuries.

Elagabalus, appointed Emperor when he was barely 15 and assassinated four years later in March of 222, was one of the most corrupt of the emperors. He showed his childishness and depravity by his life style and banquets:

"...for (Elagabalus) life was nothing except a search after pleasures....He had couches made of solid silver for use in his banqueting rooms and his bed chambers. In imitation of Apicius (gourmand who lived in the early 1st century), he frequently ate camels heels and also cocks combs taken from living birds and the tongues of peacocks and nightingales, because he was told that one who ate them was immune from the plague. He served to the palace attendants...huge platters heaped up with the viscera of mullets and flamingo brains, partridge eggs, thrush brains and the heads of parrots, pheasants and peacocks....He fed his dogs on goose livers (foie gras, a delicacy known since 2500 BC in ancient Egypt where a bas relief in the tomb of Mereruka in Saqqara shows slaves grasping geese and forcing food down their throats)....He sent grapes from Apamea (Syrian city) to his stables for his horses and he fed parrots and pheasants to his lions....he served (to his guests) peas (scattered) with gold pieces, lentils with onyx, beans with amber and rice with pearls; he also sprinkled pearls on fish and truffles in lieu of pepper.... he once overwhelmed his parasites (guests) with violets and flowers (dropped from the ceiling), so that some were actually smothered to death, being unable to crawl out to the top....As banquet favors, he gave out eunuchs or four-horse chariots or horses with saddles or mules or litters or carriages or a thousand pieces of gold or a hundred pounds of silver....He never had intercourse with the same woman (or man) twice... and he opened brothels in his house for his friends, his clients and his slaves. He never spent less on a banquet than one hundred thousand sesterces, that is, thirty pounds of silver; and sometimes he even spent as much as three million when all the cost was computed....he loved to hear the prices of the food served at his table exaggerated, asserting it was an appetizer for the banquet....At one dinner where there were many tables he brought in the heads of six hundred ostriches in order that the brains might be eaten." *Historia Augusta 2.18-30*

At the request of the 4th century Emperor Constantine the Great, the anonymous author or authors of *Historia Augusta* compiled biographies of previous emperors from the years 117-284. The author begs Constantine's "pardon for having set down in writing what I have found in various authors...I have passed over in silence many vile details...not fit to be spoken of without the greatest shame." *Historia Augusta 2.34* Even though Elagabalus was only 18 when he was assassinated, he had done such vile things that he ranks with Nero and Commodus. When he died, he was declared *damnatio memoriae* (meaning "memory of him is damned, not to be remembered") and all references to him were erased. Elagabalus knew he danced on thin ice and had prepared for his death, "but all these preparations availed him nothing...for he was slain by common soldiers, dragged through the streets, contemptuously thrust into sewers and finally cast in the Tiber." *Historia Augusta 2.33* His grandmother, Julia Maesa, had connived his ascension to the throne and Julia Maesa conspired with the Praetorian Guard, an elite corps of soldiers who guarded the emperor, to have this perverted teenage hedonist murdered. Women, though often pawns, were frequently behind the scenes puppeteers.

Elagabalus is known, among other things, for his unusual and debauched banquets but "Trimalchio's Banquet" in Petronius' *Satyricon 28-41* is the most complete description in ancient literature of the dinner parties of the super-rich. The parvenu Trimalchio, ostentatious and crude, was a freed slave, a *liberti*, who had become wealthy through trade and business deals. In spite of his wealth, Trimalchio was still ostracized from polite society and resorted to recruiting strangers on the streets for his banquets. Before going to his home for dinner, Trimalchio takes his lowlife, impromptu guests to a Bath. One of the reprobates describes the experience:

"...we entered the baths where we began sweating at once and we went immediately into the cold water. Trimalchio had been smothered in perfume and was already being rubbed down, not with linen towels, but with bathrobes of the finest wool....three masseurs sat drinking Falernian in front of him...(Later), wrapped in thick scarlet felt (Trimalchio) was put into a litter....We followed on, choking with amazement by now, and arrived at his doorway....as we were stepping forward, a slave with his back bare flung himself at our feet and began pleading with us to get him off a flogging. He was in trouble for nothing very serious...the steward's clothes, hardly worth ten sesterces, had been stolen from him at the baths....Finally, we took our places (at the dinner table). Boys from Alexandria poured iced water over our hands. Others followed them and attended to our feet, removing any hangnails with great skill....The dishes for the first course included an ass of Corinthian bronze with two panniers, white olives on one side and black on the other. Over the ass were two pieces of plate with Trimalchio's name and the weight of the silver inscribed on the rims. There were...dormice (mice) sprinkled with honey and poppy seed...steaming hot sausages on a silver gridiron with damsons and pomegranate seeds underneath....Trimalchio was carried in and set down on a pile of tightly stuffed cushions....On the little finger he wore a heavy gilt ring and a smaller one on the last joint of the next finger...studded with little iron stars. And to show off even more of his jewelry, he had his right arm bare and set off by a gold armlet and an ivory circlet....a tray was brought in with a basket on it. There sat a wooden hen....Two slaves hurried up and as the orchestra played a tune, they began searching through the straw and dug out peahens' eggs which they distributed to the guests....We took up our spoons and cracked the eggs which were made of rich pastry....I heard a guest who was an old hand say, 'There should be something good here.' So I searched the shell with my fingers and found the plumpest little figpecker (an Orphean warbler), all covered with yolk and seasoned with pepper....A young Egyptian slave carried around bread in a silver oven....four dancers hurtled forward in time to music and removed the upper part of (a) great dish, revealing underneath plump fowls, sows' udders, and a hare with wings fixed to his middle to look like Pegasus....a peppery fish sauce (ran) over some fish which seemed to be swimming in a little channel (of sauce)....a man with a carving knife and, with his hands moving in time to the music of the orchestra, sliced up the victuals....Carefully sealed wine bottles were immediately brought, their necks labeled: FALERNIAN. CONSUL OPIMIUS. 100 YEARS....(Trimalchio) said with a sigh: 'Wine has a longer life than us poor folks. So let's wet our whistles. I'm giving you real Opimian'....the next course was brought in...it was so novel that everyone stared. It was a deep circular tray with the twelve signs of the Zodiac arranged round the edge. Over each of them the chef had placed some appropriate dainty suggested by the sign. Over Aries the Ram, chickpeas; over Taurus the Bull, a beefsteak; over the Heavenly Twins, testicles and kidneys; over Cancer the Crab, a garland; over Leo the Lion, an African fig; over Virgo, a young sow's udder; over Libra the Scales, a balance with a cheesecake in one pan and a pastry in the other; over Scorpio, a sea scorpion; over Sagittarius the Archer, a sea bream with eyespots; over Capricorn, a lobster; over Aquarius, a wild goose, over Pisces, two mullets....Fresh servants entered and spread carpets before (our) couches, embroidered with pictures of fowling nets, (men) with their hunting spears and sporting gear of all kinds. We were still at a loss what to expect when a tremendous shout was raised outside the doors, and lo and behold, a pack of Laconian dogs came careening round and round the table. These were soon succeeded by a huge tray on which lay a wild boar of the largest size, with a cap on its head, while from its tusks hung two little baskets of woven palm leaves, one full of Syrian dates, the other of Theban. Round (the boar) were little piglets of baked sweetmeat, as if at suck to show it was a sow we had before us and these (piglets) were gifts to be taken home with (us)....To carve the (boar)...a great bearded fellow, wearing leggings and a shaggy jerkin (entered). Drawing his hunting knife, he made a furious lunge and gashed open the boar's flank, from which there flew out a number of birds. Fowlers stood ready with their rods and immediately caught the birds as they fluttered about the table. Then Trimalchio directed each guest to be given his bird, and this done, he added, 'Look, what elegant acorns this wildwood pig fed on.' Instantly slaves ran to the baskets that were suspended from the animal's tusks and divided the two kinds of dates in equal proportions among the diners."

It would be almost 1,000 years after the fall of Rome before such sumptuous "surprise feasts" would again be given by the rich during the Middle Ages.

Trimalchio and his eccentric entourage went to the Baths and then had their sumptuous big meal. Most Romans ate their main meal at noon and then went to the Baths. Some perhaps had their noon meal at the Baths or nibbled on slices of watermelon and a soufflé of shrimp and raisins rinsed down with a glass of diluted red wine. In the drains of ancient Roman baths bits of glass, shards from jugs and cups and even small animal bones have been found. Some archaeologists claim a large room in the Baths of Caracalla was a restaurant where diners reclined on couches, ordered their food and were served.

Anyone and everyone came to the Baths of Caracalla. But the Romans, also, had neighborhood baths called *balnea*. There were on average five of these bathhouses per block of homes and in the tenements one balneum for every thirty-five apartment buildings. These were smaller pools and grounds that serviced the immediate vicinity. It was the popularity of these communal baths that eventually led to the building of the large public Baths.

The Roman philosopher Seneca lived for a time in Baiae, a coastal resort for the wealthy on the Bay of Naples. It was popular for its hot mineral springs turned into Baths. Seneca lived in an apartment overlooking one of these small Baths. He wrote to a friend:

"I have lodgings right over a (local) bathing establishment. So picture to yourself the assortment of sounds which are strong enough to make me hate my very powers of hearing! When your strenuous gentleman, for example, is exercising himself by flourishing leaden weights; when he is working hard, or else pretends to be working hard, I can hear him grunt; and whenever he releases his imprisoned breath, I can hear him panting in wheezy and high-pitched tones. Or perhaps I notice some lazy fellow, content with a cheap rubdown and hear the crack of the pummeling hand on his shoulder, varying in sound according as the hand is laid on flat or hollow. Then, perhaps, a professional comes along, shouting out the score....Add to this the occasional boisterous person or pickpocket, the racket of the man who always likes to hear his own voice in the bathroom, or the enthusiast who plunges into the swimming pool with unconscionable noise and splashing....imagine the hair-plucker with his penetrating, shrill voice, for purposes of advertising, continually giving it vent and never holding his tongue except when he is plucking the armpits and making his victim yell instead. Then the cakeseller with his varied cries, the sausageman, the confectioner, and all the vendors of food hawking their wares....Among the sounds that din round me without distracting, I include passing carriages, a machinist in the same block, a saw-sharpener nearby, or some fellow who is demonstrating with little pipes and flutes." *Epistle 56*

Seneca's letter brings the dimension of cacophony to the experience of a Roman bath. He concludes the letter by saying he is looking for other lodgings.

The Thermae were cities within cities. There was a Bath in most major and a few minor outposts of the Empire. Some of them are still standing. The most famous of the existing Roman Baths is in Bath, England. The Roman military garrisons struck it rich when they arrived at this forlorn frontier. For thousands of years, and even today, 115 degree F. water rises from the ground at the rate of 257,000 gallons a day. The ancient Celts used the warm springs and built a shrine dedicated to their goddess Sullis at Bath long before the Romans arrived. A curse or execration tablet found at Bath attests to the fact that Celtic thieves like Roman thieves often preyed on those taking the baths:

"Solinus, to the goddess Sullis. I gave to your divinity and majesty my bathing tunic and cloak. Do not allow sleep or health to him who has done me wrong, whether man or woman, whether slave or free, unless he reveals himself and brings (my) goods to your temple."

In 60-70 the Romans began constructing a Roman Therma at Bath. Because the hot water was already there, all they had to do was build a swimming pool. Their engineers drove oak piles into the mud and then built a stone pool lined with 45 sheets of lead. Over the next 200 years, the pool was enclosed with a barreled vaulted roof and the building was decorated with stone columns and statues. As with all Roman buildings, it was built to last and is still there. The Roman plumbing and drainage systems still work. Over a million tourists visit Bath each year.

The fourth largest Bath ever built was in Odessus, Bulgaria, modern- day Varna, in c. 300. Its ruins are majestic and cause one to wonder why such a gigantic Bath for such an insignificant city. Ruins of smaller baths dot the landscapes of Algeria, Bulgaria, Germany, Romania, Spain, Turkey, the Netherlands and Lebanon. There were, of course, many emperors that built Thermae in Rome: Augustus, Nero, Titus, Domitian, Trajan, Caracalla, Diocletian and Constantine. Before the beginning of the 1st century AD, Augustus had built a Bath on the Mediterranean in Baiae by channeling the warm spring water bubbling out of the ground into a bathhouse. "Nothing is more sublime than the shores of Baiae, where it is possible to enjoy the sweetest delight and to fulfill the incomparable gift of health," says Cassiodoro five hundred years later as he was enjoying Augustus' spa at Baiae. *Variae 9. 6.6*

At the height of the Empire, Rome had 13 aqueducts, 1,352 public fountains, 962 neighborhood baths and 11 Imperial Thermae like the Baths of Caracalla. A simple basin filled with water became for the Romans plush, prodigious palaces of public pleasure. The simple joy of bathing and being clean became long afternoons of de rigueur routines, of secular ritual washings and idle languishing. The simple act of bathing was turned into a multi-purpose, multi-dimensional and multi-media recreational experience. Unlike the Jews who strove for ritual purity in their mikvehs and the Christians who believed the waters of baptism washed away sin, the Roman Baths, erected by and named for the Emperor gods who built them, were waters devoid of spiritual meaning---replete with sensual pleasure.

XIII.

"Now faith is being sure of what we hope for and certain of what we do not see....By faith Noah, when warned about things not yet seen, in holy fear built an ark to save his family.... By faith Abraham, when called to go to a place he would later receive as an inheritance, obeyed and went....For he was looking forward to the city with foundations whose architect and builder is God....All these people were still living by faith when they died. They did not receive the things promised; they only saw them and welcomed them from a distance....By faith Moses' parents hid him for three months after he was born...and they were not afraid of the king's edict. By faith Moses....regarded disgrace for the sake of Christ as of greater value than the treasures of Egypt because he was looking ahead to his reward....By faith he left Egypt, not fearing the king's anger, he persevered because he saw him who is invisible....By faith the people passed through the Red Sea as on dry land....By faith the walls of Jericho fell....By faith the prostitute Rahab, because she welcomed the spies, was not killed....I do not have time to tell about Gideon, Barak, Samson, Jephthah, David, Samuel and the prophets who through faith....shut the mouths of lions, quenched the fury of the flames...escaped the edge of the sword....women received back their dead....Others were tortured and refused to be released, so that they might gain a better resurrection. Faced jeers and flogging... were chained and put in prison. They were stoned; they were sawed in two; they were put to death by the sword....were persecuted and mistreated....They wandered in deserts and mountains and in caves and holes in the ground....Therefore, since we are surrounded by such a great cloud of witnesses, let us throw off everything that hinders and the sin that so easily entangles, and let us run with perseverance the race marked out for us." Hebrews 11:1--12:1

The Roman Baths turned getting clean into a strenuous exercise in hedonistic pleasure. They turned sporting events into amphitheaters of animal and human slaughter. They turned their spiritual bankruptcy into political and military campaigns against Jews and Christians. Whatever Rome did, she did with a fierce, unreflective dogmatism and a dogged belief that she was right.

The early Christians matched Rome's determination with intrepid faith and a tenacity of spirit that could not be broken or cracked. The more they were persecuted and killed, the stronger their numbers. They were like the mythic phoenix, the bird whose nest and self are burned to ashes and then are born again. The phoenix figured on the walls of the catacombs meant you may kill us but we will rise again. We are incapable of being destroyed.

The passage at the beginning of this chapter is a catalogue of the Old Testament Jewish heroes of the early Christian faith. The Early Church states that Paul wrote Hebrews in Hebrew to the Jews in c. 62-63. It was translated into Greek by perhaps Luke or Clement of Rome. In this passage, Paul seems to be looking back to all those before him who, like he, had suffered so much for their faith in God. Several years after this letter was disseminated among Jewish Christians, Paul would be dead, beheaded in the Neronic persecution. But his words presciently looked forward across the centuries to the hundreds of thousands of Christians who would be burned to death, crucified, torn to pieces by wild beasts, beaten to death with clubs, dragged until dead, roasted on spits, pulled apart limb by limb, speared, knifed, beheaded and hacked to death in the next two hundred and fifty years---and beyond.

By listing the Old Testament heroes who had been persecuted and had died for their faith, Paul hoped to inspire and to encourage those who would follow him up the narrow path of faith. The stories and heroes of the Old Testament of the Jews were and are the heroes of the Christians. The history of the Jews was and is their history, too. The Gentile artists in the catacombs painted these heroes of the faith on the rough walls of the underground tombs as everlasting examples of perseverance and courage in times of mortal danger.

The story of the Three Holy Children, as they are called, is prominent in catacomb paintings. The famous Babylonian King Nebuchadnezzar (reigned 605-562 BC and is mentioned over 90 times in the Old Testament) destroyed Jerusalem in 586 BC and took the young Daniel and other Jews into exile in Babylon, the largest city in the world at that time covering c. 2,500 acres. Their hometown of Jerusalem was a backwater village of c. 125 acres. The provincial Jews not only had to adjust to the different cultures and distractions of Babylon with its many people, different languages and foods, strange habits and dress, big temples and numerous gods and idols, but they had their faith in the one God tested. Three of Daniel's friends, Shadrach, Meshach and Abednego, were, like the early Christians, tormented and tortured because they refused to worship Babylonian idols:

"King Nebuchadnezzar made an image of gold, ninety feet high and nine feet wide, and set it up on the plain of Dura (modern mound called Douair southeast of Babylon) in the province of Babylon. He then summoned the satraps, prefects, governors, advisers, treasurers, judges, magistrates and all the other provincial officials to come to the dedication of the image he had set up....Then the herald loudly proclaimed, 'This is what you are commanded to do, O peoples, nations and men of every language. As soon as you hear the sound of the horn, flute, zither, harp, pipes and all kinds of music, you must fall down and worship the image of gold that King Nebuchadnezzar has set up. Whoever does not fall down and worship will immediately be thrown into a blazing furnace'....some astrologers came forward and denounced the Jews. They said to King Nebuchadnezzar, 'O king, live forever! You have issued a decree, O king, that everyone...must fall down and worship the image of gold, and that whoever does not fall down and worship will be thrown into a blazing furnace. But there are some Jews whom you have set over the affairs of the province of Babylon---Shadrach, Meshach, and Abednego---who pay no attention to you, O king. They neither serve your gods nor worship the image of gold you have set up.' Furious with rage, Nebuchadnezzar summoned Shadrach, Meshach and Abednego…and said to them, 'Is it true Shadrach, Meshach and Abednego, that you do not serve my gods or worship the image of gold I have set up?....if you do not worship the image, you will be thrown immediately into a blazing furnace. Then what god will be able to rescue you from my hand?' Shadrach, Meshach and Abednego replied to the king, 'O Nebuchadnezzar, we do not need to defend ourselves before you in this matter. If we are thrown into the blazing furnace, the God we serve is able to save us from it, and he will rescue us from your hand, O king. But even if he does not, we want you to know, O king, that we will not serve your gods or worship the image of gold you have set up.' Then Nebuchadnezzar was furious with Shadrach, Meshach and Abednego, and his attitude toward them changed. He ordered the furnace heated seven times hotter than usual and commanded some of the strongest soldiers in his army to tie up Shadrach, Meshach and Abednego and threw them into the blazing furnace. So these men, wearing their robes, trousers, turbans and other clothes, were bound and thrown into the blazing furnace. The king's command was so urgent and the furnace so hot that the flames of the fire killed the soldiers who took up Shadrach, Meshach and Abednego, and these three men, firmly tied, fell into the blazing furnace. Then King Nebuchadnezzar leaped to his feet in amazement and asked his advisers, 'Weren't there three men that we tied up and threw into the fire?' They replied, 'Certainly, O king.' He said, 'Look! I see four men walking around in the fire, unbound and unharmed, and the fourth looks like a son of the gods.' Nebuchadnezzar then approached the opening of the blazing furnace and shouted, 'Shadrach, Meshach and Abednego, servants of the Most High God, come out! Come here!' So Shadrach, Meshach and Abednego came out of the fire and the satraps, prefects, governors and royal advisers crowded around them. They saw that the fire had not harmed their bodies, nor was a hair of their heads singed; their robes were not scorched, and there was no smell of fire on them. Then Nebuchadnezzar said, 'Praise be to the God of Shadrach, Meshach and Abednego, who has sent his angel and rescued his servants! They trusted in him and defied the king's command and were willing to give up their lives rather than serve or worship any god except their own God. Therefore I decree that the people of any nation or language who say anything against the God of Shadrach, Meshach and Abednego be cut to pieces and their houses turned into piles of rubble, for no other god can save in this way.'" Daniel 3:1-29

It is obvious why this Old Testament story was painted over and over again on the walls of the catacombs where the remains of so many Christians, killed because they would not worship Caesar or the images of the Roman gods, were buried. In the Catacomb of Priscilla the three Hebrews are in the flames, their hands raised in praise like an orant. A dove hovers over them, the symbol of the Holy Spirit, the Comforter, the "one who looks like a son of the gods" in the fiery furnace. In Domitilla the son of god figure is seen in the furnace with the three. In the Cemetery Maius the hand of God is stretched down to the three from above. In Marcus and Marcellinus the three young men, dressed in Mesopotamian attire and hats, are in the act of refusing to obey Nebuchadnezzar, painted as a serious-looking man wearing, not the garb of a Babylonian king, but the toga and cape of a Roman emperor. Here, clearly, is the analogy between the three men in Babylon and the fiery deaths of Christian martyrs in Rome. The Three Holy Children burning in the fire were frequently carved on sarcophagi and painted on Christian lamps.

It was not unusual for the Romans to burn Christians alive. In the 1st Imperial persecution under Nero, he dipped Christians in pitch, impaled them on sticks, set them on fire and used them as torches to light his evening banquets.

Polycarp (c. 70-155), the 86-year-old Bishop of Smyrna (Izmir in modern Turkey), was set on fire. He was a disciple of Jesus' Apostle John. Because John lived sixty or more years after Jesus' resurrection, he was able to pass on to his disciples like Polycarp the direct teachings of Jesus. Irenaeus (c. 125-c.202) who was born and raised in Smyrna and knew Polycarp says in his book refuting Gnosticism:

"I remember events from those days (when Irenaeus was a boy) more clearly than those that happened recently....I can even picture the place where the blessed Polycarp sat and conversed, his comings and goings, his character, his personal appearance, his discourses to the crowds and how he reported his discussions with (the Apostle) John and others who had seen the Lord. He recalled their very words, what they reported about the Lord and his miracles and his teaching---things that Polycarp had heard directly from eyewitnesses of the Word of life and reported in full harmony with Scripture. I listened eagerly to these things at that time and, through God's mercy, noted them not on paper but in my heart. By God's grace I continually reflect on them, and, as God is my witness, if that blessed apostolic presbyter (Polycarp) had heard any (heretical) opinions, he would have stopped his ears and cried out characteristically, 'O good God, to what times have you preserved me that I should have to endure this?' He would have fled from wherever he was sitting or standing upon hearing such (heresy)...Polycarp not only was instructed by apostles and conversed with many who had seen the Lord, but also was appointed by apostles in Asia as Bishop of Smyrna. I (Irenaeus) also saw him in my childhood, for he lived a long time and passed away in extreme old age in glorious martyrdom. He continually taught the things he had learned from the apostles." *Against Heresies 3.3*

It should be noted that Polycarp is described here as having a similar physical reaction to heretical teaching, stopping his ears and fleeing, as did his mentor, the Apostle John. History is fortunate to have a straight line of Christian orthodox teaching from Jesus through the Apostle John to his disciple Polycarp that spans the 125 years between c. 30 AD and c. 155 AD when Polycarp was burned alive in the Circus in Smyrna.

In the 2nd century AD Smyrna was a busy port city of 100,000 people at the head of the Aegean Sea. It was the center for the inland trade route up the Hermus River Valley. An ally with Rome for hundreds of years, Smyrna was famous for its medical and scientific institutions and was devoted to the Imperial Cult. Two magnificent temples in the city were built for emperor worship. Paul, always thinking strategically, had established a church there on his 3rd missionary journey in c. 53-57, ten years before Polycarp was born.

Smyrna is one of the seven cities John addresses in the book of Revelation 2:8-10:

"To the angel (Bishop Polycarp?) of the church in Smyrna write: These are the words of him who is the First (the Alpha) and the Last (the Omega), who died and came to life again. I know your afflictions and your poverty....Do not be afraid of what you are about to suffer. I tell you, the devil will put some of you in prison to test you, and you will suffer persecution....Be faithful, even to the point of death, and I will give you the crown of life."

"The point of death" came to Bishop Polycarp and many in the Smyrnean church under the persecutions during the reign of Antoninus Pius (138-161). With precise provenance, we have *The Encyclical Epistle Of The Church At Smyrna Concerning The Martyrdom Of Polycarp* written in c. 155 right after his ordeal. This ancient document recounts the death of Polycarp and many of his parishioners:

"The Church of God which sojourns at Smyrna to the Church of God which sojourns in Philomelium (Turkey) and to all the brotherhoods of the holy and universal Church sojourning in every place....We write unto you, brothers, an account of what befell those that suffered martyrdom....noble are all the martyrdoms which have taken place.... for who could fail to admire their nobleness and patient endurance and loyalty to the Master? Seeing that when they were so torn by lashes that the mechanism of their flesh was visible even as far as the inward veins and arteries, they endured patiently, so that the very bystanders had pity and wept....none of them uttered a cry or a groan, thus showing to us all that at that hour the martyrs of Christ being tortured were absent from the flesh, or rather the Lord was standing by and conversing with them....and in the like manner also those that were condemned to the wild beasts endured fearful punishments....the right noble Germanicus encouraged their timorousness through the constancy which was in him; and he fought with the wild beasts in a singular way. For when the proconsul wished to prevail upon him and bade him have pity on his youth, Germanicus used violence and dragged the wild beast towards him....Now the glorious Polycarp at the first, when he heard of it (the persecution), so far from being dismayed, was desirous of remaining in (Smyrna); but the greater part persuaded him to withdraw. So he withdrew to a farm not far distant from the city....while praying he fell into a trance....and he saw his pillow burning with fire. And he turned and said to those that were with him: 'It must needs be that I shall be burned alive'....when (Polycarp) heard that the horsemen were come for him, he went down and conversed with them....and gave orders that a table should be spread for them to eat and drink....and he persuaded them to grant him an hour that he might pray unmolested; and on their consenting, he stood up and prayed, being so full of the grace of God that for two hours he could not hold his peace...and many repented that they had come against such a venerable old man....the hour of departure being come, they seated him on an ass and brought him into the city....(the proconsul) tried to persuade him to a denial saying, 'Have respect to your age...swear the oath and I will release you; revile the Christ.' Polycarp said, 'Fourscore and six years have I been His servant and He has done me no wrong. How then can I blaspheme my King who saved me?' But on the (proconsul's) persistence, Polycarp said ...'Do you pretend to not know who I am; hear you plainly, I am a Christian'....the proconsul said, 'I have wild beasts here and I will throw you to them, unless you repent.' (Polycarp) said, 'Call for them'....the proconsul said, 'I will cause you to be consumed by fire, if you despise the wild beasts'....But Polycarp said, 'You threaten that fire which burns for a season and after a little while is quenched, for you are ignorant of the fire of the future judgment and eternal punishment which is reserved for the ungodly. But why do you delay. Do what you will'.... the proconsul was astounded and sent his own herald to proclaim three times in the middle of the stadium 'Polycarp has confessed himself to be a Christian.' When this was proclaimed by the herald, the whole multitude both of Gentiles and of Jews who dwelt in Smyrna cried out with ungovernable wrath and with a loud shout, 'This is the teacher of Asia, the father of the Christians, the puller down of our gods, who teaches numbers not to sacrifice or worship!'....Then they thought fit to shout out with one accord that Polycarp should be burned alive. For it must needs be that the matter of the visions should be fulfilled, which was shown him concerning his pillow when he saw it on fire while praying, and turning around (Polycarp) said to the faithful who were with him, 'I must needs be burned alive'....quicker than words could tell, the crowds immediately collected from the workshops and baths timber and faggots....When the pile was made ready, divesting himself of all his upper garments and loosing his girdle....the instruments that were prepared for the pile were placed around him; and as they were going to nail him to the stake, he said, 'Leave me as I am; for He that has granted me to endure the fire will grant me also to remain at the pile unmoved!'....So they did not nail him, but tied him. Then he, placing his hands behind him and being bound to the stake, like a noble ram out of a great flock for an offering, a burnt sacrifice made ready and acceptable to God, looking up to heaven said, 'O Lord God Almighty, the Father of Thy beloved and blessed Son Jesus Christ....I bless Thee for Thou hast granted me this day and hour, that I might receive a portion amongst the number of martyrs....May I be received among these in Thy presence this day, as a rich and acceptable sacrifice....For this cause, yea and for all things, I praise Thee, I bless Thee, I glorify Thee through the eternal and heavenly High Priest, Jesus Christ, Thy beloved Son, through whom with Him and the Holy Spirit be glory both now and for the ages to come. Amen.' When he had offered up the Amen and finished his prayer, the firemen lit the fire. And a mighty flame gushed forth; we to whom it was given to see, saw a marvel, yea, and we were preserved that we might relate to the rest what happened. The fire, making the appearance of a vault, like the sail of a vessel filled by the wind, made a wall round about the body of the martyr; and (Polycarp) was there in the midst, not like flesh burning, but like a loaf in the oven or like gold and silver refined in a furnace. For we perceived such a fragrant smell, as if it were the odor of frankincense or some other precious spice. So at length the lawless men, seeing that his body could not be consumed by the fire, ordered an executioner to go up to him and stab him with a dagger. And when he had done this, there came forth a quantity of blood so that it extinguished the fire; and all the multitude marveled that there should be so great a difference between the unbelievers and the elect. In the number of these was this man, the glorious martyr Polycarp, who was found an apostolic and prophetic teacher in our own time, a bishop of the holy church which is in Smyrna....Now the blessed Polycarp was martyred on the second day of the first part of the month Xanthicus, on the seventh before the Kalends of March (Saturday, February 23, 155). He was apprehended by Herodes, when Philip of Tralles was high priest, in the proconsulship of Statius Quadratus, but in the reign of the Eternal King Jesus Christ to whom be the glory, honor, greatness and eternal throne from generation to generation. Amen."

This *Epistle* has been faithfully and carefully preserved for almost 2,000 years. The death of such an old man seems cruel and enigmatic. What harm could the preaching or the ideas of an old man in an obscure part of the Roman Empire bring to the mightiest army and power on earth? But history records that all these seemingly harmless, seemingly peaceful men, women and children were intrepid warriors who eventually toppled the temples of Rome.

In the 21st century there is an army of men, women and children who are still being burned alive for the simple confession, "I am a Christian." The *New York Times/Asia Pacific* online reported that in August of 2009 in Gojra, Pakistan, 40 Christian homes were torched by rioting Muslims and 7 Christians including two children, 6 and 13, were burned alive "just because they were Christian." The report is reminiscent of Eusebius' report of an incident in c. 303 in "a little town in Phrygia (Turkey)...all of whose inhabitants were Christians and were surrounded by armed infantrymen who set it on fire and burned to death men, women and young children as they were calling on almighty

God. The reason? All the townspeople from the mayor himself and the magistrates to the entire populace confessed their Christianity." *Church History 8.11*

In catacomb art the story of Daniel in the Lion's Den is companion to many of the paintings of the Three Holy Children in the fire. In c. 539 BC Daniel, who had been captive in Babylon for c. 60 years and was in his eighties, disobeyed a Babylonian royal decree by King Darius:

"...anyone who prays to any god or man during the next thirty days, except to you, O king, shall be thrown into the lion's den....So King Darius put the decree in writing. When Daniel learned that the decree had been published, he went home to his upstairs room where the windows opened toward Jerusalem. Three times a day he got down on his knees and prayed, giving thanks to his God, just as he had done before." Daniel 6:7, 9, 10

Daniel was discovered praying to God in open defiance of the king's decree and was thrown into a den of lions. When the King returned the next day, Daniel was alive: "My God sent his angel and he shut the mouths of the lions. They have not hurt me, because I was found innocent in his sight." (Daniel 6:22) Darius was so overwhelmed at the power of Daniel's God that he issued a decree:

"I issue a decree that in every part of my kingdom people must fear and reverence the God of Daniel. For he is the living God and he endures forever; his kingdom will not be destroyed, his dominion will never end. He rescues and he saves; he performs signs and wonders in the heavens and on the earth. He has rescued Daniel from the power of the lions." Daniel 6:26, 27

About 60 years earlier, another Babylonian King, Nebuchadnezzar, had been so astonished at God's deliverance of Shadrach, Meshach and Abednego from the fire that he had issued a decree forbidding anyone to defame Israel's God. King Darius' response to Daniel's deliverance from the lions went even further. He formally decreed that Daniel's God is a living God whose dominion and wonders will never cease. Perhaps someday archaeologists will find remnants of the decrees of these two Babylonian kings.

Daniel was an obvious Old Testament hero of the faith who, like the early Christians, had been thrown *ad bestiam*, to the lions because he would not worship a false god. Some bones found in the catacombs have teeth marks from gnawing beasts on them.

Daniel is always painted naked with his arms raised in praise. In the Catacomb of the Giordani a lion on either side of him lifts a paw toward serene Daniel. Sometimes Daniel's arms are outstretched between the lions in a "stopping" gesture. Sometimes his hands are on the mouths of the lions. Like the Holy Children in the flames, Daniel is always represented "in the midst of" his ordeal. The outcomes are not what inspired the Christian believers. It was faith in the jaws of death that gave them hope. They needed that existential immediacy.

God's deliverance of the Jews from slavery in Egypt and the final culmination and victory when the waters of the Red Sea engulf and drown the Egyptian army (Exodus 14:23-28) should have been represented often in catacomb art. It is an Old Testament story of "us against them" that would have resonated with the new persecuted. But as has been noted, there are very few crowd scenes in catacomb art and the forces of Pharaoh and the millions of Jews were an artistic challenge. However, a 4th century artist in the Via Latina did a decent painting of the scene at the Red Sea. In the middle is Moses with his rod touching the waters. He and a crowd of Jews (14) before him are looking over their right shoulders to the jumble of horses, men and spears, all topsy-turvy and drowning in the left of the painting. Whether this painting of salvation from paganism and persecution was done before or after the Edict of Milan in 313 is not known. If done before, it looked forward to Christian deliverance. If the painting was done after the cessation of persecution, it is a victory panel.

There is only one surviving painting of David in the catacombs. It is in the Catacomb of Domitilla on a panel in the ceiling. A very small David with his sling swinging from his right hand gets ready to slay a very large Goliath:

"A champion named Goliath, who was from Gath, came out of the Philistine camp. He was over nine feet tall. He had a bronze helmet on his head and wore a coat of scale armor of bronze weighing five thousand shekels (125 lbs.); on his legs he wore bronze greaves, and a bronze javelin was slung on his back. His spear shaft was like a weaver's rod and its iron point weighed six hundred shekels (15 lbs.)....David said to Saul, 'Let no one lose heart on account of this Philistine; your servant will go and fight him'....Then (David) took his (shepherd's) staff in his hand, chose five smooth stones from the stream, put them in the pouch of his shepherd's bag and, with his sling in his hand, approached the Philistine....David said to (Goliath), 'You come against me with spear and javelin, but I come against you in the name of the Lord Almighty, the God of the armies of Israel, whom you have defied. This day the Lord will hand you over to me....All those gathered here will know that it is not by sword or spear that the Lord saves, for the battle is the Lords'....Reaching into his bag and taking out a stone, (David) slung it and struck (Goliath) on the forehead. The stone sank into the forehead, and he fell facedown on the ground." I Samuel 17:4-49

For hundreds of years the early Christians faced the Goliath of Rome. They, like David, were puny and small against a formidable foe. They knew the "battle is the Lord's." By themselves, they could not defeat the might, the arms, the power of Rome and the whole ancient world. But they, like David were "at the ready," "in the act of."

In the Via Latina the strong man Samson is seen, upright, struggling with his bare hands to ward off a huge lion:

"Samson went down to Timnah (in the Sorek Valley 20 miles west of Jerusalem) with his father and mother. As they approached the vineyards of Timnah, suddenly a young lion came roaring toward him. The Spirit of the Lord came upon him in power, so that he tore the lion apart with his bare hands....Some time later...he turned aside to look at the lion's carcass. In it was a swarm of bees and some honey, which he scooped out with his hands and ate as he went along." Judges 14:5,6,8,9

Many of the faithful, before and after this painting was done, were led into arenas and had to fend off hungry lions with their bare hands. That is an important point of obvious identification made by this painting, but below the painting of Samson and the lion is something unusual in catacomb paintings, the aftermath of the story---the dead lion's gaping, rotting, honey-filled carcass with bees buzzing around it. Samson's famous riddle is prompted by the "good" that came from his "bad" experience:

"Out of the eater, something to eat:
Out of the strong, something sweet." Judges 14:14

The transcendent meaning of this little-known painting is with the dead lion. Many of them knew they would contend with lions, but would not, like the Herculean Samson, be able to kill them. They knew, however, that Christ was the slain, strong Lion of the tribe of Judah: "Do not weep! See the Lion of the Tribe of Judah, The Root of Jesse, has triumphed." (Revelation 5:5) Salvation and resurrection ("something sweet") came from that Lion's death. At Communion the bread and wine became the Body of the slain Lion of the Tribe of Judah ("something to eat...something sweet"). In the poetic, symbolic world of the early Christians, it is not unusual for their paintings to have multiple meanings. But the use of Samson's dead lion and his riddle as a symbol of the Eucharist is singular and fresh.

David facing a giant with just a sling and some stones and Samson facing a lion with only his bare hands, these paintings and others on the walls of this underground necropolis infused the persecuted Christians with courage as they, small and insignificant, faced the giant Empire of Rome and the ravenous beasts in the Colosseum. As they were being inspired to persevere by their Old Testament heroes, they were becoming the New Testament heroes of the faith for all those who would follow them on the narrow path that leads to life.

The power of the catacomb frescoes is not in the greatness of the execution but in the subject matter of the paintings. Old and New

Testament stories remain fixed upon the crumbling underground walls. Noah pleads and praises from his little ark. Complicated, morose Jonah hangs his head under the fig tree. The toddler Jesus sits upon His mother's knees with outstretched arms to receive the gifts of the Magi. Moses strikes the rock in Horeb and water gushes out to baptize Roman centurions. The Three Holy Children in the midst of the fire lift their hands in praise. The paralytic walks away with his straw pallet on his shoulder; the inquisitive woman stands at the well; the Eucharist bread is broken around a circular tripod. Thousands of paintings are silent witnesses to modern observers that these people, these events happened and meant something yesterday to a persecuted people. They have stood and will stand as crude, dark and quiet testimony to eternal truths that sustained a periled people.

Like their Jewish heroes, they had faith in the one God. In Hebrews 11:1 Paul describes what faith is: "Faith is being sure of what we hope for and certain of what we do not see." The King James Version of the Bible translates the Greek this way: "Faith is the substance of things hoped for, the evidence of things not seen." This is a more accurate translation of the verse. The Koine Greek word *upostasis*, translated in the KJV as "substance," is the reality that underlies mere appearance. *Elegchos*, translated in the KJV as "evidence," is an evident demonstration, a proof by testing. "Substance" and "evidence" are realities versus concepts or ideas. The *OED* says faith: "is a conviction practically operative on the character and will...opposed to mere intellectual assent to religious truths." Faith was and is for the Christians not an inchoate, emotional feeling but is and was a concrete, pragmatic knowledge operative on the character and will of the believer. As Paul says in II Corinthians 3:3 your faith "was not written with ink but with the Spirit of the living god, not on tablets of stone but on tablets of human hearts." Faith is as sure to the human heart as letters on stone tablets are sure to the human eye. Faith, according to Hebrews 11:1, is not a response to a subjective reality, but a fidelity to an objective reality.

The three Jews in the furnace and Daniel in the lions' den had been in the same position as the early Christians were. They were forced by Imperial decrees to choose between the State and God. Their faith was strengthened and encouraged by the experiences of fellow believers in Babylon so many centuries before them. God was and would be there in the fire with them, would be with them when they were thrown to the wild beasts in the Colosseum. He would be with them "in the midst of" whatever persecution and torture they would have to endure. Daniel and the Three Holy Children were rescued by God, but the early Christians lived what the three Hebrew children had said: "But even if (God) does not (rescue us), we want you to know, O king, that we will not serve your gods or worship the image of gold you have set up." Daniel 3:18

The untold names and numbers of graves with "M" ("martyr") marked on them witness the fact that many in the underground tombs surrounded by the frescoes were not saved from hideous deaths.

The catacombs are home to many named martyrs. One of the most famous is Saint Cecilia. The story of her marriage and martyrdom in the late 100's AD comes from a compilation of her life, the *Acts of Cecilia*, written some 200 years after her death. Cecelia was a young Christian girl of noble or patrician birth who was given in marriage by her parents to a pagan youth named Valerianus. On their wedding night, she told him she was betrothed to an angel and they could not consummate their marriage. Valerianus wanted to see the angel and she sent him to her Bishop Urbanus. He was converted. When his brother Tiburtius visited them, he, too, became a Christian. The two brothers were zealous for the faith and openly gave money to the poor and claimed and buried those who had been martyred for Christ. They attracted attention because of their high-born status and were condemned to death. A soldier, Maximus, who was to carry out their execution became converted and he, too, was beheaded. Cecilia buried the three in the Catacomb of Praetextatus. When she was apprehended, she gave her property to church members as a place of worship. Because of her nobility, she was not publicly executed. She was to be suffocated in the bath of her own home. That, however, did not kill her. The prefect ordered her decapitated at her estate. After three attempts to separate her head from her body, the executioner fled. Cecilia, bathed in her own blood, lived three days during which time she gave away all her possessions to the poor. She was buried under her family's estate in the catacomb now known as the Catacomb of St. Callixtus.

It is difficult to ascertain the truth from the many *Acta* (Latin "register of public deeds") that have been written hundreds of years after a martyr's death. But, as Heinrich Schliemann, who was a California Gold Rush banker and not an archaeologist, found the city of Troy from clues hidden in Homer's *The Iliad*, so we are able to glean kernels of truth from these *Acta*.

We know there was a wealthy young woman named Cecilia who was killed sometime in the late 100's because she was a Christian. Probably she married a pagan noble youth and he and his brother became converted. She and the others were martyred, maybe under the persecution of Marcus Aurelius (161-180) or under Septimus Severus (193-211).

We know that by the 300's, Cecilia was revered as a martyr. One thousand years later, the medieval guides to the catacombs, called *itineraria*, indicated her grave on the Via Appia in what is now the Catacomb of Callixtus. Giovanni de Rossi, the noted catacomb archaeologist, found her burial place in a crypt in the Catacomb of Callixtus in the 19th century. So there was a Cecilia. Valerianus, Tiburtius and Maximus were real people, too. Their tombs have been identified in the Catacomb of Praetextatus. The author has in her possession a 16th century prayer parchment from a church in central Italy that was dedicated to "Valerianus, Tiburtius and Maximus." The three young men as well as the young Cecilia have survived the test of time. Some call all the stories of saints and Cecilia's story "pious romances." Others believe the whole thing. Most would seek those kernels of truth.

But if one contemplates the real human trauma behind a bare bones drama like Cecilia's, it is staggering. A forced marriage and the family fights between daughter and father. An eager bridegroom and the ensuing all night struggle ending with his promise to see her priest. His conversion to a faith fraught with danger and his brother's conversion. The fights within their pagan families and the parents' fears. The young girl and her husband and brother-in-law now allies against both families. The brothers sentenced to death. Their bold proclamations of Christ before their deaths, so sincere and so persuasive that the executioner himself is converted, and the three die together. The young girl's grief and guilt and the anguish of her husbands' family and their rage. Cecilia buries them with both families dissenting and grieving. She is shortly apprehended and left to suffocate in her own bath. She suffers but does not die in the overheated room. Re-sentenced to be beheaded. But the executioner, seeing the scalded body and face of the young girl and hearing her willingness to die for her Lord, tries to steady his sword. He misses three times and flees in horror, leaving her fatally mangled. After the botched execution, she lingers for three days, suffering, bleeding and giving to her Christian brothers and sisters her possessions. She dies. Probably her stunned and mourning parents dress her in a golden gown and bury her in a sarcophagus in a soft tufa tomb below the family estate.

Cecilia's church is in the Trastevere quarter of Rome where her body was re-located by Pope Paschal I some 600 years after her ordeal. He had found her body in the Catacomb of Praetextatus where it had been hidden in the 560's from the marauding Lombards. When found, Cecilia's body was draped in gold brocade with cloths soaked in her blood lying at her feet. Pope Paschal, also, had the remains of Cecilia's husband Valerianus, his brother Tibertius and the converted Maximus transferred to the Santa Cecilia Church in Trastevere. Beneath the high altar of her church is the well-known graceful sculpture of a delicately draped and dead Cecilia, lying down, head turned to reveal the slash mark on her neck, face unseen, and hands signaling the One God in Trinity. The Renaissance sculptor Stefano Maderno (1576-1636) who was only 23 when he carved this sculpture lives on because of this masterpiece. A reproduction of the sculpture can be seen by tourists in her original burial niche in the Catacomb of St. Callixtus under the ground she walked as a child and died as a soldier.

The noble and, yes, gutsy deaths of the early martyrs not only inspired the believers, but were a powerful witness to non-believers. At Polycarp's death "all the multitude marveled that there should be so great a difference between the unbelievers and the elect." Justin Martyr, the Early Church apologist (c. 100-165), recounts how as a young man, he was drawn to the truth of Christianity by witnessing the way martyrs died. After he was intellectually convinced of the truth of the new faith, he dedicated the next 35 years of his life to defending it by writing Apologies to Emperors and other high officials. Here Justin explains to Emperor Antoninus Pius (138-161) why Christians willingly die:

"And when you hear that we look for a kingdom, you suppose, without making any inquiry, that we speak of a human kingdom; whereas we speak of that which is with God, as appears also from the confession of their faith made by those who are charged with being Christians, though they know that death is the punishment awarded to him who so confesses. For if we looked for a human kingdom, we should also deny our Christ, that we might not be slain….But since our thoughts are not fixed on the present, we are not concerned when men cut us off; since, also, death is a debt which must at all events be paid." *First Apology 11*

Justin Martyr paid that debt and was beheaded under the philosopher Emperor Marcus Aurelius in 165 after he had given a strong, cogent witness for Christ before Rusticus, the prefect of Rome.

Consider the witness and impact the Theban Legion Martyrs must have had on the whole Roman army. The Theban Legion was one of the many Legions in the Imperial army. When Rome conquered a country, a fighting force was enlisted from the citizenry, trained as Roman soldiers and dispatched, as needed, all over the Empire by the emperors. Legions were comprised of 400 to 5-6,000 men from many countries: from Britannia (England, Wales), Hispania (Spain), Raetia (Switzerland), Arabia Petraea (Jordan, Syria), Macedonia (Greece), Noricum (Austria), Germanica (Germany/France), Aegyptus (Egypt), Africa, Dalmatia (Croatia/Bosnia/Serbia) as well as from Italy itself. The Theban Legion contained 6,600 men from the ancient town of Thebes near Luxor and Karnak, Egypt. These Egyptian youths were known as a fierce group of fighters with an allegiance to Caesar. And they were, also, all Christians.

Egypt was an early hub of Christianity. In the beginning century of the faith Alexandria was as influential as Antioch in Syria, Ephesus in Turkey and Jerusalem in Israel. For hundreds of years the Egyptian Christians had acquitted themselves valiantly for their Lord:

"When Severus (reigned 193-211) was inciting persecution against the churches, champions of piety achieved glorious martyrdoms everywhere, but particularly at Alexandria. There, as if to a huge stadium, God's champions were led from the whole of Egypt and wreathed with the crowns dedicated to God." Eusebius, *Church History 6.1*

"Such was the ordeal of the Egyptians who contended so gloriously for the faith at Tyre. But those (Egyptians) who were martyred in their own land are also admirable, countless numbers of men, women and children, disdaining this passing life to endure a variety of deaths for the sake of our Savior's teaching. Some of them were scraped, racked, ruthlessly whipped and tortured in ways too terrible to describe and finally given to the flames or drowned in the sea. Others courageously bared their necks to the executioners or died of torture or hunger. Some again were crucified...while others...were nailed in the opposite way---head downward---and kept alive until they died of hunger on the cross. The outrageous agonies endured by the martyrs in the Theban area, however, defeat all description." *Church History 8.8, 9*

This last Theban persecution of Christians was under Emperor Diocletian in the years 284-305.

During the time when Diocletian and his co-regent Maximian were ravaging the Christians in Egypt, Maximian called up the Theban Legion and many other Legions to help him subdue a Burgundian insurrection in Gaul. The Theban Legion, under the command of Mauritius and his two lieutenants Candidas and Exupernis, left Egypt, landed in c. 286 near Rome and made their way up through the St. Bernard Pass to the town of Agaunum in Switzerland.

The men in the Theban Legion were steady sufferers. Many of their Christian ancestors had suffered persecution and death for hundreds of years and even then some of their families were being killed for Christ at the command of the very Emperors whom they served. It is against the background of the historic persecution of Egyptian Christians and of the ongoing persecution at home in Thebes that their story should be read.

This Letter was written by Eucharius, Bishop of Lyons (c. 380-449), about 115 years after the following events happened:

"From Eucherius to the Lord Holy and Most Blessed Bishop in Christ, Salvius (Bishop of Octodurum)

I am unfolding with my pen an account of the suffering of the holy martyrs who light up Agaunum with their glorious blood. (I am taking) especial faithfulness to the account of the martyrdom which has come down to us because forgetfulness has not yet overtaken the memory of the deed thanks to the report of successive generations....Let me now recount the very cause of their passion. During the reign of the Maximian who ruled the Roman republic together with Diocletian as his colleague, crowds of martyrs were tortured or killed throughout various provinces....(Maximian) did arm his impiety to extinguish the name of Christianity....he set his weapons directly against (Christianity) like a foreign soldier at a time of barbarian invasion. There was at that time in the army a legion of soldiers who were called the Thebaei...that contained 6,600 men under arms. When they had been summoned to his support by Maximian from the regions of the East, these men, active in battle and renowned for their courage, although more renowned for their faith, came. They strove in bravery for the emperor, but in devotion to Christ. Mindful of gospel teaching even under arms, they returned that which was God's to God and restored that which was Caesar's to Caesar. Accordingly when these men were assigned to harass the multitude of Christians in the area just like the other soldiers, they alone dared to refuse the cruel task and declared that they would not obey commands of this king. Maximian was not far off (10 miles), since, tired by his journey, he was resting near Octodurum (modern Martigny, Switzerland)....When Maximian learned the reply of the Thebaei, he burned with a fierce anger on account of their neglect of his commands and ordered every tenth person from that same legion to be executed by the sword in order that the others, terrified by fear, might more easily yield to royal injunctions; and he renewed his commands and ordered the remainder to be forced to persecute the Christians. When this repeat command reached the Thebaei and they learned that impious actions were being enjoined upon them once more, there rose indiscriminately throughout the camp the hue and cry of men declaring that they would never submit to such sacrilegious tasks, that they had always cursed the wickedness of idols, that they had been steeped in sacred rites and reared in the observation of the divine religion, that they worshipped the one eternal God and that they would suffer death rather than go against the Christian faith. When Maximian learned this, (he) ordered every tenth man to be executed once more in order that the others might be forced to those actions which they were refusing. When these commands were announced at the camp for a second time, the tenth men were chosen by lot, separated and executed, but the remaining crowd of soldiers urged each other to continue in such a distinguished effort. But the greatest incitement to faith at that time was the holy Mauritius, primicerius (commander), as it is called of that legion, who together with Exuperius and Candidus, encouraged the soldiers by exhorting and advising them individually. Setting before them the examples of their faithful fellow soldiers, now martyrs, he persuaded them all also to die on behalf of the sacrament of Christ and the divine laws, if it should prove necessary.... Accordingly, inspired by these leaders...they sent to Maximian this message...which is said to have run in the following vein: 'We are your soldiers, O emperor, but God's servants, nevertheless, a fact that we freely confess. We owe military service to you, but just living to Him; from you we have received the pay for our toil, but from Him we have received the origin of life. No way can we follow an emperor in this, a command for us to deny God our Father, especially since our Father is your God and Father whether you like it or not....We offer our hands, which we think wrong to sully with the blood of innocents against any enemy. Those right hands know how to fight against wicked enemies, not how to torture pious citizens. We remember to take arms for citizens rather than against citizens. We have always fought for justice, piety and the welfare of the innocent. These have been the prices of our dangers hitherto. We have fought for faith; what faith will we keep with you at all if we do not exhibit faith to our God? We swore oaths to God first, oaths to the king second. There is no need for you to trust us concerning the second, if we break the first. You order us to seek out Christians for punishment. You do not now have to seek out others on this charge since you have us here confessing: We believe in God the Father maker of all and God his Son Jesus Christ....Behold! we hold arms and do not resist because we well prefer to die rather than to live and choose to perish as innocents rather than to live as criminals. If you ordain any further measure against us, give any further command or direct any other measure, we are prepared to endure fire, torture and steel. We confess that we are Christians and cannot persecute Christians.' When Maximian heard these things and realized that the men's minds were resolute in their faith in Christ...he decreed in one sentence that they were all to be killed and ordered the surrounding military columns to effect the matter....(the other legions) drew their wicked swords against the holy men who did not refuse to die because of a love for life....they were indiscriminately slaughtered by the sword. They did not cry out even or fight back, but laid aside their arms and offered their necks to their persecutors, presenting their throat, or intact body even, to their executioners. Nor were they inspired by how great was their number or by the protection of their weapons, to attempt to assert the cause of justice by the sword; but, remembering this alone, that they were confessing Him who was led to His death without a cry, and like a lamb, did not open His mouth, they, the Lord's flock of sheep, so to speak, also allowed themselves to be torn by the onrushing wolves, as it were....The earth there was covered by the bodies of the pious as they fell forward into death....I, Eucherius, have sent this written account of the passion of our martyrs to your blessedness, for I was afraid lest, through neglect, time should remove from the memory of men this account of so glorious a martyrdom....I have sought the truth of this very matter from suitable sources...from the holy Isaac, Bishop of Geneva, who had learned these things in turn from the most blessed Bishop Theodore, a man of an earlier time....I offer these writings of mine, if they are deemed worthy of support."

One must consider the impact of this slaughter on the men in the Roman Legions who were forced to execute the Theban Legion. Roman soldiers had been executing Christians for hundreds of years. Individual Roman soldiers had been executed for declaring: *Christianus sum.* ("I am a Christian.") But it is a fact that Roman soldiers had never been ordered to execute an entire Roman Legion containing 6,600 men just because they were Christians. They were commanded by their Emperor to execute fellow soldiers, to execute huge numbers of armed men who laid down their swords and gave their necks one by one to their comrades in arms. One can imagine the sight of thousands of men, willingly dying for their God, praying to Him and praying for their executioners. Those Legionnaire executioners took this story of mass martyrdom back to Greece, to France, to Germany, all over the Middle East and the Empire. Around fires they must have talked of it. They confessed it to their wives and mothers and fathers and brothers. Only 27 years later, Emperor Constantine, who was c. 14 years old when the massacre occurred, declared the Edict of Milan that put an end to Christian persecution. It is likely the Legions under the Emperors were relieved they did not have to kill any more unarmed men, women, children or fellow soldiers who were praying for them.

Eucherius gives three sources as witnesses to his account: oral tradition ("local memories of successive generations"), Isaac the Bishop of Geneva and Bishop Theodore ("a man of an earlier time"). Eucherius wrote this sometime in the early 400's or about 115 years after the slaughter in c. 286. Isaac was the first Bishop of Geneva in c. 380 less than 100 years after the incident. Isaac, in turn, had heard the story from "a man from an earlier time." The only "Bishop Theodore" that fits into a prior-than-380 box is Theodore of Mopsuestia in Syria (c.350-428). He is unlikely to be that Theodore not only because he was in Syria, but because he was still alive when Eucherius wrote his letter and, therefore, could not be "a man from an earlier time." There was another Bishop Theodore in Octodurum who died in 391. He does not fit the description of "a man of an earlier time" since he was a contemporary of both Isaac and Eucherius. This Bishop Theodore, however, was the one who, in his tenure as Bishop, greatly increased the veneration of the Theban Martyrs and of their leader Maurice. It was obviously a yet unknown Bishop Theodore, who gave the account to Isaac. This Theodore, as an old man, probably told Isaac about the Theban Legion. Maybe he learned the story as a young cleric in c. 320 or earlier, only c. 40 years after the slaughter had happened. Eucherius does give us some human provenance for his information, but the strongest evidence of a major martyrdom in the Swiss Alps comes from the longevity of the story, the art and veneration inspired by the martyrdoms over the last 1,600 years and the religious prominence of the ancient and remote outpost of Agaunum.

After the massacres, a crude shrine was built on the site. As the story spread, pilgrims began coming from all over the world to the small Swiss town. They gave costly gifts of gold, silver and precious stones to the humble caretakers who used the money to build a little church in c. 390 and a monastery in 515 that is still in use. For over 1,600 years the faithful have come to the small town of Agaunum, now known as St.-Maurice-en-Valais, in Switzerland. It is named after the Christian commander, Mauritius, always pictured in battle gear with the sword of the spirit in front of him. There are 52 towns and villages in France named after him and cities in Spain, Italy and Germany claim him as their patron saint. El Greco painted *The Martyrdom of St. Maurice* in c. 1581, an astonishing work of power and technique. Maurice, seen as a Roman soldier with his lance, is grouped with three other saints. A 13th century famous statue in the Cathedral in Magdeburg, Germany depicts Maurice as a black man from Egypt. Under the altar in the modest church in St.-Maurice-en-Valais, Switzerland is a small ossuary that contains what remains of the bones of the Theban Commander Mauritius, long known as St. Maurice, who so long ago at deadly cost to him and to his men, inspired and urged his solders to render unto God the things that are God's.

The Theban Legion came from one of the very earliest cradles of Christianity---Egypt. Mark, the writer of the second Gospel and a disciple of Jesus, is said to have gone to Egypt where he founded a church in c. 62 AD in the port city of Alexandria. St. Mark's Coptic Orthodox Cathedral in Alexandria claims to be on the very site where

Mark established that first Egyptian church. Mark was dragged to death during a festival of the Egyptian god Serapis in c. 68 AD and his body was buried beneath the small church. That church has been destroyed and rebuilt many times over the last two thousand years. From 1985 to 1990 it was restored and rebuilt into the beautiful Coptic cathedral it is today.

"Coptic" is a corruption of the Greek word for "Egypt," *aigyptos* through its abbreviation *gypt*. ("Gypsy" comes from the same Greek word and they were so designated because when they first appeared in the West in c. 1000 AD, they said they were Dukes from Lower Egypt.) The Coptic Christian Church has been in continual existence from c. 30 years after the resurrection of Jesus to the present, longer than any other national or regional church. 10% of Egyptians are Coptic Christians and there are 10-12 million worldwide. Over the last two thousand years, the Coptic Church has endured not only the ravaging Roman persecutions in the first 300 years of Christianity, but, also, the savage attacks and forced conversions to the faith of Islam in the 600's.

It was in Egypt that the Desert Fathers emerged. Perhaps as early as the late 2nd century AD, these Egyptian Christian men left the pagan cities, the persecutions and the distractions of life to live as hermits in the Sahara Desert. Their purpose was to live a solitary life solely dedicated to God. A wealthy, young Christian man, Anthony of Egypt (c. 251-356), gave away all his inherited riches and retired to a hut in the desert. His very long and influential life as a hermit precipitated what has been called "the peopling of the desert." After his biographer Bishop Athanasius (293-373) published his *Vitae Antonii* extolling Anthony's life, flocks of Christian men and women came to Egypt to live the anchoritic life exemplified by St. Anthony. Soon the desert around Egypt's major cities was filled with people living in individual cells they had built with their own hands. They wove baskets to sell, formed loose-knit communities and devoted themselves to labor, solitude and prayer. With the blood persecutions over in 313, some Christians began to embrace a "white martyrdom" in which the flesh was mortified so that the spirit might live.

Another Egyptian from Thebes named Pachomius (292-348) was

one of the founders of communal monastic life. When he was 20, he was imprisoned by the Romans. Local Christians brought him and other prisoners food and other necessities every day. According to Aristides, the 2nd century apologist, Christians typically ministered not only to their brothers and sisters who were in prison for the faith, but to all prisoners as a witness to Christian charity and care:

"(Christians) help those who offend them, making friends of them; do good to their enemies....When they meet strangers, they invite them to their homes with joy....When a poor man dies, if they become aware, they contribute according to their means for his funeral; if they come to know that some people are persecuted or sent to prison or condemned for the sake of Christ's name, they put their alms together and send them to those in need. If they can do it, they try to obtain their release." *Apology 15*

Because of the kindness of Christians to people they did not even know, Pachomius became a Christian when he was released from prison in c. 314. He felt drawn to the Desert Fathers and built his cell in the desert near St. Anthony. But Pachomius saw that most of the men who desired Anthony's eremitic life could not live in such solitary isolation. He decided to build 10 to 12 room houses where men could live together in individual rooms and practice, if they so chose, certain mortifications of the flesh such as celibacy, obedience, poverty and/or self-sufficiency. These early monasteries, and soon nunneries, had no Biblical mandates or foundations but were an outgrowth of the human desire to follow God without the normal daily distractions. Even though there had been monastic groups before Pachomius, he is called the "Father of Cenobitic Monasticism." "Cenobitic" comes from the two Greek words *koinos* meaning "common, shared by many" and *bios* meaning "life." Pachomius' "communal living" was the opposite of Anthony's solitary, hermitic life. The genius was that he had combined the reclusive life of the individual cells with the communal life of corporate meals, work and worship. Pachomius remained monastic his whole life and refused to be ordained as a priest. At his death on May 9, 348 more than 3,000 of his small "monasteries" dotted the Egyptian desert.

1,700 years later there are still 11 Christian monasteries (from the Greek *monazein* meaning "to live alone") scattered throughout the Sahara Desert in Egypt. Outside of Cairo in Wadi Natroun (Coptic *natroun* meaning "salt" as in "valley of salt") there are four Coptic Orthodox monasteries that welcome visitors, Christian and Muslim. The cloistered life has always had an appeal for religious as well as philosophical people. Even in the time of Jesus, the Jewish Essenes and another group called the Therapeutae were people who lived according to strict ascetic rules outside of society in the Judean desert.

Many of the Desert Fathers in those early centuries have left golden nuggets of wisdom:

"This is the truth. If a man regards contempt as praise, poverty as riches and hunger as feast, he will never die." Macarius (d. 395)

"This is the great work of man: always to take the blame for his own sins before God and to expect temptation to his last breath." St. Anthony (251-356)

"I consider no other labor as difficult as prayer. When we are ready to pray, our spiritual enemies interfere. They understand it is only by making it difficult for us to pray that they can harm us. Other things will meet with success if we keep at it, but laboring at prayer is a war that will continue until we die." Abba Agathon (3rd century)

At the time of the Desert Fathers, the Early Church had not established the offices of nuns and monks. The tremendous attraction the Desert Fathers had on clergy and laity after the Roman persecutions were over, however, laid the foundations for the monasteries and the nunneries of the Roman church in the West from the 5th through the 10th centuries.

Some early Christians chose the white martyrdom of the anchoritic life. Large numbers of Christians relinquished their lives in blood martyrdom. Most Christians lived their lives as re-born, re-newed People of the Way, as they were called in the beginning:

"He (Saul) went to the high priest and asked him for letters to the synagogues in Damascus, so that if he found any there who belonged to the Way, whether men or women, he might take them as prisoners to Jerusalem." Acts 9:2

"Jesus answered, 'I am the way and the truth and the life. No one comes to the Father except through me.'" John 14:6

All, from all walks of life, from all countries, from all ranks and stations in society, all early Christians had faith that a Jewish carpenter named Jesus from a dusty town named Nazareth was the Old Testament predicted Messiah/Sin-Bearer who was crucified under the Roman Procurator Pontius Pilate, was dead, buried and on the third day He arose again from the dead.

The belief in the resurrection of Jesus is the catalyst for the formation, the growth and the continued presence of the Christian movement. Without the early Christian faith in the resurrection of Jesus, the movement would have been a laudatory set of pedagogic precepts. The empty tomb is the sole reason all of His timorous Apostles, hiding in a locked room in Jerusalem, turned into dauntless disciples whose faith dared the world to stop them.

The early Christians saw through Old Testament heroes and New Testament martyrs the end of their sufferings. Through faith they saw that pinpoint of light way down at the end of the tunnel. No matter what Rome did to them, they were sure of what they hoped for and certain of what they did not see.

"I consider that our present sufferings are not worth comparing with the glory that will be revealed to us....For in this hope we were saved. But hope that is seen is no hope at all. Who hopes for what he already has? But if we hope for what we do not yet have, we wait for it patiently." Romans 8:18, 24, 25

Their present sufferings were not unique. They counted them as part of the timeless struggle between good and evil, between God and Satan. Through their Scriptures and by their faith, they saw the outcome---the ultimate triumph of God. They knew the Alpha and the Omega, the Beginning and the End. They knew the end of the story.

XIV.

"As (Jesus) approached Jerusalem and saw the city, he wept over it and said, 'If you had only known on this day what would bring you peace, but now it is hidden from your eyes. The days will come upon you when your enemies will build ramparts against you and encircle you and hem you in on every side. They will dash you to the ground, you and the children within your walls. They will not leave one stone on another because you did not recognize the time of God's coming to you'....Some of the disciples were remarking about how the temple was adorned with beautiful stones and with gifts dedicated to God. But Jesus said, 'As for what you see here, the time will come when not one stone will be left on another; every one of them will be thrown down.... When you see Jerusalem being surrounded by armies, you will know that its desolation is near. Then let those who are in Judea flee to the mountains; let those in the city get out, and let those in the country not enter the city. For this is the time of punishment in the fulfillment of all that has been written. How dreadful it will be in those days for pregnant women and nursing mothers! There will be great distress in the land and wrath against this people. They will fall by the sword and will be taken as prisoners to all the nations. Jerusalem will be trampled on by the Gentiles until the times of the Gentiles are fulfilled....O Jerusalem, Jerusalem, you who kill the prophets and stone those sent to you. How often I have longed to gather your children together, as a hen gathers her chicks under her wings, but you were not willing.

Look, your house is left to you desolate.'" Luke 19:41-45; 21:5-7, 20-24; Matthew 23:37, 38

On His last visit to Jerusalem right before His crucifixion, Jesus made this doleful prophecy predicting the end of Jerusalem and the Temple. His prophecy was fulfilled 40 years later in 70 AD when the future emperor, Titus, and his Roman Legions defeated the Jews and destroyed not only their Temple but the whole city of Jerusalem.

It could be proffered that 100 years earlier in 63 BC when the Roman general Pompey (106-48 BC) was invited by the Jewish prince Aristobulus to intervene in a fight for power against his brother Hyrcanus, Jerusalem's destruction in 70 AD was a foregone conclusion. Pompey went to Jerusalem to see what this internecine fight was all about. He ended up siding with Hyrcanus and the Pharisees against his host Aristobulus. Aristobulus and the Sadducees barricaded themselves in the Temple. After a three month siege and over 12,000 dead, Pompey took the Temple, entered the Holy of Holies and his soldiers sacrificed to their gods. To the Jews these acts were blasphemy compounded. Pompey appointed Hyrcanus as high priest and that same year Rome annexed Judea and the Galilee as one of their many client states. This made neither the Pharisees nor the Sadducees happy. However, Aristobulus had invited Rome to intercede. She came. She saw. She conquered. She blasphemed. Only to the Jews was blasphemy against their God an unforgivable sin. From that time, the war between Rome and the Jews was in play.

Titus refers to this long conflict in his speech to Simon and John when the two Jewish combatants came to him to propose that Titus allow them and their families to leave Jerusalem right before it fell:

"You have been the men that have brought your people, your city and your holy house to destruction. You have been the men that have never left off rebelling since Pompey first conquered you; and you have, since that time, made open war with the Romans." Josephus, *Wars of the Jews 6.6.2*

Titus was right. The Jews never submitted to Rome. They, though small in number, chafed at the Roman yoke and rebelled against the tyranny. The people Rome conquered had to obey several rules: pay taxes to Rome and sacrifice to the emperor. From the beginning, the Jews hated the Roman taxes and because they were the only monotheists in the whole world, they refused to acknowledge the Roman gods or the emperor as a god. Other conquered nations, excepting the Gauls and Celts, were in awe of Rome, but the Jews despised Roman culture and any symbol of it. They never considered themselves a "client people." They saw themselves as a "slave nation."

The Jewish revolts against Rome were short-lived but persistent. About the time of Jesus' birth, two rabbis incited their students to remove the large golden eagle (the symbol of Rome) from a gate in the Temple. Herod the Great, appointed ruler of the Jews by the Romans, apprehended the priests and the students and burned them alive. The Roman census taken by Quirinius at Jesus' birth provoked another open revolt led by Judas of Galilee. It was violently suppressed. When Emperor Tiberias appointed Pontius Pilate Procurator of Judea in 26 AD, his soldiers marched through Jerusalem bearing standards with the head of Caesar on them. Thousands of Jews protested for five days and nights against the standards with a false/idol god on them. Pilate sent out his troops, but the Jews fell prostrate, exposed their necks to Roman swords and vowed to die rather than have any other standard but Jehovah. Pilate continued to provoke the Jews by using Temple funds to build an aqueduct; he slaughtered some Galileans who were sacrificing to God in Jerusalem; he killed Jesus of Nazareth; in 36 he so brutally suppressed a Messianic movement in Judea that Rome had him removed from office. In 41, Emperor Caligula wanted to erect a statue of himself in the Temple. Tens of thousands of Jews demanded they be slain rather than have this happen. In c. 46, another charismatic leader named Theudas said he could part the waters of the Jordan River and the Jews could exodus from Roman slavery. Roman troops beheaded him and killed his followers. There was always some sort of trouble in Judea regarding their God and their freedom.

In 66, a seemingly minor incident in Caesarea led to a series of fights and misunderstandings that eventually toppled the ancient Jewish civilization:

"Now at this time it happened that the Greeks at Caesarea had been too hard on the Jews and had obtained from Nero the government of the city....Now the occasion of this (skirmish) was by no means proportionable to those heavy calamities which it brought upon us; for the Jews that dwelt at Caesarea had a synagogue near the place (owned by) a certain Caesarean Greek. The Jews had endeavored frequently to purchase the possession of the place and had offered many times its value for the place, but the owner overlooked their offers (and) raised other buildings upon the place, as a way of affront to them, and made working shops of them and left (the Jews) but a narrow passageway (to the synagogue)...and it was very troublesome for them to go along to their synagogue; whereupon the warmer part of the Jewish youth went hastily to the workmen and forbade them to build there....on the seventh day of the week when the Jews were crowding apace to their synagogue, a certain man of Caesarea...got an earthen vessel and set it, with the bottom upward, at the entrance of that synagogue and sacrificed birds. This thing provoked the Jews to an incurable degree because their laws were affronted and the place was polluted (In Leviticus 14:5 that sacrifice was required by lepers. The Jews were being called lepers.)....(Jewish) youths were vehemently inflamed to fight. The seditious also among the Gentiles of Caesarea stood ready for the same purpose....it soon came to blows." Josephus, *Wars of the Jews 2.4.5*

The Romans under the procurator Florus, no friend of the Jews, got involved. Florus sided with the Greeks and had some of the Jews imprisoned. He next demanded 17 talents of gold (c. 1,282 lbs.) from the Temple treasury in Jerusalem "for Caesar." Knowing he was going to keep the gold for himself, in early summer of 66 zealous Jews revolted, barred the entrance to their Temple and attacked the Roman garrison in Jerusalem. The Zealots took control of Jerusalem and ceased all sacrifices for the well-being of the Roman emperor. The Jews had openly challenged Rome.

Florus arrested and crucified many. Josephus says it was "Florus who necessitated us to take up arms against the Romans." Josephus, *Jewish Antiquities 20.11.1*; "...Florus contrived another way to oblige the Jews to begin the war." Josephus, *Wars of the Jews 2.16.16*

There is always a subtle trail of little incidents that lead to a big climacteric. Hostilities escalated up the command chain until in October-November 66, Jerusalem found itself surrounded by Roman armies under General Cestius, the Roman commander in Syria.

Concurrent with the macro world of the political conflict between the Jews and the Romans was the continuing, decades-long conflict in Jerusalem between those Jewish Christians who believed Jesus was the long-awaited Messiah and the priestly class who did not. From the 30's through the 50's Stephen, the Apostle James, Paul and the other Apostles had suffered under those Jews in ecclesiastical authority who saw the Christian sect as a dangerous heresy.

Jerusalem was the Mother Church and the center of influence for the early Christians in the years leading up to 70 AD. Some of the Apostles and many who had seen and believed in Jesus as their Messiah were still living in Jerusalem. The Bishop (from Greek "*episkopos*" meaning "overseer, watcher") of Jerusalem, and the first to be called "Bishop," was James The Just, Jesus' brother, who had been appointed by the Apostles. He was called "Righteousness" and *Oblias*, in Greek meaning "Bulwark of the People." James was revered as a good man even by those in the priestly class who did not believe his brother was the Messiah. In order to keep the Nazarene sect from spreading, the priests decided to implore James to denounce his brother publicly before the people. During Passover in c. 62 with tens of thousands of pilgrims in the city:

"...they assembled and said to James: 'We call on you to restrain the people, since they have gone astray after Jesus believing him to be the Christ. We call on you to persuade all who come for the Passover concerning Jesus, since all of us trust you. We and the entire populace can vouch for the fact that you are righteous and take no one at face value. So do persuade the crowd not to err regarding Jesus….So stand on the parapet of the temple where you can be clearly seen from that height and your words be heard by all the people with all the tribes and Gentiles too who are gathered for the Passover.' So the scribes and Pharisees made James stand on the temple parapet and they shouted to him, 'O righteous one, whom we all ought to believe, since the people are going astray after Jesus who was crucified, tell us, what does the door of Jesus mean?' James replied with a loud voice, 'Why do you ask me about the Son of Man? He is sitting in heaven at the right hand of the Great Power and he will come on the clouds of heaven.' Many were convinced and rejoiced at James' testimony crying, 'Hosanna to the Son of David.' Then the scribes and Pharisees said to each other, 'We made a bad mistake in providing such testimony to Jesus, but let us go up and throw him down so that they will be afraid and not believe him.' And they cried out, 'Oh, oh, even the just one has gone astray!'….So they went up and threw down the righteous one. Then they said to each other, 'Let us stone James the Just,' and they began to stone him since the fall had not killed him. But he turned and knelt down, saying, 'I implore you, O Lord, God and Father, forgive them. They do not know what they are doing.' While they were pelting him with stones, one of the priests…cried out, 'Stop! What are you doing? The righteous one is praying for you.' Then one, a laundryman, took the club that he used to beat out clothes and hit the Just on the head. Such was his martyrdom. They buried him on the spot by the temple and his gravestone is still there by the temple (in c. 160). He became a true witness to both Jews and Gentiles that Jesus is the Christ. Shortly after, Vespasian besieged Judea, taking them captive." Hegesippus, *Historia 5*

James' manner of death is attested by Clement of Alexandria (c. 150-c. 215), the Early Church theologian and teacher of Origen:

"…Now there were two Jameses: one, James the Just who was thrown down from the parapet (of the Temple) and beaten to death with a

fuller's club; and the other James (brother of John) who was beheaded."
Outlines 7

Josephus mentions the killing of James in his *Jewish Antiquities*
20.9.1:

"...this younger Ananus, who as we have told you already, took the high
priesthood (and) was a bold man in his temper and very insolent; he was
also of the sect of the Sadducees who are very rigid in judging offenders,
above all the rest of the Jews; when, therefore, Ananus was of this
disposition, he thought he had now a proper opportunity (to exercise
his authority)....so he assembled the Sanhedrin of judges and brought
before them the brother of Jesus, who was called Christ, whose name
was James and some others; and when he had formed an accusation
against them as breakers of the law, he delivered them to be stoned; but
as for those who seemed the most equitable of the citizens and such as
were most uneasy at the breach of the laws, they disliked what was done;
they also sent to the king (Agrippa) desiring him to send to Ananus
that he should act so no more, for that what he had already done was
not to be justified."

It was four years after James' martyrdom and about the time of the
martyrdoms in Rome of Peter and Paul that the Romans under the
Syrian legate Cestius surrounded Jerusalem and began the war against
the Jews in earnest. Cestius, however, quixotically withdrew his armies
for no apparent reason. Perhaps it was because his 12th Legion had an
unsteady reputation and Cestius had seen the flint of the Jews in the
short time they were at the walls of Jerusalem. The withdrawal was a
fiasco. The Jews stormed out of the city and fell upon the retreating
12th who fled to the Pass of Beth-Horon where they were trapped.
They sneaked away in the dead of night. When the Jews attacked in
the morning, only 400 brave men had been left as decoys. They were
slaughtered. Within days, Cestius was dead. Some say by suicide, others
say he died of shame.

After the rout and defeat of the Roman army under Cestius in

66, the Jews declared an independent state. They called it Israel after Jacob, the father of the twelve tribes of the Jews, whose name God had changed from Jacob to *Israel* meaning "he struggles with God." (Genesis 32:22-32) The Jews felt so independent after Cestius' defeat that they even minted their own coins: a silver shekel has "Shekel Of Israel" in Hebrew on the obverse and "Jerusalem Is Holy" around a stem with three flowers on the reverse. There were numerous silver half shekels minted from 66-70 with "First Year Of the Revolt," "Second Year Of The Revolt," "Third Year Of The Revolt" and "Fourth Year Of The Revolt" stamped on the obverse. It was a heady time for some of the leaders in Jerusalem, but they had to have known, should have known that the defeat of a Roman army and the declaration of an independent rogue state in Judea would not be tolerated by the Romans.

It was at this time, c. November of 66, that most of the Christians left Jerusalem. They had been warned by Jesus to flee from Judea when they saw Jerusalem surrounded by armies (Luke 21:20-24). At that time a prophet warned them to leave:

"...before the war began, members of the Jerusalem church were ordered by an oracle given by revelation to those worthy of it to leave the city and settle in a city of Perea called Pella (east of the Jordan River in Jordan). Here they migrated from Jerusalem, as if, once holy men had deserted the royal capital of the Jews and the whole land of Judea, the judgment of God might finally fall on them for their crimes against Christ and his Apostles, utterly blotting out all that wicked generation." Eusebius, *Church History 3.5*

Many early Gentile Christian writers saw the destruction of Jerusalem as divine punishment on the Jews for rejecting Jesus as their Messiah:

"...while Jerusalem was still standing and whole Jewish worship celebrated in it, Jesus foretold what would befall it....But at that time there were no armies around Jerusalem, encompassing and enclosing and besieging it; for the siege began in the reign of Nero and lasted till

the government of Vespasian, whose son Titus destroyed Jerusalem on account of, as Josephus says, the killing of James The Just, the brother of Jesus who was called Christ, but in reality, as the truth makes clear, on account of Jesus Christ the Son of God." Origen, *Against Celsus 2.13*
"Moreover, I will tell you likewise concerning the temple, how these wretched men being led astray set their hope on the building and not on their God that made them." *Epistle of Barnabas 16.1*
"Now since you join the Jews in denying that their Christ has come, recollect also what is that end which they were predicted as about to bring on themselves after the time of Christ for the impiety wherewith they both rejected and slew Him.....neither in the interval from Tiberius to Vespasian did they learn repentance." Tertullian, *Against Marcion 23*

Because the Jews were, are and always will be considered God's Chosen People and because Christianity emerged from the Jews, the underlying reasons for the destruction of Jerusalem have been debated and will always be inextricably connected to spiritual and religious history.

In c. 78 AD the Jewish historian, Flavius Josephus (37-c. 100), published *Wars Of The Jews*, the only eyewitness account of the events leading up to and including the fall of Jerusalem. As the defeated Jewish commander of the Galilean town of Jotapata, Josephus had been captured and imprisoned by the Romans in 67. He was released two years later and became the Hebrew interpreter during the siege of Jerusalem for Vespasian's son, Titus, when Vespasian returned to Rome after Nero was forced to commit suicide in June of 68.

He begins his account of the fall of Jerusalem: "I, Josephus, son of Matthias, am a priest of Jerusalem who fought against the Romans in the early stages (of the war) and was an unwilling witness of (these) later events." *Wars 1.3* The following narrative relies heavily upon Josephus' account.

According to Josephus, Jesus of Nazareth was not the only person who foresaw the destruction and end of that great ancient city. A certain

Jesus, the son of Ananus, a peasant farmer, appeared in Jerusalem in c. 63 and began to cry aloud:

"'A voice from the east; a voice from the west; a voice from the four winds; a voice against Jerusalem and the holy temple; a voice against the bridegrooms and the brides; and a voice against this whole people!' This was his cry, as he went about by day and by night in all the lanes of the city. However, certain of the most eminent among the populace had great indignation at this dire cry of his and took up the man and gave him a great number of severe (beatings); yet did not he either say anything for himself, or anything peculiar to those that chastised him, but still he went on with the same words which he cried before….(he was) brought to the Roman procurator (Albinus) where he was whipped till his bones were laid bare; yet did he not make any supplication for himself, nor shed any tears, but turning his voice to the most lamentable tone possible, at every stroke of the whip, his answer was, 'Woe, woe to Jerusalem'….he every day uttered these lamentable words as if it were his premeditated vow….Nor did he give ill words to any of those that beat him every day, nor good words to those that gave him food….This cry of his was loudest at the festivals; and he continued this ditty for seven years and five months, without growing hoarse or being tired until the very time that he saw his prophecy in earnest fulfilled in our siege…as he was going round upon the wall (during the siege), he cried out with his utmost force, 'Woe, woe, to the city again, and to the people, and to the holy temple'….just as he added at the last, 'Woe, woe, to myself also,' there came a stone out of one of the Roman engines (of war) and smote him and killed him immediately; and as he was uttering the very same prophecies, he gave up the ghost." Josephus, *Wars 6.5.3*

There were other signs and omens portending the destruction of Jerusalem that most of the Jews ignored or misinterpreted:

"(the Jews)did not attend, nor give credit, to the signs that were so evident and did so plainly foretell their future desolation….there was a star resembling a sword which stood over the city, a comet, that continued a whole year (Halley's comet in March 66?)....(before Passover) at the ninth hour of the night (3:00 AM), so great a light shone round the altar and the holy house that it appeared to be bright day time; which light lasted for half an hour. This light seemed to be a good sign to the unskillful, but was so interpreted by the sacred scribes as to portend those events that followed immediately upon it....Moreover, the eastern gate of the inner court of the temple (Nicanor's Gate), which was of brass, and vastly heavy and had been with difficulty shut by twenty men and rested upon a basis armed with iron and had bolts fastened very deep into the firm floor, which was there made of one entire stone, was seen to be opened of its own accord about the sixth hour of the night (midnight)....This also appeared to the vulgar to be a very happy prodigy, as if God did thereby open them the gate of happiness. But the men of learning understood it, that the security of their holy house was dissolved of its own accord and that the gate was opened for the advantage of their enemies." Josephus, *Wars 6.5.3*

Even though some of the priests and scribes interpreted the unusual phenomena correctly, they were not the ones who held the reins of power in Jerusalem. In the years leading up to its destruction, Jerusalem was controlled by three rogues: Eleazar ben Simon, John of Giscala and Simon bar Giora. For several years before Jerusalem's fall, these Jews and their followers fought each other for the leadership of the city. By the time the Romans were actually at the gates of Jerusalem, these men had slaughtered thousands of their fellow Jews and had drastically weakened their holy city. As Josephus wrote, the wise men of Jerusalem had recognized that as a result of these internecine wars "the security of their holy house (the Temple) was dissolved of its own accord and...the gates (of Jerusalem) were opened for the advantage of their enemies."

Why, one asks, would the patriots Eleazar, John and Simon be lured into such foolishness at the very moment in time that the Romans were systematically conquering all their cities one by one? Why would they turn on each other and slaughter their own when the rulers of the world were heading for their capital? Why would these three men risk the demise of their entire civilization? The answer is an old one: the innate desire for power.

At that time the dominant group in Jerusalem were the Zealots, a militant group who opposed Roman rule as incompatible with monotheism. Their leader was Eleazar, a member of the priestly class who had successfully fought and defeated the Roman Cestius on the battlefield and who violently opposed any Jew who wanted to pacify the Romans. It was this Eleazar and his Zealots in 66 who had refused to sacrifice for the Emperor, slaughtered the Roman garrison in Jerusalem, seized control of the Temple from the priests and provoked Rome to dispatch troops under Cestius.

John came from Giscala, a city in the Galilee region. He was a natural leader, a persuasive orator and fancied himself a king. When the Romans under Vespasian's son Titus were at the gates of Giscala, John implored Titus to spare the city until the next day because that day was their Sabbath. Titus withdrew his troops several miles away to the town of Cydessa. John used the Sabbath pretense to escape in the night with his army and with their women and children. It was difficult if not impossible to travel quickly with so many people. After only three miles, they abandoned their women and children to fend for themselves. Titus later killed all 6,000 of the defenseless ones to satisfy his anger at John's deceit.

John and his army safely reached Jerusalem in November of 67. He told the anxious people that they had not fled from the Romans but had fled to Jerusalem to defend it:

"He affirmed that the affairs of the Romans were in a weak condition and extolled his own power. He also jested upon the ignorance of the unskillful, as if those Romans, although they should take to themselves wings, could never fly over the walls of Jerusalem." *Wars of the Jews 4.3.1*

The young men of Jerusalem eagerly joined John with his can-do bravado, but the older men, who believed that John had fled from the Romans, began lamenting as if Jerusalem were already fallen.

John attached himself to the Zealots and became one of their trusted leaders.

At that time (c. November 67) Jerusalem was swollen with refugees from Jewish cities already taken by the Romans. The people were divided into those who wanted to fight the tyranny and taxation of the Romans and those who wanted to sue for peace and preserve the city and Temple. Generally, the young and fit wanted to throw off the Roman yoke and the old and the rich wanted to co-exist with the Romans. The fires of youth were pitted against the waters of wisdom. Fights and factions developed. The Zealots accused the priests and the wealthy of treason. The wealthy and the priests accused the Zealots of sedition and naivete. Tempers were high on both sides. Some of the restless Zealots joined bands of robbers and began to ravage and to rob the countryside around Jerusalem. Other bands of brigands and low-lifes ran to Jerusalem to join the militant groups and to capitalize upon the chaos in the city.

The lawless men and the Zealots took over the city. They arrested and killed men of royal lineage on the pretense they had contacted the Romans in order to surrender the city. Next, they appointed base and offensive men to be high priests and cast lots for priesthoods. When they seized the innermost sanctuary of the holy Temple as their center of operations, the priests under Ananus had had enough. They exhorted the people to cleanse the Temple of these blasphemers whose "hands were still warm with the slaughter of their own countrymen." *4.3.10* The people were more numerous but were not professional soldiers. After much bloodshed on both sides, the people fought the Zealots to a standstill.

John, meanwhile, had pretended to be above the fray and moved freely throughout Jerusalem, encouraging the people by day and going by night to the Zealots with Ananus' plans. John knew the Zealots were too few against all the inhabitants of Jerusalem, so he lied to Eleazar that Ananus had sent for the Romans to come as reinforcements to their movement.

Eleazar, therefore, sent for the Idumeans to swell his ranks. Josephus says the Idumeans were "ever a tumultuous and disorderly nation, always on the watch upon every motion...and upon your flattering them ever so little, and petitioning, them, they soon take their arms and put themselves into motion and make haste to a battle as if it were to a feast." *4.4.1* They gathered an army of 20,000 men and arrived at Jerusalem in late January 68. The high priest Ananus, the same man who had Jesus' brother James killed six years earlier, saw the Idumeans approaching Jerusalem, barred the gates of the city and posted guards on the walls. A former high priest, Jesus son of Gamalas, stood on the wall and tried to reason with them. He told the Idumeans the Zealots were liars, vile, insane, robbers, murderers, and polluters of the holy Temple by their drunkenness and debauchery:

"And this place (the Temple), which is adored by the habitable world and honored by such as only know it by report as far as the ends of the earth, is trampled upon by these wild beasts born among ourselves." *4.4.2*

The battle-ready Idumeans were not persuaded. They were insulted that the gates had been barred against them, against the Idumeans who were distant relations of the Jews through Esau, Jacob's twin brother. The real villains, they said, were not the Zealots but were the ones who had closed the gates against their own relatives. The Idumeans did not want to return home without fighting, so they camped outside the walls.

That night there was an epic thunderstorm and an earthquake: "…with utmost violence and very strong winds, with the largest showers of rain, with continual lightnings, terrible thunderings, and amazing concussions and bellowings of the earth…an earthquake." *4.4.5* Under cover of the storm, the Zealots took the Temple saws and cut through the bars on the gates where the Idumeans were encamped. The hot-headed Idumeans, insulted by being barred from the city, unnerved and scared by the storm and the earthquake, burst into Jerusalem and went on an insane rampage all that night. When morning came, 8,500 citizens were dead. But that was not enough blood:

"…they plundered every house and slew everyone they met….they sought for the high priests (Ananus and Jesus son of Gamalas)….as

335

soon as they caught them, they slew them and then standing upon their dead bodies, in way of jest, upbraided Ananus with his kindness to the people….they proceeded to that degree of impiety as to cast away their dead bodies without burial….Now after these were slain (February 68), the Zealots and the multitude of the Idumeans fell upon the people as upon a flock of profane animals and cut their throats….and there were twelve thousand of the better sort who perished in this manner." *4.5.2,3*

Finally, a brave and good man, one of the Zealots, privately came to the Idumeans and upbraided them for their barbarous actions. He said they were tricked into believing that Ananus was betraying the city to the Romans; that they were "partners with the (Zealots) in shedding the blood of their own countrymen;" that they had "subverted the laws of their forefathers;" that they had "done the works of war and tyranny;" and that they should repent of their "horrid barbarity….the Idumeans complied with these persuasions, (repented) and retired from Jerusalem and went home." *4.5.5*

It seems an ironic turn of events for the descendants of Esau, Jacob's twin brother, to be injected so violently into this story of brother fighting brother. Jacob/Israel, the father of the 12 tribes of the Hebrews, had by a ruse wrested the blessing of inheritance from his brother Esau in Genesis 27. The sons of Esau, the Idumeans, came unexpectedly like the earthquake and the storm and exacted a long-delayed revenge upon the sons of Jacob. They swiftly killed over 20,000 descendants of Jacob, repented and left. Many uncanny, disturbing and enigmatic events revolve around the destruction of that holy city.

After the Idumeans left, the Zealots went on another killing spree. They slaughtered all the rich people they could find, all the bravest, all the valiant fighters, anyone who opposed them, anyone who hid from them, anyone who approached them "nor could anyone escape unless he were very inconsequential either on account of his meanness of birth or on account of his fortune." *Wars 4.6.1*

John had straddled the fence between the Zealots and the people, but after the Zealots killed so many people, John broke from them and began to set up his own duchy. Always with an eye to being a king, he acted imperious and lorded it over his former equals. Some broke away and went back to the Zealots, but many still clung to John as their savior. The people were caught in the middle:

"(The people) already had to struggle with three of the greatest misfortunes: (the impending) war with the Romans, tyranny and uprisings (in the city). It appeared upon comparison that the war was the least troublesome to the populace of them all. Accordingly they ran away from their own houses to foreigners and obtained that preservation from the Romans which they despaired to obtain from their own people." *4.7.1*

The Roman commanders under Vespasian boldly, seeing all the deserters, hearing of the infighting and divisions among the Jews, thought they should take advantage of the situation and seize Jerusalem. But General Vespasian counseled them to wait: "...if (we) now go and attack the city...(the Jews) shall...unite together....but if (we) stay a while, (we) shall have fewer enemies because they will be consumed in this sedition....God acts as general of the Romans better than (I) can do, and is giving the Jews up to (us) without any pains of (our) own." *4.6.2*

Vespasian continued to isolate Jerusalem by taking all the small cities surrounding it:

"...when he (Vespasian) had taken a city...he slew (all) the young men; but he took their families captive (as slaves) and permitted his soldiers to plunder them of their effects; after which he set fire to their houses and went on to the adjoining villages." *4.9.1*

But Vespasian's siege of Jerusalem would have to be postponed because Rome was suddenly in turmoil. Vespasian was at his base in Caesarea Maritima when he received word that Emperor Nero had been forced to commit suicide on June 9, 68. Galba, the Roman governor of Spain and a man of considerable wealth, had declared himself emperor.

He was not acceptable to the Praetorian Guard because of money disputes with them and his arrant homosexuality. They killed him in the marketplace on January 15, 69. Otho, a young noble, immediately became emperor, but he was so unpopular that he committed suicide three months later. Vitellius, a man of ignoble birth, assumed the throne, but he was not universally acclaimed as Caesar by the Roman Legions. Vespasian, waiting in the wings in Judea, saw his chance. Before Vespasian left Judea for Rome, he released from prison Josephus (who in 67 had prophesied to Vespasian that he would one day be emperor) and attached him as interpreter to his son Titus whom he appointed General in Judea. Vespasian then rallied his armies and marched into Italy. After a bloody battle that killed 50,000 of Vitellius' supporters, Vespasian had Vitellius killed on December 22, 69. His Legions in the East declared the 60-year-old Vespasian Emperor of Rome.

Unlike the previous three emperors, Vespasian ruled Rome for 10 years and brought order, respect and much-needed taxes into the treasury. He invented novel ways to tax the public by charging for the public toilets and then collecting the urine and selling it to the dry cleaners of the day called fullers who needed the ammonia salts in the urine to clean and whiten wool. The public toilets of ancient Rome, some seating up to 100 people, survive and the Italians today still call their public toilets *vespasiani* after their "I'll tax any and every thing" Emperor Vespasian. The debacle of the period in Rome between June 9, 68 and December 22, 69 is called The Year Of The Four Emperors. Rome had its savage infighting and struggles for power just like Jerusalem did.

After the Idumeans had killed the priest Ananus, a third power monger, Simon bar Gorias, headed for Jerusalem. Simon had distinguished himself as a military leader when he and his army helped rout the Romans under Cestius in 66. Rather than being honored, he was ostracized by Ananus for killing and plundering rich Jews. He and his men fled to the desert fortress of Masada where they joined a band of assassins called the Sicarii.

The Apostle Paul may have had an encounter with this same Ananus/ Ananias in the mid-50's. Ananias was high priest in Jerusalem from 47-

59 and was known for his cruelty and violence. Paul had been preaching Jesus as Messiah, was arrested and brought before the Sanhedrin:

"Paul looked straight at the Sanhedrin and said, 'My brothers, I have fulfilled my duty to God in all good conscience to this day.' At this the high priest Ananias ordered those standing near Paul to strike him on the mouth. Then Paul said to him, 'God will strike you, you white-washed wall! You sit there to judge me according to the law, yet you yourself violate the law by commanding that I be struck!' Those who were standing near Paul said, 'You dare insult God's high priest?' Paul replied, 'Brothers, I did not realize that he was the high priest; for it is written: Do not speak evil about the ruler of your people.'" Acts 23:1-5

When Paul called Ananias a "white-washed wall," he was calling him a hypocrite because as a member of the Sanhedrin, he could not order a man to be struck until he was convicted of a crime. Ananias had broken the law. But Paul acknowledged he should not have disrespected the high priest. Why Paul did not know that Ananias was the current high priest is debated.

More than a dozen years after Paul's experience when Simon bar Gorias heard his enemy Ananus was dead, he and his army left Masada for Jerusalem:

"...(Simon), affecting to tyrannize and being fond of greatness, when he had heard of the death of Ananus, left (Masada) and went into the mountainous part of the county....(proclaiming) liberty to those in slavery and a reward to those already free, and (he) got together a set of wicked men from all quarters. And as he had now a strong body of men about him, he overran the villages that lay in the mountainous country and since he was now become formidable to the cities, many of the men of power were corrupted by him; so that his army was no longer composed of slaves and robbers, but a great many of the populace were obedient to him as their king." *4.9.3,4*

In Jerusalem Eleazar and John were terrified by Simon's messianic appeal and the strength and social breadth of his army. They were afraid to openly fight him, so they laid ambushes for his men. In one of those ambushes, they captured his wife and her attendants. They thought Simon would lay down his arms as ransom for his wife. They were wrong. Simon became like a wild animal. He force-marched his army right up to the walls of Jerusalem. Any Jew who left Jerusalem for any reason, he tormented, tortured and killed. Josephus says his anger was so great that he "was almost ready to taste of the very flesh of their dead bodies." *4.9.8* He chopped off the hands of those he did not kill and sent them back to the city with bloody stumps:

"He also enjoined (the mutilated ones) to tell the people that Simon swore by the God of the universe, who sees all things, that unless they will restore him his wife, he will break down their wall and inflict the like punishment upon all the citizens, without sparing any age and without making any distinction between the guilty and the innocent." *4.9.8*

The Zealots released Simon's wife. He took his army, left Jerusalem and began to plunder Idumea. He "laid waste their whole country" *4.9.7* and forced the people from all the cities he ransacked to walk to Jerusalem. He and his army followed them and encamped around the city's walls. Simon was back.

Jerusalem, already crowded by people fleeing from the Romans, now had to absorb the refugees from Idumea. Housing and food were scarce and terror reigned. Simon was outside the walls. Eleazar's Zealots were inside the walls. And John's contingent of Galileans were defiling the city:

"murdering men…abusing women….indulging themselves in feminine wantonness…they decked their hair, and put on women's garments and were besmeared over with ointments; and that they might appear very comely, they had paints under their eyes and imitated not only the ornaments, but also the lust of women, and were guilty of such intolerable uncleanness, and they invented unlawful pleasures of that sort. And thus did they roll themselves up and down the city, as in a brothel house, and defiled it entirely with their impure actions; nay, while their faces looked like the faces of women, they killed with their right hands; and when their gait was effeminate, they presently attacked men and became warriors and drew their swords from under their finely dyed cloaks and ran everybody through whom they alighted upon." Wars *4.9.10*

Jerusalem was deteriorating from a once revered holy sanctuary set on a hill to a debased city filled with human blood and filth. The vast majority of the Jews were decent people, normal people who tried to flee from the horror, but Simon guarded the gates and killed all who ventured outside.

Up until now (69), Jerusalem was controlled by the Zealots with Eleazar as their leader in an uneasy alliance with John and his mixed band of Galileans, Idumeans and former Zealots. The priests and the people were caught in the middle of this volatile combination.

"Out of their envy at his power and hatred of his cruelty" (*4.9.11*) some of the Idumeans broke away from John, plundered his riches, slew many of the Zealots and isolated the remainder in the Temple. Zealots from all over the city rushed to the Temple to defend John and Eleazar's Zealots against the Idumeans.

A faction split from a faction, the Idumeans now formed an alliance with the priests and the people against John and the Zealots. They barnstormed ideas about how they could take back the city. They decided to admit Simon and his army of 40,00 into the city:

"Accordingly, in order to overthrow John, they determined to admit Simon and earnestly to desire the introduction of a second tyrant into the city....to beseech this Simon to come into them of whom they had so often been afraid. Those also that had fled from the Zealots in Jerusalem joined in this request to him out of the desire they had of preserving their houses and their effects. Accordingly, (Simon) in an arrogant manner, granted them his lordly protection and came into the city in order to deliver it from the Zealots. The people also made joyful acclamations to him as their savior and their preserver; but when he was come in with his army, he took care to secure his own authority and looked upon they that invited him to be no less his enemies than those against whom the invitation was intended. And thus did Simon get possession of Jerusalem in the third year of the war in the month of Nisan." *4.9.11*

In April of 69, right before Passover and a year before the Roman siege of Jerusalem would begin, the Jews invited the fox into the henhouse. Another would-be king of the Jews had entered Jerusalem and immediately attempted and lost his initial assault upon the Temple where Eleazar and his Zealots controlled the summit and the inner courts and John and his army controlled the porticoes of the outer court. From his headquarters on the heights of Zion, Simon controlled most of Jerusalem except the Temple complex. With the Romans preparing to conquer Jerusalem, there were now three Jewish factions vying for power in a city that should have been preparing for war.

They made constant sorties against each other:

"…what advantage (John) had over Eleazar in the multitude of his followers, the like disadvantage he had in the situation he was in since he had his enemies (the Zealots) over his head….(John) suffered more mischief from Eleazar and his party than he could inflict upon them yet he would not leave off assaulting them, insomuch that there were continued sallies made one against another, as well as arrows thrown at one another, and the temple was defiled everywhere with murders. Now the tyrant Simon…having in his power the upper city and a great part of the lower, did now make more vehement assaults upon John and his party….yet was (Simon) beneath (John) in position when he attacked them, as (John) was beneath the attacks of the (Zealots) above him. The same advantage that Eleazar and his party had over (John) since he was beneath them, the same advantage had John by his higher situation over Simon." *5.1.3*

The blood-related enemies were not only vying for power, they were jockeying for fighting positions to kill each other more efficiently. John, caught in the middle, had to guard his face from the Zealots above him and his back from Simon below him. If there were not human lives and the holiest city in the world at stake, the situation would seem comedic. But it was tragic.

The reckless infighting continued for a year until the unthinkable occurred. John left his headquarters near the Temple complex and sallied out to engage Simon. The two armies met in that part of the city where the stores of grain were kept. John and Simon, accidentally or on purpose, "set on fire those houses that were full of grain and all the other provisions." *5.1.4*

John and Simon had to have known that Titus and his Roman Legions were only a month's march away from Jerusalem. They had to have known that in addition to thousands of refugees, Jerusalem in 70 AD was packed with tens of thousands of foreign Jews coming to their holy city for the Passover. They had to have known these pilgrims, the refugees, the people of Jerusalem, they and their armies all needed food. They had to have known, but they did the un-thinkable. Josephus states the reason for the Roman victory at Jerusalem was the famine that resulted from the petty wars of those men:

"Accordingly, it came to pass that all the places that were about the Temple were also burned down and were become an intermediate desert space, ready for fighting on both sides. And almost all of the grain was burned which would have been sufficient for a siege of many years. So (Jerusalem and its inhabitants) were taken by the means of the famine, which it would have been impossible to do, unless (John and Simon) had not thus prepared the way for it." *5.1.5*

With little food or grain for the people and with the area around the Temple burned, the deadly infighting continued. During the fighting, the people who had come from all over the region and the world to celebrate Passover piously continued to go to the Temple to make their sacrifices:

"...yet did (John and Eleazar) still admit (into the Temple) those that desired to offer their sacrifices....(the petitioners) were often destroyed by this sedition; for those arrows that were thrown by the engines came with such force that they went all over the buildings and reached as far as the altar...and fell upon the priests and those that were about the sacred offices (the Levites), insomuch that any persons who came there with great zeal from the ends of the earth to offer sacrifices at this celebrated place which was esteemed holy by all mankind, fell down before their own sacrifices themselves and sprinkled that altar which was venerable among all men, both Greeks and Barbarians, with their own blood till the dead bodies of (pilgrims) were mingled together with those of their own country, and those of profane persons with those of the priests, and the blood of all sorts of dead carcasses stood in pools in the holy courts themselves." *5.1.3*

With Jerusalem a bloody disaster zone, the mightiest army in the world was ready to do battle with the Jews in Jerusalem. At the start of Passover in March/April of 70, Titus arrived with over 80,000 troops composed of four Legions of Roman citizens; innumerable corps of auxiliaries recruited from conquered regions who received Roman citizenships if they served for 25 years; cohorts of barbarians who were fighters from outside the Empire; 2,000 soldiers from Egypt; Syrians; 3,000 from Assyria; cavalrymen; mercenaries; road-builders; baggage handlers; siege engine operators; slaves and all those crucial to military engagements.

As Rome's empire had expanded, Roman generals increasingly used their auxiliary and Barbarian troops to do the main fighting. On Trajan's Column in Rome depicting his victory over the Dacians in 106 AD, the auxiliaries and bare-chested Barbarians lead the fight. In the rear, away from the hostilities, the Roman Legionnaires are seen lurking in fortifications or chopping and stacking wood. The war scenes on the Column are so graphic it is believed to be a replica of the war itself. Yet Legionnaires are seen fighting in just four scenes while auxiliaries and Barbarians fight in 14 scenes.

Trajan's column provides the reason for the use of auxiliary and Barbarian fighters---they were braver and fiercer. As Romans became less militant and more genteel, few wanted to risk their lives or the lives of their children in the army. Rome had to go farther and farther into the wilds of the Empire to find fearless warriors who would fight like animals in return for a monetary or Roman citizenship award. On Trajan's Column one Barbarian fighter has beheaded an opponent but both of his hands are occupied in fighting as he carries the severed head, dangling by its hair, in his teeth. The British, the Celts, the Germans and the Turks (Thracians) were known as ruthless soldiers. By the middle of the 2nd century, few of Rome's Legionnaires were recruited from Italy.

During the siege of Jerusalem, several auxiliaries were cited for bravery and got rewards and commendations. In the heat of one battle, a strong auxiliary cavalryman reached down from his saddle, picked up a Jew by his ankle and took him back to Titus head down. One senses the Romans cosseted their Legions and used them only when necessary.

This disparate but highly effective fighting machine marched toward Jerusalem in the following formation:

"...the auxiliaries...marched first....after whom followed those that were to prepare the roads and measure out the camp; then came the commander's baggage and after that the other soldiers (Barbarians).... then came Titus himself having with him another select body; and then came the pikemen (carrying 20'-30' pointed wooden poles); after whom came the horses belonging to that Legion. All these came before the engines of war; and after these engines followed the tribunes and the leaders of the cohorts with their select bodies; after these came the ensigns with the eagle; and before those ensigns came the trumpeters belonging to them; next to these came the main body of the army in their ranks, every rank being six deep; the servants belonging to every Legion came after these; and before these last their baggage; the mercenaries came last and those that guarded them brought up the rear." *5.2.1*

Eleazar, John, Simon and their men were impressed but were not terrified. It was, however, a wake-up call:

"...the (warring) factions in the city had been dashing against one another perpetually; this foreign war, now suddenly come upon them after a violent manner, put the first stop to their contentions....and as the seditious ones now saw with astonishment the Romans pitching three several camps (around them) they began to think of an awkward sort of concord." *Wars 5.2.4*

When he arrived, Titus decided to take 600 horsemen and do a reconnaissance of Jerusalem to assess its strengths and to discern whether the bulk of the people wanted to sue for peace, as he had been informed. As he was picking his way among the many walls erected around the city's gardens, the Jews suddenly jumped out of one of the gates and intercepted Titus and two of his horsemen. It was impossible for Titus to go forward because of the walls and trenches and it seemed impossible for him to turn around because the Jews were between him and his men. Nevertheless, he turned his horse around and yelled to his troops to follow him. He rode headlong into the midst of his enemies. Arrows flew around him. His two companions were killed. He was without his headpiece or his breastplate because he had gone only to view the city. He fought all those who tried to stop him with his sword and made his horse ride over the others. The Jews were so impressed by his bravery that they all "gave a great shout at his boldness and exhorted one another to rush upon him." *5.2.2* Titus' men saw their only hope of escaping was to stay with him. They all fought through the ambush and then returned to their camp. Titus had tasted the mettle of the Jews and the Jews had seen the guts of the Roman general.

The Jews were irregular guerrilla fighters, each man for himself. The Roman soldiers were team fighters in orderly formations. In the initial battles, the advantage was to the Jews. When the 10th Legion was fortifying its position on the Mt. of Olives, the Jews fell upon them:

"...(the Legion) was put into disorder unexpectedly...some left...and immediately marched off, while many ran to their arms but were smitten and slain before they could turn back upon the enemy....The disorderly way the (Jews) fought at first put the Romans also to a standstill, who had been used to fighting skillfully in good order with keeping their ranks and obeying the orders that were given them...(but) as still more and more Jews sallied out of the city, the Romans were at length brought into confusion and put to flight and ran away from their camp." *5.2.4*

Titus arrived and chided the Legion for its cowardice and began to rout the Jews. But thousands of running, yelling Jews stormed out of the city "with such mighty violence...like the most terrible wild beasts... (and) with a fury as if they had been catapulted out of an engine of war, they broke the enemies' ranks to pieces...put them to flight...and (there were) but Titus himself and a few others with him who were left in the midst of the (fray)." *5.2.4* Titus and his personal guards valiantly charged the Jews at their flank. When the soldiers saw their leader isolated, they were ashamed they had retreated, rallied to their general and drove the Jews into the Kidron Valley. The Jews and the Romans both retreated. The Jews were jubilant and buoyed up by the battle. The Romans were ashamed and mad.

It was the day of Passover, 14 Nisan 70 AD, only 40 years after the Passover associated with Jesus' crucifixion. Titus had allowed the thousands of Jewish pilgrims from all over the world to enter Jerusalem to celebrate their holiday, but he would not allow them to leave.

There was a lull in hostilities and John took advantage of it to consolidate his power. Eleazar, the leader of the Zealots, opened the gates of the inner court of the Temple for the people and the pilgrims to enter and to worship. John sent his men into the Temple disguised as worshippers. When they got in, they threw off their cloaks and killed Eleazar and many who were worshipping and sacrificing. "And thus that sedition which had been divided into three factions was reduced to two." *5.3.1* John now had control of 8,400 men composed of his own army and of Eleazar's Zealots. Simon controlled over 10,000 men plus the Idumeans. John controlled all the Temple and parts adjoining it. Simon held the upper city and parts adjoining it. With every cessation of fighting against the Romans, they "fought against each other (and) the people were their prey....But although they had grown wiser at the first onset the Romans made upon them, this lasted but a while; for they returned to their former madness....fought it out and did everything that the besiegers could desire them to do." *5.6.1*

One morning in May of 70, Titus and his good friend Nicanor were at the walls of the city with Josephus as he was trying to persuade the Jews to surrender and to save themselves and their city from destruction. They rode too close to Jerusalem's wall and an arrow struck Nicanor in his left shoulder. Titus, seeing that the Jews would not even allow those who had come in peace to speak to them, became furious and began the siege in earnest.

He had his soldiers burn all the suburbs surrounding Jerusalem. He cut down all the trees to build embankments. As his soldiers constructed the large ramps up to the walls for the battering rams to enter, the Jews continuously pummeled them with arrows and jumped out and made sorties against them. As a show of strength in contrast to the Jews' arrows, the Romans retaliated with the big bertha of catapults called the Wild Ass (*Onanger*) because of the powerful kick generated by the recoil as the machine released stones. The Onanger catapulted 75 lb. stones over 1,300 feet:

"The stones that were cast were of the weight of a talent (c. 71lbs.) and were carried two furlongs and farther. The blow they gave was no way to be sustained, not only by those that stood first in the way, but by those that were beyond them for a great space. As for the Jews, they at first watched the coming of the stone, for it was of a white color and could therefore not only be perceived by the great noise it made, but could be seen also before it came by its brightness. Accordingly when the watchmen that sat upon the towers gave them notice when the engine was let go and the stone came from it, they cried out aloud in their own country language (Aramaic), 'The son cometh.'" *5.6.3*

After the Wild Ass, the Romans brought the battering ram called Victor up the embankment to one of the walls of the city:

"This battering ram is a vast beam of wood like the mast of a ship; its forepart is armed with a thick piece of iron at the head of it which is so carved as to be like the head of a ram, whence its name is taken. This ram is slung in the air by ropes passing over its middle, and is hung like the balance in a pair of scales from another beam and braced by strong beams that pass on both sides of it in the nature of a cross. When this ram is pulled backward by a great number of men with united force and then thrust forward by the same men, with a mighty noise it batters the walls with that iron part which is prominent; nor is there any tower so strong or walls so broad that can resist any more than its first batteries." *3.7.19*

The Romans had all the conventional mechanics for war: battering rams, powerful catapults, ramps and siege towers. But they had not innovated any new military tactics or hardware. When Titus dressed up his armies and paraded them around Jerusalem to intimidate (*Wars 5.9.1*), Sennacherib's Assyrian army had employed the same strategy against Jerusalem, unsuccessfully, in c. 700 BC (2 Kings 18:19-19:35). Over a hundred years later the Babylonian king Nebuchadnezzar besieged and destroyed Jerusalem and the first Temple in 586 BC. The Romans replicated those tactics 650 years later: "(Nebuchadnezzar) encamped outside the city and built siege works against it….the famine in the city had become so severe that there was no food for the people to eat. The city wall was broken through….He set fire to the temple of the Lord, the royal palace and all the houses of Jerusalem….broke up the bronze Sea...and carried the bronze to Babylon....and (everything) made of gold or silver....took prisoners....So Judah went into captivity, away from their land." (2 Kings 25:1-21) The Romans were doing nothing new.

Even battering rams, a great invention in warfare, had been around and can be seen on ancient reliefs from the 19th century BC. The earthen ramps the Romans constructed around Jerusalem had been used for hundreds of years. Remnants of the siege mound constructed by Sennacherib in the 8th century BC during the siege of Lachish (in

Israel) are still visible as is the siege mound used by the Romans in the taking of Masada in 73-74.

The fabled Roman military's tight phalanx formations had first appeared on the world scene in c. 1200 BC at the beginning of the Iron Age. It was the evolution of these compact military ranks disciplined enough to withstand the massed chariot charges, so effective in scattering troops and causing mayhem, that eventually led to the end of armies of chariots. The chariot became a vehicle for kings and generals.

The Carthaginian Hannibal (247-183 BC), considered one of the greatest military generals of all time, overcame Rome's best military asset, its tight Legions, at the Battle of Cannae in August of 216 BC by using the pincer movement, a gradual encircling of a whole fighting force until the opponent is squeezed into defending its main fighting force, its flanks as well as its rear. Intelligent cunning will always defeat the conventional. Hannibal, who in the Second Punic War invaded Italy in 218 BC with 37 elephants and c. 43,000 soldiers and cavalry, is still studied in modern war colleges and the tactics he used against the Romans in the Battle of Trebia, the Battle of Trasimene and the Battle of Cannae have spawned many modern books: e.g. Trevor Dupuy's book *The Military Life of Hannibal: Father of Strategy* (1969); Mark Healy's book *Cannae 216 BC: Hannibal Smashes Rome's Army* (1994); Adrian Goldworthy's book *The Punic Wars* (2000).

Hannibal was a military genius and he knew it. In Plutarch's *Lives: Flamininus 21.3-4* Plutarch says Hannibal and the Roman general Scipio, who had defeated Hannibal at the battle of Zama near Carthage in October 202 BC, met after the war:

"Moreover, we are told that the two men met again at Ephesus, and...as they were walking about together, Hannibal took the side which more properly belonged to Scipio as the superior (general). Scipio suffered it and walked about without paying any heed to it, and again, when they fell to discussing generals and Hannibal declared Alexander to have been the mightiest of generals, and next to him Pyrrhus, and third himself, Scipio asked with a quiet smile, 'And what would you have said if I had not conquered you?' To which Hannibal replied, 'In that case, Scipio, I should not have counted myself third, but first among generals.'"

One of the successors of Alexander the Great, Demetrius Poliorcetes (known as "The Besieger"), had used the same engines of war during the famous Battle of Rhodes in 305-304 BC that the Romans used in the Battle of Jerusalem. But Demetrius' siege tower called *Helepolis* ("Taker Of Cities") was bigger and better than any siege tower the Romans ever built. Demetrius had brought the Athenian architect/engineer Epimachus with him to Rhodes to design and to construct this tower. Over 125' high, 60' square at the base and weighing 160 tons, each of the nine stories of the tower had battering rams and throwing machines. No ancient siege tower ever surpassed Epimachus' legendary one. The Roman's siege towers and battering rams had been de rigueur instruments of war for many centuries.

When the Jews heard the first thwack of the Victor battering ram, it was a sound millions had heard for hundreds of years in the ancient world. As the "prodigious noise" of the first blow of the battering ram against the wall echoed throughout the city, John and Simon looked at each other and "seeing the common danger they were in, contrived to make a (united) defense....on both sides they laid aside their hatred and their peculiar quarrels and formed themselves into one body." *5.7.4* The Jews rushed outside the gates, went right up to the machines and tried to set fire to the battering rams: "...the one side tried hard to set them on fire, and the other side to prevent it; on both sides there was a confused cry made and many of those in the forefront of the battle were slain. However, the Jews were now too hard for the Romans, by the furious assaults they made like madmen; and the fire caught hold of these works." *Wars 5.7.5*

Again, Titus had to come to the rescue of his crack fighting team. He rode up with the "stoutest" of his horsemen and killed 12 Jews who were in the front lines, drove the rest back into the city and then saved his siege engines from burning up. The renowned Roman Legions and their unflinching valor were not always on display in the Battle for Jerusalem.

The next night around midnight when all were sleeping, one of the 75' tall siege towers that the Romans had erected parallel to the walls came crashing down. The Roman Legions were terrified by the noise and thought the Jews were attacking. They ran for their weapons, looked all around for Jews and thought some of their own men were Jews and demanded the password from them. Titus informed his soldiers that a siege tower had collapsed and they could go back to bed.

The new 75' towers were made of wood plated with iron so the Jews could not set them on fire. With the advantage and height of the siege towers now in place, the Romans drove the Jews away from the walls. The battering rams continued unimpeded to bombard the walls. On May 25, 70 the Romans broke through the outer wall, mounted the breach, opened the city gates and "Titus pitched his camp within the city." *5.7.1,2*

The Jews retreated behind the second wall of the city. Titus had tasted victory and was relentless. He attacked the second wall, but the Jews fought "courageously (and) made violent sallies (outside the gates)...and in united bodies fought the Romans....(the Romans) being encouraged by their power joined to their skill as were the Jews encouraged by their boldness which was nourished by the fear they were in and by that hardiness which is natural to our nation under calamities." *5.7.2*

Five days later Titus breached the second wall and brought 1,000 of his choice troops into "that place where the merchants of wool, the braziers and the market for cloth (were) and where the narrow streets led obliquely to the wall." *5.8.1* But Titus did not make a huge breach in the wall. He made a small breach only because he "did not think the (Jews) would lay traps for him (because) he did not kill any of those he caught, nor set fire to their houses....(and even) promised to restore people's effects to them; for he was very desirous to preserve (Jerusalem) for his own sake and the temple for the sake of the city." *5.8.2*

While Titus and his men were resting inside that quarter of the city, the Jews encircled them and attacked. The advantage was to the Jews because they knew the city and its winding, cramped streets. The Romans had no room to fight and they could not get through the small opening in the wall. The Jews cooped them up and rushed the Romans who were beyond the walls. The Romans had assumed that with the breach of the second wall, Jerusalem was theirs. The soldiers were confused, leaped down from the walls and ran back to their camps. Titus stood within the middle of the enemy and fought them, but the Jews were too numerous and fierce. They drove the Romans out of the city and "began to think that the Romans would never venture to come into the city any more; and if they kept within it themselves, they would not be conquered." *5.8.2*

It was at this moment of victory and relief that Simon and John saw in that part of the city the effects of the growing famine: "…but now famine had for a long time seized upon the better part and a great many had died already for want of necessities." *5.8.1* They reasoned that all these dead people probably had wanted to surrender to the Romans. They wanted "none others to be preserved but such as were against a peace with the Romans." *5.8.1*

The Romans immediately made another assault upon the second wall. The Jews heroically made a wall of their own bodies and fought for four days until they retreated behind the third wall of the city. This time the Romans totally demolished the second wall, brought an entire garrison into the city and began to devise plans to take the third wall that protected the Antonia Fortress and the Temple Mount.

Titus decided to pause for a while and give the Jews time to reconsider their situation and to surrender. As a show of strength and intimidation, for four days Titus staged a parade of his forces all around Jerusalem in full military regalia with their breastplates polished and glittering in the sun. All of the inhabitants of the city crowded the walls and tops of houses to see this display of Roman Imperial might: "..a very great consternation seized upon the hardiest of Jews when they saw all the army in the same place, together with the fineness of their arms and the good order of their men." *Wars 5.9.1*

Titus simultaneously began to build embankments to reach the 75' tall Tower of Antonia because it was his access into the Temple and the rest of the city. Built by Herod the Great in c. 6 BC as a fortress, Antonia was named after Herod's patron Mark Antony. The castle overlooked the Temple area. It was connected to the northern end of the Temple area by two flights of steps mentioned in Acts 21:30-40 where Paul was rescued from a Jewish mob by Roman soldiers: "When Paul reached the steps, the violence of the mob was so great that he had to be carried (up the steps) by the soldiers." On the steps leading to Antonia and under the protection of the Roman soldiers, Paul recounted his conversion story to the angry mob:

"...Paul stood on the steps and motioned to the crowd....I am a Jew, born in Tarsus in Cilicia, but brought up in this city. Under Gamaliel I was thoroughly trained in the law of our fathers...I persecuted the followers of this Way to their death....I even obtained letters (from the Sanhedrin) to their brothers in Damascus, and went there to bring these people as prisoners to Jerusalem to be punished. About noon as I came near Damascus, suddenly a bright light from heaven flashed around me. I fell to the ground and heard a voice say to me, 'Saul! Saul! Why do you persecute me?' 'Who are you, Lord?' I asked. 'I am Jesus of Nazareth, whom you are persecuting,' he replied....'Get up,' the Lord said, 'and go into Damascus. There you will be told all that you have been assigned to do.' My companions led me by the hand into Damascus because the brilliance of the light had blinded me. A man named Ananias came to see me....He stood beside me and said, 'Brother Saul, receive your sight!' And at that very moment I was able to see him. Then he said, 'The God of our fathers has chosen you to know his will and to see the Righteous One and to hear words from his mouth. You will be a witness to all men of what you have seen and heard. And now what are you waiting for? Get up, be baptized and wash your sins away, calling on his name.'" Acts 21:40-22:1-16

The crowd was incensed by Paul's words and he was whisked away into the Antonia fortress where the Roman troops were garrisoned. Only 10 years later in 67, the Jewish historian Josephus would surrender to the Romans and would become the Hebrew interpreter for the Roman General Titus. A mere 13 years after Paul's witness on the steps of the

Tower of Antonia Titus would break into that fortification and seal the fate of Jerusalem.

While Titus was preparing the ramps and still parading his troops around the city, he sent Josephus to talk to the Jews in their own language (Aramaic) and to persuade them to surrender the city and spare its people. Josephus was not the best messenger. Many of the Jews hated Josephus because he was now aligned with the Romans and because he had deserted his command in Jotapata. It is true that Josephus was aligned with the Romans and had escaped from his responsibilities as a general in Jotapata under questionable circumstances.

Josephus has been maligned in certain academic circles ever since the early 1500's for a paragraph he wrote in *Jewish Antiquities 18.3.3*:

"Now there was about this time Jesus, a wise man, if it be lawful to call him a man, for he was a doer of wonderful works, a teacher of such men as receive the truth with pleasure. He drew over to him both many of the Jews and many of the Gentiles. He was the Christ; and when Pilate, at the suggestion of the principal men amongst us, had condemned him to the cross, those that loved him at the first did not forsake him, for he appeared to them alive again the third day, as the divine prophets had foretold these and ten thousand other wonderful things concerning him; and the tribe of Christians, so named from him, are not extinct to this day."

The sources of the Josephus problem are the three phrases: "if it be lawful to call him a man," "He was the Christ" and "for he appeared to them alive again the third day, as the divine prophets had foretold these and ten thousand other wonderful things concerning him." It is incomprehensible to Jews that the very orthodox Josephus would ever say such things about Jesus and still remain an unconverted Jew as he did his entire life. It is incomprehensible to Christians that Josephus would make that statement and still remain an orthodox Jew.

In order to solve the "Testimonium Flavianum Question," as it is called, many Jewish and Christian scholars have accused "well-meaning monks" of interpolating the phrases into an otherwise authentic text.

However, the text in *Jewish Antiquities 18:3.3* completed in c. 94-96 had not been corrupted when Eusebius wrote most of his *Church History* in c. 300 and quoted verbatim from Josephus, calling him "a reliable historian." In *Church History 1.11* Eusebius, quoting Josephus, says:

"In telling this about John (the Baptist), Josephus says the following concerning our Savior in the same historical work (*Jewish Antiquities*): 'About that time lived Jesus, a wise man, if indeed one ought to call him a man. For he was the achiever of extraordinary deeds and was a teacher of those who accept the truth gladly. He won over many Jews and many of the Greeks. He was the Messiah. When he was indicted by the principal men among us and Pilate condemned him to be crucified, those who had come to love him originally did not cease to do so; for he appeared to them on the third day restored to life, as the prophets of the Deity had foretold these and countless other marvelous things about him. And the tribe of Christians, so named after him, has not disappeared to this day.'"

When Sozomen, a Palestinian Christian historian, wrote his *Ecclesiastical History* in the 400's, it does not seem that the text had yet been interpolated because he writes:

"Josephus, the son of Matthias, also who was a priest and was most distinguished among Jews and Romans, may be regarded as a noteworthy witness to the truth concerning Christ; for he hesitates to call Him a man since He wrought marvelous works and was a teacher of truthful doctrines, but openly calls him Christ; that He was condemned to the death of the cross and appeared alive again the third day. Nor was Josephus ignorant of numberless other wonderful predictions uttered beforehand by the holy prophets concerning Christ. He further testifies that Christ brought over many to Himself both Greeks and Jews, who continued to love Him, and that the people named after Him had not become extinct. It appears to me that in narrating these things, (Josephus) all but proclaims that Christ, by comparison of works, is God. As if struck by the miracle, (Josephus) ran, somehow, a middle course, assailing in no way those who believed in Jesus, but rather agreeing with them." *Book 2.1*

Josephus' *Jewish Antiquities* and *Wars of the Jews* were wildly popular during the Middle Ages. There are still 171 Latin manuscripts from that time with Josephus' Testimony in them. One wonders when in the years after c. 94 AD when *Jewish Antiquities* was written through the 300's and 400's when his words were cited by other authors and up to the Middle Ages and the Latin manuscripts containing his Testimony, one wonders exactly where, when and by whom was the text corrupted and, most importantly, why have we not found an "uncorrupted" text.

The fact that Josephus never became a Christian, as far as one knows, weighs most heavily in the direction that something is wrong. However, it was never Josephus' intention to write anything but comprehensive historical books about the Jewish people. He judges Greek, Roman and Jew as impartially as an historian can. In spite of the many scholars who have gone to inordinate philological lengths to demonstrate contextual and subjectual inconsistencies in that small, little paragraph, modern publications of his *Jewish Antiquities* still contain the "Testimony of Flavius Josephus" in the text largely because no answer can textually be found to refute his Testimony.

The Jews disliked Josephus whom they deemed a traitor and did not preserve copies of his books. Their earliest copy is from the Middle Ages. The oldest Christian-preserved manuscript of Josephus dates from the 1000's and the questionable phrases are there as received. Eusebius, however, in the early 300's quotes Josephus' passage as it appears above and Jerome in the early 400's, relying heavily upon Eusebius, changes only three words: "He was believed to be the Christ." That "believed to be" could solve one of the problems if it really is the correct translation and some critics would stand down. But "for he appeared to them alive again the third day" still remains a problem. If one begins to question everything in ancient writings that offend or rile, we will have no history, ancient or modern. History and especially Jewish and Biblical history owe the otherwise known-to-be-reliable Josephus a great debt, even though his personal character will always be in question.

The 1st century AD Josephus can be compared to the 6th century BC prophet Jeremiah. However, Jeremiah, the Weeping Prophet, was a man of God and his character will never be impugned. But both Jeremiah and Josephus saw the super powers of their day as agents sent by God to punish the wickedness of their nation. Both men wanted the city of Jerusalem and the Temple to be preserved. Both men counseled their people to surrender to their enemies rather than to be destroyed. Jeremiah constantly begged the people of Jerusalem to surrender to the Babylonians and to save the first Temple from destruction:

"This is what the Lord says: 'Whoever stays in this city will die by the sword, famine or plague, but whoever goes over to the Babylonians will live. He will escape with his life'....And this is what the Lord says: 'This city will certainly be handed over to the army of the king of Babylon who will capture it.' Then the officials said to the king (Zedekiah), '(Jeremiah) should be put to death. He is discouraging the soldiers who are left in this city, as well as all the people, by the things he is saying to them. This man is not seeking the good of these people but their ruin.'" Jeremiah 38:2-4

At that time (c. 580's BC) the Jews had fallen into idolatry and wickedness. Jeremiah insisted God had sent the forces of Nebuchadnezzar against them to punish them. But that generation would not listen to Jeremiah. They beat him and put him in stocks (Jeremiah 20:1,2); they barred him from the Temple (36:5); and they imprisoned him in the bottom of a well. (38:6) Jerusalem fell to the Babylonians and Solomon's Temple, the first Temple, was destroyed on 9 Av 586 BC.

When Josephus was sent out to beg his own people to surrender to the Romans, they booed him and shot arrows at him. He cites Jeremiah to them:

"...when the king of Babylon (Nebuchadnezzar) besieged this very city, and our king Zedekiah fought against him, contrary to what predictions were made to him by Jeremiah, the prophet, he was at once taken prisoner and saw the city and the temple demolished....but for you to pass over what you have done within this city, which I am not able to describe as your wickedness deserves, for you to abuse me and throw arrows at me who only exhort you to save yourselves....You are quarreling about rapes and murders and inventing strange ways of wickedness. Nay, the temple itself has become the receptacle of all and this divine place is polluted by the hands of those of our own country.... After all this, do you expect Him whom you so impiously abused to be your supporter?....I believe the Jews of that age (586 BC) were not so impious as you are. Wherefore I cannot but suppose that God is fled out of His sanctuary and stands on the side of those against whom you fight...have pity upon your families, and set before every one of your eyes your children and wives and parents who will be gradually consumed by either famine or by war." *Wars of the Jews 5.9.4*

After Josephus' plea, many of the people deserted to the Romans and "Titus let a great number of them go into the country wherever they pleased. The main reasons why they were so ready to desert were these: that now they should be freed from those miseries which they had endured in that city and yet should not be in slavery to the Romans." *5.10.2*

But the growing famine was the real enemy. John and Simon scoured the city to find and to hoard food for themselves and their men. They tortured the poor and needy. If an old man held a piece of bread in his hands, they beat him and took it away. If women hid food for their families, they pulled their hair out. They tortured people whom they thought were hiding food by "stopping up the passages of their private parts...and driving stakes up their fundamentals." *5.10.3* The seditious had fallen so low they openly confessed their depravity to themselves and to others saying "they were slaves, the scum, and the spurious and abortive offspring of our nation." *5.10.5*

People risked their lives to go outside the walls to find some herbs or weeds to eat. When they were caught by the Romans, they were beaten, tortured and then crucified before the walls of the city for all to see: "...the soldiers out of the wrath and hatred they bore the Jews nailed those they caught, one after one way and another after another way to the crosses by way of jest....their multitude was so great that room was wanting for the crosses and crosses wanting for the bodies." *5.11.1*

The Romans continued to raise the ramps against the Antonia fortress. But from the beginning of their construction, the Jews, under John's leadership, had dug a tunnel under the ramps and had supported the earth with wooden beams. When the ramps were almost ready for use, John ordered wood dipped in pitch and tar to be ignited under the beams: "...as the cross beams that supported the banks were burning, the ditch yielded on the sudden, and the banks were shaken down and fell into the ditch with a prodigious noise....a consternation fell on the Romans and the shrewdness of the contrivance discouraged them.... and cooled their hopes for the time to come." *5.11.4* It was clear the Jews were going to fight the Romans for every inch of Jerusalem below ground as well as every inch above ground.

Titus had come to his wit's end. Some of his generals said they should rush the Jews with the entire army. Some said they should wait until the famine had killed most of the people. Titus, already thinking about his victory parade, was afraid the length of time it was taking to subdue Jerusalem would "diminish the glory of his success....(he determined) that they must build a wall round about the whole city.... (and) if any should think such a work to be too great...he ought to consider that it is not fit for Romans to undertake any small work." *5.12.1* In only three days the Roman army built a five-mile wall around Jerusalem. Josephus says: "...it is incredible that what would naturally have required some months was done in so short an interval." *5.12.2*

The Roman soldier was not only expected to be an excellent fighter but he was required to be a competent builder, engineer and worker. Fighting in the Roman army was competitive and done for the sake of *virtus*. Virtus, from which we get our word "virtue," was manly courage and excellence. *Disciplina*, the handmaiden of virtus, meant self-control, determination and an orderly way of doing things. Roman soldiers competed with each other for the honors and recognition conferred for virtus and disciplina. The wall was built in such a short time because each section of the wall was assigned to a specific Legion and each Legion competed with the other Legions for the awards of disciplina.

Each Legion was divided into ten cohorts. Each Legion assigned a portion of the wall to each of its cohorts. Not only were the Legions competing against each other for pay and for glory, but the individual cohorts within a Legion competed with each other. So all levels in each Legion and all the Legions in the army were competing against each other for the money, the rewards and, most importantly, for the approval of their superiors and of Titus, their supreme commander. With the wall up in record time, the Jews were walled in. There was no hope of escape.

The famine began to reap whole families, whole blocks of people and piles of rotting people were sealed away in large homes. The crooked lanes of the city were crammed with dead bodies. Heaps of bodies were scooped up and thrown over the walls into the Kidron and Hinnom valleys. Those dying had no strength to bury their dead and many died as they were burying the dead. People stumbled through the streets like the walking dead. Nobody spoke to anybody else. There were no lamentations or grief: "A deep silence…a kind of deadly night seized upon the city….and every one of these died with their eyes fixed upon the Temple." *Wars 5.12.3*

One afternoon when Titus was making his rounds, he saw the valleys filled with the dead, putrefying bodies. He groaned and raised his hands to the gods and called on them to witness that this was not his doing. The Roman soldiers, on the other hand, stood in front of the walls with food and drink, eating and jesting in front of the starving. To observe the state of his people one day, Josephus got too near a city wall and was knocked unconscious by a large stone. The Jews ran out of the city to get him, but the Romans got to him first.

Some of the deserters jumped from the city walls and ran to the Romans for food:

"…when they came first to the Romans, they were puffed up by the famine and swelled like men in a state of dropsy; after which they all of a sudden over-filled their bodies that were so empty and so burst asunder….there was found among the Syrian deserters a certain person who was caught gathering pieces of gold out of the excrements of the

dead Jews' bodies; for the deserters used to swallow such pieces of gold....
there was a great quantity of gold in the city....So the multitude of the
Arabians with the Syrians cut up those that came out as supplicants and
searched their bellies. Nor does it seem to me that any misery befell the
Jews that was more terrible than this, since in one night's time about
2,000 of these deserted were dissected." *5.13.4*

Unspeakable evil outside the city. Unspeakable suffering inside the
city.

Manneus, the son of Lazarus, was the man appointed to count and
to pay the public stipend for the bodies carried out. He defected to Titus
and told him "no fewer than 115,889 dead bodies had been carried out
(of Jerusalem)....many of the eminent citizens (who had escaped) told
Titus no fewer than 600,000 were thrown out of the gates....(and) some
persons were driven to such terrible distress as to search the common
sewers and old dung hills of cattle and to eat the dung which they got
there." *5.13.7*

The Romans thought the conditions inside the city would weaken
the resolve of the fighters. To the contrary:

"...they found the Jews' courageous souls to be superior to the multitude
of the miseries they were under....insomuch that (the Roman soldiers)
were ready to imagine that the violence of their attacks was invincible
and that the alacrity they showed would not be discouraged by these
calamities; for what would (the Jews) be able to bear if they should be
fortunate, who had turned their very misfortunes to the improvement
of their valor....the (Roman) soldiers were greatly ashamed that (Jewish)
subtlety should be quite too hard for (Roman) courage, their madness
for armor, their magnitude for skill." *6.1.2.3*

The walls around the Tower of Antonia had been weakened by
the battering rams. Using crowbars and their hands, the Romans had
removed four large stones, each weighing c. 2 ½ tons, from the base of
the Tower. Antonia's Tower was 75' high and stood on a great precipice:

"...it was the work of king Herod....the rock itself was covered over with smooth pieces of stone from its foundation, both for ornament and that any one who would either try to get up or to go down it might not be able to hold his feet upon it." *5.8*

During the night, the wall surrounding Antonia collapsed to expose yet another wall the Jews had built behind that wall. The Romans were frustrated at every turn. Thousands of Roman soldiers had already died taking walls. Before asking his soldiers to go over that makeshift wall, Titus, considering "the alacrity of soldiers in war is chiefly excited by hopes and by good words," delivers a concerted speech to his fearful troops. He extols those soldiers who under difficult and life-threatening situations like this one perform brave, valorous and courageous deeds. He emphasizes the inferiority of the Jews in comparison to the Romans "who have taken possession of almost all the world that belongs to either land or sea." *6.1.4.5* He emphasizes how cowardly it would be to wait and to let the famine rather than the Romans reap the glory.

Titus then ventures into the world of the Roman afterlife because he knows his soldiers have seen the indomitable fortitude of the Jews and they are afraid of dying while taking that wall:

"(I) speak of the immortality of those men who are slain in the midst of their martial bravery; yet cannot I forbear to imprecate upon those who are of a contrary disposition that they may die in time of peace, by some distemper or other, since their souls are already condemned to the grave, together with their bodies; for what man of Virtue is there who does not know that those souls which are severed from their fleshly bodies in battles by the sword, are received by the ether, that purest of elements, and joined to that company which are placed among the stars; that they become good demons and propitious heroes and show themselves as such to their posterity. While those souls that wear away with distempered bodies come to a subterranean night to dissolve them to nothing, and a deep oblivion takes away all remembrance of them.... therefore since fate has determined that death is to come of necessity upon all men, a sword is a better instrument for that purpose than any disease whatsoever....is it not a very little thing for us not to yield up that to the public benefit which we must yield up to fate?" *Wars 6.1.5*

Titus ends his hopeless, lackluster speech by telling them he will lavishly heap rewards on those who are first over the wall and those who fight with virtue. The speech does not encourage the troops: "Upon this speech of Titus, the rest of the multitude were affrighted at so great a danger." *6.1.6*

In ancient and in modern times it has been the duty of generals to inspire their troops to fight valiantly for home and country. Titus ends his rally by telling his troops how glorified they will be among the ether of the stars when they are dead and how ignominious it is to die of old age and disease and be consigned to eternal oblivion. At least Titus did not resort to taunting his troops as did a god in the 8th century BC Akkadian *Epic of Erra and Ishum*:

"Up, do your duty.
Why do you stay in town like a feeble old man?
How can you stay at home like a lisping child?
Are we to eat women's bread, like one who has never marched on to the battlefield?
Are we to be fearful and nervous as if we had no experience of war?
To go on to the battlefield is as good as a festival for young men!
Anyone who stays in town, even though he be a prince, will not be satisfied with bread alone;
He will be vilified in the mouths of his own people and dishonored.
How can he raise his hand against one who goes to the battlefield?
However great the strength of one who stays in town,
How can he prevail over one who has been on the battlefield?
City food, however fancy, cannot compare with what is cooked on the embers.
However sweet fine beer, it holds nothing to water from a skin.
The terraced palace holds nothing to the wayside sleeping spot!"

The warrior is manly, brave, seasoned, fearless, praised. He and his comrades prefer campfires and tents in the open air of distant battlefields to the effete comforts and amenities of city life at home. In the Akkadian epic the troops eventually rally. And at the battle for Jerusalem a puny Syrian named Sabinus who looked like he had a weak constitution but had distinguished himself on the battlefield was one of the few inspired by Titus' speech. He jumped up and told Titus that he would be the first to ascend the wall and he would choose "death voluntarily for (your) sake." *6.1.6* Eleven others ran to the wall with Sabinus. The Jews shot arrows at them and rolled stones down upon them, but Sabinus reached the top of the wall. The Jews, astonished at his ferocity and thinking there were many behind him, ran away. "And now one cannot but complain here about Fortune, envious of virtue and always hindering the performance of glorious achievements." *6.1.6* Sabinus stumbled on a large rock and fell down with a clash of his armor. The Jews looked back, noticed he was alone and pelted him with arrows until he died. The other men were killed as they got to the top of the wall. In his narrative of this famous war, Josephus has given a type of historic immortality, not promised by Titus, to the many heroic Romans and Jews who took part in the siege of Jerusalem.

Two days later at 3 o'clock in the morning, twelve soldiers from the 5th Legion took matters into their own hands. They grabbed their standard-bearer and trumpeter, climbed quietly up through the ruins of the Tower of Antonia, cut the throats of the guards as they were sleeping and ordered the trumpeter to sound his trumpet. Titus immediately ordered all the army to put on their armor and follow the twelve. The Romans ascended the fortress, but the Jews were waiting for them. A bloody 10-hour battle ensued at the crowded entrance to the Temple. The Romans tried to force their way into the Temple and the Jews tried to force them back to the Tower of Antonia. Arrows and spears were useless. It was hand-to-hand combat with swords in the dark:

"...during this battle, the positions of the men were undistinguished on both sides and they fought at random, the men being intermixed one with another, and confounded by reason of the narrowness of the place....Great slaughter was now made on both sides, and the combatants trod upon the bodies and the armor of those that were dead and dashed them to pieces....there was no room for flight, nor for pursuit....those that were in the first ranks were under the necessity of killing or being killed....those on both sides that came behind them forced those before them to go on....At length the Jews' violent zeal was too hard for the Romans' skill....the fight had lasted from the ninth hour of the night (3:00 AM) till the seventh hour of the day (1:00 PM)." *6.1.7*

The Romans fell back but took solid possession of the Tower of Antonia in mid-July 70. Now, at last, they had an entrance into the Temple and the rest of Jerusalem. Again Josephus describes a strange twist of fortune for a valiant auxiliary soldier named Julian from Bithynia (around the Black Sea). When he saw the Romans retreating, he ran after the Jews and killed many. As Titus and the soldiers watched in admiration, something happened:

"... as he had shoes all full of thick and sharp nails as had every one of the other soldiers (cleats on the soles of shoes for scaling the fortress), so when he ran on the (smooth marble) floors of the temple, he slipped and fell down upon his back with a very great noise, which was made by his armor. This made those that were running away to turn back....the Jews got about him in crowds and struck at him with their spears and with their swords on all sides....yet did (Julian), as he lay stab many of them with his sword....he pulled his neck close to his body, till all his other limbs were shattered and nobody came to defend him and then he yielded to his fate....(Titus) was deeply affected...especially since he was killed in the sight of so many (soldiers)...such as could (have helped him) but were too terrified to attempt it." *6.1.8*

The Jews barricaded the Romans in the Antonia fortress. Josephus, for the sake of history, names eight Jews who distinguished themselves in that bloody fight: Alexas and Gyphtheus of John's faction; Malachias, Judas and James of Simon's faction; "and of the zealots, two brothers, Simon and Judas, the sons of Jairus." *6.1.8*

Titus set his men the task of making a large enough breach in the walls near Antonia for his whole army to walk into the rest of Jerusalem. Because there were no lambs or no priests alive or able, on the 17 Panemus, August 6, 70 AD, the daily sacrifice was not offered to God for the first time since the second Temple was built in 538 BC. Some Jews and Christians later associated that day with the Daniel 12:11 prophecy: "From the time that the daily sacrifice is abolished and the abomination that causes desolation is set up, there will be 1,290 days."

Titus told Josephus to summon John and tell him that he could bring as many fighting men out of the city as he wished. The Romans would fight them away from the Temple and the people. But John hurled deprecations upon Josephus and said the city would never fall because it was God's city. Josephus continued to tearfully plead with John and "as Josephus spoke these words with groans and tears in his eyes, his voice was interrupted by sobs." *6.2.2*

Then Titus spoke to John and the others through Josephus: "I appeal to the gods of my own country, and to every god that ever had any regard for this place....I also appeal to my own army...that I do not force you to defile this sanctuary; and if you will but change the terrain upon which you will fight, no Roman shall either come near your sanctuary or offer any affront to it; nay, I will endeavor to preserve you your holy house, whether you will or not." *6.2.4*

John and all the militants thought Titus' words proceeded from fear of them and became insolent with the general. Titus had had enough. He had given the obdurate Jews one last chance and they had thrown it away.

Titus chose 30 of the fiercest fighters out of every hundred units, committed a thousand to each tribune, and ordered them to attack the guards in the Temple at 3 o'clock that morning. He sat on the top of the Tower of Antonia so he could assess the battle and see those who "signalized themselves in the fight" and deserved rewards. *6.2.5* The Jewish guards were not asleep this time. The fight in the dark began:

"...the confused noise that was made on both sides hindered them from distinguishing one another's voices, as did the darkness of the night hinder them from the like distinction by sight....upon the coming on of the day, the nature of the fight was discerned by the eye....here was a kind of theater of war: for what was done in this fight could not be concealed either from Titus or from those that were about him.... it appeared that this fight, which began at the ninth hour of the night (3AM), was not over till past the fifth hour of the day (11AM); and in that same place where the battle began, neither party could say they had made the other party retire; but both the armies left the victory almost in uncertainty between them." *Wars 6.2.6*

Meanwhile, the Roman Legions had opened a very wide breach in the wall for the entire Roman army to enter. The ramps up the walls to the Tower of Antonia were progressing. The Jews constantly harassed those building the ramps, but the work doggedly went on. The famine had reached Simon and John's men. They became even more bloodthirsty than they had been. They roamed Jerusalem killing for food. When they were nourished, they made surprise attacks upon the Romans: "(the) Romans showed both their courage and their skill in war; (the) Jews came on them with immoderate violence and intolerable passion. The one party was urged on by shame and the other by necessity." *6.2.8*

The Jews tried everything they could to keep the Romans holed up in the Antonia Fortress. When they set the northwest cloister of their Temple on fire, they were clearly not thinking correctly. Two days later, the Romans set fire to the cloister next to the burned one. The burning of the Temple surrounds had begun. The two armies continued to make sallies against each other and one day a Jew named Jonathan, "low of stature and of despicable appearance" *6.2.10* challenged the best Roman soldier to single combat. No one came forward. Jonathan yelled taunts and insults against the Romans until finally a cavalryman named Pudens, "out of his abomination of the other's words and of his impudence...ran out to him and was too hard for him in other respects, but was betrayed by his own ill-fortune: for as he fell down, and as he was down, Jonathan came running to him and cut his throat and then standing upon his dead body, he brandished his sword...and made many acclamations to the Roman army, and exulted over the dead man and jested upon the Romans; till at length one Priscus, a centurion, shot an arrow at him…piercing him through….and (he) fell down upon the body of his adversary." *6.2.10* The blind Roman goddess Fortuna, the goddess of good and bad luck, plagued this war with her capricious character.

The Jews were constantly inventing ingenious ways of fighting the Romans. They filled the beams and roof of the Court of the Gentiles with dry material covered with bitumen and pitch. They feigned retreat and the most naïve of the Romans ran after them. When the Court was filled with Romans, the Jews set it on fire. The inferno consumed everyone. Some soldiers threw themselves over the walls backwards into the city. Some ran to the Jews and others "leaped over the wall to their own men and broke their limbs to pieces." *6.3.1* Many were burned to death. The northwest cloister, its adjoining cloister and the Court of the Gentiles around the Temple were now destroyed by fire. The day after the fire in the Court of the Gentiles, the Romans burned down the northern cloister all the way to the eastern cloister near the Kidron Valley.

The Temple surrounds were burning and the famine was decimating the trapped Jews. People began to chew on everything: rats, dogs, cats, insects, belts, shoes, leather from shields, wisps of old hay, fibers from clothes. One woman killed her child, roasted him, ate part of him and offered the other part to the robbers who came to her house in search of food. "…those that were thus distressed by the famine were very desirous to die; and those already dead were esteemed happy, because they had not lived long enough either to hear or to see such miseries." *6.3.4*

The battering rams hammered at the walls for six days, but they would not budge because "the vast largeness and strong connection of the stones were superior…to the battering rams." *6.4.1* The Roman army needed access to the Temple. Their soldiers set fire to the 75' wide Beautiful Gate in the Temple complex where Peter had healed the crippled man in Acts 3. The silver and gold covering on the massive door melted and the wood caught fire. The flames reached the cloister nearby and before anyone knew what was happening, all the areas around the Temple were engulfed. The fire burned for two days.

John and Simon, knowing that the end was near, nevertheless mounted guerrilla attacks upon the Romans. At the end of the day, they and their men barricaded themselves in the Temple itself, the only safe place left in Jerusalem. Titus determined to storm the Temple with his whole army. The Jews came out to engage them, but the Roman army drove them back into the Temple:

"At which time one of the (Roman) soldiers, without waiting for orders, and without any concern or dread upon him at so great an undertaking, and being hurried on by a certain fury, snatched somewhat out of the materials that were still on fire, and being lifted up by another soldier, he set fire to a golden window through which there was a passage to the rooms that were round about the holy Temple." *6.4.5.*

The Romans had set fire to the holiest sanctuary in the ancient world. Josephus says Titus was very upset and ordered his men to quench the flames. His men paid no attention to him because "each soldier's passion was his commander at this time." *6.4.6* One has, also, to consider whether Titus' passion to preserve the Temple had not waned considerably under the savage struggle of the last four months.

The Romans burned the second Temple to the ground on 9 Av (July/August) 70 AD. Josephus points out that the date is a wonderment because on 9 Av 586 BC, Solomon's Temple was destroyed by the Babylonians:

"One cannot but wonder at the accuracy of this period relating to the same month and day...wherein the holy house was burned formerly by the Babylonians. Now the number of years that passed from the Temple's first foundation which was laid by king Solomon till this its destruction which happened in the second year of the reign of Vespasian are collected to be 1,130 years and 7 months and 15 days; and from the second building of it which was done by Haggai in the second year of

Cyrus the king till its destruction under Vespasian, there were 639 years and 45 days." *Wars of the Jews 6.4.8*

This second Temple, greatly augmented by Herod the Great, was originally started when the Jews returned from the Babylonian Exile in c. 538 BC and was completed in 515 BC. Since that fateful day in 70 AD when the second Temple was burned, the Jews have observed the fast of Tisha B'Av ("9th day of Av") for almost 2,000 years. Observant Jews fast and mourn for three weeks culminating on sunset the day before 9 Av until nightfall on 9 Av in memory of those two destructions of their Temple. As the centuries have progressed, however, Tisha B'Av has come to be a period of mourning for all the calamities the Jews have endured.

Over the millennia, there have been many spiritual theories about why God allowed the Temple to be destroyed. Some Christians believe it was because the Jews rejected their Messiah. They base this theory on Jesus' own words several days before His death:

"As he approached Jerusalem and saw the city, he wept over it and said, 'If you, even you, had only known on this day what would bring you peace---but now it is hidden from your eyes. The days will come upon you when your enemies will build an embankment against you and encircle you and hem you in on every side. They will dash you to the ground, you and the children within your walls. They will not leave one stone on another because you did not recognize the time of God's coming to you.'" Luke 19:41-44

Some Jews believe it was because they were so wicked at that time. In the Talmud, Mas. Yoma 9b rabbis debate why the Temples were destroyed:

"Why was the first Sanctuary destroyed (in 586 BC)? Because of three evil things which prevailed there: idolatry, immorality, bloodshed.... But why was the second Sanctuary destroyed (in 70 AD) seeing that in its time they were occupying themselves with Torah and the practice of charity? Because therein prevailed hatred without cause. That teaches you that groundless hatred is considered as of even gravity with the three sins of idolatry, immorality and bloodshed together....Rabbi Johanan and Rabbi Eleazar both say: 'The former ones whose iniquity was revealed had their end revealed, the latter ones whose iniquity was not revealed have their end still unrevealed.' Rabbi Johanan said: 'The fingernail of the earlier generations is better than the whole body of the later generations.' Said Resh Lakish to him, 'On the contrary, the latter generations are better (because) although they are oppressed by the governments, they are occupying themselves with Torah.' (Rabbi Johanan) replied: 'The Sanctuary will prove my point for it came back to the former generations, but not to the latter ones.' The question was put to Rabbi Eleazar: 'Were the earlier generations better or the later ones?' He answered: 'Look upon the Sanctuary!' Some say he answered: 'The Sanctuary is your witness in this matter.'"

A new Temple, the third, in Jerusalem has not been built again, although some Jews and Christians have been collaborating for over 50 years to build one. Orthodox Christians and some Jews believe a prayer from the traditional Jewish prayer book:

"Because of our sins we were exiled from our country and banished from our land. We cannot go up as pilgrims to worship Thee, to perform our duties in Thy chosen house, the great and Holy Temple which was called by Thy name, on account of the hand that was let loose on Thy sanctuary. May it be Thy will, Lord our God and God of our fathers, merciful King, in Thy abundant love again to have mercy on us and on Thy sanctuary; rebuild it speedily and magnify its glory."

Jews and Christians agree God allowed the two destructions of the Temple as punishment for the Jews' wickedness at those times. The two religions disagree, however, about the etiology of the wickedness in the second instance.

As the Temple was burning, the Roman soldiers plundered everything they could find. "And 10,000 of those that were caught were slain; nor was there a commiseration of any age....but children, (women) and old men and profane persons and priests were all slain in the same manner....the ground did nowhere appear visible for the dead bodies that lay on it." *Wars 6.5.1* Tens of thousands of Jews wailed and mourned when they saw the Temple in flames. The clamor and shouts of the rampaging Roman army melded with the mourning of the Jews and the hills around Jerusalem echoed with "that frightful noise."

The soldiers broke ranks and did not wait for commands. They burned the gates, the rest of the cloisters and the treasury chambers "in which was an immense quantity of money....there it was that the entire riches of the Jews were heaped up together." *6.5.2* After the conquest of Jerusalem, the Roman soldiers had to dig out all the melted gold and silver from the stones and debris. They brought the treasure back to Rome where Vespasian used the monies to build another place of blood and death, the Colosseum.

When the fighting and burning were over, the Romans "brought their ensigns to the temple and set them over against its eastern gate; and there did they offer sacrifices to them." *6.6.1* In the burned out ruins of what was then considered the holiest place on earth, the Romans committed what the Jews and Christians considered an "abomination of the desolation." (Daniel 12:11) They sacrificed to pagan images and idols right in the place where the Holy of Holies of the one God had been. Since so many of the ancients believed in auguries and omens, it is peculiar that none of them saw this act of desecration as a precursor of Rome's own demise.

Josephus chronicles all the omens, signs and predictions that, had they been heeded he believed, could have saved the Jews and Jerusalem from the devastation of those days. He writes: "Now, if any one had considered these things, he will find that God takes care of mankind, and by all ways possible foreshows to our race what is for their preservation; but that men perish by those miseries which they madly and voluntarily bring upon themselves." *6.6.4* Like so many before and after him, Josephus believed in "signs of the times."

Josephus mentions a tantalizing prediction that both Suetonius and Tacitus reference: "...what did most elevate them (the seditious Jews) in undertaking this war was an ambiguous oracle that was also found in their sacred writings, how 'about that time, one from their country should become governor of the habitable earth.' The Jews took this prediction to belong to themselves in particular and many of the wise men were thereby deceived in their determination." *Wars of the Jews 6.6.4* Perhaps this "ambiguous oracle" was the one in Genesis 49:10:

"The scepter will not depart from Judah
Nor the ruler's staff from between his feet
Until Shiloh comes to whom it belongs
And the obedience of the nations is his."

Or it could have been the 700 BC prognostication in Isaiah 9:6,7 made famous in 1741 by Handel in his oratorio *Messiah*:

"For unto us a child is born,
Unto us a son is given;
And the government will be upon his shoulder.
And his name will be called Wonderful, Counselor, Mighty God, everlasting Father, Prince of peace.
Of the increase of his government and peace there will be no end,
Upon the throne of David and over his kingdom,
To order it and establish it with judgement and justice from that time forward,
Even forever."

The Roman Suetonius, writing only 50 years after Jerusalem's destruction, records:

"There had spread over all the Orient an old and established belief that it was fated at that time for a man coming from Judea to rule the world. This prediction, referring to the emperor of Rome, as it turned out, the Jews took to themselves and they revolted accordingly." *Lives of the Caesars: Vespasian*

The pagan historian Tacitus in his *Histories 5.13* in c. 103 AD writes:

"The majority (of the Jews)were convinced that the ancient scriptures (Old Testament) of their priests alluded to the present as the very time when the Orient would triumph and from Judea would go forth the men destined to rule the world. This mysterious prophecy really referred to Vespasian and Titus, but the common people, true to the selfish ambitions of mankind, thought that this exalted destiny was reserved for them, and not even their calamities (in 70 AD) opened their eyes to the truth."

Perhaps the prophecy commonly known at that time was the one given by Balaam in Numbers 17:24: "I see him, but not now; I behold him, but not near. A star will come out of Jacob; a scepter will rise out of Israel." The catacomb Christians, as has been indicated, saw this prophecy as referring to the Star of Bethlehem and to the birth of Jesus whom they considered the Savior Messiah of the whole world. Were Tacitus and Suetonius right when they interpreted the prophecy to denote the emperors Vespasian and Titus who had destroyed Jerusalem? Were the Christians right when they interpreted the prophecy to be predictive of Jesus of Nazareth? All we know for sure from the ancient writings of Josephus, Tacitus and Suetonius is that there was an expectation throughout the whole known world that an Avatar, a god incarnate, a world ruler would appear at that time. Josephus believed the zeal of many Jews in Jerusalem had been fueled by their false belief that they were those Judean men destined to rule the world. Christians have interpreted the ancient prophecies to foretell Jesus and the Christians.

While the Temple was burning, John and Simon fled into the lower parts of the city. In spite of their dire circumstances, they proudly asked to speak to Titus face to face. Titus agreed and the two sides, both in full battle armor, met on the bridge connecting the destroyed Temple and the upper city to the rest of Jerusalem. This arched, 50' wide and 354' long bridge built by Herod the Great was called the Royal Bridge. It spanned the Tyropoeon Valley from Mt. Zion to Mt. Moriah where the Temple was located and provided a breathtaking view of the Valley 225' below.

Because Titus knew he was the conqueror, he spoke first. He upbraided them for their hubris in thinking they could win against the mightiest army in the world. He reminded them of the kindness Rome had shown to the Jews by letting them collect money for their temple and their god until "you became richer than we ourselves." *Wars 6.6.2* He recounted all their rebellions against Rome since the time of Pompey and how kind he had been in constantly asking the Jews to surrender and to save their city and Temple:

"And now, vile wretches, do you desire to treat with me by word of mouth?....What preservation can you now desire after the destruction of your temple? Yet do you stand still at this very time in your armor; nor can you bring yourselves to even pretend to be suppliants even in this your utmost extremity. Are not your people dead? Is not your holy house gone? Is not your city in my power? And are not your own very lives in my hands?....However, I will not imitate your madness. If you throw down your arms and deliver up your bodies to me, I grant you your lives....To this offer of Titus, they made this reply: That they could not accept it because they had sworn never to do so; but they desired they might have leave to go through the wall that had been made about them with their wives and children...and they would go into the desert and leave the city to him." *Wars 6.6.2.3*

Titus was furious they would even think of making terms with their conqueror "as if they had been the conquerors." *6.6.3* Titus ordered a formal proclamation to be written: "That they should no more come out to him as deserters, nor hope for any further security; for that he would henceforth spare nobody, but fight them with his whole army and they must save themselves as well as they could; for he would from that moment treat them according to the laws of war." *6.6.3* Upon dismissing them, Titus gave orders that the army should begin to sack and to burn the rest of Jerusalem.

As their last hope, John, Simon and their inner circle fled into the subterranean caves and caverns under the city. Jerusalem rests on two hills under which are white limestone caverns and a large natural cave. Some of the caverns are 30' high. In 1852 Joseph Barclay, an early explorer of Jerusalem's ruins, was walking along the north wall of Jerusalem near the Damascus Gate when his dog disappeared into an opening under the wall. He cleared away debris and found it was an entrance to an underground limestone cave that extended under the city for about 700'. He had discovered what is known as Solomon's Quarry. Solomon is said to have mined the soft white limestone in one of the large caves now called King Solomon's Quarries to build the first Temple:

"At (Solomon's) command they removed from the quarry large blocks of quality stone to provide a foundation of dressed stone for the temple.... In the building of the temple, only blocks dressed at the quarry were used, and no hammer, chisel or any other iron tool was heard at the temple site while it was being built." I Kings 5:17; 6:7

Herod the Great's engineers used the same limestone when he was rebuilding the Second Temple. King Zedekiah had fled to the underground caverns when in 586 BC Nebuchadnezzar besieged and destroyed the First Temple. For generations Jews had used these caves as secret passages of escape from war or danger.

The men who helped deliver Jerusalem to destruction hid from the Romans in those caverns. Remnants of their armies continued to fight the Romans, but they were so weak and dispirited they soon abandoned their positions and blended into the dead and the dying. When the Romans finally killed their way to the Mt. Zion area on August 30, their victory was a hollow one. There was no one to fight:

"So the Romans now become masters of the walls, they both placed their ensigns upon the towers and made joyful acclamation for the victory they had gained, having found the end of this war much lighter than its beginning....but having found nobody to oppose them they stood in doubt what such an unusual solitude could mean....

they slew those whom they overtook without mercy and set fire to the houses whither the Jews fled and burned every soul in them....when they were come to houses to plunder them, they found in them entire families of dead men and the upper rooms full of dead corpses of those who died in the famine; they then stood in horror at this sight and went out without touching anything....they made the whole city run with blood to such a degree that the fire of many of the houses was quenched with (human) blood....though the slayers left off by evening, yet did the fire greatly prevail all night; and as all was still burning, came that eighth day of the month Gorpieus (Elul) upon Jerusalem." *6.8.5*

The destruction of the city was complete 8 Elul 70 AD. Because of the conflicting calendar systems, it is impossible to calculate exactly when that was. Scholars place that date at September 7 or 25, 70 AD.

Titus ordered the wholesale killing to stop. They rounded up everyone who was still alive. They killed any who had fought against them and the "aged and infirm....of the young men (they) chose the tallest and most beautiful and reserved them for the triumphal parade (in Rome); and as for the rest of the multitude that were above seventeen years old, he put them into bonds and sent them to the Egyptian mines. Titus also sent a great number into the provinces as presents to them that they might be destroyed upon their theaters by the sword (gladiators) and by the wild beasts; but those that were under seventeen years of age were sold for slaves." *Wars 6.9.3*

Josephus says the number of captives was 97,000. The number of Jews who died during the four months of the siege was c. 1.1 million. The high number was because so many hundreds of thousands of Jews had fled to Jerusalem as refugees and then hordes had come from all over the world to celebrate Passover: "...the greater part (of our people) not belonging to the city itself and they were come up from all the countries to the feast of unleavened bread; and were on a sudden shut up by the (Roman) army." *6.9.3*

John and his men were starving to death in the caverns. He surrendered, was taken captive and spent the rest of his life in a Roman prison. Simon, on the other hand, held out until after Titus had left the city and gone to Caesarea leaving Tertius Rugus in charge of cleaning up the operation in Jerusalem. Simon's men had unsuccessfully tried to dig their way out of danger in the cavern, but the stone was unforgiving and his men were starving:

"And now Simon, thinking he might be able to astonish and delude the Romans, put on a white robe and a purple coat (symbols of royalty) and appeared out of the ground in the place where the temple had formerly been. At first, indeed, those that saw him were greatly astonished and stood still where they were; but afterward they came near to him and asked him who he was. Now Simon would not tell them, but bade them call for their captain; and when they ran to call him, Tertius Rufus… came to Simon and learned of him the whole truth and kept him in bonds, and let Titus know that he was (captured)." *7.2.1*

Both Simon and John were taken to Rome and displayed as defeated kings during Titus' triumphal procession. Those two men whose blinding ambition had been to be the rulers of Jerusalem were finally acknowledged by the despised Romans to be the "kings" of that city that the Romans dug up and plowed under until no one could tell their would-be kingdom had ever even existed. Simon was dragged with a rope around his neck through the streets of Rome during Titus' victory parade. At the Temple of Jupiter, Simon, the man who would be king, was beheaded as a sacrifice to the king of their gods.

Thus came to an end an ancient city:

"…Caesar gave orders that (the army) should now demolish the entire city and Temple….(Jerusalem) was so thoroughly laid even with the ground by those that dug it up to the foundation, that there was left nothing to make those that came there believe (the city) had ever been inhabited….Nor had anyone who had known the place before, had come on a sudden to it now, would he have known it again." Josephus, *Wars of the Jews 7.1.1*

Ancient Jerusalem was beloved by the Jews and Christians alike and its destruction by the Romans is still mourned 2,000 years later by the followers of the Jewish Lawgiver Moshe and the Jewish Messiah Yeshu'a.

XV.

"I invite the reader's attention to the much more serious consideration of the kind of lives our (Roman) ancestors lived, of who were the men, and what the means both in politics and war by which Rome's power was first acquired and subsequently expanded; I would then have (the reader) trace the process of our moral decline, to watch, first, the sinking of the foundations of morality as the old teaching was allowed to lapse, then the rapidly increasing disintegration, then the final collapse of the whole edifice, and the dark dawning of our modern day when we can neither endure our vices nor face the remedies needed to cure them." Livy, *History of Rome, Preface to Book I*

"We (Romans) can neither endure our vices nor face the remedies needed to cure them." The Roman historian Livy (59 BC-17 AD) wrote this terse, sage summary of a culture in decline when he was in his 30's and Rome was just beginning her Golden Age under Augustus. How was this young historian prescient enough to see in Augustan Rome the dark dawning of its own destruction?

Certainly the end of Jerusalem could have been foreseen in 63 BC when Pompey conquered Jerusalem and made Judea a Roman client state, and the final collapse of the Jewish state could have been predicted by the wanton evil of its leaders in the years leading up to 70 AD.

In 115, forty-five years after Jerusalem's destruction, an unknown incident between the Jews and Greeks in north Africa triggered a little-known but extremely bloody uprising called the Diaspora Rebellion. A charismatic Jewish leader called Lucuas from Cyrene, Libya led a Jewish revolt that spilled over into Alexandria, Cyprus and even into the provinces of Asia. The Jews had found their revolutionary Messiah in Lucuas and proceeded to destroy pagan temples and statues with hopes of obliterating false idols and throwing off the Roman yoke. It took the combined forces of Egyptians, Greeks and Roman Legions dispatched by Emperor Trajan to crush the rebellion in 117. The Jews had slaughtered many people and the Jews, in turn, were decimated. All the Jews in Alexandria, for hundreds of years the literary and intellectual center for Jews, were either killed or expelled.

Only 15 years later in 132-135 under another dynamic leader, Bar Kokhba, the Jews made a final attempt to retake Jerusalem. According to Justin Martyr in First *Apology 1.31*, "Bar Kokhba, the leader of the Jewish rebellion, ordered Christians (in Jerusalem) alone to be punished severely if they did not deny Jesus as the Messiah and blaspheme him." The Jews and even the famous Rabbi Akiva were convinced Bar Kokhba, meaning "Son of the Star," was the long-awaited Messiah, not Jesus of Nazareth as some claimed. The happenstance of Bar Kokhba's name as "Son of the Star" coincided with Balaam's prediction in c. 1450 BC: "I see him, but not now....A star will come out of Jacob; a scepter will rise out of Israel." Numbers 24:17

Contemporaneously, in underground Rome the catacomb Christians were claiming in their wall paintings that the Jewish Messiah had already come and his name was Jesus (Hebrew *Yeshu'a* meaning "Yahweh is Salvation") and Gentiles in Rome were being martyred for the Jewish Jesus under Emperor Hadrian. When the Romans decisively defeated Bar Kokhba in 135, the Jews averred that Bar Kokhba's name, "Son of the Star," was really "Bar Kosiba," meaning "Son of the Lie."

Emperor Hadrian began to rebuild Jerusalem in 135 and renamed the new city Aelia Capitolina after his family, the Aelia. He peopled the Roman city with Legionnaires and sundry other Romans. Hadrian wanted to create a new land, a clean territory, so he even renamed Judea *Palaestina* (a name in use to this day) after the Philistines who prior to 2000 BC had settled in the land then called Canaan. Hadrian's attempt to utterly obliterate any Jewish identity from Jerusalem was complete when he banned any and all Jews from entering the city.

With the defeat of Bar Kokhba and the rebuilding of Jerusalem as Aelia Capitolina, the Jews were scattered and for almost 2,000 years they would be the Wandering Jews always looking for a safe city or homeland. After the Jewish Holocaust in World War II, the United Nations voted 33 to 13 in favor of establishing a Jewish state in Arab Palestine. The Jews declared their independent state on May 14, 1948 and called it Israel after the name of the patriarch Jacob just as the Jews had renamed it Israel in the years of the Revolt (66-70) prior to Jerusalem's demise.

But Jerusalem called "Jerusalem" never died mainly because the burgeoning Christian population in the Roman world continued to make pilgrimages to the Holy Land and they never called its capital Aelia Capitolina. They called it Jerusalem. Even during the years after 70 when Jerusalem was in ruins, Jewish Christians lived in the destroyed city and continued their witness for Jesus. There is an unbroken line of Jewish Bishops of the Church in Jerusalem from the time of the resurrection of Jesus in c. 30 until the defeat of the Bar Kokhba's Rebellion in 135:

"...the bishops of Jerusalem...I have documentary evidence that there were fifteen up to Hadrian's siege of the Jews (135). All were said to have been Hebrews in origin who had accepted the knowledge of Christ and so were deemed worthy of the episcopal office. For the church (in Jerusalem) existed entirely of Hebrew Christians from the Apostles down to the Roman siege following the second Jewish revolt. Since bishops of the circumcision (Jews) then ceased (after 135), this is the time to give their names from the beginning. First was James, called the Lord's brother, and after him Symeon (cousin of James) was the second. Third was Justus, fourth Zaccheus, fifth Tobias, sixth Benjamin, seventh John, eighth Matthias, ninth Philip, tenth Seneca, eleventh Justus, twelfth Levi, thirteenth Ephres, fourteenth Joseph, and fifteenth, and last, Judas. These were the bishops of Jerusalem in that period (30-135), all of the circumcision (Jews)." Eusebius, *Church History*, 4.5

In addition to the Christian Jews and the Jews who lived among the ruins of old Jerusalem, Gentile pilgrims from all over the Roman Empire began flocking to Jerusalem in the first three centuries AD to see and to worship at the places where the Jew Jesus had been. The new Christians wanted to see Nazareth where He had lived as a boy, to see Capernaum where He had done so many of His miracles, to climb the Mount of Olives where He had wept over Jerusalem's coming destruction, and especially, the pilgrims wanted to go to Jerusalem where He was tried, condemned and crucified, to see the garden tomb where His body had been, to experience Jerusalem where He had resurrected. They wanted to go to Jesus' Jerusalem and the Christians always called the city Jerusalem.

In c. 320 the first Christian Emperor Constantine destroyed all of Hadrian's pagan shrines in Jerusalem and erected Christian churches over them. In c. 325 he sent his c. 76 year-old mother Helena to Jerusalem to identify and reclaim all Christian locales. When the anonymous Bordeaux pilgrim went to Jerusalem several years later in c. 333, his diary records he not only saw all the important sites, but he and the other pilgrims freely worshipped all over Palestine and Jerusalem. In name and in reverence Jerusalem was fast becoming a Christian city.

In the years leading up to Jerusalem's destruction and in the centuries following its demise, Rome and her satellites were gradually and reluctantly becoming Christianized, too. Even though the Roman historian Livy could not have foreseen that Rome would ultimately fall to a young Jewish man from the remote province of Judea who was in his early 20's when Livy died, in the preface to his *History of Rome* Livy could and did see "in these modern days (that) the might of a long paramount nation is wasting by internal decay." Livy did see in the days of Jesus' youth the "moral decline" of Rome, could and did see "the final collapse of the whole edifice" of the Roman Empire hidden in the "dark dawning" of his own day.

In Livy's time and in Jesus' youth, Rome's best days were already behind her in the wreckage of the Roman Republic. It was under the Republic (from 509 BC down to 45 BC when Julius Caesar was declared Dictator For Life) that Rome had conquered its territories; had freed the waters of the Mediterranean from pirates paving the way for peaceful trade and travel; had built its networks of roads and aqueducts; had established a code of settled law and had begun the time of peace known as the Pax Romana. The Roman Republic was the solid foundation upon which the Roman Empire built an impressive but rather vulgar structure.

When the Roman Republic was established in 509 BC, she was decidedly late to the bloody game of world domination in the ancient world. 700 years before Rome peeked out at the world, Egypt had already reached her zenith under Ramses II; 500 years before the Republic the Jews had reached their golden age under King David; and Babylon and Nineveh had ruled the world hundreds of years before the Roman Republic got on its feet. Even though Rome was late and the last of the ancient world's superpowers, she was sure-footed and over the centuries fought her way to an empire that reached from Persia and the Middle East into northern Africa and up into all of Europe including England and Scotland. At the height of its might in the 3rd century AD, Rome ruled an area encompassing 2.5 million square miles.

The Romans reckoned their city to have been founded in 753 BC by Romulus who named the little patch of land on the Palatine Hill after himself:

"The Vestal Virgin was raped and gave birth to twin boys (Romulus and Remus). Mars, she declared, was their father---perhaps she believed it, perhaps she was merely hoping by the pretense to palliate her guilt. Whatever the truth of the matter, neither gods nor men could save her or her babes from the savage hands of the king (her uncle Amulius). The mother was bound and flung into prison; the boys, by the king's order were condemned to be drowned in the river....In those days the country thereabouts was all wild and uncultivated, and the story goes that when the basket in which the infants had been exposed was left high and dry by the receding water, a she-wolf, coming down from the neighboring hills to quench her thirst, heard the children crying and made her way to where they were. She offered them her teats to suck and treated them with such gentleness that Faustulus, the king's herdsman, found her licking them with her tongue. Faustulus took them to his hut and gave them to his wife Larentia to nurse....By the time they were grown boys....they took to attacking robbers and sharing their stolen goods with their friends and shepherds." Livy, *History 1.4*

The feral children, Romulus and Remus, were eventually found to be the grandsons of Numitor, the father of the Vestal Virgin and the brother of king Amulius who had exposed the boys to death because he was jealous of Numitor. Numitor embraced his grandsons and ceded royal status to the two unruly young men. The wicked king Amulius was killed; his brother Numitor became king of Alba Longa, but, as is so often the case outside of fairy tales, the twins did not live happily ever after:

"Romulus and Remus, after the control of Alba had passed to Numitor... were suddenly seized by an urge to found a new settlement on the spot where they had been left to drown as infants....Unhappily, the brothers' plans for the future were marred by the same source which had divided their grandfather (Numitor) and (his brother) Amulius---jealousy and ambition. A disgraceful quarrel arose from a matter in itself trivial.... Angry words ensued, followed all too soon by blows, and in the course of the fray Remus was killed. There is another story, a commoner one, according to which Remus, by way of jeering at his brother, jumped over the half-built walls of the new settlement, whereupon Romulus killed him in a fit of rage, adding the threat 'So perish whoever else shall overleap my battlements.' This, then, was how Romulus obtained the sole power. The newly built city was called by its founder's name." Livy, *History 1.6,7*

Romulus was the first king of the tiny settlement on the Palatine Hill called Rome. But ancient Greek historians traced the founding of the whole Latin dynasty way back to a Trojan Greek named Aeneas who had eventually made his way to Italy in c. 1200 BC when Troy was destroyed. Votive statues of Aeneas from the 6th century BC and dozens of 5th and 4th century BC vases depicting Aeneas carrying his father Anchises on his back from burning Troy have been found in the ancient ruins of Veii north of Rome, so there is an Aeneas connection. Virgil (70-19 BC), the author of the classic Roman epic *The Aeneid*, promoted the Greek origin of Rome and tied his hero Aeneas genealogically to his friend and patron Caesar Augustus. The origin, dates and mingling of the peoples who eventually became the Romans will never be known for sure. But it is likely that Romulus was the eponymous founder of the Rome that dominated the world in the first centuries of the Christian Era. Roman mythology conveniently placed Romulus and Remus in the family tree stemming from Aeneas.

Romulus founded Rome sometime in the 7th century BC. 753 BC is the beginning of the Roman AUC calendar, the *Ab Urbe Condita* ("From The Founding Of The City") calendar, from which the Roman's calculated time. After Romulus founded Rome, he realized he did not have a very populous city, so "he threw (the city) open…as a place of asylum for fugitives. Hither fled for refuge all the rag-tag-and-bobtail from the neighboring peoples…all wanting nothing but a fresh start. That mob was the first real addition to the City's strength, the first step to her future greatness." Livy, *History 1.8* Livy admires this hardened rag-tag mob, sees them as the necessary aggressive seed for the type of people who had to be produced in order to bring Rome to hegemony in Italy and the world.

Next Romulus created the Senate and chose 100 men of rank to help him rule. The men were called "patricians" from the Latin *patres* meaning "fathers." With policy and population now in place, Rome was strong enough to challenge and overcome any adversaries, "but great though she was, her greatness seemed likely to last only for a single generation. There were not enough women." Livy, *History 1.9*

Romulus first tried to encourage neighboring people to allow intermarriage with his men:

"Romulus' overtures were nowhere favorably received; it was clear that

everyone despised the new community, and at the same time feared…
the growth of this new power in their midst. More often than not his
envoys were dismissed with the question of whether Rome had thrown
open her doors to female, as well as to male, runaways and vagabonds
as that would evidently be the most suitable way for Romans to get
wives. The young Romans naturally resented this jibe, and a clash
seemed inevitable. Romulus, seeing it must come, set the scene for it
with elaborate care." Livy, *History 1.9*

Romulus invited all surrounding settlements to a festival in Rome
to celebrate Consus, the ancient god of the granary. Much later Romans
would build the Circus Maximus for their chariot races on the exact
site on the Marcian plain between the Aventine and Palatine hills
where Romulus provided horse races as entertainment for his guests
that day:

"On the appointed day crowds flocked to Rome, partly, no doubt, out
of curiosity to see the new town….all the Sabines were there too, with
their wives and children. Many houses offered hospitable entertainment
to the visitors; they were invited to inspect the fortifications, layout
and numerous buildings of the town, and expressed their surprise at
the rapidity of growth. Then the great moment came; the show (the
horse races) began and nobody had eyes or thoughts for anything else.
This was the Romans' opportunity; at a given signal all the able-bodied
men burst through the crowd and seized the young (Sabine) women.
Most of the girls were the prize of whoever got hold of them first, but
a few conspicuously handsome ones had been previously marked down
for leading senators, and these were brought to their houses by special
gangs….By this act of violence the fun of the festival broke up in panic.
The girls' unfortunate parents made good their escape, not without
bitter comments on the treachery of their hosts….The young women
were no less indignant and full of foreboding for the future. Romulus,
however, reassured them. Going from one to another he declared that
their own parents were really to blame, in that they had been too proud
to allow intermarriage with their neighbors; nevertheless they need not

fear; as married women they would share all the fortunes of Rome, all the privileges of the community, and they would be bound to their husbands by the dearest bond of all, their children. He urged them to forget their wrath and give their hearts to those to whom chance had given their bodies....The men, too, played their part: they spoke honeyed words and vowed that it was passionate love which had prompted their offense. No plea can better touch a woman's heart." Livy, *History 1.9*

It is certain that most of the Sabine women were not swayed by the honeyed words of Romulus or their rapists. But it was a badge of pride to their Roman posterity that their progenitors had procured wives in such a resourceful, forceful and cunning way. For hundreds of years after this incident, Romans carried their brides over the thresholds of their new homes to honor their brave Sabine mothers. Today in the West this custom is still in use.

"The Rape of the Sabine Women," as it came to be called, was a powerful and popular story in the ancient world. It has been equally inspiring to artists all over the Western world. The 16th century statue by Giambologna of the Rape depicts an anguished father pinned under the feet of the Roman who is trying to abduct his distraught daughter. In the 17th century Nicholas Poussin did two paintings of the Rape and Reubens in 1640, with his full-bodied and fleshy people, did an impressive painting of the lust, anguish and confusion attendant upon the abduction. Even Picasso near the end of his life attempted a Cubist rendering of the Rape in 1962.

Most of the small tribes who had been invited by Romulus to the mock festival subsequently attacked and were defeated by the Romans. Eventually the Romans became masters of central Italy. Within a generation, it was time for the Sabine tribe to exact revenge for the abduction of their daughters. By means of a ruse, the Sabines surreptitiously entered Rome. They took the unprepared Romans by surprise and reached the Forum near the gate of the Palatine. "Comrades," one of the Sabine leaders cried, "we have beaten our treacherous hosts--- our feeble foes. They know now that catching girls is a different matter from fighting against men!" Livy, *History 1.12* After this boast, the Sabines faltered and it seemed the Romans would win:

"This was the moment when the Sabine women, the original cause of the quarrel, played their decisive part....With loosened hair and rent garments they braved the flying spears and thrust their way in a body between the embattled armies. They parted the angry combatants; they besought their fathers on the one side, their husbands on the other, to spare themselves the curse of shedding kindred blood. 'We are mothers now,' they cried, 'our children are your sons---your grandsons; do not put on them the stain of parricide. If our marriage, if the relationship between us is hateful to you, turn your anger on us. We are the cause of the strife; on our account our husbands and fathers lie wounded or dead, and we would rather die ourselves than live on either widowed or orphaned.' The effect of the appeal was immediate and profound. Silence fell and not a man moved. A moment later the rival captains stepped forward to conclude a peace. Indeed, they went further: the two states were united under a single government, with Rome as the seat of power. Thus the population of Rome was doubled....Romulus, moreover, marked his own special awareness of this deepened feeling (between the Sabines and the Romans) by giving the women's names to the thirty wards into which he then divided the population." Livy, *History 1.13*

In 1799 the French painter Jacques-Louis David painted a sequel to Poussin's *Rape of the Sabine Women* and called it *The Intervention of the Sabine Women*. Filled with fighting men, spears, rearing horses and women saving babies and imploring husbands and fathers, David's painting evokes the anguish the Sabine women felt as they saw husbands and fathers and sons and grandfathers killing each other.

It was inevitable that a people born of the resentments and grit of raped women and the predilections and gall of outlaw men would be hard to govern. Romulus' system of rule by a King and patrician Senators lasted for 244 years after Rome's founding. During that time, Rome consolidated its grip on the Italian peninsula, but the oligarchy was in constant tension with the people who had built Rome and had fought the wars and skirmishes that brought the city wealth and renown. The patricians became corrupt and abusive to the people. As Lord Acton wrote in 1887, "Power tends to corrupt and absolute power corrupts absolutely." The Roman plebeians were not a passive populace. In 509 BC a revolt of the masses against the rulers erupted:

"The chief cause of the dispute was the plight of the unfortunates who were bound over to their creditors for debt. These men complained that while they were fighting in the field to preserve their country's liberty and to extend her power, their own fellow-citizens at home had enslaved and oppressed them; the common people, they declared, had a better chance of freedom in war than in peace; fellow Romans threatened them with worse slavery than a foreign foe....Debtors of all conditions—some actually in chains—forced their way into the streets and begged for popular support; everywhere men flocked to join the rising, until every street was packed with noisy crowds making their way to the Forum....An explosion was only just avoided by the arrival of the absent Senators, who had been unable to decide whether they ran the greater risk by staying away or coming....On top of this highly critical situation came the alarming news...that a Volscian army was marching on Rome. So deeply was the country divided by its political differences that the people...hailed the prospect of invasion with delight. For them it seemed like an intervention of providence to crush the pride of the Senate....Let the Patricians, they argued, do the fighting...if there were war, let those face its dangers who alone reaped its profits." Livy, *History 2.23. 24*

One of the Roman Consuls appeared before the people and issued an edict: from that moment on it was illegal to fetter or imprison a Roman citizen and prevent him from enlisting in the army and it was illegal to seize or to sell the property of any soldier who was in active service to Rome. The people rejoiced; debtors were released from prison; all able-bodied men enlisted in the army; the Romans routed the Volscians and the Roman Republic was founded.

These last two laws completed The Twelve Tables of Roman Law that became the legal foundation of the Roman Republic (the *Res Publica* "matters of the public"). The laws were a response to the continuing frictions between the patricians and the public called the Struggle of the Orders. The early Roman plebeians always exercised non-passive resistance but when they felt oppressed, they would not be denied. They forced their will upon the patricians by a show of numbers in the streets and by refusing to work or to fight Rome's battles. The Roman State was the preeminent value to all Romans. To cause its downfall by civil violence would have been unthinkable for both the plebeians and the patricians. This non-violent tension and confrontation between the two classes resulted in both a strong citizenry and a strong aristocracy. Both classes ceded power to the other. In those early days of the Republic, Rome had pounded out and perfected the compromises that would serve her so well in the days of her expansion and subsequent Empire.

In the next centuries the Romans developed a uniquely mixed form of government composed of checks and balances on power praised even by the 2nd century BC Polybius who had been abducted by the Romans from his native Greece and forced to live in Rome:

"The three kinds of government that I spoke of...all shared in the control of the Roman state. And such fairness and propriety in all respects was shown in the use of these three elements for drawing up the constitution and in its subsequent administration that it was impossible even for a native to pronounce with certainty whether the whole (Roman) system was aristocratic, democratic or monarchical. This was indeed only natural. For if one fixed one's eyes on the power of the consuls, the constitution seemed completely monarchical and royal; if on that of the senate it seemed again to be aristocratic; and when one looked at the power of the masses, it seemed clearly to be a democracy." *The Histories 6.11.11.12*

Polybius believed all systems of government were cyclical. Monarchy, born from mob rule and lack of leadership, is the first form and degenerates into hereditary Kings who become corrupt and are deposed by an Aristocracy that degenerates into an Oligarchy. When the rule of the few becomes corrupt, the people overthrow the regime. When the dust of mob rule and anarchy settles, Democracy is born:

"But when a new generation arises and the democracy falls into the hands of the grandchildren of the founders, they become accustomed to freedom and equality (and) they no longer value them....they begin to lust for power....And when by (democracy's) foolish thirst for reputation they have created among the masses an appetite for gifts and the habit of receiving them, democracy in its turn is abolished and changes into a rule of force and violence. For the people, having grown accustomed to feed at the expense of others and to depend for their livelihood on the property of others, as soon as they find a leader who is enterprising... institute a rule of violence...and uniting their forces massacre, banish and plunder until they degenerate again into perfect savages and find once more a master and Monarch. Such is the cycle of political revolution, the course appointed by nature in which constitutions change, disappear and finally return to the point from which they started....in the case of the Roman state will this (cyclical) method enable us to arrive at a knowledge of its formation, growth and greatest perfection, and likewise of the change for the worse which is sure to follow some day?" Polybius, *The Histories 6.7-9*

That day, that Polybius-predicted day of "change for the worse," arrived about 70 years after Polybius wrote those words when a 51-year-old Roman general named Gaius Julius Caesar illegally crossed the River Rubicon with his troops and declared himself Monarch, dictator of Rome. The pre-determined cycle from Monarch (Romulus) to Monarch (Julius Caesar) was complete.

Polybius is, also, remembered for a method of encryption called the Polybius Square that pioneered a way of sending messages 2,000 years before the Morse code or semaphores. He meant it to be used with torches in lighthouses, but it has been used for millennia to encrypt messages. Prisoners of war in Vietnam used Polypius' Square to communicate with each other. It is a simple 5x5 grid:

	1	2	3	4	5
1	A	B	C	D	E
2	F	G	H	I/J	K
3	L	M	N	O	P
4	Q	R	S	T	U
5	V	W	X	Y	Z

Under this encryption, "MORSE" would be tapped or sent as 32, 34, 42, 43, 15 (M is 3rd line down and 2nd line across; O is 3rd line down and 4th line across, etc.). "CODE" is 13 (1st line down and 3rd line across), 34, 14, 15. Because of his Square, Polybius, the Greek historian, is often called a "mathematician." His Square has inspired many cipher systems over the centuries including the Bifed Cipher in 1901 and the ADFGX cipher used by the German military in World War I.

Even though Livy did not share Polybius' theory about the inexorable march of governments, Livy did see the "change for the worse" that was coming to the Roman State. Unlike Polybius who saw no exit from the forward and inevitable turn of the wheel of governance, Livy felt that Rome could recover the former glory of the Republic if she would only go back to the values and virtues of her past. In the following passage one can hear Livy's nostalgia for Rome's past and a strong warning, a faint hope that his book will demonstrate to Rome the folly of her ways:

"I hope my passion for Rome's past has not impaired my judgment; for I do honestly believe that no country has ever been greater or purer than ours or richer in good citizens and noble deeds; none has been free for so many generations from the vices of avarice and luxury; nowhere have thrift and plain living been for so long held in such esteem. Indeed, poverty, with us, went hand in hand with contentment. Of late years wealth has made us greedy, and self-indulgence has brought us, through every form of sensual excess, to be, if I may so put it, in love with death both individual and collective." *History, Preface to Book I*

To Livy and other Roman historians "Rome's past" under the Republic was a time of good morals and virtues when men and women were industrious (*Industria*), frugal (*Frugalitas*), dutiful (*Pietas*) and brave (*Virtus*). For hundreds of years Roman mothers and fathers had inculcated into their children Roman Republican values through the story of their great hero Horatius the Brave who in c. 500 BC single-handedly saved Rome from destruction by the Etruscans:

"Some parts of Rome were secured (against the 90,000 Etruscans) by walls; other parts by the barrier of the Tiber; but the Sublician Bridge afforded a passage to the enemy had there not been one man, Horatius Cocles...who chanced to be posted as a guard on the bridge. When he saw...the enemy charging with full onset, while his friends in terror and confusion were actually casting away their arms...he appealed to them in the name of gods and men....if they fled their posts, if they once left the bridge behind them, there would soon be foes on the Palatine hill and the Capitol. He therefore urged and enjoined them to hew down the bridge, by sword, fire or any means and he would stand the brunt of the foe, so far as one man might....Then casting his eyes sternly with threatening mien upon all the Tuscan chiefs, he now challenged them singly, now taunted them all....For some little time they hesitated.... then mere shame put their host in motion; they raised their war shout, and from every side hurled in their arrows on their lone adversary. But all these arrows stuck fast in his shield, and with a firm stand he held the bridge. Then they strove by a single push to thrust him down, but the crashing noise of the falling bridge and the cheers of the Romans checked their fury with a sudden panic. Thereupon Horatius spoke, 'Holy Father Tiber, I pray that thou do receive these my arms and this thy soldier in thy benignant stream.' All in his armor he sprang down into the river and while arrows showered around him, he swam across quite safely to his friends….The state was not ungrateful for his valor. A statue was erected to him in the Forum and as much land was given to him as he was able to plow around in a single day." Livy, *History 2.9.10*

The Sublician Bridge defended by Horatio was rebuilt and in 312 AD was called the Milvian Bridge where the Roman Emperor Constantine won a battle under the banner of Christ and ushered in the Christian Era. The 18th century poem, "Horatio At The Bridge," begins *The Lays Of Ancient Rome* by the poet Lord Thomas Macaulay. Horatio's uncommon valor and sacrifice in battle still inspire.

The Sabine Romans with their austerity and asceticism were the stock that built Rome's Republic. Their nascent and pristine society had strict roles for women and for men. Plus they had poverty. Poverty and rigid gender roles bred a Spartan warrior race that conquered the world. It was the Roman Empire in the 1st century AD with its luxuries, its money, its idleness and ease that had weakened and enervated Rome, had sapped her of her moral fiber and fostered the break down of the traditional Roman family. Romans of the past were the ideals of martial manhood and chaste womanhood. The good old days was a time when men protected and enlarged the Roman State and women stayed at home to raise good Romans. Nobody castigates the decline in the morals of Roman women and its effects upon Roman life more than the 1st century AD Tacitus:

"In the good old days, every man's son born in wedlock was brought up not in the chamber of some hireling nurse, but in his mother's lap and at her knee. And that mother could have no higher praise than that she managed the house and gave herself to her children religiously and with the utmost delicacy she regulated not only the serious tasks of her youthful charges, but their recreations also and their games…. Nowadays (c. 100 AD), on the other hand, our children are handed over at their birth to some silly little Greek serving-maid, with a male slave, who may be anyone to help her, quite frequently the most worthless member of the whole establishment, incompetent for any serious service. It is from the foolish tittle-tattle of such persons that the children receive their earliest impressions, while their minds are still pliant and unformed…Yes, and the parents themselves make no effort to train their little ones in goodness and self-control; they grow up in an atmosphere of laxity and pertness, in which they gradually lose all sense of shame and all respect both for themselves and for other people." *A Dialogue on Oratory 29*

It is not a popular notion but William R. Wallace's nineteenth century quotation is a sure one: "the hand that rocks the cradle rules the world." Women and their ideas, proclivities and morals either uphold the household and the State or they undermine the household and the State. Women have always been the dominant influence over children; have always been the sex that nurtures morality and corrects behavior; have always been the civilizing influence upon men and consequently on the body politic. When the women in a society become corrupt, the men and the children follow.

Rome's women at the end of the Republic had become morally lax. But they were simply harbingers of what the rustic Roman's conquest and subjugation of most of the known world would bring to Rome. It is impossible to say exactly what caused Rome to shed her old Spartan ways at the end of the Republic and direct her passions to money, ostentation and loose morals. It is likely that the conquests by her military, the ever-increasing assimilation of the conquered, the tales of other cultures more wealthy than Rome and the opulent trophies of war displayed for all to see in public triumphs caused the provincial people of Rome, female and male, to marvel at and then covet other lifestyles less stringent and simple than their own.

When the 1st century BC Roman General Lucullus, best remembered for his sumptuous and extravagant "Lucullan feasts," brought back to Rome a small taste of the opulence of the Turkish ruler Mithridates' kingdom, all Rome was stunned:

"…a golden image of Mithridates six feet high, a shield set with precious stones, twenty loads of silver vessels, and thirty-two of golden cups, armor and money all carried by men. Besides which, eight mules were laden with golden couches, fifty-six with gold bullion, and a hundred and seven with coined silver, little less than two million seven hundred thousand pieces." Plutarch, *Lives: Life of Lucullus*

Mithradates VI, called Mithridates the Great, was one of the richest rulers and strongest foes of the Romans in the late Republic. From 88-63 BC four Roman generals, Sulla, Lucinius, Lucullus and Pompey, were sent against him. After 25 years of war, Pompey finally defeated him and threatened to take him to Rome as the prime trophy in his triumphal parade:

"Mithridates tried to make away with himself and after first removing his wives and remaining children by poison, he swallowed all that was left; yet neither by that means nor by the sword was he able to perish by his own hands. For the poison, although deadly, did not prevail over him since he had inured his constitution to it, taking precautionary antidotes in large doses every day; and the force of blow from his sword was lessened on account of the weakness of his hand caused by his age (71) and present misfortunes, and as a result of taking the poison.... When therefore he failed to take his own life through his own efforts and seemed to linger beyond the proper time, those whom he had sent against his son fell upon him and hastened his end with their swords and spears. Thus Mithridates, who had experienced the most varied and remarkable fortune, had not even an ordinary end to his life. For he desired to die, albeit unwillingly, and though eager to kill himself was unable to do so; but partly by poison and partly by the sword he was at once self-slain and murdered by his foes." Cassius Dio, *Roman History 37.13*

For almost 2,000 years after his death, a potion called Antidatum Mithridaticum aka Theriac was used as a panacea for serious ailments. Mithridates' daily dose of poison worked on the same principle as our modern vaccines. To combat smallpox, inject smallpox. The Asian

King Mithridates' daily dose of poison to ward off death by poisoning worked.

Roman historians saw "Asiatic influence" like that of Mithridates as a corrupting force on the morals, dress, ideas and gods of Rome. It was not Rome's contact with the Barbarians who lived in northern Europe's hibernal huts and forests that influenced Rome. It was her contact with the advanced civilizations in the Mediterranean and the East.

The protracted period of wars with the Tunisian city of Carthage known as the Punic Wars (264-146 BC) exposed the Latin peasants to a sophisticated, wealthy and powerful city. Carthage, unlike land-locked Rome, was on the Mediterranean Sea. With their superior navy they had conquered many of their maritime neighbors. Carthage was the glue that held together the intricate trading alliances between the kingdoms from northern Africa and Spain to Syria and Lebanon. In the 1st century AD Rome would call the Mediterranean *mare nostrum*, "our sea," but when it was fighting the Carthaginians in the 2nd century BC, it was definitely "their sea" (*mare suum*).

The Romans, especially the women, were not immune to the fashions and fantastics they had seen in these more elevated cultures. It was during the second Punic War in 218-201 BC that the Lex Oppia was enacted by the Roman Senate. It was a sumptuary law designed ostensibly to save money during wartime. The law was directed entirely against women. It specified that no woman could wear more than half an ounce of gold or wear a garment of expensive mingled colors or drive her carriage and horses within a mile of Rome's city limits unless she was attending a religious rite. In 195 BC, 20 years after the Law was passed, the war was over and Rome was drenched in Carthaginian riches, but the law was still in effect. This time the emboldened Roman women took to the streets for its repeal. Cato the Elder (234-149 BC), a defender of the good old days, argued passionately before the Senate for the Law's enforcement:

"…it was with something like a blush of shame that I made my way just now to the Forum through the midst of an army of women….if modesty restrained matrons within the limits of their own rights, it would not become these women to be concerned about the question of what laws should be passed or repealed in this (Senate)....Citizens of Rome, if each one of us had set himself to retain the rights and the dignity of a husband over his own wife, we should have less trouble with women as a whole sex....It is because we have not kept them under control individually that we are now terrorized by them collectively.... Our ancestors refused to allow any woman to transact even private business without a guardian to represent her; women had to be under the control of fathers, brothers or husbands. But we, heaven preserve us, are now allowing them even to take part in politics....Give a free rein to their undisciplined nature, to this untamed animal, and then expect them to set a limit to their own license...What they are longing for is complete liberty, or rather, if we want to speak the truth, complete license. Indeed, if they carry this point (to repeal Lex Oppia), what will they not attempt? Run over all the law relating to women whereby your ancestors curbed their license and brought them into subjection to their husbands. Even with all these bonds, you can scarcely restrain them....The very moment they begin to be your equals, they will be your superiors." Livy, *History 34.2.3*

"The very moment (women) begin to be your equals, they will be your superiors." Ancient Cato's argument still persists in parts of our modern world and in the secret recesses of minds. That day in ancient Rome the women won the day and the Lex Oppia was overwhelmingly repealed by the men in the Senate. The women, bedecked in all their finery, celebrated by parading through the streets and around the Forum.

The ever-enlarging empire of Rome under the Republic brought into her city the rare and the exotic from all over the world: silk from China, fine glassware from Egypt, perfumes from Persia, emeralds from Scythia, new foods, novel dress fashions and hair styles, exotic ideas and customs. As Rome grew, her appetites grew. Markets and shops filled the small side streets with goods from afar and people from afar crowded the streets of Rome. Aelius Aristides (117-181), a popular Greek orator, in his *Oration To Rome* praises the plenitude the conquests had brought to Rome:

"Whatever the seasons make grow and whatever countries and rivers and lakes and arts of Hellenes and non-Hellenes produce are brought from every land and sea, so that if one would look at all these things, he must needs behold them either by visiting the entire civilized world or by just coming to Rome. For whatever is grown and made among each people cannot fail to be (in Rome) at all times and in abundance. And here the merchant vessels come carrying these many products from all regions in every season…so that the city appears a kind of common emporium of the world."

At the beginning of the 1st millennium AD, Rome's conquests, foreign influences and the immigration of conquered people had subtly turned Rome from a small city with a provincial populace into a grand cosmopolitan metropolis. The very virtues that had brought Rome to its height were beginning to be subverted by the wealth, ease and iniquity that would soften and sap Rome's might.

But the greatest influence on Rome and the whole ancient world at that time was Greece. In 334 BC a 22-year-old, sandy-haired Greek king named Alexander began a conquest that would change history. Alexander, later given the appellation "the Great," conquered Egypt, the entire Middle East, the Persian Empire and then forced his reluctant army on to vanquish Central Asia as far as the Indus Valley in India. As they conquered, he and his soldiers spread Greek culture, habits, babies and, most importantly, a language across a huge swath of the world. Several hundred years after Alexander's conquests, the world's first written languages, Mesopotamian cuneiform and the Egyptian hieroglyphs, both had become lost languages and would be unintelligible for almost 2,000 years until they were deciphered by linguists in the West in the 19th century. By the time Alexander the Great died in 323 BC in Babylon at the age of 33, he had Hellenized his world, had united and tied the literate from all countries to Greek philosophy and art and had enabled the world to communicate with each other in one language, Koine Greek, the common Greek dialect of the people of Greece.

Even before Alexander the Great's exploits, Greece was renowned for its thinkers and playwrights. In the 4th century BC, the three great tragedians Aeschylus, Sophocles and Euripides taught the ancient and the modern world how to write plays. At the same time Socrates taught Plato and Plato taught Aristotle and the three of them taught the whole world how to think philosophically. The Greek rhetorician and orator Isocrates (436-338 BC) was contemporary with most of those men in that potent time in the history of Western thought: "So far has Athens left the rest of mankind behind in thought and expression that her pupils have become the teachers of the world, and she has made the name of HELLAS (Greece) distinctive no longer of race but of intellect, and the title of HELLENE is a badge of education rather than common descent." *Panegyricus 50*

Ironically, history pens the period from Alexander's conquests to the rise of Christianity as the Greco-Roman Period (c. 300 BC-c. 300 AD), as though Rome is a book propped up by the two calendrical bookends of Greece and Christianity. Greece on one end gave her an ideological core. On the other end after 300 AD, Christianity gave her a spiritual core. Rome was not a civilization. She was a force that needed a civilization. Ancient Rome's civilization was Greek. Greek thought, art, architecture and language prevailed. Even though Latin was the language of Rome and of Imperial officialdom, the language spoken throughout her Empire was Greek. Greek was the lingua franca that bound the Roman Empire together as English is the lingua franca that binds our world together.

Even before Rome conquered Greece in the 2nd century BC, the Roman upper class had been fascinated with everything Greek. The Greeks themselves were fascinated with the Greeks. Pericles, (495-429 BC), statesman and orator, was the most outstanding of the ancient Greeks and raised his culture to such a height that today his reign of influence is called the Age of Pericles. His proud and impressive funeral oration praising the virtues of the war dead and of Athens survives through Thucydides in *The Peloponnesian War 2.40*:

"We (Greeks) love beauty with simplicity, and we love the pursuit of knowledge without effeminacy. We employ wealth properly, for use rather than for noisy display, and we do not consider poverty to be a disgrace but do regard it as shameful for someone not to seek to escape poverty through labor. We citizens of Athens care for both our own domestic concerns and for the affairs of state; those of us engaged in business are not lacking in understanding of public matters. For we alone consider those who avoid engagement in public affairs not as 'uninvolved' but as useless. And we, as we judge and reflect carefully on matters, do not consider words to be a hindrance to actions. Rather, the real hindrance to action is to enter into whatever must be done without taking forewarning through discussion."

The Greeks were the superior people of the ancient world. The Romans, whose long suit was war and construction, tried with their Republic to emulate Athenian democracy. Rome even took the Greek gods and put Roman names on them: Zeus became Jupiter; Ares became Mars, etc. Latin literature was created in the 3rd century BC by appropriating Greek models. When the Greeks perfected mosaics that mimicked paintings, the Romans either copied the procedure or imported Greek artisans. Greeks perfected metalworking and the Romans imported Greek silversmiths to create for them elaborate silverware such as was found in 1895 near a villa in Boscoreale one mile away from Mt. Vesuvius. The villa's 1st century AD owner had buried the treasure during or before the eruption of Vesuvius in August of 79. His villa, his treasures and perhaps he and his family were buried in the ashes. Fashioned in the Greek style, the 109 silver pieces in the Boscoreale collection include silverware, mirrors, bowls, vases, dishes, cups and two famous silver wine goblets embossed with skeletons holding masks interspersed with sayings about the futility of life: "Life is a theater;" "Enjoy life while you can, for life is uncertain;" "Honor filth." On the goblets Clotho, one of the Greek fates, gazes laconically at the skeletons of Euripides, Sophocles, Monimus the Cynic and other Greek philosophers while skeletons of Zeno the Stoic and Epicurus the

Epicurean confront each other before two mating dogs. The goblets are outstanding representations of Greek handiwork and their Greek subject matter as well as their subjects in repousse on the wine goblets are ultimate depictions of the pagan world's cynicism and hopelessness in the face of death.

The engaging poet of the Augustan Age, Horace the Epicurean (65-8 BC), would have agreed with the sentiments on the Skeleton Goblets:

"...whether Jupiter grants us additional winters or whether this is our last....Be wise, strain the wine; and since life is brief, prune back far-reaching hopes! Even while we speak, envious time has passed; seize the day (*carpe diem*), putting as little trust as possible in tomorrow!" *Odes 1.11*

Horace's famous *carpe diem* phrase has survived for millennia and is understood and quoted in its Latin form in most modern languages. With no hope for a life after death, the Romans and the pagan world lifted their goblets to the present. The Epicureans believed man should "eat, drink and be merry for tomorrow we die." There were no after-death consequences for a life lived well or ill. There was only the eternity of non-entity.

Horace was aware of his age and of the debt Romans owed to Greece. He had been educated in Athens and sent his son to Athens to learn the mind and art of the Greeks. Horace realized that Rome had physically conquered Greece, but in reality Greece had conquered Rome. In one of his letters he comments: "When Greece was taken, she took control of her rough invader and brought the arts to rustic Latium." *The Epistles 2.1.ll.156-57* Horace suggests a sexual metaphor with Greece as the conquered, cultivated woman who took control of the crude Roman man.

Pliny the Elder (23-79 AD), the proud Roman historian and natural philosopher who died during the eruption of Mt. Vesuvius, advises his son Marcus to be leery of Greeks:

"In due course, my son Marcus, I shall explain what I found out in Athens about these Greeks, and demonstrate what advantage there may be in looking into their writings, while not taking them too seriously. (The Greeks) are a worthless and unruly tribe. Take this as a prophecy: When those folk give us their writings, they will corrupt everything. All the more if they send their doctors here. They have sworn to kill all barbarians with medicine---and they charge a fee for doing it....They call us barbarians, too, of course, and *'Opici'* (peasant farmers), a dirtier name than the rest." *Natural History 29.13.14*

As if to recover from the affront of being called "barbarians" and "peasant farmers," Pliny the Elder praises the refining results of Roman imperialism:

"(Our) land....chosen by the providence of the gods to render even heaven itself more glorious, to unite the scattered empires of the earth, to bestow a polish upon men's manners, to unite the discordant and uncouth dialects of so many nations by the powerful ties of one common language, to confer the enjoyments of discourse and of civilization upon mankind, to become, in short, the mother-country of all the nations.... (The Roman) genius is its manners, its men and the nations whom it has conquered by eloquence and the might of arms. The very Greeks—a folk fond mightily of spreading their own praises—have given ample judgment in favor of Italy whom they named simply a small part of *Magna Graecia* (Larger Greece)." *Natural History 3.8*

In spite of Pliny's enumerations of Rome's prowess, he cites the judgment of the ultimate people, "the very Greeks." If the Greeks called Rome "simply a small part of Magna Graecia," it is difficult to fathom the compliment.

By the 2nd century AD, the Roman's love affair with the Greeks was waning. Rome was ruler of the world, yet her statues, her buildings, her fashions, her ideas and her gods were Greek-inspired, not Roman. Juvenal, the ultimate Roman satirist of the 1st and 2nd centuries, wrote extensively of his hatred for the Greeks, of their obsequious insinuation into Roman society and about their corrupting influence:

"And now let me speak at once of the race which is more dear to our rich men, and which I avoid above all others; no shyness shall stand in my way. I cannot abide...a Rome of Greeks; and yet what fraction of our dregs comes from Greece?....He has brought with him any character you please: grammarian, orator, geometrician, painter, trainer, or rope-dancer, augur, doctor or astrologer....Must I not make my escape from purple-clad gentry like these....who have been wafted to Rome by the wind that brings us our damsons and our figs? Is it to go so utterly for nothing that as a babe I drank in the air of the Aventine and was nurtured on the Sabine berry?" *Satires 3.58-81*

Juvenal goes only so far as to ask the question, Does it not count for anything that I am a native-born Roman, a Sabine-bred Roman who has from my birth inhaled the fresh air of the Aventine Hill and been nurtured on the fruit of the olive tree? To ask the question, Why is the whole world in love with everything Greek rather than everything Roman, would have been too reflective a question for the sardonic Juvenal. For the Romans, in general, and often in particular were not a race given to thought or reflection or spirituality. William Stearns Davis in his book *Readings in Ancient History: Rome and the West pg. 97* says: "Few great peoples have more strictly excluded the spiritual and ideal from their lives than did the Romans."

Rome was pragmatic, practical, knew what she did well. She could fight and win better than anyone else; could build aqueducts, walls, sewers, roads, buildings and bath houses better than anyone else; she could govern conquered people better than anyone else. Rome was master of the physical. Rome had a body, but like the Tin Man in *The Wizard Of Oz* she did not have a heart, a soul. Like the Straw Man Rome did not have a brain.

The *Epistle of Mathetese to Diognetus 6*, one of the earliest of Christian writings in the first half of the 100's, explains what Christians are and would be to the Roman world:

"In a word, what the soul is in a body, this the Christians are in the world. The soul is spread through all the members of the body, and Christians through the divers cities of the world. The soul has its abode in the body and yet it is not of the body. So Christians have their abode in the world and yet they are not of the world. The soul which is invisible is guarded in the body which is visible: so Christians are recognized as being in the world, and yet their religion remains invisible. The flesh hates the soul and wages war with it....so the world hates Christians though it receives no wrong from them because they set themselves against it pleasures. The soul loves the flesh which hates it...so Christians love those that hate them. The soul is enclosed in the body and yet itself holds the body together; so Christians are kept in the world as in a prison-house and yet they themselves hold the world together. The soul though itself immortal dwells in a mortal tabernacle; so Christians sojourn amidst perishable things while they look for the imperishability which is in the heavens. The soul hardly treated in matter of meats and drinks is improved; so Christians when punished increase more and more daily. So great is the office for which God has appointed them and which it is not lawful for them to decline."

The pagan world needed humanity, heart and holiness. It needed a soul. It was about to get one.

At the very beginning of the Roman Empire appeared a Jewish man, a miracle worker, who had new ideas, ideas that moved the heart, spiritual ideas, fiat ideas, ideas not open to question, ideas He said were the Truth, not the many small "t" truths of the pagan world, not the "you have your views and we have our views" syncretism, but dogmatic, obdurate, uncompromising Truths with a capital "T." He was crucified on a cross on a hill in Jerusalem with a thief on either side of Him. A rich friend of His, Joseph of Arimathea, claimed His body and buried it in a tomb he had purchased for himself. According to His followers and 500 other people who saw Him, He came alive again three days later, talked and ate with His friends for forty days before He was taken up into the sky. He claimed to be the Jewish Messiah, the Christ as the

Greeks called Him. He claimed He was God incarnate. He claimed He was the Way, the Truth, the Life; that He was the Water of life; the Bread of life; the Light of the world; the Resurrection and Life and anyone who believed in Him would live eternally.

Because His followers saw Him and talked with Him and touched Him and ate with Him after He had resurrected from the dead, they knew He had done what no other had ever done. They became radical, fervent, zealous in their desire to obey His last command to them: "Go and make disciples of all nations, baptizing them in the name of the Father and the Son and the Holy Spirit and teaching them to obey everything I have commanded you. And surely I am with you always, to the very end of the age." (Matthew 28:18) This small cadre of men fanned out throughout the Roman Empire and beyond preaching this Jesus as the long-prophesied Christ, the Savior of the world, the One, the only One.

The only ancient description we have of Jesus is the prognostication of the Messiah in Isaiah 9:6; 52:13,14; 53:2-7, 9-11:

"For to us a child is born, to us a son is given, and the government will be on his shoulders. And he will be called Wonderful Counselor, Mighty God, Everlasting Father, Prince of Peace....See, my servant will act wisely; he will be raised and lifted up and highly exalted. Just as there were many who were appalled at him---his appearance was so disfigured beyond that of any man and his form marred beyond human likeness....He had no beauty or majesty to attract us to him, nothing in his appearance that we should desire him. He was despised and rejected of men, a man of sorrows and acquainted with grief....he took up our infirmities and carried our sorrows….he was pierced for our transgressions, he was crushed for our iniquities; the punishment that brought us peace was upon him, and by his wounds we are healed…. the Lord has laid on him the iniquity of us all….He was oppressed and afflicted, yet he did not open his mouth; he was led like a lamb to the slaughter, and as a sheep before her shearers is silent, so he did not open his mouth….He was assigned a grave with the wicked, and with the rich in his death....the Lord makes his life a guilt offering....my righteous servant will justify many, and he will bear their iniquities." c. 740 BC

The modern world reckons time from the birth of Jesus Christ. AD (*Anno Domini*) means "in the year of the Lord." BC, "Before Christ," means all that happened before His birth. Even those who dislike the AD/BC designations reckon time dating from the birth of Christ---CE, the Common Era and BCE, Before Common Era. When, however, CE and BCE were first introduced, the designations meant "Christian Era" and "Before the Christian Era." Because of sensitivities to non-Christians, late 20th century academic publications began using CE/BCE to mean Common (to all) Era and Before Common Era. No matter what one calls the era in which one lives, the connected world divides time into only two periods---one before Christ and one after Christ. This man arrived when Rome was at her apex of conquest and nearing her nadir of morality. Rome could "neither endure (her) vices nor face the remedies needed to cure them." The seeds of her destruction were sprouting; the foundation of her empire was showing hairline cracks; the faint odor of putridity was wafting over her seven hills. Time was running out.

Even though Rome appeared to be on the ascendancy, she was ripe to be taken. She could not have fallen to a stronger army for she had conquered the world and appropriated all their men. Rome had to slowly marinate, had to linger, to languish in her own depravity before she could be vanquished. Rome, the master of the heathen world, was the culmination of and the perfect personification of the whole pagan world---the tired, worn-out silly gods and the despicable, libertine behaviors they fostered, the fatuous concentration on the material world and the vapid ideas of the good life. The pagan world had long lost its savor. It was ebbing, was softening, was disintegrating and would gradually be replaced by that man from whom we have reckoned time for the last 2,000 years.

There was another man, another JC, assassinated 40 years before Jesus was born, who reckoned how we calculate time. This man, Julius Caesar, founded the Roman Empire and created the world in which

Jesus would live, die and resurrect. Suetonius gives the only physical description of Caesar:

"He was tall, of a fair complexion, round limbed, rather full faced, with eyes black and piercing....kept the hair of his head closely cut and had his face smoothly shaved. His baldness gave him much uneasiness... he used to brush forward the hair from the crown of his head, and of all the honors conferred on him by the Senate and People, there was none which he either accepted or used with greater pleasure than the right of constantly wearing a laurel crown." *Lives Of The Caesars: Julius Caesar 45*

What is known from ancient texts is that Caesar increased his fortunes by plundering cities that were not enemies of the State, that he was unrestrained in sexual indulgences, but was almost a teetotaler in regard to wine. There was a joke that circulated in Rome that Caesar was the only man who undertook to overthrow the State when sober. Julius Caesar believed he was a man of destiny. He fought and bludgeoned his way to supreme rule in Rome. When he had finally killed his path to power, he declared himself a dictator. His friend, the Roman historian Sallust (86-35 BC), had helped him come to power but grew increasingly anxious about Caesar's road to tyranny. In his *Speech to Caesar 5-7* Sallust implores his friend to embrace the ideals of the Republic and to "call men back to the old standards, which from the corruption of our morals have long since been a farce....keep depraved practices and evil passions far from our youth....(do not) allow them a temporary gratification at the expense of inevitable evil in the near future....our young men (should) cultivate honesty and industry, not extravagance and the pursuit of wealth."

Caesar was not a man to be moved by words of a glorious past. From his youth he was intent upon building a glorious future with him as its ruler. Throughout his years of public service, the suspicious Senate correctly saw in the young man's each political move an unbridled ambition that could lead to a dictatorship. They frustrated his every grab for power. But the people and his armies loved him because he gave them gifts, privileges and victories.

Caesar left Rome and spent his 40's subduing Gaul and Britain where he amassed great wealth and vast public acclaim. Julius was an intelligent man and such a brilliant military strategist that his *Gallic Wars* are still studied at some military schools. To frustrate attempts to intercept his military correspondence, he invented a secret substitution code called "The Caesar Shift" cipher. He shifted the order of the alphabet so that it started on the letter E and continued F, G, H, I, etc. down to Z and then continued with A, B, C, D. Under this algorithm, his message, "Need More Legions," would read, "Riih Qsvi Pikmsrw." The Caesar Shift is a very simple code and would be easy to break by modern cryptanalysts, but Caesar's idea of a substitution cipher, a polyalphabetic cipher, has dictated the basic form of encryption for 2,000 years.

The *Chiffre Indechiffrable*, the Indecipherable Code, popularized by the French diplomat Blaise de Vigenere (1523-96), was based on Caesar's encryption code. It was made as a *tabula recta*, a square table of letters of the alphabet from A-Z extending down to 26 lines of letters. The 1st row begins with A and goes to Z; 2nd row begins with B and ends with A; the 3rd row begins with C and ends with B, the 4th row begins with D and ends with C, etc. Vignenere's code was so secure that it was used successfully until the beginning of the 20th century.

Caesar, also, sent messages in Greek when he was in Barbarian territories because he knew they did not know Greek. During the war in the Pacific in 1942, it was sure the Japanese did not know the Navajo Indian language. A Marine, son of Christian missionaries to the Navajo Indians, proposed using the Navajo language in codes. 420 Navajos were trained in signals. The messages from these "Windtalkers" were never decoded by the Japanese. Most modern encryption methods, however, usually use mathematical algorithms to create their codes.

During his command in Gaul, Julius Caesar had become the most popular man in Rome, had become dangerous to a democratic Republic. The Senate called upon him to resign his command, disband his army and return to Rome. It was now or never for the ambitious 51-year-old general. He made his move. An ancient law declared it was an act of war for a Roman general to cross into Rome's boundaries with a standing army:

"...at the river Rubicon, the boundary of his province, (Caesar) paused for a while (with his army), and realizing what a step he was taking, he turned to those about him and said, 'Even yet we may draw back; but once cross yonder little bridge and the whole issue is with the sword.' As he stood in doubt....on a sudden there appeared...a wondrous (man) who sat and played a reed....(he) snatched a trumpet (from one of the soldiers), rushed to the river and sounding the war-note with a mighty blast, strode to the opposite bank. Then Caesar cried: 'We take the course which the signs of the gods...point out. The die is cast (*alea jacta est*),' he said." Suetonius, *Lives Of The Caesars: Julius Caesar 31.32*

That cold January 10 in 49 BC Julius Caesar declared war on Rome. He proceeded to methodically march his battle-tested armies around the world. He defeated all actual or potential opposition to his power: Lucius Domitius in Italy, Pompey in Greece, King Ptolemy in Egypt, King Pharnaces who was the son of Mithridates the Great in Turkey, Scipio in north Africa and the sons of Pompey in Spain. All these victories made him even more popular with the people. Caesar had himself declared Dictator for Life and Divine Julius. The Senate grudgingly acquiesced. His youthful ambitions had been realized far beyond his ken, for he had changed the course of history by ushering in the days of the Roman Empire. His last name, Caesar, would become synonymous with Ruler and is the etymological origin of the German word "Kaiser" and the Russian word "Czar." Caesar would live on in many languages and literatures, but his dictatorship was short-lived. Less than two years after declaring himself Dictator for Life, Republicans in the Senate assassinated the 56-year-old man.

Even though his time of infallible power was brief, Julius Caesar, like Jesus Christ, became a man after whom time is computed. Our month of July is named after Julius whose birthdate was July 13, 100 BC and August is named after Caesar Augustus, the first of Rome's emperors.

While in Egypt with Cleopatra, Caesar recognized the superiority of the Egyptian way of calculating time based on the movements of the sun rather than the Roman AUC calendar based on lunar movements. Our calendar still calls a "month" a *maenon* from the ancient word for "moon" as a measurement of time. The advanced Egyptians determined the tropical year at 365 days, very close to the actual calculation of 365.24219 days. His year spent with the Egyptian queen Cleopatra and her astronomer Sosigenes convinced him to institute a calendar based on Alexandrian reckonings when he returned to Rome.

The 52-year-old Caesar spent enough time with the 22-year-old Cleopatra to have a child by her named Caesarion, but unlike his luckless cousin Mark Antony, Caesar was not to be deterred from his destiny by the considerable charms of Cleopatra. Antony was a staunch supporter and loyal friend to Caesar. When Caesar was assassinated, he was appointed to give the eulogy made famous by Shakespeare in his play *Julius Caesar*:

"Friends, Romans, countrymen, lend me your ears;
I come to bury Caesar, not to praise him.
The evil that men do lives after them;
The good is oft interred with their bones…."

For a non-poetic and ancient rendering of what Antony actually said, read *The Roman History 2.143-147* by Appian (95-165 AD).

After Caesar's murder, Antony and two other generals formed a triumvirate to rule Rome. In 41 BC, while in Paul the Apostle's hometown of Tarsus in modern-day Turkey, Antony summoned Cleopatra from Egypt. Some say he had known her in Rome when she was with Caesar and wanted to renew the acquaintance. Others say he was hoping her money would finance his invasion of Parthia. It would be a fateful rendezvous for both. In relating the meeting of the 44-year-old Antony and the 28-year-old Cleopatra, Plutarch, who was born in 46 AD when much about Cleopatra was still au courant, describes the attractions of this femme fatale of the ancient world:

"She received several letters, both from Antony and from his friends, to summon her, but she paid no attention to these orders; and at last, as if in mockery of them, she came sailing up the river Cydnus in a barge with gilded stern and outspread sails of purple, while silver oars beat time to the music of flutes....She herself lay stretched along under a canopy of cloth of gold, dressed as Venus....The perfumes diffused themselves from the vessel to the shore....the people...running out of the city to see the sight....and Antony at last was left alone sitting upon the tribunal....the word went through all the multitude that Venus had come to feast with Bacchus for the common good of Asia....For her actual beauty, it is said, was not in itself so remarkable that none could be compared with her, or that no one could see her without being struck by it; the contact of her presence, if you lived with her, was irresistible; the attraction of her person, joining with the charm of her conversation and the character that attended all she said or did was something bewitching. It was a pleasure merely to hear the sound of her voice with which, like an instrument of many strings, she could pass from one language to another; so that there were few of the barbarian nations that she answered by an interpreter; to most of them she spoke herself, as to the Ethiopians, Troglodytes, Hebrews, Arabians, Syrians, Medes, Parthians and many others whose language she had learned... Plato admits four sorts of flattery, but Cleopatra had a thousand. Were Antony serious or disposed to mirth, she had at any moment some new delight or charm to meet his wishes. She played at dice with him, drank with him, hunted with him; and when he exercised in arms, she was there to see." *Lives: Life of Antony*

The Roman General Antony and Queen Cleopatra eventually allied themselves against the might of Rome commanded by the Roman General Octavian, the future Caesar Augustus. At the Battle of Actium in 31 BC, they were defeated. Antony stabbed himself and was carried to Cleopatra. He died in her arms. Antony and Cleopatra had spent more than 10 years together and had three children even though he had a wife in Rome for much of that time. When Cleopatra tried to negotiate with General Octavian the terms for her survival and that of her children, he refused. At the age of 39 in 31 BC she committed suicide by the bite of a poisonous asp brought to her in a basket of figs.

The victorious Octavian, Julius Caesar's adopted son, then killed Caesar's only living son, the 16-year-old Caesarion, son of Cleopatra and Caesar. With that final act, all pretenders to the throne after Caesar's death were gone. Octavian appropriated the title Caesar, and on January 16, 27 BC he became Caesar Augustus (meaning "The Revered One"), first Emperor of the Roman Empire.

Unlike Antony, Julius Caesar had been able to escape the charms and arms of Cleopatra. When he returned to Rome, he initiated the Egyptian calendar in 45 BC. The Roman AUC calendar had been so inaccurate that even though Caesar had crossed the Rubicon on January 10, 49 BC, several years later that date fell in mid-Autumn. The Egyptian calendar was a simple one of 365 days with an extra day (an intercalary leap year day) every fourth year in order to make up for the drift of the vernal equinox. Caesar wanted the new calendar to begin with his rule, but the Senate had always started a new year on January 1, the month named after the god Janus who had two faces, one looking ahead to the future and the other looking back to the past. The Senate won that fight and modern New Years always commence on January 1. The Julian calendar and its ease of use were an immediate success in the Roman world. Only nine years after its initiation, the Roman scholar and writer Varro (116-27 BC) was using the system to fix dates for the start of seasons. Within a hundred years after its introduction, the Julian calendar was the staple of time in the Roman Empire and would be used by the civil world for almost 1,600 years.

But the Christian Church had for centuries used a different calendar for its main celebration, Easter aka Pascha (meaning "Passover"). The Church Calendar, based on a lunar system, had been devised at The First Council of Nicea in 325 to ensure the Church celebrated Easter on the exact Sunday of the resurrection. The Church in Alexandria had always celebrated Easter on the 14th day of the moon that falls on or after the vernal equinox. By the 900's most Christian churches celebrated Easter according to the Alexandrine method. But the vernal equinox drifts. By the 1500's the lunar calendar was off and Easter was being celebrated on the wrong day.

Pope Gregory XIII and the learned ecclesiastics were determined to fix the problem of equinox drift and the confusion over the date of Easter once and for all. To remedy the drift problem, the Gregorian calendar dropped 10 days from the year 1582. On Thursday October 4, 1582 the Church adopted what would be called the Gregorian calendar by a papal bull entitled *Inter Gravissimas* ("Among The Greatest Concern"). The Christian Church may have had grave concerns about the date of Easter being astronomically inaccurate on the church lunar and Julian solar calendars, but the secular world was not obligated by a papal bull. The Catholic countries of Spain, Italy, Portugal and the Polish-Lithuanian Commonwealth, however, adopted the new calendar immediately. Scotland and most Protestant countries adopted Gregory's calendar in the 1700's. England and colonial America adopted it in 1752. When Alaska was purchased by the United States from Russia in 1867, the Alaska Territory began to keep Gregorian time. Russia remained on the Julian calendar until 1917 after the Russian Revolution and Greece held on to Julian until 1923. Some tribes and isolated peoples still use the Julian calendar. Today, internationally, the Gregorian calendar is the only one used. It is so accurate it has an infinitesimal error of gaining only one day every 3,325 years. The Christian concern over the date of Easter has prevailed even though most of the secular world had no idea there had been a problem.

This divine obsession in the Christian Church on fixing the exact date for the Paschal Celebration had led Dionysius Exiguus in 525 to invent the AD/BC designations used in the Julian and Gregorian calendars. The monk Exiguus devised an arcane and confusing Paschal Table to project from the past into the future the exact dates of Easter. His Table was so mathematically and astronomically correct it became the basis for not only prognosticating Easter for generations but also for designating with AD/BC everything after and before the birth of Christ.

Calendars were traditionally invented and used to facilitate agricultural plantings and harvests, religious events, the start of seasons, tribal migrations and to chronicle the past. But since the advent of Jesus of Nazareth, the Christian Western world has been fixated on refining and correctly ascertaining the exact Sunday in each year when Christians are to celebrate His resurrection. Countries with no Christian backgrounds have recognized the Gregorian calendar. Japan adopted it January 1, 1873; Korea on January 1, 1895 and China in 1912. It may be for some an uncomfortable reality, but it is true that for over 2,000 years the world has had to reckon with a young Jewish rabbi who taught, lived, died and, according to His followers and their Bible, resurrected from the dead. The dates on our 21st century calendars are reckoned from Him.

XVI.

"Petrifaction is of two sorts. There is petrifaction of the understanding and also of the sense of shame. This happens when a man obstinately refuses to acknowledge plain truths and persists in maintaining what is self-contradictory. Most of us (in Rome) dread mortification of the body and would spare no pains to escape anything of that kind. But of mortification of the soul we are utterly heedless....And mortification of the sense of shame and modesty we go so far as to dub strength of mind!" Epictetus, *The Golden Sayings 23*

The Greek Epictetus (55-135 AD) was a Roman slave who became a philosopher and lived in Rome during the rise of the Christian Church. He compares the moral depravity of his day to petrifaction, the process that gradually turns an organic material into stone. It is a bromide that one becomes what one beholds. The pagan world had for thousands of years worshipped gods hand-made of wood and stone:

"Our God is in heaven....But their idols are silver and gold, made by the hands of men. They have mouths, but cannot speak, eyes, but cannot see; they have ears, but cannot hear, noses, but they cannot smell; they have hands, but cannot feel, feet, but they cannot walk; nor can they utter a sound with their throats. Those who make them will be like them, and so will all who trust in them." Psalm 115:3-8

The pagan world became what they beheld. Like their mute idols, they were unseeing, without understanding. The Roman conscience was so calcified they praised their lack of shame as a sign of strong minds capable of withstanding mortification. To them the contempt for a moral compass was a sign of frigid strength, not weakness.

Epictetus and his contemporary the Apostle Paul (c. 2-67) agree in their assessments of 1st century Rome. They both describe the Roman nonchalance toward depravity, their lack of shame and their obdurate defense of immorality. Epictetus cannot fathom reasons for the petrified hearts of his contemporaries. In his letter to the Romans, the theist Paul is more explicit in his comments than Epictetus and presents causality:

"For although they knew God, they neither glorified him as God nor gave thanks to him, but their thinking became futile and their foolish hearts were darkened. Although they claimed to be wise, they became fools and exchanged the glory of the immortal God for images made to look like mortal man and birds and animals and reptiles....Because of this, God gave them over to shameful lusts. Even their women exchanged natural relations for unnatural ones. In the same way the men also abandoned natural relations with women and were inflamed with lust for one another....(God) gave them over to a depraved mind, to do what ought not to be done. They have become filled with every kind of wickedness, evil, greed and depravity....Although they know God's righteous decree that those who do such things deserve death, they not only continue to do these very things but also approve of those who practice them." Romans 1:21-32

It cannot be over-emphasized that during the moral and spiritual declines of civilizations there are always decent, wise people who eschew the predominant values of the culture and hew to decency and sanity. Goodness does not always speak up for itself and the writings and words of those with admirable beliefs and warnings like Epictetus and Paul do not always survive the tramp of history. It is a truism that evil acts and lack of morals have been found in every day and age. But when the practices of the few in darkness become the accepted common currency of a culture in daylight, that civilization is in its dotage, on the slippery path to either irrelevancy or destruction.

Such was Rome and the pagan world in the 1st century AD. Those who would destroy Rome and inherit her Empire, the Christian Church, began to come of age in the nexus of time prior to the impending demise of the Roman Empire and the pagan world in the West.

Christianity was born on an early Sunday morning in c. 30 AD on the outskirts of Jerusalem in a cave near a hill called Golgotha, the Place Of The Skull. A group of women among whom were Mary Magdalene and Mary the mother of James, Joanna and Susanna (Luke 8:2,3; 23:55; 24:10) went to the cave tomb to anoint with oils and spices the body of their friend and rabbi, Jesus of Nazareth, who had been crucified on Friday. The tomb was empty. Angels asked them, "Why do you look for the living among the dead? He is not here. He has risen. Remember how he told you while he was still with you in Galilee: 'The Son of Man must be delivered into the hands of sinful men, be crucified and on the third day be raised again.'" (Luke 24:5-8) Christianity, named after the man who would wear the mantle of "the Messiah, the Christ," was founded that Sunday on the proclaimed truth of the resurrection of Jesus of Nazareth.

It is rare to have in ancient manuscripts the genesis and the spread of an idea or a religion. In the Gospels of the New Testament, in the book of Acts and in the Epistles written by Paul are chronicled the beginnings and the growth of Christianity. The New Testament was written before 100 AD and most of the books date before the destruction of Jerusalem in 70, so the value of having certified documents that register the historical and geographical progress of Christianity from its inception in c. 30 until 70 is immense.

The women were the first to see the resurrected Jesus early in the morning on Sunday. (John 20:10-18; Matthew 28:1-10) They believed, ran and told the Apostles who "did not believe the women because their words seemed to them like nonsense." (Luke 14:11) Jesus then appeared in His resurrected body to His disciples:

"On the evening of that first day of the week (Sunday), when the disciples were together, with the doors locked for fear of the Jews, Jesus came and stood among them and said, 'Peace be with you!' After he said this, he showed them his hands and side. The disciples were overjoyed when they saw the Lord....Now Thomas...one of the twelve was not with the disciples when Jesus came. So the other disciples told him, 'We have seen the Lord!' But (Thomas) said to them, 'Unless I see the nail marks in his hands and put my finger where the nails were, and put my hand into his side, I will not believe it.' A week later his disciples were in the house again, and Thomas was with them. Though the doors were locked, Jesus came and stood among them and said....to Thomas, 'Put your finger here; see my hands. Reach out your hand and put it into my side. Stop doubting and believe.' Thomas said to him, 'My Lord and my God!' Jesus told him, 'Because you have seen me, you have believed; blessed are those who have not seen and yet have believed.'" John 20:19-29

Thomas' epithet, Doubting Thomas, has become the archetype of all those who hear and will not believe until they have empirical evidence. Perhaps Thomas later recalled Isaiah's verse: "See, (the Lord says) I have engraved you on the palms of my hands." (49:16) Thomas spread the word of what he had seen in the hands and on the side of Jesus to all those who had not seen all the way to India where pagan priests had him killed. Thomas, who had to see for himself the wounds in Jesus' hands became the archetype of the converted: "One will say, I belong to the Lord....still another will write on his hand, 'The Lord's.'" Isaiah 44:3,5

After the conversion of the Apostles, "...(Jesus) appeared to more than five hundred of the brothers at the same time, most of whom are still living (in c. 51) though some have fallen asleep.....Then he appeared to (his brother) James, then to all the apostles, and last of all he appeared to me also, as to one abnormally born" according to Paul in I Corinthians 15:6, 7. Jesus had four brothers, James, Joseph, Simon and Judas, none of whom had believed in Him before His resurrection. John 7:5 states: "even his own brothers did not believe in him." Later,

Jesus' brothers would travel and spread the word about their brother's resurrection (I Corinthians 9:5). Other members of His family and extended family, called the *desposyni* meaning in Greek "of or belonging to the Master or Lord," were active in the days of the Early Church.

In the 40 days following the Resurrection and before His Ascension, Jesus appeared at least 12 times to His disciples and other people. About a month after the Sunday resurrection, there were already at least 500-600 people in Judea who had become believers because they had seen the resurrected Jesus with their own eyes.

The Christian movement took a significant leap forward nine days after Jesus' Ascension when observant Jews and some Gentiles, called "God fearers," who had converted to Judaism, flocked to Jerusalem from all over the world to celebrate Shavuot called Pentecost in Greek, a festival commemorating the giving of the 10 Commandments to Moses and the First Fruits of the Harvest. According to Acts 2:8-11, at Pentecost in 30 AD there were people from the kingdom of Parthia then encompassing parts of Iran, Afghanistan, Pakistan and some of India; people from Media (parts of Iran, Azerbaijan, Kurdistan in Iraq); Elamites from the regions north of the Persian Gulf; Mesopotamians from parts of Iraq, Iran, Syria, and Turkey; worshippers from Cappadocia, Pontus, Asia, Phrygia, Pamphylia and all the countries in the stretch of land going from Turkey to the Black Sea; from Egypt; from the island of Crete and from Libya in north Africa. Arabs who inhabited the areas of the Red Sea extending up into Jordan were in Jerusalem and there were people from Rome at Pentecost, both Jews who lived there and Romans who had converted from paganism to the one God. Passover, the most popular Jewish festival, drew hundreds of thousands of Jews to Jerusalem, but tens of thousands of the faithful came for all the minor festivals like Pentecost.

The ancient parchments say that on the day of Pentecost, a core group of new converts "numbering about 120" met together in an upper room (called the Cenacle) in Jerusalem for prayer. Some of the 120 people were the 12 Apostles (Matthias had been chosen to replace Judas in Acts 1:12-26)). The Twelve were Jesus' most intimate companions but Jesus, also, had 70-72 disciples who had been with Him from the beginning of His ministry. (Luke 10:1-24) It is logical that some of the 120 people in the room were these disciples and perhaps some converts from the group of 500 who had seen Him after the resurrection. We are told the 120 included the women who had followed Jesus from Galilee and "Mary the mother of Jesus…with his (recently converted) brothers." Acts 1:13-15

In the early morning on the day of Pentecost these people:

"…were all together in one place. Suddenly a sound like the blowing of a violent wind came from heaven and filled the whole house where they were sitting. They saw what seemed to be tongues of fire that separated and came to rest on each of them. All of them were filled with the Holy Spirit and began to speak in other tongues as the Spirit enabled them. Now there were staying in Jerusalem God-fearing Jews from every nation under heaven. When they heard this sound, a crowd came together in bewilderment, because each one heard them speaking in his own language. Utterly amazed, they asked: 'Are not all these men who are speaking Galileans? Then how is it that each of us hears them in his own native language?….We hear them declaring the wonders of God in our own tongues!' Amazed and perplexed, they asked one another, 'What does this mean?' Some, however, made fun of them and said, 'They have had too much wine.' Then Peter stood up with the Eleven, raised his voice and addressed the crowd: 'Fellow Jews and all of you who live in Jerusalem, let me explain this to you; listen carefully to what I say. These men are not drunk, as you suppose. It's only nine in the morning! No, this is what was spoken by the prophet Joel: In the last days, God says, I will pour out my Spirit on all people….Even on my servants, both men and women….and they will prophesy….and everyone who calls on the name of the Lord will be saved. Men of Israel, listen to this: Jesus of Nazareth was a man accredited by God to you by miracles, wonders and signs, which God did among you through him, as you yourselves know. This man was handed over to you by God's set purpose and foreknowledge, and you, with the help of wicked men, put him to death by nailing him to the cross. But God raised him from the dead, freeing him from the agony of death, because it was impossible for death to keep its hold on him....let all Israel be assured of this: God has made this Jesus, whom you crucified, both Lord and Messiah.' When the people heard this, they were cut to the heart and said to Peter and the other apostles, 'Brothers, what shall we do?' Peter replied, 'Repent and be baptized every one of you in the name of Jesus Christ for the forgiveness of your sins'....With many other words he warned them and he pleaded with them, 'Save yourselves from this corrupt generation.' Those who accepted his message were baptized and about 3,000 were added to their number that day." Acts 2:1-41

Fifty days, less than two months, after the Passover associated with Jesus' death and resurrection, there were at least 3,620 converts to Christianity. The 3,000 converts harvested at Pentecost encompassed the known world from India throughout the Middle and Near East to Africa, to Crete in the Mediterranean Sea and up to Rome. We are told that these 3,000 became grounded in the new faith before they went back to their homes: "They devoted themselves to the apostles' teaching and to the fellowship, to the breaking of bread (Eucharist) and to prayer." (Acts 2:42) Stemming from the conversions at Pentecost, numerous home churches, including the church in Rome, were founded throughout the Roman Empire. After Pentecost, "...the Lord added to their numbers daily those who were being saved." Acts 2:47

At 3:00 one afternoon Peter and John:

"...were going up to the temple at the time of prayer....a man crippled from birth was being carried to the temple gate, called Beautiful, where he was put every day to beg from those going into the temple courts. When he saw Peter and John about to enter, he asked them for money. Peter looked straight at him, as did John. Then Peter said, 'Look at us!' So the man gave them his attention, expecting to get something from them. Then Peter said, 'Silver and gold I do not have, but what I have I give you. In the name of Jesus Christ of Nazareth, walk.' Taking him by the right hand, he helped him up, and instantly, the man's feet and ankles became strong. He jumped to his feet and began to walk. Then he went with them into the temple courts, walking and jumping and praising God. When all the people saw him walking and praising God, they recognized him as the same man who used to sit begging at the temple gate…and they were filled with wonder and amazement at what had happened to him. While the beggar held on to Peter and John, all the people were astonished and came running to them in the place called Solomon's Colonnade. When Peter saw this, he said to them: 'Men of Israel….Why do you stare at us as if by our own power or godliness we had made this man walk? The God of Abraham, Isaac and Jacob, the God of our fathers, has glorified his servant Jesus. You handed him over to be killed….You disowned the Holy and Righteous One….You killed the author of life, but God raised him from the dead. We are witnesses of this. By faith in the name of Jesus, this man whom you see and know was made strong….Now, brothers, I know that you acted in ignorance as did your leaders. But this is how God fulfilled what he had foretold through all the prophets, saying that his Christ would suffer'….many who heard the message believed, and the number of men grew to about 5,000." Acts 3:1-18—4:4

Not just women. Not just a handful. Not just 100's, but 1,000's of Jews in Jerusalem were being converted to Christ less than six months after the resurrection.

The first of the persecutions of the new faith occurred on that day when Peter healed the crippled man. A religious sect called the Sadducees who did not believe in the resurrection of the dead were offended at the Apostles for preaching the resurrection from the dead. That evening they had Peter and John imprisoned. The next day the rulers, elders and teachers of the law in addition to the high priest Annas and "Caiphas….began to question (Peter and John)….Then Peter, filled with the Holy Spirit, said to them, 'Rulers and elders of the people. If we are being called to account today for an act of kindness shown to a cripple and are asked how he was healed, then know this, you and all the people of Israel: It is by the name of Jesus Christ of Nazareth, whom you crucified but whom God raised from the dead, that this man stands before you healed….Salvation is found in no one else, for there is no other name under heaven given to men by which we must be saved.'

When they saw the courage of Peter and John and realized that they were unschooled, ordinary men, they were astonished and took note that these men had been with Jesus." Acts 4:6-13

The assembly of ruling elders in Jerusalem was called the Sanhedrin, meaning "council" in Hebrew. It was composed of 71 influential and/or promising younger men and modeled after Moses' 70 elders plus Moses (Numbers 11:16.17). During New Testament times the Sanhedrin had a mix of aristocratic Sadducees, priests and learned but lay Pharisees who adjudicated cases involving Jewish law and, some maintain, the Sanhedrin had considerable authority in cases even involving capital punishment. The supreme court of Jerusalem decided they had to release the two Apostles because all the people were praising God for the miraculous healing of the beggar. But they "called them in again and commanded them not to speak or teach at all in the name of Jesus. But Peter and John replied, 'Judge for yourselves whether it is right in God's sight to obey you rather than God. For we cannot help speaking about what we have seen and heard.'" (Acts 4:18-20) At the very inception of the new faith in 30 AD is that bold, stubborn and unshakeable belief in the resurrection of Jesus that would be seen by unbelievers in the courtrooms, in the catacombs and in the Colosseum and other arenas all over the Roman Empire in the next three hundred years.

The Apostles in Jerusalem continued preaching the resurrection of Jesus and confirmed their words with miracles: "…more and more men and women believed in the Lord and were added to their number…. Crowds gathered also from the towns around Jerusalem, bringing their sick and those tormented by evil spirits, and all of them were healed." Acts 5:14-16

The number of believers became so great that the new religion had long abandoned the private upper room that held 120 people and began meeting in public on Solomon's Porch in the Temple. (Acts 3:11; 5:12) The Portico, a popular gathering place for rabbis and their students, was a massive colonnade covered with a ceiling of engraved cedar wood. 50' high polished white marble pillars and two 30' wide aisles punctuated the open space. Solomon's Porch contained the only remnant of the original Temple built by Solomon in c. 950 BC and had a beautiful eastern view overlooking the Kidron Valley, the Mt. of Olives and the Garden of Gethsemane.

Herod the Great, known for his prodigious building projects and for his attempt to kill the infant Jesus, had built the magnificent Temple and its surrounds frequented by Jesus and His disciples. The Idumean Herod wanted to build a Jewish Temple site that would be better and bigger than any other religious complex in the world and, as Josephus says in *Jewish Antiquities 15.11.1*, "…would be sufficient for an everlasting memorial of him." His 35-acre Temple complex dwarfed in size and grandeur one of the Seven Wonders of the Ancient World, the 425' long, 225' wide and 60' high splendid but small Temple of Diana, the many-breasted goddess, at Ephesus. The modest 90' by 30' and 60' high holy Temple itself was situated within the northwest area of the vast compound. One thousand Jews from the priestly classes built the sacred precinct according to the specifications the Lord had given in I Kings 6, 7 and II Chronicles 3, 4. It had been such an honor to be chosen to construct the Second Temple that an ossuary found in a tomb in the Old City of Jerusalem bears the simple engraving: "Simon The Temple Builder."

The rest of the 35-acre complex on top of Mt. Moriah was composed of courts, sacrificial areas, and gathering places like Solomon's Porch. Unlike every other temple in the ancient world, the entire area had no statues, no graven images of any kind anywhere. Herod began the architectural wonder in c. 19 BC, but all the polish and ornamentation on the site was not finished until c. 63 AD, 67 years after Herod's death, and only seven years before its destruction in 70 AD.

The rhomboid-shaped Temple compound could hold 150,000 people. At one entrance was the Court of the Gentiles, a giant bazaar of money changers and sellers of souvenirs, sacrificial animals and birds. It was so vast that 50,000 people could mingle. This area is where Jesus used physical force to throw out the money changers both at the beginning and at the end of His ministry:

"(At the beginning of His ministry in c. 27) Jesus went up to Jerusalem. In the temple courts he found men selling cattle, sheep and doves, and others sitting at tables exchanging money. So he made a whip out of cords and drove all from the temple area, both sheep and cattle; he scattered the coins of the money changers and overturned their tables. To those who sold doves he said, 'Get these out of here! How dare you turn my Father's house into a market!'" John 2:13-16

"(Near the end of His ministry in c. 30) On reaching Jerusalem, Jesus entered the temple area and began driving out those who were buying and selling there. He overturned the tables of the money changers and the benches of those selling doves, and would not allow anyone to carry merchandise through the temple courts. And as he taught them, he said, It is written: 'My house will be called a house of prayer for all nations;' (Isaiah 56:7) But you have made it a den of robbers." Mark 11:15-17

Clearly, Jesus of Nazareth was a revolutionary and fearless man to interrupt the patterns at Passover in such a violent way. It appears that His ire was kindled by the mix of worship and merchandising. God and Mammon (Aramaic *mamon* meaning "money").

Beyond the vast Court of the Gentiles where Jesus overturned tables and drove all animals from the area were numerous 75' tall gold-gilted doors and gates leading to other parts of the enclosure. Imported white marble covered the acres of pavements. The small Temple containing the Holy of Holies was almost completely covered and furnished in solid gold. Solid gold spikes lined the roof to prevent birds from landing and defiling the Temple. All this white and gold beauty on Mt. Moriah could be seen glistening 2,430' high against the sky by travelers approaching the city of Jerusalem. The Christian believers who met in Solomon's Porch after His resurrection were gathering in one of the most famous, imposing and resplendent complexes ever created in the ancient world. Pliny the Elder called Jerusalem "the most splendid city in the whole East" *Natural History 5.15.70* and the Temple Compound was its crown.

The new Christians met often "in Solomon's Colonnade....(and) more and more men and women believed in the Lord and were added to their numbers." (Acts 5:12-14) To the Sadducees, who did not believe in the resurrection of the dead and whose sect, ironically, completely disappeared after the destruction of Jerusalem in 70AD, this preaching of the resurrection of Jesus was anathema. Because they were influential in the Sanhedrin, the Sadducees again had all the Apostles arrested and put in the public jail. But "during the night an angel of the Lord opened the doors of the jail and brought them out. 'Go, stand in the temple courts,' he said, 'and tell the people the full message of this new life.' At daybreak (the Apostles) entered the temple courts, as they had been told, and began to teach the people." (Acts 5:19-21) The Sadducees were livid, brought the apostles before the Sanhedrin and castigated them for disobeying their orders. When Peter replied, "We must obey God rather than men! The God of our fathers raised Jesus from the dead---whom you killed by hanging him on a tree....We are witnesses of these things," the Sadducees were "furious and wanted to put them to death." Acts 5:29-33

But:

"a Pharisee named Gamaliel, a teacher of the law, who was honored by all the people, stood up in the Sanhedrin and ordered that the men be put outside for a little while. Then he addressed (the Sanhedrin): 'Men of Israel, consider carefully what you intend to do to these men. Some time ago Theudas appeared, claiming to be somebody, and about four hundred men rallied to him. He was killed, all his followers were dispersed and it all came to nothing. After him, Judas the Galilean appeared...and led a band of people in revolt. He too was killed and all his followers were scattered. Therefore in the present case, I advise you: Leave these men alone! Let them go! For if their purpose or activity is of human origin, it will fail. But if it is from God, you will not be able to stop these men; you will only find yourselves fighting against God.' His speech persuaded them. They called the apostles and had them flogged....ordered them not to speak in the name of Jesus and let them go. The apostles left the Sanhedrin, rejoicing because they had been counted worthy of suffering disgrace for the Name. Day after day, in the temple courts and from house to house, they never stopped teaching and proclaiming the good news that Jesus is the Christ." Acts 5:34-42

Gamaliel, a Pharisee who believed in the resurrection of the dead and whose sect was the only one to survive after the destruction of Jerusalem in 70 AD, was the most respected rabbi in 1st century Judaism. He was the grandson of the legendary Hillel the Elder (c.110 BC-10 AD), founder of the House of Hillel whose rabbis and sages dominated Jewish thought into the 5th century AD. Hillel, like Moses, died at the age of 120 and for the last 40 years of his life (c.30 BC-10 AD) he led the Sanhedrin in Jerusalem. When he died, his son Simeon assumed his position, but Simeon died shortly after he took office and in 10 AD Simeon's son Gamaliel (c. 20 BC-c. 52 AD) took office and became the most respected rabbi in the Sanhedrin during the years of Jesus' life and the rise of the Early Church. It is interesting to speculate whether Gamaliel, his father Simeon and/or his grandfather Hillel were among the rabbis that reasoned in the Temple with the 12-year-old Jesus in c. 6 AD:

"Every year (Jesus') parents went to Jerusalem for the Feast of the Passover. When (Jesus) was twelve years old, they went up to the Feast according to the custom. After the Feast was over, while his parents were returning home, the boy Jesus stayed behind in Jerusalem, but they were unaware of it. Thinking he was in their company, they traveled on for a day. Then they began looking for him among their relatives and friends. When they did not find him, they went back to Jerusalem to look for him. After three days they found him in the temple court, sitting among the teachers, listening to them and asking them questions. Everyone who heard him was amazed at his understanding and his answers. When his parents saw him they were astonished. His mother said to him, 'Son, why have you treated us like this? Your father and I have been anxiously searching for you.' 'Why were you searching for me?' he asked. 'Didn't you know I had to be in my Father's house?' But they did not understand what he was saying to them. Then he went down to Nazareth with them and was obedient to them. But his mother treasured all these things in her heart. And Jesus grew in wisdom and stature and in favor with God and men." Luke 2:41-52

We will never know whether Hillel, Simeon or Gamaliel were there during that three day post-Passover period in c. 7 AD when the precocious young Jesus was listening to, answering questions and being taught in the Temple by teachers of the Law, but it is a chronological possibility that Jesus and one or more of the three rabbis may have met and conversed together.

It is tantalizing to speculate the effect Gamaliel's caution had on the other priests gathered in the Sanhedrin that day when Gamaliel saved the lives of the Apostles. The Bible does record that "a large number of priests (had become) obedient to the faith." Acts 6:7 We know that at least two of the 71 men in the Sanhedrin that day had already acknowledged Jesus as the Messiah: Nicodemus and Joseph of Arimathea (Mark 15:43). Previously, Nicodemus had come to Jesus under the cloak of night and revered Him by calling Him "Rabbi," meaning "master." They had a discussion in which Jesus told Nicodemus, "...no one can see the kingdom of God unless he is born again." (John 3:3) Another time during the Feast of Tabernacles (early Autumn), Nicodemus spoke up for Jesus when the Sanhedrin wanted to have Him arrested: "Nicodemus, who had gone to Jesus earlier and (was a member of the Sanhedrin) asked, 'Does our law condemn anyone without first hearing him to find out what he is doing?' (The priests) replied, 'Are you from Galilee, too. Look into it, (Nicodemus), and you will find that a prophet does not come out of Galilee.'" (John 7:50-52) Nicodemus had tried to intervene, but tepidly. The last Biblical mention of Nicodemus is when Joseph of Arimathea came boldly in broad daylight to Pilate and asked for permission to claim and bury Jesus' body:

"Later, Joseph of Arimathea asked Pilate for the body of Jesus. Now Joseph was a disciple of Jesus, but secretly because he feared the Jews. With Pilate's permission, he came and took the body away. He was accompanied by Nicodemus, the man who earlier had visited Jesus at night....Taking Jesus' body, the two of them wrapped it with the spices, in strips of linen." John 19:38-40

Both Nicodemus and Joseph of Arimathea were afraid to outwardly proclaim their beliefs in Jesus as the Messiah. "Yet at the same time many even among the leaders believed in him. But because of the Pharisees they would not confess their faith for fear they would be put out of the synagogue; for they loved the praise from men more than praise from God." (John 12:42,43) Prominent Jews in the synagogues and the Sanhedrin did believe Jesus was the Messiah, but were afraid of being publicly castigated or of being expelled from the synagogues and the Sanhedrin. Perhaps Gamaliel felt that way.

Gamaliel's supposed sympathy to the Apostles in the Book of Acts has prompted numerous references to him as a covert Christian. The Clementine Literature dating from c. 100-300 asserts Gamaliel was a silent Christian in order to help his fellow Christians. *Recognitions of Clement 1.65-67* Some early manuscripts aver that Gamaliel and his son Simeon (named after Gamaliel's father) were baptized by Peter and John. There is no ancient Jewish textual evidence that Gamaliel was a convert to Christianity. However, it is noted that Gamaliel, this most celebrated leader of the school of Hillel in Jerusalem, is not represented as the one who continued the Mishnaic tradition of his grandfather Hillel. In the chain of tradition given in the Mishnah (Avot i.,ii) Johanan b. Zakkai is given that mantle. It can be deduced that for some unknown reason Gamaliel did not deserve, could not or did not want to inherit the authority of his grandfather Hillel. Gamaliel is seldom mentioned in the Halakhah, but Johanan b. Zakkai, the successor to Gamaliel's grandfather, does comment that when Gamaliel died in c. 52, "the honor of the Torah ceased and purity and piety became extinct." Sotah 15:18

There is a long history in the Christian church that claims Gamaliel was a Christian. His purported remains, as well as the relics of Nicodemus, are in the Duomo in Pisa, Italy. The Early Church claimed Gamaliel in the August 3 celebration in the *Roman Martyrology* (300's) and a superb Renaissance painting by a student of Carlo Saraceni, assuming the truth of Gamaliel as a Christian, was done as late as 1615. It is called *St. Stephen Mourned by Gamaliel and Nicodemus* and is in the Museum of Fine Arts in Boston. Whether he was a Christian or not, on that day in c. 33 before the Sanhedrin Rabban ("our master") Gamaliel gave a reasonable, historically-based argument that prevented the deaths of the Apostles. But neither the elders, rulers, scribes, Pharisees nor Sadducees could stop the steady growth of this "Nazarene sect" (Acts 24:5) among the Jews.

Most of the religious ruling class had not been receptive to Jesus' message and considered His Messianic claims blasphemous. They had pressed Pilate for Jesus' death and were not pleased when Peter and the other Apostles constantly accused them of killing their Messiah. Most of them sincerely believed that Jesus was a blasphemer and deserved to die because He had claimed to be God:

(During the Feast of Dedication, now called Hanukkah, when Jesus was teaching in the Temple, He said) "I and the Father are one." John 10:30

(During the trial in front of the Sanhedrin on the Thursday night before His death) "...Jesus remained silent. The high priest (Caiaphas) said to him, 'I charge you under oath by the living God: Tell us if you are the Christ, the Son of God.' 'Yes, it is as you say,' Jesus replied. 'But I say to all of you: In the future you will see the Son of Man sitting at the right hand of the Mighty One and coming in the clouds of heaven.' Then the high priest tore his clothes and said, 'He has spoken blasphemy! Why do we need any more witnesses? Look, now you have heard the blasphemy. What do you think?' 'He is worthy of death,' they answered. Then they spit in his face and struck him with their fists. Others slapped him and said, 'Prophesy to us, Christ, who hit you?'" Matthew 26:63-68

Many of these members of the Sanhedrin were honorable men. They simply could not believe that Jesus of Nazareth was the Messiah as He claimed to be. After the resurrection, these same men were irate and alarmed at the spread of this new sect and of their presumptive use of the Temple to teach the resurrected Jesus. They wanted this unorthodox and heretical group gone from Jerusalem. In c. 34 they made a serious attempt to amputate this new arm of Judaism.

Stephen, a Hellenized Jew, was the first Christian martyr. In spite of the fact that members of the Sanhedrin "saw that his face was like the face of an angel," they had him stoned to death at the instigation of the Synagogue of Freedmen composed of former Jewish slaves from Rome, North Africa or Asia Minor. The mob "laid their clothes at the feet of a young man named Saul....And Saul was there, giving approval to (Stephen's) death. On that day a great persecution broke out against the church in Jerusalem and all except the apostles were scattered." Acts 7:58; 8:1

The scattering of believers, like the breaking open of a milkweed pod, facilitated the spread of the Gospel out of Jerusalem into all of Israel and beyond because "those who had been scattered preached the word wherever they went." Acts 8:4

In Acts 9 Luke the physician (Colossians 4:14) tells the story of Saul's conversion from a rabid and murderous Pharisee to a rabid and zealous Christian. Saul's name in Hebrew means "asked for, inquired of God" and a derivative of his name, *sheol*, means "hell." He was (as of Acts 13:9) and still is called by his Greek name *Paulos* meaning "small." A pivotal point in Christian history was when that small, insignificant and often frail 40-year-old man began to target and to pursue all Gentile nations for Christ with the same dogged hell-fire-and-brimstone enthusiasm and conviction with which he had persecuted and jailed Christians for five years. It is to that signatory conversion that Christians in the West owe their faith. After Paul's metanoia in c. 35, the church "enjoyed a time of peace and grew in numbers, living in the fear of the Lord." (Acts 9:31)

In c. 39, Peter went on a pastoral visit to towns north of Jerusalem where he encouraged and taught new believers. When he healed a paralytic in Lydda, all those who lived in Lydda and the nearby town of Sharon "turned to the Lord." (Acts 9:35) Farther north in the port city of Joppa (modern-day Jaffa), a believer by the name of Tabitha had died. When Peter raised her from the dead, "this became known all over Joppa and many believed in the Lord." (Acts 9:42) Because Joppa was the main port of Judea, it is probable that many took the news of the resurrected Tabitha and the risen Christ to ports and cities all over the Mediterranean.

During his stay in Joppa at Simon the Tanner's seaside home, Peter received a call from God to preach to a Roman centurion named Cornelius stationed in another important port city, Caesarea Maritima, the Roman headquarters in Palestine. It was in Caesarea, 35 miles north of Joppa, that Italian archaeologists in 1961 found a 2' by 3' block of limestone incised with an inscription mentioning Pontius Pilate. It is important because it provides concrete proof of the historicity of Pontius Pilate and gives additional credence to the Biblical citations of him. The stone and inscription are damaged but on the 2nd and 3rd lines the letters *TIUS PILATUS* and *ECTUS JUDA* can clearly be seen. The 1st line has a dedication to *TIBERIUM* (TIBERIAS). The reconstructed letters would have read: *PONTIUS PILATUS PRAEFECTUS JUDAEAE*, "PONTIUS PILATE, PREFECT OF JUDEA." During Peter's visit, perhaps he had seen this dedication stone at the base of the temple in Caesarea that Pontius Pilate had built to honor his patron Tiberias. Tiberias Caesar had abruptly terminated Pontius Pilate's prefecture in 36, three years before Peter's visit to Cornelius.

Cornelius' conversion at Caesarea is the first known penetration of the Gospel into the Legions of the Roman army. The army would become a fertile ground for the new faith and many named martyrs in the catacombs and in early writings were Roman soldiers, including the martyrs of the entire Theban Legion.

The conversion of the Roman centurion Cornelius and other Gentiles was big news: "The apostles and the brothers throughout Judea heard that the Gentiles also had received the word of God. So when Peter went up to Jerusalem, the circumcised believers (Jews) criticized him." (Acts 11:1,2) The mother church in Jerusalem was underwhelmed by these conversions. Cornelius was not only a symbol of Rome's military boot on the neck of Israel but he and his family were also pariahs, were Gentiles. When Peter and the six men who went with him to Cornelius' house, explained the supernatural events surrounding the conversion of Cornelius and the others (Acts 10,11), the leaders in Jerusalem were persuaded that God intended His salvation in Christ to extend to all nations and peoples. Ancient texts show that by 40 AD, just 10 years after the resurrection, converts to the new faith were diffused all over the world, came from all ranks of society, were of all colors and spoke all languages.

Years before Paul's three missionary journeys (c. 46-c. 58), there was a solid core of believers in Israel and in Gentile countries and cities: in Damascus (Acts 9:2) and Samaria (8:5) and North Africa (8:27) and in all the countries represented at Pentecost (2:9-11) and in Syrian Antioch (11:19). Antioch was one of the leading and largest cities in the ancient world with a diverse population of over 500,000 people. Called "Antioch the Beautiful," its favorable position on a plain between the Mediterranean and the East made it a center of commercial activity that attracted businessmen and their families from all over the Roman Empire.

Since the persecution after the stoning of Stephen in c. 34, many believers had migrated to Antioch and were "telling the message only to Jews." However, some Jews from the island of Cyprus and from Cyrene in modern-day Libya "began to speak to Greeks also, telling them the good news about the Lord Jesus. The Lord's hand was with them and a great number of people believed and turned to the Lord." (Acts 11:19-21) Over the years the growing number of Gentile as well as Jewish converts in Antioch prompted the Jerusalem church in c. 42 to send a Levite from Cyprus to Antioch to find out what was happening in that early base of Christianity. That man, Barnabas, is called an "Apostle" at least twice in Scripture (Acts 14:4,14; 15:33) and is one of the lynchpins who facilitated the growth and stability of the Early Church.

The reader of history first meets Barnabas in Acts 4:36 shortly after the resurrection: "Joseph…whom the apostles called Barnabas which means Son of Encouragement, sold a field he owned and brought the money and put it at the apostles' feet." His given name *Josef*, meaning in Hebrew "he will add," had already been changed to the Greek name *Barnabas* meaning "son of consolation or encouragement." Names and name changes in the Bible always have had direct textual or prognostic meanings. In Genesis 17:5 God signaled Abraham's destiny by changing the father of the Jews and the Arabs name from *Abram* meaning "exalted father" to *"Abraham"* meaning "father of many" even though his wife Sarah was still barren. Barnabas' name change was precipitated by his amplifying, encouraging and generous nature seen in every passage where he is mentioned.

When Barnabas arrived in Antioch in c. 42 and "...saw the evidence of the grace of God, he was glad and encouraged them all to remain true to the Lord with all their hearts. (Barnabas) was a good man, full of the Holy Spirit and faith and a great number of people were brought to the Lord." (Acts 11:23,24) Barnabas assessed the scope of the work in Antioch and made a decision that would contribute to the depth of teaching in the New Testament and would change the course of Christian history: "...he went to Tarsus to look for Saul." (Acts 11:25) Even though Saul ("inquired of God") had his name changed to Paul ("small"), this Apostle, coming from the Greek word *apostolos* meaning "messenger," did not inquire of God, but God required him as a messenger, a missionary and made sure his ego was kept in check so he would remain humbled, small. II Corinthians 12:7-10

After Paul's conversion in c. 35, he had left Damascus and spent three years in Arabia where Mt. Sinai is located and where the Jews wandered in the wilderness for 40 years. Paul's reasons for this self-imposed exile on the greater Arabian Peninsula are not given, but it can be conjectured that Paul had been shaken to his foundations by his encounter with God on the road to Damascus. He needed to be alone with God and his own thoughts in a place where he could discern the next steps in his new life as a Christian Jew instead of a Pharisaic Jew.

After three years in Arabia, Paul returned to Damascus. Damascus was and still is the capital of Syria. For thousands of years this city, situated in the fertile valley along the Barada River, has had continual occupation and was a significant hub of early Christianity. The great Umayyad Mosque in Damascus has for 2,000 years been a worship temple. As the centuries morphed, the original Roman temple on the site was rebuilt into a Christian church dedicated to John the Baptist. After the Arab conquest in 634 the Basilica of John the Baptist was refashioned into a Moslem mosque that still has a "Minaret of Jesus" and an inscription on an insignificant, unused gate that says, "Jesus is the Messiah." The Mosque, also, preserved the Christian shrine, supposedly with the Baptist's head in it, because they believe John the Baptist was a prophet of Allah. Muslims revere John the Baptist:

"Yusufali: While he (Zachariah father of John) was standing in prayer in the chamber, the angels called unto him: 'Allah doth give thee glad tidings of Yahya (John), witnessing the truth of a Word from Allah, and (be besides) noble, chaste and a prophet, of the goodly company of the righteous.'
Pickthal: And the angels called to him as he stood praying in the sanctuary 'Allah giveth thee glad tidings of (a son whose name is) John (who cometh) to confirm a word from Allah lordly, chaste, a prophet of the righteous.'
Shakir: Then the angels called to him as he stood praying in the sanctuary: 'That Allah gives you the good news of Yahya (John) verifying a Word from Allah, and honorable and chaste and a prophet from among the good ones.'"
Quran 3:39 (Three English translations of the same verse in the Quran)

Muslims believe that *Isa* (Jesus) or *Mashi* (Messiah) will return to the Umayyad Mosque during the End Times to help the *Mahdi*, "the rightly guided one," fight against the "false messiah," *al-Dajjal*. Isa will kill al-Dajjal at the Battle of Armageddon and all will eventually believe in the one god Allah:

Narrated by Abu Hurairah (a close companion of Mohammed): "The Hour (End Times) will not be established until the son of Mary descends amongst you as a just ruler, he will break the cross, kill the pigs, and abolish Jizya tax." *Sahih al-Bukhari. Vol.3, Book 43, Kitab-ul-'ilm, Hadith No. 656*

Muslims highly revere Jesus/Isa. He is mentioned in their Scriptures over 25 times and they call Jesus and other prophets like Muhammud *al-Masih* ("messiah"). The perfect state of self-purification and self-annihilation for the sake of Allah is called *Iswiyyah*, literally meaning "Jesushood." The Quran imbues Isa/Jesus with the term *kalimat Allah*, meaning "word of God." (Surah 3:45) They believe He was virgin-born when God spoke into Mary's womb at Jesus' conception: "She said: 'O my Lord! How shall I have a son when no man hath touched me?' He said: 'Even so: Allah createth what He willeth: When He had decreed a plan, He but saith to it, Be and it is.'" Quran 3:47

There is a confused, complex, tortured but definitely shared relationship between the sons of Abraham through his wife Sarah (the Jews and the Christians) and the sons of Abraham through Sarah's handmaiden Hagar (Arabs and Muslims). The Umayyad Mosque in Damascus is just one of many examples of this tight Gordian knot.

When 1st century Paul began to preach in all the synagogues of Damascus that Jesus was the Jewish Messiah, risen from the dead (the Muslims do not believe that), the Roman temple that would become a Christian church that would become the Umayyad Mosque was just a Roman temple and its pagan worshipers were a target for the missionary Paul. Everyone knew Paul had previously come to Damascus to "…raise havoc…among those who call on this name," and the more he preached, the more the traditional Jews resented him. They conspired to kill Paul, but "his followers took him by night and lowered him in a basket" down the walls of Damascus. He escaped to Jerusalem and "tried to join the disciples, but they were all afraid of him, not believing he was a disciple." (Acts 9:21-28) Barnabas intervened and pleaded Paul's case. With most of the Christians in Jerusalem leery of Saul/Paul, it is certain that only Barnabas' words and character prevailed over the reservations of both Peter and James (Galatians 1:18, 19):

"…(Barnabas) told them how Saul on his journey had seen the Lord and that the Lord had spoken to him, and how in Damascus he had preached fearlessly in the name of Jesus. So Saul stayed with them and moved about freely in Jerusalem, speaking boldly in the name of the Lord. He talked and debated with the Grecian Jews, but they tried to kill him. When the brothers learned of this, they took him down to Caesarea and sent him off to Tarsus." Acts 9:27-30

Paul had to be secreted in a basket in the dead of night to escape death in Damascus. In Jerusalem he was almost killed by Grecian Jews. Christian brothers took provocative Paul to Caesarea and shipped him back home to Tarsus in modern-day Turkey where he spent the next five years planting churches and teaching in Syria and in his home territory of Cilicia. Then in c. 43, eight years after Paul's conversion, Barnabas, who had always believed in the potential of Paul, appeared in Tarsus and persuaded Paul to return to Antioch to help him with the work. It was in Antioch at this time, about 13 years after the resurrection, that new converts began to be called "Christians."

Several years later, the predominantly Gentile church in Antioch sent Paul and Barnabas, accompanied by Barnabas' cousin John Mark, on what would become known as Paul's 1st Missionary Journey from c. 46-48. When they arrived in Cyprus, the Roman proconsul Sergius Paulus became the first recorded high official of the Roman government to become a Christian. (Acts 13:4-12) From Cyprus they sailed to Perga in Pamphylia (southern Turkey) "where John left them to return to Jerusalem." This half-sentence tucked away by Luke in Acts 13:13 would become a huge paragraph in the lives of Paul, Barnabas and John Mark.

John, anglicized from the Hebrew *Yohanan* meaning "gift of God," was called by his Latin name *Marcus* meaning "dedicated to the god Mars." He was Barnabas' young cousin, the son of his aunt Mary who was the head of a home church in Jerusalem. (Acts 12:12) We are not told directly, but it can be inferred that Mary had suggested Mark accompany his older cousin Barnabas and Paul on the missionary journey. Barnabas, always the encourager of others, persuaded Paul to allow the young man to come with them in order to toughen his faith and to give him experience in planting churches. We do not know why Mark decided to go home. Perhaps he was homesick or found the rigorous ministry too taxing. We are not told. But we are told of the argument several years later between Paul and Barnabas precipitated by Mark's exit at the port city of Perga, capital of Pamphylia:

"Some time later (after the Council in Jerusalem in c. 50) Paul said to Barnabas, 'Let us go back and visit the brothers in all the towns where we preached the word of the Lord (on the 1st Missionary Journey) and see how they are doing.' Barnabas wanted to take John, also called Mark, with them, but Paul did not think it wise to take him because he had deserted them in Pamphylia and had not continued with them in the work. They had such a sharp disagreement that they parted company. Barnabas took Mark and sailed for Cyprus, but Paul chose Silas and left, commended by the brothers to the grace of the Lord. He went (on this 2nd Missionary Journey) through Syria and Cilicia, strengthening the churches." Acts 15:36-41

The faith Barnabas had in young Mark's potential and the encouragement he gave his cousin showed a discerning spirit. At the time of the argument Paul could never have imagined that the young "Mama's boy" would not only write one of the four Gospels, but would end up journeying across the Mediterranean and founding the Coptic Church in Egypt.

It is, however, interesting that not long after the disagreement with Barnabas when Paul and Silas came to Lystra in Turkey: "...where a disciple named Timothy lived, whose mother was a Jewess and a believer....Paul wanted to take (the young Timothy) along on the journey, so he circumcised him." (Acts 16:1-3) The young Timothy, a protege of Paul, like the young Mark, a protege of Barnabas, would turn out to be one of Paul's most beloved and faithful disciples. Perhaps it was through Barnabas' devotion to Mark that Paul came to realize the importance of fostering young men in the faith and giving them the experience of spreading the Gospel?

In c. 60 AD when Paul was in prison in Caesarea, he ended his letter to the church in Colossae near Ephesus: "My fellow prisoner Aristarchus sends you his greetings, as does Mark, the cousin of Barnabas." (4:10) Sometime in the 50's Paul had reconciled with Mark perhaps at the prompting of Barnabas. At the end of Paul's life, he is in prison again in Rome, awaiting his beheading. He writes to his own young disciple Timothy: "Only Luke is here with me. Get Mark, and bring him with you because he is helpful to me in my ministry." (II Timothy 4:11) "Mark...is helpful to me in my ministry." Hopefully, Barnabas, the Son of Encouragement, lived to see the abundant fruit of his labors with his young cousin Mark. Legend says Barnabas who came from Cyprus was burned to death in the hippodrome on that island. Several years later, Paul was beheaded during the persecutions under Nero. And many years after a young Mark left Paul and Barnabas in Perga, he was dragged to death by horses on the streets of Alexandria because of his witness for Christ. Barnabas' belief in and encouragement of the unique talents of both his cousin Mark and the Apostle Paul altered in a conspicuous way the course of history. The three Christian men are a triad of redemption, forgiveness and encouragement.

After Barnabas brought Paul to Antioch in c. 43, the Good News of Jesus' resurrection began to spread like wildfire throughout Gentile cities. Paul would travel constantly and intrepidly for over 20 years to make sure the major cities, ports and byways in his world knew that Jesus had resurrected from the dead and was the Jewish Messiah, the Christ in Greek.

"The word of God continued to increase and spread" in Israel even though Herod Agrippa I, the grandson of Herod, had killed John's brother James, the first of the 12 Apostles to be martyred. (Acts 12:1,2) When Paul was in the synagogue in Pisidian Antioch "many of the Jews and devout converts to Judaism (Gentiles)" believed. (13:43) In Iconium "Paul and Barnabas went as usual into the Jewish synagogue. There they spoke so effectively that a great number of Jews and Gentiles believed." (14:1) As Paul and Silas "traveled from town to town....the churches were strengthened in the faith and grew daily in numbers." (Acts 16:4,5) When they came to Thessalonica there was a Jewish synagogue. "As his custom was, Paul went into the synagogue and on three Sabbath days he reasoned with them from the Scriptures, explaining and proving that the Christ had to suffer and rise from the dead. 'This Jesus I am proclaiming to you is the Christ,' he said. Some of the Jews were persuaded and joined Paul and Silas as did a large number of God-fearing Greeks and not a few prominent women." (17:1-4) In the synagogue at Berea "many of the Jews believed as did also a number of prominent Greek women and many men." 17:12

"Prominent Greek women" were women who came from rich and influential families in the towns. Women, Jew and Gentile, were some of the most fervent and unwavering followers of Jesus from the beginning of His ministry into the early years of Christianity's growth and continue to be so in our modern world. It can be extrapolated from Scripture that without the steady acceptance of the resurrected Christ by Gentile women worshiping in Jewish synagogues, the growth of the Early Church would not have been so rapid.

There was a proliferation of synagogues outside of Israel ever since the 7th century BC when Northern Israel was taken into captivity by the Assyrians. None of the ten northern tribes ever returned to Israel. Over the centuries, Jews from this diaspora and Jews, for business, family or personal reasons, were living in most of the cities and towns of the Roman Empire. Paul preached in Jewish synagogues in such diverse cities as Damascus, Antioch, Salamis, Pisidian Antioch, Iconium, Thessalonia, Berea, Athens, Corinth and Ephesus. The Jews were never shy about their belief in one God and about the holiness of their Scriptures. In the 1st century AD the entire Hellenized world knew that the worship of one God was what distinguished the Jews from the rest of the world. Their one God, their 10 Commandments and their hope for a coming Messiah attracted to Judaism many Gentiles from all walks of life who had recognized the folly of paganism. Josephus recounts the story of Izates, the 1st century AD Persian king of Adiabene (Arbil, Iraq), who was converted to Judaism by a Jewish merchant whose name was Ananias. The women in Izates' harem were catalysts for his conversion :

"Ananias got among the women that belonged to the king (his harem) and taught them to worship God according to the Jewish religion. (Ananias) became known to Izates and persuaded him, in like manner, to embrace the religion....his mother Helena about the same time was instructed by a certain other Jew and went over to (Judaism).... When Izates perceived that his mother was highly pleased with the

Jewish customs, he made haste to change and embrace (all the customs) entirely; and as he supposed that he could not be thoroughly a Jew unless he were circumcised, he was ready to have it done. But when his mother understood what he was about, she endeavored to hinder him from doing it....as he was a king, he would thereby bring himself into great odium among his subjects....and they would never bear to be ruled over by a Jew." *Jewish Antiquities 20.2-4*

Izates was so fervent he eventually sent for his surgeon and was circumcised. His mother and his spiritual mentor Ananias were horrified and feared Izates would lose his kingdom. But "it was God Himself who hindered what they feared from taking effect; for He preserved both Izates himself and his sons." Most male converts to Judaism were not circumcised and Gentile converts usually did not follow all the Pharisaic and Jewish prohibitions and customs.

Gentile converts to Judaism were called "God-fearers" (*theosebeis*). They believed in Jehovah, the Law and the Prophets and they looked forward to the predicted Messiah. Some scholars had doubted the existence of a people the New Testament calls "God-fearers" (Acts 10:2; 13:16). But a New York University team excavating in Aphrodisias, Turkey in 1976 found a 16' high marble pillar, part of a Jewish memorial building or a synagogue built in the early 200's, with two lists of names engraved on it. There were 69 Jewish names denoted *ktistai* or donors to the building and 54 Greek names under the phrase *kai hosoi theosebeis* meaning "and those who are God-fearers." These Gentile believers worshipped with the Jews and contributed financially to a building they considered theirs, also. It cannot be over-emphasized the role that Biblical archaeology, used as a hermeneutical tool, has not only confirmed Biblical assertions but has expanded and explained so many Old and New Testament passages. Over and over again archaeologists confirm the historical truths of the Bible. Dr. Yigael Yadin, the late Professor of Archaeology at Hebrew University, said his modus operandi was "to hold the Bible in one hand and a spade in the other" to find out what the ruins he was uncovering were and what they meant.

In the first 40 years of Christianity, the Jews and especially the

Jewish synagogues that were sprinkled all over the Roman world were one of the main springboards used to launch the news of the resurrected Jesus into the Gentile world.

In concert with the Jews, Rome, also, facilitated the rapid growth of Christianity. The Roman Republic had succeeded in spreading Alexander's Greek language throughout the world. Koine Greek had begun as a commercial language and became the language of common communication. No longer was there the Babel-effect where no one could understand any one from a different territory. Most of the world spoke and understood Koine Greek. The entire Old Testament had been translated into Greek in the several centuries preceding the birth of Jesus and the New Testament was being written in Koine Greek. A common language united the world and the Early Church had the advantage of being universally understood.

Rome had united the world under one ruler, Caesar. No longer would a traveler enter a different oligarch's territory every 20 or 30 miles and have to explain himself to a suspicious satrap. Paul would never have been able to spread the Gospel so swiftly if he would have had to pass muster every step of his way across Asia Minor and Greece. Rome did allow "client kings" who held the title at the discretion of Rome such as King Herod in Palestine. These regional kings could rule internal affairs as long as their edicts did not countermand Rome. They were responsible for maintaining order, protecting the trade routes and, most importantly, collecting and paying taxes to Rome.

The mass Roman citizenships given to many tribes and peoples had united the world under one acknowledged supreme ruler. Rome had eliminated most of the bandits who preyed on travelers so Paul's journeys were not constantly threatened by robbers and thugs. Sea travel was safe because the Roman navy had fought and won the battle with the pirates. Paul suffered shipwrecks, but he never had to worry about buccaneers. Rome had provided the unity and safety, the Pax Romana, needed for the unimpeded spread of the new faith.

The universality of Roman law was another aid to the spread of Christianity. The laws were fair and protected the increasing number of Roman citizens from the whims and petty quarrels of insular tribes.

When he appealed to Caesar, Paul unequivocally believed the Roman courts would be more equitable to him than the Jewish Sanhedrin. (Acts 25:1-12) Under Roman law the accused could confront his accusers and if the accuser lost, he was subject to the punishment sought against the accused. This equanimity brought stability and transparency to legal proceedings in the 1st century AD.

The c. 50,000 miles of Roman roads, also, augmented the number of Christian converts. It was true that all those roads led to Rome. A traveler could begin in Rome, travel north up through Switzerland and Germany, go through France, skirt the Atlantic into and all around Spain, cross into France on the Mediterranean side of Spain, travel along the Cote D'Azur into Italy and go back to Rome. If one traveled from northwest Africa along the roads and crossed the Mediterranean, he could disembark in Israel and take the Roman roads that went north all through Asia Minor, Greece, down into Italy and ended in Rome again. The constant and easy travel on these connecting highways greatly expedited the spread of the Gospel.

The fervor and evangelical zeal of thousands of early Jewish converts to Christianity and the strategic locations of hundreds of synagogues where the Gospel could be preached dove-tailed with the societal and physical mechanics the Romans had put in place to produce the "fullness of time." The Avatar, the God Incarnate, could be born: "...we were in slavery under the basic principles of the world. But when the fullness of time had come, God sent his Son, born of a woman, born under the law, to redeem those under the law." (Galatians 4:3,4) Jesus of Nazareth entered history at a time when two great civilizations, one spiritual and one secular, were on their way out. The Jews and the Romans had served their time in the sun and helped to establish the time of the Son of Man. It is difficult, if not impossible, to imagine Christianity's lightning growth in the 1st century AD without the unwitting assistance of the Jews and the Romans.

Paul, the man who wrote the previous quote to the Christians in Galatia (Turkey), was the supernaturally appointed messenger to announce to pagan peoples in the Middle East, Greece and Rome the birth and resurrection of the Christ, the Redeemer. He let nothing deter him from his divine ordination. Even after the fight with Barnabas over John Mark, Paul took Silas and they began the walk north from Antioch on one of the best of the Roman roads, the Via Sebaste, a magnificent 10' to 19' wide, straight road that lead from Antioch up into and through central Turkey. It was built in 6 BC by Augustus Caesar to connect important military posts. Along the Roman roads were inns where horses could be fed and people could be lodged. The public inns had a terrible reputation for filth and thievery, so many travelers probably carried tents. Silas' and Paul's was made no doubt by Paul who was a tentmaker. (Acts 18:3) He and Silas traveled on foot. There is no evidence in the Bible that Paul ever used a horse except when he was whisked away by Roman authorities in Jerusalem. (Acts 23:24) The two missionaries walked about 20 miles a day either alone or with groups of travelers who were going to Tarsus, Iconium, Pisidian Antioch, Laodicea, Ephesus, Troas or one of the little towns along the Sebastian Way. It was in Troas, a port city on the Aegean Sea 840 miles from Antioch, that Paul had a vision:

"During the night Paul had a vision of a man of Macedonia (Greece) standing and begging him, 'Come over to Macedonia and help us.' After Paul had seen the vision we (Luke, the physician who authored the Book of Acts and the Gospel of Luke, has now joined Paul and gives personal testimony) got ready at once to leave for Macedonia, concluding that God had called us to preach the gospel to them. From Troas we put out to sea and sailed straight for Samothrace, and the next day on to Neapolis. From there we traveled to Philippi, a Roman colony and the leading city of that district of Macedonia. And we stayed there several days." Acts 16:9-12

Paul's interpretation of and obedience to that night vision is the reason Christianity is the nominal religion of Europe and the Americas. If Paul had not crossed the Aegean onto the European continent in the early 50's AD, all that is encompassed in the phrase "Western Civilization" would be, perhaps, moot.

When Paul landed in Greece, he walked to Philippi on the Via

Egnatia, the Roman post road that spanned the c. 700 mile East/West corridor across Albania, Greece and Turkey from the Aegean Sea to Byzantium (modern Istanbul). Silas and Paul were imprisoned in Philippi because of a troubling event:

"...we (here Dr. Luke, Paul's travel companion, includes himself in the narrative) were met by a slave girl who had a spirit by which she predicted the future. She earned a great deal of money for her owners by fortune telling. This girl followed Paul and the rest of us shouting, 'These men are servants of the Most High God, who are telling you the way to be saved.' She kept this up for many days. Finally Paul became so troubled that he turned around and said to the spirit, 'In the name of Jesus Christ I command you to come out of her!' At that moment the spirit left her. When the owners of the slave girl realized that their hope of making money was gone, they seized Paul and Silas and dragged them into the marketplace to face the authorities. They brought them before the magistrates and said, 'These men are Jews, and are throwing our city into an uproar by advocating customs unlawful for us Romans to accept or practice.' The crowd joined in the attack against Paul and Silas, and the magistrate ordered them to be stripped and beaten. After they had been severely flogged, they were thrown into prison." Acts 16:16-23

One wonders what happened to the prescient slave girl and one wonders how Paul and Silas, beaten, skin flayed open by cat 'o nine tails, had the physical strength to lead their jailer and his family to Christ that night. One wonders from what reserve well did Paul draw the gumption to castigate his captors the next day: "(You) beat us publicly without a trial, even though we are Roman citizens and threw us into prison. And now do (you) want to get rid of us quietly? No!...come (yourselves) and escort us out!" (Acts 16:37) With official escorts, Paul and Silas left Philippi and went to Thessalonica where Paul caused another riot. (17:2-9) In Berea there was another ruckus and "the brothers immediately sent Paul to the coast....(and) escorted him to Athens." (17:14,15) Saul/Paul whom God knocked off his high horse had the temperament and the nerve required to confront, protest, profess and proclaim the resurrected Christ anytime, anywhere to anyone and he was not daunted by the physical repercussions.

By the time Paul reached Athens in c. 52, he had already preached to thousands and had walked thousands of miles. Athens was a stopover for Paul while he waited for Silas and Timothy to join him, but he redeemed the time: "He reasoned in the synagogues with Jews and the God-fearing Gentiles, as well as in the marketplace with those who happened to be there." (Acts 17:17) As Paul was redeeming the time in the agora, he must have seen and kept track of his time by the 47' tall horologion (clock) in the marketplace. It is called the Tower of the Winds because on each of its sides is carved a personification of the eight wind variables. The octagonal white Pentelic marble Tower is one of the very few buildings from antiquity that is still virtually intact. On the inside was the water clock, on the outside was a sundial and the weathervane on top was of Triton holding a wand indicating the prevailing winds. The beautiful Tower of the Winds in Athens was reputedly designed and built by the Greek astronomer Andronikos of Kyrrhos in c. 50 BC about 100 years before Paul saw it in the marketplace and 2,000 years before the modern visitor sees it.

When he arrived in a town, Paul's modus operandi was always a combination of church preaching and street evangelism. In the Athenian market, he disputed with a group of Epicurean and Stoic philosophers. Some said he was a "babbler" and others were titillated because he was advocating a new religion. Luke says in Acts 17:21 that "all Athenians and the foreigners who lived there spent their time doing nothing but talking about and listening to the latest ideas," so they invited Paul to present his novelty to the philosophers who reasoned on the Areopagus or Mars Hill, a rocky outcrop near the Acropolis where the Athenians had temples to their many gods. Paul gave his famous speech about the "unknown god" to whom the Athenians, hedging their bets, had dedicated an altar on the Acropolis. He shows his knowledge of Greek philosophy by interspersing quotes from the poet Epimenides and the Stoic Cleanthes, "but when they heard about the resurrection from the dead, some of them sneered, but others said, 'We want to hear you again on this subject.'" (17:32) He garnered a few converts, but Athens never became a center of early Christianity.

The modern visitor sees a bronze plaque fixed to a large rock near the stairs leading up to Mars Hill. On it is the Greek text of the entire address Paul delivered to the Athenians in Acts 17:22-31. One of the few converts to Christianity as a result of Paul's speech was "Dionysius, a member of the Areopagus." (Acts 17:33) A street in modern Athens is called "Dionysius the Aereopagite" and one of Athen's prominent churches is named St. Dionysius the Aereopagite. Legend says he became the first Bishop of Athens and was martyred in c. 95. Good seed.

Paul was the unique combination of an itinerant preacher and a dedicated pastor. When he left Athens, he walked the 56 miles to Corinth where he established a church. Strabo (c. 63 BC-c.24 AD), describing Corinth in Paul's day, said it was a wealthy port city not only because of its fortunate location on the isthmus connecting Asia and Italy but:

"...(its) temple of Aphrodite (goddess of love) was so rich that it owned more than 1,000 temple slaves, courtesans, whom both men and women had dedicated to the goddess. And therefore it was also on account of these women (temple prostitutes) that the city was crowded with people and grew rich; for instance, the ship captains freely squandered their money (in the temple brothels) and hence the common proverb: 'Not for every man is the voyage to Corinth.'" *Geography 8.6.20*

So notorious for its licentiousness was Corinth that one of the Greek words for "fornication" was *korinthiazomai*. The American School of Classical Studies in Athens began excavations in Corinth in the late 1800's and, in addition to uncovering the Agora, a Greek theater and the temple of Apollo, they found a marble lintel of a door on which was inscribed "Synagogue of the Hebrews." Perhaps it was the same 1st century Corinthian synagogue where Paul "reasoned in the synagogue every Sabbath and persuaded the Jews and the Greeks." (Acts 18:4) Paul labored in Corinth for a year and a half trying rather unsuccessfully to stabilize the new church. (18:11) Pastor Paul passionately pleaded his case and ministry to the Corinthians with words that would not only show his love and vulnerability to them but would sum up his entire ministry:

"We put no stumbling block in anyone's path, so that our ministry will not be discredited. Rather, as servants of God we commend ourselves in every way: in great endurance; in troubles, hardships and distresses; in beatings, imprisonments and riots; in hard work, sleepless nights and hunger; in purity, understanding, patience and kindness; in the Holy Spirit and in sincere love; in truthful speech and in the power of God; with weapons of righteousness in the right hand and in the left; through glory and dishonor, bad report and good report; genuine, yet regarded as impostors; known, yet regarded as unknown; dying, and yet we live on; beaten and yet not killed; sorrowful, yet always rejoicing; poor, yet making many rich; having nothing, and yet possessing everything. We have spoken freely to you, Corinthians, and opened wide our hearts to you. We are not withholding our affection from you, but you are withholding yours from us. As a fair exchange---I speak as to my children---open wide your hearts also." II Corinthians 3-13

Some of the believers in that iniquitous city came out of lifestyles and habits that were hard to break. They were constantly backsliding and required constant upbraiding: "Do you not know that the wicked will not inherit the kingdom of God? Do not be deceived: Neither the sexually immoral nor idolaters nor adulterers nor male prostitutes nor homosexual offenders nor thieves nor the greedy nor drunkards nor slanderers nor swindlers will inherit the kingdom of God. And that is what some of you were." (I Corinthians 6:9, 10) The Corinthians had such calcified and unstable hearts they required two long letters of encouragement and admonishment from Paul and after Paul's death, his disciple Clement wrote two censorious letters to them. Clement's first *Letter to the Corinthians* (c. mid-late 1st century) is the oldest surviving Christian document outside of the New Testament. In spite of Paul's love for and agony over the Corinthians, the church never flourished.

He, also, spent a lot of time in Ephesus, a major port city for all of

Asia Minor. Paul chose port cities because people from all over the world could be reached and ports of call were influential in disseminating not only goods but also ideas across the Empire. For almost three years he pastored the church in Ephesus. Paul did door to door evangelism there: "(he) taught publicly and from house to house….(he) declared to both Jews and Greeks that they must turn to God in repentance and have faith in the Lord Jesus." Acts 20:20, 21

By teaching for two years "daily in the lecture hall (school) of Tyrannus," (Acts 19:9) Paul seems to have temporarily abandoned the synagogues and gone straight to the intellectual heart of this pagan city. There are many theories about the "lecture hall of Tyrannus." Was it owned by a private man called Tyrannus who was sympathetic to the Gospel and given to or leased by Paul? Was it a public building open to orators and philosophers of all persuasions? A notation in the margin of the *Codex Bezae,* a very early 5th century manuscript containing parts of the New Testament including the book of Acts, says Paul lectured daily from 11 o'clock in the morning until 4 o'clock in the afternoon in that school. We will never know for sure how Paul got access to this facility nor will we ever know for sure whether the School was owned by the city or an individual. What is sure is that Paul "had discussions daily in the lecture hall of Tyrannus. This went on for two years, so that all the Jews and Greeks who lived in the province of Asia heard the word of the Lord." (Acts 19:9,10) Those two years of daily lectures and discussions in the port city of Ephesus were Paul's most fruitful years of ministry because "all the Jews and Greeks in the province of Asia heard (either personally or by word of mouth) the word of the Lord."

After many years of lectures, miracles, renunciations of idols and conversions, Paul was expelled from Ephesus by the silversmiths who made their living making idols of Diana, their Queen of Heaven who was also called "the queen bee." Her priests were "her drones" and the priestesses were temple prostitutes, her "worker bees." Paul had been so successful spreading the Gospel of Jesus the Christ that few were buying their silver idols. (Acts 19:23-20:1) But Pastor Paul's years in Ephesus (c. 54-57) firmly established that church. It became home to the Apostle John and perhaps to Mary, the mother of Jesus, who was under the care of John (John 19:26, 27). Ephesus continued to flourish as a center of Christianity for over 600 years.

After his expulsion from the city, Paul would never see Ephesus again, but on his way from Greece to Jerusalem, he asked the Ephesian elders to meet him for a final farewell in Miletus, a port city on the Aegean about 50 miles from Ephesus:

"...I know that none of you among whom I have gone about preaching the kingdom will ever see me again....Keep watch over yourselves and all the flock of which the Holy Spirit has made you overseers. Be shepherds of the church of God, which he bought with his own blood....Now I commit you to God and to the word of his grace, which can build you up and give you an inheritance among all those who are sanctified.... When he had said this, he knelt down with all of them and prayed. They all wept as they embraced him and kissed him. What grieved them most was his statement that they would never see his face again. Then they accompanied him to the ship. After we had torn ourselves away from them we put out to sea." Acts 20:25-21:1

After Paul left the Ephesian elders on the shores of Miletus, he would testify to the faith before the whole Sanhedrin in Jerusalem, before two Roman governors of Palestine, before King Agrippa II, before Publius, the chief Roman official of Malta, and before the ultimate tribunal in Rome who sentenced him to death in c. 64-67. Paul, more than any other recorded 1st century Christian, began the work of chipping away at the stony heart of paganism and of rebuilding the world in the image and likeness of his God and Savior.

By c. 70 AD, word of the risen Messiah had been taken to India by the Apostles Thomas and Nathaniel; had been taken to Africa by the Ethiopian eunuch, John Mark and others; had been proclaimed throughout the Middle East by the Jews; had been pleaded all over Europe after Paul's travels; had been accepted even in the British Isles according to the legends of Joseph of Arimathea's travels. As Paul wrote in c. 62 AD, "This is the gospel that you heard and that has been proclaimed to every creature under heaven." Colossians 1:23

As a result of Pentecost and early evangelism, Christianity had circumnavigated the entire connected world in less than 40 years. The "people of God" were no longer just the Jews, nor were they defined by national and ethnic boundaries. By 70 AD the people of God were a worldwide potpourri blended and united by their belief in the resurrection and redeeming power of a Jewish carpenter from Nazareth. The petrified heart of paganism was beginning to dissolve like rock salt in water.

XVII.

"(Rome's) primeval state, such as she might appear in a remote age…has been delineated by the fancy of Virgil. This Tarpeian rock was then a savage and solitary thicket: in the time of (Virgil), it was crowned with the golden roofs of a temple; the temple is overthrown, the gold has been pillaged, the wheel of fortune has accomplished her revolution, and the sacred ground is again disfigured with thorns and brambles. The hill of the Capitol, on which we sit, was formerly the head of the Roman empire, the citadel of the earth, the terror of kings, illustrated by the footsteps of so many triumphs, enriched by the spoils and tributes of so many nations. This spectacle of the world, how is it fallen! How changed! How defaced! The path of victory is obliterated by vines, and the benches of the senators are concealed by a dunghill. Cast your eyes on the Palatine hill, and seek among the shapeless and enormous fragments, the marble theater, the obelisks, the colossal statues, the porticoes of Nero's palace; survey the other hills of the city, the vacant space is interrupted only by ruins and gardens. The Forum of the Roman people, where they assembled to enact their laws and elect their magistrates, is now enclosed for the cultivation of pot-herbs, or thrown open for the reception of swine and buffaloes. The public and private edifices, that were founded for eternity, lie prostrate, naked, and broken like the limbs of a mighty giant; and the ruin is the more visible, from the stupendous relics that have survived the injuries of time and fortune." Poggio Bracciolini (1380-1459), *On The Vagaries Of Fortune's Wheel 1*

Poggio, as he is known, was an Italian historian who lived in the days of the early Renaissance. On one of his many travels, he sat with a friend on Capitoline Hill overlooking the ruins of Rome and penned the above reminiscences and observations on the vagaries of the wheel of fortune in the lives of civilizations. As Poggio observed 600 years ago, the rock and marble structures of Rome have outlasted both time and the men who designed and built them. Like the pyramids, the statues at Abu Simbel, the circle at Stonehenge, the mute memorials on Easter Island, it is the mass, the sheer weight and might of the rocky elements of nature, that attest to long ago human existence and hints, as through a glass darkly, at their lives and their character.

The belief in a cosmic wheel of destiny for civilizations is found in ancient as well as modern writings. As individuals are born, mature and die, so civilizations rise, crest and fall. Rome, the last in the cycle of ancient empires in the West, was the best of the pagan breed. At its apex, it embodied and combined most perfectly in its gods and goddesses man's unregenerate demiurges with man's innate capacity for conquest and structure. If Jerusalem nursed two of the mightiest spiritual empires ever known on earth, Rome fathered the mightiest secular empire ever known.

Rome's fall began in 45 BC when Julius Caesar had himself declared "dictator for life." His presumption was quickly followed by his assassination in 44 BC. When the dust of the ensuing civil war settled 17 years later, Caesar's grandnephew Augustus, son of Caesar's niece and adopted son of Julius, ironically became "dictator for life" of Rome. He declared Julius Caesar "divine" and was himself declared a god. The idea of a divine ruler, a man as god, had been broached. Each consecutive Caesar was declared a god. The Olympian deities had an earthly equal.

The pagan world has always known that this world, the universe and man were not created by man. They have always known that the creator of all was "other" than man. According to the Bible, monotheism, the worship of one God Who is spirit, deteriorated into polytheism, the worship of many gods who are physical. Stephen Langdon (1876-1937), the American-born Professor of Assyriology at Oxford University, found cuneiform tablets in Iraq while digging at Kish, one of the world's oldest cities, that indicated the original god of the Babylonians was a sky god from whom all their other gods had descended. Langdon wrote: "In my opinion, the history of the oldest religion is a rapid decline from monotheism to extreme polytheism and wide-spread belief in evil spirits. It is in a very true sense the history of the fall of man." The monotheism to polytheism question will always be debated in academic circles, but what is not debatable is man's innate longing to worship a creator god.

For thousands of years, the pagan world has fashioned gods out of wood, stone and, often, stubble. Man wants, needs to worship a concrete reality made of matter. At the height of Western paganism under the Roman Empire came the apotheosis---"man is god." God was not "other." God was "man." The logical culmination of pagan worship, "man is god," had finally arrived in their Caesar and was universally accepted across the Roman Empire.

Rome's pantheon of deities were self-indulgent, capricious, petty and self-absorbed. The Caesars mirrored them and the Romans of the Empire Period reflected in their behaviors and their desires both their celestial gods and their human god. Had a time-traveler from the West in the 21st century been able to observe the everyday life of Romans in the first centuries of the Christian Era, he or she would, even in the days of our own decline, have been shocked at the coarse and heedless treatment of humans and the lack of, to permit the word, morals and its correlatives---guilt and shame.

The Greeks in their mythology made a stab at remorse with the Eumenides, the Furies, who were three sisters created when the god Chronos castrated his father Uranus and his blood splattered the earth. Called the goddesses of revenge, the Furies are depicted as old crones with snakes for hair, smelling of dried blood and barking like dogs. *Eumenides* in Greek means "kindly ones." It is sure the kindly name for these Furies was an attempt to keep them at a distance. These blood-spewing celestial avengers pursued those who had murdered a relative until the person went insane or died. Little is known of these Furies in ancient literature except in Aeschylus' play *The Eumenides* when the curse on the ill-fated House of Atreus is finally exacted and expunged. The creation of the Furies is the closest the pagan world ever came to a consciousness of guilt in the Biblical sense. They knew it was wrong to kill a member of your family. Pagans knew the nuances of the inevitable and the ironic. They understood taboo and anathema.

The gods and goddesses of the pagan world required rote outward acts of animal and human sacrifices and complicated rituals in order to curry their favor or pacify their quixotic behavior. The essence of pagan religion is what the Romans called *do ut des*, "I give that you may give." It was built on reciprocity between man and god. Man gave the god or gods something and the god or gods gave him back something. The pagan did not have to think about righteousness or the integrity of his thoughts, his words or his deeds. There were no injunctions in those areas, no encouragements or commandments directed inward, only outward acts and practices.

The Christian God was just the opposite. He directed all actions, words and deeds inward to the heart and mind: ""The kingdom of God does not come with your careful observation, nor will people say, 'Here it is' or 'there it is,' because the kingdom of God is within you." (Luke 17:20, 21) The Christian God bid His followers to think and to dwell on only good thoughts: "Finally, brothers whatever is true, whatever is noble, whatever is right, whatever is pure, whatever is lovely, whatever is admirable---if anything is excellent or praiseworthy---think about such things." (Philippians 4:8) The Christian God knew that most of man's life is lived internally, lived inside himself. Man lives inside out and not outside in. That was the reason Jesus said when talking about prohibited foods, "It is not what goes into a man's mouth that defiles him, but what comes out of him." (KJV Matthew 15:11) The pagan gods recognized only the physical life of man, encouraged only outward acts.

The Christian's King Jesus required different minds and hearts than existed at that time. In His Sermon on the Mount, He said revolutionary things: He said a person was blessed if she/he was "poor in spirit" or "was mourning" or was "meek, docile" or "persecuted because of righteousness." (Matthew 5:3-10) He pronounced judgment on inward feelings as well as outward idle words and actions:

"You have heard that it was said to the people long ago (in the Ten Commandments), Do not murder, and anyone who murders will be subject to judgment. But I tell you that anyone who is angry with his brother will be subject to judgment. Again, anyone who says to his brother 'Raca' (Hebrew word of contempt) is answerable to the Sanhedrin. But anyone who says, 'You fool!' will be in danger of the fires of hell." Matthew 5:21, 22

Jesus intimidated when He said: "You have heard that it was said (in the Ten Commandments), 'Do not commit adultery.' But I tell you that anyone who looks at a woman lustfully has already committed adultery with her in his heart." (Matthew 5:27, 28) He commanded His followers: "Do not resist an evil person. If someone strikes you on the right cheek, turn to him the other also. And if someone wants to sue you and take your tunic, let him have your cloak as well." Matthew 5:39, 40

Most revolutionary to the pagan world of tribes and loyalties was Jesus' command to "Love your enemies:" "You have heard that it was said, 'Love your neighbor and hate your enemy.' But I tell you: Love your enemies and pray for those who persecute you, that you may be sons of your Father in heaven....If you love those who love you, what reward will you get?...And if you greet only your brothers, what are you doing more than others? Do not even pagans do that? Be perfect, therefore, as your heavenly Father is perfect." Matthew 5:43, 46-48

It was clear from the counter-cultural and counter-intuitive New Testament teachings that the Christian's God was out to change the minds and hearts of the world. The perfection of behavior He demanded could only be achieved by a new mental and spiritual way of looking at man and his world, a conversion, by an overhaul, a serious cleansing of the intellectual, cultural, political and moral mind and heart, the whole zeitgeist of paganism.

Under paganism, religion was something man did for the gods. The Christian message proclaimed what God had done for man. Man was so puny, so self-full and so sin-full that there was nothing he could give to or do for his Creator. God, the Christians said, had showered something called "grace" on man. Christian "grace" was "unearned, unmerited mercy." They said the one and only God had sent His Son, a man named Jesus, to die a bloody death on a cross in Judea, to be the final sacrifice for the sin-full-ness of man. One of their Scriptures written in c. 60-69 said: "He did not enter by means of the blood of goats and calves; but he entered the Most Holy Place once and for all by his own blood, having obtained eternal redemption." (Hebrews 9:12) Christians claimed this long-predicted Sin-Bearer/Messiah had resurrected from the dead, validating all He had said about Himself and all the ancient Scriptures had written of Him.

The consciousness of individual sin and the sense of shame and guilt, so long repressed by paganism, cracked out of its stony cocoon in the 1st century AD. Men, women and children everywhere were embracing this Savior, repenting of their sins, being baptized, were telling others about Him and were, as it turned out, willing to die for Him. Jesus had predicted that after He was gone, the world would be convicted of individual sin:

"I tell you the truth: It is for your good that I am going away. Unless I go away, the Counselor (Holy Spirit) will not come to you; but if I go, I will send him to you. When he comes, he will convict the world of guilt in regard to sin and righteousness and judgment." John 16:7,8

Rome's rulers intuited, and they were dead-right, that this message, this Redeemer, this so-called Sin-Bearer, this man born at just the right time would eventually erode and assume the Roman Empire if something was not done.

Rome, for all its might and majesty, had no resources to combat Christianity. It was powerless against ideas embodied in a man who had no earthly kingdom to defend or boundaries to invade. Rome's wealth could not bribe believers nor could her Caesar god command them. When he commanded them to worship him, they refused and said there is only one God. But where was their one God? Caesar could not see or touch Him. Only one God? Corporate worship and collective belief in the gods whose statues were right there in the temples for all to see had always united Romans to the State. Christians must be atheists with only one God who, by the way, could not be seen. Caesar said he would kill them if they did not acknowledge him as a god. They still refused and he killed them. They died by the droves, singing hymns, forgiving their murderers, rejoicing that they could partake of their God's sufferings and proclaiming they would live forever with their God. Live after the body was dead? Everyone knew that when you died, the candle went out and that was it—nonentity. Christians were deluded into believing there was something in each man that would never die, something that was eternal, something they called "spirit." It was hard to stamp out a people who believed they would survive death and whose God was invisible. Caesars had never had to deal with this type of problem involving intangibles and abstractions.

Christians were, in addition, unpatriotic because they had no allegiance to the Roman State. Patriotism was the sine qua non for Romans. The State was their mother, their father, their pride and their god. But Roman citizenship was unimportant to Christians because their citizenship was in their heaven. They were not a tribe or a nationality that could be rounded up and destroyed or neutered. They were a multi-ethnic, multi-cultural, supranational people sprinkled all over Caesar's world who were composed of all different languages and traditions, all different colors of skin, all races and tribes who were united by their "faith" which was a non-concrete, immaterial belief, a belief in the resurrection of an obscure Galilean. They were definitely a threat, a peculiar threat, and Rome always killed threats.

Christianity answered age-old, perplexing questions, questions of ontology---where did I come from? Questions of eschatology---what's going to happen when I die? The fact of consciousness and the objectivity of matter have always provoked metaphysical questions. The Judeo-Christian Scriptures declared fiatly that there was a Creator, only one Creator God, who had fashioned each individual and all matter on earth and in the universe. He was the Alpha of creation. After a person died, the candle did not go out. The essence of you would live on in a spiritual body. You were created and you would not be destroyed. The new faith declared that the universe and you were not a cosmic accident or joke.

Christians were spreading and teaching ideas, new ideas that would, if unchecked, subvert the State. Everywhere they went the Christians, like salt shakers, were sprinkling the word of the risen Christ and the words of His Gospel (Old English *godspel* from *god* meaning "good" and *spel* meaning "story"). Parallel with and underneath the juggernaut of Rome the Good Story was subtly introducing the world to a new and pleasing flavor. Nevertheless, it was preposterous to believe as Christians did that there is no difference between a Roman and a Barbarian or between a man and a woman or between a slave and his master. Everyone had always known, in fact it was a law of Nature, that a Roman, a man and a slave master were superior to a Barbarian and a woman and a slave. And who could ever believe the absurd idea that a slave was freed the minute he accepted their Christ? Yes, the Christians answered that question saying the slave was free inside. They constantly talked all that inside/mind/spirit/faith nonsense. Christians said their God created and loved everyone in the world and allegiance should only be given to their King Jesus. They were saboteurs of all local and national gods and were bent on undermining the authority of the Roman State.

In his only surviving work *Octavius*, the early Christian apologist Felix Minucius (c. 160-250) records an extensive exposition of the pagan point of view regarding Christians. *Octavius* is clearly intended to be heard and read by Romans since there is in this rhetorical work a prolonged debate between two historical people: the early 2nd century Caecilius Natalis of Cirta (in Algeria) who argues for paganism against Christianity and his contemporary Octavius Januarius of Saldae (in Algeria) who advocates Christianity over paganism. Minucius was the judge. Probably, though not certainly, because he was a converted Christian, Minucius chose the Christian argument as the winner of the debate and has the pagan Caecilius acquiesce to Christian argument if not to the Christian viewpoint. It is a fascinating colloquy between two intelligent men. Some think they actually had this debate and Minucius captured it in *Octavius*. The pagan Caecilius' depictions of Christian practices and assessments of the Christian God reflect, no doubt, what was heard and believed about Christianity by dedicated pagans in the 2nd century. Caecilius argues:

"...since the consent of all nations concerning the existence of the immortal gods remains established, although their nature or their origin remains uncertain, I suffer nobody swelling with such boldness and with I know not what irreligious wisdom, who would strive to undermine or weaken this religion, so ancient, so useful, so wholesome....why is it not a thing to be lamented that men...of a reprobate, unlawful and desperate faction should rage against (our) gods? (Men) who, having gathered together from the lowest dregs of society the more unskilled and women, credulous and, by the facility of their sex, yielding, establish a herd of profane conspiracy (Christianity) which is leagued together by nightly meetings and solemn fasts and inhuman meats---not by a sacred rite, but by that which requires expiation---a people who skulk and shun the light, silent in public but garrulous in corners. (Christians) despise the temples as dead-houses; they reject the gods; they laugh at sacred things....half naked themselves, they despise honors and purple robes. Oh, wondrous folly and incredible audacity! They despise present torments....they do not fear to die for the present; so does a deceitful hope soothe their fear with the solace of revival....these abominable shrines of an impious assembly are maturing themselves throughout the whole world. Assuredly this confederacy ought to be rooted out and execrated. They know one another by secret marks and insignia and they love one another almost before they know one another. Everywhere also there is mingled among them a certain religion of lust, and they call one another promiscuously brothers and sisters....I hear that they adore the head of an ass, that basest of creatures....Some say that they worship the virilia (male sex organs) of their pontiff and priest and adore the nature, as it were, of their common parent (Jesus). I know not whether these things are false....(some) explain their ceremonies by reference to a man (Jesus) punished by extreme suffering for his wickedness and to the deadly wood of the cross, appropriate and fitting altars for reprobate and wicked men, let them worship what they deserve. Now the story about the initiation of young novices is as much to be detested as it it is well known. An infant covered over with grain that it may receive the unwary, is placed before him who is to be stained with their rites; this infant is slain by the young pupil who has been urged on as if to harmless blows on the surface of the meal, with dark and secret wounds. Thirstily---O horror!---they lick up its blood; eagerly they divide its limbs. By this victim they are pledged together; with this consciousness of wickedness they are covenanted to mutual silence. Such secret rites as these are more foul than any sacrileges....I purposely pass over many things for those I have mentioned are already too many; and that all these, or the greater part of them, are true, the obscurity of their vile religion declares.... Why have they no altars, no temples, no acknowledged images?.... whence or who is he, or where is their one God, solitary, desolate, whom no free people, no kingdoms and not even Roman superstition, has known? The lonely and miserable nationality of the Jews worshipped one God, and one peculiar to itself....he who is the Christian's God, whom they can neither show nor behold, inquires diligently into the character of all, the acts of all and into their words and secret thoughts; he runs about everywhere and is everywhere present; they make him out to be troublesome, restless, even shamelessly inquisitive, since he is present at everything that is done, wanders in and out in all places, although, being occupied with the whole, he cannot give attention to particulars, nor can he be sufficient for the whole while he is busied with particulars....(they believe in) old women's fables; they say that they will rise again after death...and with I know not what confidence, they believe by turns in one another's lies....Deceived...they promise to themselves, as being good, a blessed and perpetual life after their death; to others, as being unrighteous, eternal punishment. Many things occur to me to say in addition, if the limits of my discourse did not hasten me." *Octavius 8-11*

From Minicius one can understand the normal heathen's suspicions of Christians. The half-truths, lies and misinterpretations of Christian doctrines and practices were rightly unsettling to the outside pagan world. Christianity's true doctrines, practices and their God Who was spirit and not material were totally other, foreign to the cement and stone and concrete realities where Rome lived and had her being.

The collective worship of wooden or stone statues of gods and goddesses united people to each other and to the State. Romans, tribes, nationalities in the ancient world were constructed around and drew their cohesion from the collective, the State, the tribe. Judeo-Christian beliefs in individual liberties and proclivities were not even imagined. All was subordinated to the community. Only the State and its well-being, its growth and its survival mattered.

Rome had always held the presentiment that she was special and would last forever. As Ovid said at the end of Augustus' reign: "The land of other nations has a fixed boundary, but the space of Rome is the space of the world." *Fasti 2* Emperor Hadrian (76-138), who lived in the time of the Apostle John and his disciple Polycarp, struck a gold coin depicting Rome as a seated woman holding in one hand the sun and in the other the moon, both symbols of eternity. Above her head is the legend *Roma Aeterna* ("Rome Eternal"). Romans were convinced that Rome was indestructible. How dare these revolutionary Christians presume another kingdom and corrupt the Roman State with their newfangled God and their upstart ideas.

No matter what Rome did or did not do over the first three centuries of the Christian Era, she could not eradicate Christianity. From its inception Rome had lived in the material, the empirical. Every thing was seen as and subject to the outside world of the five senses. She had even borrowed her gods, her governing structure, her ideas and her architecture from Greece and had no ability to combat metaphysical theses or realities and no skills or inclinations to philosophically engage the tight theology of both the Old and the New Testaments and no armor against the non-material faith of the Christians. Starting in the early 100's, Greek and Latin Christian apologists barraged the Caesars with learned, well-wrought theses entreating the case for Christianity and pleading that the persecutions stop.

Aristides, a 2nd century intellectual who lived in Athens, addressed the first extant *Apologia* (Defense) of Christianity to Emperor Hadrian in c. 126. Because of Emperor Hadrian's initiation into the Eleusinian

Mysteries in Athens in 124, there had been an outbreak of Christian persecution by proud pagans. Aristides' Apology is a brief, elevated response to this persecution followed by a calm argument appealing to the righteous behavior of Christians and the inherent reasonableness of Christian tenets opposed to the illogical beliefs and corrupt practices of the major religions of his day.

Hadrian (76-138) was a practical man not given to subjects detailing doctrines and philosophies. He is best known for Hadrian's Wall, a 73 miles long stonewall in northern England built to separate Romans from Barbarians. In 136, Hadrian quashed the last gasp of the Jewish state in the Bar Kokhba rebellion, demolished the remains of Jerusalem and rebuilt the city as Aelia Capitolina. He was a Roman demolisher and builder. He is, also, remembered for his homosexual relationship with one of his Greek slaves, Antinous, who drowned in the Nile on a visit to Egypt. Hadrian was so distraught he deified Antinous, made people worship him as a god, fashioned statues of him, built temples dedicated to him, struck coins with his head on them, built the city of Antinopolis in his honor and tried, unsuccessfully, to name a constellation after him. The Senate declined that proposal. It was to a jaded, battle-tested emperor that the apologist Aristides appealed:

"To the all-powerful Caesar Titus Hadrianus Antoninus, venerable and merciful, from Marcianus Aristides, an Athenian philosopher…. The Christians…trace the beginning of their religion from Jesus the Messiah; and he is named the Son of God Most High. And it is said that God came down from heaven, and from a Hebrew virgin assumed and clothed himself with flesh; and the Son of God lived in a daughter of man. This is taught in the gospel, as it is called, which a short time was preached among them; and you (Hadrian) also if you will read (the Gospel), may perceive the power which belongs to it. This Jesus, then, was born of the race of the Hebrews; and he had twelve disciples….But he himself was pierced by the Jews, and he died and was buried; and they say that after three days he rose and ascended to heaven. Thereupon these twelve disciples went forth throughout the known parts of the world, and kept showing his greatness with all modesty and uprightness.

And hence also those of the present day who believe that preaching are called Christians, and they are become famous." *Apology 2*

Aristides mentions that Christians had become "famous" in the Empire less than 100 years after the resurrection of Jesus.

Shortly after Aristides wrote his *Apology*, the *Epistle of Mathetes to Diognetus* was written in c. 150 AD. Both the writer Mathetes meaning "disciple" and the recipient Diognetus are unknown. The *Epistle of Mathetes to Diognetus* is considered by J. B. Lightfoot (1828-1889) to be one of the earliest and "noblest of early Christian writings." The Disciple explains to his non-believer friend Diognetus exactly who and what Christians are:

"For Christians are not distinguished from the rest of mankind either in locality or in speech or in customs. For they dwell not somewhere in cities of their own, neither do they use some different language, nor practice an extraordinary kind of life. Nor again do they possess any invention discovered by any intelligence or study of ingenious men, nor are they masters of any human dogmas as some are....They dwell in their own countries, but only as sojourners; they bear their share in all things as citizens, and they endure all hardships as strangers. Every foreign country is a fatherland to them and every fatherland is foreign. They marry like all other men and they beget children, but they do not cast away their offspring. They have their meals in common, but not their wives. They find themselves in the flesh and yet they live not after the flesh. Their existence is on earth, but their citizenship is in heaven....they are put to death and yet they are endued with life. They are in beggary and yet they make many rich....They are reviled and they bless; they are insulted and they respect. Doing good they are punished as evil-doers; being punished they rejoice as if they were thereby quickened by life." *Epistle of Mathetes to Diognetus 5*

This is a quite beautiful and gentle apologetic for the faith. Philip Schaff (1819-1893), a contemporary of J. B. Lightfoot, ranks it "with the great unknown authors of Job and Hebrews, who are known only to

God." *History of the Christian Church 2.699-700* These early apologists not only affirm and defend Apostolic beliefs, but they attest to the rapid population of the Roman world by Christians.

Writing about the same time, Tertullian says: "(All countries) cry aloud that the state is besieged by Christians, that even in the country districts, in the walled villages, in the islands, you will find Christians. (Pagans) mourn as for a loss that all, without distinction of sex, age, circumstances or even position are deserting to Christ's name." *Apology 1*

With the expansion of the seditious Christians, Rome could only do what it always did when threatened---go to war against the threat. Christian apologists seemed at times to be losing the battle, but their constant and consistent apologies inevitably introduced a subset of new ideas into the Roman vocabulary.

The Church was exponentially expanding in the 2nd century and the apologists were forced to wage an intellectual war on two fronts. They had to defend the integrity of the Scriptures and to rebuke heresies like Montanism, Docetism and Gnosticism that were creeping inside the Church. On another front they had to pacify local and Imperial persecutions outside the Church. Tertullian in *Apologeticus 47,* addressing Roman magistrates, argues that Christians are not strange and unnatural people, but are in many ways like "normal" Romans:

"...we live with you, eat with you, wear the same clothes, follow the same way of living and have the same necessities of life. We remember to give thanks to God, our Lord and Creator, and do not refuse any fruit of his work. There is no doubt that we make use of things with moderation and not in an evil or unrestrained way. We live together with you and often attend the forum, the market place, the baths, the shops and workshops, the stables, taking part in all activities. We also are at sea together with you, we serve in the army, we till the land, we carry on trade, we exchange goods and put on sale...the fruits of our work....And finally, you will never find any Christian in prison, unless he be there for religious reasons. We have learned from God to live honest lives."

Tertullian testifies to the ubiquity and normalcy of Christians in the

2nd century. He is called the "Father of Western Theology" because he not only formed much of Christianity's dogma but because all his many works jump with the vitality of a man who was converted late in life and raced to put his "born-again" enthusiasm into written parchments. He who said "Christians are made, not born" (*Apologeticus 18*) crafted seminal Christian writings that are still studied and critiqued almost 2,000 years later.

Justin Martyr (103-165) was one of the most gifted intellectual advocates of his time. He was born a pagan in Palestine. From his youth Justin had sought truth and spent his early years among the Peripatetics, the Pythagoreans and the Platonists. When he went with friends to the amphitheaters and saw:

"Christians slandered, and saw them fearless of death and of all other things which are counted fearful, (I) perceived that it was impossible that they could be living in wickedness and pleasure (a common Roman accusation). For what sensual or intemperate man or one who counts it good to feast on human flesh (an early charge against them relating to transubstantial Communion) could welcome death that he might be deprived of his enjoyments, and would not rather continue always the present life and attempt to escape the observation of the rulers; and much less would such a man denounce himself when the consequence would be death?" *Second Apology 12*

The heroic ways that Christians died in the arenas made an impression on young Justin as it did on many pagans. It was while he was studying Plato in Ephesus that Justin met an old man on a deserted beach who opened up to him the Old Testament prophecies of the coming Messiah and explained to him how Jesus had fulfilled all of them. Justin was converted then and there: "Straightway a flame was kindled in my soul and a love of the prophets and those who are friends of Christ possessed me." *Dialogue with Trypho 8*

When he found the truth in Christianity, Justin immediately began to exercise his well-honed rhetorical skills for the defense of the faith. Many of his writings have been lost, but two Apologies and *The Dialogue with Trypho* have been preserved. His *First Apology*, written when he was 47 in c. 150 AD, was addressed to Hadrian's adopted son and heir the 64-year-old Antoninus. Emperor Antoninus Pius, like Hadrian his adoptive father, did not initiate an Imperial persecution, but many Christians were killed during his reign, notably Polycarp the disciple of John the Apostle. Justin took the death of Polycarp and other Christians in Smyrna and Asia as an opportunity to address the continuing number of Christian deaths: "To the Emperor Titus Aelius Adrianus Antoninus Pius Augustus Caesar, and to his son Verissimus the Philosopher, and to Lucius the Philosopher, the natural son of Caesar and the adopted son of Pius, a lover of learning, and to the sacred Senate with the whole People of the Romans." *First Apology 1* It is likely, but not inevitable, that Justin's *Apology* was circulated in the Roman Senate. It should not go unnoticed that Justin, who had founded a school for philosophers in Ephesus and in Rome and who always wore his philosopher's robe in public, was making a peer on peer, philosopher to philosopher appeal to Antoninus' 29-year-old adopted son Verissimus aka Marcus Aurelius the Philosopher and to his other adopted son, the 20-year-old Lucius the Philosopher, both of whom would be co-emperors when Antoninus died 11 years later.

It was in this *First Apology* that Justin issued his famous challenge to the Roman State: "You, you can kill us, but you cannot hurt us." The killing of Christians, in fact, did not hurt the Church. Each death, each round of deaths not only strengthened Christian resolve, but also garnered more pagan converts as they saw how Christians died praying for their enemies and exhibiting an obvious superiority to revenge and hate that was enigmatic and attractive to pagans: "Though beheaded and crucified and thrown to wild beasts and chains and fire and all other kinds of torture, we do not give up our confession, but the more such things happen, the more do others in larger numbers become faithful." *Dialogue With Trypho 10*

Justin's task in his *First Apology* was to attempt to stop the killing of Christians by appealing philosophically to a common link between Hellenist writers and Christian thinkers. He spent time in both of his Apologies on the concept of the Greek word *logos* meaning "word" that

John mentions in the beginning of his Gospel: "In the beginning was the Word and the Word was with God and the Word was God. He was with God in the beginning. Through him all things were made; without him nothing was made that has been made." (John 1:1-3) King David, way back in c. 1000 BC had, like John, denoted the Word, the Logos as the means of creation:

"By the word of the Lord were the heavens made, their starry host by the breath of his nostrils....For he spoke and it came to be; he commanded and it stood firm." Psalm 33:6,9

Heraclitus in the 6th century BC was the first to enunciate philosophically the concept of Logos that he defined as the principle of reason and associated it with fire. Plato (c. 428–c. 348 BC) identified the Logos as that which is formed in the mind and expressed through the mouth. Philo (20 BC-50 AD), a devout Jewish philosopher from Alexandria, elevated Plato's mental forms, the Logos, into the eternal, ineffable thoughts of God. Justin links pagan philosophers with John's quote and announces Christ as the embodiment of Logos. Emperor Antoninus may not have understood Justin's emphasis on the Logos, but the two young philosophers, schooled in Platonic and Greek thought, surely did. Throughout Justin's writings he mentions Homer, Euripides, Menander, Xenophon and especially Plato not only because he knew them so well, but because he was trying to demonstrate that Christianity was not some exotic, foreign religion totally unrelated to Hellenistic thinking. He spends time on the Old Testament prophecies of the coming Messiah and ties them precisely and inevitably to Jesus of Nazareth. He explains why Christians will not worship idols; why Christ is the Incarnate Word; why Christians die for Christ; what Christians believe and what they do in worship and why they are atheists: "We confess we are atheists so far as gods of this wickedness and impiety are concerned, but not with respect to the most true God." *First Apology 6*

Justin pleads the changed, transformed-by-the-Spirit life as proof of the truth of Christianity:

"We who formerly delighted in fornication now strive for purity. We who used magical arts, have dedicated ourselves to the good and eternal God. We who loved the acquisition of wealth more than all else, now bring what we have into a common stock and give to every one in need. We who hated and destroyed one another, and on account of their different manners would not receive into our houses men of a different tribe, now, since the coming of Christ, live familiarly with them. We pray for our enemies, we endeavor to persuade those who hate us unjustly to live conforming to the beautiful precepts of Christ, to the end that they may become partakers with us of the same joyful hope of a reward from God, the Ruler of all." *First Apology 14*

Justin was the first to defend the faith with such conviction, erudition and daring.

Found attached to a copy of Justin's *First Apology* was a letter written in 174 by then Emperor Marcus Aurelius who had heard Justin's *Apology* in 150. Aurelius recounts an incident that occurred in the old Austrian city of Carnuntum where the Emperor lived from 172-175 while fighting the Marcommani and Quadi, German tribes. The letter, *Epistle To The Roman Senate*, recounts what happened when he was imperiled, stranded without his Legions and almost forced to surrender because he and his men had no water:

"...in consequence of the circumstance that I was surrounded by the enemy....being shut up in Carrnuntum with 74 cohorts nine miles away. And the enemy being at hand, the scouts pointed out to us and our general Pompeianus showed us that there was close on us a mass of a mixed multitude of 977,000 men, which indeed we saw; and I was shut up by this vast host, having with me only a battalion composed of the first, tenth, double and marine legions. Having then examined my own position, and my host, with respect to the vast mass of barbarians and of the enemy, I quickly betook myself to prayer to the gods of my country. But being disregarded by them, I summoned those who among us go by the name of Christians. And having made inquiry (in his army), I discovered a great number and vast host of (Christians) and I raged against them, which was by no means becoming; for afterwards I learned their power. Wherefore they began the battle, not by preparing weapons, nor arms, nor bugles; for such preparation is hateful to them, on account of the God they bear about in their conscience. Therefore it is probable that those whom we suppose to be atheists have God as their ruling power entrenched in their conscience. For having cast themselves on the ground, they prayed not only for me, but also for the whole army as it stood, that they might be delivered from the present thirst and famine. For during five days we had got no water, because there was none; for we were in the heart of Germany, and in the enemy's territory. And simultaneously with their casting themselves on the ground and praying to God---a God of whom I am ignorant---water poured from heaven upon us refreshingly cool, but upon the enemies of Rome a withering hail. And immediately we recognized the presence of God following on the prayer---a God unconquerable and indestructible. Founding upon this, then, let us pardon such as are Christians, lest they pray for and obtain such a weapon against ourselves.....But if any one be found laying to the charge of a Christian that he is a Christian, and accused of nothing else than only this, that he is a Christian.... he who accuses him must be burned alive. And I further desire that he who is entrusted with the government of the province shall not compel the Christian, who confesses and certifies such a matter, to retract.... And I command that this my edict to be published in the Forum of Trajan (area in Rome where public business was conducted)...The prefect Vitrasius Pollio will see that it be transmitted to all the provinces round about."

Mention has been made of the early receptivity of Roman soldiers to the message of Christianity and of the Theban Legion composed of all Christians. Marcus Aurelius was surprised to find such a host of Christians in his own army there in Carnuntum.

Aurelius' *Epistle to the Roman Senate* is not the only place in ancient literature where his story of miraculous rain is told. Christian and pagan writers were fascinated by such an unusual tale, especially because it was told by an Emperor. Tertullian tells it in his *Apology 5*; Eusebius recounts it in his *Church History 5.5*; Orosius in *Seven Books Of History Against The Pagans 7.15*; Gregory of Nyssa in *Oration*; Cassius Dio in *Roman History 71.8*. The weight of so much retelling of the narrative by Christian and pagan writers certainly points to the historicity of an unusual, miraculous rain event as a result of Christian prayer witnessed by Marcus Aurelius at Carnuntum. It was so impressive to Aurelius that he had the miraculous storm event depicted on his column that is still standing in the Piazza Colonna in Rome. Some pagan writers attribute the miracle to Jupiter or an Egyptian god.

If one certifies Aurelius' *Epistle* as true, it is ironic that this Philosopher King presided over one of the bloodiest persecutions of Christians---the mass murders in Lyons and Vienne during his reign have been described in Chapter VI of this book. In the fourth year of Aurelius' reign in 165, Justin Martyr who had pleaded the Christian case to the 29-year-old Aurelius was arrested with six of his students, brought before Rusticus, the prefect of Rome and confessed, "I am a Christian." He was commanded to offer sacrifice to the gods and replied, "No right-thinking person falls away from piety to impiety," whereupon he and his students were "scourged and led away to suffer punishment by decapitation according to the laws." Anonymous Eyewitness, *The Acts Of Martyrdom Of St. Justin And Companions*

Perhaps Marcus Aurelius, who had warned in his Stoic *Meditations*, "Take heed not to be transformed into a Caesar, not to be dipped in the purple dye" persecuted Christians because, as most of his admirers argue, he was just following Roman law like a good, dyed-in-the purple Caesar. Or maybe he answered one of his own rhetorical questions: "Is it not strange that ignorance and complaisance are stronger than wisdom?" It is likely Aurelius, a self-described "citizen of the Universe," lived with the same superiority and detachment from earthly matters he displays in his quote: "The Universe is change. Life is an opinion."

Another very poetic *Apology* by Melito, Bishop of Sardis in Turkey, was written to Marcus Aurelius after Justin's death in 165. It has been lost but we have quotes preserved by Eusebius and Tertullian. He explained to Aurelius that Jesus was:

"...born as a son, led forth as a lamb, sacrificed as a sheep, buried as a man, he rose from the dead as a God, for he was by nature God and man. He is all things: he judges and so he is Law; he teaches and so he is Wisdom; he saves and so he is Grace; he begets and so he is Father; he is begotten and so he is Son; he suffers and so he is Sacrifice; he is buried and so he is man; he rises again and so he is God. This is Jesus Christ, to whom belongs glory for all ages....This is he who was made flesh in a virgin, whose bones were not broken upon the tree, who in burial was not resolved into earth, who arose from the dead and raised man from the grave below to the heights of the heavens. This is the lamb that was slain; this is the lamb that was dumb; this is he that was born of Mary; the fair ewe."

The writer of the *Meditations* must have been pleased by the words and phrases of Melito even if he did not believe them. Marcus Aurelius died in 180 while on campaign near the Danube frontier. His 19-year-old son Commodus succeeded him as Emperor. Unlike the philosophic Aurelius, Commodus' entire universe revolved around the physical. Handsome and muscular, he declared himself the god Hercules and often fought naked in the Colosseum. Even the jaded Romans were offended and rumored he was not Aurelius' son but the son of a gladiator by his adulterous mother. Wounded soldiers and Roman citizens who had lost their feet were rounded up and brought into the arena for the evil Commodus to kill or to club to death. On one occasion he slew 100 lions and had statues of himself made as Hercules carrying a club and draped in a lion's skin. He even charged the Roman treasury one million sesterces for each of his appearances as Hercules. In 192 at the age of 31 Commodus was strangled to death by his wrestling partner Narcissus, probably provoked by the Senate. Instead of mourning the god-king, the Roman Senate declared him *damnatio memoriae*. Many Caesars before Commodus had done damnable things, but Commodus was flagrantly public with his offenses. The arena had always been for the worthless to fight and to die for Roman pleasure. For a royal to engage in such carnage highlighted the utter helplessness of victims and made the public uneasy. Roman sensibilities were changing.

The Roman State was changing, too. At the dawn of the 3rd century, her Empire was far-flung. The rising cost of defending and maintaining order on her borders, the incorporation of more and more Barbarians into her army and the welfare given to all the immigrants flooding into her cities from her many client states began to destabilize the economy. With so many extra responsibilities, the Roman State needed money and began to raise taxes precipitously. The number of people eligible for doles of grain and goods had increased exponentially. Marcus Aurelius had added free pork and wine to those on the dole and later Severus would add olive oil. In addition to paying Barbarian chieftains huge bribes to keep them from attacking Rome, the State was spending an increasing amount of money on "bread and circus" to keep the plebeians from rioting. The Roman historian Ammianus Marcellinus in *The History 28.4.28* laments the effects of too much Roman state welfare. He writes that the plebs on the dole:

"…devote their whole life to drink, gambling, brothels, shows and pleasure in general. Their temple, dwelling, meeting-place, in fact the center of all their hopes and desires, is the Circus Maximus. (They swear) that the country will go to the dogs if in some coming race the driver they fancy fails to take a lead from the start, or makes too wide a turn round the post with his unlucky team. Such is the general decay of manners that on the longed-for day of the races, they rush headlong to the course before the first glimmering of dawn as if they would outstrip the competing teams, most of them having passed a sleepless night distracted by their conflicting hopes about the result."

It was at this time of "decay in manners" and of turbulence in the Roman Empire that two formidable Christian theologians and apologists arose in North Africa: Tertullian (160-220) from Carthage and Origen (185-253) from Alexandria. Both were born and lived their lives under periods of Christian persecution. Tertullian converted to Christianity when he was a young man and spent the rest of his life defending the faith against persecutions by the State and attacks by pagan philosophers. He, like the apologists before him, addressed and sent his *Apology* to the emperors of Rome:

"Rulers of the Roman Empire, if, seated for the administration of justice on your lofty tribunal under the gaze of every eye and occupying there all but the highest position in the state, you may not openly inquire into and sift before the world the real truth in regard to the charges made against Christians; if in this case alone you are afraid or ashamed to exercise your authority in making public inquiry with the carefulness which becomes justice; if, finally, the extreme severities inflicted on our people…stand in the way of our being permitted to defend ourselves before you, you cannot surely forbid the Truth to reach your ears by the secret pathway of a noiseless book (this Apology)." *Apology 1*

The early Christian apologists seem to have had a rather naïve belief that the force of their intellects and the cogency of their arguments would surely be recognized by the rulers who ran Rome. Tertullian (who some speculate may have helped with Perpetua's *Diary* and who may have been there on March 7, 203 when Perpetua and her friends were martyred in Carthage) did see the utter intolerance and anti-intellectualism of the Roman State. It was in Tertullian's address to the rulers of Rome that the phrase "religious liberty" first came into Western vocabulary:

"Let one man worship God, another Jupiter; let one lift suppliant hands to the heavens, another to the altar of Fides; let one, if you choose to take this view of it, count in prayer the clouds and another the ceiling panels; let one consecrate his own life to his god and another to a goat. See that you do not give a further ground for the charge of irreligion by taking away *religious liberty* and forbidding free choice of deity so that I may no longer worship according to my inclination, but am compelled to worship against it….It is well that there is a God of all, whose we all are whether we will or no. But with you (Rome) liberty is given to worship any god but the true God, as though He were not rather the God all should worship and to whom all belong." *Apology 24*

In Tertullian's *Apology*, he admitted allegiance to the State and its ideals, to the military and even to the political sphere of the emperors, but he broached for the first time the idea of religious freedom separate from State veneration, of individual religious freedom for each person according to his/her conscience to worship God or a goat or clouds or ceiling panels. Tertullian's historic phrase, "religious liberty," has been the cry of millions over the millennia. In our modern world more than half the people on earth, under penalty of persecution or death, are denied "religious liberty" and are compelled by the State to worship a certain god or are not allowed to worship any god. Even in the West where religious liberty is assumed, it requires constant vigilance and attentiveness by Jews and Christians to negotiate the balance between coercive mandates of the State and explicit doctrines of the Old and New Testaments.

Before the Edict of Milan in 313 giving Christians the religious freedom to worship their God, the brilliant and most gifted of the Early Church Fathers was Origen, a contemporary of Tertullian. In *Contra Celsus (Against Celsus)* he broached the idea of religious freedom in a subtle way. He makes it clear to Rome and his readers that Christianity will not owe its victory to coercion but to the power of truth. He explains how Jesus draws men to Him rather than forces men to Him:

"...this man (Jesus), in addition to his other merits, is an object of admiration both for his wisdom, and for his miracles, and for his powers of government. For he persuaded some to withdraw themselves from their laws and to secede to him, not as a tyrant would do, nor as a robber who arms his followers against men; nor as a rich man, who bestows help upon those who come to him; nor as one of those who confessedly are deserving of censure; but as a teacher of the doctrine regarding the God of all things, and of the worship which belongs to Him, and of all moral precepts which are able to secure the favor of the Supreme God to him who orders his life in conformity therewith." *1.30*

Unlike Tertullian, Origen was raised in a Christian home in Alexandria. In his teens, his father Leonides and many other Alexandrians were imprisoned under the persecutions of Emperor Severus (192-211). The impetuous Origen was ready to follow his father into prison, but his mother hid all his clothes. His father and others were beheaded and had their properties confiscated. The young Origen became a teacher to support his mother and six younger brothers. Over the years his Catechetical School in Alexandria and later his school in Caesarea became renowned for scholarship and attracted many young philosophers, some of whom were martyred. Origen devoted himself to study and self-denial. When he was continually plagued by lust for women, he castrated himself, an act known as an orchiectomy. Eusebius says of this young man's act:

"While Origen was teaching in Alexandria, he did something that gave proof enough of his young and immature mind, but also of his faith and self-control. He took the saying, 'There are those who have made themselves eunuchs for the kingdom of heaven's sake' (Matthew 19:12) in too literal and absurd a sense and he was eager to fulfill the Savior's words and also to forestall any slander on the part of unbelievers for despite his youth, he held forth on religious matters before women as well as men. So he quickly carried out the Savior's words, trying to do so unnoticed by most of his students. But however much he wished it, he could not possibly hide such a deed. Demetrius learned of it later, since he presided over the community there. He was astonished at Origen's rash act." *Church History 6.8*

Origen's youthful and reckless audacity gave way over the years to a mature and disciplined mind. He produced a body of over 6,000 works that laid a firm foundation for Christian theology, apologetics and homiletics. This "Genius Of The Early Church" traveled all over the ancient world and taught and debated with the best pagan minds as their acknowledged superior. One of those minds was an Epicurean Greek philosopher named Celsus who had written the earliest known philosophical attack on Christianity called *A True Discourse*. None of the original book survives, but because Origen wrote his famous rebuttal to it called *Against Celsus* in which he quoted Celsus word for word and then rebutted his ideas, most scholars think we have all of Celsus' original ideas in Origen's book. In reply to one of Celsus' postulations, Origen gave a prescient peek into the future of paganism:

Celsus argues: "If all men were to act like you...the affairs of the earth would fall into the hands of the wildest and most lawless barbarians; and then there would no longer remain among men any of the glory of your religion or of the true wisdom."
Origen replies: "If all do as I do, then it is evident that even the barbarians when they yield obedience to the word of God will become most obedient to the law and most humane. And every form of worship will be destroyed except the religion of Christ which will alone prevail. And indeed it will one day triumph, as its principles take possession of the minds of men more and more every day." *8.68*

Origen, writing in the midst of Christian persecutions in 248 AD, saw the Twilight of the Pagan Gods approaching and the final triumph in the West of the one God. He saw the tired, fin de siecle gods of Rome fading in the twilight dusk and saw the flickering, tentative glimpses of the new day and the new age of the Son of Man.

Origen's father had been martyred and many of Origen's students had lost their lives in persecutions. Because of his fame as a Christian scholar, in his 60's Origen was targeted in the systematic persecution of Christians under Emperor Decius (249-251):

"In this persecution the evil demon (Decius) attacked Origen, in particular, with all the weapons in his arsenal, making him endure chains and torture for the Word of Christ as he lay in irons in the depths of his dungeon. Day after day his legs were stretched apart four paces in the stocks, but he courageously endured threats of fire and every other torment devised by his enemies." Eusebius, *Church History 6.39*

Origen was not killed, but shortly after his release, he died at the age of 69 from the effects of torture and was buried in Tyre. The Romans could kill and torture Christians and their leaders, but they could not quench with their blood the fire that was slowly and surely licking away at their Empire in Rome, in the East, in the South and way up to their distant outposts where most of their Legions had never even seen Rome, spoke a babble of languages and had no sense of duty or devotion to Latin culture.

The Roman Legions, once composed of Roman citizens, were increasingly conscripted from conquered tribes who had no loyalty to Rome. So numerous were recruits from barbarian tribes that contemporary writers from the 3rd century on began to use the word *miles* meaning "soldier" interchangeably with *barbarus* meaning "barbarian." Polybius in c. 140 BC had explained why Rome under the good old days of the Republic had come to dominate the world:

"Carthaginians bestow all their attention upon their (navy)....and wholly neglect their infantry....The reason for this is that they employ foreign mercenaries (while) the Romans use native and citizen levies. It is in this point that the Roman polity is preferable to the Carthaginian. (Carthaginians) have their hopes of freedom ever resting on the courage of mercenary troops; the Romans on the valor of their own their citizens....The result is that even if the Romans have suffered a defeat at first, they renew the war with undiminished forces....For, as the Romans are fighting for country and children, it is impossible for them to relax the fury of their struggle; but they persist with obstinate resolution until they have overcome their enemies." *Histories 52*

Rome's armies were no longer Roman. Their soldiers had no real skin or kin in Rome's wars. By the end of the 3rd century less than 1% of Rome's Legions were actually Roman. One remembers the 1st century Juvenal's lament that he could not abide a Rome of Greeks. By the 3rd century, Rome and its armies were not only Greek but were Egyptian, Syrian, African, Romanian, Celtic, Gothic and especially "German," from the word *Germanus* first used by Julius Caesar during his wars in 58-50 BC to describe all northern European tribes.

Power had shifted from Rome and the Senate to the commanders and their non-Roman armies in remote provinces. Because they were the armed defenders of Rome, the soldiers knew they were the de facto power of Rome and could be ruled by a Caesar of their own choosing. After the death of Commodus in 192, Rome entered a chaotic time called The Year Of The Five Emperors. The Praetorian Guard installed Pertinax as Caesar to replace Commodus. He cut their pay and they threatened to kill him. To raise the money to mollify them, Pertinax sold the concubines and young boys Commodus had kept for his pleasure and gave the Praetorians the money. They killed Pertinax anyway. Glutted with power and the lust for money, the soldiers decided to auction off the Roman Empire to the highest bidder:

"When this proclamation was known, the more honorable and weighty Senators and all persons of noble origin and property would not approach the military barracks to offer money in so vile a manner for a besmirched sovereignty. However, a certain Julianus…was holding a drinking bout late that evening at the time the news came of what the soldiers proposed. He was a man notorious for his evil living; and now it was that his wife and daughter and fellow feasters urged him to rise from his banqueting couch and hasten to the barracks….they pressed it on him that he might get the sovereignty for himself, and that he ought not to spare the money to outbid any competitors with great gifts to the soldiers. When he came to the wall of the camp, he called out to the troops and promised to give them just as much as they desired, for he had ready money and a treasure room full of gold and silver….they lowered a ladder and brought Julianus into the fortified camp; for they would not open the gates until they had made sure of the amount of the money they expected….(Julianus)…promised to give the soldiers the same lax discipline they had enjoyed under Commodus. Also he promised the troops as large a sum of money as they could ever expect to require or receive. The payment should be immediate and he would at once have the cash brought over from his residence. Captivated by such speeches and with such vast hopes awakened, the soldiers hailed Julianus as Emperor….with a great escort of guards, Julianus went out.

It was against the will and intention of the people…what a shameful and unworthy stain upon the public honor that he had bought the Empire….then (the Praetorian Guard) brought him to the palace with no man of the multitude daring to resist; but just as little was there any cheer of welcome….On the contrary, the people stood at a distance and hooted and reviled him as having the throne with lucre at an auction." Herodian (c. 170-c. 240), *History Of The Roman Empire Since The Death Of Marcus Aurelius 2.6*

Julianus was emperor for only 86 days before the soldiers assassinated him. Septimus Severus was then declared Caesar by his troops along the Rhine and Danube. After the fiascos of Commodus, Pertinax and the auctioning off of the Empire to Julianus, every general with an ambition and an army declared himself emperor. In Antioch General Niger had his troops declare him Emperor, but he was later pursued and killed by the forces of Septimus Severus. The troops in Britain were loyal to their Albinus, so Severus made a deal with Albinus that he could be called Caesar and would inherit the throne at Severus' death. That was, for the time being, sufficient for Albinus. Meanwhile Severus consolidated his grip on the monarchy when Egypt recognized him as emperor. But Albinus wanted more recognition than Severus had given him and marched his armies into France. Severus declared Albinus an enemy of the State and in 197 in Lyons Severus defeated Albinus. Albinus committed suicide. Severus had his naked body laid on the ground and rode his horse over it, severed his head, sent it to Rome and then killed his entire family. In 193 there had been five emperors of Rome all of whom had come to power through their military and had been deposed by military might. Herodian's *History* describes not only this chaotic Year of the Five Emperors but also the Year of the Six Emperors in 238.

Herodian is one of the most accessible historians. His stated aim in this interesting *History* "is to write a systematic account of the events within a period of 70 years, during the reigns of several emperors, of which I have personal experience." *2.15.7* Herodian had lived during this time of upheaval in the 3rd century when in only 45 years Rome had 17 emperors: only one of them died a natural death; one of them was a boy of 13; one a very old man and one was even a priest of the Syrian sun god. Most of Rome's emperors during this time were not Roman and some of them lived and died without ever visiting Rome. They were often foreign-born men from the lower castes of society who had distinguished themselves in battle and rose up the ranks to be proclaimed emperor by their troops and the Praetorian Guard. During these years of crisis, Barbarian emperors were leading the Roman army that consisted of Barbarians in battles against Barbarians. Between 235-284, there were at least 14 of these "Barracks Emperors" who lead Roman troops under the aegis of the Roman eagle. They exploited the Roman treasury to pay and regale their troops while buildings, repairs, public concerns and even the Senate in far-away Rome went begging. Inflation, high taxes, sporadic riots and a general feeling of malaise hung over Rome.

Reports of military victories by emperors that no one in Rome knew or had rarely seen arrived by royal couriers. The Illyrian-born (Balkans) emperor Claudius II wrote a letter to Rome extolling his stunning victory over the Goths in 269 AD:

"We have destroyed 320,000 of the Goths; we have sunk 2,000 of their ships. The rivers are bridged over with shields, the shores are covered with lances and with swords. The fields are hidden under the superincumbent bones, no road is free from them. We have taken so many women that each soldier can have two or three allotted to him."

No one in Rome proposed a victory parade or festival or round of games in the Colosseum. There was no jubilation, but the Senate did allow the unroman title of *Gothicus* to be added to Claudius' name and they pronounced him "a god."

Claudius II is associated with one of the most enduring of martyrs, St. Valentine. Very little is known from antiquity about the Valentine that is celebrated in the West every February 14th on St. Valentine's Day. What is probably true is that he was a presbyter/priest in Rome at the time of Emperor Claudius II and was beheaded because of his faith in Christ in c. 280 AD. Because he has been associated with love and lovers for hundreds of years, legends and myths have grown up about him. There is, of course, always a kernel of truth in myths and legends and perhaps this Valentine did marry Christian couples when it was forbidden to do so. Supposedly, that drew the attention of Claudius and he was arrested and imprisoned. His jailer had a blind daughter and Valentine prayed for her and she was healed. She, the jailer and all their household became Christians. Legend says before Valentine was beheaded, he left a note to the jailer's daughter signed, "Your Valentine." Kernels of truth or the lies of history? There is an ancient basilica dedicated by Pope Julius I in the early 300's, very close to the date of Valentine's death, on the Via Flaminia called St. Valentini Extra Portam. We know there was a Valentine and he was martyred under Emperor Claudius Gothicus and he likely had something to do with love.

After Claudius' Gothic victory, "Rome's" army was happy to receive into its Barbarian ranks many of the defeated Goths. Rome and Rome's military had gradually become two different entities separated over the years by distance and different imperatives. Rome and her Empire were splitting apart and were sporadically but surely, slowly sliding downhill.

In July of 283 fourteen years after Claudius II's letter was written, the penultimate of the Barracks Emperors, Carus, was found dead in his tent in Persia after a horrific storm. He had been emperor for less than a year. It was reported he died by lightning, but it is possible and probable that he was poisoned. His sons Numerian and Carinus succeeded him, but Numerian was murdered by the Praetorian prefect Arrius Aper who, it must be noted, had been in camp when Carus had died under mysterious circumstances. Aper, as head of the Praetorian Guard and advisor to Emperor Carus, obviously had hoped to have himself declared emperor. But the army passed over him as well as Numerian's brother Carinus and declared Diocletian who was Commander of the Cavalry Rome's next Emperor in November of 284. The first thing he did was to kill the perfidious Arrius Aper with his sword and then pursue and defeat the pretender Carinus.

Emperor Diocletian was the culmination of the merit-in-battle choices made by the Praetorian Guard during the Barracks Emperors' years. Since most Roman Emperors historically had come from the patrician class of Italy, Diocletian, the son of slaves from the ancient city of Solona (near modern Split, Croatia), started off at the bottom of the social barrel and rose to be sovereign ruler of a kingdom that encompassed most of the known world during his time.

After all the unpredictability of the 3rd century, all the plots against and abrupt assassinations of emperors and all the problems emperors had encountered policing Rome's porous borders, in 293 Diocletian decided to split the Roman Empire into a more manageable size and provide a safer haven for an orderly succession of its rulers.

Diocletian broke Rome. He divided the Empire into a Western section that included Italy, Gaul, Britannia and Spain and an Eastern section that included Syria, Palestine and Egypt.

Diocletian smashed Rome's traditional governing structure. Each division of the Empire was to be ruled by an absolute despot called an "Augustus" whose power was limited to a 20-year term of office. Each Augustus/Emperor would have an Emperor-in-waiting called a "Caesar." No longer, Diocletian supposed, would ambitious younger men attempt to overthrow the Emperor because the waiting Caesars would know that with patience they would rule in 20 years. No longer would the Empire go to a blood relative of the Augustus. Each Caesar would be hand-picked by the Augustus from the best and brightest.

Diocletian divided the entire empire into 12 districts called dioceses from the Greek word *dioikensis* meaning "management of a household or government." Each diocese had a *vicarius*, meaning "deputy" over it. It is not enigmatic to see how the Early Church rescued and received, and some within the modern Church have retained, a few of Rome's ruling structures.

Diocletian appointed Maximian as Augustus to rule the Western Empire with his Caesar Constantius who, the plan was, would become Emperor when Maximian either died or retired in 20 years. Diocletian, as the Augustus, ruled the Eastern Empire with his successor, the evil and ill-fated Caesar Galerius.

The young rabbi from Galilee had warned: "Every kingdom divided against itself will be ruined, and every city or household divided against itself will not stand." (Matthew 12:25) Rome's hairline cracks had become seismic fissures. Diocletian and his innovative Tetrarchy would be the last desperate gasp for air of the Roman Empire and the pagan world.

XVIII.

"And now, when Galerius (who co-ruled with Emperor Diocletian) was in the eighteenth year of his reign (311 AD), God struck him with an incurable plague. A malignant ulcer formed itself low down in his secret parts and spread by degrees. The physicians attempted to eradicate it and healed up the places affected. But the sore, after having been skinned over, broke out again; a vein burst and the blood flowed in such quantity as to endanger his life. The blood, however, was stopped.... The physicians had to undertake their operations anew, and at length they cicatrized the wound. In consequence of some slight motion of his body, however, Galerius received a hurt and the blood streamed more abundantly than before. He grew emaciated, pallid and feeble, and the bleeding then stanched. The ulcer began to be insensible to the remedies applied, and gangrene seized all the neighboring parts. It diffused itself the wider the more the corrupted flesh was cut away, and everything employed as the means of cure served but to aggravate the disease.... Then famous physicians were brought in from all quarters; but no human means had any success. Apollo and Aesculapius (gods) were besought importunately for remedies: Apollo (through an oracle) did prescribe but the distemper augmented. Already approaching to its deadly crisis, it had occupied the lower regions of his body: his bowels came out and his whole seat putrefied. The luckless physicians, although without hope of overcoming the malady, ceased not to apply fomentations and administer medicines. The humors having been repelled, the distemper attacked his intestines and worms were generated in his body. The stench was so foul as to pervade not only the palace, but even the whole city; and no wonder, for by that time the passages from his bladder and bowels, having been devoured by the worms, became indiscriminate and his body, with intolerable anguish, was dissolved in one mass of corruption....They applied warm flesh of animals to the chief seat of the disease, that the warmth might draw out those minute worms; and accordingly, when the dressings were removed, there issued forth an innumerable swarm; nevertheless the prolific disease had hatched swarms much more abundant to prey upon and consume his intestines. Already, through a complication of distempers, the different parts of his body had lost their natural form: the superior part was dry, meager and haggard and his ghastly-looking skin had settled itself deep amongst his bones while the inferior, distended like bladders, retained no appearance of joints. These things happened in the course of one complete year; and at length, overcome by calamities, he was obliged to acknowledge God, and he cried aloud, in the intervals of raging pain, that he would re-edify the Church which he had demolished, and make atonement for his misdeed; and when he was near his end, he published an Edict of the tenor following:

'Amongst our other regulations for the permanent advantage of the commonweal, we have hitherto studied to reduce all things to a conformity with the ancient laws and public discipline of the Romans.

It has been our aim in an especial manner, that the Christians also, who had abandoned the religion of their forefathers, should return to right opinions. For such willfulness and folly had, we know not how, taken possession of them, that instead of observing those ancient institutions, which possibly their own forefathers had established, they, through caprice, made laws to themselves, and drew together into different societies many men of widely different persuasions.

After the publication of our edict, ordaining the Christians to betake themselves to the observance of the ancient institutions, many of them were subdued through the fear of danger, and moreover many of them were exposed to jeopardy; nevertheless, because great numbers still persist in their opinions, and because we have perceived that at present they neither pay reverence and adoration to the gods, yet worship their own god, therefore we, from our wonted clemency in bestowing pardon on all, have judged it fit to extend our indulgence to those men, and to permit them again to be Christians, and to establish the places of their religious assemblies; yet so as that they offend not against good order. By another mandate we purpose to signify unto magistrates how they ought herein to demean themselves.

Wherefore it will be the duty of the Christians, in consequence of this our toleration, to pray to their god for (my) welfare, and for that of the public, and for their own; that the commonweal may continue safe in every quarter, and that they themselves may live securely in their habitations.'

This edict was promulgated at Nicomedia on the day preceding the kalends of May (April 30, 311), in the eighth consulship of Galerius.... Then the prison-gates having been thrown open....the confessors for the faith were set at liberty....Galerius, however, did not, by publication of this edict, obtain the divine forgiveness. A few days after, he was consumed by the horrible disease that had brought on a universal putrefaction." Lactantius (c. 250-320), *De Mortibus Persecutorum (On The Deaths of the Persecutors) 33-35*

It is difficult to hear or to read about gruesome deaths especially when described, like Galerius' contemporary Lactantius has, in such minute detail. It does not go unnoticed that the decaying, putrefying body of Galerius was symptomatic of Rome's entire Empire at the beginning of the 4th century. Galerius' agony lasted about a year. It was a slow, painful death for this Caesar who in concert with his Emperor Diocletian hastened the decay and demise of the Roman Empire and the pagan world in the West.

When civilizations slowly decline and die like the Romans did, it is impossible for people living at the time to know if the decline has started or when it started, how far they are into the decline or if their civilization has, indeed, died. Some countries, however, lose their hegemony abruptly like Britain did after World War II. Before the Second World War, "the sun never set on the British Empire." In the

19th century, British world maps highlighted its imperial power with red and pink countries all over the globe that were under its dominion. The sun never set on Britain's territories, meaning it was always daylight somewhere on the planet earth that was "owned" by the British. After World War II as part of a decolonization movement by Europe, most British territories were given independence and two years after the war in 1947, India, Britain's most valuable possession, was granted its freedom. Britain went into the war an Empire, but a few years later, she was just a country with a few possessions. England had obtained its hegemony in 1588 at the Battle of the Gravelines in the North Sea when it defeated the Armada of the super-nation Spain. Spain delivered its supremacy to Britain. After winning World War II, America became the world's super power.

In ancient history there were even more precipitous downfalls of civilizations. The Book of Daniel in the Bible describes the fall in just one night of one of the greatest ancient powers, Babylon. One of the seven Wonders of the Ancient World was Babylon's Hanging Gardens built for his wife by Nebuchadnezzar in c. 600 BC when young Daniel was the king's chief governor. Babylon was an impregnable city. Its 300' high and 80' thick walls surrounded the city and even extended 35' below the ground to prevent enemies from tunneling under it. The wall was protected by wide and deep canals filled with water. 250 watch towers dotted the walls and 100 brass gates were closed and bolted every night. Babylon's kings and people felt very safe. But one night in early October 539 BC:

"King Belshazzar gave a great banquet for a thousand of his nobles and drank wine with them. When Belshazzar was drinking his wine, he gave orders to bring in the gold and silver goblets that Nebuchadnezzar... had taken from the temple in Jerusalem (586 BC), so that the king and his nobles, his wives and concubines might drink from them....As they drank the wine, they praised the gods of gold and silver, of bronze, iron, wood and stone. Suddenly the fingers of a human hand appeared and wrote on the plaster of the wall near the lamp stand in the royal palace.

The king watched the hand as it wrote. His face turned pale and he was so frightened his knees knocked together and his legs gave way.

The king called out for the enchanters, astrologers and diviners to be brought and said to these wise men of Babylon, 'Whoever reads this writing and tells me what it means will be clothed in purple and have a gold chain placed around his neck, and he will be made the third highest ruler in the kingdom.'

Then all the king's wise men came in, but they could not read the writing or tell the king what it meant. So King Belshazzar became even more terrified and his face grew pale. His nobles were baffled.

The queen (Belshazzar's mother), hearing the voices of the king and his nobles, came into the banquet hall. 'O king, live forever!' she said. 'Don't be alarmed! Don't look so pale! There is a man in your kingdom who has the spirit of the holy gods in him. In the time of your (ancestor Nebuchadnezzar) he was found to have insight and intelligence and wisdom like that of the gods. King Nebuchadnezzar...appointed him chief of the magicians, enchanters, astrologers and diviners. This man Daniel, whom the king called Belteshazzar, was found to have a keen mind and knowledge and understanding and also the ability to interpret dreams, explain riddles and solve difficult problems. Call for Daniel, and he will tell you what the writing means.'

So Daniel (now in his 80's) was brought before the king, and the king said to him, 'Are you Daniel, one of the exiles my father the king brought from Judah? I have heard the spirit of the gods is in you and that you have insight, intelligence and outstanding wisdom. The wise men and the enchanters were brought before me to read this writing and tell me what it means, but they could not explain it. Now I have heard that you are able to give interpretations and to solve difficult problems. If you can read this writing and tell me what it means, you will be clothed in purple and have a gold chain placed around your neck, and you will be made the third highest ruler in the kingdom.'

Then Daniel answered the king, 'You may keep your gifts for yourself and give your rewards to someone else. Nevertheless, I will read the writing for the king and tell him what it means.

O king, the Most High God gave your (ancestor) Nebuchadnezzar sovereignty and greatness and glory and splendor. Because of the high position he was given, all the peoples and nations and men of every language dreaded and feared him. Those people the king wanted to put to death, he put to death; those he wanted to spare, he spared; those he wanted to promote, he promoted; and those he wanted to humble, he humbled. But when his heart became arrogant and hardened with pride, he was deposed from his royal throne and stripped of his glory. He was driven away from people and given the mind of an animal (clinical lycanthropy); he lived with the wild donkeys and ate grass like cattle; and his body was drenched with the dew of heaven, until he acknowledged that the Most High God is sovereign over the kingdoms of men and sets over them anyone he wishes.

But you his son, O Belshazzar, have not humbled yourself, though you knew all this. Instead, you have set yourself up against the Lord of heaven. You had the goblets from his temple brought to you, and you and your nobles, your wives and your concubines drank wine from them. You praised the gods of silver and gold, of bronze, iron, wood and stone, which cannot see or hear or understand. But you did not honor the God who holds in his hand your life and all your ways. Therefore he sent the hand that wrote the inscription. This is the inscription that was written:

Mene, Mene, Tekel, Upharsin

This is what the words mean:

Mene: God has numbered the days of your reign and brought it to an end.

Tekel: You have been weighed on the scales and found wanting.

Upharsin: Your kingdom is divided and given to the Medes and Persians.'

Then at Belshazzar's command, Daniel was clothed in purple, a gold chain was placed around his neck, and he was proclaimed the third highest ruler in the kingdom.

That very night Belshazzar, king of the Babylonians, was slain, and Darius the Mede took over the kingdom at the age of sixty-two." Daniel 5:1-30

There have been many scholarly and linguistic discussions over the millennia about the interpretation of the four Aramaic words written on the wall of the palace. The historical consensus is that *Mene* and *Tekel* refer to Hebrew and Mesopotamian terms of measurements and divisions. The "U" in *Upharsin* means "and;" *Pharsin* is the plural of *Peres* meaning "Persians." Thus the interpretation: "(You) Numbered, Numbered, Divided, And (You) Given To Persians."

The history of the interpretations of ancient writings belongs to a small band of patient, dogged and skilled men who have given their minds and lives to breaking the codes of undecipherable scribbles on ancient walls, shards, stones and parchments. We owe to this relatively recent group (c. 1700's to the present) of linguists and philologists our understanding of Egyptian hieroglyphs, of Minoan scripts and of Sumerian *cuneiforms* (Latin "wedge-shaped").

To illustrate their indefatigable persistence: they have shown the world that the original Sumerian word for "Babylon" was *ka-dingir-ra KI*. *Ka* was an ideogram meaning "gate." *Dingir* was an ideogram for "god." *Ra* was a phonogram indicating that an "R" sound followed. *KI* was the sign for "land, earth" and served as a determinative. Under this linguistic scenario, the Sumerian name for Babylon" meant "Gate Of God Land." Babylon came to be pronounced "Babylon" when the Akkadians and Babylonians conquered the city in the 2nd millennium BC and gave Babylonian pronunciations to Sumerian words. The Babylonian for "gate" was *babum* and for "gate of" was *bab*. Their word for "god" was *ilu*. The same signs that the Sumerians pronounced *kadingirraki* were pronounced *babilu* by the Babylonians which pronunciation came into Hebrew as *babel* in the Hebrew Bible and is how we get our modern pronunciation of the word "Babylon," meaning in Akkadian/Babylonian "Gate of God." According to the Bible (Genesis 11:1-9), it was at prehistoric Babylon/Babel that God split mankind into different language groups so they could not understand each other. "Babel" sounds like the Hebrew word for "confused," and the word resonates in English as the word "babble" meaning "to utter sounds or words without meaning; to chatter or prattle." As can be gleaned from this small paragraph, every word we speak and write has an awesome and complicated oral and written history.

The Biblical narrative of the Fall of Babylon was written by Daniel mostly in Aramaic, the common language of Babylon, in c. 530 BC shortly after Babylon fell the night of October 10, 539 BC to Cyrus the Persian who appointed his uncle Darius the Mede as its temporary ruler. Daniel's account is an inside-the-Babylonian-palace view of the night of the fall and precedes all the other historical narratives of Babylon's fall by a hundred or more years. The Greek historian Herodotus of Halicarnassus in c. 430 BC gives the narrative of impregnable Babylon's fall an outside historical and military perspective:

"Cyrus on his way to Babylon came to the banks of the Gyndes (Diyalah River in Iraq)....When Cyrus reached the stream which could only be passed in boats, one of the sacred white horses accompanying his march, full of spirit and high mettle, walked into the water and tried to cross by himself; but the current seized him, swept him along with it and drowned him in its depths. Cyrus, enraged at the insolence of the river, threatened so to break its strength that in the future even women should cross it easily without wetting their knees. Accordingly he put off for a time his attack on Babylon, and dividing his army into two parts, he marked out by ropes one hundred and eighty trenches on each side of the Gyndes, leading off from it in all directions, and setting his army to dig, some on one side of the river, some on the other, he accomplished his threat by the help of so great a number of hands, but not without losing thereby the whole summer season.

Having, however, thus wreaked his vengeance on the Gyndes by dispersing it through three hundred and sixty channels, Cyrus, with the first approach of the ensuing spring (of 539 BC), marched forward against Babylon. The Babylonians, encamped without their walls, awaited his coming. A battle was fought at a short distance from the city, in which the Babylonians were defeated by the Persian king, whereupon they withdrew within their defenses in Babylon. Here they shut themselves up, and made light of his siege, having laid in a store of provisions for many years in preparation against this attack; for when they (had seen)

Cyrus conquering nation after nation, they were convinced that he would never stop and that their turn would come at last.

Cyrus was now reduced to great perplexity, as time went on and he made no progress against the place. In this distress either some one made the suggestion to him or he bethought himself a plan which he proceeded to put into execution.

He placed a portion of his army at the point where the river (Euphrates) enters the city, and another body at the back of the place where it issues forth, with orders to march into the town by the bed of the stream as soon as the water became shallow enough. He then himself drew off with the unwarlike portion of his host, and made for the place where Nitocris (Babylonian queen c. 550 BC) had dug the basin for the river, where he did exactly what she had done formerly. He turned the Euphrates by a canal into the basin, which was then a marsh, on which the river sank to such an extent that the natural bed of the stream became fordable.

Hereupon, the Persian soldiers who had been left for that purpose at Babylon by the riverside, entered the stream which had now sunk so as to reach about midway up a man's thigh and thus got into the town.

Had the Babylonians been apprised of what Cyrus was about, or had they noticed their danger, they would never have allowed the Persians to enter the city, but would have destroyed them utterly; for they would have made fast all the street gates which gave upon the river, and mounting upon the walls along both sides of the stream, would so have caught the enemy, as it were, in a trap.

But, as it was, the Persians came upon them by surprise and so took the city. Owing to the vast size of Babylon, the inhabitants of the central parts (where the palace was located) long after the outer portions of the town were taken, knew nothing of what had chanced, but as they were engaged in a festival, continued dancing and reveling until they learned the capture but too late. Such, then, were the circumstances of the taking of Babylon." *Inquiries* aka *The Histories 1.189-191*

Herodotus, called "The Father Of History," confirms Daniel's account of the drunken revelry of the king and his commanders the night Babylon was caught off guard and conquered.

Another historian and Biblical prophet named Isaiah foresaw the fall of Babylon 200 years before the event. Isaiah, son of Amoz, was a prophet in Israel from c. 740-700 BC. The themes of his book are the coming captivities of northern and southern Israel, prophecies regarding the coming Messiah, pleas to repent and words of comfort. But interspersed with these themes are prophetic "oracles," are weighty utterances of doom. Babylon in Isaiah's time was a major city, but it did not enter its Golden Age and dominate the Near East until c. 625 BC, about 100 years after Isaiah wrote this prophecy of its eventual fall:

"An oracle concerning Babylon that Isaiah son of Amoz saw....
See, the day of the Lord is coming,
A cruel day, with wrath and fierce anger,
To make the land desolate
And destroy the sinners within it....
Babylon, the jewel of kingdoms,
The glory of the Babylonians' pride,
Will be overthrown by God
Like Sodom and Gomorrah.
She will never be inhabited
Or lived in through all generations;
No Arab will pitch his tent there;
No shepherd will rest his flocks there.
Her time is at hand,
And her days will not be prolonged." Isaiah 13:1, 9, 19, 20, 22

After its fall, Babylon, 53 miles south of Baghdad in Iraq, was never again an influential city. In the 21st century, no Arabs pitch their tents there.

Unlike Babylon that fell without a fight, most ancient super powers died when a more provincial people defeated them in battle. Nineveh, the Assyrian super power of the Near East in the 7th century BC, was defeated and destroyed after a long siege in July 612 BC by an amalgam of semi-nomadic tribes composed of Medes and Babylonians. Most, if not all, civilizations primed for fall have existed for some time and have accrued the corruptions and weaknesses that necessitate and facilitate their demises. Nineveh was no exception. Her king at the time of her destruction was:

"Sardanapallus, the 13th in succession from Ninus, who founded the empire and the last king of the Assyrians who outdid all his predecessors in luxury and sluggishness....he was not seen by any man residing outside the palace; he lived the life of a woman and spending his days in the company of his concubines and spinning purple garments and working the softest of wool, he assumed the feminine garb and so covered his face and indeed his entire body with whitening cosmetics and the other unguents used by prostitutes, that he rendered it more delicate than that of any luxury-loving woman. He also took care to make even his voice to be like a woman's and at his carousals not only to indulge regularly in those drinks and viands which could offer the greatest pleasure, but also to pursue the delights of love with men as well as women; for he practiced sexual indulgence of both kinds without restraint, showing not the least concern for the disgrace attending such conduct....he composed a funeral dirge for himself...to be inscribed upon his tomb after his death:

'Knowing full well that thou wert mortal born,
Thy heart lift up, take thy delight in feast;
When dead no pleasure more is thine. Thus I,
Who once o'er mighty Ninus (Nineveh) ruled, am naught
But dust. Yet these are mine which gave me joy
In life---the food I ate, my wantonness,
And love's delights. But all those other things
Men deem felicities are left behind.'" Diododrus Sicullus (1st century BC), *Library of History 2.23*

As the enemy was at the gates of Nineveh that July of 612 BC, Sardanapallus "in order that he might not fall into the hands of the enemy...built an enormous pyre in his palace, heaped upon it all his gold and silver as well as every article of the royal wardrobe, and then, shutting his concubines and eunuchs in the room which had been built in the middle of the pyre, he consigned both them and himself and his palace to the flames." Diodorus, *Library of History 2.27*

Archaeologists have found in the ruins of Nineveh a tiny tablet 5.1" long by 2.7" wide on which is inscribed the fall of Nineveh. It is called the *Fall of Nineveh Chronicle* and is part of a larger chronicle that describes the final years of the Assyrian Empire. The scribe whose job it was to chronicle events in Assyria from 616 to 607 BC gave a rather indifferent account of the fall of its major city:

"From the month Simanu until the month Abu---for three months--- they (Babylonians and Medes) subjected the city to heavy siege. On the Nth day of the month Abu they inflicted a major defeat upon a great people. At that time Sinsariskun (Sardanapallus), king of Assyria, died. They carried off the vast booty of the city and the temple and turned the city into a ruin heap." *Fall of Nineveh Chronicle 3* or *ABC3*

The destruction of Nineveh, and even the name "Nineveh," was so complete that 200 years later in c. 401 BC when the Greek soldier Xenophon and his 10,000 troops on their *anabasis* ("march up country") passed by the mounds of rubble, they thought it was the ruins of a Parthian city. In 331 BC Alexander the Great fought the Battle of Arbela near the site and had no idea there had ever been a city there. Many scholars over the centuries had doubted the Biblical references to a city called Nineveh, but when in 1845 Henry Austin Layard and other archaeologists discovered Nineveh near the modern city of Mosul, Iraq and began to uncover the site, the hundreds of thousands of inscriptions and shards they found in the ruins of the magnificent palaces confirmed not only the existence of a Biblical Nineveh but the names the Bible had given their kings.

The Biblical prophet Nahum had prophesied Nineveh's fall in c. 630 BC about 20 years before its destruction:

"This is what the Lord says....An attacker advances against you, Nineveh. Guard the fortress. Watch the road. Brace yourselves. Marshal all your strength!....The chariots storm through the street, rushing back and forth through the squares. They look like flaming torches; they dart about like lightning. He summons his picked troops, yet they stumble on their way. They dash to the city wall; the protective shield is put in place. The river gates (Tigris River) are thrown open and the palace collapses. It is decreed that the city be exiled and carried away. Its slave girls moan like doves and beat upon their breasts. Nineveh is like a pool, and its water is draining away. 'Stop! Stop!' they cry, but no one turns back. Plunder the silver! The supply is endless, the wealth from all its treasures! She is pillaged, plundered, stripped! Hearts melt, knees give way, bodies tremble, every face grows pale. Where now is the lions' den, the place where they fed their young, where the lion and lioness went, and the cubs, with nothing to fear? (The lion was the symbol of the Assyrian kingdom.)....'I am against you.' declares the Lord Almighty. 'I will burn up your chariots in smoke, and the sword will devour your young lions. I will leave you no prey on the earth. The voices of your messengers will no longer be heard. Woe to the city of blood....Nothing can heal your wound; your injury is fatal. Everyone who hears the news about you will clap their hands at your fall, for who has not felt your endless cruelty?'" Nahum 2:1-13; 3:1,19

Assyrian Nineveh fell to the Babylonians after a three-month siege in 612 BC and Babylon, in turn, fell in one night to the Persians and the Medes in 539 BC. Everyone from Greece and north Africa to India came under the rule of the Hellene Alexander's conquests in 334-324 BC and gracious Greece's tenuous hold on the reins of power were yanked away from her by the rustic Romans at the Battle of Corinth in 146 BC. The cycles of the rise and fall of world powers are an unending forward progression of decisive battles, sieges, ambushes, intrigues, bloodsheds, rapes, enslavements, power-brokerings, gougings, slashings, burnings, pillagings and the other usual execrables. If history is wooden shoes clattering upstairs and silken stockings floating down, man's history is short on silk and long on wood.

The fall of Rome was not the result of a stunning military victory or a stealth attack. Rome did not fall to a Barbarian horde from the East or from a challenger in the West. She fell from within. The fullness of time had come. At the beginning of the 300's, Rome's Empire was now divided and decentralized. Rome was not even the titular administrative capital of the Empire any more nor were most Romans Roman. Diocletian and Galerius were Dacians (from modern Rumania). Galerius particularly hated Rome and "at the very time of his obtaining sovereign power, he had avowed himself the enemy of the Roman name; and he proposed that the empire should be called, not the Roman but the Dacian Empire." Lactantius, *On The Death Of The Persecutors 27* From the middle of the 200's to the time of the Great Persecution in 303-313, most of the Caesars of Rome were not Roman but Barbarian. The Roman Empire and its rulers had become a melting pot for the known world and Roman identity, once prized and respected, had become despised and rejected by many.

Diocletian as the Empire's Augustus had to bow to certain Roman formalities. He built a huge Bath in Rome, known as Diocletian's Bath, to denote a connection to Rome. (The central hall of his Bath is now part of the S. Maria degli Angeli church.) But Diocletian only visited Rome once and ruled Thrace, Egypt and Asia from Nicomedia (modern Izmit, Turkey). Diocletian's Caesar Galerius ruled the borders of the Danube from modern Sremske Mitrovica, Serbia. The Augustus in the West, Maximian, ruled Italy and Africa not from Rome but from Mediolanum (modern Milan, Italy) and his Caesar Constantius ruled Spain, Gaul and Britain from modern Trier, Germany. The Roman Empire had become so vast and diverse that 4th century rulers chose capitals central to their areas of influence. Rome had become just another city among many in the Empire. Rome and the soldiers and the emperors who had made Rome Rome had nothing in common and rarely saw each other. The cracks in her body politic and the persistent wafts of moral putrefaction, usually powerful warning signs of degeneration, had gone unheeded for centuries. By the time the stench was intolerable and the body structure was breaking apart, it was too late.

At the beginning of the 4th century, Christianity, Rome's persistent and internal nemesis, was not a nascent religion but was now a mature, robust legion of seasoned soldiers ready to marshal its spiritual resources whenever Rome attacked. Over the past centuries, the Roman Empire had been the whetstone on which Christianity, destined to be the new world order, had sharpened its sword. Every thing was in place for paganism's final and concerted attack upon its sworn enemy, the Christian Church.

Christianity had been Rome's arch enemy since 30 AD when Roman believers in Judaism (both Jew and Gentile) went to Jerusalem for the festival of Pentecost (Acts 2:10,11), heard the news of Jesus' resurrection, believed in the Jewish Messiah and brought their conversions back home to Rome. The Empire had plenty of space for and gave license to gods of all peoples as long as their adherents recognized Rome's Caesar as a god. But from the very beginning, Christians, like the Jews whom Rome tolerated, stubbornly insisted there was only one God and that the Roman gods and the Roman emperor-god were fake, false idols. At the beginning, Rome had nudged back calling Christians *prava et immodica*, "wicked and unbridled" as did Pliny the Elder in *Letters 10.96.97* and as early as 35 AD the Roman Senate had declared the new religion *strana et ellicita* "strange and unlawful." Rome's attacks in the first decades of the faith were anecdotal and aimed at its low class believers, but when Nero blamed the Christians for burning Rome in 64 AD and killed Christians wholesale, war was openly declared. Over the next 250 years Rome fought many wars against external enemies while sporadically dealing in deadly ways with its most fatal foe, Christianity. During the long, drawn-out centuries, Rome intuited she was slowly but surely losing ground to a new god, one God, who, in spite of the edict that had declared His followers null and void---*non licet vos esse*, "you have no right to exist"---persisted through harassments, persecutions and executions.

With Diocletian and Galerius Rome decided to wage war, its final war as it turned out, against this intractable enemy within. Once and for all, Diocletian reasoned, Rome's many gods, not the Christian one God, would be acknowledged and worshipped and Rome would recover its quondam glory. The pagan idols and gods would again unify the Empire.

What he did not realize was the pagan gods were has-beens, were weak and out-dated specters and could never be the cement needed to cobble together and hold up the dying Empire. Let no one be misinformed. This final battle was an inevitable clash between thousands of years of paganism personified by the Roman Empire and thousands of years of monotheism personified by Judaism and Christianity. It was a clash of the titans of the West, an ageless war in the hearts and minds of humans between idols created by man and man's Creator. No sane and impartial judge could adjudicate this last war in any other way.

The persecution of Christians under Diocletian and Galerius, called by some the Great Persecution (303-313), was not undertaken lightly. Diocletian knew that Rome had tried to stamp out Christianity for hundreds of years and he was well aware that in spite of the Imperial persecutions and often because of them, the Christian population within the Roman provinces had increased almost daily over the centuries. Diocletian knew, as the son of slaves, that slaves like his parents were some of the earliest followers of Christ. When he was a boy in his hometown of Solona, there was even a shrine, called the Manastirine, dedicated to 2nd century local martyrs for Christ. As a Roman soldier, Diocletian had seen and admired the mettle and morals of Christian soldiers and he trusted believers so much that he had hired only Christians as his personal bodyguards. His wife Prisca and daughter Valeria were Christian sympathizers. Why would Diocletian, the Supreme Augustus, risk a war he did not want and intuitively knew he could not win?

The answer is because he had become by 303 a superstitious, timorous, semi-senile man. The Diocletian who 19 years previously had confidently assumed the throne and invented the Tetrarchy was now afraid of losing his grip on Imperial power and was duped and persuaded by his underling, the hapless Galerius, that wiping out the Christians is what would restore the good old gods and the good old days of the early Roman Empire. When the first Augustus Caesar (27 BC-14 AD) had bemoaned the loss of the good old days of the Roman Republic and tried to restore its morals and might, he could not even control the morals of his own household. When Augustus Diocletian three hundred years later tried to restore the halcyon days of Augustus Caesar, Rome was in a tailspin morally and fiscally.

When he divided the Empire into two parts under four rulers, Diocletian created a money monster that increasingly destabilized the Empire's solvency. The two Augusti and the two Caesars each increased their individual armies to such a large force that each force was greater than the entire army of the Roman Empire had been. They each built great temples and buildings in their sections of power. This continual, incremental augmentation of men and memorials, of course, drained the royal treasury because there were eventually fewer men in Rome who paid taxes than there were those in the Empire who received wages. Rome was broke and in debt, so they raised taxes. Large land owners were often targeted with false law suits in order to confiscate their properties and many who would not pay the prohibitive taxes on their estates abandoned Rome and settled with their families in distant provinces. Under the spiraling tax rates in Rome, many farmers no longer found it profitable to grow and to sell their crops and abandoned their farms. This created food scarcity and inflation. With inflation running rampant, Diocletian tried to stem it by price fixing, but that failed, so he reversed the policy.

The Supreme Augustus Diocletian, living in Nicomedia, would not curtail his own spending on his palaces and estates or on public buildings: new temples for the old gods, circuses, factories to make arms and triremes, mints to print money. He wanted Nicomedia to rival Rome. His many projects cost money and the over-taxed inhabitants of Nicomedia, also, started to abandon that city: "Presently, great parts of (Nicomedia) were quitted, and all men removed with their wives and children, as from a town taken by enemies." *Lactantius, On The Deaths Of The Persecutors 7*

But cities, states and empires have had, have and will have monetary crises. The real problem Diocletian and the Roman Empire had was Diocletian's son-in-law, the Caesar right under his august nose--- Galerius. When Diocletian had instituted the Tetrarchy, he cemented the union by giving Galerius his daughter Valeria in marriage and then adopting him as his son. The Western Augustus Maximian gave his daughter Theodora to his Caesar Constantius who had to divorce his wife Helena, mother of Constantine the Great, in order to assume his place in Diocletian's Tetrarchy. In St. Mark's Basilica in Venice, Italy there is a porphyry sculpture of the four men, each Augustus embracing his Caesar and all four clotted together into a stiff, phlegmatic mass. It is striking as an example of Roman art because it has none of the Grecian grace or subtlety associated with other Roman sculptures. All four men have the same frozen face, the same dress, the same swords and are of the same height. *The Tetrarchs* sculpture (c. 300) was obviously meant to convey sameness, equality of rule, united strength, the many are one. The union of the four men was to be strengthened by those marriages and adoptions among the four, but divided power is often divisive power.

The devolution of the Tetrarchy was part of this last, and some say the most virulent, of the persecutions of Christians. The killings started in 303 and lasted until the Edict of Milan in 313. Before that time, the Church had been at peace with Rome for about 30 years and had been accepted throughout the Empire. Diocletian and the other three men in the Tetrarchy had many Christians in their palaces and in high places in their administrations.

The seed of the persecution started innocuously enough when the highly superstitious Diocletian was having animals slain and their entrails examined for readings about future events. This ritual, called extispicy, was performed over the millennia by haruspices, priests who divined the meanings through entrails of animals. We get our word "auspices" meaning "prophetic signs" from these men who looked at the livers or intestines of animals or birds (and sometimes babies) for anomalies that had meanings relating to future events. As the priest was sacrificing that day in Nicomedia, some attendants of his who were Christians put the sign of the cross on their foreheads to protect them from the evil spirits of divination. The priest sacrificed over and over again and finally said he could not divine anything because there were "profane unbelievers," meaning Christians, who interrupted the rites. Diocletian who was a strong believer in these divinations was furious and caused everyone in his palace and Empire to sacrifice to the gods or be flogged. In case there were any Christians in his army, he commanded all of his soldiers to sacrifice and any who would not sacrifice should be thrown out of the army.

The Christian historian Eusebius of Caesarea who lived through the Diocletian persecution illustrates the confusion Diocletian's edict commanding sacrifice to the idols caused throughout the Empire and the complicated and sinister ways this first edict was carried out:

"the governors...and the military prefects who were incited by edicts, letters and public ordinances, and the magistrates, together with generals and the city clerks in all the cities (rushed) to fulfill the Imperial edicts which commanded that the altars of the idols should be rebuilt with all zeal and that all the men, together with the women and children, even infants at the breast, should offer sacrifice and pour out libations; and these officials urged them anxiously (and were) careful to make the people taste of the sacrifices; and (they caused) the meats in the markets to be polluted by the libations of the sacrifices and had watchmen... stationed before the Baths so as to defile those who washed in these with the all-abominable sacrifices." *Martyrs of Palestine 9*

The patience and forbearance of Christians had been so great that the pagans, in their impotence and rage, went so far as to sprinkle sacrificial wine on all meats in the marketplaces and to pollute the waters of the Baths with water that had been used in idol sacrifices. The Christians would be defiled one way or another.

This first edict commanding all to sacrifice to idols created a small rumble, but the Empire-wide explosion did not come until Diocletian had spent three months, from November and December of 302 through January of 303, with his Caesar Galerius in Bithynia (a part of modern Turkey).

The Christian writer Lactantius (c. 250-c. 325) was born a pagan and was brought to Nicomedia's court by Diocletian as a professor of rhetoric. He became a Christian there and his book, *On The Deaths Of The Persecutors,* is a first-hand account of all that transpired during the last great persecution. He knew Galerius and describes him: "The form of Galerius corresponded with his manners. Of stature tall, full of flesh and swollen to a horrible bulk of corpulency; by his speech, gestures and looks, he made himself a terror to all that came near him. His father-in-law (Diocletian) dreaded him excessively." *On The Deaths Of The Persecutors 9* Galerius complained publicly that Diocletian was old and should retire and hand over the title of Augustus to him. He who had been a herdsman scorned the title of Caesar as a title for mere clerks.

Galerius hated Christians because his mother Romula, a priestess of the pagan gods of the mountainous region east of the Danube River, constantly railed against them as enemies of her gods. It enflamed her as a priestess that the Christians in her household refused to eat the meat she had sacrificed to her idols. Meat sacrificed to idols in the Greco-Roman world was then eaten by the devotees. In Corinth the Temple of Ascelpius had three temple "restaurants," each seating 11 people. Temples dedicated to Demeter, the goddess of grain, as well as ones dedicated to Egyptian gods and Roman emperors had similar eating places in their temples. Romula, as a priestess, was entitled to bring the sacrificed meat home to her palace and to feed it to her guests. Some, but not all Christians (e.g. I Corinthians 8), considered meat sacrificed to idols unclean and offensive.

When Galerius and Diocletian were in Bithynia that winter, they met together alone many times and the servants and dignitaries in the palace spread the word that the meetings were "of the most momentous affairs of the empire." Lactantius, *On The Deaths Of The Persecutors 11* Galerius fulminated against Diocletian's unwillingness to start another persecution of the Christians:

"The (59 year) old man (Diocletian) long opposed the fury of (the 43-year-old) Galerius and showed how pernicious it would be to raise disturbances throughout the world and to shed so much blood; and that the Christians were wont with eagerness to meet death; and that it would be enough for him to exclude persons of that religion from the court and army. Yet he could not restrain the madness of that obstinate man (Galerius). Diocletian resolved, therefore, to take the opinion of his friends....Some, through personal ill-will toward the

Christians were of the opinion that they ought to be cut off as enemies of the gods and adversaries of established religious ceremonies. Others thought differently, but having understood the will of Galerius, they, either from dread of displeasing or from a desire of gratifying him, concurred in the opinion given against Christians. Yet not even then could (Diocletian) be prevailed upon to yield his assent. He determined above all to consult his god....he dispatched a soothsayer to inquire of Apollo at Miletus whose answer was such as might be expected from an enemy of the divine religion. So Diocletian....could struggle no longer against his friends and against Gallerius and Apollo, yet still he attempted to observe such moderation as to command the business to be carried through without bloodshed; whereas Galerius would have had all Christians burnt alive who refused to sacrifice." *On The Death Of The Persecutors 11*

The seers of the god Apollo at Miletus or Delphi usually gave ambiguous or cryptic responses such as "Know thyself." When the Lydian King Croesus, known for his wealth, asked the oracle at Delphi whether he should go to war with Persia, the oracle replied, "a great kingdom will fall." Emboldened, he went to war and was defeated by Cyrus the Great in 546 BC. If the questions were about Christians, the oracle usually began with "the impious on this earth..." When, however, in the 1st century AD Emperor Augustus sought advice from the oracle, he was given none. He asked, "Why is the Oracle silent?" He received an interesting, prescient response from the priest of Apollo: "A Hebrew boy, a god who rules among the blessed bid me leave this house and go back to Hades. So go in silence from my altars." *Chronicle Of John Malalas 9* By the 4th century when Diocletian asked advice from Apollo, many of the centers of oracular readings had been abandoned, but this seer at Miletus apparently gave Diocletian permission to begin the persecution.

Before dawn on February 23, 303 with Galerius and Diocletian watching from a nearby tower, tribunes and soldiers approached the church building in Nicomedia, forced open the gates, burned the Scriptures, destroyed everything in the church and then leveled it to the ground. The next day an edict ordained that all Christians should be stripped of high positions and were to be denied all rights in the courts of law. But Galerius was not satisfied unless there was blood. He had his servants set fire to a part of the palace. The Christians and the eunuchs were accused of trying to kill Diocletian and Galerius. Diocletian was scared and furious. He commanded his servants should be tortured until they confessed. None confessed, but Galerius had made sure none of his servants were subjected to torture. Fifteen days later in early March of 303 Galerius again had a part of the palace set on fire. It was quickly extinguished. Galerius furthered his plot by hastily leaving the palace at Nicomedia with all his retinue, loudly proclaiming he was escaping only with his life.

Diocletian was humiliated and raged against all Christians. He forced his wife Prisca and his daughter Valeria whom he had always suspected of being Christians to sacrifice to idols. Peter, a Christian official of high rank, refused to sacrifice. He was beaten, had salt and vinegar rubbed into his wounds and his limbs were burned one after the other. Diocletian killed all the eunuchs, all the Christian presbyters and other officers of the Church together with every member of their family with no respect to age or sex. They were herded together in groups and burned alive. He sent mandates to the Western Augustus Maximian and to his Caesar Constantius for all his edicts to be carried out in their regions. Maximian, who had ordered the slaughter of the entire Theban Legion in c. 286, started killing Christians immediately but Constantius, father of Constantine the Great, had always been tolerant of Christians and did not kill them but destroyed portions of their churches. Everyone in Diocletian's Nicomedia as well as in his territories and all in Galerius' provinces had to sacrifice to the idols or be killed. Galerius' plan to inaugurate blood martyrdoms had worked. His own persecutions were personal, particular and ghastly:

"...he kept bears, most resembling himself in fierceness and bulk, whom he had collected together during the course of his reign. As often as he chose to indulge himself, he ordered some particular bear to be brought in and men were thrown to that savage animal, rather to be swallowed up than devoured; and when their limbs were torn asunder, he laughed with excessive complacency; nor did he ever have dinner without being spectator of the effusion of human blood. Men of private station were condemned to be burnt alive; and he began this mode of execution by edicts against the Christians, commanding that, after torture and condemnation, Christians should be burnt over a slow fire. They were fixed to a stake and first a moderate flame was applied to the soles of their feet until the muscles, contracted by burning, were torn from the bones; then torches, lighted and put out again, were directed to all the members of their bodies, so that no part had any exemption. Meanwhile cold water was continually poured on their faces and their mouths moistened, lest, by reason of their jaws being parched, they should expire. At length they did expire when, after many hours, the violent heat had consumed their skin and penetrated into their intestines. The dead carcasses were laid on a funeral pile and wholly burnt; their bones were gathered, ground to powder and thrown into the river or into the sea." Lactantius, *On The Deaths Of The Persecutors 21*

It is ironic, and some would say just, that Galerius, whose death is described at the beginning of this chapter, lingered in horrendous agony daily for a whole year before he died.

The Christian historian Eusebius (269-339) who was eyewitness to this last great persecution (303-313) records:

"I myself was there when this was happening....to luminaries in Palestine and those in Tyre of Phoenicia...who under countless lashes and perseverance displayed (they were) champions of godliness: at the contests with man-eating beasts that followed the floggings, when they were attacked by leopards, bears of all kinds, wild boars and bulls goaded with hot irons....(and there was) incredible courage of these noble people in facing each of the beasts....You would have seen a youth not yet twenty (in front of lions) standing unchained, his arms spread in the form of a cross and his mind at ease, in leisure prayer to the Deity....You would also have seen others...thrown to a maddened bull.... in Egypt....others courageously bared their necks to the executioners or died of torture or hunger. Some again were crucified as criminals usually are, while others, even more cruelly, nailed in the opposite way, head downward, and kept alive until they died of hunger on the cross....Need I cite the names or numbers of the rest of the varieties of their martyrdoms? Sometimes they were killed with an axe, as was the case in Arabia, or had their legs broken, as those in Cappadocia (part of modern Turkey). At other times they were hung upside down over a slow fire, so that smoke rising from the burning wood suffocated them, as in Mesopotamia. Sometimes noses, ears and hands were mutilated and the other parts of the body butchered, as was the case in Alexandria.... At Antioch they were roasted on hot gridirons for prolonged torture and seared to death....In Pontus (area in Turkey around the Black Sea), others suffered things horrifying to hear: sharp reeds were driven into their fingers under the nail ends, or molten lead was poured down their backs, scalding the vital parts of their bodies. Others endured shameful, pitiful, unmentionable suffering in their private parts and intestines, which the noble, law-abiding judges eagerly invented, trying to outdo one another in devising new tortures as if contending for a prize. These tortures came to an end when their gruesome wickedness wore them out. Tired of killing and sated with blood, they turned to what they deemed mercy and humanity in no longer harming us.... Instead, orders were now issued that their eyes be gouged out and one of their legs maimed---which was 'humanity,' in their opinion and 'the lightest of punishments.' As a result of such philanthropy on the part of godless men, it is now impossible to report the vast number of people who first had their right eye sliced out with a sword and cauterized with fire and the left foot rendered useless by branding irons applied to the joints. After this they were condemned to the copper mines in the provinces, less for work there and more for the abuse and hardship they would receive, as well as other ordeals too numerous to report. Their dauntless deeds exceed all calculation. In all these trials the magnificent martyrs of Christ were so distinguished throughout the (Roman) world that eyewitnesses of their courage under torture were astounded. (The martyrs) provided in themselves clear proof (to the heathen) that the power of our Savior is divine and ineffable indeed....they preferred to suffer for the faith rather than transfer to idols the reverence due to God. As for the women, inspired by the Divine Word, they showed themselves as manly as the men. Some were subjected to the same ordeals as the men and won the same prizes for valor." *Church History 8.7.8.12.14*

There were so many martyrs in Africa at this time that the Coptic Churches of Egypt and Abyssinia (Ethiopia) still date their calendars from the accession of Emperor Diocletian to the throne in 284. Eusebius describes one governor in Palestine as being so eager to kill Christians that in one day, November 2, 307, he had a man Dominus burned alive, some young men castrated, sent three virgins to the brothels and three young men to the gladiators, had a minister of the gospel exposed to wild animals and imprisoned a priest, a scholar and an apologist for the faith. *Martyrs of Palestine 7.3.7*

The most famous martyr to emerge from the Diocletian persecution is St. George of St. George and the Dragon fame. There is little that is known for sure about George, but it seems he was a young Christian tribune from Palestine chosen to guard Diocletian. We know that Diocletian trusted only Christians to guard him, so that part is maybe true. When Diocletian's edict for all soldiers to perform the sacrifice to the pagan gods was issued in early 303, George refused, denounced the pagan edict and confessed himself a Christian in front of Diocletian's court. The legend goes that Diocletian was very fond of George and offered him money and lands to renounce Christ. George refused and Diocletian had no recourse but to have him executed. He was decapitated at Nicomedia April 23, 303 and his body was returned to his hometown of Lydda (modern-day Lod southeast of Tel Aviv) where about 20 years later, Emperor Constantine built a church consecrated to him. Ancient textual and historical evidence indicates there was a soldier named Georgios (George) executed in Nicomedia at the time of the Diocletian persecution, that George was from Lydda and that Constantine built a church there honoring him shortly after his death.

St. George, however, is not known for these scant historical facts. He is known as St. George the Dragon Slayer from the medieval *Golden*

Legend, a compilation (in c. 1260) of all that was then known, and perhaps embellished over the centuries, of famous early Christian martyrs and lore. In the *Golden Legend* a "dragon" was terrorizing a village and would only be appeased by the offering of a daily sheep for its feast. When no sheep could be found, lots were cast for a maiden to sacrifice and the lot fell to the monarch's daughter. Her father's money and power could not save her, so she went to the lake where the dragon lived and awaited her fate. George, on his horse and in military garb, came upon the scene and after making the sign of the cross, killed the dragon and the princess was saved. All the pagans in the town became Christians.

What bits of truth can be gleaned from this story? George was a soldier; he was a Christian; and perhaps was able to kill or overcome something that was threatening a town or his hometown. There may have been a young girl involved, or this may be medieval romantic fantasy. He became a hero and many people gave their lives to Christ because of his bravery or his example. Due to the medieval *Golden Legend*, however, George has become the archetype of all who through holy physical prowess save and slay.

Whatever may be glimpsed from the *Golden Legend* and the historical information on St. George is dwarfed by the impact of his life on the ages. The church Constantine erected to honor his martyr's death in the early 300's has been continually destroyed and rebuilt over the last 1,700 years and the one erected over the site in 1870, the Church of Saint George in Lod, Israel, is still standing. St. George has been able to unite Christians, Jews and Muslims. In Muslim Sufi literature George is called Khidr and is one of the four prophets Islam believes are still alive and immortal. The other three are Idris (Enoch), Ilyas (Elijah) and Isa (Jesus). Muslims, Christians and Jews to this day go to the rather shabby Eastern Orthodox shrine of St. George at Beit Jala near Bethlehem. Jews believe Elijah is buried there. Christians believe it to be the birthplace of St. George and Muslims come to ask Khidr, St. George, to help them with illnesses, mainly mental problems.

Even though George has no connection to Britain that can be validly ascertained, the English have particularly embraced St. George.

He is the patron saint of England and the St. George flag, a red cross on a field of white, is the official emblem of England and of the Most Noble Order of the Garter. St. George Day, April 23 the day on which he was martyred, is still celebrated all over the world: in Hungary, Lebanon, Syria, Spain, Canada, Russia, Albania, Bosnia, Serbia, Bulgaria and, of course, in the Caucasus country of Georgia named after St. George. The Christians of India reverence him and the Hindus pray to St. George the Dragon Slayer believing he will protect their children from cobras. The Mormon Latter Day Saints have a temple in St. George, Utah called the St. George Utah LDS Temple. Both town and Temple are named after George. It causes amazement that one little life and one heroic death so long ago and so far away can have such an historical impact on so many religions in so many places for so many centuries.

Over the centuries and especially during the Renaissance, painters have been drawn to the martyrdoms of early Christians. Veronese's large oil painting *The Martyrdom of St. George* adorns the high altar of the church of San Giorgio in Braida in Verona. Michelangelo painted many martyrs on the ceiling and walls of the Sistine Chapel. The early 15th century Il Sodoma's famous painting of St. Sebastian pierced with arrows is in the Uffizi Gallery in Florence; the painting by Caravaggio (1571-1610) called *The Martyrdom of St. Matthew* is in the Contarelli Capel, San Luigi dei Francesi in Rome;; *The Martyrdom of St. Philip* by the 16th century Spanish artist Jusepe de Ribera hangs in the Prado Museum in Madrid; and the famous academic painting by the 19th century French artist Jean-Leon Gerome, *The Christian Martyrs' Last Prayer* in the Walters Art Gallery in Baltimore, Maryland, portrays Christians in the Colosseum kneeling in prayer as they await their gnawing by an at-the-ready lion while their brothers, burning on crosses in the background, ring the amphitheater.

After the Christians won the right for religious liberty in 313, Lactantius in *On the Deaths of the Persecutors 16* wrote to his friend Donatus, who had been imprisoned and tortured for his faith:

"How pleasing the spectacle to God when He beheld you a conqueror, yoking in your chariot not white horses nor enormous elephants, but those very men who had led captive the nations! After this sort to lord it over the lords of the earth is triumph indeed!....No violence could bereave you of your fidelity and persevering resolution. This it is to be a disciple of God and this it is to be a soldier of Christ; a soldier whom no enemy can dislodge or world snatch from the heavenly camp; no artifice ensnare or pain of body subdue or torments overthrow."

There is no question that by 303-313 the martyrdom of Christians by the Tetrarchy was not sanctioned by the bulk of the Roman people who had over the centuries become sympathetic to Christians and their ideas. Some officials who were charged with making Christians perform the sacrifices or killing them would seize the hands of Christians, put the sacrifice in their hands and force their hands to throw the sacrifice on the fire. Some officials told Christians they had already sacrificed and dismissed them. But most, like so many before and after them, did not intervene or protest the treatment of Christians as long as their own lives were not affected.

Money affects people's lives and when the Tetrarch rulers, especially Galerius, imposed grueling taxes on all citizens, the people did protest and became irate. The methods of assessing taxes were a reflection of the despotic and dictatorial nature of the men who made up the Tetrarchy. A capitation tax, poll tax, was enacted on each person in the Empire. Surveyors would arrive on a person's property and measure every spot of land, number all the vines and fruit trees and make lists of all animals and their kinds in order to tax the assets of a landowner. Slaves were beaten to extract information on hidden assets of their masters. Wives were tortured to bear witness against their husbands and sons were strapped to the rack to force them to reveal their fathers' assets. Imaginary assets given under torture were entered into the books and were taxed as real assets. The head tax was imposed on a sliding scale on every one in the Empire including children and babies. The people were further outraged when the rulers levied a "death tax" not only on those who had died but, also, on their dead animals. It was said, "We cannot live or cease to live without being subject to taxes." When Galerius was confronted with mendicants who could not pay any tax, he caused them to be assembled in groups, put them in boats and sunk the boats because, as he said, he had compassion on them and did not want them to remain indigent. This draconian action, also, insured that none, under the pretext of poverty, should elude the capitation tax. There were riots in Rome and Carthage. The Roman Empire and its olio of peoples were worn out by centuries of constant fighting and imperial vagaries and were worn down by the weight of taxes, quixotic laws and the personal tolls exacted by just being "the Roman Empire."

In 305 Diocletian in the East and Maximian in the West were pressed by Galerius to take their retirement and allow their Caesars, Galerius and Constantius, to become supreme rulers. Both Augusti seemed relieved after 20 years of rule (285-305) to live lives of ease and luxury in posh palaces and extravagant villas. The Tetrarch plan seemed to have worked. Both Augusti were replaced by their Caesars.

But the structure began to fall apart when the new Augustus in the East, Galerius, insisted on naming both of the Caesars who would serve under the new Augusti. He elevated his nephew Daia who as a youth had looked after cattle in the forests of Dacia to be Caesar (Maximinus II) under him and he installed an old military friend, Severus, as Caesar under Constantius. There was outrage that Maxentius, the son of Maximian, was not named Caesar when his father retired and that Constantine, the son of Constantius, was not named Caesar under his father. The idea of the Tetrarchy had been there would be no hereditary heirs, but the real power of Rome, the troops, wanted the heirs. July 25, 306 Constantius died and his son Constantine was proclaimed Emperor by his troops. As a result, Maxentius, son of the retired Maximian, went to Rome and was proclaimed Emperor by his troops. Galerius ignored Constantine and his troops and elevated Severus into the Augustus position vacated by Constantius. Thirteen years after the institution of the Rule by Four, there were five rulers on thrones: Galerius, Maximinus Daia, Flavius Valerius Severus, Constantine and Maxentius.

In order to bring the number of rulers back to four, Galerius dispatched Severus and his troops to Rome to kill Maxentius. Severus was not successful and was permitted to commit suicide. Now there were four again. But Galerius made it five again when he appointed a childhood friend, Licinius, to be Augustus in the West in 308. Even though Maxentius in Rome had defeated Severus, he had a precarious hold on the throne, so he summoned his father Maximian, the former Augustus in the West, out of retirement to bolster his power. Maximian came and became inflamed with power declaring himself Augustus again. And now there were six rulers: Galerius and Daia in the East and Licinius, Maxentius, Maximian and Constantine in the West. It was a mess.

By 312 there were only four rulers. Maximian, twice an Augustus, was forced to commit suicide in 310 about 20 years after he had ordered the Theban Legionnaires killed at St.-Maurice-en-Valais, Switzerland, and Galerius died a painful death in 311 after which Daia co-ruled the East with Licinius. Maxentius and Constantine battled in the West. There were now four men, a Tetrarchy again, who should have been trying to rule jointly and harmoniously but were instead each ruling their territories independent of each other and each vying to become the Supreme Augustus of the Roman Empire. The united Tetrarchy imagined by Diocletian had fractured and that old demon, the primordial desire for power, was prowling. Would Polybius' cycle from monarchy to monarchy be completed?

During the ten years the rulers were coveting and maneuvering for the sovereignty of the Empire (303-313), untold thousands of Christians all over the Empire were being martyred. Heathenism was exhausting its powers with every death. The pagan world had nothing to throw against Christianity but brute force. It had no gods, no ideology, no internal power or energy to match the force of the vibrancy of the Christian God and of His steady, suffering servants. The *Liber Pontificalis 1.162*, a collection of biographies of the popes from the 1st century Peter through the 15th century, asserts that 17,000 were martyred during a 31-day period at this time. On his deathbed in 311 in Nicomedia, Galerius had signed an Edict of Toleration rescinding the persecution of Christians, designating Christianity as a *religio lecita* ("legitimate religion") and asking the Christians to pray for his health. But in spite of his "death-bed conversion," Galerius and his power were dead. Christians were still pursued, tortured and killed by all the rulers except Constantine. In the areas under his sovereignty, Christians were tolerated as they had been under Constantine's father.

In early 312 the usurper Maxentius in Rome declared war on Constantine by having all statues of him in Italy destroyed. Maxentius had been warned by soothsayers to remain inside the walls of Rome if he wanted to stay alive. If his enemy would not come to Constantine, Constantine would go to his enemy. In the Spring of 312, Constantine with c. 40,000 troops and 15,000 cavalry began the long march south to Rome. Along the way he took city after city, most of which opened their gates to him and received him joyously. He had adopted the policy of forgiveness for citizens of the cities so none were raped or killed nor were their cities plundered. By October of 312 Constantine was outside Rome on the Via Flaminia, the road that led northeast from Rome over the Apennine Mountains to Rimini on the Adriatic Sea. The surveyors and engineers who had mapped out the Flaminian road in 220 BC were so accurate in assessing the easiest way north from Rome to the Adriatic that the SS3 and SP3 parallel the original Via Flaminia.

With Constantine at the gates of Rome, Maxentius, feeling very secure in the well-fortified city, was ready to celebrate the sixth year of his reign with chariot races in the Circus Maximus. At the races the people shouted, "Constantine cannot be overcome!" In terror Maxentius fled from the Circus, assembled some senators and ordered the Sibylline Books to be consulted. Maxentius and most pagans in the ancient world were highly superstitious and consulted seers, tried to devise prophetic meanings from sacrifices and omens and if they were a ruler or patrician, they could have access to the Greek Sibylline Books, an ancient compilation of oracular sayings from the 600's BC. The legend was that Tarquin the Proud, the last King of Rome whose tyrannical rule led to the establishment of the Roman Republic in 509 BC, had purchased the oracles from a Greek sibyl for an enormous amount of money. At the time of Maxentius, the Sibylline Books were kept in the Temple of Apollo on the Palatine (the etymological origin of the words *palace*, Italian *palazzo* and French *palais*).

The verses in the Sibylline Books were cryptic, ambiguous and often inane. Livy in *History 10.47* writes that during a plague in 293 BC, the Books said vapidly, "Aesculapius (god of healing) must be brought to Rome from Epidaurus." In 216 BC when Hannibal defeated the Romans at Cannae, the Sibyls said two Gauls and two Greeks had to be buried alive in the marketplace. Tacitus in his *Annals 1.76* recounts a time when a sensible Caesar did not want to consult the oracles, preferring instead to keep prophecy a secret: "In the same year (15 AD) the Tiber, swollen by continuous rains, flooded the level portions of Rome. Its subsidence was followed by destruction of buildings and of life. Thereupon Asinius Gallus proposed to consult the Sibylline books. Tiberius refused, veiling in obscurity the divine as well as the human." Tiberius Caesar understood that the "rain falls on the just and the unjust." Matthew 5:45

Maxentius had been told by a soothsayer to stay shut up in Rome, but on that day in October of 312 the Sibylline Books read: "On the same day the enemy of the Romans shall perish." Buoyed on to victory over Constantine by this prophecy, Maxentius decided to go out of Rome with his troops and engage Constantine near the Milvian Bridge, today called the Ponti Milvio, on the Via Flaminia. In order to facilitate the crossing of the Tiber River for his tens of thousands of troops, Maxentius caused another wooden bridge or a pontoon bridge overlaid with planks to be hurriedly built near the Milvian Bridge.

Years after the battle, Constantine the Great related to Eusebius, Bishop of Caesarea, the miraculous event that happened to him shortly before that battle:

"He said that about noon, when the day was already beginning to decline, he saw with his own eyes a trophy of a cross of light in the heavens, above the sun, and bearing the inscription, 'Conquer By This Sign.' At this sight he himself was struck with amazement, as was his whole army also, which followed him on this expedition, and witnessed the miracle. (Constantine) said, moreover, that he doubted within himself what the import of this apparition could be. And while he continued to ponder and reason on its meaning, night suddenly came on; then in his sleep the Christ of God appeared to him with the same sign which he had seen in the heavens, and commanded him to make a likeness of that sign which he had seen in the heavens and to use it as a safeguard in all engagement with his enemies....the victorious emperor himself long afterwards declared (this) to this writer of history when he (Eusebius) was honored with his acquaintance and society, and (Constantine) confirmed his statement by an oath." Eusebius, *Life of Constantine 28.29*

Eusebius wrote his biography of Constantine in Greek and Constantine saw three Greek letters in the sky: *In Touto Nika*, "In This (Sign) Conquer." (Raphael's early 16th century painting *Vision of the Cross* in the Apostolic Palace of the Vatican clearly shows *In Touto Nika* across the sky, so the painter and his assistants used information from Eusebius' Greek text.) The same phrase, more familiar to us when translated into Latin, is: *In Hoc Signo Vinces*, "In This Sign Conquer" or just *In Hoc Signo*, "In This Sign." The meaning of "IHS" has been expanded over the centuries: it is the first three letters of the spelling of "Jesus" in Greek (*iota, eta, sigma*); in Latin "IHS" is *Iesus Hominum Salvator* meaning "Jesus, Savior of Mankind;" and in modern English "IHS" is often used by Christians to mean "In His Service."

When Constantine saw Christ in a dream that night, Christ commanded him to put a "likeness of that sign which he had seen in the heavens...as a safeguard in all engagement with his enemies." Most assume the sign was a conventional cross, but we are not told in this narrative exactly what "a likeness of that sign" was. Were the three words in the sky or the signs of the words (e.g. IHS) or "a trophy of a cross of light" to be emblazoned? The old Greek word *tropaion* meaning "trophy" meant "a monument of an enemy's defeat." The word as a noun or adjective was always associated with the rout or the defeat of an enemy. The "trophy" Constantine saw had several meanings: it was a sign of Christ as the text indicates as well as a harbinger of defeat to his enemy as the word "trophy" indicates. Was this "sign" to be signified on the shields or the helmets of his soldiers or on the military standards of the army? Lactantius, who later became an advisor to Constantine, is the only other contemporary footprint in parchment to this pivotal historical phenomenon. He gives us more specific information:

"Constantine was directed in a dream to cause the heavenly sign to be delineated on the shields of his soldiers, and so to proceed to battle. He did as he had been commanded and he marked on their shields the (Greek) letter X (Chi), with a perpendicular line drawn through it turned around thus at the top (a Rho), being the cipher of CHRIST. Having this sign, his troops stood to arms." *On the Deaths of the Persecutors 44*

Lactantius says "the heavenly sign" was a "Chi-Rho" and it was to be marked on the shields of the soldiers. That makes sense as the Chi-Rho had been a Christogram for Christ since the 1st century AD as Lactantius indicates when he calls it "the cipher of Christ." To spell the name "Christ" in Greek, one begins with Chi-X (for Ch) and Rho-P (for R). Chi-Rhos had been inscribed by early Christians on walls and in the catacombs for hundreds of years. XP was their discreet designation for Christ. More meaning and resonance is achieved when the vertical Rho (in Greek a P) is centered and superimposed over the Chi (X which looks like an unconventional St. Andrew's-type cross) to form a more conventional-looking cross. In the cautious world of the early Christians, if the uninitiated saw that monogram, it would have had no meaning to them. The pagan Constantine, confused and doubting, did not understand this monogram until, no doubt, some Christians in his army explained it to him.

After Constantine's dream, the next day he had the Chi-Rho symbol painted over the pagan symbol on all his soldiers' shields. (*Scutum* was the name given to this long rectangular shield that covered the front and part of the sides of his soldiers.) His troops were willing to carry the Christian shield because, as Eusebius recounts, most of the army had seen the same phenomenon in the sky Constantine had seen.

Roman armies carried upright metal standards called *signum* into battles. From the time of the Republic most standards had *SPQR* on them. The letters in Latin are the first letters of the four words *Senatus Populus Que Romanus* standing for (in the name of) "The Senate And The People Of Rome." (Modern manholes in Rome enigmatically bear "SPQR" on their covers.) Often the symbol of Rome, an Eagle, topped the Roman military standard. (The USA has had the bald eagle as a symbol of its nation since 1782.) Under the traditional Roman symbol on top of the standard was a flag with the emperor, often with his children, depicted and embroidered on it. Eusebius confirms that Constantine had the Chi-Rho on top of the military standard as well as a banner of himself and his children configured under it:

"Now it was made in the following manner: A long spear, overlaid with gold, formed the figure of the cross by means of a transverse bar laid over it. On the top of the whole was fixed a wreath of gold and precious stones, and within this, the symbol of the Savior's name, two letters indicating the name of Christ by means of its initial characters, the letter P being intersected by X in its center, and these letters the emperor was in the habit of wearing on his helmet at a later period. (A silver medallion struck in 313 in Ticinum shows Constantine with a small Chi-Rho on his helmet above his right eye.) From the crossbar of the spear was suspended a cloth, a royal piece, covered with a profuse embroidery of most brilliant precious stones which, being also richly interlaced with gold, presented an indescribable degree of beauty to the beholder. This banner was of a square form, and the upright staff, whose lower section was of great length, bore a golden half-length portrait of the pious emperor and his children on its upper part, beneath the trophy of the cross (the Chi-Rho) and immediately above the embroidered banner. The emperor constantly made use of this standard (now called the *labarum*) as a safeguard against every adverse and hostile power and commanded that others similar to it should be carried at the head of all his armies." *Life of Constantine 31*

Constantine and his c. 40,000 troops and cavalry, flashing the Chi-Rho Christian symbol on their shields, went into battle as the first Christian army on October 28, 213 against Maxentius and his c. 100,000 troops and cavalry. Constantine's troops were outnumbered two to one, but they were better trained, had seen the phenomenon in the sun, bore its sign on their shields and were eager for the enemy. Maxentius had decided to defend the stone Milvian Bridge leading into Rome. If the defense failed, he and his troops could always retreat behind the gates and walls of the city. Constantine's troops held the high ground. When both cavalries charged and scattered troops, Maxentius' troops were pushed down toward the Tiber River. Many were pushed into the water. Maxentius panicked and decided to call a retreat. The tens of thousands of soldiers and cavalrymen who were crowding the damaged Milvian Bridge and the temporary wooden bridge nearby caused chaos. Soldiers with their shields, arms and shirts of mail were pushed into the Tiber and sunk to the bottom. Maxentius on his horse tried to cross the river on either the temporary wooden bridge or the damaged Milvian Bridge. He was indiscriminately crushed and pushed by his retreating troops into the Tiber where he drowned. Lactantius writes: "The bridge in his (Maxentius') rear was broken down. At sight of that the battle grew hotter. The hand of the Lord prevailed, and the forces of Maxentius were routed. Maxentius fled towards the broken bridge; but the multitude pressing on him, he was driven headlong into the Tiber." *On The Deaths Of The Persecutors 44* History is filled with ironies. The Tiber River was named after Tiberinus, a 9th century BC pagan king of the area around Rome, who drowned in its waters. Over a thousand years later the last pagan king to rule over the city of Rome drowned, also, in the muddy waters of the Tiber.

The victory at Milvian Bridge gave Constantine total control over the Roman Empire in the West and was the decisive event in the Christianization of greater Europe and by extension of all of North and South America. The next day, October 29, 312, Constantine entered Rome and was received with jubilation. He had the body of Maxentius fished out of the Tiber, beheaded and sent to Carthage. Africa as well as Rome then declared Constantine sole ruler of the Western Empire. After being in Rome for less than a month, he left for Milan to meet with the Augustus Licinius from the East and to solemnize the nuptials of his half-sister Constantia's marriage to him. He told Licinius the miraculous circumstances of his victory over Maxentius and about the God Who had directed his battle.

There were now three men in contest for the Roman Empire. The third, Daia, resented the meeting of the two men in Milan and took that opportunity to invade Licinius' territory. Licinius, caught off guard, quickly cobbled together a small army as he marched to Tzirallum in modern Turkey where he and Daia prepared to battle for the supremacy of the East. Daia had decided to vow to Jupiter that he would erase Christians from the face of the earth if the god would favor his side. Licinius, no doubt influenced by Constantine's miraculous story and victory, saw:

"an angel of the Lord standing before him while he was asleep, admonishing him to arise immediately and with his whole army to put up a prayer to the Supreme God...to obtain victory....(Licinius) sent for his secretaries and dictated these words exactly as he had heard them: 'Supreme God, we beseech Thee; Holy God, we beseech Thee; unto Thee we commend all right; unto Thee we commend our safety; unto Thee we commend our empire. By Thee we live, by Thee we are victorious and happy. Supreme Holy God, hear our prayers; to Thee we stretch forth our arms. Hear, Holy Supreme God.' Many copies were made of these words and distributed amongst the principal commanders, who were to teach them to the soldiers under their charge. At this all the men took fresh courage, in the confidence that victory had been announced to them from heaven....A barren and open plain, called Campus Serenus, lay between the two armies. They were now in sight of one another. The soldiers of Licinius placed their shields on the ground, took off their helmets and, following the example of their leaders, stretched forth their hands towards heaven. The emperor (Licinius) uttered the prayer and they all repeated it after him. (Daia)...heard the murmur of the prayers of their adversaries. And now, the ceremony having been performed three times, the soldiers of Licinius became full of courage, buckled on their helmets again and resumed their shields....the two armies drew nigh; the trumpets gave the signal; the military ensigns advanced; the troops of Constantine charged. But the enemies, panic struck, could neither draw their swords nor yet throw their javelins....Then were the troops of Daia slaughtered, none making resistance....After great numbers had fallen, Daia perceived that everything went contrary to his hopes...he threw aside the purple of royalty...put on the clothes of a slave and hastened across the Thracian Bosphorus." Lactantius, *On The Death Of The Persecutors 46.47*

Whether Daia, dressed as a slave, fled to Nicomedia on horseback or on foot, we are not told. But he is remembered in some history books as one of the fastest people ever: "Before the expiration of the kalends of May (May 1, 313), Daia arrived at Nicomedia, although distant 160 miles from the field of battle." Lactantius, *On The Deaths Of The Persecutors 47* One has to assume he went on horseback. He traveled 160 miles in less than two days because the Battle was on April 30, 313. A good horse and rider can travel 30-40 miles a day in relatively smooth terrain. Daia, assuming he appropriated a horse, had to ride day and night through mountainous terrain with no relays or rests. That little sentence in Lactantius' book has caused quite a stir over the centuries. In Nicomedia he gathered up his wife, children and some followers and fled, incognito, to Cappadocia in central Turkey where he again assumed the purple robe of Emperor.

Meanwhile, Licinius bolstered by his victory over Daia, acknowledged that the Christian God had handed him the battle. Licinius and Constantine, both having won battles under the aegis of Christ, had a summit in June of 313 in Milan, Italy where they composed and sent out to all in the Empire a letter, called the Edict of Milan, giving Christians "religious liberty:"

"We have long intended that freedom of religion should not be denied but that everyone should have the right to practice his religion as he chose. Accordingly, we have given order that both Christians and all others should be permitted to keep the faith of their own sect....When under happy auspices I, Constantine Augustus, and I, Licinius Augustus, had come to Milan and were discussing all matters that concerned the public good, among the other items of benefit to the general welfare... we decided to issue such decrees as would assure respect and reverence for the Deity, namely, to grant the Christians and all others the freedom to follow whatever form of worship they pleased....Here, therefore, is the decision we reached by sound and prudent reasoning: no one at all was to be denied the right to follow or choose the Christian form of worship or observance....we have granted to these same Christians free and limitless permission to practice their own form of worship....this permission has also been given to others who wish to follow their own observance and form of worship....This we have done so that we might not appear to have belittled any rite or form of worship in any way....(all their places of worship) must be handed over to the body of the Christians immediately, through zealous action on your part and without delay.... (all private property confiscated from Christians) you will order restored without any question whatever to these same Christians....in order that our generosity and enactment may be known to all, what we have written should be announced...published everywhere, and brought to the attention of all, so that the enactment incorporating our generosity may escape the notice of no one." Eusebius, *Church History 10.5*

The State-mandated Edict of Milan in 313 was the first ever to proclaim the "religious liberty" Tertullian had demanded over 100 years earlier in his *Apology 24* and the young Carthaginian martyr Perpetua had shouted out to the Roman procurator Hilarian in 203: "For this cause we came willingly that our liberty might not be obscured." At last, not only Christians but all pagans had the right to choose to worship whatever god their consciences and convictions dictated without interference from the State. Christians, by their faith and constancy under persecution and death, had at last triumphed. They could shout to all, *A Crux Nostra Corona*! "The Cross Is Our Crown!" Their invisible, non-material faith had proved stronger and more invincible than all the might and muscle of the Roman Empire. "This is the victory that has overcome the world, even our faith." (I John 2:2) The Church historian Eusebius, who had lived through the years of the Diocletian persecution and had read the records of all those who had been martyred before he lived, rejoiced:

"'Sing to the Lord a new song, for he has done marvelous things; His right hand and his holy arm have wrought salvation...His righteousness He has revealed in the sight of the heathen.' (Psalm 98:1,2) Accordingly, let me now sing the new song, since after those grim and horrifying scenes and narratives (of martyrs), I was now privileged to see and to celebrate what many righteous men and martyrs of God before me desired to see but did not see, and to hear but did not hear....From now on, a cloudless day, radiant with rays of heavenly light, shined down on the churches of Christ throughout the world." *Church History 10.1*

The Christians' triumph over the State in 313 was not just for them. Their victory was for people of all faiths in the West and in the East. The cry for "religious liberty" resounds today throughout the world.

There is, however, no indication that Constantine was a Christian before he saw the sign in the sky or even after he saw it and crafted the Edict of Milan. He, like all pagans, was superstitious and the fact he had won the battle against Maxentius under the sign of the Christian God and had acknowledged that fact did not mean that he was a Christian. But he certainly was a man with the power and the will to change the Roman State's stance toward Christianity. Over the next 25 years of his reign Constantine step by step molded and allowed Christians to mold the Roman Empire into a Christian Empire.

Rome did not fall like Babylon or disappear without a trace as did Nineveh. The Christians rescued Rome as they had rescued Jerusalem. The Christian Church resuscitated the dying embers of the Roman civilization into not only a powerful flame but into a holy fire that 2,000 years later shows no signs of abating. Every seed of Christian life that was tortured, burned, scraped to death, beheaded or torn to pieces by wild beasts spawned many seeds of faith that were blown by the wings of winds to every part of the world.

In the end, Constantine, the pagan/Christian Emperor fully embraced the Christian faith. On his deathbed, he asked to be baptized as a Christian. Eusebius in *The Life of Constantine 4.62.4* records that some bishops "performed the sacred ceremonies according to custom" in May of 337. After he was baptized, he said, "Now all ambiguity vanishes." *The Life Of Constantine 6.62* Constantine, called the Great, died on the last day of Pentecost May 22, 337 at age 65.

What took the Emperor who had transformed the Roman world

into a Christian world so long to be baptized into the faith he had so assiduously imbedded in the old Roman Empire? One will never know for sure because we have no textual evidence. Maybe he held back because he did not want to offend the sensibilities of the many who were still pagan. "Now all ambiguity vanishes" would favor that hypothesis. Maybe he was not totally sure of his own faith. We know, however, Constantine had been exposed to Christian influences from his boyhood. His mother Helena was a strong Christian and his father Constantius never killed Christians and seemed to revere, if not worship, the Christian God. Sozomen, the 5th century Christian historian, tells an interesting, if perhaps apocryphal, story about Constantius:

"Constantius, the father of Constantine, accorded the Christians the right of worshiping God without fear. I know of an extraordinary thing done by him which is worthy of being recorded. He wished to test the fidelity of certain Christians...who were attached to his palaces. He called them all together and told them that if they would sacrifice to idols as well as serve God, they should remain in his service and retain their appointments; but if they refused compliance with his wishes, they should be sent from the palaces and should scarcely escape his vengeance. When difference of judgment had divided them into two parties, separating those who consented to abandon their religion from those who preferred the honor of God to their present welfare, the emperor determined upon retaining those who had adhered to their faith as his friends and counselors; but he turned away from the others whom he regarded as unmanly and impostors, and sent them from his presence, judging that they who had so readily betrayed their God could never be true to their king." *Ecclesiastical History Book 2.6*

Constantine is plagued by modern historians who either challenge the reliability and impartiality of the two contemporary accounts of him, Eusebius' *Life of Constantine* and Lactantius' *On The Death of the Persecutors*, as too biased toward Christianity or they bemoan the purely political and military accounts as omitting mentions of Constantine's religion. Since the 19th century there has been a concerted effort in academia to paint Constantine as a hypocrite. The attacks on Constantine give false alternatives: he was either a total Christian or a total hypocrite and liar. He, like most who try to learn about and follow a faith, was not a perfect man and many contrary things exist in the heart of most people. Perhaps Constantine was not only personally drawn to Christianity but as a ruler saw its vitality as the salt needed to preserve the Roman State from the putrefaction of paganism. The real historical and academic interest in Constantine should not be only as an Emperor, warrior, hypocrite, liar or man of God but as a man who had the power to change the face of the pagan world into a Christian image regardless of his motives.

Constantine did just that---slowly but surely. After his victory at the Milvian Bridge, he did not go to the Temple of Jupiter in Rome and offer sacrifices as was the custom of conquerors. He tore down the stables of the Imperial cavalry and erected the Lanteran Basilica, now home to the offices of the Vicariate of Rome and the living quarters of the Vicar general of the diocese of Rome. In c. 313, he commissioned in Rome a 40' high statue of himself with a Chi-Rho in his right hand and an inscription: "By this salutary sign, the true proof of valor, I have freed your city and saved it from the yoke of the tyrant." Eusebius, *Church History 9.9.11* All that remains of the colossus are his over 7' high handsome head now in the Musei Capitolini in Rome, his hands, a 6' long foot complete with callouses on it, fragments of the left and right kneecaps and other body fragments.

From 313 on, Constantine lavished money and land on Christian churches and banished crucifixion as a means of capital punishment because Christ was killed on a cross. Criminals could no longer be branded on their forehead because the face was a reflection of God's creation and heavenly beauty and should not be defaced. This last seemingly irrelevant law was actually founded upon the Christian principle of the dignity of man, a principle totally foreign to paganism but important in the Judeo-Christian Bible. Infanticide, practiced for thousands of years, was forbidden and he encouraged the freeing of slaves who were some of the earliest followers of Christ. The anti-slavery law, the first in man's history, required the manumission of slaves to take place in a church ceremony in the presence of a priest. The freeing of a slave was considered a holy act.

In order to make Christianity Roman-wide, Constantine used the word, *catholic* meaning "universal," to describe the desired scope of the Christian church. "Catholic" comes from the Greek word *katholikos* meaning "on the whole" and the Latin word *catholicus* meaning "general, universal." In the 1st century Early Church the word was used to differentiate the Church in Jerusalem or the Church in Rome or the Church in Alexandria from the Catholic Church, meaning the Church of Christ as a whole. The *Muratorian Fragment* from c. 170 uses the word "catholic" in the sense of "whole body of believers": "... And John too, indeed, in the Apocalypse, although he writes only to seven churches, yet addresses all. (Paul) wrote...one to Philemon, and one to Titus and two to Timothy....these are hallowed in the esteem of the catholic church." In the 2nd century the word "catholic" began to be used to differentiate groups of heretics from the orthodox, the catholic church. In the early 16th century when Luther, Zwingli and Calvin wanted to reform the Universal Church, they had no intention of leaving it and starting a new Christian movement. Their desire was to return the Church to a firm Biblical and Apostolic footing. But history has a way of defining words and the word "Protest-ant" has been attached to those sects and denominations who eventually broke away from the Catholic Church. And "catholic" has since been affixed to the Roman Catholic Church, not designating the Church in Rome but all who adhere to that denomination world-wide.

A Protestant (Latin *protestari* meaning "to profess") was originally one who "avowed" or "confessed" certain things. "Protestant" in the sense of an ecclesiastical denomination was first used at the Diet of Speyer in 1529 to characterize those Catholics who had become members of congregations that wished to reform the Catholic Church. The Diet of 1529 prohibited all present and future reformations of the Church. Philip of Hesse, Johann of Saxony and other German princes whose 14 cities had become "reformed" composed a "Letter of Protestation" against that decision. Those Luther and Zwingli-influenced men who had issued the *protestatio* (the "profession, declaration") were called

"Protest-ants." The word did not morph into one who "objects or dissents" until the 1700's. The early Christians, it must be stated, were not Catholic or Protestant. All were simply Christians, *Christianoi*.

Constantine continued his reformations of pagan society by consecrating Sunday, the day of the resurrection of Jesus, as a Sabbath day of rest in the Empire. Sunday was, also, the day of the Sun god, Sol Invictus, so Constantine straddled his position between paganism and Christianity as he would do in other areas of governance. But when he enacted laws banning abortion and the exposure of children, Constantine was acting as a Christian ruler. When many parents sold their children during a famine in 321, Constantine banned that long-standing practice. If parents were verifiably destitute, the State would give them money. One of the most important things Constantine did was to commission in 331 the writing of 50 Bibles for the Church in his new capital in the East called Byzantium (which name would in the 400's be changed to Constantinople which name would be changed to Istanbul in 1930 when modern Turkey was established). These Bibles, like most early Christian Bibles, were written on leaves of parchment stitched and bound together (a codex) to create a facsimile of a modern book. It is surmised, but not proven, that the two oldest Greek Bibles extant, the Codex Vaticanus and the Codex Sinaiticus both of which were written in the 300's, are two of those Bibles commissioned by Constantine.

Constantine sent his then c. 76 year-old devout mother Helena to Palestine to ferret out relics and recover Christian memorials. Jerusalem, destroyed in 70 AD by Titus, had been rebuilt by Emperor Hadrian in 135 AD as a Roman city named Aelia Capitolina. Constantine tore down all of Hadrian's heathen temples and destroyed all pagan idols in the city. He called it officially "Jerusalem" again. Helena was in charge of rebuilding churches at important Christian sites. Eusebius credits her with finding the birthplace of Jesus and then building a church, the Church of the Nativity in Bethlehem, over the site. When she found what she believed was the cross on which Jesus was crucified, Constantine commissioned the building of the Church of the Holy Sepulcher on the site. Whether it was the exact cross on which Jesus was crucified or not is open to speculation. However, St. Helena is always painted or sculpted with a cross in her hand. The Andrea Bolgi sculpture of Helena in the shrine dedicated to her in St. Peter's Basilica has her holding with her right hand a cross that is taller than she is. She walked all over Palestine identifying, through local people and traditions, the supposed places where Jesus or His Apostles had done important things. Almost two thousand years later, most of her discoveries are still acknowledged as probable or valid. She died in August of 330 with her son Constantine at her bedside. Her ornate Egyptian porphyry sarcophagus can be seen in the Museo Pio-Clementino in the Vatican.

Constantine had to navigate his Christian faith or feelings carefully because most of his Empire was still pagan. Of c. 50-75 million people in the Roman Empire in the early 300's, it is estimated that 10-15% were Christians, though many were Christian sympathizers. That was a sizable number of people considering Christianity started with 120 people in an upstairs room in 30 AD. Constantine had once worshipped Sol Invictus and coins struck of him before 312 indicate that fact. Sol Invictus was an Asiatic god who had been worshipped by Emperor Marcus Aurelius (121-180) and had been used on coins by every emperor thereafter as a symbol of Roman strength and a bow to tradition. Removing the image of Sol Invictus from Roman coins in 313 would have been tantamount to removing the eagle from American coins starting in 2015. After 313, there are some coins minted with Constantine on the obverse and the labarum, the Christian standard, on the reverse. Most of his coins, however, have Sol Invictus on the reverse until the Council of Nicea in 325 when all pagan signs on Roman coins disappeared.

The Arch of Constantine built in c. 313 to celebrate Constantine's victory over Maxentius is still standing between the Colosseum and the Palatine hill. Its ornamentations are a hodgepodge of scenes gouged out of earlier memorials dedicated to Trajan, Hadrian and Marcus Aurelius and plastered into Constantine's Arch. Rome had for so many years been a minor city in Rome's Empire that competent sculptors and artists had taken up residence in the important cities to the East and few were left to memorialize Constantine. It was a public building and Constantine did not choose to put overt Christian symbols on it. In the dedication "To the Emperor Caesar Flavius Constantius, the greatest, pious and blessed Augustus" there are the words: "...because he, inspired by the divine and by the greatness of his mind, has delivered the state from the tyrant." The phrase, "inspired by the divine," rather than "through Jupiter" is a tactful hint of Constantine's changing allegiances. His dilemma as ruler of a mainly pagan people to whom he had, also, given in the Edict of Milan total religious freedom was to negotiate with equanimity his own growing belief in Christianity and his obligations to and genuine feelings for a pagan populace. Constantine did not want a religious civil war, nor did he want to coerce his subjects into beliefs foreign to their ancestry or far from their minds and hearts. He was a pragmatic man and knew he had to remain a relatively neutral force in order to unite a citizenry who had been torn apart by years of internecine wars.

The Edict of Milan essentially ended the last Imperial persecution of Christians. Unlike Galerius' hostile, chastising and begrudging Edict of Toleration before his lurid death in 311, the Edict of Milan was an embracing, friendly and wholehearted endorsement of Christianity with the full rights and protections of the Roman Empire behind it.

In spite of and because of the Edict, Daia continued to kill and persecute Christians in his provinces in the East. He published an edict encouraging every city to expel all its Christians. (Three copies of this edict survive at Tyre, Colbasa and Aykiricay, Turkey.)

Licinius continued to pursue Daia from town to town. Daia came at last to Tarsus, the hometown of the 1st century Paul the Apostle:

"...There, (Daia) in anguish and dismay of mind, sought death as the only remedy of those calamities that God had heaped on him. But first he gorged himself with food and large draughts of wine...and then swallowed poison. However, the force of the poison, repelled by his full stomach, could not immediately operate, but it produced a grievous disease, resembling the pestilence....the poison soon began to rage and to burn up everything within him so that he was driven to distraction with the intolerable pain; and during a fit of frenzy which lasted four days, he gathered handfuls of earth and greedily devoured it. Having undergone various and excruciating torments, he dashed his forehead against the wall and his eyes started out of their sockets. And now, become blind, he imagined that he saw God with His servants arrayed in white robes sitting in judgment on him. He roared out as men on the rack are wont and exclaimed that not he, but others, were guilty. In the end, as if he had been racked into confession, he acknowledged his own guilt and lamentably implored Christ to have mercy upon him. Then, amidst groans, like those of one burnt alive, did he breathe out his guilty soul in the most horrible kind of death (summer of 313)." Lactantius, *Deaths of the Persecutors 49*

And now there were two, a dyarchy: Licinius in the East and Constantine in the West.

With Daia's death, Licinius began in 315 to seek out and to kill all who could possibly be a threat to his throne. After Galerius' death in 311, Galerius' wife Valeria, Galerius' illegitimate son Candidianus whom Valeria had adopted and Valeria's mother Prisca, wife of Diocletian, refused to go to Licinius as Diocletian had suggested when he retired in 305. Instead, they took up residence in Daia's court. Daia lusted Valeria and as the daughter of an emperor, Diocletian, and the wife of a previous emperor, Galerius, she would have given great legitimacy to Daia's rule. She spurned him and he exiled her and her mother Prisca to a nondescript town in Syria. When the civil war between Licinius and Daia erupted in 313, Valeria and Prisca spent the next year in hiding. Diocletian died that year either of old age or of suicide. Licinius ordered that both Valeria and Prisca be found and killed. They were discovered in Thessalonica, beheaded and their bodies thrown into the sea. The two women, innocent pawns in deadly games of power, are both revered as Christian martyrs. The face of Empress Prisca can still be seen in the medallions depicting her and Didocletian in the Cathedral of Split, Croatia. Licinius next killed Daia's wife, eight-year-old son and seven-year-old daughter. He then killed Galerius' illegitimate son Candidianus and finally the late Emperor Severus' surviving son. He was sweeping the slate clean of any blood lines or rivals to power. Now there was only one more to eliminate before Licinius could be supreme Monarch of the Roman Empire---Constantine.

In spite of the fact that Licinius had won the war against Daia under prayers offered to the one God of the Christians, he became increasingly hostile to his brother-in-law Constantine whom he saw as too Christian. All the people in the West and in Licinius' East loved Constantine and sang the praises of his reforms, peace-making efforts and statesmanship. Licinius began to feel that the Christians and Christian priests were praying only for Constantine and not for him. He disapproved of many of Constantine's laws favoring Christians and finally purged his army and his government of Christians and installed staunch heathens. He forbade the assemblies of bishops in his territories and banished Christians from their churches to open fields. Mocking them, he said the fresh air would be more wholesome for such large assemblies of people. He began to close churches, to confiscate church property and finally to kill Christians. The most notable martyrs at that time were The Forty Martyrs of Sebaste in c. 320. According to St. Basil's *Homily on The Forty Marty*rs delivered 50 years after their martyrdom:

"These holy martyrs suffered at Sebaste, in the Lesser Armenia, under the Emperor Licinius in 320. They were of different countries, but enrolled in the same troop....were of the Thundering Legion, so famous under Marcus Aurelius for the miraculous rain and victory obtained by their prayers....on orders of the emperor Licinius for all to sacrifice, these forty went bold up to (their commander Lysias) and said they were Christians and that no torments should make them ever abandon their holy religion....The governor, finding them all resolute, caused them to be torn with whips and their sides to be rent with iron hooks....the governor, highly offended at their courage and that liberty of speech with which they accosted him, devised an extraordinary kind of death, which, being slow and severe, he hoped would shake their constancy. The cold in Armenia is very sharp, especially in March and toward the end of winter...there was also at that time a severe frost. Under the wall of the town stood a pond that was frozen so hard that it would bear walking upon with safety. The judge ordered the saints to be exposed quite naked on the ice; and in order to tempt them the more powerfully to renounce their faith, a warm bath was prepared at a small distance from the frozen pond for any of this company to go to who were disposed to purchase their temporal ease and safety on that condition. The martyrs, on hearing their sentence, ran joyfully to the place and without waiting to be stripped, undressed themselves, encouraging one another in the same manner as is usual among soldiers in military expeditions attended with hardships and dangers, saying that one bad night would purchase them a happy eternity....The guards in the meantime ceased not to persuade them to sacrifice....of the whole of the number only one had the misfortune to be overcome....A sentinel was warming himself near the bath....While he was attending, he had a vision of blessed spirits descending from heaven on the martyrs....The guard, being struck with the celestial vision and the apostate's desertion, was converted....threw off his clothes and placed himself in his stead amongst the thirty-nine martyrs. In the morning the judge ordered both those that were dead with the cold, and those that were still alive, to be laid on carriages and cast into a fire....Their bodies were burned and their ashes thrown into the river; but the Christians secretly carried off or purchased part of them with money."

The Forty Martyrs were soldiers in the Roman 12th Legion called *Fulminata*, The Lightning or Thundering Legion, and some believe the Legion was given that name by Marcus Aurelius after he experienced "the miraculous rain" event in c. 169.

The deaths of The Forty Martyrs have attracted veneration and artistic representation from the time of their martyrdoms until the present day. These very young men, only one was married, and their icy deaths was the last famous mass martyrdom of Christians. Forty naked, pale, shivering, stoic young men crowded together are painted on a wooden icon from the 4th century in the Musee des Beaux Arts in Paris. The small exquisite painting is signed by an unknown painter named Nikitarea. In the Forum in Rome is a small building called the Oratory of the Forty Martyrs. Dating from the 600's, its walls are frescoed with the slim bodies of the young men whose arms are raised in praise like orants. The years when martyred heroes adorned the underground walls of the catacombs in Rome subsided in the late 300's, but in Syracuse, Sicily under the 4th century Church of St. John are hollowed out and hallowed catacombs where the Forty Martyrs grace the walls with their naked faith. The Forty Martyrs, like the martyrs on the walls of the catacombs in Rome and the sculptures and paintings of martyrs for the last 2,000 years, represent all Christian martyrs, past and present, whose willing martyrdoms and faithful renderings unto God the things that are God's inspire the creative spirit.

The persecuted and dying Christians in the East looked to their champion Constantine for rescue. Licinius had been harassing and killing them for years after their freedom of worship was conferred on them. Licinius had been plotting against and provoking Constantine to battle for years. Constantine finally moved against his brother-in-law in a series of battles in July through September of 324. Constantine took with him Christian priests to pray for him and his men. His troops had the Christian sign on their shields and the labarum as their standard. Licinius gathered around him Egyptian diviners, Roman soothsayers, priests and prophets from all the pagan regions in the East. Every one proclaimed he would win the battle. The night before the first of the battles on July 3, 324 Licinius gathered in a grove with his idols, pagan priests, bodyguards and friends:

"After lighting tapers and performing the usual sacrifices in honor of the gods, (Licinius) is said to have delivered the following speech: 'Friends and fellow-soldiers! These are our country's gods and these we honor with a worship derived from our remotest ancestors. But he who leads the army now opposed to us (Constantine) has proved false to the religion of his forefather, and adopted atheistic sentiments, honoring in his infatuation some strange and unheard-of deity with whose despicable standard (the labarum) he now disgraces his army and confiding in whose aid he has taken up arms, and is now advancing, not so much against us as against those very gods whom he has forsaken. However, the present occasion shall prove which of us is mistaken in his judgment and shall decide between our gods and those whom our adversaries profess to honor. For either it will declare the victory to be ours, and so most justly evince that our gods are the true saviors and helpers; or else, if this god of Constantine's, who comes we know not whence, shall prove superior to our deities, who are many, and in point of numbers, at least, have the advantage, let no one henceforth doubt which god he ought to worship, but attach himself at once to the superior power and ascribe to him the honors of victory. Suppose then this strange god, whom we now regard with ridicule, should really prove victorious; then indeed we must acknowledge and give him honor, and so bid a long farewell to those for whom we light our tapers in vain. But if our own gods triumph, as they undoubtedly will, then, as soon as we have secured the present victory, let us persecute the war without delay against these despisers of the gods.'" Eusebius, *Life of Constantine 2.5*

It had taken many millennia for paganism in the West to say its "long farewell" to the pagan gods to whom they had "lit their tapers in vain." With the Edict of Milan, a dam had burst. The towns and hamlets of the Empire were filled with the white robes of the baptized, the churches of the Christians were flooded with worshippers and the pagan temples stood empty. But there still remained Emperor Licinius. Clinging with desperate uncertainty to the old stone gods, he sallied forth.

These last three battles at Adrianople (aka Hadrianopolis), Hellspont and finally at Chrysopolis on September 18, 324 were seen by the participants, and have been historically seen, as the final military battles between paganism and Christianity. Constantine's forces won all three battles. During the final battle at Chrysopolis, Licinius, who had won a decisive battle against Daia under the name of the Christian God only eleven years earlier, absolutely forbade his troops to even look at Constantine's standard with the image of the Chi-Rho on it. Licinius lost 25,000-30,000 troops at Chrysopolis. He fled with a vestige of his army to Nicomedia. Constantine demonstrated he had either embraced the concept of Christian mercy or took the advice of his Christian counselors to "love your enemies" (Matthew 5:44) because he spared the lives of many of Licinius' soldiers and when his troops went on wanton rampages, "(Constantine) repressed their fury by a largess of money, rewarding every man who saved the life of an enemy with a certain weight of gold...so that great numbers even of the barbarians were thus saved and owed their lives to the emperor's gold." Eusebius, *Life of Constantine 2.13*

Licinius persuaded his wife, Constantine's half-sister, to beg her brother to spare his life. She did and he did, but Licinius kept plotting against Constantine and in the spring of 325 Constantine had him hanged.

And now there was one. Polybius' cycle had been completed.

Constantine was sole Emperor, not of Rome, but of what would be the Christian world. Christianity had triumphed over paganism. The centuries of the Christian God begin.

"It was written in the book of fate that this great city of ours (Rome) should arise and the first steps be taken to the founding of the mightiest empire the world has known---second only to God's." Livy, *History 1* (Translation by Aubrey de Selincourt, Penguin Books, 1960)

BIBLIOGRAPHY

Abercius, *Epitaph*—google—Abercius Epitaph

Acts of Martyrs and Saints: Acta Sanctorum, (Volume 1) (Syriac Edition), Paul Bedjan, Claude Detienne, Gorgias Press LLC, Piscataway, New Jersey 2009.

Aeschylus, *The Eumenides*—google—internet classics archive aeschylus eumenides

Africanus, *Narrative of Events Happening in Persia on the Birth of Christ*—google—new advent africanus narrative

Ambrose, *De virginibus*—google—crossroadsinitiative ambrose agnes
   On the Sacraments—google—crossroadsinitiative ambrose sacraments

Ammianus, Marcellinus, *The History*—google—penelope.uchicago.edu Ammian history

Appian, *The Roman History*—google—lacuscurtius appian

Apuleius, *The Golden Ass* aka *Metamorphoses*—google—gutenberg.org/files apuleius

Aristides, *Apology*—google—early christian writings aristides
   Oration to Rome—google—aristides oration to rome online

Aristotle, *Nicomachean Ethics*—google—classics.mit.edu/aristotle/ nicomachean
   Politics—google—internet classics archive aristotle politics

Athanasius, *Vita Antonii*—google—essene.com vita

Augustine, *The City of God*—google—new advent city of god

Augustus, Caesar, *Deeds of the Divine Augustus*—google—augustus caesar deeds online

Aurelius, Marcus, *Epistle to the Roman Senate*—google—ccel.org/lxxi
    Meditations—google—internet classics archive aurelius

Basil of Caesarea, *Homily on the Forty Martyrs*—google—ewtn.com/library forty martyrs

Bible, Douay-Rheims Catholic Bible—google—drbo.org
    King James Version—google—kingjamesbibleonline.org
    New American Standard Bible—google—biblegateway.com/NAS
    New International Version—google—biblegateway.com/NIV Bible

Bordeaux Pilgrim Itinerary—google—christusrex.org/pilg/bord

Bossio, Antonio, *Underground Rome* (EBM book) Harvard Bookstore, Cambridge, MA.

Butler, Alban, *Lives of Saints*—google—bartleby.com/210/

Caesar, Julius, *Gallic Wars*—google—internet classics archive gallic wars

Cassiodorus, *Variae*—google—gutenberg.org/files18590

Cassius Dio, *Roman History*—google—lacuscurtius cassius

Cato the Elder, *De Agricultura*—google—Cato the elder de agricultura

Cicero, *Letters*—google—gutenberg.org/files letters of cicero
    On The Laws—google—Cicero's treatise on the laws online

Clement of Alexandria, *Pedagogues*—google—early christian writings clement
    Stromata—google—early christian writings clement

Clement of Rome, *First Epistle to Corinthians*—google—early christian writings 1 clement

Codex Bezae: An Early Christian Manuscript and its Text—google— Amazon.com books

Cyprian, Bishop of Carthage, *Epistles*—google—new advent cyprian epistles

Cyril of Jerusalem, *Catechetical Lecture*—google—early christian writings cyril of jerusalem

Davis, William Stearns, *Readings in Ancient History: Rome and the West*— google—Amazon.com books

Didache: The Teaching of the Twelve Apostles—google—early christian writings didache

Diocles, *Monument Inscription CIL VI, no. 10048*—google—inscription CIL VI no.10048

Dionysius of Alexandria, *Letter to Hermammon*—google—aren.org epistles dionysius

Edersheim, Alfred, *The Life and Times of Jesus the Messiah (1883)*—google—Amazon.com books

Egeria, *The Pilgrimage of Egeria*—google—ccel.org egeria

Epictetus, *The Golden Sayings*—google—internet classics archive golden

Epistle of Barnabas—google—newadvent.org epistle barnabas

Epistle of Mathetes to Diognetus—google—new advent mathetes

Epitome of the Definition of the Iconoclastic Conciliabulum—google—fordham.edu epitome

Euripedes, *Bacchae*—google—internet classics archive bacchae

Eusebius, *Church History*—google—new advent eusebius history
    Martyrs of Palestine—google—people.ucalgary.ca/eusebius martyrs of palestine
    The Life of Constantine—google—new advent eusebius constantine

Fall of Nineveh Chronicle—google—fall of nineveh chronicle

Festus, *Brevarium of the Accomplishments of the Roman People*—google—roman emperors.org festus

Foxe, John, *Book of Martyrs*—google—ccel.org foxe martyrs

Frontinus, Sextus Julius, *The Aqueducts of Rome*—google—frontinus aqueducts

Gaius, *Institutes*—google—faculty.cua.edu gaius

Goebbels, Joseph, *Diaries*—google—Amazon.com books

Golden Legend—google—fordham.edu/golden legend

Gregory of Nyssa, *Oratorio*—google—sag.edu gregory of nyssa oration

Hammurabi's Code—google—internet history sourcebook hammurabi

Hegesippus, *Historia*—google—early christian writings hegesippus

Herodian, *History of the Roman Empire Since the Death of Marcus Aurelius*—google—livius.org herodian history

Herodotus, *The Histories* aka *The Inquiries*—google—internet classics archive herodotus

Historia Augusta—google—penelope.uchicago.edu historia

Horace, *Epistles*—google—poetry in translation horace epistles
Odes—google—poetry in translation horace odes

Ignatius, *Martyrdom of Ignatius* aka *Martyrium Colbertinus*—google—new advent martyr ignatius
Seven Letters—google—early christian writings ignatius

Irenaeus, *Against Heresies*—google—new advent against heresies

Isocrates, *Panegyricus*—google—classicpersuasion.org panegyricus

Ixtlilxochitl, Fernando de Alva Cortes, *Codex Ixtlilxochitl*—google—famsi. org ixtlilxochitl

Jerome, *Book of Illustrious Men*—google—new advent illustrious men
St. Jerome: Commentary on Ecclesiastes—google—Amazon.com books

Josephus, Flavius, *Against Apion*—google—sacred-texts.com josephus
Jewish Antiquities—google—sacred-texts.com josephus
Wars of the Jews—google—sacred-texts.com josephus

Juvenal, *Satires*—google—tertullian.org/juvenal satires online

Koran aka Quran—google—quran.com/1

Lactantius, *On The Deaths of the Persecutors*—google—newadvent.org/ fathers/0705.htm

LaRousse Encyclopedia of Mythology—google—Amazon.com books

Letter of Barnabus aka *Epistle of Barnabas*—google—early christian writings barnabas

Letter from Eucherius to Bishop Salvius—*The Passion of St. Maurice and the Theban Legion*—google—ucc.ie/milmart/BHL5740

Livy, *History of Rome*—google—mcadams.posc livy

Lucian of Samosata, *Dialogues of the Gods*—google—sacred-texts.com lucian
The Death of Peregrinus—google—tertullian.org peregrinus

Malalas, John, *The Chronicle of John Malalas*, translation by Elizabeth

Jeffreys, Michael Jeffreys and Roger Scott, Australian Association for Byzantine Studies, Sydney, Australia 1986.

Martial, *Epigrams*—google—tertullian.org/fathers/martial_epigrams
  On The Spectacles—google—tertullian.org public shows domitian

Martyr, Justin, *Dialogue with Trypho*—google—early christian writings justin martyr dialogue
  First Apology—google—early christian writings first apology
  Second Apology—google—early christian writings second apology

Martyrdom of Lawrence—google—catholic.org/saints/366

Martyrdom of Polycarp—google—early christian writings martyrdom polycarp

Melito, Bishop of Sardis, *Apology*—google—aren.org/prison/documents melito

Minucius, Felix, *Octavius*—google—early christian writings octavius

Mishneh—google—chabad.org/library/article_cdo/aid/682956

Modern Catholic Dictionary, 1999—google—therealpresence.org/dictionary/dict

Mumford, Lewis, *The City in History*—google—Amazon.com books

Origen, *Against Celsus*—google—new advent 0416

Orosius, *Seven Books of History Against the Pagans*—google—Amazon.com books

Ovid, *Fasti*—google—poetry in translation ovid fasti
  The Loves—google—sacred-texts.com ovid loves

Pectorius, *Inscription*—google—new advent Pectorius

Perpetua, *The Passion of St. Perpetua, St. Felicitas and their Companions*—google—newadvent.org/fathers/perpetua

Petronius, *Satyricon*—google—sacred-texts.com satyricon

Philocalus, *Chronographia of 354*—google—tertullian.org/fathers/chronography of 354

Plato, *The Republic*—google—classics.mit.edu/Plato/republic.html

Pliny the Elder, *Natural History*—google—lacuscurtius pliny the elder natural

Pliny the Younger, *Letters*—google—internet history sourcebook pliny letters

Plutarch, *Lives*—google—Plutarch parallel lives online

Morals—google—attalus.org/info/moralia

Poggio, *On the Vagaries of Fortune's Wheel* aka *De Varietate Fortunae* c.1440—
google—Amazon.com Two Renaissance Book Hunters

Polybius, *The Histories*—google—lacuscurtius polybius histories

Prudentius, *Liber Peristephanon*—Roberts, Michael, *Poetry and the Cult of the Martyrs:*
The Liber Peristephanon of Prudentius—google—Amazon.com books
Prudentius: Against Symmachus 2—google—Amazon.com books

Recognitions of Clement—google—new advent.org/fathers/080401.htm

Roman Martyrology—google—archive.org/stream/romanmartyrology00cathuoft

Sallust, *Speech to Caesar*—google—lacuscurtius speech to caesar

Schaff, Philip, *History of the Christian Church*—google—ccel.org/schaff/history

Senatus Consultum de Bacchanalibus—google—ancient history sourcebook
consultum

Seneca, *Moral Letters*—google—stoics.com/books
On Anger—google—stoics.com/seneca_essays

Siculus, Diodorus, *Library of History*—google—lacuscurtius siculus

Socci, Antonio, *I Nuovi Perseguitati (The New Persecuted: Inquiries Into*
Anti-Christian Intolerance in the New Century of the Martyrs) 2002.
(not translated into English)

Sozomen, *Ecclesiastical History Book*—google—new advent history sozomen

Stevenson, *The Catacombs: Rediscovered Monuments of Early Christianity*—
google—Amazon.com books

Strabo, *Geography*—google—lacuscurtius strabo

Suetonius, *Lives of the Caesars*—google—lacuscurtius suetonius

Tacitus, *A Dialogue on Oratory*—google—gutenberg.org/files dialogue oratory
The Annals—google—lacuscurtius tacitus annals
The Histories—google—lacuscurtius tacitus histories

Talmud—google—jewish virtual library talmud

Tertullian, *A Treatise on the Soul*—google—early christian writings treatise
on the soul
Against Marcion—google—early christian writings tertullian
against marcion

Apology—google—early christian writings tertullian apology

Demurrer Against The Heresies—google—new advent against heresies

On Baptism—google—early christian writings tertullian baptism

Tertullian's Treatises, Concerning Prayer—google—tertullian.org
   treatises on prayer

To The Nations—google—tertullian.org ad nationes

The Acts of Cecilia—google—ewtn.com/library/cecilia

The Acts of Martyrdom of St. Justin and Companions—google—
   earlychristians.org/testimonies_martyrs/justin

The Acts of Paul and Thecia—google—new advent 0816

The Acts of Peter and Paul—google—new advent 0815

The Acts of St. Sebastian—google—ewtn.com/library/mary/sebastn

The Book of Pontiffs (Liber Pontificalis)—google—Amazon.com books

*The Encyclical Epistle of the Church at Smyrna Concerning the Martyrdom of
   Polycarp*—google—new advent 0102

Theophilus, *Apology to Autolycus*—google—logoslibrary.org/theophilus/
   autolycus/index.html

Thucydides, *The Peloponnesian War*—google—classics.mit.edu/thucydides

Virgil, *Eclogues*—google—classics.mit.edu/virgil/ecologues
   The Aeneid—google—classics.mit.edu/virgil/aeneid
   The Georgics—google—classics.mit.edu/virgil/georgics

VOM's Persecuted Church Global Report 2009-12, The Voice of the
   Martyrs, VOM Books.com

Wurmband, Richard, *Tortured For Christ*—google—Amazon.com books

547

INTERNET SOURCES

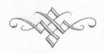

For Most Greek, Roman and Early Christian Authors

Early Christian writings (c. 50-250 AD)—google—earlychristianwritings.com

Early Christian writers—google—newadvent.org/fathers/

Roman/Greek classics in English online—google—lacuscurtius

The Internet Classics Archive (western/eastern ancient writers)—google—
internet classics archive

INDEX

557

Made in the USA
Middletown, DE
15 July 2020